Mental Health: Law and Practice

Mental Health: Law and Practice

Second Edition

Professor Philip Fennell
Cardiff Law School, Cardiff University

Published by
Jordan Publishing Limited
21 St Thomas Street
Bristol BS1 6JS

British Library Cataloguing-in-Publication Data

A catalogue record for this book is available from the British Library.

ISBN 978 1 84661 240 4

Typeset by Letterpart Ltd, Reigate, Surrey

Printed in Great Britain by CPI Antony Rowe, Chippenham and Eastbourne

DEDICATION

To my remarkable wife Vic,
to our children Danielle and James,
and to our wonderful dogs Bridie and Phoebe.

PREFACE

The amendments introduced by the Mental Health Act 2007 ('MHA 2007') to the Mental Health Act 1983 ('MHA 1983'), the Mental Capacity Act 2005 ('MCA 2005') and the Domestic Violence, Crime and Victims Act 2004 ('DVCVA 2004') have now been brought fully into force. A consolidated version of the MHA 1983 is provided in the Appendix.

The Deprivation of Liberty safeguards in Schedule A1 to the MCA 2005 came into force in April 2005. Unlike the first edition, this book does not contain the full text of the Deprivation of Liberty provisions of the MCA 2005, nor does it contain the amended provisions of the DVCVA 2004. However, the deprivation of liberty procedures and the relevant case law are discussed in detail in chapter 6, and the impact of the DVCVA 2004 is discussed in chapters 7 and 9. Mental health law has now attained a level of complexity unrivalled since the days prior to the Mental Health Act 1959, which swept away the tangled body of law in the Lunacy and Mental Treatment Acts, and the Mental Deficiency Acts. Between them the MHA 1983 and the MCA 2005 provide a comprehensive code of mental health legislation, each providing powers to deprive people of their liberty and treat without consent, each based on distinct eligibility criteria for compulsion, and each with its own Code of Practice.

To add to this complexity England and Wales now each have separate regulations dealing with detention, consent to treatment, community treatment and guardianship,[1] conflict of interests,[2] designation of nurses eligible to exercise the holding power under s 5(4),[3] Independent Mental Health Advocates[4] and Approved Mental Health Professionals.[5] England and Wales have separate Directions on eligibility to be an Approved Clinician for the

---

[1]   Mental Health (Hospital, Guardianship and Treatment) (England) Regulations 2008, SI 2008/1184; the Mental Health (Hospital, Guardianship, Community Treatment and Consent to Treatment) (Wales) Regulations 2008, SI 2008/2439 (W 212).

[2]   Mental Health (Conflicts of Interest) (England) Regulations 2008, SI 2008/1205; the Mental Health (Conflicts of Interest) (Wales) Regulations 2008, SI 2008/2440 (W 213).

[3]   Mental Health (Nurses) (England) Order 2008, SI 2008/1208; the Mental Health (Nurses) (Wales) Order 2008, SI 2008/2441 (W 214).

[4]   Mental Health (Independent Mental Health Advocates) (Wales) Regulations 2008, SI 2008/2437 (W 210); the Mental Health Act 1983 (Independent Mental Health Advocates) (England) Regulations 2008, SI 2008/3166.

[5]   Mental Health (Approved Mental Health Professionals) (Approval) (England) Regulations 2008; SI 2008/1206; the Mental Health (Approval of Persons to be Approved Mental Health Professionals) (Wales) Regulations 2008, SI 2008/2436 (W 209).

purposes of the Mental Health Act 1983,[6] and each has a separate Code of Practice on the Mental Health Act 1983.[7]

In England the jurisdiction previously exercised by Mental Health Review Tribunals has been vested in the Health, Education and Social Care Chamber of the First-tier Tribunal, whilst in Wales the jurisdiction remains with the Mental Health Review Tribunal for Wales. Each has separate Tribunal Rules.[8]

England and Wales each have separate regulations on the Deprivation of Liberty safeguards.[9]

Not only do England and Wales have separate subordinate legislation, there will soon also be significant differences between the primary legislation applicable in the respective jurisdictions. The Welsh Assembly has now passed the Mental Health (Wales) Measure 2010 which will add 56 new sections and two Schedules to the Mental Health Act 1983 as it applies in Wales. The Measure also contains extensive rule making powers. The intent is to entitle mental health service users to early intervention and to entitle all patients, not just those subject to compulsion, to an Independent Mental Health Advocate.[10] These rights were originally enshrined in the Mental Health National Service Framework for Wales, and were, after various 'refocussings' (postponements) to have been brought into effect by 2010. The likely effect of the new measure is difficult to assess, as at the time of writing the regulations are out for consultation. A preliminary analysis suggests that the measure provides little by way of enforceable rights for service users, the rule making process seems likely to be protracted, and the rules themselves are complex and voluminous. It is doubtful whether this supposed 'rights-based' approach will succeed where the policy levers of the National Service Framework have so

---

[6]   Mental Health Act 1983 Approved Clinician (General) Directions 2008 Issued under ss 7, 8 and 273 of the National Health Service Act 2006 http://www.dh.gov.uk; Mental Health Act 1983 Approved Clinician (Wales) Directions 2008 issued under ss 12, 13 and 203 of the National Health Service (Wales) Act 2006.

[7]   Department of Health, Code of Practice: Mental Health Act 1983 (2008) http://www.doh.gov.uk; Welsh Assembly Government, Mental Health Act 1983 Code of Practice for Wales (2008) http://www.wales.nhs.uk.

[8]   Tribunal Procedure (First-tier Tribunal) Health, Education and Social Care Chamber) Rules 2008, SI 2008/2699; the Mental Health Review Tribunal for Wales Rules 2008, SI 2008/2705 (L 17).

[9]   In England the regulations are: the Mental Capacity (Deprivation of Liberty: Standard Authorisations, Assessments and Ordinary Residence) Regulations 2008, SI 2008/1858; the Mental Capacity (Deprivation of Liberty: Appointment of Relevant Person's Representative) Regulations 2008, SI 2008/1315; and the Mental Capacity (Deprivation of Liberty: Appointment of Relevant Person's Representative) (Amendment) Regulations 2008, SI 2008/2368. In Wales the relevant regulations are: the Mental Capacity (Deprivation of Liberty: Assessments, Standard Authorisations and Disputes about Residence) (Wales) Regulations 2009, SI 2009/783 (W 69); and the Mental Capacity (Deprivation of Liberty: Appointment of Relevant Person's Representative) (Wales) Regulations 2009, SI 2009/266 (W 29).

[10] The text of the Measure, which has now received Royal Assent, may be found at http://www.assemblywales.org/bus-home/bus-legislation/bus-leg-measures/business-legislation-measures-mhs-2.htm.

conspicuously failed, but it is to be hoped that the measure will lead to more than a further protracted delay in achieving what ought to have been achieved by last year at the latest. The amendments to the MHA 1983 introduced by the Measure have not been included in this edition.

The aim of this book is to explain mental health legislation and the relevant case law in a way which is accessible not only to professionals and students of mental health law, but also to service users, carers, and interested lay readers. Heartfelt thanks are due to my good friends and colleagues Professor Luke Clements and Professor Richard Jones of Cardiff Law School, John Horne of Northumbria University, and Chris Curran of the University of Lincoln. All have shown endless patience in discussing MHA and MCA issues with me, and Chris's excellent Mental Health Network Updates are an invaluable treasure trove. The book is intended to provide an outline of mental health law as it stood on St Patrick's Day 2011.

Phil Fennell
17 March 2011

CONTENTS

Chapter 6
Powers of detention under the Mental Health Act 1983 and the Mental
Capacity Act 2005

TABLE OF CASES

References are to paragraph numbers.

TABLE OF STATUTES

References are to paragraph numbers.

TABLE OF STATUTORY INSTRUMENTS

References are to paragraph numbers.

TABLE OF INTERNATIONAL AND EUROPEAN LEGISLATION

References are to paragraph numbers.

LIST OF ABBREVIATIONS

AC	Approved Clinician
ACUS	After-care under Supervision
AMHP	Approved Mental Health Professional
ANH	Artificial Nutrition and Hydration
ASBO	Anti-social Behaviour Orders
ASW	Approved Social Worker
BNF	British National Formulary
CAMHS	Child and Adolescent Mental Health Services
CCfW	Care Council for Wales
CPA	Care Programme Approach
CPRD	UN Convention on the Rights of Persons with Disabilities
CPS	Crown Prosecution Service
CPT	European Committee for the Prevention of Torture and Inhuman or Degrading Treatment
CQC	Care Quality Commission
CRC	UN Convention on the Rights of the Child 1989
CSA 2000	Care Standards Act 2000
CTO	Community Treatment Order
DoH	Department of Health
DoL	Deprivation of Liberty
ECHR	European Convention on Human Rights
ECT	Electro Convulsive Therapy
FTT	First Tier Tribunal
GSCC	General Social Care Council
HRA 1998	Human Rights Act 1998
IMCA	Independent Mental Capacity Advocate
IMHA	Independent Mental Health Advocate
IPCC	Independent Police Complaints Commission
JCHR	Parliamentary Joint Committee on Human Rights
LSSA	Local Social Services Authority
MAPPA	Multi-Agency Public Protection Arrangements
MCA 2005	Mental Capacity Act 2005

MHA 1959	Mental Health Act 1959
MHA 1983	Mental Health Act 1983
MHA 2007	Mental Health Act 2007
MHAC	Mental Health Act Commission
MHT	Mental Health Tribunal
MHRT	Mental Health Review Tribunal
NHS	National Health Service
NHSFT	National Health Service Foundation Trust
NICE	National Institute of Clinical and Public Health Excellence
NR	Nearest Relative
PCT	Primary Care Trust
PVS	Permanent Vegetative State
RC	Responsible Clinician
RMO	Responsible Medical Officer
SCT	Supervised Community Treatment
SOA 2003	Sexual Offences Act 2003
SOAD	Second Opinion Appointed Doctor

Chapter 1

BACKGROUND

THE MENTAL HEALTH ACT 2007 AND THE MENTAL CAPACITY ACT 2005: TWO DIFFERENT TYPES OF MENTAL HEALTH LEGISLATION

1.1   The Mental Health Act 2007 ('MHA 2007') was the Government's third attempt this century to introduce major reform of the Mental Health Act 1983 ('MHA 1983'). The MHA 2007 also amends the Mental Capacity Act 2005 ('MCA 2005') to introduce new procedures for deprivation of liberty, and the amendments to that Act are as significant as those to the MHA 1983. The 2007 Act also significantly amends the Domestic Violence, Crime and Victims Act 2004, increasing the rights of victims of crimes committed by mentally disordered offenders, and underlining the position of the MHA 1983 at the intersection between the health and criminal justice systems.

1.2   The MHA 2007 and the MCA 2005 are both mental health statutes in the sense that each provides authority to detain and to treat for mental disorder without consent, albeit in different ways and subject to different safeguards. The MCA 2005 operates on the basis of incapacity due to any impairment of, or disturbance in the functioning of, the mind or the brain and best interests. Decisions about admission to hospital or treatment may be taken on a person's behalf if the person lacks capacity, which means 'unable to make a decision for himself in relation to the matter because of an impairment of, or disturbance in the functioning of, the mind or brain'. Decisions under the MCA 2005 must be made in the incapacitated person's best interests.

1.3   The MHA 2007 operates on the basis of mental disorder and risk to self or others. The definition of mental disorder is 'any disorder or disability of the mind'. People with mental disorder may be detained and treated without consent if their mental disorder is of a nature or degree justifying detention and detention is necessary for their health or safety or for the protection of others. There are limits to 'mental disorder' under the 2007 Act, such as that learning disability is not a mental disorder for the purposes of long-term detention, unless there is abnormally aggressive or seriously irresponsible conduct, and addiction to alcohol or drugs are not themselves to be regarded as mental disorders. However, for many mentally disordered people there will be two alternative legal frameworks under which decisions about their care and treatment may be taken out of their hands and exercised by others. Any disorder or disability of the mind for the purposes of the MHA will necessarily include an impairment of, or disturbance in the functioning of, the mind.

Where the MCA extends further is by extending to impairments or disturbances caused by drugs or alcohol and by allowing deprivation of liberty for longer than 28 days for people with learning disability who are not abnormally aggressive or seriously irresponsible in their conduct.

1.4 This raises the problem of the interface between these two codes, each containing as it does powers to detain and to treat without consent, and the question:

> 'When is it appropriate for someone to be given treatment without consent under the Mental Health Act, and when should the Mental Capacity Act be used?'

The interface between the two statutes is discussed in chapter 6 in relation to deprivation of liberty and in relation to treatment without consent in chapter 10. Since the passage of the MCA 2005 and the MHA 2007, the United Kingdom has ratified the UN Convention on the Rights of Persons with Disabilities ('CPRD'), which purportedly prohibits legislation authorising detention which is linked to disability. The potential impact of the CPRD on mental health and mental capacity legislation is discussed in chapter 2 (at **2.57–2.83**).

MENTAL HEALTH LEGISLATION

1.5 A basic difference between psychiatry and other branches of medicine, which provides a key *raison d'etre* of mental health legislation is that, in some cases, patients may be forced, in their own interests or for the protection of others, to accept admission to hospital or treatment without consent. That lack of consent may arise because the patient lacks capacity to consent, or because he or she refuses intervention. Mental health legislation provides authority for intervention without consent. It legitimises detentions carried out in accordance with correct procedure. It provides safeguards against arbitrary deprivation of liberty and arbitrary interference with physical integrity, in accordance with the positive obligations of states to provide effective review under Arts 5 and 8 of the European Convention on Human Rights.[1] The different functions performed by mental health legislation are discussed further below (at **2.1** below), but a core function is to strike a fair balance between, on the one hand, individual rights to liberty and physical integrity and, on the other, society's presumed entitlement to impose therapy without consent, whether that lack of consent arises from incapacity or refusal.

1.6 The Mental Health Act 1959 ('MHA 1959') still provides the basic framework of contemporary mental health legislation. The MHA 2007 is the fifth significant amendment to the 1959 Act, which conferred discretionary powers on doctors and social workers to detain and treat compulsorily persons suffering from mental disorder where necessary for their health or safety or for

---

[1]   As laid down by the European Court of Human Rights in *Storck v Germany (Application No 61603/00)* (2005) 43 EHRR 96.

the protection of others. The MHA 1959 broke with the past by abolishing 'judicial certification' prior to admission as the safeguard against wrongful detention of non-offender patients. 'Certification' by judicial personnel was replaced with 'sectioning' by mental health experts, with the patient enjoying a right to seek review of the need for detention before a Mental Health Review Tribunal ('MHRT'). 'Sectioning' meant an application made by a social worker supported by two medical recommendations presented to, and formally received by, someone acting on behalf of the managers of the receiving hospital.

1.7 The first substantial amendment was by the Mental Health (Amendment) Act 1982, consolidated with the MHA 1959 into the Mental Health Act 1983 ('MHA 1983'), which placed more emphasis on safeguards for patients' rights to seek review of detention and compulsory treatment, and the right to be treated in the setting which imposed the minimum necessary restrictions on freedom. The 1982 amendments were also motivated by a desire to comply with the ruling of the European Court of Human Rights in *X v United Kingdom*[2] that there had been a breach of Art 5(4), which entitles people detained on grounds of unsoundness of mind to speedy review of the lawfulness of detention before a court that must have the power to order discharge. The MHA 1983 extended the right to apply to the tribunal to patients detained under s 2 for assessment, and to offender patients subject to restriction orders. It also gave the MHRT the power to direct discharge of a restriction order patient. Previously the MHRT's role was confined to advising the Home Secretary on fitness for discharge. The MHA 1983 introduced a Mental Health Act Commission to supervise the operation of the Act and to protect the rights of detained patients. It also required that an application for detention could come only from the patient's nearest relative or an Approved Social Worker with special training in the implementation of compulsory powers under the Act.

1.8 The MHA 1983 was further amended by the Mental Health (Patients in the Community) Act 1995 to introduce arrangements for supervised discharge of patients who had been detained under the Act. This Act effectively marked the turning of the tide away from a rights-based focus towards an approach based on risk management, public protection, and ensuring compliance with medication. The 1995 Act was a response to concern about high profile homicides committed by mentally disordered people in the community. However, the powers of supervised discharge introduced by the 1995 Act were rarely used, being seen as bureaucratic and ineffective in ensuring compliance.

1.9 The third significant reform illustrates the effect of the Human Rights Act 1998 ('HRA 1998') on mental health legislation. The HRA 1998 requires public authorities to act compatibly with Convention rights. A public authority includes any court or tribunal. It also includes any 'body or person certain of whose functions are of a public nature', which can include people exercising

---

[2]   *(Application No 7215/75)* (1981) 4 EHRR 188, ECtHR.

functions relating to detention and compulsory treatment.³ Section 6(1) of the HRA 1998 makes it 'unlawful for a public authority to act in a way which is incompatible with a Convention right.' Under s 7(1):

> 'A person who claims that a public authority has acted (or proposes to act) in a way which is made unlawful by section 6(1) may –
>
> (a)   bring proceedings against the authority under this Act in the appropriate court or tribunal, or
> (b)   rely on the Convention right or rights concerned in any legal proceedings.'

The Human Rights Act has produced a significant body of case-law on the MHA 1983. In *R (on the application of H) v London North and East Region Mental Health Review Tribunal (Secretary of State for Health intervening)*,⁴ the Court of Appeal granted a declaration of incompatibility under s 4 of the HRA 1998, holding that s 72 of the MHA 1983 was incompatible with the right to review of detention under Art 5(4) of the European Convention on Human Rights ('ECHR'). Section 72 provided that a Mental Health Review Tribunal ('MHRT') only came under a duty to discharge if satisfied that the patient was **not** suffering from mental disorder of a nature or degree warranting detention. The Court of Appeal held that the positioning of the burden of proof on the applicant to satisfy the tribunal of the absence of detainable mental disorder was incompatible with Art 5(4) the effect of which was that the review body had to satisfy itself that the conditions were met in order for detention to be continued. Section 10(2) of the HRA 1998 allows primary legislation to be amended by ministerial order by the minister. This power was used to introduce the Mental Health Act 1983 (Remedial) Order 2001⁵ which amended the MHA 1983 so that a tribunal is now under a duty to discharge if it is not satisfied that the patient is suffering from mental disorder of a nature or degree justifying detention.

1.10 The fourth major change was the removal from the MHA 1983 to the Mental Capacity Act 2005 of the jurisdiction of the Court of Protection over those who lack capacity because of mental disorder to manage their own property and affairs, and the extension of that jurisdiction to cover health and personal welfare decision-making.

1.11 The Mental Health Act 2007 emphasises public protection and risk management. It extends powers of compulsion, introduces compulsory community treatment orders, broadens the definition of detainable mental disorder, increases the range of different professional/occupational groups eligible to exercise powers of compulsion, and entrenches new legislative concepts of compliance with medication as a key goal of mental health legislation. Whilst the MHA 1983 represented a turn towards patients' rights,

---

3   Human Rights Act 1998, s 6(3). See also *R (on the application of Wilkinson) v Responsible Medical Officer Broadmoor Hospital* [2001] EWCA Civ 1545, CA.
4   [2001] 3 WLR 512, CA.
5   SI 2001/3712.

the main emphasis of the MHA 2007 is on duties of service users to accept medication, to reside in specified places, and to desist from specified conduct, and duties of professionals and Mental Health Tribunals in their decision-making to have regard to risk and non-compliance. There are some provisions which arguably increase detained patients' rights of self-determination, such as the prohibition on giving Electro Convulsive Therapy ('ECT') to a patient (detained or not) who retains decision-making capacity and refuses treatment. There are also new provisions relating to patient advocacy, and treatment of children in age appropriate environments, but overall the emphasis is on public protection and risk management.

1.12 The MHA 2007 amends the MCA 2005 to introduce a procedure to be employed to detain adults who lack mental capacity and who are not actively resisting detention. In *HL v United Kingdom*[6] the European Court of Human Rights ruled that procedural safeguards are needed where anyone lacking mental capacity is subject to control over their residence, movement, and treatment which reaches a sufficient degree and intensity to amount to a deprivation of liberty. The MHA 2007 repeals the prohibition on deprivation of liberty under the MCA 2005 and introduces two new Schedules to the MCA 2005 (Schs 1A and A1) providing a complex procedure to authorise deprivations of liberty of mentally incapacitated adults. This will allow deprivation of liberty to be authorised not just in hospital but also in a privately run residential care home, and even in a private residence.

POLICY CONTEXT: MENTAL HEALTH LAW REFORM

Mental health services

1.13 Since the 1950s there has been a marked shift of mental health care from a primarily hospital-based model to community care. Between 1954 and 2004 the total number of in-patient beds in psychiatric hospitals fell from a peak of 154,000 to 32,400.[7] During the same period the population increased from 45m to over 53m.[8] These bed reductions have led to a massive upsurge in the numbers of people with severe and enduring mental illness being looked after in the community. Although bed numbers have been decreasing, admissions of psychiatric patients to hospital run at approximately 250,000 per year. Compulsory admissions have been steadily increasing from less than 20,000 per year in the 1960s and 1970s to over 30,000 in 2009–2010. In 2009–2010 there were 30,774 admissions under powers of detention in the Mental Health Act 1983, 2,191 of which were under the offender provisions of the Act. A further 18,643 people were detained under the Act following admission as an informal patient. On 31 March 2010 there were 16,622 patients detained in

---

6 *(Application No 45508/99)* (2004) 40 EHRR 761, 81 BMLR 131, ECtHR.
7 L Warner *Beyond the Water Towers: The Unfinished Revolution in Mental Health Services 1985–2005* (2005), pp 37–47, especially at p 37.
8 National Statistics (2009–10) http://www.ic.nhs.uk/webfiles/publications/005_Mental_Health/inpatientdetmha0910/KP90_final_report.pdf.

hospital, of whom 77.2 per cent were in National Health Service hospitals and 22.8 per cent in private hospitals. If there are no more than 32,000 psychiatric beds and at any one time 16,500 detained patients are detained, this suggests the percentage of the in-patient psychiatric population at any one time who are detained is much greater than the level of 10 per cent between the 1950s and 1990s. During the year 2009–2010, 4,103 community treatment orders were made, and on 31 March 2010 there were 3,325 patients on CTOs.

1.14 Private sector hospitals now provide over 20 per cent of beds for detained patients. Private sector residential care homes have taken over the provision of non-hospital care for elderly people with mental illness and for adults with learning disabilities. There is no power under the Mental Health Act 1983 to detain people in residential care homes. They may be required to reside there, under guardianship, but Mental Health Act guardianship has not, until now, given the power to deprive someone of their liberty, which is the province of powers of detention. Many elderly patients who would previously have been admitted informally to long-stay NHS hospitals are now being looked after in private residential care homes. Some will be deprived of their liberty, and will require authorisations under the new power to detain people in residential care homes under Schs A1 and 1A to the Mental Capacity Act 2005 introduced by s 50 of the MHA 2007.

1.15 Direct care outside institutions, both physical and emotional, is now provided largely by informal/unpaid carers, 1.5m of whom provide over 20 hours unpaid care per week and 985,000 of whom provide over 50 hours.[9] Cost savings to the State have clearly been a major driver of policy in this area. The average annual cost of a psychiatric bed has increased from £17,500 in 1983 to £70,000 in 2005, and is currently £100,000.[10] The Association of the British Pharmaceutical Industry claims that the ability of psychiatric medication to maintain people in the community resulted in savings from reduced use of hospital beds in 2001–2002 of £7,434m.[11] The shift towards care in the community and the reduction in hospital beds has led to a desire to ensure that patients may be subject to an effective obligation to take their medication, and carers are expected to play a vital role in ensuring that patients take their medication.

Debate about mental health law reform

1.16 There are three principal drivers of mental health law and policy:

*   reducing stigma and promoting social inclusion;

---

[9]   Commission for Social Care Inspection *The State of Social Care 2005–2006* (2006) (available at http://www.csci.org.uk/PDF/state_of_social_care.pdf).
[10]   Answer by John Bowis (Minister for Health) to question from Alan Milburn, House of Commons *Hansard* Written Answers (12 February 1996, p 16) (available at http://www.mind.org.uk/News+policy+and+campaigns/Policy/MindandMA1Advocacy.html).
[11]   See http://www.abpi.org.uk.

- management of risk to the public and to sufferers themselves; and

- protection of human rights.[12]

Since the 1990s successive governments have pursued a public safety agenda in relation to mental health services responding to concerns about homicides by mentally disordered people. These fears have had a profound impact on mental health law and policy and produce tensions between the agendas of public safety and social inclusion.[13] The New Labour Government followed its immediate predecessors in pursuing a legislative agenda of increased control over mentally disordered people in the community whilst at the same time, through the National Service Frameworks for England and Wales, promoting policies of social inclusion, combating stigma, and user and carer involvement in decisions about care.[14] The National Service Frameworks for England have now been replaced by *New Horizons: a Shared Vision for Mental Health.*[15] Although Convention compliance has been a major issue in mental health law since the 1981 decision of the Strasbourg Court in *X v United Kingdom*, since the Human Rights Act 1998 it has become a direct issue in the courts, and has also come to be a major focus of ethical debate about law reform.

1.17 The risk management/public protection agenda has come to prominence as a result of inquiries into homicides by people who have been receiving psychiatric services. Most notable among these were the killing of Jonathan Zito by a stranger, Christopher Clunis, who suffered from schizophrenia, and the conviction in 1996 of Michael Stone, who had a personality disorder and was addicted to drugs and alcohol, for the murders of Lyn and Megan Russell. Since 1992 health authorities have had a duty to carry out an independent inquiry in any case of homicide or suicide by a mentally disordered person in their care. The inquiry into the care of Christopher Clunis[16] identified a woeful catalogue of failure to provide adequate supervision, that there had been no s 117 after-care plan, and that the authorities had failed to manage or oversee provision of health and social services for the patient. The *Report of the Independent Inquiry into the Care and Treatment of Michael Stone* carried out on behalf of the South East Coast Strategic Health Authority was completed in 2002 but not published until September 2006.[17] The Stone case has been used in support of the argument for removal of the so-called 'treatability test', the

---

[12] House of Lords, House of Commons Joint Pre-Parliamentary Scrutiny Committee *Report on the Draft Mental Health Bill* (HL Paper 79(1), HC Paper 95(1), Session 2004–2005), paras 18–22.

[13] P Fennell 'Reforming the Mental Health Act 1983: 'Joined Up Compulsion'' (2001) *Journal of Mental Health Law* (Jun) 5–20.

[14] Department of Health *National Service Framework for Mental Health: Modern Standards and Service Models* (2000); Welsh Assembly Government *Strategy Document for Adult Mental Health Services in Wales: Equity, Empowerment, Effectiveness, Efficiency* (2001).

[15] Department of Health *New Horizons: A Shared Vision for Mental Health* http://www.dh.gov.uk/en/Publicationsandstatistics/Publications/ PublicationsPolicyAndGuidance/DH_109705.

[16] Ritchie et al (2004) at p 106.

[17] South East Coast Strategic Health Authority (2006).

precondition of detention of people with personality disorder, that medical treatment in hospital must be likely to alleviate or prevent deterioration in the patient's condition. These and other homicide inquiries have led to a desire on the part of the Government to strengthen the powers of mental health professionals to require patients with mental illness to accept medication in the community, and to reduce the obstacles to detention of people with personality disorder who pose a risk to other people.

1.18　The MHA 2007 marked the culmination of a lengthy period of debate which began in July 1998 when then Secretary of State for Health, Frank Dobson, declared that community care had failed, and that 'a third way' in mental health was necessary.[18] The third way would steer a path between reliance on putting all mentally ill people in institutions – 'out of sight – out of mind' – and community care where people with mental health problems could be 'left off the books' thereby putting themselves and other people 'at risk. The third way was not greatly different from the policy proclaimed by Stephen Dorrell in the last years of John Major's Conservative Government, replacing community care by a 'Spectrum of Care'.[19] Like 'Spectrum of Care', the 'third way' involves developing a range of services, from the top-security special hospitals which provide care for patients with dangerous or violent proclivities to community provision. This would include:

> 'specialist regional secure units in every NHS Region; accommodation in every locality to provide short-term round the clock nursing care and supervision; assertive outreach teams to keep tabs on people who have been discharged and make contact with people who shy away from getting help; and changes to enable carers and professionals to respond promptly and effectively to the needs of mentally ill patients in the community.'

1.19　The 'third way' included a promise of 'root and branch review' of mental health law:[20]

> 'to reflect the opportunities and limits of modern therapies and drugs … It will cover such possible measures as compliance orders and community treatment orders to provide a prompt and effective legal basis to ensure that patients get supervised care if they do not take their medication and their condition deteriorates.'

The Secretary of State subsequently appointed a Committee chaired by Professor Genevra Richardson to consider reform of the Mental Health Act 1983. The Minister, Paul Boateng, at the Department of Health press conference launching the Richardson Committee left them in no doubt that,

---

[18]　During the last years of the Major Conservative Government policy was packaged in 'point-plans' (usually ten-point plans), for the Blair Government the mantra was 'the third way'.

[19]　*The Spectrum of Care – A summary of comprehensive local services for people with mental health problems* and the *NHS Patient's Charter for Mental Health Services* (NHS Executive – EL(97)1).

[20]　Department of Health *Press Release 98/311* (29 July 1998).

whilst they were at liberty to consider 'root and branch reform', they should remember the Government's key imperative was to 'make clear that non-compliance with agreed treatment plans is not an option'. From the very outset it became clear that imposing an obligation on community patients to comply with treatment, and making that obligation enforceable in some way, were to be the key goals of law reform.

The Richardson Committee

1.20 The Richardson Committee recommended a system that employed a broad definition of mental disorder, but narrower accompanying criteria for compulsion, provided for a single pathway to compulsion regardless of whether compulsion was to be in hospital or in the community, and placed the Mental Health Tribunal at the centre of the system of safeguards, authorising compulsion, hearing applications for review of compulsion, and approving the compulsory treatment plan. Under their proposals, after 28 days compulsory assessment, tribunal authorisation would be required for compulsory treatment either in hospital or in the community. The Committee sidestepped the issue of how compulsory powers in the community would be enforced. Clear undertakings had already been given by Minister Boateng at the committee launch, that compulsory treatment in the community did not mean forcibly injecting people on their kitchen tables. The Committee did not say anything about enforcement in the event of non-compliance with medication in the community.

1.21 The Richardson Committee was concerned that the broad concept of mental disorder might lead to a potential 'net widening' effect. Because of this, and their concern to produce a non-discriminatory and principled framework for intervention in the absence of consent, the Committee recommended the introduction of strict accompanying conditions of compulsion, including a capacity test.[21] Under their proposals anyone who lacked capacity could be subject to compulsion if necessary for their own health, or safety, or for the protection of others. Anyone retaining capacity could be subject to compulsion only if there was a substantial risk of serious harm to the health or safety of the patient or to the safety of others. The Committee also proposed a further condition of compulsion that there must be positive clinical measures, which were likely to prevent deterioration or secure an improvement in the patient's condition. Without this, they said, healthcare professionals might be forced 'to engage in activities they would regard as inappropriate and possibly unethical'.[22]

1.22 Richardson attached great importance to the inclusion of principles on the face of the Act which in their view would be educative and would provide a guide as to how provisions should be interpreted. The Committee recommended that some principles should be spelt out on the face of the

---

[21] Department of Health *Report of the Expert Committee: Review of the Mental Health Act 1983* (1999), para 5.96.
[22] Ibid, para 5.99.

legislation, whilst others should be reflected in the Code of Practice.[23] They regarded the principle of non-discrimination on grounds of mental health as central to the provision of treatment and care to those suffering from mental disorder. However, they also recognised that it would not be appropriate to express the principle within the legislation itself. Instead, they endorsed the approach of giving considerable emphasis in the Code of Practice to the principle that wherever possible the principles governing mental health care should be the same as those which govern physical health.

1.23   The Committee also recommended that the legislation should state one of its main purposes as recognising and enhancing patient autonomy. They then went on to list ten principles, noting at the outset that they did not intend them to be susceptible of specific enforcement on the part of individuals. The principles advocated included the least restrictive alternative, that necessary care, treatment and support be provided both in the least invasive manner and in the least restrictive manner and environment compatible with the delivery of safe and effective care, taking account of the safety of other patients, carers, and staff. The other principles recommended included that there should be a preference for informal and consensual care, reciprocity, participation, equality, respect for diversity, recognition of carers, provision of information, and effective communication.

The Mental Health Bills 2002 and 2004

1.24   In 2000, the Government issued a two-volume White Paper, *Part 1: The New Legal Framework and Part 2: High Risk Patients,*[24] following which the Department of Health ('DoH') and the Home Office together produced the Draft Mental Health Bill 2002, heralded as an example of 'joined-up government'.[25] The 2002 Bill rejected many of the Richardson Committee proposals, among them that the legislation should include a requirement to have regard to principles such as non-discrimination and proportionality. The Government published a Draft Bill based on the White Paper in 2002. The partnership between the Department of Health and the Home Office is the key to understanding the prominence of the public safety agenda in the process of reform. The 2002 Bill retained the proposal for a Tribunal authorised community treatment order, and contained special procedures for detaining so-called 'high risk patients', who had not yet committed an offence but might do so.

1.25   The Government identified the following failings in the MHA 1983:[26]

23   Ibid, paras 2.14–2.25.
24   *Reforming the Mental Health Act, Part 1 The New Legal Framework and Part 2 High Risk Patients* Cm 5016–1 and Cm 5016–2 (2000).
25   P Fennell 'Joined Up Compulsion: The White Paper on Reform of the Mental Health Act 1983' (2001) *Journal of Mental Health Law* (Jun) 5–20.
26   Cm 5016–1 (2000), para 1.15.

'The 1983 Act ... fails to address the challenge posed by a minority of people with mental disorder who pose a significant risk to others as a result of their disorder. It has failed properly to protect the public, patients or staff. Severely mentally ill patients have been allowed to lose contact with services once they have been discharged into the community. Such patients have been able to refuse treatment in the community. And it is the community as well as those patients which has paid a heavy price. We also need to move away from the narrow concept of treatability which applies to certain categories of mental disorder in the 1983 Act. New legislation must be clearly framed so as to allow all those who pose a significant risk of serious harm to others as a result of their mental disorder to be detained in a therapeutic environment where they can be offered care and treatment to manage their behaviour.'

The Mental Health Act 1983 was described as 'outmoded, based on treatment within hospitals, complex, confusing and lacking in explicit statements of its underlying principles'. There were two primary policy goals behind the White Papers and the 2002 Bill. The first was to introduce more effective compulsory community powers than guardianship or supervised discharge to ensure that patients in the community are subject to an effective undertaking to carry on with medication. The second was to ensure that dangerous severely personality disordered patients can be subject to detention in the mental health system. Both these policy goals have been achieved by the MHA 2007.

1.26 So widespread was the opposition to the public order ethos of the Government's proposals that an umbrella organisation was formed to oppose them, the Mental Health Alliance. The alliance included all the major stakeholders outside the Government, service user organisations, carer groups, the major mental health charities, the Royal Colleges of Psychiatry and Nursing, the British Psychological Society, UNISON, the British Association of Social Workers, the Law Society, the BMA and organisations representing children in mental health care. In broad terms the Mental Health Alliance agenda was to seek restoration of the Richardson Committee proposals, which had largely been taken up in Scotland by the Millan Committee.[27] The Millan Committee recommendations led to the Mental Health (Care and Treatment) (Scotland) Act 2003. The Scottish Act adopts a broad definition of mental disorder, and the model of tribunal authorised compulsion with a community treatment order option. It sets out principles on the face of the Act. It adopts as conditions of compulsion that the judgment of the patient in relation to decisions about the provision of medical treatment is significantly impaired by their mental disorder, and it is a condition of compulsion that medical treatment is available which would either prevent the disorder from worsening or alleviate any of the symptoms or effects of the disorder.

1.27 Meanwhile, in England the Government remained resistant to these ideas. The consultation on the 2002 Bill elicited over 2,000 responses, and the result was a resounding thumbs-down from stakeholders and from the Mental

---

[27] *New Directions: Report on the Review of the Mental Health (Scotland) Act 1984* – laid before the Scottish Parliament by the Scottish Ministers (SE/2001/56, January 2001). Available at http://www.scotland.gov.uk/health/mentalhealthlaw/millan/Report/rnhs-00.asp.

Health Alliance. The Department of Health and the Home Office rejected the evidence of the key stakeholders in their document *Improving Mental Health Law: Towards a New Mental Health Act*[28] which accompanied the Draft Mental Health Bill 2004. The 2004 Bill was introduced in substantially in the same form as the 2002 version, and was subject to strong criticism by the Joint Pre-Parliamentary Scrutiny Committee. Initially, the Government expressed determination to proceed with the 2004 Bill, but later opted to introduce an amending measure rather than a comprehensive new code.[29] One of the main reasons for this decision appears to have been concern that the Mental Health Tribunal would be unable to deal with the caseload engendered by authorising each use of long-term compulsion rather than exercising the function of reviewing detention already authorised by either a court or by application by a social worker supported by two doctors. The tribunal has retained its review function following the 2007 Act. The Mental Health Act 2007 is an amending Act, grafted on to the basic framework of the Mental Health Act 1983, rather than a comprehensive new code.

The Mental Health Act 2007

1.28 The MHA 2007 introduced a broader definition of mental disorder, recast the criteria for compulsion, established new powers of Supervised Community Treatment (community treatment orders – CTOs), and created the statutory roles of Approved Mental Health Professional ('AMHP') (to replace the Approved Social Worker ('ASW')), Responsible Clinician ('RC') (to replace the Responsible Medical Officer ('RMO')), as well as the completely new role of Independent Mental Health Advocate ('IMHA'). The MHA 2007 also made changes in relation to nearest relatives, prompted by the ruling of the European Court of Human Rights in *JT v United Kingdom*,[30] introduced into the MCA 2005 new procedures to authorise deprivation of liberty of mentally incapacitated people to comply with the ruling in *HL v United Kingdom*,[31] and changed the process of automatic referral of patients' cases to Mental Health Tribunals. The MHA 2007 introduced extra safeguards in relation to Electro Convulsive Therapy ('ECT') and new powers (new Part 4A) to give treatment in the community. The 2007 Act puts limits on the use of ECT to treat children, and entitles children to age appropriate accommodation subject to clinical need.

1.29 If a person diagnosed with mental disorder needs hospitalisation and treatment in their own interests but also for the protection of others, and they are resisting admission, that person is likely to be detained under the

---

[28]   Department of Health and Home Office *Improving Mental Health Law: Towards a New Mental Health Act* (2004).

[29]   House of Lords, House of Commons Joint Pre-Parliamentary Scrutiny Committee *Report on the Draft Mental Health Bill* (HL Paper 79(1). HC Paper 95(1), Session 2004–2005); P Fennell 'Protection! Protection! Protection! The Government's response to the Joint Parliamentary Scrutiny Committee on the Mental Health Bill 2004' (2005) *Journal of Mental Health Law* (Nov) 1–13.

[30]   (2000) 30 EHRR CD 77, ECtHR.

[31]   *(Application 45508/99)* (2004) 40 EHRR 761, ECtHR.

MHA 1983. If a person with mental disorder needs treatment for mental disorder in their own best interests, and they lack capacity to consent to in-patient admission, their care is more likely to be managed under the MCA 2005, particularly if they have a diagnosis of learning disability or a mental illness of old age.

POLICY CONTEXT: MENTAL CAPACITY LAW REFORM

1.30 The process of mental capacity law reform effectively began in 1989 with two events. One was the House of Lords ruling in *Re F (Sterilisation: Mental Patient)*[32] enunciating the common law doctrine of medical necessity that doctors have the power and, in certain cases, the duty to give a mentally incapacitated patient treatment which is necessary in her or his best interests. The Lords ruling in *Re F (Sterilisation: Mental Patient)*[33] also established the jurisdiction of the Family Division to grant declarations in the best interests of mentally incapacitated adults. The other key event was that the Law Commission began its consideration of decision-making on behalf of mentally incapacitated adults, which culminated in proposals for a Mental Incapacity Bill. Following the recommendations of the Pre-Parliamentary Scrutiny Committee, the Bill was renamed the Mental Capacity Bill to emphasise the presumption that adult patients are capable and the principle of personal autonomy.

1.31 The Mental Capacity Act 2005 and its accompanying rules, regulations and Code of Practice provide a complete legislative framework of decision-making for mentally incapacitated adults. The common law doctrine of necessity enabling treatment without consent and restraint has been codified by ss 5 and 6 which allow a range of steps to be taken on behalf of a mentally incapacitated person by carers, health and care professionals, indeed anyone where it is reasonable for that person to take action and the action is in the patient's best interests. The jurisdiction to grant declarations and to appoint deputies will be taken over by the Court of Protection.[34] The Act recognises the binding nature of 'valid and applicable' advance decisions made by a person, who is capable, to refuse specified treatments should they lose capacity in the future. It provides for a person who is still capable to grant a lasting power of attorney to a person of their choice to take decisions about their property and affairs health and personal welfare, in the event that they become incapable in the future. It confers jurisdiction on the Court of Protection to appoint a deputy, who is a proxy decision maker on matters concerning property and affairs, or health and personal welfare, depending on the scope of the order of appointment.

---

[32]   [1990] 2 AC 1, HL.
[33]   *Re F (Sterilisation: Mental Patient)* sub nom *F v West Berkshire Health Authority (Mental Health Act Commission intervening)* [1990] 2 AC 1, [1989] 2 All ER 545, [1989] 2 WLR 1025, [1989] 2 FLR 376, HL.
[34]   MCA 2005, ss 15–19.

'The *Bournewood* Gap'

1.32 Unlike the MHA 1983, which operates by a procedure requiring applications and supporting medical evidence on statutory forms, like the common law before it, the MCA 2005 operates by providing in ss 5 and 6 a defence in respect of acts of care and treatment done for a person where reasonable steps have been taken to assess capacity, where the person is reasonably believed to lack capacity and where the intervention is reasonably believed to be in the person's best interests. The MCA 2005 as originally drafted could not be used to authorise deprivation of liberty. Under the Mental Health Act 1959 and the MHA 1983 it was accepted practice that patients who lacked capacity and did not resist admission to hospital should be admitted informally, without using Mental Health Act powers of detention. It was only if the incapacitated person 'persistently and purposefully' attempted to leave hospital, or refused to go there in the first place, that powers of detention should be used. This raised the question whether it was lawful to subject a person to 'de facto detention' without the rights of review which attach to the legal status of detained patient, if they would be prevented from leaving if they tried to do so, such as might be the situation of an elderly patient with dementia on a locked ward.

1.33 The legality of this approach was not questioned until the late 1990s when the case of *R v Bournewood Community and Mental Health NHS Trust, ex parte L (Secretary of State for Health and others intervening)* was taken to the House of Lords, and then, as *HL v United Kingdom,*[35] to the European Court of Human Rights. In *HL v United Kingdom,* the Strasbourg Court held that HL, who lacked mental capacity because of autism, and who had been admitted informally to a hospital run by the Bournewood Trust, should have been detained using a procedure prescribed by law.

1.34 Mr L had autism and profound intellectual disability. He lacked capacity to consent or dissent to being in hospital. He had lived with his carers, the Es, for three years. One day he became agitated and disturbed at a day centre, was given valium, and was taken to the learning disability hospital run by the Bournewood Trust and kept there. His doctor instructed staff that he was to be stopped from leaving if he tried to do so. Although he never did attempt to leave the hospital, his carers, the Es, were prevented from visiting, in case he might want to go home with them. He showed symptoms of abandonment, withdrawing, becoming sad, and losing weight. He was also on higher doses of sedative medication in hospital than were ever necessary in the community. His psychiatrist admitted him under the common law doctrine of necessity, rather than using the powers of detention under the Mental Health Act 1983.

1.35 The carers challenged the common law detention on the grounds that the procedure prescribed by law under the Mental Health Act 1983 had not been followed. Their application for habeas corpus failed at first instance, but the Court of Appeal held that L had been detained and that his detention was

---

[35]   *(Application 45508/99)* (2004) 40 EHRR 761, ECtHR.

unlawful because it had not been carried out in accordance with the Mental Health Act. Following this ruling, L was discharged from hospital and returned to the care of Mr and Mrs E, where he has continued to make steady progress ever since. The House of Lords in *Bournewood*[36] ruled by a 3:2 majority that HL had not been detained for the purposes of the law of false imprisonment. They also ruled unanimously that, even if he had been detained, there was a power at common law to restrain and detain a mentally incapacitated person in their best interests. The common law doctrine of necessity was extended by the House of Lords to confer a power on a doctor to restrain and detain a mentally incapacitated adult if it was necessary in his or her best interests. The House of Lords decided *Bournewood* just before the Human Rights Act 1998 came into force.

1.36 An application was made on L's behalf to the Strasbourg Court, which held in *HL v United Kingdom* that, where a compliant incapacitated patient is to be deprived of his liberty, this must be done in accordance with a procedure prescribed by law. Whatever the position under English law, the Strasbourg Court held that removal of HL to the hospital, and his retention there without access to his carers, amounted to a deprivation of liberty under the Convention, and had to be carried out in accordance with a procedure prescribed by law, as required by Art 5(1)(e) of the Convention. Moreover, he was entitled, under Art 5(4), to the opportunity, by himself, or through a proxy, to challenge the lawfulness of that detention. The Strasbourg Court refused to treat compliant incapacitated patients as on a par with capable patients who were consenting, and reaffirmed the importance of the right to liberty:

> 'The right to liberty in a democratic society is too important for a person to lose the benefit of Convention protection simply because he has given himself up to detention, especially when it is not disputed that that person is legally incapable of consenting to, or disagreeing with, the proposed action.'

The ruling in *HL v United Kingdom* came at a very late stage in the Parliamentary passage of the Mental Capacity Bill. The Mental Capacity Act 2005 originally provided that the power to restrain a person under s 6 of that Act does not authorise 'deprivations of liberty'.[37] Various last minute amendments to the Mental Capacity Bill intended to fill 'the *Bournewood* Gap' were introduced and then abandoned. The ill-fated Mental Health Bill 2004 was beginning its Pre-Parliamentary Scrutiny. The Government felt that the problem could be addressed in a considered way by waiting for the introduction of mental health legislation, which could either provide for deprivations to take place under a Mental Health Act procedure or could introduce a new procedure by amendment of the Mental Capacity Act. The MHA 2007 introduced amendments into the Mental Capacity Act 2005[38] to plug 'the

---

[36] *R v Bournewood Community and Mental Health NHS Trust, ex parte L (Secretary of State for Health and others intervening)* [1998] 3 All ER 289, HL.

[37] Originally s 6(5) of the MCA 2005, now repealed.

[38] MHA 2007, s 50, and Mental Capacity Act 2005, Schs A1 and 1A. This came into force in March 2009.

Bournewood Gap' with a procedure to authorise deprivations of liberty of mentally incapacitated adults. '*Bournewood* patients' are be deprived of their liberty under the Mental Capacity Act rather than the Mental Health Act.

CONCLUSION

1.37 The Mental Health Act 1983 (as amended by the MHA 2007) provides for detention and treatment without consent on grounds of mental disorder and risk to self or to others. The Mental Capacity Act 2005 authorises deprivation of liberty in a hospital if the patient has a mental disorder, lacks capacity, is not resisting admission, and deprivation of liberty is necessary in her or his best interests. The MCA 2005 also authorises deprivation of liberty in a residential care home of someone who is incapable of consenting, even if they are resisting admission.

Divergence between England and Wales

1.38 An important change flowing from the 2007 Act reforms is that England and Wales now each have separate regulations dealing with detention, consent to treatment, community treatment and guardianship,[39] conflict of interests,[40] designation of nurses eligible to exercise the holding power under s 5(4),[41] Independent Mental Health Advocates[42] and Approved Mental Health Professionals.[43] England and Wales have separate Directions on eligibility to be an Approved Clinician for the purposes of the Mental Health Act 1983,[44] and each has a separate Code of Practice on the Mental Health Act 1983.[45] In England the jurisdiction of Mental Health Review Tribunals has been vested in the Health, Education and Social Care Chamber of the First-tier Tribunal, whilst in Wales the jurisdiction remains with the Mental Health Review

---

[39] Mental Health (Hospital, Guardianship and Treatment) (England) Regulations 2008, SI 2008/1184; the Mental Health (Hospital, Guardianship, Community Treatment and Consent to Treatment) (Wales) Regulations 2008, SI 2008/2439 (W 212).

[40] Mental Health (Conflicts of Interest) (England) Regulations 2008, SI 2008/1205; the Mental Health (Conflicts of Interest) (Wales) Regulations 2008, SI 2008/2440 (W 213).

[41] Mental Health (Nurses) (England) Order 2008, SI 2008/1208; the Mental Health (Nurses) (Wales) Order 2008, SI 2008/2441 (W 214).

[42] Mental Health (Independent Mental Health Advocates) (Wales) Regulations 2008, SI 2008/2437 (W 210); the Mental Health Act 1983 (Independent Mental Health Advocates) (England) Regulations 2008, SI 2008/3166.

[43] Mental Health (Approved Mental Health Professionals) (Approval) (England) Regulations 2008; SI 2008/1206; the Mental Health (Approval of Persons to be Approved Mental Health Professionals) (Wales) Regulations 2008, SI 2008/2436 (W 209).

[44] Mental Health Act 1983 Approved Clinician (General) Directions 2008 Issued under ss 7, 8 and 273 of the National Health Service Act 2006 http://www.dh.gov.uk; Mental Health Act 1983 Approved Clinician (Wales) Directions 2008 issued under ss 12, 13 and 203 of the National Health Service (Wales) Act 2006.

[45] Department of Health *Code of Practice: Mental Health Act 1983* (2008) http://www.doh.gov. uk; Welsh Assembly Government, Mental Health Act 1983 Code of Practice for Wales (2008) http://www.wales.nhs.uk.

Tribunal for Wales. Each has separate Tribunal Rules.[46] England and Wales each have separate regulations on the Deprivation of Liberty safeguards.[47]

1.39 Not only do England and Wales have separate subordinate legislation, there will soon also be significant differences in the provisions of the primary legislation between the two jurisdictions. The Welsh Assembly has now passed the Mental Health (Wales) Measure 2010 which will add 56 new sections and two Schedules to the Mental Health Act 1983 as it applies in Wales. The Measure also contains extensive rule making powers. The intent is to entitle mental health service users to early intervention and to entitle all patients, not just those subject to compulsion, to an Independent Mental Health Advocate.[48]

1.40 Chapter 2 summarises the reforms introduced by the Mental Health Act 2007 to the Mental Health Act 1983, to the Domestic Violence, Crime and Victims Act 2004 and to the Mental Capacity Act 2005, and the functions that they are designed to perform within the mental health system. Chapter 2 will conclude with a consideration of the potential impact of the United Nations Convention on the Rights of Persons with Disabilities.

---

[46] Tribunal Procedure (First-tier Tribunal) Health, Education and Social Care Chamber) Rules 2008, SI 2008/2699; the Mental Health Review Tribunal for Wales Rules 2008, SI 2008/2705 (L 17).

[47] In England the regulations are: the Mental Capacity (Deprivation of Liberty: Standard Authorisations, Assessments and Ordinary Residence) Regulations 2008, SI 2008/1858; the Mental Capacity (Deprivation of Liberty: Appointment of Relevant Person's Representative) Regulations 2008, SI 2008/1315; and the Mental Capacity (Deprivation of Liberty: Appointment of Relevant Person's Representative) (Amendment) Regulations 2008, SI 2008/2368 which correct a minor defect in the earlier regulations: they prevent supervisory bodies from selecting paid representatives from amongst their own employees, thus avoiding any conflicts of interest. In Wales the relevant regulations are: the Mental Capacity (Deprivation of Liberty: Assessments, Standard Authorisations and Disputes about Residence) (Wales) Regulations 2009, SI 2009/783 (W 69); and the Mental Capacity (Deprivation of Liberty: Appointment of Relevant Person's Representative) (Wales) Regulations 2009, SI 2009/266 (W 29).

[48] The text of the new Measure, which has yet to receive Royal Assent, may be found at http://www.assemblywales.org/bus-home/bus-legislation/bus-leg-measures/business-legislation-measures-mhs-2.htm.

Chapter 2

OVERVIEW OF THE
MENTAL HEALTH ACT 2007

FUNCTIONS OF MENTAL HEALTH LEGISLATION

2.1 Since the Mental Health Act (MHA) 1959 English and Welsh mental health legislation has performed a number of functions, and has followed the same essential framework. The basic structure of powers remains following the amendments to the Mental Health Act 1983 introduced by the Mental Health Act 2007, and the 1983 Act as amended continues to perform the following functions:

(a) defining mental disorder;

(b) providing powers to detain and treat without consent;

(c) providing compulsory community powers;

(d) providing safeguards against arbitrary detention or unnecessary treatment (particularly upholding Convention Rights under Arts 3, 5 and 8);

(e) setting out principles for the treatment of mentally disordered people;

(f) providing powers and safeguards in relation to treating children for mental disorder;

(g) providing a framework for transfer of patients in lawful custody from one jurisdiction to another; and

(h) providing effective protection for mentally disordered people under the criminal law.

The function of providing a framework for managing property and affairs of mentally disordered people has been removed from Part 7 of the Mental Health Act 1983 and is now dealt with under the Mental Capacity Act 2005. This chapter concludes by examining the potential impact of the UN Convention on the Rights of Persons with Disabilities which purportedly prohibits specialist mental health legislation as discriminatory on grounds of disability.

DEFINING 'MENTAL DISORDER'

2.2   The first function of mental health legislation is to define the scope of the term 'mental disorder' and thereby delineate broadly the population who may be subject to detention. Part 1 of the MHA 1983 defined 'mental disorder'. It followed the pattern of the MHA 1959 by having a general definition of mental disorder for the (up to) 28 day power of admission for assessment (mental illness, psychopathic disorder, arrested or incomplete development of mind and 'any other disorder or disability of mind'). A narrower, more elaborate system of subcategories applied to admission for treatment for up to six months: mental illness, and severe mental impairment (sometimes referred to as the major disorders), and mental impairment and psychopathic disorder. All of these, bar mental illness, required an association with abnormally aggressive or seriously irresponsible conduct. Someone with a learning disability or a personality disorder unaccompanied by abnormally aggressive or seriously irresponsible conduct could not be detained for treatment, but could be detained for up to 28 days' assessment.

2.3   A further drawback of the subcategories was that detention on grounds of mental impairment or psychopathic disorder could only take place if the patient was 'treatable' in the sense that medical treatment in hospital was likely to alleviate or prevent deterioration in his condition. This requirement was construed broadly by the courts. In *Reid v Secretary of State for Scotland*[1] the House of Lords held that the term was wide enough to include treatment which alleviates or prevents deterioration in the symptoms of the disorder, even though it did not necessarily produce such an impact on the disorder itself, and that anger management classes in the structured environment of a high security hospital were likely to be preventing deterioration in the patient's mental condition. This was because they resulted in the patient being less physically aggressive, and if he were not in hospital he would probably commit criminal offences which would lead to an inevitable deterioration in his condition. As Richard Jones put it, the interpretation in the case law of the treatability test was so broad that it was 'difficult to imagine the circumstances that would cause a patient to fail it'.[2] In *Reid v Secretary of State for Scotland*[3] Lord Hope held that the provision gives effect to the policy that people with psychopathic disorder or mental impairment 'should only be detained under compulsory powers if there is a good prospect that the treatment they will receive there will be of benefit'. His Lordship went on to hold that the term 'treatment' was 'wide enough to include treatment which alleviates or prevents deterioration of the symptoms of the mental disorder'.[4] Lord Hutton[5] held that the test could be satisfied where 'anger management in the structured setting of the State Hospital in a supervised environment resulted in the patient being less physically aggressive'. Despite the breadth of the treatability test, the

---

1   [1999] 1 All ER 481, HL.
2   RM Jones *Mental Health Act Manual* (Sweet and Maxwell, 10th edn, 2006), p 42.
3   [1999] 1 All ER 481 at 493, HL.
4   [1999] 1 All ER 481 at 497, HL.
5   [1999] 1 All ER 481 at 515, HL.

Government saw it as a fault-line in the legislation which enables psychiatrists to decide that a person with psychopathic disorder who might be dangerous to others should not be detained because they are not treatable. The effect of the case-law was that a person being contained as a detained patient in the structured environment of a hospital might be held to be treatable, depending on the production of a suitably worded therapeutic rationale for such 'milieu therapy' Nevertheless, in the MHA 2007, in addition to adopting a general definition of mental disorder – 'any disorder or disability of the mind' – for all durations of detention, the Government replaced the treatability test with a new requirement in s 4 of the MHA 2007 that treatment must be available for the patient which is 'appropriate in his case, taking into account the nature and degree of the mental disorder and all other circumstances of his case'. This is discussed further below in chapter 3 at **3.59–3.71**.

2.4 The MHA 1983 now applies one broad definition – 'any disorder or disability of the mind' – to all types of detention whether as an offender or a non-offender patient. This new definition is modeled on the 'catch all' definition previously used for admission for assessment: 'any other disorder or disability of mind'. The scope of admission for assessment under s 2 has not been not significantly altered. A person with a learning disability unaccompanied by abnormally aggressive or seriously irresponsible conduct can still be admitted under s 2. It remains the case following the 2007 Act changes that a person with a learning disability[6] can only be detained for treatment under s 3 if the disability is associated with abnormally aggressive or seriously irresponsible conduct on his part. But the term psychopathic disorder disappears from the Act. By broadening and simplifying the definition of mental disorder to 'any disorder or disability of the mind', the 2007 Act has removed many of the perceived obstacles to detention of people with personality disorder. No longer is abnormally aggressive or seriously irresponsible conduct necessary before people with a personality disorder may be detained. They may be detained for treatment if appropriate treatment including nursing and psychological treatment is available and provided detention is deemed necessary for their health or safety or for the protection of others. There is no longer any requirement that medical treatment must be likely to alleviate or prevent deterioration in the patient's condition.

2.5 The MHA 2007 also removed from the MHA 1983 all exclusions other than 'dependence on alcohol or drugs' neither of which may be considered to be a disorder or disability of the mind. By removing the sexual deviancy exclusion the Government intended to bring paraphilia (and hence paedophilia) clearly within the scope of detainable mental disorders. The concern was that the sexual deviancy exclusion enabled paedophiles to avoid detention under mental health legislation, where this might be otherwise deemed necessary on grounds of risk to others. The changes to the definition of

---

6   Learning disability is defined as a state of arrested or incomplete development of the mind which includes significant impairment of intelligence and social functioning: MHA 1983, s 1(4), as inserted by MHA 2007, s 2(3).

mental disorder and the impact of the change from treatability to availability of appropriate treatment are discussed in full in chapter 3.

PROVIDING POWERS TO DETAIN AND TREAT WITHOUT CONSENT

2.6   The second function of mental health legislation is providing a framework of powers whereby health and social care professionals may detain and treat mentally disordered people without consent. Powers to detain non-offender patients are provided in Part II of the Act, powers to detain offenders in Part III. The first key task of a framework of compulsory powers is to specify which professional groups are eligible to exercise those powers, and who is eligible to provide the evidence necessary to justify detention. The second is to set the criteria for detention or compulsory powers in the community. Chapter 4 explains and discusses the statutory roles of the Approved Mental Health Professional ('AMHP') and the Responsible Clinician ('RC'). Chapter 5 deals with the role of relatives, carers, Independent Mental Health Advocates and Hospital Managers. Chapter 6 deals with powers to detain patients under Part II of the Mental Health Act 1983, and the power to deprive mentally incapacitated adults of their liberty under the changes introduced to the Mental Capacity Act 2005 by the MHA 2007.

Who may exercise compulsory powers? The statutory roles: Approved Mental Health Professionals, Responsible Clinicians, Nearest Relatives and Independent Mental Health Advocates

2.7   Although it was and still is possible for an application for detention or guardianship to come from the patient's nearest relative, under the original MHA 1983 an application would normally come from a specially trained Approved Social Worker, whose role was to ensure that the necessary treatment could not be provided without detention, to see that the section was effectively carried out, medical recommendations were obtained, and the patient was safely 'taken and conveyed' in legal custody (with police support if necessary) to the hospital. In response to concerns about poor decision-making by social workers under the MHA 1959, the MHA 1983 required an increased mandatory statutory period of training before a person could become an Approved Social Worker ('ASW') and thus entitled to apply for a person's detention under the Act.

Approved Mental Health Professional ('AMHP')

2.8   The MHA 2007 opened the power to apply for detention to 'Approved Mental Health Professionals' who need not be a social worker but may be a nurse, psychologist, or occupational therapist with appropriately recognised training. The 1983 Act still requires an application for non-emergency admission to be supported by two medical recommendations, to the effect that the patient is suffering from mental disorder of a nature or degree warranting detention in the interests of his health or safety or for the protection of others. One of the recommending doctors must be approved under s 12 of the MHA 1983 as having special experience in the diagnosis or treatment of mental disorder. The evidential requirement of medical recommendations from doctors remains.

Responsible Clinician

2.9   The second major professional role change affects those eligible to be the person in charge of decisions about treatment without consent and prolongation of detention, who, under every Act since 1959 has been 'the responsible medical officer' ('RMO'), who had to be a doctor. The RMO has been replaced by the 'responsible clinician' ('RC') who need not be a doctor but may be a nurse, psychologist, an occupational therapist, or a social worker, provided they have undergone responsible clinician training. The MHA 1959 devolved the functions of being in charge of treatment and renewing detention from the Medical Superintendent to the RMO, but at the same time preserved the medical monopoly of power. The MHA 2007 dismantles that monopoly, by potentially conferring the power to be in charge of the management of the case of a detained or community patient on other professions. The legal effects of these changing professional roles will be discussed in detail in chapter 4.

Nearest Relative

2.10   The MHA 2007 has also introduced reforms affecting the non-professional role of the 'nearest relative' who has the power to apply for compulsory admission, to seek discharge and challenge the patient's detention before a Mental Health Tribunal ('MHT'). The identity of the nearest relative is determined according to a statutory list, beginning with husband or wife, father or mother, son or daughter. The 2007 Act modifies that list to recognise civil partners, as well as same or opposite sex couples living together as man and wife.[7] The rights of the nearest relative remain essentially unchanged by the 2007 Act. The Act does however introduce a new possibility for the patient to seek displacement of an unsuitable nearest relative. This is necessitated by successful challenges in the European Court of Human Rights and in the English Courts under the Human Rights Act 1998.

2.11   The nearest relative has a right under Art 8 of the European Convention on Human Rights to respect for their family life with the patient and vice versa. But the patient also has the right to respect for privacy under Art 8. In *JT v United Kingdom*[8] the applicant complained was that her nearest relative according to the statutory formula was her mother, who was living with a man who JT alleged had abused her in the past. Each time JT applied for discharge from detention to a MHRT, the tribunal rules required that her mother, as

---

[7]   See *R (on the application of SSG) v Liverpool City Council* at http://www.dh.gov.uk/en/Policyandguidance/Healthandsocialcaretopics/Mentalhealth/DH_4077674.

[8]   (2000) 30 EHRR CD 77, ECtHR.

nearest relative, be informed. JT objected to her mother being given information about her life. The European Commission on Human Rights held that the absence in the MHA 1983 of any possibility for a patient to apply to the county court to change her nearest relative was an interference with her right to respect for her private life under Art 8(1) of the European Convention and could not be justified under Art 8(2). A friendly settlement was reached whereby the UK Government undertook to:

(a)   enable a patient to apply to the court to replace his nearest relative where there were reasonable grounds to object to a particular individual acting in that capacity; and

(b)   prevent certain persons from acting as the nearest relative of the patient.

Subsequently, the English High Court in *R (on the application of M) v Secretary of State for Health*[9] granted a declaration of incompatibility under the Human Rights Act 1998, holding that the absence of a right for a patient to seek displacement of a nearest relative was incompatible with Art 8.

2.12 Following the MHA 2007 the nearest relative has retained the rights set out in the MHA 1983, and the patient will have the right to apply to the county court to displace a nearest relative on grounds of unsuitability, as necessitated by the friendly settlement in *JT v United Kingdom*. In *R (on the application of E) v Bristol City Council*[10] the Court held that in order to ensure compatibility with Art 8 the Approved Social Worker's duty to consult the nearest relative about compulsory admission 'if practicable' does not apply if the patient objects to that person being consulted as the nearest relative. This is still the position. The AMHP does not have a duty to consult the NR if the patient is capable and objects to the consultation of that person, but the NR remains the NR until displaced or until they confer their function on someone else. The Nearest Relative is discussed in chapter 5.

Independent Mental Health Advocates

2.13 Section 30(2) of the MHA 2007 introduced new ss 130A–130D to the MHA 1983, placing a duty upon the Secretary of State (or Welsh Assembly) to provide advocacy services for all detained patients (except those held under s 4, 5, 135 or 136), guardianship patients and patients subject to community treatment orders. Advocacy must include help in obtaining information about and understanding the provisions of the Act which subject him to compulsion, any conditions or restrictions, what medical treatment is being given or is proposed and why, and the requirements of the Act which apply in relation to that treatment. Advocacy must also include help in obtaining information about and understanding any rights which may be exercised by or in relation to him and help by way of representation or otherwise in exercising those rights.

---

9   [2003] EWHC 1094 (Admin).
10   [2005] EWHC 74 (Admin), [2005] MHLR 83.

Section 130D places a duty upon hospital managers and in certain cases responsible clinicians to provide qualifying patients with information that advocacy services are available. Advocates have the right to meet patients in private, and to meet professionals. They have access to patient records only where a capable patient gives consent, or, in the case of an incapable patient, where access would not conflict with a decision of a health care attorney, a deputy, or the Court of Protection, and the person holding the records agrees that the records are relevant to the matter at issue and access is 'appropriate'. Advocacy services are discussed in chapter 5.

The criteria for detention in hospital

Human rights

2.14 The second key aspect of a system of compulsory powers is that it sets the criteria which must be satisfied before detention may take place. Article 5(1) of the Convention on Human Rights protects against arbitrary detention. Article 5(1)(e) reflects the attitudes of the 1950s, authorising detention on grounds of unsoundness of mind, alcoholism, addiction to drugs, vagrancy, or to prevent the spread of infectious diseases, provided that detention takes place in accordance with a procedure prescribed by law. The Strasbourg Court has built additional safeguards through its jurisprudence. In 1979 in *Winterwerp v Netherlands*[11] the Court laid down three important substantive and procedural requirements for lawful detentions of persons of unsound mind:

(a)   except in emergencies, the individual must reliably be shown to be suffering from a true mental disorder on the basis of objective expertise;

(b)   the mental disorder must be of a kind or degree justifying confinement;

(c)   those carrying out the detention must satisfy themselves at intervals that the criteria for detention continue to be met.[12]

Winterwerp also established that mere deviancy from society's norms is not to be regarded as mental disorder, and detention must be a proportionate response to the patient's circumstances.[13]

2.15   *Winterwerp* laid down two procedural requirements. The first is that the objective medical evidence must be presented to a competent authority. In the case of non-offender patients the competent authority is the hospital managers, with offenders it is the sentencing court. The second requirement is that the detaining authority must at intervals review the continued need for detention.

---

[11]   *(Application 6301/73)* Series A, No 33, p 16, para 37, ECtHR.
[12]   *Winterwerp v The Netherlands* ibid; *X v United Kingdom (Application 7215/75)* (1981) 4 EHRR 188, ECtHR; and *Van der Leer v Netherlands (Application 11509/85)* (1990) 12 EHRR 567, ECtHR.
[13]   *Litwa v Poland (Application 26629/95)* (2000) 63 BMLR 199, ECtHR.

Non-offender patients

2.16 The *Winterwerp* requirements are met in the detention procedures for non-offenders under the Mental Health Act 1983. Admission is by administrative process, based on professional expertise and checks and balances. Only an Approved Mental Health Professional ('AMHP') (with specialised mental health training) or the patient's nearest relative may apply for detention, supported by two medical recommendations, one from a person with psychiatric expertise. The AMHP presents objective medical evidence (the medical recommendations) of a true mental disorder of a kind or degree warranting detention to a competent authority, the hospital managers. The competent authority has the duty to review the detention at reasonable intervals and to discharge if the criteria are not met. An application may only be made if the treatment cannot be provided without detention, reflecting the principle of proportionality. Nothing in Art 5 or the case-law requires admission to be authorised by a court or tribunal, so the current admission procedures are Convention compliant.[14]

2.17 The criteria which must be met for detention for treatment of a non-offender patient under s 3 of the MHA 1983 now are:

(a)   that the patient is suffering from mental disorder of a nature or degree which makes it appropriate for him to receive medical treatment in a hospital;

(b)   that it is necessary for the health or safety of the patient or for the protection of other persons that he should receive such treatment and it cannot be provided unless he is detained; and

(c)   that appropriate medical treatment is available to him.

The major differences introduced by the MHA 2007 were:

(a)   the removal of the subcategories of mental disorder which previously applied to detention for treatment under s 3; and

(b)   the replacement of the so-called 'treatability test' with the test of availability of appropriate treatment.

Appropriate treatment is available

2.18 Medical treatment for mental disorder is redefined in s 145. It includes nursing and also psychological intervention and specialist mental health habilitation, rehabilitation and care. Psychological interventions are expressly mentioned for the first time. These include psychotherapy and other interactive treatments requiring co-operation from the patient, often the main treatments

---

[14]   *HL v United Kingdom* (2004) 40 EHRR 761, ECtHR.

used for people with personality disorders. The 'treatability test' under the MHA 1983 applied to psychopathic disorder and mental impairment. The doctor had to certify that medical treatment was likely to alleviate or prevent deterioration in the patient's condition, which would be hard to do if the patient was resolutely not co-operating. This might happen if a person with a personality disorder refused to engage with cognitive behaviour therapy, which requires active participation. Treatment might be available and appropriate but unlikely to make any difference if the patient were refusing to participate. The MHA 2007 requires only that appropriate treatment is available. Treatment must have the *purpose* of alleviating or preventing 'a worsening of the disorder or more of its symptoms or manifestations'.[15] But it need not be likely to achieve those purposes, although it is difficult to envisage a doctor prescribing treatment which s/he does not think is likely to benefit the patient. The patient's refusal to accept treatment can no longer be an obstacle to detention, as long as the treatment is available.

2.19 The 'treatability issue' has generated massive debate for more than a decade. It is not overdramatic to say that opinion leaders within the psychiatric profession saw the issue as crucial in preserving their role as doctors rather than agents of state policies of preventive detention. Service users see the issue in terms of entitlement to therapeutic intervention rather than containment. The Government perceived the treatability test as a serious fault-line in mental health legislation which gave psychiatrists discretion not to detain people with personality disorders who pose a risk to others, or to themselves.

2.20 The general definition of mental disorder means the welcome disappearance of the stigmatising term psychopathic disorder from the face of the Act. It also preserves and arguably extends the possibilities to detain people with a personality disorder, who are believed to pose a risk to self or others. If violent conduct is a manifestation of their disorder, available appropriate treatment of that manifestation might include nursing supervision, as well as psychological interventions such as anger management or cognitive behaviour therapy. It could also include specialist mental health habilitation, rehabilitation and care. These changes have set the legal scene for increased use of mental health legislation to detain people who have not yet committed a crime but who have a personality disorder and pose a risk to self or to others. This has been done by removing various sources of discretionary power not to detain, such as the treatability test, and the exclusions in relation to sexual deviancy and other immoral conduct.

The Bournewood Gap: deprivation of liberty of mentally incapacitated adults

2.21 Section 50 of the MHA 2007 was intended to take the consequences of *HL v the United Kingdom*. Section 50(4) repeals the provisions in the MCA 2005 prohibiting deprivations of liberty. It inserts new ss 4A, 4B and 16A

---

[15] MHA 1983, s 145(4), as inserted by MHA 2007, s 7(3).

into the Mental Capacity Act 2005. These provisions make it lawful to deprive a person of their liberty only if a standard or urgent authorisation (under the new Schs A1 and 1A to the 2005 Act) is in force or the Court of Protection has ordered a deprivation of liberty in deciding a personal welfare matter, or if an application has been made to court and it is immediately necessary to save the person's life or to perform a vital act. Standard or urgent authorisations may be sought after the person has already been deprived of his or her liberty. The procedures for DoLs authorisations as they have come to be known, apply to deprivations of liberty in hospitals and care homes. They extend the scope of powers of detention considerably and bring into the system many patients who would hitherto have been dealt with informally. It is open to debate whether the new procedures meet the requirements of the case-law from the Strasbourg Court and from the English Courts under the Human Rights Act 1998. It is also suggested that a more effective system might be to have built on the reforms to guardianship in the 2007 Act and to use guardianship to authorise deprivation of liberty. These complex procedures are explained and discussed in chapter 6 which deals with all the Procedures for Detention of Non-offender Patients under the Mental Health Act and the Mental Capacity Act.

Offender patients

2.22   Part III of the MHA 1983 provides a framework of powers to sentence to a hospital order with or without restrictions, to remand to hospital for reports or treatment, and to transfer mentally disordered prisoners from prison to hospital. The main changes flow from the definition of mental disorder – remand for treatment, sentencing and transfer powers were limited to patients suffering from various subcategories of mental disorder. These limitations have been removed by the substitution of 'any disorder or disability of mind' for references to the subcategories wherever they appeared under the 1983 Act. As is the case with non-offenders, the scope of powers to detain mentally disordered offenders is further increased by replacing the 'treatability test' with the test of 'availability of appropriate treatment'.

2.23   Section 37 of the MHA 1983 enables offenders with mental disorder to be sentenced to hospital orders for six months renewable. The new wide definition of mental disorder and the test of availability of appropriate treatment apply to this power. Section 41 provides that a Crown Court judge who considers it necessary may impose restrictions on discharge. One significant change introduced by the MHA 2007 is that whilst previously under the MHA 1983 these restrictions could be time limited or without limit of time, henceforth they are automatically without limit of time. The restrictions are that the patient may not be granted leave of absence or discharge from hospital, nor may he be transferred to another hospital without the leave of the Mental Health Unit in the Ministry of Justice, acting on behalf of the Secretary of State. The reforms to Part III of the 1983 Act are discussed in chapter 7 which deals with mentally disordered offenders.

The criteria which must be met for compulsory powers in the community

2.24 Under the Mental Health Act 1983 there were three compulsory powers over patients in the community:

(a) extended leave under s 17;

(b) guardianship under s 7;

(c) after-care under supervision under ss 25A–25J.

Neither guardianship nor after-care under supervision were much used.[16] Section 17 leave was the most frequently used vehicle for imposing control over patients in the community. The reason for its attractiveness was its simplicity. It is granted and may be revoked on the authority of a single clinician. The ultimate sanction for non-compliance is detention, if the clinician considers continued non-compliance will make it necessary to recall the patient for the patient's health or safety or for the protection of others. The difficulty is that, in order for recall to be an effective sanction, there must be a bed available for the patient to be recalled to.

2.25 Under the MHA 1959 and the MHA 1983, s 17 leave was granted by the Responsible Medical Officer, usually a consultant psychiatrist, and this power was used to provide the equivalent of a community treatment order, by granting leave subject to a condition of compliance with medication. Following the MHA 2007 amendments, s 17 leave is granted by the responsible clinician ('RC'), who need not be a doctor. A patient may be granted leave subject to such conditions as the RC thinks necessary in the interests of the patient or for the protection of other persons. Under the 1959 and 1983 Acts this power has been exercised by the Responsible Medical Officer, following the 2007 Act it passed to the Responsible Clinician. The patient remains liable to be detained. This means that the patient is still subject to the section authorising detention, and may be returned to hospital and to detained patient status if deemed necessary by the Responsible Clinician for the patient's own health or safety or for the protection of others. The case-law on s 17 leave centres around the need, if this is arrangement is to be long-term, for renewal of the section authorising the patient's detention, raising questions about the lawfulness of renewing a section allowing detention when the patient is living in the community. Current case-law holds that the patient's liability to detention may be renewed

---

[16] At any time about 1,000 people are subject to Mental Health Act guardianship in England and Wales. Jonathan Bindman's *Evaluation of Supervised Discharge and Guardianship* (published by the Department of Health in 2002) found that: 'Both measures continue to be used only for a very small proportion of patients under the care of mental health services and their apparent effectiveness is likely to be a consequence of careful selection of patients.' The numbers under supervised discharge went from 160 in 1997 to 596 in 1999 (Department of Health Research Findings Register – see http://www.refer.nhs.uk/ViewRecord.asp?ID=703).

repeatedly while he or she continues to live in the community, so long as the patient needs some treatment in hospital, not necessarily as an in-patient.[17]

2.26 Chapter 4 of the MHA 2007 repeals ss 25A–25J of the MHA 1983 on after-care under supervision and replaces them with new ss 17A–17G introducing the new 'community treatment orders' ('CTOs') or supervised community treatment ('SCT'). After-care under supervision ('ACUS') was introduced by the Mental Health (Patients in the Community) Act 1995 in a climate of concern about homicides by people receiving treatment for mental disorder in the community, and whilst the practice of renewing detention of patient on s 17 leave was subject to challenge in the courts. After-care under supervision was limited to detained patients who were not subject to Home Office (now Ministry of Justice) restrictions, and who had been detained following admission for treatment for up to six months, renewable under a hospital order, or following transfer from prison. Such a patient could be placed under supervised discharge and could be subject to various requirements including residing at a specified place and attending a specified place to receive medical treatment. A patient who did not attend could be 'taken and conveyed' in custody to that place. The patient could then be held at that place while a decision was taken whether they could be given treatment under common law using reasonable force, or whether they needed to be detained under the 1983 Act. ACUS was not widely used.

2.27 The low use of after care under supervision was generally attributed to the fact that, by comparison with s 17 leave, the procedural requirements were onerous, and there was a lack of clarity about what should happen when a patient was taken and conveyed to the place of treatment and still refused the treatment. The ultimate sanction – re-detention – could be employed if the professionals went through the sectioning procedure afresh. By contrast, under s 17 re-detention by recall requires the authority of one clinician. Scarcely surprising then, that s 17 remained the favoured option. Particularly so, once the case-law recognised the lawfulness of renewing the authority to detain a patient living in the community, as long as some of the treatment required is received in hospital, not necessarily as an in-patient. Under the MHA 2007, s 17 leave remains, but it is intended that its role will be reduced and supplanted by the community treatment order ('CTO') under s 17A. To reinforce this policy, a responsible clinician considering granting leave for more than seven days must first consider whether the patient should be 'dealt with' under s 17A instead. Compulsory community powers are dealt with in chapter 8.

SAFEGUARDS

2.28 The third function of mental health legislation is to provide a system of safeguards to ensure that powers to detain or to treat compulsorily are not misused, and that fundamental rights of freedom from arbitrary detention and

---

[17] *R (on the application of DR) v Mersey Care NHS Trust* [2002] EWHC 1810 (Admin).

physical integrity are not interfered with. These matters are dealt with in Parts IV, IVA and V of the Mental Health Act 1983. Part V deals with review of detention. Mental Health Review Tribunals (MHRTs) established under the MHA 1959 fulfill the function of providing, as required by Art 5(4) of the European Convention on Human Rights, access to a court with power to review the lawfulness of detention and direct discharge if detention is not warranted. Provisions authorising treatment without consent for mental disorder, subject to a statutory second opinion, are contained in Part IV (introduced by the MHA1983) for in-patients, and in Part IVA (introduced by the MHA 2007) for patients on a community treatment order ('CTO').

Review of compulsory powers by hospital managers

2.29 The managers of the detaining hospital perform an important role in reviewing the need for detention. The application and reports authorising compulsory admission are forwarded to the managers, who are the detaining authority. Detention is renewed by the Responsible Clinician furnishing to the managers a report to the effect that the patient still suffers from mental disorder of a nature or degree justifying detention in the interests of his health or safety or for the protection of others, and that appropriate treatment is available. The hospital managers have a power to discharge the patient which may be exercised at any time during the patient's detention and on any grounds. The Act enables NHS trusts and PCTs (but not NHS foundation trusts) to delegate functions to committees or subcommittees whose members need not be directors of the trust. The MHA 2007 enables the power to discharge in a NHS foundation trust to be exercised by any three or more persons authorised by the board of the trust in that behalf, each of whom is neither an executive director of the board nor an employee of the trust.[18] The role of the hospital managers is discussed in chapter 5.

Mental Health Tribunals

2.30 Part V of the MHA 1983, which is amended by chapter 5 of the Mental Health Act 2007, deals with Mental Health Tribunals. Mental Health Review Tribunals (MHRTs) were first established under the MHA 1959 to provide patients with an opportunity to seek review by a judicial body of the continued need for their detention. In England MHRTs have been renamed Mental Health Tribunals, but Wales retains the name Mental Health Review Tribunal for the body which reviews the continued need for detention. Article 5(4) of the European Convention on Human Rights entitles detainees to take proceedings by which the lawfulness of detention must be decided speedily by a court and release ordered if it is not lawful. In *X v United Kingdom*,[19] the Strasbourg Court held that the court must be able to review the applicability of the *Winterwerp* criteria.[20] If those criteria are not met, the court must have the

---

18 MHA 1983, s 23(6), as inserted by s 45(1) of the MHA 2007.
19 (1981) 4 EHRR 188, ECtHR.
20 (1981) 4 EHRR 188 at 189, ECtHR. See also *Hutchison Reid v United Kingdom* (2003) 37 EHRR 211, ECtHR.

power to direct the patient's discharge. Review of the 'lawfulness' of detention must be carried out in light of domestic legal requirements, the Convention, and the principle of proportionality. Article 5(4) review is carried out jointly by the High Court and by Mental Health Tribunals ('MHTs'). The High Court reviews the formal legality of decisions to detain and renew detention via judicial review and habeas corpus. Review of the continued applicability of the *Winterwerp* criteria is done by MHTs, which have the power to direct discharge.

2.31 Mental Health Tribunals have been affected by the MHA 2007 and the Tribunals, Courts and Enforcement Act 2007 in five main ways. First, the organisation has been changed so that Wales has its own MHRT with its own Chairman and the panels for each individual hearing are presided over by a president. In England the MHT has been subsumed into the Health, Education and Social Care Chamber of the First Tier Tribunal established under the Tribunals, Courts and Enforcement Act 2007. There is a National President and the panel for each hearing is presided over by a tribunal judge, not a President. Second, the discharge criteria are altered by the new broad definition of mental disorder, the removal of the exclusion for sexual deviancy, and the condition that appropriate treatment must be available. Third, the jurisdiction to reclassify as suffering from a different form of disorder is abolished. Fourth, a new jurisdiction over CTO patients is introduced. Fifth, changes to the Domestic Violence, Crime and Victims Act 2004 mean that victims of certain crimes committed by mentally disordered offenders are entitled to make representations to MHTs. The jurisdiction and functioning of Mental Health Tribunals are fully discussed in chapter 9.

Consent to treatment and statutory second opinions

2.32 Part IV provides a system of statutory second opinion safeguards in relation to certain treatments for mental disorder. No patient may be given psychosurgery or hormone implants to reduce male sex drive without a certificate from a panel of three people appointed by the Care Quality Commission ('CQC') that the patient is capable and has consented. Moreover, the doctor member of the panel must certify that the treatment ought to be given having regard to the likelihood that it will alleviate or prevent deterioration in the patient's condition. The new test for the second stage of this process and for the decision under ss 58 (medicines) and 58A (Electro Convulsive Therapy – ECT) will be that it is appropriate for the treatment to be given. It is appropriate for treatment to be given to a patient if the treatment is appropriate in his case, taking into account the nature and degree of the mental disorder from which he is suffering and all other circumstances of his case.[21]

2.33 Under the MHA 1983, ECT or medicines for mental disorder could be given without consent to a detained patient, subject to a written statement from a Second Opinion Doctor ('SOAD') appointed by the Mental Health Act Commission ('MHAC') certifying that the treatment ought to be given. The

---

[21]   MHA 1983, s 64(3), as inserted by MHA 2007, s 6(3).

functions of the MHAC have been taken over by the Care Quality Commission Following the changes introduced by the MHA 2007 there is a separate regime for medicines which remain under s 58 and may (subject to a second opinion), be given without consent to a capable patient who is refusing them. Medicines may be given if the responsible clinician certifies that the patient is capable of understanding the nature purpose and likely effects of the treatment and has consented. A patient does not become eligible to seek a second opinion for psychiatric medication given without consent until three months have elapsed since the first occasion during that period of detention when medication was administered. So for three months medicines may be given without consent under the direction of the responsible clinician. Thereafter, if they are to be given without consent, a second opinion must be obtained. It does not make any difference whether the SOAD certifies the patient to be incapable of understanding the nature purpose and likely effects of the treatment, or to be refusing it. In either case the medicine may be given subject to the test of appropriateness outlined above. ECT will in future be dealt with by a separate procedure under s 58A, and may not be given to a capable patient who is refusing the treatment. If the patient lacks capacity to consent and it is appropriate to give ECT, it may be authorised by a SOAD. The second opinion procedures are fully discussed in chapter 10.

2.34 Section 35 of the MHA 2007 adds a new Part IVA to the MHA 1983 comprising ss 64A–64K. These provisions authorise 'relevant treatment' to be given to a community patient who has not been recalled to hospital. They set out the circumstances in which medication for mental disorder may be given to a community patient in the community (not necessarily in a hospital or clinic). They apply parts of the decision-making framework of the Mental Capacity Act 2005 to treatment under the Mental Health Act and authorise treatment in the community without the consent of an incapable patient:

(a) if there is consent from someone authorised under the MCA 2005 to make decisions on the patient's behalf;

(b) if the patient lacks capacity and force is not necessary to secure compliance; or

(c) if emergency treatment needs to be given, using force if necessary, to a patient who lacks capacity.

Their general intent is to clarify the circumstances in which treatment may be given in the community without consent if necessary. Parts IV and IVA are explained in chapter 10.

Care Quality Commission

2.35　The Mental Health Act Commission ('MHAC') was established by the MHA 1983.[22] The MHAC was a multidisciplinary body appointed by the Secretary of State for Health, with a general duty to oversee the use of compulsory powers under the 1983 Act. Scrutiny of admission documents remains the province of hospital managers. The jurisdiction to discharge remained with MHRTs. The MHAC had specific duties of investigating the handling of complaints made by or on behalf of detained patients. It was required to report biennially to Parliament, and assisted the Secretary of State in preparing a Code of Practice. Commissioners visited hospitals regularly, usually with advance warning, but sometimes not, and interviewed patients under detention.[23] The MHAC also appointed and oversaw the operation of the system of second opinions in Part IV and now Part IVA of the Act.

2.36　The functions of the MHAC were assumed by the Care Quality Commission ('CQC') in April 2009 and in November 2010 the CQC issued its first report on the exercise of its functions under the Mental Health Act 1983.[24] The role and function of the CQC in relation to the Mental Health Act are discussed in chapter 10.

Victims' rights

2.37　The Mental Health Act 2007 significantly amended chapter 2 of Part 3 of the Domestic Violence, Crime and Victims Act 2004. These provisions entitle a victim or any person acting for a victim of a sexual or violent offence where the offender is subject to a restriction order or and restriction direction, to be notified of their right to make representations to the local probation board about whether the patient should be subject to any conditions in the event of his conditional discharge from hospital and if so what those conditions should be. Schedule 6 to the MHA 2007 extends this right to victims of sexual or violent offences where the offender is sentenced to a hospital order without restrictions, or is given a transfer direction without restrictions. In such cases the victim or representative is entitled to make representations as to what conditions he should be subject to in the event of his discharge from hospital under a community treatment order.[25] The victim or representative is entitled to receive information about any conditions that are imposed on discharge.[26] Furthermore, where the offender is subject to a hospital order without restrictions, the victim may ask to make representations or to receive information, and if they do so the probation board must notify the victim of the hospital's name and address and the hospital must be notified of the

---

[22]　The establishment of a Commission was recommended by *The Report of The Review of Rampton Hospital* Cmnd 8073 (1980), para 4.7.

[23]　MHA 1983, ss 119–121.

[24]　Care Quality Commission, Monitoring the Use of the Mental Health Act in 2009/10, www.cqc.org.uk.

[25]　Domestic Violence, Crime and Victims Act 2004, s 36(5).

[26]　Ibid, s 36(6)

victim's address.[27] The probation board is required to forward any representations made to the person responsible for determining matters to do with discharge, ending of restrictions, conditional discharge or discharge subject to a community treatment order. The changes to the 2004 Act require responsible clinicians, Mental Health Tribunals ('MHTs'), and the Secretary of State (in the case of a restricted patient) when considering whether to discharge to notify the hospital managers who must notify the local probation board, and give victims the chance to make representations and information about discharge and conditions. Since the 2004 Act came into force MHTs have been granting rights to victims to make representations in relation to discharge and conditions of discharge. The changes to the Domestic Violence, Crime and Victims Act 2004 are significant in that they require responsible clinicians of all offender patients who have committed sexual or violent offences to consider the victim's representations before discharging either conditionally or under a community treatment order. Tribunals too must consider the victim's representations. The rights of victims are discussed in chapter 7 (powers of discharge of mentally disordered offenders) and chapter 8 (powers to send on extended leave, to make community treatment orders, and to conditionally discharge offender patients who are subject to restrictions). They are also discussed in relation to the Mental Health Tribunal in chapter 9.

PRINCIPLES AND CODES OF PRACTICE
Principles

2.38 The idea behind principles and Codes of Practice is that they should offer guidance on how the legislation is to be implemented, but that they should also promote respect for the individual human dignity of the mentally disordered person. Both the Mental Capacity Act and the Mental Health Act have fundamental principles. Each has its own statutory Code to guide professionals on using of their powers and discharging their responsibilities. The Mental Capacity Act has statutory principles set out in the Act. The Mental Health Act has principles in its Code of Practice. This prompts the question what practical differences there are in the status of principles under each regime. There has been a trend in mental health law reform to argue for the adoption of statutory principles to guide the way in which the Act is implemented. There was much debate, following Richardson, about including principles on the face of the Mental Health Act, such as non-discrimination, least restrictive alternative, respect for autonomy and diversity, reciprocity and consensual care. Including principles in the Act was a key goal of the Mental Health Alliance. The Mental Health (Care and Treatment) (Scotland) Act 2003 includes principles in s 1 to which professionals must have regard. These include respect for the past and present wishes of the patient, the importance of full patient participation, minimum restriction of freedom of the patient necessary in the circumstances, encouragement of equal opportunities, and the views, needs and circumstances of the patient's carer.

---

[27]   Ibid, s 36A.

2.39 The Parliamentary Joint Committee on the Draft Mental Health Bill 2004 recommended that principles should appear on the face of the Act, and that it was not appropriate to 'leave fundamental guiding principles to the Code of Practice'.[28] In the Code is where they have been left by the MHA 2007, the main victory being in securing the appearance in the statute of a list of 'matters' to be reflected in the principles. Generally, the principles have been intended to promote treating mentally disordered people and their carers with respect.

MCA 2005 Principles

2.40 The Mental Capacity Act 2005 sets out five statutory principles. They are:

(a) a person must be assumed to have capacity unless it is established that they lack capacity;

(b) a person is not to be treated as unable to make a decision unless all practicable steps to help him to do so have been taken without success;

(c) a person is not to be treated as unable to make a decision merely because he makes an unwise decision;

(d) an act done, or decision made, under this Act for or on behalf of a person who lacks capacity must be done, or made, in his best interests;

(e) before the act is done, or the decision is made, regard must be had to whether the purpose for which it is needed can be as effectively achieved in a way that is less restrictive of the person's rights and freedom of action.[29]

Section 1 merely says that the following principles apply. It does not say that those making decisions must have to have regard to them. Richard Jones argues that:[30]

> 'Although there is no legal duty placed on persons or bodies to apply the principles, a failure to do so could be cited in legal proceedings as evidence of unlawful conduct.'

2.41 The emphasis of the MCA 2005 and its accompanying Code is on empowerment and personal autonomy, enabling people to plan for future incapacity. This might be done by a valid and effective advance decision refusing treatment which is binding, or an advance statement requesting specific treatment which is not binding but which must be considered by doctors in determining what is in the patient's best interests. Or it might be

---

28 House of Lords, House of Commons Joint Pre-Parliamentary Scrutiny Committee *Report on the Draft Mental Health Bill* (HL Paper 79(1), HC Paper 95(1), Session 2004–2005), para 64.
29 Mental Capacity Act 2005.
30 RM Jones *Mental Capacity Act Manual* (Sweet and Maxwell, 2005), para 9/9.

done by appointing a treatment proxy using the lasting power of attorney. If no proxy has been appointed, interventions be carried out by others without consent in the patient's best interests, but only after reasonable steps have been taken to assess capacity, the person is reasonably believed to lack capacity. The ethos of both the 2005 Act and the Code is based on upholding dignity while protecting the best interests of vulnerable people. The power to make an advance decision refusing treatment or the power to appoint a proxy with instructions to refuse it raises the question when an advance refusal of psychiatric treatment is binding, and when it may be overridden by detention and compulsory treatment under the Mental Health Act 1983. These issues are governed by ss 5, 6, 28 and 37 of the Mental Capacity Act 2005, and are discussed in full in chapter 10 which deals with consent to treatment for mental disorder. The principles in the Mental Capacity Act 2005 reflect a presumption of autonomy, of the least restrictive alternative, and of regard for the best interests of patients.

Mental Health Act 1983

2.42   The original Mental Health Act 1983 did not contain principles, but the Code of Practice did. Since the passage of the MHA 2007 new separate Codes of Practice have been issued for England and Wales respectively. The legal status of the guidance in the Mental Health Act Code remains that whilst the '[1983] Act does not impose a legal duty to comply with the Code but as it is a statutory document, failure to follow it could be referred to in legal proceedings'. Chapter One of the 1998 Code was entitled 'Guiding Principles'. Paragraph 1.1 said that:[31]

'The detailed guidance in the Code needs to be read in the light of the following broad principles, that people to whom the Act applies (including those being assessed for possible admission should:

- Receive recognition of their basic human rights under the European Convention on Human Rights (ECHR).
- Be given respect for their qualities, abilities and diverse backgrounds as individuals and be assured that account will be taken of their age, gender, sexual orientation, social ethnic, cultural and religious background, but that general assumptions will not be made on the basis of any of those characteristics.
- Have their needs full taken into account, although it is recognised that, within available resources, it may always not be practicable to meet them in full.
- Be given any necessary treatment or care in the least controlled or segregated facilities compatible with ensuring their own health or safety or the safety of other people.
- Be treated and cared for in such a way as to promote the greatest practicable degree their self determination and personal responsibility, consistent with their own needs and wishes.

---

[31]   Department of Health and Welsh Office *Mental Health Act 1983 Code of Practice* (1999), para 1.1.

- Be discharged from detention or other powers provided by the Act as soon as it is clear their application is no longer justified.'

This list was then followed by five further principles.

2.43 First, was that patients should be treated in accordance with the Care Programme Approach ('CPA'). All service users, whether or not they have been detained, who have been in contact with the specialist psychiatric service are entitled to be dealt with under the CPA. The CPA requires a risk assessment, a needs assessment, a written care plan which will be regularly reviewed and a key worker (now known as a 'care co-ordinator'). In 1996 the CPA was extended to all patients receiving care from the specialist psychiatric services.[32] In 2003 new guidance *Modernising the Care Programme Approach*[33] was produced providing for two levels of CPA, standard and enhanced. Standard CPA was for people whose mental illness is less severe or who had low risk factors or had an active informal support network. Although it is unlawful to do so, some social services authorities tried to limit community services to both patients and carers to those who were on enhanced CPA. People were on enhanced CPA if their mental disorder is assessed as posing a potential risk to their own safety or to that of other people. Resources follow risk. From October 2008 new guidance has applied in England whereby the two tiers have been abolished and 'New CPA' will be available to manage complex and serious cases who according to the DoH guidance should not be significantly different from those currently needing the support of enhanced CPA[34] (see **8.5** below).

2.44 The second principle emphasised the responsibility of staff to make sure that effective communication takes place between themselves and patients, and to do everything possible to overcome any barriers to communication. The third principle was patient confidentiality, that information about a patient should not be disclosed without a patient's consent, unless it is necessary to pass on information 'in the public interest, for instance where personal health or safety is at risk'. Then information should be revealed on a 'need to know' basis. The fourth principle was recognition of the rights of victims of crimes committed by mentally disordered offenders. These rights have been significantly strengthened since the Code was issued by the Domestic Violence, Crime and Victims Act 2004, and the amendments to that Act introduced by the Mental Health Act 2007. The final principle was recognition of the duty of hospital managers to give information about rights to patients and nearest relatives, and to collect information about ethnicity of all patients admitted under the Act.

---

[32]   NHS Executive (1996).
[33]   Care Programme Approach Association *The Care Programme Approach Handbook* (Chesterfield Care Programme Approach Association, 2003).
[34]   *Refocusing the Care Programme Approach* Department of Health, March 2008.

The principles introduced by the Mental Health Act 2007

2.45 Section 8 of the Mental Health Act 2007 (cross-heading 'fundamental principles') lists a number of matters which must be addressed, but requires the principles to be stated in the Code of Practice. Section 118 of the 1983 Act, which governs preparation of the Code of Practice, is amended to require the Codes of England and Wales to include a statement of the principles which the Secretary of State/Welsh Ministers think should 'inform decisions under this Act'.[35] The new concept of principles which 'should inform decisions' is different from the principles that professionals must have regard to. In preparing the statement of principles the Secretary of State must, in particular, ensure that 'each of the following matters is addressed':

(a)   respect for patients' past and present wishes and feelings;

(b)   respect for diversity generally including, in particular, diversity of religion, culture and sexual orientation (within the meaning of s 35 of the Equality Act 2006);

(c)   minimising restrictions on liberty;

(d)   involvement of patients in planning, developing and delivering care and treatment appropriate to them;

(e)   avoidance of unlawful discrimination;

(f)   effectiveness of treatment;

(g)   views of carers and other interested parties;

(h)   patient well-being and safety; and

(i)   public safety.

Section 118(2C) requires the Secretary of State and the Welsh Ministers also to have regard to the desirability of ensuring:

(a)   the efficient use of resources; and

(b)   the equitable distribution of services.

2.46 This is a good deal weaker than a statutory requirement to have regard to principles spelt out in statute, and crystallises the difference between the MCA 2005 and the MHA 1983. Respect for human rights and confidentiality have disappeared from the list. The practical impact on patients' rights may be small, since under the Human Rights Act 1998, all public authorities are under a legal duty to act compatibly with Convention Rights. But this is scant

---

[35]   MHA 1983, s 118(2A)–(2B), as inserted by MHA 2007, s 8.

justification for removing the Code's emphasis to mental health professionals of the need to respect Convention rights. The principles now clearly include public safety for the first time, as well as the effectiveness of treatment, will certainly include emphasis on compliance with medication. In line with Government policy announced by ministers Dobson and Boateng in 1998, the Mental Health Act 2007 and the principles mark a shift towards seeking to impose obligations on patients to comply with medication, and on professionals to manage risk.

2.47 There are now separate Codes for England and Wales. The Department of Health, *Code of Practice on the Mental Health Act 1983*[36] applies to England, and sets out five principles: (1) the purpose principle, (2) the least restriction principle, (3) the respect principle, (4) the participation principle and (5) the effectiveness, efficiency and equity principle. The purpose principle is that 'Decisions under the Act must be taken with a view to minimising the undesirable effects of mental disorder, by maximising the safety and wellbeing (mental and physical) of patients, promoting their recovery and protecting other people from harm.' The least restriction principle requires people taking action without a patients consent to 'keep to a minimum the restrictions they impose on the patient's liberty, having regard to the purpose for which the restrictions are imposed.' The respect principle requires those taking decisions under the Act to avoid unlawful discrimination and to 'respect the diverse needs, values and circumstances of each patient, including their race, religion, culture, gender, age, sexual orientation and any disability. They must consider the patient's views, wishes and feelings (whether expressed at the time or in advance), so far as they are reasonably ascertainable, and follow those wishes wherever practicable and consistent with the purpose of the decision.' The participation principle requires patients to 'be given the opportunity to be involved, as far as is practicable in the circumstances, in planning, developing and reviewing their own treatment and care to help ensure that it is delivered in a way that is as appropriate and effective for them as possible. The involvement of carers, family members and other people who have an interest in the patient's welfare should be encouraged (unless there are particular reasons to the contrary) and their views taken seriously.' Finally, the effectiveness, efficiency and equity principle requires people taking decisions under the Act to 'seek to use the resources available to them and to patients in the most effective, efficient and equitable way, to meet the needs of patients and achieve the purpose for which the decision was taken.'[37] The principles in the Welsh Assembly Government *Mental Health Act 1983 Code of Practice* are based on those in the Welsh Assembly Government Mental Health Strategy *Adult Mental Health Services for Wales*, namely (1) Empowerment, (2) Equity, (3) Effectiveness, and (4) Efficiency.[38] Although they are set out in more detail than their English equivalents, the Welsh principles cover broadly the same ground. One interesting example of the greater detail of the Welsh Code is that it

---

[36]   Department of Health *Code of Practice: Mental Health Act 1983* (2008) www.dh.gov.uk.
[37]   Ibid, paras 1.2–1.6.
[38]   Welsh Assembly Government Mental Health Act 1983 Code of Practice www.wales.nhs.uk, paras 1.8–1.28.

requires 'careful consideration of the potentially stigmatising effect assessment and admission processes may have on patients, their carers and families', giving as a particular example the way in which a patient is taken to hospital.[39] Both Codes use the same form of words in explaining how the principles are to be used, stating that:[40]

> 'The principles inform decisions, they do not determine them. Although all the principles must inform every decision made under the Act, the weight given to each principle in reaching a particular decision will depend on the context.'

Hence the principles may not be ignored. They must be applied, but they may be balanced in very different ways depending on the circumstances and the degree of risk, and the English Code in particular gives examples of scenarios illustrating how they might be applied.

The legal status of the Codes: seclusion, and restraint

2.48 In performing functions under the Act persons mentioned in subsection (1)(a) or (b) must have regard to the Code. The persons mentioned in s 118(1)(a) and (b) are doctors, approved clinicians, managers and staff of hospitals, independent hospitals and care homes and AMHPs in relation to admission guardianship and CTOs. The Code also provides guidance to doctors and members of other professions in relation to treatment for mental disorder. Para iv of the Code of Practice for England and the Code of Practice for Wales each state that 'the Act does not impose a legal duty to comply with the Code but departures from the Code could give rise to legal challenge and a court, in reviewing any departure from the Code, will scrutinise the reasons for the departure to ensure there is sufficiently convincing justification in the circumstances. It is good practice to ensure any such reasons are appropriately evidenced.' The Code of Practice gives guidance on how the Act should be implemented. It also provides guidance on interventions which find no mention in the legislation. Seclusion and restraint provide an important example of interventions which potentially breach the right of physical integrity in Art 8. No provisions in the MHA 1983 expressly justify seclusion. It is, however, subject to guidance under the MHA Code of Practice, where it is defined as:[41]

> 'the supervised confinement of a patient in a room, which may be locked to protect others from significant harm. Its sole aim is to contain severely disturbed behaviour which is likely to cause harm to others.'

The Code requires that seclusion should only be used as a last resort and for the shortest period possible, a reflecting common law necessity and the Convention principle of proportionality. The Code goes on to say that seclusion should not be used as a punishment or a threat, or because of a shortage of staff or as part of a treatment programme. It should never be used 'solely as a means of

---

[39]   Ibid, para 1.13.
[40]   English MHA Code of Practice, paras 1.8–1.9, Welsh MHA Code of Practice, para 1.28.
[41]   Department of Health *Code of Practice: Mental Health Act 1983* (2008), para 15.43.

managing self-harming behaviour. Where the patient poses a risk of self-harm as well as harm to others, seclusion should be used only when the professionals involved are satisfied that the need to protect other people outweighs any increased risk to the patient's health or safety and that any such risk can be properly managed.'[42] Although there have at various points in recent history been calls to ban seclusion, it has retained its place as an accepted psychiatric practice. The 1998 version of the Code of Practice on the Mental Health Act 1983, whilst not regarding seclusion as 'a treatment technique', described it as falling within the broad legal definition of 'medical treatment' in s 145. Although this paragraph no longer appears in the 2008 Codes, judicial dicta in the Court of Appeal and the House of Lords in *R (on the application of Munjaz) v Mersey Care NHS Trust; R (on the application of S) v Airedale NHS Trust* suggested that the term medical treatment for mental disorder in s 145 is broad enough to include seclusion.[43] Even though it may not be a 'treatment technique' or may not be part of a treatment programme, it is a form of treatment meted out to psychiatric patients which is authorised by law under defined circumstances.

2.49 The applicants in *Munjaz* and *S v Airedale* challenged their seclusion in breach of the MHA Code of Practice.[44] The cases established that legal powers to seclude exist under the MHA 1983 and outlines the impact of Arts 3 and 8 of the Convention on those powers. The effects had not reached the level of severity necessary to engage the prohibition in Art 3 against inhuman or degrading treatment. However, there was a potential breach of the right to respect for private life (physical integrity) in Art 8. The European Court had already held in *Raininen v Finland*[45] that respect for privacy under Art 8(1) includes:

> 'the physical and moral integrity of the individual, and extends to deprivations of liberty ... affording a protection in relation to conditions of detention that do not reach the level of severity required by Article 3.'

2.50 The Court of Appeal upheld both challenges to seclusion, holding that Ashworth were only entitled to depart from the Code if they had good reason to do so on the facts of the individual case, and that Airedale were not justified in keeping S in seclusion from the time when it ceased to be a necessary and proportionate response to the risk he presented to others. The Court of Appeal held that Convention rights obliged them to afford a status and weight to the Code consistent with the State's obligation to avoid ill-treatment of patients detained by or on the authority of the State. Seclusion would infringe Art 8 unless justified under Art 8(2) to protect health or the rights and freedoms of others. Since the justifications under the MHA 1983 were very broad, the Code

---

42 Ibid, para 15.45.
43 [2003] EWCA Civ 1036. See now [2005] UKHL 58. Lord Bingham (at para [20]) said that 'medical treatment is in my opinion an expression wide enough to cover nursing and caring for a patient in seclusion, even though seclusion cannot properly form part of a treatment programme'.
44 [2003] EWCA Civ 1036.
45 (1997) 26 EHRR 563, ECtHR.

of Practice had an import
necessary degree of predicta

2.51 There was no appeal _____ case, but the House of Lords
overturned the Court of Appeal's ruling on the status of the Code in *Munjaz,*
holding that the Code has the status of guidance which should be followed
unless there was a good reason for departing from it, and that a good reason
need not be because of the facts of the individual case. A good reason might be
a policy reason arise from the exigencies of running a high security hospital
which might justify differences in the seclusion policy, relating for example to
frequency of medical review, to contend with the fact that the hospital exists to
treat people who need treatment in conditions of security on grounds of their
violent or dangerous proclivities.

2.52 After 1999, the National Institute of Clinical and Public Health
Excellence ('NICE') assumed responsibility for issuing guidance on psychiatric
treatment. NICE was initially set up with two functions:[46]

(a) promoting 'clinical excellence and the effective use of available resources
in the National Health Service ('NHS') through the development and
dissemination of guidelines for the management of certain diseases or
conditions, guidance on the appropriate use of certain interventions, audit
methodologies and the dissemination of these to support frontline staff
and patients';

(b) advising on 'good clinical practice in the use of existing treatment options,
appraising evidence on new health interventions, and advising the NHS
on how they can be implemented and on how best they fit alongside the
range of existing treatments. The Institute will promote the appropriate
use of treatments which offer good value to patients, and will discourage
the use of those that do not'.

NICE has issued a range of guidance on psychiatric treatment, including ECT,
anti-psychotic medication, the use of cholinesterase inhibitor drugs in the
treatment of dementia, interventions to prevent self-harm, and on the
management of violence in psychiatric patients.[47] Each piece of guidance is
prefaced by a standard statement that:

---

[46] National Institute of Clinical Excellence *Framework Document*, paras 3.1 and 3.2 (see further
www.nice.org.uk).

[47] National Institute of Clinical Excellence *Dementia: the treatment and care of people with
dementia in health and social care* (2001); *Guidance on the use of newer (atypical) antipsychotic
drugs for the treatment of schizophrenia* (Technology Appraisal Guidance 43, June 2002);
Guidance on the Use of Electro Convulsive Therapy (Technology Appraisal Guidance 59, April
2003); *Self-Harm: The Short Term Physical and Psychological Management and Secondary
Prevention of Self-Harm in Primary and Secondary Care* (Clinical Guideline 16, July 2004);
*Violence: The Short-Term Management of Disturbed/Violent Behaviour in In-Patient Psychiatric
Settings* (Clinical Guideline 25, February 2005). All guidance available at www.nice.org.uk.

into account when exercising
~~ot override the individual
decisions appropriate to the
circumstances of the individual patient, in consultation with the individual patient
and or guardian or carer.'

In relation to management of violence the guidance provides that:[48]

> 'Failure to act in accordance with the guideline may not only be a failure to act in
> accordance with best practice, but in some circumstances may have legal
> consequences. For example, any intervention required to manage disturbed
> behaviour must be a reasonable and proportionate response to the risk it seeks to
> address.'

2.53 NICE Guidance on the management of violence in psychiatric settings
refers to both seclusion and restraint. It states that: 'These interventions are
management strategies and are *not* regarded as *primary treatment techniques*'.[49]
Although legally these are 'treatments for mental disorder', in reality they are
legally sanctioned treatments *of mentally disordered people*. The courts have
been willing to accept that treatment designed to prevent harm to others can be
in the best interests of the patient. The law on restraint and seclusion is
explained in chapter 10.

CHILDREN

2.54 Children may be detained under the Mental Health Act 1983, with
parental consent, or under the Children Act 1989. The MHA 2007 introduces
new provisions affecting children including a 'requirement' of age appropriate
accommodation, provisions restricting the use of ECT on children under new
s 58A, and new provisions governing treatment in the community of child
community patients. Chapter 11 outlines the basic framework of powers of
detention and compulsory treatment of children and the effect of the changes
introduced by the 2007 Act.

TRANSFERRING PATIENTS SUBJECT TO COMPULSION ACROSS JURISDICTIONS

2.55 Part VI entitled 'Removal and return of patients within the United
Kingdom' introduces a new range of reciprocal arrangements enabling
restricted patients, detained patients and community patients to be transferred
in custody of necessary from any part of the United Kingdom, Channel Islands
or the Isle of Man. Until now there has been little co-ordination between the
different legal regimes involved. The new provisions are designed to rectify this

---

[48]   National Institute for Clinical Excellence *Violence: The Short-Term Management of
       Disturbed/Violent Behaviour in In-Patient Psychiatric Settings* (Clinical Guideline 25, February
       2005), p 10.
[49]   Emphasis added.

problem, by providing a coherent regime of powers to take and retake patients, to remove them from one jurisdiction and convey them in custody to another, and to ensure that they are subject to lawful compulsion when they reach their destination.

OFFENCES AGAINST MENTALLY DISORDERED PEOPLE

2.56 Mentally disordered people may need special protection from the criminal law, either because they are not in a position because of their mental disorder to complain about their treatment in an institution, or where consent is a defence to an offence, such as a sexual offence, and the victim suffers from mental disorder which renders her or him incapable of consenting, or vulnerable to undue influence. Mental health legislation must provide effective protection via the criminal law of the rights of mentally disordered people, and the Mental Health Act sets out a number of special offences in relation to mentally disordered people. The transfer provisions, together with the offences under the Mental Health Act, are discussed in chapter 12.

THE UN CONVENTION ON THE RIGHTS OF PERSONS WITH DISABILITIES (CPRD)

Aims of the CPRD

2.57 As we have already seen, lawyers, policy-makers and practitioners in the United Kingdom have become used to measuring mental health law and practice against the yardstick of the European Convention on Human Rights ('ECHR'). The ECHR accepts the existence of specialist mental health legislation. The UN Convention on the Rights of Persons with Disabilities purportedly prohibits legislation which allows detention based on any grounds linked to disability, including mental disorder. The purpose of the Convention is described in Art 1 as being:

> 'to promote, protect and ensure the full and equal enjoyment of all human rights and fundamental freedoms by all persons with disabilities, and to promote respect for their inherent dignity.'

'Persons with disabilities' are defined inclusively rather than exhaustively in Art 1, by way of a description rather than a definition.[50]

> 'Persons with disabilities include those who have long-term physical, mental, intellectual or sensory impairments which in interaction with various barriers may hinder their full and effective participation in society on an equal basis with others.'

---

[50]   http://www.un.org/disabilities/convention/conventionfull.shtml.

This clearly includes people who would be described by UK mental health legislation as suffering from 'mental disorder', or who are subject to 'psychosocial disability' to use the term preferred by service users and survivors.

2.58 'Persons with disabilities' are a diverse group. Many with physical, mental, intellectual or sensory impairments will retain the mental capacity to make decisions about their life and their care. Many may not, and the Convention as interpreted by the Committee and the High Commissioner raises questions which go the core of even the most recent mental capacity and mental health legislation such as the MCA 2005 and the MHA 1983.

Effect of Ratification of the CPRD and the Optional Protocol

2.59 The UK ratified the Convention on 8 June 2009 and ratified the Optional Protocol on 7 August 2009. The effects of ratifying the Convention are specified in Arts 4 and 33. Article 4 sets out the obligations of states 'to ensure and promote the full realisation of all human rights and fundamental freedoms for all persons with disabilities without discrimination of any kind on the basis of disability'.

2.60 Article 4 also sets out a fidelity obligation requiring states to 'refrain from engaging in any act or practice that is inconsistent' with the Convention and 'adopt all appropriate legislative, administrative and other measures for the implementation of the rights recognised in the ... Convention'. Finally, under Art 4, signatory states must:

'take all appropriate measures, including legislation, to modify or abolish existing laws, regulations, customs and practices that constitute discrimination against persons with disabilities.'

2.61 Article 33 relates to the specific machinery which states must put in place to ensure implementation. It imposes a duty on states to designate one or more focal points within government for implementation of the Convention. It requires them to 'give due consideration to the establishment or designation of a coordination mechanism.' It also requires states, in accordance with their legal and administrative systems to provide one or more independent mechanisms, as appropriate, to promote, protect and monitor implementation. Finally, it places a duty on signatory states to ensure that civil society, in particular persons with disabilities and their representative organisations, shall be involved and participate fully in the monitoring process.

2.62 Article 1 of the Optional Protocol effectively recognises a right of individual or group petition to the Committee on the Rights of Persons with Disabilities. It simply states that:

'A State Party to the present Protocol ("State Party") recognises the competence of the Committee on the Rights of Persons with Disabilities ("the Committee") to receive and consider communications from or on behalf of individuals or groups of individuals subject to its jurisdiction who claim to be victims of a violation by that State Party of the provisions of the Convention.'

The UN High Commissioner has stated that:[51]

'In order to adequately implement the Convention, one of the first steps that States need to undertake is a comprehensive review of the national legislation and policy framework.'

Reservations and Declarations

2.63 Article 46 of the CPRD allows parties to lodge reservations provided that such reservations are not 'incompatible with the object and purpose of the present Convention.' Article 2, para 1(d), of the Vienna Convention on the Law of Treaties defines a 'reservation' as:

'a unilateral statement, however phrased or named, made by a State when signing, ratifying, accepting, approving or acceding to a treaty, whereby it purports to exclude or to modify the legal effect of certain provisions of the treaty in their application to that State.'

Australia and Canada have entered interpretive declarations and reservations in relation to Art 12, and Australia has entered a declaration of its 'understanding that the Convention allows for compulsory assistance or treatment of persons, including measures taken for the treatment of mental disability, where such treatment is necessary, as a last resort and subject to safeguards.'

2.64 The United Kingdom Government considered whether to enter any declaration or reservation in relation to mental capacity law or mental health legislation, and ultimately decided that none was necessary. The challenges to mental capacity and mental health legislation come particularly from Arts 12 and 14 of the CPRD.

Article 12, Mental Capacity Legislation, and Substitute Decision-Making

2.65 Article 12 of the Convention affirms the right of persons with disabilities to recognition everywhere as persons before the law, and has important implications for laws relating to decision-making for those who lack capacity. Article 12(2) acknowledges the centrality of the concept of legal capacity in legal thought and practice by requiring States Parties to 'recognise that persons with disabilities enjoy legal capacity on an equal basis with others in all aspects of life.' This prompts the question whether a State might comply with this

---

[51] *Annual Report of the United Nations High Commissioner for Human Rights and Reports of the Office of the High Commissioner and the Secretary-General* Thematic Study by the Office of the United Nations High Commissioner for Human Rights on enhancing awareness and understanding of the Convention on the Rights of Persons with Disabilities, para 30. http://www2.ohchr.org/english/bodies/hrcouncil/docs/10session/A.HRC.10.48.pdf.

obligation by allowing substitute decision-making, but proscribing status and outcome based approaches to capacity, employing instead a functional test. In other words would the Mental Capacity Act (MCA) 2005 survive scrutiny against the yardstick of Art 12? The UK Government clearly thought so, because they did not enter any, reservations or declarations in respect of the MCA 2005.

The Functional Approach to Capacity

2.66   The MCA 2005 seeks to proscribe a status based approach to incapacity by emphasising the pre-existing common law presumption[52] of capacity – 'A person must be assumed to have capacity unless it is established that he lacks capacity.'[53] This is further reinforced by s 2(3) which provides that:

> 'A lack of capacity cannot be established merely by reference to –
>
> (a)   a person's age or appearance, or
> (b)   a condition of his, or an aspect of his behaviour, which might lead others to make unjustified assumptions about his capacity.'

The 2005 Act provides that outcome may not determine capacity by stating the principle that 'A person is not to be treated as unable to make a decision merely because he makes an unwise decision.' The presence of the word 'merely' indicates that this principle does not completely rule out consideration of outcome based factors. Indeed, in the real world, it is likely that capacity will only be assessed if the person's own choice or their inability to make a choice is likely to lead to an unfavourable outcome for their own health or welfare or for the protection of the safety of others. Nevertheless, the fact that this is the likely outcome may not be used to determine the issue of incapacity.

2.67   The modern approach to capacity is the functional approach. The case law of the European Court of Human Rights shows that this is not yet fully accepted among Council of Europe Member States.[54]

2.68   The English MCA 2005 seeks to adopt the functional approach by stating that 'a person lacks capacity in relation to a matter' (capacity is task specific) if at the material time (capacity may fluctuate) he is unable to make a decision for himself in relation to the matter because of an impairment of, or a disturbance in, the functioning of, the mind or brain. Note that the Mental Capacity Act 2005 does not use a concept of mental disorder but instead that of an impairment of or disturbance in the functioning of the mind or the brain. That impairment may be temporary, and it may be induced by alcohol, drugs, brain injury, toxic confusional state, stroke, or other cause. It is not

---

52   *Re C (adult: refusal of treatment)* [1994] 1 WLR 290, *Re MB (an adult: medical treatment)* [1997] 2 FLR 426, [1997] Fam Law 542, CA.
53   Mental Capacity Act 2005, s 1(2).
54   *Shutkaturov v Russia* Judgment of 27 March 2008.

confined to mental disorder, although we should note that in recent years the scope of the concept of mental disorder has widened considerably.

2.69 The MCA 2005 goes on to list the functional domains of capacity/incapacity stating that a person is unable to make a decision for himself if he is unable:

(a) to understand the information relevant to the decision;

(b) to retain that information;

(c) to use or weigh that information as part of the process of making the decision; or

(d) to communicate his decision (whether by talking, using sign language or any other means).

It is clear that (a) and (b) are primarily cognitive abilities which might be affected by profound intellectual disability, Alzheimer's, dementia, or florid psychosis, and that (c) goes to the ability to communicate, which might be removed by such conditions as locked-in-locked-out syndrome. However, (c) is more about evaluative ability and emotional competence, and it is here that issues of outcome may be smuggled in to what is on its face a functional test. If, for example, someone is profoundly depressed or has a diagnosis of personality disorder and makes a decision which will result in his life being shortened because they set a low value on remaining alive, does that mean that there is a disturbance of the mind which results in them being unable to weigh information as part of the process of making a decision? Does this mean that functional tests should concentrate on cognitive abilities otherwise they risk discriminating against persons with psychosocial disability? But then conditions which attack cognitive ability, such as advanced Alzheimer's would be psychosocial disabilities.

The Requirements of Article 12 CPRD

2.70 Article 12(3) of the CPRD requires States Parties to take appropriate measures to provide access by persons with disabilities to the support they may require in exercising their legal capacity. One of the principles of the MCA 2005 is that 'A person is not to be treated as unable to make a decision unless all practicable steps to help him to do so have been taken without success.' Decisions to give 'serious treatment' or to place in long term residential or hospital care require input from an Independent Mental Capacity Advocate, if there is 'no-one other than a paid carer to consult about the decision.'

2.71 Article 12(4) requires States Parties to ensure that all measures relating to the exercise of legal capacity ensure appropriate and effective safeguards to prevent abuse which must:

- accord with international human rights law;

- respect the rights, will and preferences of the person;

- be free of conflict of interest and undue influence;

- be proportional and tailored to the person's circumstances;

- apply for the shortest time possible;

- be subject to regular review by a competent, independent and impartial authority or judicial body;

- be proportional to the degree to which such measures affect the person's rights and interests.

2.72 The MCA 2005 provides that decisions may be made on behalf of mentally incapacitated adults and requires that these shall be in the best interests of the incapacitated person,[55] and that before any act is done, regard must be had to whether the purpose for which it is needed can be as effectively achieved in a way that is less restrictive of the person's rights and freedom of action. Section 4(6) of the MCA requires anyone deciding what is in a person's best interests to consider, so far as is reasonably ascertainable:

(a) the person's past and present wishes and feelings (and, in particular, any relevant written statement made by him when he had capacity);

(b) the beliefs and values that would be likely to influence his decision if he had capacity; and

(c) the other factors that he would be likely to consider if he were able to do so.

2.73 The intent here is to retain best interests based decision-making but to inject an element of substituted judgment into the process. In my opinion these provisions and the supporting Code of Practice are sufficient to meet the requirement in Art 12(4) to 'respect the rights, will and preferences of the person.'

2.74 As to safeguards, the MCA 2005 provides that the Court of Protection can review decisions about incapacity and best interests, and can make orders concerning the care and treatment of mentally incapacitated adults.

---

[55]   MCA 2005, s 1(5).

Does Article 12 require supported decision-making to replace substitute decision-making in all cases?

2.75 The key question here is whether, as has been asserted, all substituted decision making for adults who lack capacity should be replaced by supported decision-making. Whilst supported decision-making may be possible in many cases, in others, a person's mental disability may be so profound that supported decision-making is impossible and substituted decision-making becomes necessary. As Kämpf has pointed out, although substituted decision-making was extensively debated in the CPRD drafting process, it is not mentioned in the final text of Art 12. Kämpf concludes that this silence indicates that substituted decision-making must be seen as a last resort. The Government of Canada was sufficiently concerned about the possibility that the CPRD might be interpreted to so as to proscribe substitute decision-making that it entered a declaration and two reservations in relation to Art 12:

> 'Canada recognises that persons with disabilities are presumed to have legal capacity on an equal basis with others in all aspects of their lives. Canada declares its understanding that Article 12 permits supported and substitute decision-making arrangements in appropriate circumstances and in accordance with the law.'

To the extent Art 12 may be interpreted as requiring the elimination of all substitute decision-making arrangements, Canada reserves the right to continue their use in appropriate circumstances and subject to appropriate and effective safeguards. With respect to Art 12(4), Canada reserves the right not to subject all such measures to regular review by an independent authority, where such measures are already subject to review or appeal.

2.76 Australia too entered a declaration in similar terms, declaring its understanding that the CRPD allows for fully supported or substituted decision-making arrangements, which provide for decisions to be made on behalf of a person, only where such arrangements are necessary, as a last resort and subject to safeguards.

2.77 As noted (in **2.65**) above, the United Kingdom Government considered whether to enter any declaration or reservation in relation to mental capacity law or mental health legislation, and ultimately decided that none was necessary. The Minister of Disabled People Anne McGuire MP wrote to the Chair of the Joint Committee on Human Rights in 2008 reporting:[56]

> 'that possible compatibility issues in respect of choice of residence and aspects of mental health legislation have been resolved and reservations and interpretative declarations will not be required.'

---

[56] Report of the Joint Committee on Human Rights The UN Convention on the Rights of Persons with Disabilities First Report of Session 2008–2009 HL Paper 9 HC 93 Letter of 24 September 2008. http://www.publications.parliament.uk/pa/jt200809/jtselect/jtrights/9/9.pdf.

Ultimately the only reservation entered in relation to Art 12 was to make clear that there was not yet a system in place for regular review of whether appointees (people who are given the right to deal with benefits on behalf of a disabled person) should continue in that role.

2.78 In conclusion, whilst the silence in Art 12 on the issue of substitute decision-making may indicate a preference for supported decision-making over substituted decision-making, the provision does not prohibit substitute decision-making as a last resort, as long as all practicable steps are taken to support decision-making by the disabled person, whether by advocacy or by recognition of mechanisms such as advance decisions or lasting powers of attorney for health and welfare.

Article 14 of the CPRD: A direct challenge to Specialist Mental health legislation?

2.79 It is Art 14 which poses the direct challenge to the existing rights paradigm in relation to detention on grounds of mental disorder. Article 14(1) requires States Parties to ensure that persons with disabilities, on an equal basis with others: (a) Enjoy the right to liberty and security of person; and (b) Are not deprived of their liberty unlawfully or arbitrarily, and that any deprivation of liberty is in conformity with the law, and that the existence of a disability shall in no case justify a deprivation of liberty.

2.80 Article 14(2) requires States Parties to ensure that if persons with disabilities are deprived of their liberty through any process, they are, on an equal basis with others, entitled to guarantees in accordance with international human rights law and shall be treated in compliance with the objectives and principles of this Convention, including by provision of reasonable accommodation.

2.81 The key phrase here is 'the existence of a disability shall in no case justify a deprivation of liberty'. Australia has entered a declaration of its 'understanding that the Convention allows for compulsory assistance or treatment of persons, including measures taken for the treatment of mental disability, where such treatment is necessary, as a last resort and subject to safeguards.' Any thought that states such as Australia might interpret this as meaning that the existence of a disability shall not of itself justify detention is dismissed by the following trenchant interpretation offered by the United Nations High Commissioner for Human Rights in his 2009 *Thematic Study by the Office of the on enhancing awareness and understanding of the Convention on the Rights of Persons with Disabilities* which states that the effect of Art 14 is to completely proscribe traditional mental health legislation:

> A particular challenge in the context of promoting and protecting the right to liberty and security of persons with disabilities is the legislation and practice related to health care and more specifically to institutionalisation without the free and informed consent of the person concerned (also often referred to as

involuntary or compulsory institutionalisation). Prior to the entrance into force of the Convention, the existence of a mental disability represented a lawful ground for deprivation of liberty and detention under international human rights law. The Convention radically departs from this approach by forbidding deprivation of liberty based on the existence of any disability, including mental or intellectual, as discriminatory. Article 14, paragraph 1(b), of the Convention unambiguously states that "the existence of a disability shall in no case justify a deprivation of liberty". Proposals made during the drafting of the Convention to limit the prohibition of detention to cases "solely" determined by disability were rejected.[57] As a result, unlawful detention encompasses situations where the deprivation of liberty is grounded in the combination between a mental or intellectual disability and other elements such as dangerousness, or care and treatment. Since such measures are partly justified by the person's disability, they are to be considered discriminatory and in violation of the prohibition of deprivation of liberty on the grounds of disability, and the right to liberty on an equal basis with others prescribed by article 14.[58]

Hence, according to the High Commissioner, all legislation:

'authorising institutionalisation of persons with disabilities on the grounds of their disabilities without free and informed consent must be abolished.'

This necessarily entails repeal of provisions authorising detention for the person's own care and treatment, as well as preventive detention on grounds of danger to self or others, 'in all cases where such grounds of care, treatment and public security are linked in legislation to an apparent or diagnosed mental illness.' The Report emphasises that this was not to say that 'persons with disabilities cannot be lawfully subject to detention for care and treatment or to preventive detention.' What it does require however, was that 'the legal grounds upon which restriction of liberty is determined must be de-linked from the disability and neutrally defined so as to apply to all persons on an equal basis.

Article 19 of the CPRD: Independent Living

2.82 Article 14 should be read together with Art 19 which provides the right to independent living, stating that:

'States Parties to the present Convention recognise the equal right of all persons with disabilities to live in the community, with choices equal to others, and shall

---

[57] During the third session of the Ad Hoc Committee on a Comprehensive and Integral International Convention on the Protection and Promotion of the Rights and Dignity of Persons with Disabilities, proposals were made to add the word 'solely' to then draft article 10, paragraph 1 (b), so it would read 'any deprivation of liberty shall be in conformity with the law and in no case shall be based solely on disability'. This amendment was not adopted.

[58] *Annual Report of the United Nations High Commissioner for Human Rights and Reports of the Office of the High Commissioner and the Secretary-General* Thematic Study by the Office of the United Nations High Commissioner for Human Rights on enhancing awareness and understanding of the Convention on the Rights of Persons with Disabilities http://www2.ohchr.org/english/bodies/hrcouncil/docs/10session/A.HRC.10.48.pdf Para 48.

take effective and appropriate measures to facilitate full enjoyment by persons with disabilities of this right and their full inclusion and participation in the community, including by ensuring that:

(a)   persons with disabilities have the opportunity to choose their place of residence and where and with whom they live on an equal basis with others and are not obliged to live in a particular living arrangement;

(b)   persons with disabilities have access to a range of in-home, residential and other community support services, including personal assistance necessary to support living and inclusion in the community, and to prevent isolation or segregation from the community;

(c)   community services and facilities for the general population are available on an equal basis to persons with disabilities and are responsive to their needs.'

Between them Arts 14 and 19 state the aspiration of ending non-consensual institutional care as the cornerstone of the system of care of people with psychosocial disabilities.

The Rhetoric of the CPRD: 'A Paradigm Shift'

2.83   As is repeatedly emphasised in the UN supporting literature, this will involve a significant 'paradigm shift',[59] whose magnitude and difficulty should not be underestimated. The dimensions of this shift are medical, social and legal. In assessing them it is important to bear in mind that international human rights law exists in a political context. Its implementation, even by courts such as the European Court of Human Rights, has a strong political component, where the European Court of Human rights allows a significant 'margin of appreciation to Member States. It is also important to realise that the Disability Rights movement in mental health care has achieved much greater political success at the level of the UN institutions than it has achieved in any signatory state.

2.84   To bring the rights of mentally disordered people under the umbrella of disability rights will not be an easy task, either in technical legal terms, or in political terms, since Governments seem strongly committed to specific mental health legislation authorising detention on grounds of mental disorder plus the presence of risk to own health or safety or the safety of others. The Joint Parliamentary Scrutiny Committee on the English Mental Health Bill 2004 expressed the view that:[60]

'The primary purpose of mental health legislation must be to improve mental health services and safeguards for patients and to reduce the stigma of mental disorder.'

---

[59]   Thomas Kuhn coined the term in his seminal work *The Structure of Scientific Revolutions* (1962). Since then the term has become much used (some might say over-used) to connote a change in the fundamental assumptions on which a body of knowledge or discourse is founded.

[60]   House of Lords House of Commons Joint Committee *Report on the Draft Mental Health Bill*, Session 2004–2005 HL Paper 79–1, HC 95–1. Session 2004–2005, Summary, 5.

The UK Government's Response was dismissive and blunt: 'The Bill is not about service provision, it is about bringing people under compulsion.'[61]

2.85 England and Wales have recently introduced two statutes authorising detention: the Mental Capacity Act 2005 where the person has a mental disorder (defined as any disorder or disability of the mind), and lacks capacity to decide where to reside, and deprivation of liberty is necessary in the person's own best interests; and the Mental Health Act 2007 which amends the 1983 Act and allows detention where the person has mental disorder of a nature or degree warranting detention in the interests of their own health or safety or for the protection of others. Despite these changes, the UK Government did not see fit to enter any reservations or declarations along the lines entered by Australia and Canada.

2.86 The CPRD 'paradigm shift' approach involves nothing less than the wholesale implantation of the social model of disability in mental health care, dismantling the medical model of mental disorder and replacing it with a model based on psychosocial disability. Great strides have been made in achieving such a shift in relation to intellectual disability, referred to in the international diagnostic manuals as mental retardation or mental handicap. There can be no doubt that much has been achieved in this regard in the United Kingdom, including the almost complete closure of the large learning disability hospitals and their replacement with smaller supported living homes, and care homes for those with higher levels of dependency. There has been a progressive movement to remove learning disability from the scope of mental health legislation unless it is accompanied by abnormally aggressive or seriously irresponsible conduct. The experience with learning disability shows that much can be achieved. However, even these types of reforms would not go far enough to meet the interpretation of Art 14 promulgated by the High Commissioner.

2.87 These attitudinal and policy shifts will not be so easily achieved in relation to mental illness, where pharmacological approaches to treatment are much more firmly entrenched, and the medical model of treatment predominates.[62] Whilst pharmacological approaches to treatment of psychosocial disability are hotly contested by service users and others, their efficacy is generally accepted by national policy makers. Indeed, across the globe, and certainly in these islands, compliance with medication and the minimisation of risk to self and to others are among the principal goals pursued by Governments in their mental health legislation. Moreover there is an increasing trend for mental health NGOs to promoting 'recovery programmes' where great emphasis is laid on (admittedly voluntary) compliance with medication.

2.88 As is acknowledged by the UN High Commissioner, the proposed shift involves not only supplanting medical hegemony but also jettisoning existing

---

[61] Government Response to the Report of the Joint Committee on the Draft Mental Health Bill (Cm 6624) 2005, para 10.

[62] For a critique of the Age of Psychopharmacology see for example E Valenstein Blaming the Brain: The Truth About Drugs and Mental Illness (1998) Free Press New York.

human rights paradigms such as the 1991 UN Principles for the Protection of Persons with Mental Illness and the Improvement of Mental Health Care,[63] the European Convention on Human Rights Article 5, and Recommendation Rec (2004)10 of the Council of Europe Committee of Ministers to Member States concerning the protection of the human rights and dignity of persons with mental disorder, particularly those subject to involuntary placement or involuntary treatment. This Recommendation emphasises the need for decisions to detain or treat without consent to be based on objective medical expertise and that treatment must have a therapeutic purpose. Article 5 of the European Convention on Human Rights protects against arbitrary detention. Article 5(1)(e) allows detention on grounds of unsoundness of mind provided detention is based on objective medical evidence of a true mental disorder, is a proportionate response and is carried out in accordance with a procedure prescribed by law.[64]

2.89   There is a less extensive but nonetheless important jurisprudence of the ECtHR on the right of respect for private life under Art 8 of the European Convention on Human Rights. Private life includes physical and psychological integrity, which may only be interfered with in accordance with law and necessary to meet one of the legitimate aims listed in Art 8(2). These include health, prevention of crime and protecting the rights and freedoms of others. In *Storck* v *Germany* the European Court of Human Rights held that states have positive obligations under both Art 5 and Art 8 to provide effective supervision and review of interferences with the right to liberty and the right to personal integrity.[65] The case law of the European Court of Human Rights on Art 5 and unsoundness of mind was developed in a context of concerns about the abuse of psychiatry for political ends, hence the requirement in *Winterwerp* of objective medical evidence of a true mental disorder, and the proscription of detention on grounds of 'mere deviance from society's norms' falling short of criminality. In the context of a Council of Europe where many states struggle to meet the requirements even of this case law, the danger is that the UN CPRD will lead to the baby being thrown out with the bathwater.

2.90   However worthy the aim, there would seem to be little immediate prospect of new legislation authorising therapeutic detention on the basis of risk to own health or safety or the safety of others which is 'de-linked from the disability and neutrally defined so as to apply to all persons on an equal basis.' And we might question whether it is wise to abandon over thirty years of Convention jurisprudence for an unknown future. Official UN publications acknowledge the potential legitimacy of legislation authorising preventive detention (which is by no means politically uncontroversial) or detention for care and treatment as long as it is de-linked from mental illness or mental disorder. Yet these documents, and those who have written in support of

---

[63]   Adopted by General Assembly resolution 46/119 of 17 December 1991 <http://www 2.ohchr.org/english/law/principles.htm>.
[64]   *Winterwerp v the Netherlands* (1979) 2 EHRR 387.
[65]   [2005] ECHR 406.

implementing the High Commissioner's interpretation of Art 14,[66] are conspicuously vague about what such legislation might look like. The danger is that states will wish to retain the right to exercise the police and parens patriae powers of the state to prevent risk to self or to others, and that delinked legislation might well lead to vulnerable people with psychosocial disabilities ending up in the prison system in greater numbers than currently is the case. It is a fact of life that many people with mental disabilities such as dementia, severe psychosis, or depressive illness require residential care in an institution with medical support.

2.91 Might it be the case that a statute allowing detention on grounds of decision-making incapacity would satisfy the requirement of de-linkage from disability. The question which then arises is whether the issue of capacity must be 'de-linked' from any concept of mental disorder or impairment of mental functioning in order to comply with the CPRD. For example the English MCA 2005 requires that a person will only lack capacity as a result of an impairment of or disturbance in the functioning of the mind or the brain. This may be permanent or temporary and may include intoxication by alcohol or drugs. Is requiring incapacity to result from such a condition discriminatory on grounds of disability, or is it simply recognition of the fact that the concept of informed consent generally requires decision–making capacity, and decision-making incapacity generally results from impairments of mental functioning? One danger of this is that given the political premium placed on managing risk to self or to others, the concept of decision-making incapacity will be expanded via the highly subjective component of 'inability to appreciate' or to weigh treatment information as part of the process of arriving at a decision. Alternatively, those making decisions about detention might under assess incapacity resulting in people who need care and treatment in their own interests or those of others being denied it. It is important to remember that there are positive obligations under the European Convention to protect vulnerable people from exploitation and to uphold their dignity, as well as to protect their right to liberty.[67]

CONCLUSION

2.92 Notwithstanding the UN Convention on the Rights of Persons with Disabilities England and Wales have two mental health statutes: the Mental Health Act 1983 and the Mental Capacity Act 2005. The MCA 2005 has statutory principles. Its ethos is based on the welfare and 'best interests' of the individual. It employs the paternalist power of the State as *parens patriae* for the individual's benefit. The lead Department is the Ministry of Justice. The MHA 1983 provides for intervention on paternalist grounds in the interests of the patient's health, and also where it is necessary for the patient's safety. The

---

[66] See for example Tina Minkowitz, 'Abolishing Mental Health Laws to Comply with CPRD' in Mc Sherry and Weller (eds) *Re-Thinking Rights-Based Mental Health Laws* (2010) 151–177, at 167–168.

[67] *Re F (Adult Patient: Court's Jurisdiction)* [2001] Fam 38.

significant difference is that the MHA 1983 also deploys the police power of the State where someone's mental disorder warrants their detention for treatment and detention is necessary for the protection of other people. The lead department is the Department of Health. A more overt emphasis on public protection is found in Part III of the MHA 1983, which provides for the sentencing of mentally disordered offenders, and transfers from prison. The Home Office used to be the lead department for mentally disordered offenders. Its functions in this regard have now been transferred to the Ministry of Justice, but the key goals of protecting the public and preventing re-offending remain. This goal is reflected in the inclusion of public safety alongside patient well-being among the matters to be addressed in drawing up the principles for the Code. This means that there are two Government Departments involved in policy-making, the Department of Health, and the Ministry of Justice. Although a person may be detained under the MHA 1983 in the interests of their own health or safety, the key difference from the MCA 2005 is the availability under the 1983 Act of detention for the protection of others. Hence the Mental Health Act marks the intersection between the health system and the criminal justice system.

2.93 Little wonder then, that when the Joint Parliamentary Scrutiny Committee considered the Mental Health Bill 2004, Lord Rix and Mrs Angela Browning MP were anxious in their questions to witnesses to ensure that people with learning disabilities and people with Autism or Asperger's should not be treated as mentally disordered for the purposes of the Mental Health Act. Their view was that if decisions need to be taken about admission to hospital or treatment of patients in these diagnostic groups these should be made within the statutory framework of the Mental Capacity Act 2005. This is now reflected in the amended MHA 1983 by the exclusion of learning disability from powers of long-term detention unless there is abnormally aggressive or seriously irresponsible conduct. For people with learning disabilities and autistic spectrum disorder, being admitted and treated as a mentally disordered person under mental health legislation is to be avoided as stigmatising. There is a general perception that the Mental Capacity Act is for people with mental illness of old age, or for people with learning disability. They should only be dealt with under mental health legislation if abnormally aggressive or seriously irresponsible in their conduct. The Mental Health Act is seen by the Government as being for other groups of people with mental disorders, such as younger adults with psychotic illnesses or personality disorders, who may be articulating resistance to treatment, and, perhaps most important, who may pose a risk to others.

2.94 The Mental Health Act 2007 is a radical reform in mental health legislation for a number of reasons, but perhaps most notably for its complexity and its greater emphasis on patient obligations, particularly community obligations to accept medication and to behave in accordance with conditions. A person on a community treatment order ('CTO') may be obliged to accept medication and to desist from certain conduct. If they do not comply, they may be recalled to hospital. They may be detained there for up to 72 hours. If they accept medication within that time they will probably be released into the community still subject to the CTO. If will not accept treatment and they meet the criteria for detention for treatment under s 3 of the MHA 1983, their CTO may be revoked and they become a detained patient again. Emergency treatment for mental disorder may be given in limited circumstances without consent in the community using reasonable force if necessary, where the patient lacks capacity (or is a *Gillick* incompetent minor). Non-emergency treatment may be given if the patient is capable and consents. Treatment may be given even if there is reason to believe the patient is refusing it as long as force is not necessary. So in a non-emergency situation the patient may be told that if s/he does not consent to the treatment s/he may be recalled to hospital and held for up to 72 hours while professionals decide whether to allow the section to be reinstated. Patients who are aware of this power dynamic are likely to comply with the obligation to accept treatment without force being necessary even though there is reason to believe they are resisting treatment.

2.95 The Mental Health Act 1983 and the Mental Capacity Act 2005 are companion mental health statutes. If they are to be placed on a spectrum between health and criminal justice statutes, the Mental Capacity Act is a health and welfare statute, whereas the Mental Health Act marks the intersection between the health care system and the penal system. Between them they provide a framework for detaining mentally incapacitated patients where necessary in their best interests and mentally disordered people whether they retain capacity or not, where it is necessary for the health or safety of the patient or for the protection of others. Part III provides the link with the criminal justice system. The new community treatment orders are intended to provide an equivalent to conditional discharge for non-offender patients and for mentally disordered offenders who have been sentenced to hospital orders without restrictions. The Mental Health Act offers powers to detain people adjudged to present a risk to public safety without the need to arrest them for any offence. In the chapters which follow the effect of the MHA 2007 is examined in the context of the European Convention on Human Rights and the Human Rights Act 1998. At the core of the changes introduced by the 2007 Act are the new broad definition of mental disorder and the test of availability of appropriate treatment. Chapter 3 below explains and discusses the definition of mental disorder and the conditions of compulsion.

Chapter 3

'MENTAL DISORDER' AND THE AVAILABILITY OF APPROPRIATE TREATMENT

INTRODUCTION

3.1   At the core of the changes introduced by the MHA 2007 are the new broad definition of mental disorder and the test of availability of appropriate treatment. As the Joint Parliamentary Committee put it in their scrutiny of the 2004 Bill:[1]

> 'Not only will vital decisions about people's lives be directly based upon them, but the remainder of the Bill depends on and is shaped by them ... Any legislation designed to deprive individuals who have committed no offence of their personal liberty and autonomy requires Parliament to go to considerable lengths to satisfy itself that the Government has got the balance right and is creating a framework in which mental health professionals can more appropriately exercise their judgment.'

The MHA 2007 has widened the definition of mental disorder so that it now includes 'any disorder or disability of the mind', the intention being to create an effective legal framework within which risk to self and others may be managed.

The definition of 'mental disorder'

3.2   The MHA 2007 abolishes the four separate categories of mental disorder applicable to longer-term admission for treatment under the MHA 1983, and introduces a single simplified definition of mental disorder that applies throughout the Act. It is 'any disorder or disability of the mind.' Previously a person could only be detained for treatment for up to six months if classified as suffering from mental illness, psychopathic disorder, mental impairment or severe mental impairment. Now a person may be detained if suffering from 'any disorder or disability of the mind', regardless of whether the detention is for a short or a long period.

3.3   The new broad definition, which is basically the 'catch all' at the end of the broad definition of mental disorder in the old s 1(2), extends the scope of

---

[1]   House of Lords, House of Commons Joint Pre-Parliamentary Scrutiny Committee *Report on the Draft Mental Health Bill* (HL Paper 79(1), HC Paper 95(1), Session 2004–2005), para 81.

powers of detention, particularly in relation to personality disorder, the group causing most concern to the Government, perceived as high risk for offending behaviour, particularly sex offences. The original MHA 1983 classification of such people would have been psychopathic disorder, which required abnormally aggressive or seriously irresponsible conduct. A person with a diagnosis of personality disorder may now be detained without such conduct being a requirement. The Government saw three major 'fault lines' in the 1983 Act:

(i)   the definition of psychopathic disorder;

(ii)   the exclusion that no-one may be treated as mentally disordered by reason only of sexual deviancy; and

(iii)   the 'treatability' test.

These 'flaws' represented an unacceptable obstacle to using powers of detention under the Mental Health Act to protect society against the risk from sex offenders with personality disorders emerging from prison at the end of determinate sentences. They could not be rearrested until they committed an offence. In the Government's view, the MHA 1983 put too many obstacles in the way of detaining them under the Mental Health Act on grounds of personality disorder if they were assessed as high risk for re-offending.

3.4   In 1995 Dr Jim Higgins summarised the implications of a diagnosis of psychopathy as often being that:[2]

> 'the patient is untreatable, has no proper place in a hospital and is disliked by clinical staff. It is often employed in order to reject patients for treatment and for this purpose may be deliberately applied to patients with other psychiatric disorders such as schizophrenia or hypomania.'

3.5   The Reed Committee – which examined the issue in 1994 – emphasised this point, stating that:[3]

> 'As a consequence people who might benefit from medical care were, at times, denied it and remained in prison or be left unsupported in the community. The implications for public safety were clearly matters of concern.'

The Reed committee recommended replacement of the stigmatising term 'psychopathic disorder' with 'personality disorder'. In fact neither term now appears in the MHA 1983. Personality disorder falls within 'any disorder or disability of the mind'. The treatability test has been removed, as has the exclusion for sexual deviancy. The Government has invested considerably in

---

2   'Crime and Mental Disorder: Forensic Aspects of Psychiatric Disorder' in D Chiswick and R Cope (eds) *Practical Forensic Psychiatry* (Gaskell Royal College of Psychiatrists, 1995), at pp 65–66.

3   Department of Health and Home Office *Report of the Department of Health and Home Office Working Group on Psychopathic Disorder* (HMSO, 1994), para 10.16v.

developing services for offender patients and has established special units for Dangerous People with Severe Personality Disorder in Broadmoor and Rampton High Security Hospitals and Whitemoor Prison, the aim being to develop effective treatment programmes for this group.[4]

Treatability and appropriate treatment

3.6   For patients suffering from psychopathic disorder or mental impairment detention for treatment under s 3 or under a s 37 hospital order was only possible if medical treatment for mental disorder was likely to alleviate or prevent deterioration in their condition – the 'treatability' test. It could therefore be to a patient's advantage to be reclassified under the MHA 1983 from 'mental illness' or 'severe mental impairment' (which used to be known as the 'major disorders' and where it was assumed that treatment would be of benefit) to 'psychopathic disorder' or 'mental impairment' (which used to be known as the 'minor disorders' where a treatability test applied). If not treatable, a patient with a minor disorder would be entitled to discharge.[5] The numerous provisions relating to reclassification under the MHA 1983 have now been rendered obsolete by the new broad definition of mental disorder and these provisions were repealed by the MHA 2007.

The rejection of significantly impaired judgment as a condition of compulsion

3.7   The Richardson Committee recommended that capacity play a part in the conditions of compulsion, to the extent that a higher threshold of risk to self or others would be required to impose compulsion on a capable person. This was rejected by the Government in 2000. The Millan Committee, whose recommendations formed the basis of the Mental Health (Care and Treatment) (Scotland) Act 2003, learned from the experience of Richardson and proposed the intermediate concept of significantly impaired decision-making ability. The Scottish Act requires as a condition of compulsion that the person's judgment *in relation to the decision to accept treatment* must be significantly impaired. The Scottish Code of Practice emphasises that it is a separate concept to incapacity, even though similar factors are taken into account, including consideration of:

> 'the extent to which the person's mental disorder might affect adversely affect their ability to believe, understand and retain information concerning their care and treatment, to make decisions based on that information, and to communicate those decisions to others.'

The question is whether judgment is significantly impaired, not whether the person lacks capacity. A person's judgment might be significantly impaired if

---

[4]   The website of the DPSPD projects is http://www.dspdprogramme.gov.uk, where will be found the slogan: 'Ensuring the public is protected from some of the most dangerous people in society'.

[5]   *Reid v United Kingdom* (2003) 37 EHRR 9, ECtHR.

they lacked insight into the fact that they had a mental illness, or where their ability to use information and weigh it in the balance to make a decision was impaired by a depressive illness.

3.8   The Department of Health and the Home Office successfully fought off attempts to install the concept of significantly impaired judgment in the MHA 2007. They were concerned that:[6]

> 'it is possible that people who are at very great risk to themselves or to others would nonetheless retain the ability to make unimpaired decisions about treatment.'

Dawson, in his excellent comparative survey of community treatment orders, suggests that the decision-making of people with less severe personality disorders would probably not be sufficiently impaired to meet the test, and that:[7]

> 'This is one principled way to exclude most persons with a personality disorder from cover by an involuntary patient regime.'

The Government's agenda was to remove all obstacles to mental health detention of people with personality disorder where there is risk, so it was little surprise that the significantly impaired judgment test was rejected.

THE EUROPEAN CONVENTION ON HUMAN RIGHTS AND DETENTION ON GROUNDS OF UNSOUNDNESS OF MIND

3.9   Article 5(1) of the European Convention on Human Rights provides that no-one shall be deprived of his liberty unless the deprivation is carried out in accordance with a procedure prescribed by law and is necessary in a democratic society on one of a number of grounds. One of those grounds, set out in Art 5(1)(e), is deprivation of liberty on grounds of unsoundness of mind. In order for a non-emergency detention on grounds of unsoundness of mind to conform to the requirements of Art 5(1)(e) of the ECHR there must be reliable evidence of a true mental disorder.

Unsoundness of mind

3.10   In *Winterwerp v Netherlands* the European Court of Human Rights laid down the substantive and procedural requirements for lawful detention of persons of unsound mind. Three minimum conditions ('the *Winterwerp* criteria') must be satisfied:

---

[6]   *Government Response to the Report of the Joint Committee on the Draft Mental Health Bill* Cm 6624 (2005), response to recommendation 26, p 16.

[7]   John Dawson 'Community Treatment Orders: International Comparisons' (May 2005) *Law Foundation New Zealand*, p 100.

(a)   Except in emergency cases, the individual must reliably be shown to be of unsound mind. This has been held to entail the establishment of a true mental disorder on the basis of objective expertise.

(b)   The mental disorder must be of a kind or degree justifying compulsory confinement.

(c)   The validity of continued confinement depends on the persistence of such a mental disorder. This implies that it is for those carrying out the detention to satisfy themselves at intervals that the criteria for detention continue to be met.[8]

The court in *Winterwerp* declined to define 'unsoundness of mind' as it was a term whose meaning is constantly evolving as research in psychiatry progresses, an increasing flexibility in treatment is developing, and society's attitude to mental illness changes.[9] Although this confers broad discretion on clinicians, there are two limiting factors. There must be a true mental disorder, and it must be of a kind or degree warranting confinement.

A true mental disorder

3.11   Psychiatrists might view a true mental disorder as being one which appears in either the Diagnostic and Statistical Manual of Mental Disorders of the American Psychiatric Association ('DSM-IV-R' soon to be replaced by the 'DSM-V')[10] or the International Classification of Diseases of the World Health Organisation ('ICD-10').[11] The DSM-IV is a 900-page reference book classifying 300 different disorders, each one containing a list of symptoms some or all of which must be present for the specific diagnosis. In the United States, a DSM IV diagnosis is the key to insurance coverage. All mental health professionals must list a diagnostic label from the DSM together with a code number in order to obtain insurance reimbursement for treatment.[12] Both DSM-IV and ICD-10 contain many conditions ranging from psychotic illnesses such as bipolar illness and schizophrenia, to depression or Alzheimer's, to personality disorders, disorders of sexual preference, and addictions ranging from addiction to alcohol and drugs to nicotine and caffeine related disorders. In psychiatry there is much greater reliance on the clinician's observation rather than scientific tests, and hence greater subjectivity in the diagnostic process.

---

[8]   *Winterwerp v Netherlands (Application 6301/73)* (1979) 2 EHRR 387, ECtHR; *X v United Kingdom (Application 7215/75)* (1981) 4 EHRR 188, 1 BMLR 98, ECtHR; and *Van der Leer v Netherlands (Application 11509/85)* (1990) 12 EHRR 567, ECtHR.

[9]   *Winterwerp v Netherlands* (1979) 2 EHRR 387, at para 37.

[10]   *Diagnostic and Statistical Manual of Mental Disorders* (American Psychiatric Association, 4th edn (DSM-IV), 1994).

[11]   World Health Organisation *Tenth Revision of the International Classification of Disease (ICD-10)*; *Classification of Mental and Behavioural Disorders* (1992).

[12]   H Kutchins and S Kirk *Making us Crazy: DSM – The Psychiatric Bible and the Creation of Mental Disorders* (Constable London, 1997).

3.12 For these reasons, it is important to note DSM-IV's cautionary reminder that:[13]

> '[I]n most situations the clinical diagnosis of a DSM-lV mental disorder is not sufficient to establish the existence for legal purposes of a "mental disorder" … In determining whether an individual meets a specified legal standard (e.g. for competence, criminal responsibility or disability), additional information is usually required beyond that contained in the DSM-1V diagnosis. This might include information about the individual's functional impairments … [A]ssign-ment of a particular diagnosis does not imply a specific level of impairment or disability.'

Broad as the scope of DSM disorders is, the Government did not wish to be tied down by the need for a disorder to appear in its pages in order to be a true mental disorder. In the debates during the Public Bill Committee stage, the Minister of State Rosie Winterton MP said it 'cannot be said that something that is not in any classification is not a mental disorder'.[14]

Distinguishing between deviancy from society's norms and mental disorder

3.13 There is great sensitivity about the boundary between mental disorder and deviant conduct. This is due in part to the history of abuses of psychiatry, particularly in the Soviet Union, where dissidents were detained in psychiatric hospitals, their alleged illness being their dissident views and conduct.[15] These concerns persist to the present day. China, for example, does not have effective legal protections to prevent psychiatric detention of dissidents.[16] It is also due to the desire on the part of psychiatrists to be seen primarily as therapists rather than agents of social control. Decisions to detain on grounds of unsoundness of mind must be free from arbitrariness. The Strasbourg Court has held that Art 5(1)(e) cannot be taken to permit the detention of a person simply because his views deviate from the norms prevailing in a particular society.[17]

3.14 Both ICD-10 and DSM-IV are keen to emphasise the distinction between mental disorder and deviance, but offer only imprecise boundaries between the two. Each offers a clinical definition of mental disorder. In DSM-IV mental disorder is:[18]

> 'A clinically significant behavioural or psychological syndrome or pattern that occurs in an individual and that is associated with present distress (e g a painful

---

13   See p xxiii.
14   Public Bill Committee, col 16.
15   See for example Zhores and Roy Medvedev, *A Question Of Madness*, Penguin Books 1971.
16   See 'Assertive Chinese Face the Risk of Being Locked Up as Insane' New York Times November 21 2010
17   *Winterwerp v Netherlands* (1979) 2 EHRR 387, at para 37.
18   DSM-IV, p xxi.

symptom) or disability (ie impairment in one or more important areas of functioning) with a significantly increased risk of suffering death, pain, disability or an important loss of freedom.'

DSM-IV emphasises the importance of distinguishing between mental disorder and behaviour which might be expected in legitimate response to traumatic events. To be regarded as a mental disorder the syndrome or pattern of behaviour cannot be:[19]

'[A]n expectable and culturally sanctioned response to a particular event, for example, the death of a loved one. Whatever its original cause, it must currently be considered a manifestation of a behavioural, psychological, or biological dysfunction in the individual. Neither deviant behaviour (e.g. political religious or sexual) nor conflicts that are primarily between the individual and society are mental disorders unless the deviance or conflict is a symptom of a dysfunction in the individual as described above.'

3.15 ICD-10 too lays emphasis on the concept of individual dysfunction as the means of distinguishing between deviance and mental disorder in these terms:[20]

'Disorder is used to imply the existence of a clinically recognisable set of symptoms or behaviour associated in most cases with distress and with interference with personal functions. Social deviance alone, without personal dysfunction, should not be included in mental disorder as defined here.'

These concerns are also reflected in the English Code of Practice on the MHA 1983 which provides as follows:[21]

'Difference should not be confused with disorder. No-one may be considered to be mentally disordered solely because of their political, religious or cultural beliefs, values or opinions, unless there are proper clinical grounds to believe that they are the symptoms or manifestations of a disability or disorder of the mind. The same is true of a person's involvement, or likely involvement, in illegal, anti-social or "immoral" behaviour. Beliefs, behaviours or actions which do not result from a disorder or disability of the mind are not a basis for compulsory measures under the Act, even if they appear unusual or cause other people alarm, distress or danger.'

The exclusions

3.16 There were exclusions in s 1(3) of the MHA 1983 that a person should not be treated as suffering from mental disorder by reason only of promiscuity or other immoral conduct, sexual deviancy, or dependence on alcohol or drugs. The Government's concern was that people whose disorder manifested itself in sexual behaviour, and who were adjudged high risk to commit sex offences,

---

[19] DSM-IV, p xxii.
[20] ICD-10, 5.
[21] Department of Health *Code of Practice: Mental Health Act 1983* (2008), para 3.6.

might avoid detention under mental health legislation by availing themselves of one of these exclusions. The original Mental Health Bill 2006 removed the exclusions, except those for addiction. The House of Lords amended the Bill to provide that a person should not be considered to have a mental disorder solely on the grounds of:

(a)   his substance misuse (including dependence on alcohol or drugs);

(b)   his sexual identity or orientation;

(c)   his commission or likely commission of illegal or disorderly acts; or

(d)   his cultural, religious or political beliefs.

This amendment was overturned in the Commons Public Bill Committee and replaced by a single provision (now s 1(3) of the MHA 1983) stating that dependence on alcohol or drugs is not considered to be a disorder or disability of the mind.

Dependence on alcohol or drugs

3.17   The exclusion refers to dependence and so extreme intoxication is not prevented from being a mental disorder by this provision. The Department of Health Code of Practice emphasises that other mental disorders relating to the use of alcohol or drugs are not excluded, and these include withdrawal state with delirium or associated psychotic disorder, organic mental disorders association with prolonged abuse of drugs or alcohol, and even severe acute intoxication (drunkenness) provided all the relevant criteria are met.[22]

3.18   Dependence on alcohol or drugs appears in the diagnostic manuals as a mental disorder. Addiction is a separate ground of detention under Art 5(1)(e). Use of alcohol or drugs is not, by itself, regarded clinically as a disorder or disability of the mind, but the Government considers that 'the effects of such use may be'.[23] The effect of the statement in s 3 of the MHA 2007 that 'dependence on alcohol or drugs is not considered to be a disorder or disability of the mind' is that:[24]

> 'no action can be taken under the 1983 Act in relation to people simply because they are dependent on alcohol or drugs (including opiates, psycho-stimulants or some solvents), even though in other contexts their dependence would be considered clinically to be a mental disorder.'

3.19   The exclusion does not mean that addicts are excluded entirely from the scope of the MHA 1983. A person may have a mental disorder which is

---

22   Ibid, para 3.11.
23   Department of Health, Ministry of Justice, Welsh Assembly Government *Mental Health Act 2007 Explanatory Notes* (2007), para 25.
24   Ibid, para 26.

completely unrelated to their dependence on alcohol or drugs. Excess consumption of alcohol or drugs may precipitate recognised forms of mental illness such as Korsakoff's Syndrome, drug induced psychoses, delirium consequent on withdrawal, or depression. The Explanatory Notes also point out that the exclusion does not mean that:

> '[P]eople may never be treated without consent under the 1983 Act for alcohol or drug dependence. Like treatment for any other condition which is not itself a mental disorder, treatment for dependence may be given under the 1983 Act if it forms part of treatment for a condition which is a mental disorder for the purposes of the 1983 Act.'

This might occur where the dependence is a consequence of the mental disorder and treatment may therefore be given under s 63 of the MHA 1983.[25]

Promiscuity, other immoral conduct, or sexual deviancy

3.20 The Government considers that deletion of the exclusion for promiscuity or 'other immoral conduct' makes no practical difference, since 'clinically … neither by itself is regarded as a mental disorder', and 'sexual orientation (homo-, hetero- and bi-sexuality) alone is not regarded as a mental disorder'.[26] Removing the sexual deviance exclusion is intended to have an effect and the Explanatory Notes make clear what it is – to allow detention of paedophiles under the Act:[27]

> 'some disorders of sexual preference are recognised clinically as mental disorders. Some of these disorders might be considered "sexual deviance" in the terms of the current exclusion (for example paraphilias like fetishism or paedophilia). On that basis, the amendment would bring such disorders within the scope of the 1983 Act.'

3.21 The arguments which the Government intend to eliminate by this change are exemplified in the case of *R (on the application of MN) v Mental Health Review Tribunal*[28] where the patient was detained as suffering from psychopathic disorder where a necessary component is abnormally aggressive or seriously irresponsible conduct. The patient argued that the only such conduct of this nature which he had engaged in was directed towards pursuing his sexually deviant urges as a paedophile. Therefore he argued he was entitled to discharge by the Mental Health Review Tribunal ('MHRT') as the only behavioural components of his disorder were acts in pursuit of his sexual deviancy. The MHRT rejected his argument, viewing it as fallacious. The tribunal's decision was upheld by Calvert-Smith J because it had taken into account not only the sexual deviancy, but also other symptoms which stood outside the actual sexual deviancy.

---

[25] *B v Croydon Health Authority* [1995] 1 All ER 683, CA.
[26] Department of Health, Ministry of Justice, Welsh Assembly Government *Mental Health Act 2007 Explanatory Notes* (2007), para 24.
[27] Ibid.
[28] [2007] EWHC 1524 (Admin).

3.22 The tribunal considered it wrong to exclude consideration of abnormally aggressive behaviour or seriously irresponsible behaviour in pursuit of sexual deviancy. If the conduct of a paedophile, while he is pursuing his sexual gratification, was abnormally aggressive or seriously irresponsible then such behaviour could amount to psychopathy. In other words, diagnosis of psychopathy can be based on the way a paedophile conducts his sexual assaults. The tribunal was satisfied that N's behaviours included serious manipulative lying outside his sexual pursuits, fantasies of using violence to gratify his desires and concerns that he might strangle someone to achieve his sexual desires clearly. Also N's serious lying, outside his sexual pursuits, to manipulate others cannot be discounted altogether by reason of his institutionalisation. The tribunal was satisfied that there was a seriously aggressive nature which existed as well as his sexual needs.[29] The High Court upheld their decision. These lines of argument will no longer be possible. The MHA 2007 has done away with them by abolishing the sexual deviancy exclusion and the requirement that anyone who suffers from personality disorder must be abnormally aggressive or seriously irresponsible in their conduct. There is now no obstacle to detaining N under the MHA 1983 on grounds of personality disorder.

3.23 Considerable concern was expressed by the Joint Committee on Human Rights about gender identity dysphoria and transvestic fetishism, given that transsexualism may be regarded as falling within the right to personal development and physical and moral integrity under Art 8.[30] The Government's response was that both conditions may be regarded as mental disorders, since 'gender dysphoria is a disorder of gender identity, not sexuality', and hence has never been excluded from the MHA 1983. Transvestic fetishism, by contrast, would be considered clinically to be an abnormality of sexual preference. The Government thinks that a court might consider transvestic fetishism 'sexual deviancy' for the purposes of the MHA 1983, and so removing that exclusion brings it within the scope of the 1983 Act.[31] However:[32]

> '15.   While very different from one another, gender dysphoria and transvestic fetishism are like very many other mental disorders which are in theory covered by the 1983 Act, but which in practice would not be expected to lead to people being detained. Other examples include mild depression and anxiety, phobia of flying and various forms of sexual dysfunction.
>
> 16.   On the other hand, if a person did meet the criteria for detention as a result of gender identity or transvestic fetishism (or any other equally unlikely disorder) and needed to be detained for their own sake or to protect others then it is right that mental health legislation should enable appropriate

---

[29]   [2007] EWHC 1524 (Admin) at [26]–[28].

[30]   House of Lords, House of Commons Joint Committee on Human Rights *Legislative Scrutiny: Mental Health Bill: Fourth Report of Session 2006–07* (HL Paper 40, HC Paper 288), paras 14 and 15; *Legislative Scrutiny: Seventh Progress Report: Fifteenth Report of Session 2006–07* (HL Paper 555, HC Paper 112), paras 1.4–1.6.

[31]   Ibid, Seventh Progress Report, p 19.

[32]   Ibid.

action to be taken. But for that to happen there would have to be wholly exceptional – and very hard to envisage – circumstances.'

3.24 The JCHR argued for express exclusions, beyond simply those for addiction, to be included in the legislation, to reflect human rights obligations:[33]

'Obligations under EU law have made it necessary to provide express legal protection against employment discrimination on grounds of sexual orientation or gender reassignment.[34] The European Court of Human Rights has held that sexual identity is protected by virtue of the right to respect for private life under Article 8. Freedom of religion (Article 9), freedom of association and freedom of expression of religious, cultural or political beliefs are protected by Articles 10 and 11 of the Convention. Discrimination in the way rights (including the right to protection against arbitrary detention under Article 5) are protected on grounds of ethnicity, religious, cultural or political beliefs, age or any other status is also proscribed by Article 14 of the Convention.'

Their argument was rejected, but this summary serves as a salutary reminder to the Government and clinicians of the human rights context in which the Mental Health Act operates, and where the boundary between mental disorder and deviancy from society's norms may lie.

Clinically recognised mental disorders

3.25 The Department of Health Code of Practice contains the following non-exhaustive list of clinically recognised conditions which could fall within the concept of mental disorder:

- affective disorders, such as depression and bipolar disorder;

- schizophrenia and delusional disorders;

- neurotic, stress-related and somatoform disorders, such as anxiety, phobic disorders, obsessive compulsive disorders, post-traumatic stress disorder and hypochondriacal disorders;

- organic mental disorders such as dementia and delirium (however caused);

- personality and behavioural changes caused by brain injury or damage (however acquired);

- personality disorders;

- mental and behavioural disorders caused by psychoactive substance use;

---

[33]   Ibid, para 1.6.
[34]   Employment Equality (Sexual Orientation) Regulations 2003, SI 2003/1661; Employment Equality (Sexual Orientation) (Amendment) Regulations 2003, SI 2003/2827; and Sex Discrimination (Gender Reassignment) Regulations 1999, SI 1999/1102.

- eating disorders, non-organic sleep disorders and non-organic sexual disorders;

- learning disabilities;

- autistic spectrum disorders (including Asperger's syndrome);

- behavioural and emotional disorders of children and adolescents.[35]

The Explanatory Notes to the Bill give the following examples of 'clinically recognised mental disorders':[36]

> '[M]ental illnesses such as schizophrenia, bipolar disorder, anxiety or depression, as well as personality disorders, autistic spectrum disorders and learning disabilities. Disorders or disabilities of the brain are not regarded as mental disorders unless (and only to the extent that) they give rise to a disability or disorder of the mind as well.'

If a brain injury or a brain tumour, for example, causes a mental disorder or a mental disability, or manifests itself in a disturbance of mental functioning, then there will be a disability or disorder of the mind. We now consider the examples given in the Explanatory Notes.

Bipolar disorder

3.26 Bipolar disorder (also known as 'manic depressive illness') is a form of affective (mood) disorder where the sufferer suffers oscillations in mood or affect between profound depression and elation. The elated state may be described as hypomania or mania, hypomania being a lesser degree of mania. It involves mild elevation of mood increased energy and activity. The person may be extremely talkative, over-familiar, and may show increased sexual energy. Mania is where the person's mood has been elevated out of keeping with their circumstances for at least one week and is so severe as to disrupt ordinary social and work activities more or less completely. The signs are rapid fire speech, grandiosity, and decreased need for sleep. Bipolar illness may entail manic episodes of four to five months followed by depressions of six months or more, or it may be more rapid cycling.[37] Bipolar illness may be accompanied by psychotic features. The term 'psychotic' indicates the presence of hallucinations, delusions, abnormalities of behaviour, such as gross excitements and over-activity, marked psychomotor retardation, disorganised speech or disorganised or catatonic behaviour.[38]

---

[35] Department of Health *Code of Practice: Mental Health Act 1983* (2008), para 3.3.
[36] *Mental Health Act 2007 Explanatory Notes*, para 17.
[37] ICD-10, categories F30–F39; Mood (Affective) Disorders, p 112.
[38] ICD-10, pp 5–6; DSM-IV, p 273.

Schizophrenia

3.27 The most common psychotic illness is schizophrenia which, together with schizotypal and other delusional disorders, is grouped in ICD-10, ss F20–F29. These disorders are characterised by 'fundamental and characteristic distortions of thinking and perception, and by inappropriate or blunted affect (mood)'.[39] The characteristic distortions of thinking and perception include hallucinations, visual and auditory, delusions, attaching grossly disproportionate importance to minor and irrelevant matters, and developing an unshakable belief in the importance of bizarre ideas. As ICD-10 evocatively describes it:[40]

> 'The disturbance involves the most basic functions that give a normal person a feeling of individuality, uniqueness and self-direction. The most intimate thoughts, feelings, and acts are often felt to be know to or shared by others, and explanatory delusions may develop, to the effect that natural or supernatural forces are at work to influence the afflicted individual's behaviour or thoughts.'

Paranoid schizophrenia is the commonest type of schizophrenia in most parts of the world. Its classic symptoms include delusions of persecution, exalted birth, special mission, bodily change or jealousy, hallucinatory voices that threaten the patient or give commands, or auditory hallucinations without verbal form. There may also be hallucinations of smell, or taste or of sexual or other bodily sensations. Schizoaffective disorders are a hybrid of schizophrenia and bipolar illness where the symptoms of both illnesses are present at the same time or within a few days of each other.

Anxiety

3.28 Both ICD-10[41] and DSM-IV[42] include stress-related and anxiety disorder. These include post traumatic stress disorder, phobic anxiety disorders (agoraphobia, social phobias, animal phobia, examination phobia), other anxiety disorders manifested in panic attacks, or disorders where patients repeatedly present physical symptoms requesting medical investigations, in spite of repeated negative findings and reassurance from doctors. It is rare for patients with anxiety disorders to be detained under mental health legislation, their affliction rarely being of a nature or degree warranting detention. Obsessive compulsive disorder can on occasion produce disabling effects to the requisite nature or degree. Here obsessive thoughts enter the patient's head again and again, and this is followed by ceaseless repetition of compulsive acts or rituals of stereotyped behaviour.

---

[39] ICD-10, p 86.
[40] ICD-10, pp 86–87.
[41] ICD-10, categories F40–F48.
[42] DSM-IV, p 393.

Depression

3.29 Depressive disorder is where the person is profoundly depressed in mood, involving loss of interest or pleasure in nearly all activities, and may be accompanied by feelings of worthlessness or guilt which may reach delusional proportions. In severe cases there may be thoughts of suicide or self harm, or the person may be beyond communication or refusing food and fluids.

Learning disability

3.30 The term currently favoured in the United Kingdom to describe people with intellectual impairment is 'learning disability', reflecting a move away from medical models of treatment in hospitals towards an emphasis on small residential units, integrated into the community, where the skills of residents can be developed and their individuality can be better respected.

3.31 New s 1(4) of the MHA 1983 defines learning disability as:[43]

'a state of arrested or incomplete development of the mind which includes significant impairment of intelligence and social functioning.'

This broadly corresponds with the ICD-10 and DSM-IV category of 'mental retardation', defined in ICD-10 as:[44]

'A condition of arrested or incomplete development of mind especially characterised by impairment of the skills manifested during the developmental period, which contribute to the overall level of intelligence, ie cognitive, motor language and social abilities.'

For there to be a learning disability there must be a state of arrested or incomplete development of the mind, and it must include significant impairment of intelligence and social functioning.

Arrested or incomplete development of the mind

3.32 The Department of Health Mental Health Act 1983 Code of Practice states that an adult with arrested or incomplete development of mind is one who has experienced a significant impairment of the normal process of maturation of intellectual and social development that occurs during childhood and adolescence. Hence:[45]

'The Act embraces the general understanding that features which qualify as a learning disability are present prior to adulthood. For the purposes of the Act, learning disability does not include people whose intellectual disorder derives from

---

43 Inserted by s 2(3) of the MHA 2007.
44 ICD-10, categories F70–F79 at p 226. See also DSM-IV, 3.17–3.19.
45 Department of Health *Code of Practice: Mental Health Act 1983* (2008), para. 34.4.

accident, injury or illness occurring after they completed normal maturation (although such conditions do fall within the definition of mental disorder in the Act).'

People with learning disability will remain ineligible for long term detention or guardianship unless they have abnormally aggressive or seriously irresponsible conduct. This will not apply to people with 'acquired learning disability' since, following the Code's approach, they do not suffer from 'learning disability'. They are eligible for long term detention or guardianship, provided the other criteria are met, even if their conduct is not abnormally aggressive or seriously irresponsible.

Significant impairment of intelligence and social functioning

3.33 Diagnosis is based on a combination of arrested or incomplete development of intelligence and lack of social competence. Some IQ tests can disadvantage people whose education has been interrupted, or people from different ethnic backgrounds, and verbal tests may disadvantage people with communication problems. Standardised IQ tests, although an important indicator, do not determine the question whether a person is suffering from arrested or incomplete development of mind, or of its level of severity, and a full social assessment is required.

3.34 Whether the impairment is considered to be 'significant' is a matter for clinical judgment. The DSM-IV and ICD-10 state that the diagnosis of 'mental retardation' may be made for someone who has an IQ score of 70 or below. However, IQ scores are not determinative. In *Meggary v Chief Adjudications Officer*, where the issue was whether a child with autistic disorder had a 'severe impairment of intelligence and social functioning' and was therefore entitled to disability living allowance, Simon Brown LJ made clear that intelligence included insight and sagacity as well as intellectual intelligence. He said this:[46]

> 'In most cases, no doubt, the measurement of IQ will be the best available method of measuring intelligence. But among the dictionary definitions of intelligence one finds the reference not merely to the functions of understanding and intellect but also to the qualities of insight and sagacity. It seems to me that in the case if an autistic child those qualities may well be lacking and to the extent that they are there will be a functional impairment which overlaps both limbs of the regulation, ie both intelligence and social functioning.'

3.35 In *R v Hall* the Court of Appeal considered the meaning of the words 'severe impairment of intelligence and social functioning' in the context of an appeal against conviction for unlawful sexual intercourse with a 'defective' contrary to the Sexual Offences Act 1956. A person was a mental defective for the purposes of the 1956 Act if she suffered from 'severe impairment of intelligence and social functioning'. The Court of Appeal held that these were 'not terms of art' but 'ordinary English words', and that on a natural reading of

---

[46]   (1999) *The Times*, 11 November, CA.

the words 'severe impairment' was to be measured 'against the standard of normal persons', not by comparison with other people with learning disabilities.[47] The same must be true of significant impairment.

Autistic spectrum disorders

3.36 The DSM-IV category of 'Disorders Usually first Diagnosed in Infancy, Childhood or Early Adolescence' includes a category of Pervasive Developmental Disorders, which includes autistic disorder and Asperger's disorder, as well as mental retardation. The essential features of autistic disorder according to the DSM-IV are the presence of markedly abnormal or impaired development in social interaction, communication or awareness of others, leading to gross and sustained impairment in reciprocal social interaction, failure to develop peer relationships. The Department of Health Mental Health Act Code states that while it is possible for someone on the autistic spectrum to meet the conditions for treatment under the Mental Health Act without having any other form of mental disorder, even if it is not associated with abnormally aggressive or seriously irresponsible behaviour, this is likely to happen only very rarely.[48] The Code suggests that 'Compulsory treatment in a hospital setting is rarely likely to be helpful for a person with autism, who may be very distressed by even minor changes in routine and is likely to find detention in hospital anxiety provoking. Sensitive, person-centred support in a familiar setting will usually be more helpful.'[49] The Code further urges that assessment should take place by specialists in autistic spectrum disorders and that, where appropriate, someone who knows the service user should be present at initial assessment, provided it can be done without breaching the person's confidentiality. Knowledge of the person's early development history and usual pattern of behaviour will help prevent someone with an autistic spectrum disorder from being wrongly brought under compulsion.[50] The Code warns against construing as mental disorder warranting detention eccentricity or repetitive behaviour which might be a coping mechanism.

3.37 Asperger's Disorder entails severe and sustained impairment in social interaction and the development of restricted, repetitive patterns of behaviour interests and activities, causing clinically significant impairment in social, occupational or other areas of functioning. It is distinguished in the DSM-IV from autistic disorder, by the lack of clinically significant delays in acquisition of language, or in cognitive development or development of age-appropriate self-help skills.[51] A person with Aspergers might have a high IQ and therefore fall outside the definition of learning disability.

---

47 (1987) 86 Cr App R 159, per Parker LJ at 162, CA.
48 Department of Health *Code of Practice: Mental Health Act 1983* (2008), para 34.18.
49 Ibid.
50 Ibid, para 34.25.
51 DSM-IV, p 75.

3.38 Although people with high measured IQ can still have these diagnoses, where the person has an IQ below 70, they may be counted as learning disabilities for the purpose of the Act, so an association of the disability with abnormally aggressive or seriously irresponsible conduct will be needed for long-term detention, a community treatment order, guardianship, a mental health disposal by a criminal court, or transfer to hospital.

The requirement that learning disability be associated with abnormally aggressive or seriously irresponsible conduct for long-term detention, guardianship or a CTO, or in relation to the offender provisions of the MHA 1983

3.39 For the most part people with learning disabilities are ineligible for detention under long-term powers of detention, under guardianship, or under the offender provisions in Part 3 of the MHA 1983 unless their learning disability was associated with abnormally aggressive or seriously irresponsible conduct. This provision was introduced in relation to learning disability in the 1983 Act. It was lifted from the definition of psychopathic disorder in the MHA 1959. Lord Rix explained to the House of Lords during the debates on the 2006 Bill that these words represented the:[52]

> 'best compromise we could then reach between the Government's position that people with a learning disability should come under the scope of the Act, and my position that people with a learning disability are not ill and should not be treated as if they were.'

This argument has worked for learning disability but not for personality disorder, which might equally be said not to be an illness. The MHA 2007 preserves the position under the MHA 1983 for people with learning disability, but it removes the requirement of abnormally aggressive or seriously irresponsible conduct if someone is to be detained on grounds of personality disorder.

3.40 New s 1(2A) and (2B) provide that for the purposes of detention for treatment (s 3), guardianship and guardianship orders (ss 7 and 37), community treatment orders (s 17A), detention under a hospital order (s 37), detention under a hospital direction (s 45A) transfer from prison (ss 47 and 48), use of remand powers and interim hospital orders (ss 35–38), and making a hospital order where it is impracticable or inappropriate to bring the offender to court (s 51) a person may not be considered to be suffering from a mental disorder simply as a result of having a learning disability, unless that disability is associated with abnormally aggressive or seriously irresponsible conduct on the part of the person concerned. This also applies to the power to renew

---

[52] *Hansard*, HL Deb, vol 687, col 662.

detention, guardianship or a community treatment order (ss 20 and 20A), and to the Mental Health Tribunal's power of discharge (s 72). As the Explanatory Notes to the MHA 2007 put it:[53]

> 'In those cases where the 1983 Act as it stands now effectively precludes the use of detention or other compulsory measures on the basis of a learning disability which is not associated with abnormally aggressive or seriously irresponsible conduct, the same will be true of the Act as amended.'

The phrase requires the learning disability to be associated with the abnormally aggressive or seriously irresponsible conduct. Although this does not necessarily imply a cause-effect relationship, any such conduct which arises from other sources such as a physical disorder or severe toothache, is excluded.

3.41 In *R v Trent Mental Health Review Tribunal, ex parte Ryan*, Nolan LJ said that whether conduct amounts:[54]

> 'to seriously irresponsible or abnormally aggressive behaviour seems to me … to raise questions other than of a purely clinical nature.'

The Mental Health Act Code of Practice states that in assessing whether a patient's learning disability includes abnormally aggressive behaviour, relevant factors may include:

- when such aggressive behaviour has been observed, and how persistent and severe it has been;

- whether it has occurred without a specific trigger or seems out of proportion to the circumstances that triggered it;

- whether, and to what degree, it has in fact resulted in harm or distress to other people, or actual damage to property;

- how likely, if it has not been observed recently, it is to recur; and

- how common similar behaviour is in the population generally.[55]

3.42 In assessing whether conduct is seriously irresponsible, according to the Department of Health Code, relevant factors to be taken into account may include:[56]

- whether behaviour has been observed that suggests a disregard or an inadequate regard for its serious or dangerous consequences;

---

53   Department of Health, Ministry of Justice, Welsh Assembly Government *Mental Health Act 2007 Explanatory Notes* (2007), para 22.
54   [1992] COD 157.
55   Department of Health *Code of Practice on the Mental Health Act 1983* (2008), para 34.8.
56   Ibid. para 34.9.

- how recently such behaviour has been observed and, when it has been observed, how persistent it has been;

- how seriously detrimental to the patient, or to other people, the consequences of the behaviour were or might have been;

- whether, and to what degree, the behaviour has actually resulted in harm to the patient or the patient's interests, or in harm to other people or to damage to property; and

- if it has not been observed recently, how likely it is to recur.

3.43 Such conduct on the part of the person need not be current nor have been particularly recent. The requirement will be met if the learning disability has been associated with such conduct in the past and that there is a real risk that, if treatment in hospital is discontinued, that conduct will manifest itself in the future. In *Lewis v Gibson*, Thorpe LJ said this:[57]

'To make a balanced assessment of the patient's present state some regard must be had to the past history and the future propensity. A conclusion based only on the recent past, which might represent a transient phase of quiescence, would be superficial.'

3.44 In *R (on the application of P) v Mental Health Review Tribunal (East Midlands and North East Region)*[58] the issue was whether a person could still be suffering from psychopathic disorder even though there had been no recent abnormally aggressive or seriously irresponsible conduct. P's index offence was at a pub in 1992. It was not in dispute that he suffered from psychopathic disorder at the time of his index offence, manslaughter of a young man whom he had ferociously assaulted. But there had been no abnormally aggressive or seriously irresponsible conduct for some years. Pill LJ said this:[59]

'The extent to which abnormally aggressive or seriously irresponsible conduct now occurs may throw light on whether there is psychopathic disorder, but the disorder may still exist even though there has been no such conduct for years. I have no difficulty in accepting that the tribunal were entitled to decide that a disorder which admittedly existed in 1992 still existed in 2000, even though, because of successful management of the condition, no abnormally aggressive or seriously irresponsible conduct has occurred for years.'

3.45 A number of cases have considered the issue of seriously irresponsible conduct. In *Re F (Mental Health Act: Guardianship)*,[60] the issue was whether a learning disabled 17-year-old was exhibiting seriously irresponsible conduct by wanting to return to a home where she had suffered neglect and possible sexual abuse. If her conduct was seriously irresponsible, she would be eligible for

---

57 [2005] EWCA Civ 587, [2005] MHLR 309, para 31.
58 [2002] EWCA Civ 697, CA.
59 [2002] EWCA Civ 697 at [23]–[26].
60 [2000] 1 FLR 192, CA.

Mental Health Act guardianship. The Court of Appeal held that guardianship could not be used as she was not behaving seriously irresponsibly since the urge to return to one's home and family is 'almost universal'.

3.46 *Re F* was applied in *Newham London Borough Council v S (adult: court's jurisdiction)*,[61] Wall J held that guardianship could not be used in S's case to remove her from the care of her father who was having serious difficulty coping with her to residential care, because:[62]

> 'the only example of "seriously irresponsible conduct" on S's part was her total lack of road sense and a tendency to rush into the road without looking.'

This was not enough to satisfy the statutory test. In each case although guardianship was held not to be available, the court achieved the same effect by using its inherent jurisdiction to determine where an incapacitated person should live. However, the Newham case precedent was not followed by King J in *R (GC) v Managers of the Kingswood Centre of Central and North West London NHS Foundation Trust*.[63] The patient suffered from obsessive Compulsive Disorder and had a compulsion to pick up litter, even if that litter was in the road. Although he had caused road accidents, he thought himself invincible. The hospital managers considered that this conduct could be considered to be seriously irresponsible conduct. The court upheld the managers' view that GC was likely to act in a dangerous manner so they were right not to discharge. The judge declined to follow *London Borough of Newham v BS*[64] where lack of road sense and tendency to rush suddenly into the road had been held not to be seriously irresponsible conduct.

3.47 Although the *Kingswood* case is cause for optimism, these differing interpretations of the abnormally aggressive or seriously irresponsible conduct exclusion risk closing off the possibility of using guardianship to rescue people with learning disabilities from abusive situations where it is the irresponsible conduct of *others* which is putting *them* at risk and they are passively enduring abuse. Jones has rightly been critical of the preservation of the status quo as having little to commend it, a monument to the effectiveness of the learning disability lobby, but little else.[65] In 1989 Beverley Lewis, a young woman with a profound learning disability, who starved to death in her mother's living room. Beverley's mother was herself mentally ill and was severely neglecting Beverley, who was passively enduring neglect, but whose own conduct was not seriously irresponsible. Therefore, guardianship or admission for treatment under the Mental Health Act could not be used to rescue her from this fate.[66]

---

61 [2003] EWHC 1909 (Fam).
62 [2003] EWHC 1909 (Fam) at [11].
63 [2008] EWHC (Admin) (CO/7784/2008).
64 [2003] EWHC 1909 (Fam), para 11.
65 RM Jones *Annotations to the Mental Health Act 2007*, section 2.
66 P Fennell 'Blaming the Law: Lessons from the Case' (1989) *The Guardian*, 3 November, p 38; 'Beverley Lewis – Was the Law to Blame?' (1989) 139 NLJ 1557–1558; 'Falling through the legal loopholes' (1989) *Social Work Today*, 30 November, pp 18–20.

3.48 Nowadays an application could be made to the Court of Protection on the grounds that Beverley lacked capacity and removal was in her best interests or she could be deprived of her liberty under a Mental Capacity Act DoLs authorisation. These are cumbrous procedures by comparison with guardianship, which has a procedure which is currently in use and readily understood. Under the MHA 2007, a completed guardianship application authorises a person to be taken and conveyed to their required place of residence, to be required to reside there and grant access to professionals, to be returned there if they abscond, and to attend specified places for treatment education or training. This is capable of amounting to the complete and effective control over residence, treatment, movement of the degree and intensity required to amount to a deprivation of liberty.[67]

3.49 Removal of the abnormally aggressive or seriously irresponsible conduct requirement for guardianship in cases of learning disability would provide a means of rescue for many people with learning disabilities from abusive situations, without complex legal process, and with effective redress via the Mental Health Tribunal.

Personality disorders

3.50 In *Koniarska v United Kingdom*[68] the Strasbourg Court gave a strong indication that psychopathic disorder and personality disorder amount to unsoundness of mind for the purposes of Art 5(1)(e). The applicant was a juvenile suffering from psychopathic disorder which had been deemed untreatable. Her detention was found necessary as there was a danger of her injuring herself or other persons. There could thus be said to be both medical and social reasons for her detention, and the court considered the detention might have been justified under Art 5(1)(e) on grounds of unsoundness of mind. In the event no ruling on the Art 5(1)(e) point was necessary as the detention was justified under Art 5(1)(d) since it was the detention of a minor for the purposes of educational supervision. However, it is clear from this case and the later decision in *Reid v United Kingdom*[69] that personality disorder is unsoundness of mind for Convention purposes.

3.51 Under the MHA 1983 a person with a personality disorder could only be detained if they had a diagnosis of 'psychopathic disorder', meaning 'a persistent disorder or disability of mind (whether or not including significant impairment of intelligence) which *results in* abnormally aggressive or seriously irresponsible conduct'. As the Reed Committee noted in 1994 the group labelled as 'psychopathically disordered' is 'extremely heterogeneous', covering:[70]

---

[67]   *HL v United Kingdom* (2004) 40 EHRR 761, ECtHR.
[68]   *(Application 33670/96)* Decision of 12 October 2000, ECtHR.
[69]   (2003) 37 EHRR 9, ECtHR.
[70]   Department of Health and Home Office *Report of the Department of Health and Home Office Working Group on Psychopathic Disorder* (HMSO, 1994), para 10.16(iii).

'at one end of the spectrum highly dangerous serial murderers and rapists, and at the other disturbed young women whose disorder mainly manifested itself in repeated self-harm.'

The MHA 2007 removes the requirement of abnormally aggressive or seriously irresponsible conduct in cases of personality disorder.

3.52 Personality disorders are grouped together in ICD-10 categories F60-69 'Disorders of Adult Personality and Behaviour', and defined as:[71]

'Clinically significant conditions and behaviour patterns which tend to be persistent and are characteristic of an individual's characteristic lifestyle and mode of relating to self and others. They are deeply ingrained and enduring behaviour patterns, manifesting themselves as inflexible responses to a broad range of personal and social situations. They represent either extreme or significant deviations from the away the average individual in a given culture perceives, thinks, feels, and particularly relates to others.'

3.53 The DSM-IV gives the following diagnostic features of personality disorder in general, assuming there is no other mental disorder, substance abuse, or head trauma to explain them:[72]

'An enduring pattern of inner experience and behaviour that deviates markedly from the individual's culture. This is manifested in two or more of the following areas:

(1)   cognition (ie ways of perceiving and interpreting self, other people and events)
(2)   affectivity (ie the range, intensity, lability and appropriateness of emotional response)
(3)   interpersonal functioning
(4)   impulse control.'

The enduring pattern must be inflexible and pervasive across a wide range of personal and social situations, and must lead to clinically significant distress or impairment in social, occupational or other important areas of functioning. The pattern must also be stable and of long duration and its consent must be traceable back at least to adolescence or early adulthood.

3.54 The DSM-IV lists ten types of personality disorder:[73]

•   paranoid personality disorder is a pattern of distrust and suspiciousness interpreting others' motives as malevolent;

•   schizoid personality disorder manifested in a pattern of detachment from social relationships and a restricted range of emotional expression;

---

[71]   ICD-10, p 200.
[72]   DSM-IV, p 633.
[73]   DSM-IV, p 629.

- schizotypal personality disorder is a pattern of acute discomfort in close relationships, cognitive or perceptual distortions and eccentricities of behaviour;

- antisocial personality disorder is a pattern of disregard for and violation of the rights of others;

- borderline personality disorder is a pervasive pattern of instability of interpersonal relationships, self-image and affects and marked impulsiveness that begins in early adulthood, is present in a variety of contexts, and is manifested in frantic efforts to avoid real or imagined abandonment, including self-mutilation or self harm;

- histrionic personality disorder is a pattern of excessive emotionality and attention seeking;

- narcissistic personality disorder is a pattern of grandiosity, need for admiration and lack of empathy;

- avoidant personality disorder is a pattern of social inhibition feelings of inadequacy and hypersensitivity to negative evaluation;

- dependent personality disorder is a pattern of submissive and clinging behaviour relating to an excessive need to be taken care of;

- obsessive compulsive personality disorder is a pattern of preoccupation with orderliness, perfectionism and control.

There is an eleventh category of personality disorder not otherwise specified, which covers (inter alia) the situation where a person meets the general criteria for personality disorder, but traits of several different types of personality disorder are evident.

3.55 The now legally obsolete psychopathic disorder equates broadly to the DSM-IV category of Anti-Social Personality Disorder or the ICD-10 category of Dissocial Personality Disorder which usually comes to attention because of a gross disparity between behaviour and the prevailing social norms. According to the ICD-10 dissocial personality disorder is characterised by the following:[74]

'(a)   callous unconcern for the feelings of others;
(b)   gross and persistent attitude of irresponsibility and disregard for social norms, rules and obligations;
(c)   incapacity to maintain enduring relationships, although having no difficulty in establishing them;
(d)   very low tolerance to frustration and a low threshold for discharge of aggression, including violence;

---

[74]   ICD-10, F60.2, p 204.

(e) incapacity to experience guilt and to profit from experience, particularly punishment;

(f) marked proneness to blame others, or to offer plausible rationalisations, for the behaviour which has brought the individual in conflict with society.'

3.56 Psychopathic disorder required a cause effect relationship between the disorder and any abnormally aggressive or seriously irresponsible conduct. This is no longer necessary. It will in most cases be aggressive or irresponsible behaviour which will bring the individual to the attention of the psychiatric services, but it is not necessary to show that the conduct is caused by the disorder. So a patient with a diagnosis of one of the above listed personality disorders, who meets the other statutory criteria will be liable to compulsion. Removal of the term 'psychopathic disorder' and its key component of abnormally aggressive or seriously irresponsible conduct from the Act broadens considerably the scope of powers to detain people with personality disorder. One of the Government's key concerns is to ensure that sex offenders with personality disorders emerging from prison following determinate sentences will be detainable under the non-offender provisions of the MHA 1983. This is a key reason for the change to a single broad definition of 'mental disorder', coupled with the removal of the sexual deviancy exclusion (see **3.20–3.25** above), and the replacement of the treatability test (see **3.59–3.66** below).

Mental disorder of a kind or degree warranting confinement

3.57 Not only must a person be suffering from mental disorder but it must be of a kind or degree warranting confinement, reception into guardianship or a community treatment order. Determining whether mental disorder is of the relevant nature or degree warranting treatment in hospital depends on whether the relevant admission criteria (necessity for own health or safety or for the protection of others, and availability of appropriate treatment) are met. The disorder must be of a nature or degree making it appropriate for the person to receive treatment in hospital. As the Explanatory Notes state, 'nature' refers to the particular mental disorder from which the patient is suffering, its chronic nature, its prognosis, and the patient's previous response to receiving treatment for disorder. 'Degree' refers to the current manifestation of the patient's disorder.[75]

3.58 Treatment in hospital must be necessary in the interests of the person's own health or safety or for the protection of other persons. Appropriate treatment must be available. *Winterwerp* also established that detention must be a necessary and proportionate response to the patient's circumstances. Other less severe measures must have been considered and found to be insufficient to safeguard the individual or public interest, leaving no alternative to detention.[76]

---

[75] Department of Health, Ministry of Justice, Welsh Assembly Government *Mental Health Act 2007 Explanatory Notes* (2007), para 31; *R v Mental Health Review Tribunal for the South Thames Region, ex parte Smith* [1999] COD 148, QBD.

[76] *Litwa v Poland* (2001) 33 EHRR 53, (2000) 63 BMLR 199, ECtHR.

REPLACING TREATABILITY WITH AVAILABILITY OF APPROPRIATE TREATMENT

3.59 The 'treatability test' under the MHA 1983 applied to psychopathic disorder and mental impairment. For detention or renewal the doctor had to certify that medical treatment was likely to alleviate or prevent deterioration in the patient's condition, which would be hard to do if the patient was resolutely not co-operating. This might happen if a person with a personality disorder refused to engage with cognitive behaviour therapy or some other psychological treatment. Treatment might be available and appropriate but unlikely to make any difference if the patient refused to participate.

3.60 The MHA 1983 now requires only that appropriate treatment be available regardless of whether the patient accepts it. Section 3(4) of the MHA 1983 states that:[77]

> 'references to appropriate medical treatment, in relation to a person suffering from mental disorder, are references to medical treatment which is appropriate in his case, taking into account the nature and degree of the mental disorder and all other circumstances of his case.'

'All the circumstances of the case' would require consideration of, inter alia, the patient's age, gender, cultural background, family and social circumstances, and living accommodation, as well as medical considerations.

3.61 In addition to replacing the treatability test, the MHA 2007 has introduced the test of availability of appropriate treatment where it had not existed hitherto, in s 36 (remand for treatment), s 48 (transfer of unsentenced prisoners) and s 51(6) (hospital orders where it is impracticable or inappropriate to bring a detainee before the court).[78]

3.62 The Government's intention is:[79]

> 'to remove ground for argument about the efficacy or likely efficacy of a treatment which can be used to prevent detention of people who present a risk to themselves or others.'

The concern was that if the 'treatability test' required clinicians to predict whether treatment would work for a particular patient, which might not always be possible, a decision might be taken not to detain under civil powers in the Mental Health Act even though the patient posed a significant risk to self or to others.[80] The second aim is to ensure that people with personality disorders are

---

[77] Inserted by MHA 2007, s 4(3).

[78] Ibid, s 5.

[79] Joint Committee on Human Rights *Legislative Scrutiny: Mental Health Bill Fourth Report of Session 2006–07* (HL Paper 40, HC Paper 288, 4 February 2007), p 45; Appendix 1 – Letter of 17 November 2006 from The Rt Hon Rosie Winterton MP, Minister of State, Department of Health to the JCHR, para 8.

[80] *Hansard*, HL Deb, vol 688, col 319.

not too readily ruled out as being beyond help, and interventions should be developed to treat these afflictions, which can cause great distress to sufferers and their loved ones.

3.63 The Minister of State, Rosie Winterton, took the unusual step of writing to the Joint Committee on Human Rights prior to its scrutiny of the Mental Health Bill 2006 to explain the basis of the Government's view that the Bill was 'Convention compliant'. In relation to treatability the Government's position was based on *Reid v United Kingdom*[81] where the European Court of Human Rights said that Art 5(1)(e) imposed no requirement that detention in a mental hospital was conditional on the illness or condition being of a nature or degree amenable to medical treatment. The Court held (at para 51) that confinement under Art 5(1)(e) may be necessary not only where a person needs therapy, medication or other clinical treatment to cure or alleviate his condition, but also where the person needs control and supervision to prevent him, for example, causing harm to himself or other persons.

3.64 The Joint Committee on Human Rights noted the strongly held views of psychiatrists during the Committee stage in the House of Lords, that if the treatability test was to be abolished, it should be replaced with the test that treatment is available which is likely to be of therapeutic benefit to the patient. This was to avoid a perceived risk of psychiatrists becoming mere custodians rather than therapists, and psychiatric detention becoming perceived as preventive detention. The Committee considered that there was nothing in the European Convention on Human Rights to prevent abolition of the treatability test. They also noted Art 17(1)(iii) of Council of Europe Recommendation No (2004)10 of the Committee of Ministers to member states concerning the human rights and dignity of persons with mental disorder, which requires that detention has a 'therapeutic purpose.' This is broadly defined (in Art 2(3)) as 'including prevention, diagnosis, control, cure or treatment'.

3.65 Chris Bryant, a Labour MP, tabled an amendment to address concerns about the absence of a test of therapeutic benefit, and which has brought England and Wales into compliance with this provision of the Recommendation. New s 145(4) requires treatment to have a 'therapeutic purpose':

> 'Any reference in this Act to medical treatment, in relation to mental disorder, shall be construed as a reference to medical treatment the purpose of which is to alleviate, or prevent a worsening of, the disorder or one or more of its symptoms or manifestations.'

As Baroness Royall put it on behalf of the Government:[82]

---

81   (2003) 37 EHRR 9, ECtHR.
82   *Hansard*, HL Deb, vol 693, col 835.

'"Symptoms" is intended to cover the consequences of which patients themselves complain while "manifestations" more obviously covers the evidence of the disorder as seen by other people.'

So a manifestation could be violent conduct, sex offending, or self-harming. Treatment must have the *purpose* of alleviating or preventing 'a worsening of the disorder or one or more of its symptoms or manifestations'.[83] But it need not be likely to achieve those purposes. The intention was to ensure that a patient's refusal to accept treatment can no longer be an obstacle to detention, as long as the treatment is available. The Minister of State at the Department of Health, Rosie Winterton, went so far as to say that she had been informed that:[84]

'lawyers have advised their patients not to engage with treatment because if it can be proved that they are not treatable they have to be released.'

3.66 Medical treatment for mental disorder is redefined in s 145. It includes nursing and also psychological intervention and specialist mental health habilitation, rehabilitation and care. Psychological interventions are expressly mentioned for the first time. These include psychotherapy and other interactive treatments requiring co-operation from the patient, often the main treatments used for people with personality disorders. A key issue is the extent to which therapeutic interventions are required which go beyond presence in what is sometimes referred to as 'a structured environment' Chapter 6 of the Department of Health Code of Practice gives guidance on the appropriate medical treatment test, and seeks to distinguish between nursing and specialist day to day care in a safe and secure therapeutic environment and mere preventive detention:[85]

'Appropriate medical treatment does not have to involve medication or individual or group psychological therapy – although it very often will. There may be patients whose particular circumstances mean that treatment may be appropriate even though it consists only of nursing and specialist day-to-day care under the clinical supervision of an approved clinician, in a safe and secure therapeutic environment.

Simply detaining someone – even in a hospital – does not constitute medical treatment.'

The line between simply detaining someone, and keeping them in a safe and secure therapeutic environment with nursing care may be hard to draw in practice and given the breadth of the concept of medical treatment for mental disorder the threshold of availability of appropriate treatment is a very low one.

3.67 Not surprisingly, the issue of availability of appropriate treatment has already been raised in two cases following the 2007 Act, and in each case in relation to personality disorder. The crucial question in each has been whether

---

[83] MHA 1983, s 145(4), as inserted by MHA 2007, s 7(3).
[84] Public Bill Committee, cols 121–122.
[85] Department of Health *Code of Practice: Mental Health Act 1983* (2008), paras 6.16–6.17.

the new wording has secured the Government's policy intention that a patient's refusal to engage with psychological treatment should not be an obstacle to detention, since appropriate treatment is available. Both decisions are by Judge Jacobs in the Upper Tribunal. The first was *MD* v *Nottinghamshire Health Care NHS Trust.*[86] MD was a patient with a diagnosis of psychopathic personality disorder who had been subject to transfer under a ss 47 and 49 restriction direction, but whose sentence had now expired and was treated as if detained under a s 37 hospital order without restrictions. The First Tier Tribunal ('FTT') had decided not to discharge, finding that MD had a psychopathic personality disorder and that he was at risk of violent re-offending. The FTT concluded that, taking a long term view, 'appropriate positive psychotherapeutic treatment is available here', taking account of the responsible clinician's long experience and rejecting evidence to the contrary. Alternatively, the tribunal concluded that the patient had been, in Judge Jacobs' words 'engaging in and benefiting from the specialist nursing care and 'milieu' therapy on the ward. The latter is professional shorthand for nursing and specialist day to day care under clinical supervision of an approved clinician, in a safe and secure therapeutic environment with a structured regime. That, as the tribunal acknowledged, is the language of Code paragraph 6.16.'[87] The FTT also found that, although MD's psychological defence mechanisms prevented him from engaging with therapy, he had the potential to benefit from the milieu of the ward, both for its short term effects and for the possibility that it would break through the defence mechanisms and allow him later to engage in therapy.

3.68   The key issue in the Upper Tribunal was whether appropriate treatment was available. Judge Jacobs accepted that there was a crucial distinction between containment, which was 'a matter for the criminal courts and prisons' and treatment which was a matter for hospitals subject to the supervision of the First Tier and the Upper Tribunal. The distinction between containment and treatment and the definition of 'available' and 'appropriate' were 'matters of fact and judgment for the tribunal ... [which] is an expert body and ... has to use that expertise to make its findings and exercise its judgment.' In doing so, the tribunal:[88]

'has to grapple with difficult issues of evidence and principle that affect the liberty of the subject. That can only be done, as the tribunal did in this case, on the evidence before the tribunal and in the circumstances of a particular patient's case at the time of the hearing before the First-tier Tribunal.'

3.69   The first argument raised on MD's behalf was that in order to qualify as treatment for the purposes of s 145(4) the treatment had to offer the possibility of reduction of the risk posed by the patient otherwise it was mere containment. Judge Jacobs rejected this contention, stating that it was sufficient if the treatment was 'for the purpose of preventing a worsening of the symptoms or manifestations and that envisages that the treatment required may

---

[86]   [2010] UKUT 59 (AAC), [2010] AACR 34.
[87]   Ibid, paras 25–26.
[88]   Ibid, para 48.

not reduce the risk posed by the patient.' It was also sufficient if it 'will alleviate but one of the symptoms or manifestations, regardless of the impact on the risk posed by the patient'.[89]

3.70   Judge Jacobs held that the line between treatment and containment would be crossed 'if there was no prospect of the patient progressing beyond milieu, his detention would become mere containment' and then there might come a point at which detention was no longer appropriate, but in this case the facts found by the tribunal showed that the patient had not reached that position as there was the potential for the milieu to benefit the patient in both the short and longer term.[90] The ward manager gave evidence to the effect that the patient had improved. He no longer needed seclusion as he had in 2007. It was argued for MD that the tribunal was not entitled to accept the evidence of the ward manager in preference to that of the responsible clinician. Judge Jacobs was not convinced that there was any conflict between the ward manager's evidence and that of the RC, but in any event 'the tribunal was entitled to accept the evidence of the ward manager as someone who had more, and more regular, contact with the patient than any other witness and who was able to speak to the patient's progress and, based on that, his ability to progress further.'[91] Judge Jacobs emphasised that 'appropriateness is an important additional criterion for detention' and is 'not surplus verbiage', and that there might come a point at which continuing treatment for a patient (in this case milieu therapy), even viewed in the long term, would no longer be appropriate. Nevertheless, on the evidence that point had not been reached for MD, as there was still the potential for the milieu to benefit him both in the short term and the long term. This is not a very exacting standard.

3.71   *DL-II* v *Devon Partnership NHS Trust*[92] was decided by Judge Jacobs on the basis of the inadequacy of the reasons given by the tribunal which had simply recorded that 'We accept the opinion of Dr Parker that continued treatment in hospital provides alleviation or prevention of a deterioration in his condition. Appropriate medical treatment is available on C Ward with the hope that he will begin to engage in treatment.' This was too general a formulation to deal with the issue and it ignored evidence to the contrary. It begged the question of whether the patient could be persuaded to engage. The patient had been transferred to another hospital and was back on antipsychotic medication. Judge Jacobs directed a rehearing. He also went on to offer guidance on how tribunals should approach the questions of fact and judgment involved in deciding whether appropriate treatment is available. After quoting extensively from the NICE Guidance on Treatment of Anti- Social Personality Disorder which emphasises the need for treatment approaches to take into account sufferers' needs and preferences, Judge Jacobs acknowledged that this 'presents a problem when patients refuse to engage in treatment. Some may

---

[89]   Ibid, para 34.
[90]   Ibid, para 35.
[91]   Ibid, para 41.
[92]   [2010] UKUT 102 (AAC).

argue that there is no treatment available'.[93] Treatment is so broadly defined in s 145 that it can include attempts by nursing staff to encourage the patient to engage, which is not difficult to satisfy. This in turn produced a further 'danger that a patient for whom no appropriate treatment is available may be contained for public safety rather than detained for treatment.' In Judge Jacobs' view the solution lay 'in the tribunal's duty to ensure that the conditions for continued detention are satisfied', which placed it under a duty to 'investigate behind assertions, generalisations and standard phrases.' This could be done by making an individualised assessment for the particular patient focusing on the following 'specific questions':

- What precisely is the treatment that can be provided?

- What discernible benefit may it have on this patient?

- Is that benefit related to the patient's mental disorder or to some unrelated problem?

- Is the patient truly resistant to engagement?

The tribunal's reasons then need only reflect what it did in the inquisitorial and decision-making stages. The tribunal in this case had given inadequate reasons.

CONCLUSION

3.72 The new single broad definition of 'mental disorder' has broadened the scope of compulsory powers. The combined effect of the changes to the definition, the removal of all exclusions save those for addiction, and the replacement of the treatability test with appropriate treatment, is to remove areas of discretion not to use compulsory powers. There will be many fewer legitimate reasons for clinicians not to use compulsory powers under the Act with relation to people with personality disorder. In addition to broadening the scope of compulsory powers, the MHA 2007 also extends the power to use them to new professional groups beyond the medical and social work professions. Chapter 4 discusses the statutory roles conferred by the MHA 2007 on Approved Mental Health Professionals, 'Section 12 approved doctors', Approved Clinicians, and Responsible Clinicians. Chapter 5 considers the role of Nearest Relatives, Independent Mental Health Advocates and Hospital Managers.

---

[93]   Ibid, para 32.

Chapter 4

STATUTORY POWERS AND RESPONSIBILITIES: THE POWERS AND DUTIES OF MENTAL HEALTH STAFF

OVERVIEW

4.1　This chapter deals with the statutory roles conferred by the MHA 1983 on Approved Mental Health Professionals ('AMHPs'), doctors who provide medical recommendations in support of compulsory powers, Responsible Clinicians ('RCs'), and Approved Clinicians ('ACs'). The reforms introduced by the MHA 2007 allow the key roles in imposing and managing compulsory powers to be performed by a wider range of professionals than at present. The 'approved social worker' ('ASW') is replaced by the 'approved mental health professional' ('AMHP'), and the 'responsible medical officer' ('RMO') by the 'responsible clinician' ('RC').

Approved Mental Health Professionals ('AMHPs')

4.2　Under Part II of the MHA 1983 an application for detention or guardianship could be made only by an approved social worker or the patient's nearest relative.[1] The 2007 Act amendments open the role of applicant for detention to anyone who is an 'Approved Mental Health Professional' ('AMHP'), who may be a social worker, a nurse, psychologist, or occupational therapist as long as they have recognised training.[2]

4.3　The MHA 1983 requires an application for admission to be made to the managers of the receiving hospital. Each non-emergency application must be supported by two doctors' recommendations, to the effect that the patient is suffering from mental disorder of a nature or degree warranting detention in the interests of his health or safety or for the protection of others. One of the recommending doctors must be approved under s 12 of the MHA 1983 as having special experience in the diagnosis or treatment of mental disorder. The AMHP also acquires the new responsibility of agreeing the appropriateness of, and the terms of, a community treatment order ('CTO') proposed by the RC.[3]

---

[1]　MHA 1983, s 11(1).
[2]　Mental Health (Approved Mental Health Professionals) (Approval) (England) Regulations 2008; SI 2008/1206; Mental Health (Approval of Persons to be Approved Mental Health Professionals) (Wales) Regulations 2008, SI 2008/2436 (W 209).
[3]　MHA 1983, s 17A, as inserted by MHA 2007, s 32(2).

Section 12 approved doctors

4.4 A 'section 12 doctor' is approved under s 12 of the MHA 1983 as having special experience in the diagnosis or treatment of mental disorder. The evidential requirement of medical recommendations from doctors for detention remains following the MHA 2007. Where two recommendations are necessary for compulsory admission under ss 2 or 3, one must come from a section 12 approved doctor.

4.5 Previously, once detained under the MHA 1983, a patient was assigned a responsible medical officer ('RMO') to be in charge of treatment, and the RMO was usually a consultant psychiatrist. Following the 2007 Act reforms, the RMO is replaced by the responsible clinician ('RC') who need not be a doctor and is 'the approved clinician with overall responsibility for the patient's case'.[4]

Approved Clinicians ('ACs') and Responsible Clinicians ('RCs')

4.6 RCs replace RMOs, and need not be medically qualified, provided they have undergone approved clinician ('AC') training. Previously under the 1983 Act, the RMO was the registered medical practitioner in charge of the treatment of the patient, and had extensive powers. These powers have now been vested in RCs. They include the power to send the patient on leave, and to recall from leave (s 17), the power to renew detention (s 20), the power to discharge (s 23), the power to block discharge by the nearest relative (s 25) and the power to direct the patient to accept treatment, subject to the second opinion safeguards in Part IV.

4.7 Following the MHA 2007 changes, the RC (who need not be a doctor as long as the person is an 'Approved Clinician' ('AC')) takes over most of the functions of the RMO. As the Explanatory Notes point out 'some functions currently reserved to RMOs may be taken instead by another AC, not just the RC'.[5] This includes such matters as the prescription of drug treatment where the RC is from a profession which does not have prescribing rights, so another AC who is a doctor may be in charge of that part of treatment for the purposes of Part IV of the 1983 Act. Approval as an AC is not restricted to medical doctors, and may be extended to practitioners from other professions, such as nursing, psychology, occupational therapy and social work. In addition to assuming the functions previously exercised by RMOs, RCs also have the power to initiate, with the agreement of an AMHP, a Community Treatment Order.[6]

---

[4]   MHA 1983, s 34(1).
[5]   Department of Health, Ministry of Justice, Welsh Assembly Government *Mental Health Act 2007 Explanatory Notes* (2007), para 48.
[6]   MHA 1983, s 17A, as inserted by MHA 2007, s 32(2).

The impact of the Human Rights Act 1998

4.8   The Human Rights Act (HRA) 1998 requires public authorities to act compatibly with Convention rights. A key question is whether AMHPs, doctors recommending detention, RCs, and others carrying out functions under the Mental Health Act will be 'public authorities' for the purposes of the HRA 1998. A public authority includes 'any body or person certain of whose functions are functions of a public nature.'[7] Section 6(1) of the HRA 1998 makes it 'unlawful for a public authority to act in a way which is incompatible with a Convention right.' Under s 7(1):

> 'A person who claims that a public authority has acted (or proposes to act) in a way which is made unlawful by s 6(1) may –
>
> (a)   bring proceedings against the authority under this Act in the appropriate court or tribunal, or
> (b)   rely on the Convention right or rights concerned in any legal proceedings.'

In *R (on the application of Wilkinson) v Responsible Medical Officer Broadmoor Hospital*, Hale LJ said this:[8]

> 'Health authorities and NHS trusts and their staff are clearly public authorities. Under section 6(3), a public authority includes "a person certain of whose functions are functions of a public nature": this is apt to cover the actions of private doctors and others carrying out statutory functions under the Mental Health Act.'

Although this statement was obiter, it is a strong indication that anyone exercising statutory functions which engage the Convention rights of service users is a public authority.

4.9   The rights most likely to be engaged are the protection against arbitrary deprivation of liberty (Art 5) and the right to respect for private life (Art 8) which includes physical integrity and confidentiality. In order to comply with Art 5 an AMHP, for example, must ensure that the detention is carried out in accordance with correct procedure under the Mental Health Act, with objective medical evidence of a true mental disorder which is of a nature or degree warranting detention, and that detention is strictly necessary, that is:[9]

> 'that other less severe measures have been considered and found to be insufficient to safeguard the individual or public interest which might require that the person concerned be detained.'

4.10   In order to comply with Art 8 an AMHP would have to ensure that any disclosure of confidential information can be justified under Art 8(2) as being in accordance with the law and necessary in a democratic society (a

---

7   HRA 1998, s 6(3).
8   [2001] EWCA Civ 1545 at [61].
9   *Litwa v Poland* (2001) 33 EHRR 53, ECtHR.

proportionate response) in the interests of national security, public safety or the economic well-being of the country, for the prevention of disorder or crime, for the protection of health or morals, or for the protection of the rights and freedoms of others.

Section 139 of the Mental Health Act 1983

4.11 Section 139 of the MHA 1983 provides a defence and a procedural hurdle in respect of actions brought against people purportedly acting pursuant to the Act:[10]

> 'No person shall be liable ... to any civil or criminal proceedings to which he would have been liable apart from this section in respect of any act purporting to be done in pursuance of this Act or any regulations or rules made under this Act, unless the act was done in bad faith or without reasonable care.'

The procedural hurdle is that leave of the High Court is required for civil proceedings and the leave of the Director of Public Prosecutions for criminal prosecutions.[11] The procedural hurdle does not apply to proceedings against the Secretary of State, the National Assembly for Wales, a Strategic Health Authority, Health Authority, Special Health Authority, or Primary Care Trust or against a National Health Service trust. Under the MHA 1959 the applicant needed to show substantial grounds for the contention of bad faith or negligence before leave could be granted. This is no longer necessary. The defence that a person acted in good faith and with reasonable care remains under the 1983 Act, although where the right to compensation for unlawful detention under Art 5(5) is engaged and there has been an unlawful detention without negligence or bad faith, s 139 may be 'read down' to allow compensation even in the absence of negligence or bad faith.[12]

4.12 Section 139 does not apply to habeas corpus or judicial review. In *R v Governor of Pentonville Prison, ex parte Azam*[13] Lord Denning MR held that if Parliament was to suspend habeas corpus express words of clear implication would be necessary. In *R v Hallstrom and another, ex parte W*, the Court of Appeal applied this principle and held that the requirement of leave does not apply to public law applications for judicial review.[14] Since then, in *R (on the application of Wilkinson) v Responsible Medical Officer Broadmoor Hospital* Brooke LJ said, obiter, that a civil claim under s 7 of the Human Rights Act 1998 would be caught by the language of s 139(1) and would require leave.[15] Hale LJ expressed herself 'inclined to agree' emphasising that:

---

[10]   MHA 1983, s 139(1).
[11]   MHA 1983, s 139(2).
[12]   *TTM v LB Hackney East London NHS Foundation Trust and the Secretary of State for Health* [2011] EWCA Civ 4, paras 66–67.
[13]   [1974] AC 18 at 31, CA.
[14]   [1985] 3 All ER 775, CA.
[15]   [2001] EWCA Civ 1545 at [54].

'proceedings under s 7(1) are not confined to judicial review, and indeed it would be most surprising if they were'. Her Ladyship then went on to say that:[16]

> 'Section 8(1) provides that "In relation to any act (or proposed act) of a public authority which the court finds is (or would be) unlawful, it may grant such relief or remedy, or make such order, within its powers as it considers just and appropriate." In some cases, for example where delegated legislation or the policy of a public authority is in question, then the appropriate remedies will only be available in judicial review. But in others, where specific invasions of individuals' rights are in question, an ordinary action would be more appropriate.'

The position would appear to be that no leave is required for habeas corpus or judicial review, including a judicial review application under s 7. But where Convention Rights are being upheld by ordinary action under s 7 of the HRA 1998 leave may be required. Hale LJ stressed that the court had not heard argument on this point, and there might be a case for drawing a distinction between 'ordinary actions in tort' and ordinary actions under s 7 of the HRA 1998.[17] Actual liability may still only arise if bad faith or want of reasonable care is established in the main action, but leave may now be granted without the plaintiff having to show substantial grounds for the contention. For criminal proceedings, the leave of the Director of Public Prosecutions is now required. Whether the defendant acted in bad faith or without reasonable care is a question of fact, and the burden is on the applicant to establish this.[18] In *R (Wilkinson) v Responsible Medical Officer Broadmoor Hospital and others*,[19] Hale LJ (as she then was) suggested that the qualified immunity does not protect a defendant who has made 'a negligent mistake of law as to the extent of legal authority under the Act.'

4.13 In *Winch v Jones*, a negligence action, the Master of the Rolls held that a plaintiff is entitled to leave if he or she can show that the case deserves further examination.[20] However, this was thrown into doubt by Farquharson LJ's subsequent statement in *James v Mayor and Burgesses of Havering* that the purpose of section was to protect professionals from actions in respect of mere error, and that a prima facie case of bad faith or lack of reasonable care should be made out before leave would be granted.[21]

4.14 If leave is not obtained, any proceedings are a nullity.[22] In *Seal v Chief Constable of South Wales*[23] Mr Seal, was a litigant in person who wished to claim for damages for false imprisonment after having been detained under

---

[16] [2001] EWCA Civ 1545 at [61].

[17] [2001] EWCA Civ 1545 at [61].

[18] *Richardson v London County Council* [1957] 1 WLR 751.

[19] [2001] EWCA Civ 1545, [2002] 1 WLR 419 at para [57].

[20] [1986] QB 296, [1985] 3 All ER 97, CA.

[21] (1992) 15 BMLR 1, CA.

[22] *R v Bracknell JJ, ex p Griffiths* [1976] AC 314, *Seal v Chief Constable of South Wales* [2007] UKHL 31 [2007] 4 All ER 177.

[23] *Seal v Chief Constable of South Wales* [2007] UKHL 31, [2007] 4 All ER 177.

s 136 by South Wales Police. The claim was made without the leave of the High Court. It appeared that Mr Seal did not know of the leave requirement. However, the failure to obtain leave meant that his case, in so far as it was based on the unlawful use of the police officer's power of arrest under s 136 of the Mental Health Act under s 136, was struck out. The House of Lords decided by a majority of three to two that the section should be interpreted so as to nullify any case brought without permission, and this failure could not be rectified by a successful application for permission after proceedings have commenced.

4.15 In *Seal* Lord Bingham held that the provisions of s 136 do not infringe the patient's right to a fair trial under Art 6 of the European Convention on Human Rights.[24] Baroness Hale of Richmond gave a powerful dissenting speech, in the course of which she concluded that s 139 represented a disproportionate interference with the fundamental right of access to the courts. Her Ladyship said this:[25]

'To restrict the right of access to the courts of people who have previously abused that right obviously bears a rational connection with the aim of protecting defendants against vexatious claims. But it is not obviously rational to brand every person who is or has been subject to the compulsory powers in the Mental Health Act as a potential vexatious litigant. There are some compulsory patients who suffer from paranoid delusions; there are some who suffer from psychopathic disorders who may be more inclined than others to make trouble. But the blanket restriction in section 139(2) takes no account of these subtleties. It assumes that everyone who has ever been subject to Mental Health Act compulsion is automatically suspect. This is not only empirically unproven. It certainly cannot be taken for granted when Mental Health Act powers may be exercised by people with no mental health expertise whatsoever.'

Lord Simon's statement in *R v Bracknell JJ, ex p Griffiths* that 'Patients under the Mental Health Act may generally be inherently likely to harass those concerned with them by groundless charges and litigation'[26] was seen by Baroness Hale, and by the Mental Health Act Commission as based on an unacceptably stereotyped and prejudicial view of mentally disordered people, as well as a disproportionate interference with the right of access to the courts.[27] There can be little doubt that s 139 creates a technical and often unprincipled obstacle to litigation which is blanket in its effects, and therefore potentially breaches Art 6(1). Support for this view is found in the decision of the European Court of Human Rights in *Salontaji-Drobnjak v Serbia*,[28] where the court held that such a restriction would breach Art 6(1) if it was disproportionate and if it was not based on the propensity of the patient to be a vexatious litigant. Despite Baroness Hale's spirited dissent, the position

---

[24] Ibid, para [20].
[25] Ibid; para [57].
[26] *Pountney v Griffiths* [1975] 3 WLR 140, p 141.
[27] Mental Health Act Commission, *12th Biennial Report 2005–2007 Risks, Rights and Recovery*, paras 2.153–2.154.
[28] Judgement of 13 October 2009, para [134].

remains that any case brought without permission is a nullity, and this cannot be rectified by a successful application for permission after proceedings have commenced.

4.16 In *TTM v London Borough of Hackney* the AMHP had formed the honest but unreasonable belief that the nearest relative was not objecting to detention under s 3. An objection by the nearest relative is a bar to detention under s 3 by virtue of s 11(4). Habeas corpus was granted, on the grounds that the test was not whether the AMHP's belief was honest, but whether it was reasonable for her to have reached that conclusion on the facts. In a subsequent application for judicial review and damages under s 7 of the Human Rights Act 1998, Collins J held that there was no prospect of succeeding in an action based on the negligence of the AMHP or on the grounds that she had acted in bad faith, and his Lordship refused leave under s 139(2). The Court of Appeal reversed the decision at first instance. Toulson LJ, delivering the leading judgment of a unanimous Court of Appeal, reversed Collins J's decision, holding that because the AMHP had proceeded with the application when she ought reasonably to have concluded that the nearest relative had objected to detention for treatment, that M's rights under Article 5 had been infringed and that he was entitled to compensation. This result could be achieved by 'reading down' s 139(1) by virtue of s 3 of the Human Rights Act so as to permit a claim by M for compensation from the local authority.[29] Toulson LJ concluded that Collins J had been wrong to dismiss the application for judicial review, even though there had been no bad faith and Toulson LJ did not consider it necessary to make a finding that the social worker had been negligent. The judge should have found that:[30]

> 'M was unlawfully detained, both as a matter of domestic law and within article 5, by reason of the AMHP's contravention of s 11(4), and he should have given M leave under s 139(2) to pursue a claim for compensation against the local authority.'

Hence in light of the decision of the Court of Appeal, where the applicant for judicial review and damages is a victim of an unlawful deprivation of liberty contrary to Art 5, s 139 should be read down to allow leave to be given even if there is no negligence or bad faith on the part of those acting pursuant to the MHA 1983.

THE APPROVED MENTAL HEALTH PROFESSIONAL

4.17 Section 18 of the MHA 2007 has replaced the role of ASW with that of Approved Mental Health Professional ('AMHP'). Only an AMHP or the patient's nearest relative may make an application for detention or guardianship. AMHPs are defined in s 114(10). An AMHP who is 'acting on

---

[29]   *TTM v LB Hackney East London NHS Foundation Trust and the Secretary of State for Health* [2011] EWCA Civ 4, para 66.

[30]   Ibid, para 69.

behalf of' local social services authority ('LSSA') in England must be approved by any LSSA whose area is in England, and if 'acting on behalf' of a LSSA in Wales must be approved by any LSSA whose area is in Wales.

Approval as an AMHP

4.18   A LSSA may approve a person to act as an AMHP as long as the person is not a doctor. Doctors are specifically excluded by s 114(2). The Mental Health (Approval of Persons to be Approved Mental Health Professionals) Regulations 2008 provide that only the following can be approved:

(a)   a social worker registered with the General Social Care Council (or in Wales the Care Council for Wales;

(b)   a first-level nurse, registered in subpart 1 of the Nurses' Part of the Register established and kept by the Nursing and Midwifery Council, with a recordable qualification in mental health nursing;

(c)   a first-level nurse, registered in subpart 1 of the Nurses' Part of the Register established and kept by the Nursing and Midwifery Council, their field of practice being learning disabilities nursing;

(d)   an occupational therapist registered with the Health Professions Council;

(e)   a chartered psychologist listed in the British Psychological Society's Register of Chartered Psychologists.[31]

The LSSA must be satisfied that any candidate for approval has 'appropriate competence in dealing with persons who are suffering from mental disorder'.[32] The person must also comply with any regulations issued by the Secretary of State for Health if the authority is located in England, or the Welsh Ministers if the authority is located in Wales.[33] The regulations will set out conditions for approval, factors as to competency, and requirements for training. The question of what is appropriate competence is addressed in Sch 2 to the Mental Health (Approved Mental Health Professionals) (Approval) (England) Regulations 2008.[34]

4.19   There are separate regulations for England and Wales. The Explanatory notes state that:[35]

---

[31]   Mental Health (Approved Mental Health Professionals) (Approval) (England) Regulations 2008; SI 2008/1206; Mental Health (Approval of Persons to be Approved Mental Health Professionals) (Wales) Regulations 2008, SI 2008/2436 (W 209).
[32]   MHA 1983, s 114, as inserted by MHA 2007, s 18.
[33]   MHA 1983, s 114(4)–(8), as inserted by MHA 2007, s 18.
[34]   SI 2008/1206.
[35]   Department of Health, Ministry of Justice, Welsh Assembly Government *Mental Health Act 2007 Explanatory Notes* (2007), para 67.

'[A]n AMHP approved by a LSSA in England may only act on behalf of an English LSSA, and an AMHP approved by a Welsh LSSA may only act on behalf of a Welsh LSSA. This means that a Welsh LSSA cannot arrange for an English-approved AMHP to act on their behalf and vice versa. However, it does not mean that a Welsh-approved AMHP cannot make an application to admit a patient in England or convey a patient in England and vice versa. It is also possible for an AMHP with the appropriate competencies to be approved in both territories.'

Training courses for English and Welsh AMHPs from all professional backgrounds are approved by the General Social Care Council ('GSCC') and the Care Council for Wales ('CCfW'), the statutory bodies set up to regulate the social work profession.[36] Although an AMHP can ony be approved by one LSSA, the regulations provide for her or him to exercise AMHP functions in the area of another LSSA if that LSSA has authorised the AMHP to perform such functions on its behalf. The AMHP is required to notify the approving LSSA if such authorisation is given.[37]

4.20 The Department of Health Reference Guide to the Mental Health Act 1983 states that:[38]

'Being approved by a LSSA to be an AMHP is not the same thing as being permitted by a LSSA to act on its behalf. It is for each LSSA to establish its own arrangements for determining which AMHPs may act ... on its behalf and when they may do so. A LSSA may arrange for AMHPs to act on its behalf even though they are approved by another authority.'

For an AMHP to act on behalf of a Welsh LSSA, the AMHP must be approved by a Welsh LSSA under the Welsh regulations However, an AMHP acting on behalf of an English LSSA may apply for admission of patient to a hospital in Wales or for a warrant under s 135 and vice versa, provided that the Welsh statutory admission forms[39] are used for admission to a Welsh hospital and the English ones[40] for admission to an English hospital or for an application to the magistrates in the relevant jurisdiction.

Professional regulation of AMHPs

4.21 Part 4 of the Care Standards Act 2000 ('CSA 2000') requires the GSCC and CCfW to provide codes of practice for social care workers, which includes 'a person who engages in relevant social work'. 'Relevant social work' is defined as 'social work which is required in connection with any health, education or

---

36   MHA 1983, s 114A, as inserted by MHA 2007, s 19.

37   SI 2008/1206, r 5.

38   Department of Health Reference Guide to the Mental Health Act 1983, (London) TSO 2008 para 32.5.

39   Mental Health (Hospital, Guardianship, Community Treatment and Consent to Treatment) (Wales) Regulations 2008, SI 2008/2439 (W 212).

40   Mental Health (Hospital, Guardianship and Treatment) (England) Regulations 2008, SI 2008/1184.

social services provided by any person'. To ensure that AMHPs from different professional backgrounds continue to be regulated by their own professional bodies, new s 114A(4) states that the functions of an approved mental health professional shall not be considered to be 'relevant social work' for the purposes of Part 4 of the CSA 2000. The GSCC and CCfW codes of practice will continue to apply to social workers when carrying out AMHP functions, and these bodies are given a new statutory power to lay down standards of conduct and practice expected of social workers when carrying out the functions of an approved mental health professional.[41]

The role of the AMHP

4.22 AMHPs take over the key function in the compulsory admission process previously performed by ASWs. Where a LSSA have reason to think that an application for admission to hospital or a guardianship application may need to be made in respect of a patient within their area, they must make arrangements for an AMHP to consider the patient's case on their behalf.[42] LSSAs are also under a duty, if so required by the nearest relative of a patient residing in their area, to direct an AMHP as soon as practicable to consider a patient's case with a view to making an application for compulsory admission.[43] The AMHP is then under a duty to make an application for compulsory admission, but only if s/he is satisfied that such an application ought to be made in respect of the patient, and is of the opinion – having regard to any wishes expressed by relatives or any other relevant circumstances – that it is necessary or proper for the application to be made by him/her.[44]

4.23 The duty on LSSAs to direct an AMHP to consider compulsory admission or guardianship is not confined to cases where the nearest relative has requested it, as it may arise from the request of someone else, who gives the LSSA reason to believe that an application may be necessary. Where the AMHP has considered a case as the result of a request by the nearest relative, and decides not to make an application for compulsory admission, s/he must inform the nearest relative of the reasons in writing.

4.24 The AMHP takes over the ASW role to:[45]

'arrange and co-ordinate the assessment, taking into account all factors to determine if detention in hospital is the best option for a patient or if there is a less restrictive alternative'.

Since the AMHP assumes the existing powers and duties of the ASW under the MHA 1983, the law governing the role remains broadly the same.

---

[41] CSA 2000, s 62(1A), as inserted by MHA 2007, s 20.
[42] MHA 1983, s 13(1), as inserted by MHA 2007, Sch 2, para 5(2).
[43] MHA 1983, s 13(4), as amended by MHA 2007, Sch 2, para 5(5).
[44] MHA 1983, s 13(1B), as amended by MHA 2007, Sch 2, para 5(2).
[45] Department of Health, Ministry of Justice, Welsh Assembly Government *Mental Health Act 2007 Explanatory Notes* (2007), para 71.

The personal responsibility of the AMHP

4.25 The Department of Health Code of Practice on the MHA 1983 Code of Practice emphasises the individual professional responsibility of the AMHP and states that:[46]

> 'Although AMHPs act on behalf of a LSSA, they cannot be told by the LSSA or anyone else whether or not to make an application. They must exercise their own judgement, based on social and medical evidence, when deciding whether to apply for a patient to be detained under the Act. The role of AMHPs is to provide an independent decision about whether or not there are alternatives to detention under the Act, bringing a social perspective to bear on their decision.

The AMHP has overall responsibility for coordinating the assessment and has a professional responsibility for ensuring that the patient is taken and conveyed to hospital (see **4.39** below) unless different policies agreements apply at local level.[47] SInce the AMIIP acts on behalf of the LSSA, the authority is vicariously liable for any negligence or bad faith on the AMHP's part.[48]

4.26 Whereas ASWs were employed by LSSAs, there is no longer a requirement that an AMHP be an officer (employee) of an LSSA.[49] AMHPs do, however, 'act on behalf of the LSSA'. The phrase 'acting on behalf of the LSSA' does not signify that the LSSA can direct AMHPs in their individual decision making. Now s 13(1A) retains the individual personal responsibility of the AMHP by requiring that the AMIIP must be:

(a)   satisfied that such an application ought to be made in respect of the patient; and

(b)   of the opinion, having regard to any wishes expressed by relatives of the patient or any other relevant circumstances, that it is necessary or proper for the application to be made by him, he shall make the application.[50]

This is in effectively identical terms to the old s 13(1) of the MHA 1983 which, as Judge LJ in *St George's Healthcare NHS Trust v S* said:[51]

> 'makes clear that the social worker must exercise her own independent judgment on the basis of all the available material, including her interview and assessment of the patient, and personally make the appropriate decision. When doing so she is required to take account of the recommendations made by the medical practitioners.'

---

[46]   Department of Health *Code of Practice: Mental Health Act 1983* (2008), para 4.51.

[47]   Department of Health *Mental Health Act 1983 Draft Revised Code of Practice* (2007), para 10.13. See http://www.dh.gov.uk/en/Consultations/Liveconsultations/DH_079842.

[48]   *TTM v London Borough of Hackney* [2010] EWHC 1349 (Admin), para 35; [2011] EWCA Civ 4.

[49]   Department of Health, Ministry of Justice, Welsh Assembly Government *Mental Health Act 2007 Explanatory Notes* (2007), para 65.

[50]   Inserted by MHA 2007, Sch 2, para 5.

[51]   [1998] 3 All ER 673 at 694, CA.

Since the AMHP acts on behalf of the LSSA, the authority is vicariously liable for any negligence or bad faith on the AMHP's part.[52]

4.27 The intention of the phrase 'acting on behalf of the LSSA' is to make clear that AMHPS carry out their functions on behalf of the LSSA and, as Baroness Royall put it, thereby 'underline the independence of the AMHP from the trust that may employ the doctors who also examine a patient's case for admission'.[53] The original scheme of the MHA 1959 and MHA 1983 was that the applicant was employed by social services and the recommending doctors would be employed by the NHS. As the Explanatory Notes state, 'unlike with ASWs, there is no longer a requirement that an AMHP be an officer (employee) of an LSSA'.[54] There is now nothing to stop both AMHP and the doctors recommending detention being employed by the same NHS trust, but for the purposes of the application for detention, the AMHP acts not for the trust, but on behalf of the LSSA. The aim is to provide 'a mix of professional perspectives at the point in time when a decision is being made regarding a patient's detention'. Although all those involved may be employed by the NHS, 'the skills and training required of AMHPs aim to ensure that they provide an independent social perspective'.[55]

4.28 Another reason for stating that the AMHP acts on behalf of the LSSA is to ensure, in Baroness Royall's words:[56]

> 'that the responsibility for providing that an AMHP service is in place clearly lies with the LSSA, whether or not it chooses to enter into arrangements with another body, such as a trust, to provide the service.'

Under the original s 114 of the MHA 1983 a clear statutory duty did lie with social services to appoint a sufficient number of ASWs. The MHA 2007 has repealed this provision. However, the Department of Health *Code of Practice on the Mental Health Act 1983* states that:[57]

> 'LSSAs are responsible for ensuring that sufficient AMHPs are available to carry out their roles under the Act, including assessing patients to decide whether an application for detention should be made. To fulfil their statutory duty, LSSAs must have arrangements in place in their area to provide a 24-hour service that can respond to patients' needs.'

---

[52]   *TTM v London Borough of Hackney* [2010] EWHC 1349 (Admin), para 35; [2011] EWCA Civ 4.

[53]   *Hansard*, HL Deb, vol 688, col 681.

[54]   Department of Health, Ministry of Justice, Welsh Assembly Government *Mental Health Act 2007 Explanatory Notes* (2007), para 65.

[55]   Department of Health, Ministry of Justice, Welsh Assembly Government *Mental Health Act 2007 Explanatory Notes* (2007), para 67.

[56]   Hansard, HL Deb, vol 688, col 682.

[57]   Department of Health *Code of Practice: Mental Health Act 1983* (2008), para 4.33. Similar provisions are found in the Welsh Assembly Government Mental Health Act 1983 Code of Practice 2008, paras 2.72–2.73.

The assessment

4.29 Before making an application for compulsory admission, it is the duty of the AMHP to interview the patient '*in a suitable manner*' and satisfy him/herself that detention in hospital is in 'all the circumstances of the case, the most appropriate way of providing the care and treatment which the patient needs'.[58] The Department of Health Code of Practice states that:[59] 'Patients should usually be given the opportunity of speaking to the AMHP alone. However, if AMHPs have reason to fear physical harm, they should insist that another professional is present.' And it goes on to say that it is not desirable for patients to be interviewed through a closed door or window, and this should be considered only where other people are at serious risk. The duty to interview in a suitable manner was considered in *R (M)* v *The Managers Queen Mary's Hospital*[60] where Underhill J at first instance considered that the purpose of the interview was achieved where, despite the AMHP's attempts to communicate with the patient, the patient 'fails to respond or responds inappropriately, in a manner suggesting that she does indeed require treatment.' In the Court of Appeal Richards LJ confirmed that the duty to interview in a suitable manner left a degree of flexibility to the AMHP when he said that there was no set minimum time limit for such an interview, and that what was required was a matter for the professional judgment of the AMHP.[61]

4.30 In *Re GM (Patient: Consultation)*[62] the patient was interviewed by the ASW prior to an emergency application under s 4 for detention for up to 72 hours. During the currency of the s 4, an application for admission for treatment under s 3 was made without a fresh interview. Burton J held that a fresh interview would only be necessary for the purposes of the s 3 application if the s 4 had expired before the decision to detain under s 3 was made. The purpose of the phrase 'in a suitable manner' is to ensure that the AMHP conducts the interview so as to take account of the particular needs of all groups such as children, people with communication difficulties, or people whose first language is not English. The Department of Health Code of Practice provides guidance on overcoming barriers to communication in the case of people with learning disabilities.[63]

4.31 'All the circumstances of the case' include the past history of the patient and his or her disorder, his or her present condition and social and family factors relevant to it; the wishes of the family; and medical opinion. In order to assess the relevant options, the AMHP will need to be informed of the availability and suitability of other ways of giving the patient the care and treatment needed, such as informal admission, day care, out-patient treatment,

---

[58] MHA 1983, s 13(2).
[59] Department of Health *Code of Practice: Mental Health Act 1983* (2008), paras 4.53–4.54.
[60] [2008] EWHC 1959 (Admin); [2008] MHLR 303, para [14].
[61] [2008] EWCA Civ 1112; [2008] MHLR 306, para [25].
[62] [2000] MHLR 41.
[63] Department of Health *Code of Practice: Mental Health Act 1983* (2008), para 34.13.

crisis intervention centres, community psychiatric nursing and social work support, primary health care support, support from family, friends or voluntary organisations.

4.32 The Department of Health Code of Practice (at para 4.5) states that in judging whether compulsory admission is appropriate, those concerned should consider not only the statutory criteria but also:[64]

- the patient's wishes and view of their own needs;

- the patient's age and physical health;

- any past wishes or feelings expressed by the patient;

- the patient's cultural background;

- the patient's social and family circumstances;

- the impact that any future deterioration or lack of improvement in the patient's condition would have on their children, other relatives or carers, especially those living with the patient, including an assessment of these people's ability and willingness to cope; and

- the effect on the patient, and those close to the patient, of a decision to admit or not to admit under the Act.

Informing and consulting the Nearest Relative

4.33 Section 11(3) of the MHA 1983 places an AMHP under a duty – either before or within a reasonable time after making an *application for admission for assessment* – to take all such steps as are practicable to inform the person appearing to be the nearest relative that an application is about to be or has been made, and that the nearest relative has the power (subject to the limitations in s 25) to direct the discharge of the patient. The words 'person appearing to be the nearest relative' were held by Laws J (as he then was) in *R v Managers of South Western Hospital ex parte M*[65] not to 'embrace a situation where on the facts known to the [AMHP], the person in question is legally incapable of being the nearest relative having regard to the terms of section 26.' (see **5.8** below). In *R(WC) v South London and Maudsley NHS Trust* Scott Baker LJ held that s 11(3) does not require the AMHP to 'don the mantle of Sherlock Holmes' in making inquiries as to the identity of the nearest relative.[66] His Lordship further held that the court would not interfere with an AMHP's decision unless the AMHP had failed to apply the test in s 26 or acted in bad faith or in some way reached a conclusion that was plainly wrong.[67]

---

[64]   Department of Health *Code of Practice: Mental Health Act 1983* (2008), para 4.5.
[65]   [1994] 1 All ER 161 at 175.
[66]   [2001] EWHC Admin 1025; [2001] MHLR 187, para [28].
[67]   Ibid, para [27].

4.34 When the AMHP is making an application for admission for treatment or for guardianship, s 11(4) requires that the nearest relative be consulted – unless it appears to the AMHP that in the circumstances such consultation is not practicable or would involve unreasonable delay. There is no duty to consult if it is not practicable. The word 'practicable' was interpreted in *R (on the application of E) v Bristol City Council*[68] to take account of the wishes, health and well-being of the patient. The Code of Practice had said that 'practicability' refers to the availability of the nearest relative and not to the appropriateness of informing or consulting the person concerned. Bennett J held that the Code was 'wrong' and contrary 'to common sense' on this point. Impracticability could be invoked where here it was known that the NR intensely disliked the patient, or where, as here, the patient was competent and had strongly expressed her wish that the NR not be consulted. Bennett J counselled caution before removing the important role of the NR on grounds of practicability. However, the relative should not be consulted if it were likely to be detrimental to the patient or an infringement of their right to respect for private life under Art 8 of the European Convention on Human Rights.

4.35 The issue of reasonable delay was considered in *CV* v *South London and Maudsley NHS Foundation Trust*.[69] In this case the patient was a 44-year old man whose diagnosis was unclear, but was most recently considered to have either schizotypal personality disorder or Asperger's Syndrome. He was detained under s 3 of the MHA 1983, but Bethlem Royal hospital itself discharged that detention because they considered the section papers defective. When the Claimant indicated that he would leave the ward, he was re-detained under s 5(2) of the Act. He was subsequently re-detained under s 3, but the social worker took the view that it would be unreasonable to delay to consult the nearest relative. Wyn Williams J held that the AMHP was 'plainly wrong' to take the view that it would be unreasonable to delay to consult the Nearest Relative at a time when she thought that at least 7 hours of lawful detention under s 5(2) remained.

4.36 If the nearest relative objects to an application for admission for treatment or a guardianship application, the AMHP cannot proceed with it. The consultation must be genuine. In *GD v Hospital Managers of Edgware Community Hospital and London Borough* Barnet Burnett J concluded that:[70]

> '[I]n seeking to protect the best interests of GD the [mental health professionals] calculated that they should do no more than nod in the direction of consultation as contemplated by section 11(4). They set in motion a course of events which was designed to leave consultation with GD's father to the very last moment, and thus seriously inhibit the chances of his having any effective input into the process and the chances of his having an opportunity to make an objection. In those circumstances, what in my judgment they contemplated could not properly be considered consultation at all.'

---

[68] [2005] EWHC 74 (Admin), [2005] MHLR 83.
[69] (2010) CO/943/2010.
[70] [2008] EWHC 3572.

His Lordship held that this amounted to a misuse of power, albeit for the best of motives, which had infected the application process from beginning to end. In this case the nearest relative was the patient's father, who was away in Wales, and who was consulted by mobile phone when he was on a mountainside.

4.37   In *TTM v London Borough of Hackney*[71] it was held that in deciding whether there is an objection, the question is not whether the AMHP honestly believed that there was no objection, but whether that belief was reasonable. Habeas corpus was granted because although the AMHP honestly believed that the patient's nearest relative was agreeing to the sectioning, he in fact had not and the AMHP should not reasonably have concluded that he had. Burton J granted habeas corpus on the grounds that the AMHP had failed to acknowledge that the patient's nearest relative was in fact objecting to detention under s 3. In a subsequent action for damages, Collins J dismissed the action, but supported the view adopted by Burton J who had said that the question which the court had to ask itself was 'What was the reasonable belief of the AMHP? Given that the nearest relative had voiced an objection, and there had been no subsequent indication of a change of mind it was not reasonable for the AMHP to have formed the view that she did, and hence the admission was unlawful.[72]

4.38   An unreasonable objection by a nearest relative is one of the grounds in s 29(3) on which the court may order the transfer of the powers of nearest relative to another person. An AMHP is on the list of potential applicants for such an order.

The power to 'take and convey'

4.39   Applicants for compulsory admission under Part 2, whether they are an AMHP or the nearest relative, are authorised by s 6(1) to 'take and convey', or to authorise others to take and convey the patient to hospital. Even if delegation takes place, the AMHP inherits the ultimate responsibility of the ASW 'to ensure that the patient is conveyed in a lawful and humane manner, and should give guidance to those asked to assist' and if the patient is likely to be violent or dangerous, police assistance should be requested.[73] Section 137 of the Act provides that any person who is required or authorised by the Act to be conveyed to any place, kept in custody or detained in a place of safety or at any place specified by the Secretary of State under s 42(6), shall be deemed to be in legal custody. Any person authorised under the Act to take and convey a patient to any such place has all the powers of a constable whilst so acting, including the power of arresting a person who is wilfully obstructing a police officer in the execution of his duty, and the power to use reasonable force in effecting an arrest.

---

71   [2010] EWHC 1349 (Admin).
72   [2010] EWHC 1349 (Admin), paras [22]–[23].
73   Department of Health and Welsh Office *Code of Practice on the Mental Health Act 1983* (TSO, 1999), paras 11.4–11.7.

The power to retake

4.40 By virtue of s 138(1)(a), where a patient escapes, the person who had the patient in legal custody – an AMHP or a constable – is empowered to retake the patient. With regard to absconding patients, AMHPs have the power under s 18 – also conferred on the police and hospital staff, to take into custody and return to hospital any patient who has absented him or herself from the hospital without leave, or who has failed to return to the hospital on the expiry of the leave. This power also applies in the case of patients who have absconded from hospitals or compulsory community powers in Scotland, Northern Ireland, the Channel Islands or the Isle of Man (see Part VI of the MHA 1983). Where an offender patient is subject to a hospital order made under Part III of the MHA 1983, an AMHP is one of the persons authorised under s 40(1) to take and convey the patient to hospital.

Application for a warrant to enter premises

4.41 An AMHP has the power under s 135 of the Act to lay an information on oath before a justice of the peace to the effect that there is reasonable cause to suspect that a person believed to be suffering from mental disorder:

(a)   has been or is being ill-treated, neglected, or being kept otherwise than under proper control; or

(b)   is living alone and is unable to care for him or herself.

The magistrate may then issue a warrant authorising a police officer to enter the premises (using force if necessary) accompanied by an AMHP and a doctor. If the social worker and the doctor think fit, the patient may be removed to a place of safety with a view to making an application for compulsory admission.

Duty to assess person detained under s 136

4.42 Where a constable has found a person in a public place who appears to be suffering from mental disorder and to be in immediate need of care and control, s/he may remove that person to a place of safety under s 136 if he or she considers it necessary in the interests of that person or for the protection of others. The purpose of removal is to enable the patient to be examined by a medical practitioner and assessed by an AMHP, and to enable any necessary arrangements for his or her care to be made.

Powers of entry and inspection

4.43 Section 115 is amended to empower an AMHP to enter at all reasonable times and inspect any premises other than a hospital in which a mentally disordered person is living, if he or she has reasonable grounds to believe that the person is not under proper care. Under the MHA 1983 this power could only be exercised within the area of the employing local authority. Under the new s 115 there is no geographical limitation on where the power may be exercised.[74] The AMHP may be required to produce a duly authenticated document to show that he or she is an AMHP.

Role on making, renewal and revocation of a community treatment order

4.44 Unless an AMHP states in writing that he agrees with the responsible clinician's (RC's) opinion that the statutory criteria are met, and that it is appropriate, the RC may not make, renew or revoke a community treatment order.[75] The AMHP must also agree the conditions to be applied. The role of the AMHP is set out in the Department of Health Code of Practice, which states that:[76]

> 'The AMHP must decide whether to agree with the patient's responsible clinician that the patient meets the criteria for SCT, and (if so) whether SCT is appropriate. Even if the criteria for SCT are met, it does not mean that the patient must be discharged onto SCT. In making that decision, the AMHP should consider the wider social context for the patient. Relevant factors may include any support networks the patient may have, the potential impact on the rest of the patient's family, and employment issues.'

The Code of Practice states that the AMHP may be a member of the patient's multi-disciplinary team, but this is not essential:[77]

> 'The Act does not specify who this AMHP should be. It may (but need not) be an AMHP who is already involved in the patient's care and treatment as part of the multi-disciplinary team. It can be an AMHP acting on behalf of any willing LSSA, and LSSAs may agree with each other and with hospital managers the arrangements that are likely to be most convenient and best for patients. But if no other LSSA is willing, responsibility for ensuring that an AMHP considers the case should lie with the LSSA which would become responsible under section 117 for the patient's after-care if the patient were discharged.'

The Code then goes on to emphasise that the need for the AMHP's agreement is seen as an important safeguard. The AMHP must reach an independent professional view:[78]

> 'If the AMHP does not agree with the responsible clinician that the patient should go onto SCT, then SCT cannot go ahead. A record of the AMHP's decision and the full reasons for it should be kept in the patient's notes. It would not be appropriate for the responsible clinician to approach another AMHP for an alternative view.'

---

[74]   Inserted by MHA 2007, Sch 2, para 8.
[75]   MHA 1983, ss 17A(4)(b), 20A(8), 17F(4)(b), as inserted by MHA 2007, s 34(2) and (3).
[76]   Department of Health *Code of Practice: Mental Health Act 1983* (2008), para 25.24.
[77]   Ibid, para 25.26.
[78]   Ibid, para 25.27

4.45 It is difficult to see how an AMHP who is a member of the multi-disciplinary team can be seen as bringing sufficient independence to the process to amount to a significant safeguard, especially if the AMHP is to be responsible for the patient's after care under s 117. Article 20(2) of Council of Europe Recommendation Rec (2004)10 of the Committee of Ministers to member states concerning the protection of the human rights and dignity of persons with mental disorder recommends that the decision to subject a person to involuntary treatment should be taken by a court or another competent body. Assuming that an order to comply with medication in the community falls within this provision, the fact remains that under the MHA 2007 a CTO may be imposed on a patient with restrictive conditions as to behaviour potentially interfering with rights under Art 8, on the authority of a RC and an AMHP without a legal requirement to seek the authority of the hospital managers or another competent body. The court or other competent body authorising involuntary treatment should, according to Art 20(2), take into account the opinion of the person concerned, and act in accordance with procedures provided by law based on the principle that the person concerned should be seen and consulted. Although the Government has reserved its right not to comply with all or part of this recommendation, this would not prevent the European Court of Human Rights from using this provision as an aid to interpretation of the scope of this procedural obligation in Art 8 regarding the right to respect for private life.

Conflicts of interest

4.46 Section 22 replaces s 12(3)–(7) of the MHA 1983, which specified when a medical practitioner may not provide a medical recommendation, because of their position either in relation to the applicant, the patient or the other recommending doctor. These provisions are replaced by a power to enable regulations to be made setting out when, because of a potential conflict of interest, an AMHP may not make an application for admission to hospital or guardianship; or a doctor may not provide a medical recommendation accompanying such an application.[79] The regulation making power is broader than the old provisions in s 12, as it covers conflicts of interest involving AMHPs as well as doctors. This extension is necessitated because the AMHP may now be employed in the same trust as the recommending doctors, and it will be important that regulations ensure the requisite degree of independence when the AMHP is making an application.

MEDICAL RECOMMENDATIONS AND S 12 APPROVED DOCTORS

4.47 Applications for compulsory admission for assessment under s 2 or for treatment under s 3 require two medical recommendations from doctors who

---

[79]   MHA 1983, s 12A, as introduced by MHA 2007, s 22. The regulations are Mental Health (Conflicts of Interest) (England) Regulations 2008, SI 2008/1205; Mental Health (Conflicts of Interest) (Wales) Regulations 2008, SI 2008/2440.

are fully registered under the Medical Act 1983. One medical recommendation must be given by a practitioner approved under s 12(2) as having special experience in the diagnosis or treatment of mental disorder. Unless that practitioner has previous acquaintance with the patient, the other such recommendation must, if practicable, be given by a doctor who has such previous acquaintance. The issue of reasonable practicability was raised in *TTM* v *London Borough of Hackney*.[80] The nearest relative had sought to exercise his power to discharge the patient, and the RC had failed, despite reminders to issue a barring certificate preventing discharge on grounds of dangerousness to self or others within the requisite 72 hour period. A a resut the patient was discharged. A subsequent application was made under s 3 and habeas corpus was granted on grounds that the AMHP had failed to acknowledge the nearest relative's objection. In the subsequent action for damages a further contention was raised, namely that the requirements of s 12(2) had not been met. There was a disagreement between the two psychiatrists who had been treating the patient as to whether detention was appropriate, and so the hospital Trust decided to approach two forensic psychiatrists both of whom were approved under s 12 as having special experience in the diagnosis or treatment of mental disorder, but neither of whom had previous acquaintance with the patient. Collins J held that s 12 had not been infringed:[81]

'I think that the decision to use two professionals who came afresh and who, of course, had access to all the hospital notes and could question nurses or other doctors was reasonable and a proper exercise of judgment of what was in the claimant's best interests. Thus there was no breach of s 12(2).'

Emergency admissions for assessment for up to 72 hours under s 4 require only one medical recommendation, which should, if practicable, be given by a doctor who has previous acquaintance with the patient. As Jones points out, for s 4, 'There is no legal requirement for the recommending doctor to be approved under s 12'.[82]

4.48   The medical recommendations required for an application for admission or a guardianship application must be signed on or before the date of the application, and must be given by doctors who have personally examined the patient either together or separately. If they have examined the patient separately, not more than five days must have elapsed between the days on which the separate examinations took place.[83]

4.49   Section 6(1) provides that a duly completed application is sufficient authority for the applicant, or any person authorised by the applicant, to take the patient and convey him to the hospital within the 14 days following the date

---

80   [2010] EWHC (Admin) 1349.
81   Ibid, para [33].
82   RM Jones *Mental Health Act Manual* (Sweet and Maxwell, 13th edn, 2010), p 50.
83   MHA 1983, s 12(1).

on which the patient was last examined by a doctor giving a medical recommendation. For emergency applications the period is 24 hours.

4.50 As with the AMHP, a doctor giving medical recommendations is exercising functions of a public nature in an area where Art 5 is engaged, providing the necessary objective medical evidence of a true mental disorder which is of a nature or degree warranting detention, and that detention is strictly necessary, ie:[84]

> 'that other less severe measures have been considered and found to be insufficient to safeguard the individual or public interest which might require that the person concerned be detained.'

The report must focus on the patient's actual current state of mental health and not past events.[85]

4.51 Jones submits that the AMHP and the recommending doctors:[86]

> 'have assumed personal responsibility towards the patient to take reasonable care to avoid an inappropriate and/or unlawful detention. It follows that an action for negligence could be brought.'

Perhaps the most persuasive argument for this view is s 139 of the MHA 1983 which states that no-one shall be liable to any civil or criminal proceedings in respect of any act purporting to be done in pursuance of the Act unless the act was done in bad faith or without reasonable care. This clearly suggests there can be liability in negligence for acts done in pursuance of the Act. Equally persuasive is Lord Atkin's famous statement in *Everett v Griffiths* that:

> '[I]t is just as it is convenient that the law should impose a duty to take reasonable care that such persons, if sane, should not suffer the unspeakable torment of having their sanity condemned and their liberty restricted; and I am glad to record my opinion, ineffectual though it may be, that for such an injury the English law provides a remedy.'

Doctors providing medical recommendations must act compatibly with Convention rights, in good faith and with reasonable care. In *TTM* v *London Borough of Hackney* Collins J said that he could see no reason in principle why an AMHP should not owe a duty of care to the patient.[87]

4.52 Interestingly, the Minister of State – Rosie Winterton – in her evidence to the Joint Committee on Human Rights would not accept that there is any 'requirement in relation to the European Court of Human Rights for doctors to decide about initial detention'. The minister stated that 'as a matter of policy:

---

[84] *Litwa v Poland* (2001) 33 EHRR 53, ECtHR.
[85] *Varbanov v Bulgaria* [2000] MHLR 263.
[86] RM Jones *Mental Health Act Manual* (Sweet and Maxwell, 13th edn, 2010), p 92.
[87] [2010] EWHC 1349, at para 36.

'[W]e decided to keep doctors as making the decision because at initial detention, some patients are not known to services or have disengaged from services, so a patient's clinical needs may not be known at that point. We felt that it was practical that doctors, with their broad diagnostic skills should decide whether people should be detained.'

The Minister recorded the Government's acceptance of:[88]

'the case for a medical expert's opinion where someone of unsound mind is to be detained, but we do not agree that it gives authority for the proposition that a psychiatrist must provide the necessary medical expertise in each case.'

This view is difficult to square with Art 20(4) of Council of Europe Recommendation (2004)10 of the Committee of Ministers to member states concerning the protection of the human rights and dignity of persons with mental disorder that:

'Involuntary placement, involuntary treatment, or their extension should only take place on the basis of examination by *a doctor having the requisite competence and experience*, and in accordance with valid and reliable professional standards.'

The Government has reserved its right not to comply with all or part of this recommendation, but this would not prevent the European Court of Human Rights from using this provision as an aid to interpretation of Art 5.

4.53 The Government relied on the Commission decision in *Schuurs v the Netherlands*[89] involving complaints about the detention of the patient on the basis of a certificate by a general practitioner. The patient's complaints were about the fact that the GP did not properly examine her and that she was not allowed to make representations to the District Court that ordered her detention in hospital for six months. Her complaints did not raise any objection to the examination being carried out by a general medical practitioner rather than a psychiatrist. The Commission did not rule on this matter. The decision is therefore weak authority for the proposition that the evidence need not come from someone with psychiatric expertise. The only circumstance where an application for admission would be made on the basis of a recommendation from a GP would be the emergency procedure under s 4. Since the *Winterwerp* requirement of objective medical evidence applies 'otherwise than in emergencies'. This would not infringe Art 5.

4.54 In any event detention requires medical recommendations from doctors. Section 16 of the MHA 2007 has amended s 12 of the MHA 1983 so that a

---

[88]	House of Lords, House of Commons Joint Committee on Human Rights *Legislative Scrutiny: Seventh Progress Report: Fifteenth Report of Session 2006–2007* (HL Paper 555, HC Paper 112), para 1.9.

[89]	41 D & R 186.

registered medical practitioner who has been approved as an AC is also approved for the purposes of s 12. The Explanatory Note to the Act states that:[90]

> 'It is expected that the competencies a registered medical practitioner will require in order to be approved as an AC will be such that they will have the "special experience in the diagnosis or treatment of mental disorder" required for section 12 approval. ACs who are not registered medical practitioners will not be deemed to be section 12 approved.'

The other professional eligible to be approved clinicians ('ACs') will not be eligible to provide medical recommendations for detention or guardianship.

APPROVED CLINICIANS ('ACS') AND RESPONSIBLE CLINICIANS ('RCS')

4.55 The 'responsible clinician' ('RC') is defined in s 34 of the MHA 1983 as:

(a) in the case of a patient who is liable to be detained for assessment or treatment or who is a community patient the approved clinician ('AC') with overall responsibility for the patient's case;

(b) in relation to a patient subject to guardianship, the AC authorised by the responsible local social services authority to act (either generally or in any particular case or for any particular purpose) as the RC;

(c) for a person under guardianship of someone other than a local authority, the patient has a 'nominated medical attendant', who must be a doctor and who acts as the AC for various purposes.[91]

In order to be a responsible clinician, a person must be an approved clinician.

Approved Clinicians ('ACs')

4.56 Approval is not restricted to medical practitioners, and may be extended to practitioners from other professions, such as nursing, psychology, occupational therapy and social work. Approved clinicians acquire some of the powers previously reserved to doctors. For example, s 9 of the MHA 2007 has amended s 5(2) and (3) of the MHA 1983 so that an AC, in addition to a registered medical practitioner, may hold an inpatient for up to 72 hours from the time a report is furnished to the hospital managers, if the AC thinks an application for admission under the Act should be made.

4.57 Any AC may be authorised under s 24 by the nearest relative ('NR') to visit and examine a patient in private for the purposes of advising about

---

[90] *Explanatory Notes*, para 62.
[91] Inserted by MHA 2007, s 9(10).

exercising the NR's power of discharge, or for the purpose of a reference (s 67) or an application (s 76) to the Mental Health Tribunal ('MHT'), or if authorised by the Care Quality Commission ('CQC') under s 120(4). An AC is empowered to visit and examine the patient in private, and is entitled to the production of the patient's medical records. It is an offence under s 129 wilfully to obstruct an AC in carrying out these functions, or to refuse to produce records where the AC has authority to ask for them.

4.58 An AC may give evidence in court in certain cases under Part III. An AC may furnish a report to a criminal court following remand for reports under s 35, provide evidence to a criminal court on which the remand for reports can be extended,[92] may give evidence as to the availability of a bed for an offender patient who is to be remanded for reports or treatment or to be given a hospital order, interim hospital order, or hospital direction,[93] give evidence on the basis of which a patient transferred from prison may be remitted to prison.[94] An AC is eligible to provide a mental condition report on the basis of which an accused person may apply for remand for reports or treatment to be terminated.[95]

4.59 In order to be eligible for approval as an AC, a person must be:

(a)   a registered medical practitioner;

(b)   a chartered psychologist listed in the British Psychological Society's Register of Chartered Psychologists;

(c)   a first-level nurse, registered in subpart 1 of the Nurses' Part of the Register established and kept by the Nursing and Midwifery Council, with a recordable qualification in mental health or learning disabilities nursing. This means that the nurse must be a specialist practitioner or a nurse prescriber;

(d)   an occupational therapist, registered with the Health Professions Council;

(e)   a social worker, registered with the General Social Care Council.

The person must then demonstrate the competencies listed in Sch 2. Separate Directions on the required competencies have been issued for England and Wales.[96]

---

[92]   MHA 1983, s 35(5). Section 36(4) provides that extension of the period of remand for treatment under s 36 may only be done on the evidence of the RC.

[93]   MHA 1983, ss 35(4), 36(3), 37(4), 38(4), 44(2) and 45A(5).

[94]   MHA 1983, ss 50(1) and 53(2).

[95]   MHA 1983, ss 35(8) and 36(7).

[96]   Mental Health Act 1983 Approved Clinician (General) Directions 2008 Issued under ss 7, 8 and 273 of the National Health Service Act 2006 http://www.dh.gov.uk; Mental Health Act 1983 Approved Clinician (Wales) Directions 2008 issued under ss 12, 13 and 203 of the National Health Service (Wales) Act 2006.

Understanding of the AC and RC Roles

4.60 The competencies require an AC to demonstrate a comprehensive understanding of the role of the approved clinician, including the role of the responsible clinician, legal responsibilities and key functions.

Ability to carry out an assessment

4.61 The person must demonstrate ability to identify the presence or absence of mental disorder and the severity of the disorder, to undertake a broad mental health assessment and formulations incorporating biological, psychological, cultural and social perspectives. The person must also demonstrate 'broad understanding' of all mental health related treatments, ie physical, psychological and social interventions. The person must show an advanced level of skills in making and taking responsibility for complex judgments and decisions, without referring to supervision in each individual case. An AC must be able to assess, manage and take responsibility for decisions relating to complexity, at all levels of clinical risk, and the safety of the patient and others within an evidence based framework for risk assessment and management. Finally, an AC must be able to assess the capacity of patients with regard to consent to treatment.

Leadership & multi-disciplinary team working

4.62 An AC must be able to effectively lead a multi-disciplinary team and assimilate and respect the (potentially diverse) views and opinions of other professionals, service users, and carers, weigh evidence appropriately, seek consensus, and make informed decisions if no consensus can be reached within the team. An AC must demonstrate respect for the opinions of others, but be 'able to reach a balanced decision from a variety of stakeholder contributions'. The person must be able to take an independent view, including the ability to take dispassionate decisions and to weigh up evidence, including the views of others, objectively. Finally they must understands the limits of their own skills and know when to delegate.

Treatment

4.63 In relation to treatment an AC must show ability to formulate and appropriately review treatment in the context of a multi-disciplinary team, and to clarify the aims of the treatment, both to the service user and carer and the team. The AC must also show a broad understanding of the different treatment approaches and their applicability to different patients.

Reciprocal recognition of approval in England and Wales

4.64 New s 142A of the MHA 1983, gives the Secretary of State, jointly with Welsh Ministers, the power to specify in regulations the circumstances in which s 12 approval in England and approval as an AC should be considered to mean approval in Wales as well, and vice versa.[97]

Responsible Clinicians ('RCs')

4.65 The definition of the RC is the AC with 'overall responsibility for the patient's case'[98] RCs have a number of powers and duties under Parts 2, 3, 4, and 5 of the MHA 1983. The RC's powers are set out below.

Power to grant leave of absence to a patient who is liable to be detained (s 17)

4.66 The RC may grant either indefinite leave or leave for a specified period, subject to such conditions as he or she considers necessary in the interests of the patient or for the protection of others (see **8.23–8.29** below). Before granting leave of more than seven days, the RC must consider whether the patient should be dealt with under a s 17A community treatment order ('CTO') instead.[99]

Supervised Community Treatment (SCT) and the power to initiate a community treatment order (s 17A)

4.67 Section 17A(1) gives the RC the power, 'by order in writing' to 'discharge a detained patient from hospital subject to his being liable to recall in accordance with section 17E'. This is called a 'Community Treatment Order' ('CTO'), but is referred to in the *Code of Practice on the Mental Health Act 1983* as Supervised Community Treatment.[100] (see **8.30–8.40** below).[101]

Power to recall to hospital from s 17 leave or from a community treatment order (ss 17 and 17E)

4.68 Patients on s 17 leave from a hospital may have their leave revoked and be recalled to the hospital where they were detained if the RC considers it necessary in the interests of the patient's health or safety or for the protection of other persons. Revocation and recall are by the RC giving notice in writing 'to the patient or to the person for the time being in charge of the patient'.[102]

4.69 A community patient may be recalled to any hospital[103] if in the RC's opinion:

---

[97] Inserted by the MHA 2007, s 17. The Secretary of State for Health and the Welsh Ministers have made the Mental Health (Mutual Recognition) Regulations 2008, SI 2008/1204.

[98] MHA 1983, ss 34(1), 55(1), 64(1) and 79(6), as inserted by MHA 2007, ss 9–12.

[99] MHA 1983, s 17(2A) and (2B), inserted by MHA 2007, s 33(2).

[100] Department of Health *Code of Practice: Mental Health Act 1983* (2008), Chapter 25.

[101] MHA 1983, s 17A(3).

[102] MHA 1983, s 17(4).

[103] MHA 1983, s 17E(3) provides that: 'The hospital to which a patient is recalled need not be the responsible hospital.'

(a)   the patient requires medical treatment in hospital for his mental disorder; and

(b)   there would be a risk of harm to the health or safety of the patient or to other persons if the patient were not recalled to hospital for that purpose.

A patient may also be recalled for breach of a condition of a CTO, although this is not a necessary condition of recall provided the other criteria for recall are met (see **8.41–8.45** below).

Power to revoke a community treatment order (s 17F)

4.70   Recalling a patient from leave under s 17(4) automatically revokes the leave and the patient resumes detained patient status in the hospital from which they were granted leave. By contrast, recalling a community patient means that the patient may be detained in a hospital for up to 72 hours immediately following return to hospital. A separate decision under s 17F is necessary to revoke a CTO. The RC may revoke a CTO by order in writing if of the opinion that the conditions for detention under s 3(2) are satisfied in respect of the patient. An AMHP must agree with that opinion and that it is appropriate to revoke the order. If a CTO is revoked, the patient reverts to detained patient status and is treated for the purposes of renewal of detention as if they had been admitted for treatment on the date of the order being revoked (see **8.46** and **8.47** below).[104]

Power to renew the authority to detain patients detained under ss 3 or 37 (s 20)

4.71   The RC must examine a patient who is detained for treatment during the last two months of the current period of detention, with a view to deciding whether the authority to detain should be renewed. If it appears to the RC that the conditions of detention under s 3 are met, he or she is under a duty to furnish a report to that effect to the managers, and the act of furnishing the report has the effect of renewing the authority to detain the patient. The conditions are:

(a)   the patient is suffering from mental disorder of a nature or degree which makes it appropriate for him to receive medical treatment in a hospital; and

(b)   it is necessary for the health or safety of the patient or for the protection of other persons that he should receive such treatment *and* that it cannot be provided unless he continues to be detained; and

(c)   appropriate medical treatment is available for him.[105]

---

[104]   MHA 1983, s 17G.
[105]   MHA 1983, s 20(4), as inserted by MHA 2007, s 4(4) and Sch 1, para 4.

Before furnishing a report renewing the authority to detain, the RC is required to consult one or more other persons who have been professionally concerned with the patient's medical treatment), and to secure the written agreement of another person who belongs to a different profession from the responsible clinician that the renewal conditions set out in subsection are satisfied.[106]

4.72 The Joint Committee on Human Rights took the view that the requirement in *Winterwerp v Netherlands*[107] of objective medical evidence of a true mental disorder, coupled with the ruling in *Varbanov v Bulgaria*[108] indicated that the opinion justifying renewal of detention should come from a medically qualified expert who has recognised skills in psychiatric diagnosis and treatment. The Government took the view that the term 'medical expertise' in *Winterwerp* was:

> 'used in the wider sense and the court was not seeking to lay down which sort of qualifications available in a national system would be acceptable and which would not.'

In light of the need to modernise the workforce, the Government's view is that *Winterwerp* must be broadly interpreted and that what is required is a person who is able to make a decision as to whether or not the person in question is of unsound mind.

4.73 The competencies for a person to become an AC include the ability to identify the presence and severity of mental disorder. The Government has contended that such a person will have the objective medical expertise required by Art 5. It is open to argument whether the Strasbourg Court would support the Government's contention that it is for national authorities to decide which professionals possess the required expertise to perform functions under the Act. The Government argues that this comes within the 'margin of appreciation' allowed to national authorities to have when applying the ECHR. The JCHR countered that:

> 'Despite the Government's belief that the precise qualifications for providing medical expertise are a matter for the Member States, there are equally grounds for considering that the requirement of medical expertise has a minimum content in European law.'

That minimum content was suggested to be a medical qualification or a chartered clinical psychologist.[109] Although the Government initially reserved its right not to comply with Council of Europe Recommendation (2004)10 on the protection of the human rights and dignity of persons with mental

---

[106]   MHA 1983, s 20(5), (5A); MHA 2007 s 9(4).
[107]   (1979) 2 EHRR 387, ECtHR.
[108]   [2000] ECHR 31365/96, [2000] MHLR 263, ECtHR.
[109]   House of Lords, House of Commons Joint Committee on Human Rights *Legislative Scrutiny: Seventh Progress Report: Fifteenth Report of Session 2006–2007* (HL Paper 555, HC Paper 112), paras 1.7–1.14.

disorder, Art 20(4) of that recommendation represents a consensus as to the importance of medical expertise from a doctor when it states that:

> 'Involuntary placement, involuntary treatment, or their extension should only take place on the basis of examination by *a doctor having the requisite competence and experience.*'

Power to renew a community treatment order (s 20A)

4.74 Within the last two months of a community treatment order the RC must:

(a) examine the patient; and

(b) consult 'one or more other persons who have been professionally concerned with the patient's medical treatment'; and

(c) if there is a written statement from an AMHP agreeing that the conditions for making a CTO are met, and it is appropriate to do so, submit to the hospital managers a report renewing the CTO.

Furnishing the report has the effect of renewing the CTO for six months if it is the first renewal, and for 12 months in the case of the second or subsequent renewals.[110]

Power to discharge a patient from detention, guardianship or a community treatment order (s 23)

4.75 The RC has the power under s 23(2) to discharge a patient from detention, guardianship or SCT by order in writing. This does not apply to patients who are subject to restrictions on discharge under Part III of the Act. Before the decision is taken to discharge, the RC is responsible for ensuring, in consultation with the other professionals concerned, that the patient's needs for health and social care are fully assessed and the care plan addresses them. The RC is also responsible for ensuring that a proper assessment is made of risks to the patient or other people and that plans, services and support are available to manage those risks. In the case of offender patients, the circumstances of any victim and their families must be taken into account. Consideration should be given to the after care needs of the patient under s 117 and whether a patient being discharged from detention meets the criteria for guardianship or a CTO.

4.76 In *R (C)* v *Mental Health Review Tribunal and South West Region* Scott Baker J held that the RC has a continuing duty to consider whether the admission criteria remain satisfied.[111] The Department of Health Code of

---

[110] MHA 1983, s 20A, as inserted by MHA 2007, s 34(3).
[111] [2000] MHLR 220, at para 20.

Practice on the Mental Health Act 1983 further emphasises that RCs must keep under review the appropriateness of exercising the discharge power:[112]

> 'Because responsible clinicians have the power to discharge patients, they must keep under review the appropriateness of using that power. If, at any time, responsible clinicians conclude that the criteria which would justify renewing a patient's detention or extending the patient's SCT (as the case may be) are not met, they should exercise their power of discharge. They should not wait until the patient's detention or SCT is due to expire.'

4.77 In *Winterwerp v Netherlands* the Court held that the validity of continued confinement depends on the continued existence of mental disorder of a nature or degree warranting compulsion. It is part of the RC's role to keep this under review. The English and the Welsh regulations require that a RC's order for discharge must, as soon as practicable after it is made, be sent to the hospital managers (if the patient is detained), to the responsible hospital if the patient was subject to a CTO, or to the LSSA if the patient was subject to guardianship.[113] In *R (Wirral Health Authority and Wirral Borough Council)* v *Dr Finnegan and DE Scott* Baker J observed that:[114]

> 'There are no statutory criteria governing the exercise of this power. Its exercise is wholly within the [RC's] discretion subject ... to the usual restrictions of lawfulness and so forth ... If ... exercised for reasons based on error of law it is subject to challenge by judicial review.'

Power to prevent discharge by the nearest relative by issuing a 'barring certificate' to the managers of the hospital (s 25)

4.78 Where the nearest relative wishes to discharge a detained patient, 72 hours notice must be given.[115] The RC may then, within that period, forward to the managers a 'barring certificate', if he or she considers that the patient if discharged, would be likely to act in a manner dangerous to self or others.

Duty to report to the Ministry of Justice on the condition of offender patients subject to restrictions

4.79 The RC is required by s 41(6) to examine, at intervals not exceeding one year (or more frequently if required by the Minister of Justice), any patient in his or her care who is subject to a restriction order. A report must then be furnished to the Minister of Justice on the patient's condition. A similar obligation exists under s 49(3) with patients who have been transferred from prison subject to restriction directions.

---

[112] Department of Health *Code of Practice: Mental Health Act 1983* (2008), para 29.16, para 22.10(a).

[113] Mental Health (Hospital, Guardianship and Treatment) (England) Regulations 2008, SI 2008/1184, r 18; Mental Health (Hospital, Guardianship, Community Treatment and Consent to Treatment) (Wales) Regulations 2008, SI 2008/2439 (W 212), r 7.

[114] [2001] EWHC (Admin) 312, [2001] MHLR 66, para [68].

[115] MHA 1983, s 23.

Powers and duties under Parts IV and IVA with relation to the administration of medical treatment

4.80 For the purposes of Part IV, the RC means the AC 'with overall responsibility for the case of the patient in question'.[116] Section 12 of the MHA 2007 amends Part IV so that powers and duties previously limited to doctors may now be exercised by either the RC or an AC. For example, s 63 now provides that a patient's consent is not required for treatment for mental disorder which is not covered by the second opinion procedures in ss 57, 58 and 58A, provided 'it is given by or under the direction of the approved clinician in charge of the treatment'. Thus for the purposes of Part IV the RC with overall responsibility for the patients case will not be the AC in charge of treatment if that RC does not have prescribing rights The AC in charge of treatment is responsible for signing a certificate that the patient is capable and is consenting to medicines or ECT for mental disorders, for authorising emergency treatment of detained and community patients, for assessing capacity and authorising treatment of adult and child community patients who lack capacity to consent, and for deciding that treatment of detained or recalled community patients ought not to be discontinued, pending a second opinion, because it is necessary to prevent serious suffering on the patient's part.[117]

4.81 The Explanatory Notes clarify the reason for the frequent use in Parts IV and IVA of the phrase 'approved clinician in charge of treatment' rather than 'responsible clinician':[118]

> 'In the majority of cases the AC in charge of the treatment will be the patient's RC, but where, for example, the RC is not qualified to make decisions about a particular treatment (e g medication if the RC is not a doctor or a nurse prescriber) then another appropriately qualified professional will be in charge of that treatment, with the RC continuing to retain overall responsibility for the patient's case.'

Parts IV and IVA are discussed in detail in chapter 10.

CONCLUSION

4.82 The MHA 2007 introduces significant changes to the roles of mental health staff responsible for implementing compulsory powers under the MHA 1983, widening the range of occupational groups who are eligible to implement compulsory powers. Chapter 5 examines the role of the nearest relative ('NR'), the Independent Mental Health Advocate ('IMHA') and the hospital managers.

---

[116] MHA 1983, s 64(1).
[117] MHA 1983, ss 58(3)(a), 58A(3)(c), 62(1), 64G, 64D, 64F, 62(2) and 62A(5) respectively.
[118] *Explanatory Notes*, para 57.

Chapter 5

RELATIVES, INDEPENDENT MENTAL HEALTH ADVOCATES, AND HOSPITAL MANAGERS

INTRODUCTION

5.1 This chapter deals with the role of Nearest Relatives ('NRs'), Independent Mental Health Advocates ('IMHAs'), and Hospital Managers. All three perform key functions in safeguarding the rights of patients. The 2007 Act introduced key changes in relation to NRs, and new entitlements to the services of an Independent Mental Health Advocate ('IMHA'). This chapter also explains the role of the 'hospital managers' in relation to detained and community patients.

The Nearest Relative

5.2 The nearest relative of a patient exercises important functions in relation to compulsory powers under Part II (see **5.6** below). The nearest relative for the purposes of the MHA 1983 is defined in s 26, which is amended to give the legal standing of nearest relative to a civil partners as well as spouses. This provision is already in force. In order to comply with the ruling of the European Court of Human Rights in *JT v United Kingdom*,[1] the MHA 2007 also introduces a new power for the patient to apply to the county court to displace the nearest relative on the grounds that the person is unsuitable to act in that capacity.

Independent Mental Health Advocates

5.3 New ss 130A–130D place a duty upon the Secretary of State (in Wales on the Welsh Assembly) to provide advocacy services for all detained patients (except those held under ss 4, 5, 135 or 136), guardianship patients and patients subject to community treatment orders.. Advocacy must include help in obtaining information about and understanding the provisions of the Act which subject the patient to compulsion, any conditions or restrictions, what medical treatment is being given or is proposed and why, as well as the requirements of the Act which apply in relation to that treatment; advocacy must also include help in obtaining information about and understanding any

---

[1]   (2000) 30 EHRR CD 77, [2000] 1 FLR 909.

rights which may be exercised by or in relation to him, and help by way of representation or otherwise in exercising those rights.

5.4 Section 130D places a duty upon hospital managers and, in certain cases, RCs to provide qualifying patients with information that advocacy services are available. Advocates have the right to meet patients in private, and to meet professionals. They have access to patient records only where a capable patient gives consent, or, in the case of an incapable patient, where access would not conflict with a decision of a health care attorney, a deputy, or the Court of Protection, and the person holding the records agrees that the records are relevant to the matter at issue and access is 'appropriate'.

Hospital Managers

5.5 The hospital managers are the detaining authority for patients who are not subject to restrictions.[2] Applications for admission are addressed to the hospital managers, the managers receive the report from the Responsible Clinician ('RC') which renews detention, the managers have the power to direct discharge, and the managers have duties to give information to patients about their rights under the Act. The main changes introduced by the MHA 2007 in relation to managers are:

(a) the introduction of a duty on hospital managers to ensure that an age appropriate environment is provided to patients who are under 18;

(b) changes in the provisions requiring the managers to refer a patient's case to a Mental Health Tribunal; and

(c) introduction of a provision enabling foundation trusts to delegate their discharge power to a subcommittee in the same way as is already the case with other NHS bodies.

THE NEAREST RELATIVE ('NR')

5.6 The MHA 2007 has introduced changes in relation to the 'nearest relative' ('NR') who has the power to apply for compulsory admission, to seek discharge and challenge the patient's detention before a Mental Health Tribunal ('MHT'). The NR has various functions with relation to patients detained under Part 2 of the Act. These include the right to:

(a) apply for compulsory admission or guardianship (s 11(1));

(b) be consulted, if practicable, before any such application is made by an AMHP (s 11(3));

---

[2] MHA 1983, s 11(2), which provides that every application for admission must be addressed to the managers of the hospital to which admission is sought, and s 6(2) which says that the application is sufficient authority for the managers to detain the patient in the hospital.

(c)   object to and block an application for guardianship or admission for treatment (s 11(4));

(d)   discharge the patient from detention or guardianship (ss 23 and 25); and

(e)   apply for a Mental Health Review Tribunal hearing to determine the patient's fitness for discharge (s 66(1)(g) and (h));

(f)   information about the patient's and nearest relative's rights (s 132(4)) and to be informed if the patient is discharged from detention (s 133). These rights are not available if the patient objects.

NRs may not exercise their rights in respect of patients subject to special restrictions under Part III of the MHA 1983.

5.7   The identity of the NR is determined according to a statutory list, beginning with husband or wife, father or mother, son or daughter. The MHA 2007 has modified that list to recognise civil partners, as well as same or opposite sex couples living together as man and wife.[3] The rights of the nearest relative remain essentially unchanged by the MHA 2007. The Act does, however, introduce a new possibility for the patient to seek displacement of an unsuitable nearest relative. This is necessitated by successful challenges in the European Court of Human Rights and in the English Courts under the Human Rights Act 1998 (see **5.14**).

5.8   Section 26(1) as amended provides that 'relative' means any of the following persons:

(a)   husband, wife or civil partner;

(b)   son or daughter;

(c)   father or mother;

(d)   brother or sister;

(e)   grandparent;

(f)   grandchild;

(g)   uncle or aunt;

(h)   nephew or niece.

---

[3]   See *R (on the application of SSG) v Liverpool City Council* at http://www.dh.gov.uk/en/Policyandguidance/Healthandsocialcaretopics/Mentalhealth/DH_4077674.

5.9 The 'nearest relative' is the person who appears first on this list and, if there is more than one relative coming into the same category, the eldest is to take priority. The definition of 'husband', 'wife' or 'civil partner' includes a person with whom the patient has been living as husband or wife or civil partner for not less than six months, although such a person cannot take precedence over a legal spouse or civil partner unless there has been a separation or desertion. In *R (Robinson) v Hospital Managers of Park Royal Hospital*[4] the cohabitant partner of the patient purported to exercise the nearest relative's power to discharge him under s 23 of the MHA 1983, contending that she, and not the patient's aunt, was the nearest relative. The hospital declined to discharge on the grounds that they did not accept that the cohabitant qualified as nearest relative. Stanley Burnton J refused habeas corpus and judicial review, but said that:

> 'Although it might be difficult to identify when a period of cohabitation began, a hospital had a duty to try as it had a duty to investigate whether a six month cohabitation period had altered the identity of the nearest relative. Whether or not a period apart would bring a cohabitation to an end would depend on the nature and duration of the relationship when the interruption took place.'

5.10 Any person who has resided with the patient for five years or more or is caring for the patient is counted as a relative.[5] A non-relative who is caring for the patient is treated as a relative by virtue of s 26(4). Where a relative is caring for a patient they will take precedence over any other relative, even a spouse. In *Re D (Mental Patient: Habeas Corpus)*[6] the Court of Appeal held that the words 'caring for' have their ordinary meaning, and that although services need not have been provided over a long period, they must be more than minimal and must have a quality of continuity.

5.11 The nearest relative of a child who is in care is determined in accordance with s 27 whereby the nearest relative will be the local authority unless the patient is married in which case it will be the spouse. If the child is subject to guardianship under s 5 of the Children Act 1989, s 28 of the MHA 1983 applies, the nearest relative will be the guardian, and no spouse can take precedence. If a child is a ward of court an application for compulsory admission requires the leave of the court, as does any application by the nearest relative to the MHT. If the patient is ordinarily resident in the UK and the person who would be the nearest relative is ordinarily resident abroad, that person is ineligible to be nearest relative by virtue of s 26(5)(a). This exclusion does not apply in a case where the patient him or herself is ordinarily resident abroad.

5.12 Section 132(4) of the Act requires the managers of any hospital or mental nursing home where a patient is detained to take 'such steps as are

---

4   Unreported, November 26, 2007 Stanley Burnton J; see L Davidson, Nearest relative Consultation and the Avoidant Approved Mental Health Professional [2009] JMHL 70–80.
5   MHA 1983, s 26, as amended by MHA 2007, s 26.
6   [2000] 2 FLR 848, CA.

practicable' to inform the relative of the patient's rights under the Act, and of his or her powers and duties under the Act. This duty applies unless the patient has requested that the relative not be informed of the fact that the admission has taken place. If the patient lacks capacity to request that the information should not be copied to the nearest relative, the information should be provided, unless either the patient has, whilst capable, refused to allow the information to be imparted, or if to do so would be likely to harm the patient.[7]

5.13 In certain circumstances a nearest relative may authorise another person to perform the functions of nearest relative under the Act. The nearest relative must give written notice of such authorisation to the person authorised and to the hospital managers or, in the case of a patient under guardianship, to the local social services authority and the guardian. The authority may be revoked at any time.[8]

Displacing the Nearest Relative

5.14 The nearest relative has a right under Art 8 of the European Convention on Human Rights to respect for their family life with the patient and vice versa. But the patient also has the right to respect for privacy under Art 8. In *JT v United Kingdom*[9] the applicant complained that her nearest relative according to the statutory formula was her mother, who was living with a man who JT alleged had abused her in the past. Each time JT applied for discharge from detention to a MHRT, the tribunal rules required that her mother, as nearest relative, be informed. JT objected to her mother being given information about her life. The European Commission on Human Rights held that the absence in the MHA 1983 of any possibility for a patient to apply to the County Court to change her nearest relative was an interference with her right to respect for her private life under Art 8(1) of the European Convention and could not be justified under Art 8(2). A friendly settlement was reached whereby the UK Government undertook to:

(a) enable a patient to apply to the court to replace his nearest relative where there were reasonable grounds to object to a particular individual acting in that capacity; and

(b) prevent certain persons from acting as the nearest relative of the patient.

---

[7] See *R (E) v Bristol City Council* [2005] EWHC 74 (Admin), [2005] MHLR 83 where it was held for the purposes of s 11(4) that it would not be 'reasonably practicable' to consult the nearest relative if it would cause harm to the patient and therefore breach his or her rights under Art 8 of the European Convention on Human Rights.

[8] Mental Health (Hospital, Guardianship and Consent to Treatment) Regulations 2008, SI 2008/1184, reg 24 which allows the NR to grant or revoke in writing, authority to exercise the functions of the NR.

[9] (2000) 30 EHRR CD 77.

Subsequently, the English High Court in *R (on the application of M) v Secretary of State for Health*[10] granted a declaration of incompatibility under the Human Rights Act 1998 that the absence of a right for a patient to seek displacement of a nearest relative was incompatible with Art 8.

5.15 Section 29 of the 1983 Act empowers a county court to make an order directing that the functions of nearest relative be exercised by another person or by the local social services authority. Section 23 of the MHA 2007 amends s 29 and introduces the possibility for the patient him or herself to seek displacement of an unsuitable nearest relative. An application for such an order may be made by the patient, any relative of the patient, any other person with whom the patient is residing (or was last residing before admitted to hospital), or by an AMHP. A relative or person residing with the patient may apply for the functions of nearest relative to be conferred on him or her personally or on any other willing person whom the court considers suitable. If the applicant is an AMHP, the effect of a successful application will be that the local social services authority will be appointed as acting nearest relative. An application may be made on any of the following grounds in s 29(3):

(a) that the patient has no nearest relative within the meaning of the Act, or that it is not reasonably practicable to ascertain whether he or she has such a relative, or who that relative is;

(b) that the nearest relative is incapable of acting as such by reason of mental disorder or other illness;

(c) that the nearest relative of the patient unreasonably objects to the making of an application for admission for treatment or guardianship;

(d) that the nearest relative has exercised, without due regard to the welfare of the patient or the interests of the public, his or her power to discharge the patient from hospital or guardianship, or is likely to do so.

5.16 The MHA 2007 has introduced an additional ground in new s 29(3)(e) 'that the nearest relative is otherwise unsuitable to act'. The patient may apply for displacement on any of the above grounds. Section 29 of the MHA 1983 now provides that where the person nominated by the applicant is, in the court's opinion, not 'suitable' or there is no nomination, the court can appoint any other person it thinks is 'suitable'.

5.17 The MHA 2007 introduced into s 30 of the MHA 1983 a new right for the patient or (with prior leave of the court) the displaced NR to apply to discharge or vary an order appointing an acting NR. Currently, court appointments of acting NRs are only for a limited period. In future, the court may make an appointment for an indefinite period.

---

10   [2003] EWHC 1094 (Admin).

5.18   Section 25 of the MHA 2007 has amended s 66 of the MHA 1983 and limits applications to the Mental Health Tribunal (MHT) from displaced NRs. Such an application may be made only by a NR displaced on grounds of unreasonable objection to admission or exercising the power of discharge without due regard to the welfare of the patient or the protection of the public. A person displaced as the NR because he or she is too ill to act, or unsuitable to act, will not have the right to apply to the MHT.

THE INDEPENDENT MENTAL HEALTH ADVOCATE

5.19   Section 30 of the MHA 2007 introduced new ss 130A–130D into the MHA 1983. Section 130A(1) places a duty on the Secretary of State and the Welsh Ministers to make such arrangements as they consider reasonable to enable independent mental health advocates ('IMHAs') to be available to help 'qualifying patients'. Section 130A(4) requires that:

> 'the appropriate national authority shall have regard to the principle that any help available to a patient should, so far as practicable, be provided by a person who is independent of any person who is professionally concerned with the patient's medical treatment.'

The detail of qualifications to be an IMHA and the conditions of approval are provided in regulations made under s 130A(2).

5.20   The Mental Health Act 1983 (Independent Mental Health Advocacy) Regulations 2008 provide that no-one may be appointed to act as an IMHA unless they are of integrity and good character, have appropriate experience or training or an appropriate combination of experience and training, and are able to act independently of both professionals and any person who has requested them to visit and interview the patient. The person must undergo a criminal record check. Regard must be had to whether the person has an appropriate advocacy qualification although the absence of such a qualification does not preclude appointment.[11] The Codes of Practice for England and Wales also contain individual chapters on the role of the IMHA.[12]

Duties

5.21   The help to be provided by IMHAs is listed in s 130B(1) and (2). It is to include help in obtaining information about and understanding:

(a)   the provisions of the Act under which he is subject to compulsion;

---

[11]   Mental Health (Independent Mental Health Advocates) (Wales) Regulations 2008, SI 2008/2437 (W 210); the Mental Health Act 1983 (Independent Mental Health Advocates) (England) Regulations 2008, 2008/3166.

[12]   Department of Health *Code of Practice: Mental Health Act 1983* (2008), Chapter 20 http://www.doh.gov.uk; Welsh Assembly Government, Mental Health Act 1983 Code of Practice for Wales (2008), Chapter 25 http://www.wales.nhs.uk.

(b)   any conditions or restrictions to which he is subject by virtue of this Act;

(c)   what (if any) medical treatment is given to him or is proposed or discussed in his case;

(d)   why it is given, proposed or discussed;

(e)   the authority under which it is, or would be, given;

(f)   the requirements of this Act which apply, or would apply, in connection with the giving of the treatment to him;

(g)   help in obtaining information about and understanding any rights which may be exercised under this Act by or in relation to him.

Finally, help is to be made available (by way of representation or otherwise) in exercising those rights. The Department of Health *Reference Guide to the Mental Health Act 1983* states that:[13]

> 'The help which independent mental health advocacy services must provide also includes helping patients to exercise their rights, which can include representing them and speaking on their behalf. But independent mental health advocacy services are not designed to take the place of advice from, or representation by, qualified legal professionals.'

5.22   Richard Jones argues that '[T]here is nothing to stop IMHAs from accompanying patients to tribunals and hospital managers hearings and speaking on their behalf'. In relation to Mental Health Tribunals, there is no express provision in the 1983 Act or the Code which entitles IMHAs to attend tribunal hearings. However, if the patient wishes to be accompanied by an IMHA, and indicates this to the tribunal, it is difficult to see how refusal on the part of the tribunal could be squared with the overriding objective in the English and the Welsh Tribunal Rules which requires the hearing to be conducted '(c) ensuring, so far as practicable, that the parties [in this case the patient] are able to participate fully in the proceedings.'[14]

5.23   The Department of Health Code of Practice states that the role of the IMHA 'also includes helping patients to exercise their rights, which can include representing them and speaking on their behalf.'[15] If an IMHA is representing a patient difficulties may arise in relation to applications for non disclosure of documents which may only be disclosed to the patient's representative on condition that the representative undertakes not to disclose it to the patient, which the IMHA may feel conflicts with the IMHA role. If so it would be

---

[13]   Department of Health *Reference Guide to the Mental Health Act 1983* TSO 2008, para 34.11.
[14]   Tribunal Procedure (First-tier Tribunal) (Health, Education and Social Care Chamber) Rules 2008, SI 2008/2699, r 2; the Mental Health Review Tribunal for Wales Rules 2008, SI 2008/2705 (L 17), r 1.
[15]   Department of Health *Code of Practice: Mental Health Act 1983* (2008), para 20.

preferable for the patient to have a legal representative as well as an IMHA. The IMHAs may also have an important role in helping to clarify points arising in evidence and helping to reformulate questions so that the patient can understand them. If the patient has both an IMHA and a legal representative, and it will be important for the legal representative and the IMHA together to clarify their respective roles, and if there is any point in the hearing where they wish to confer, they should ask to be allowed to withdraw from the hearing room to do so.

5.24 For the purpose of providing help to a patient in accordance with the arrangements, an IMHA is under a duty to comply with any reasonable request from the person appearing to be the NR, the RC, or an AMHP. The patient remains entitled to decline help under the arrangements.[16]

Powers

5.25 The powers of IMHAS are listed in s 130B(3). For the purposes of providing help, an IMHA may:

'(a)   visit and interview the patient in private;
(b)   visit and interview any person who is professionally concerned with his medical treatment;
(c)   require the production of and inspect any records relating to his detention or treatment in any hospital or registered establishment or to any after-care services provided for him under section 117 above;
(d)   require the production of and inspect any records of, or held by, a local social services authority which relate to the patient.'

5.26 The IMHA is not entitled to require production of records unless either:[17]

'(a)   in a case where the patient has capacity or is competent to consent, he does consent; or
(b)   in any other case, the production or inspection would not conflict with a decision made by a donee or deputy or the Court of Protection, and the person holding the records, having regard to such matters as may be prescribed in regulations under section 130A above, considers that—
      (i)   the records may be relevant to the help to be provided by the advocate; and
      (ii)   the production or inspection is appropriate.'

The Codes of Practice give guidance on IMHAs' access to patients' records.[18] The Welsh code is much less detailed. In April 2009 the English Code was supplemented by Supplementary Guidance on Access to Patient Records under

---

16   MHA 1983, s 130B(5) and (6).
17   MHA 1983, s 130B(4).
18   Department of Health *Code of Practice: Mental Health Act 1983* (2008), paras 20.25–20.33 http://www.doh.gov.uk; Welsh Assembly Government, Mental Health Act 1983 Code of Practice for Wales (2008) paras 25.31–25.34 http://www.wales.nhs.uk.

s 130B of the Mental Health Act 1983, which states that record holders may
not withhold information from IMHAs simply because it would not be
disclosed to the patient under the Data Protection Act, either on grounds that it
is provided by or relates to a third party, or that its disclosure would be likely to
cause serious harm to the patient or to someone else. The Guidance does
acknowledge that there may be exceptional circumstances where third party
information should not be disclosed. Information holders should tell IMHAs if
information they are disclosing would not have been disclosed to the patient.
Generally, where the information is of a confidential nature, IMHAs should
not disclose information about third parties without their consent, although
there might be exceptional circumstances. Finally, IMHAs must not pass on
information which would not have been passed on to the patient because of a
risk of serious harm to the patient or to others.[19]

Qualifying patients

5.27 Qualifying patients are defined in s 130C(2) and (3): They include
patients who are:

(a)   liable to be detained under the MHA 1983 (otherwise than under ss 4,
       5(2), (5)(4), 135 or 136);

(b)   subject to guardianship under this Act; or

(c)   community patients.

A patient is also a qualifying patient according to s 130C(3) if:

> '(a)   not being a qualifying patient falling within subsection (2) above, he
>   discusses with a registered medical practitioner or approved clinician the
>   possibility of being given a form of treatment to which section 57 above
>   applies; or
> (b)   not having attained the age of 18 years and not being a qualifying patient
>   falling within subsection (2) above, he discusses with a registered medical
>   practitioner or approved clinician the possibility of being given a form of
>   treatment to which section 58A above applies.'

This basically means that the duty to provide an IMHA applies to informal
adult patients who discuss the possibility of neurosurgery for mental disorder
or the surgical implantation of hormones to reduce male sex drive, and it also
applies to informal child ptients under 18 who discuss having ECT.
Section 130C(4) provides that where such a patient is informed that the
treatment concerned is proposed in his case, he remains a qualifying patient
falling within that subsection until either:

(a)   the proposal is withdrawn; or

---

[19]   Department of Health Supplementary Guidance on Access to Patient Records under s 130B of
        the Mental Health Act 1983 issued in April 2009, p 4.

(b)   the treatment is completed or discontinued.

Duty to provide information about IMHAs

5.28   A 'responsible person', defined in s 130D(2), has a duty under s 130D(1) to take such steps as are practicable to ensure that:

(a)   the patient understands that help is available to him from an IMHA; and

(b)   how he can obtain that help.

5.29   Where the patient is detained the 'responsible person' means the hospital managers, and the information is to be given as soon as practicable after the patient becomes liable to be detained. If the patient is a community patient the managers of the responsible hospital are the responsible person, and the information is to be given as soon as practicable after the patient becomes a community patient. Where the patient is a conditionally discharged restricted patient, the responsible person is the RC and the information is to be given as soon as practicable after the conditional discharge. If the patient is subject to guardianship, the responsible person is the LSSA and the information is to be given as soon as practicable after the patient becomes subject to guardianship. In any case, where the patient is a qualifying patient because of treatment proposed to be given, the responsible person is the registered medical practitioner or approved clinician with whom the patient first discusses the possibility of being given the treatment concerned.

5.30   Section 134 of the Act is amended by s 30(3) of the MHA 2007 to ensure that hospital managers cannot withhold correspondence between patients and their IMHAs.

HOSPITAL MANAGERS

5.31   The hospital managers are the detaining authority in law.[20] The Department of Health Code describes their general role as follows:[21]

> 'It is the hospital managers who have the authority to detain patients under the Act. They have the primary responsibility for seeing that the requirements of the Act are followed. In particular, they must ensure that patients are detained only as the Act allows, that their treatment and care accord fully with its provisions, and that they are fully informed of, and are supported in exercising, their statutory rights.'

5.32   Section 145 defines the hospital managers. As the Department of Health Code explains:[22]

---

[20]   MHA 1983, ss 6(2) and 40(1).
[21]   Department of Health *Code of Practice: Mental Health Act 1983* (2008), para 30.3.
[22]   Ibid, para 30.2.

'In England, NHS hospitals are managed by NHS trusts, NHS foundation trusts and primary care trusts (PCTs). For these hospitals, the trusts themselves are defined as the hospital managers for the purposes of the Act. In an independent hospital, the person or persons in whose name the hospital is registered [under the Health and Social Care Act 2008] are the hospital managers.'

If a hospital in Wales is vested in a Local Health Board, the managers are the members of that Board. If an independent hospital is in Wales the managers are the persons registered under the Care Standards Act 2000 The three high security special hospitals in England are owned by the Secretary of State and managers' functions are exercised on behalf of the Secretary of State by the Special Health Authorities set up to manage those hospitals.

5.33 If an establishment is registered in England under the Health and Social Care Act 2008, or in Wales under Part 2 of the Care Standards Act 2000 as an independent hospital in which treatment or nursing (or both) are provided for persons liable to be detained under the MHA 1983, the managers are the person or persons registered in respect of the establishment.[23]

5.34 For community patients the managers are those of the responsible hospital where the patient was detained immediately before becoming subject to the CTO, or to which responsibility for the patient has subsequently been assigned.

5.35 Most of the hospital managers' responsibilities may be delegated to officers of the body Trust or Hospital Authority but the power to discharge patients may only be delegated in accordance with s 23. The Department of Health Code states that:[24]

'Hospital managers (meaning the organisation, or individual, in charge of the hospital) may arrange for their functions to be carried out, day to day, by particular people on their behalf. In some cases, regulations say they must do so.

The arrangements for who is authorised to take which decisions should be set out in a scheme of delegation. If the hospital managers are an organisation, that scheme of delegation should be approved by a resolution of the body itself. Unless the Act or the regulations say otherwise, organisations may delegate their functions under the Act to any one and in any way which their constitution or (in the case of NHS bodies) NHS legislation allows them to delegate their other functions.'

The power to discharge may only be delegated in accordance with s 23 of the 1983 Act.

5.36 Section 23 of the 1983 Act gives managers the power to discharge patients from detention. This power can be delegated by NHS Trusts to three or more people who are either non-executive directors of the trust or members

---

[23] MHA 1983, ss 34 and 145.
[24] Department of Health *Code of Practice: Mental Health Act 1983* (2008), paras 30.8–30.9.

of a committee or subcommittee of the trust. The subcommittee may include outside people, but may not include employees of the trust. The Department of Health Code emphasises that:[25]

> 'Hospital Managers retain responsibility for the performance of all delegated duties and must ensure that those acting on their behalf are competent to undertake them.'

5.37 The Department of Health Code points out that NHS bodies which have contracted with independent hospitals to treat NHS patients as in-patients or to act as responsible hospitals for them as community patients retain the power to discharge those patients. 'This is in addition to the power of the managers of the independent hospitals themselves. The NHS body concerned is the one which has contracted with the independent hospital in respect of the patient.'[26]

5.38 The Code goes on to say that:[27]

> 'As a general rule, NHS bodies are entitled to expect that the managers' panel arrangements in independent hospitals will be sufficient. They do not need to arrange a panel hearing of their own simply because they are requested to do so. But they (or a panel on their behalf) must consider whether there are any special circumstances which would make it unfair to a patient for them not to hold a hearing. As a result, NHS bodies contracting with independent hospitals should take steps to satisfy themselves that the independent hospital's own arrangements for taking discharge decisions are adequate to protect the rights of NHS patients.'

The managers of independent hospitals and NHS bodies are advised, where possible, to co-operate over exercising their respective functions in relation to the discharge of NHS patients detained in independent hospitals, but are reminded that they must all take their own decisions, not defer to those of another body.

Duties in relation to the receipt of admission documents

5.39 Applications for compulsory admission are addressed to the managers of the receiving hospital. As the detaining authority, it is the Hospital Managers' duty to ensure that the grounds for admitting the patient are valid and that all relevant admission documents are in order. Chapter 13 of the Department of Health Code of Practice deals with the receipt and scrutiny of documents authorising detention, guardianship or Supervised Community Treatment ('SCT'). The Hospital Managers are responsible for detained patients and patients on SCT. Social Services Authorities are responsible for patients under guardianship. Each should monitor the receipt and scrutiny of documents on a regular basis. The Code of Practice distinguishes between receiving the documents and scrutinising them:[28]

---

[25]   Ibid, para 30.10.
[26]   Ibid, para 31.45.
[27]   Ibid, para 31.47.
[28]   Ibid, para 13.6.

'For these purposes, receipt involves physically receiving documents and checking that they appear to amount to an application that has been duly made (since that is sufficient to give the managers the power to detain the patient). Scrutiny involves more detailed checking for omissions, errors and other defects and, where permitted, taking action to have the documents rectified after they have already been acted on.'

5.40 The managers must therefore delegate the authority to receive the statutory documents to a limited number of officers who may include staff on the wards. Paragraphs 13.7–13.10 provide as follows:[29]

'Hospital managers should formally delegate their duties to receive and scrutinise admission documents to a limited number of officers, who may include clinical staff on wards. Someone with the authority to receive admission documents should be available at all times at which patients may be admitted to the hospital. A manager of appropriate seniority should take overall responsibility on behalf of the hospital managers for the proper receipt and scrutiny of documents.

Hospitals should have a checklist for the guidance of people delegated to receive documents ("receiving officers"), to help them detect those errors which fundamentally invalidate an application and which cannot be corrected at a later stage in the procedure.

When a patient is being admitted on the application of an approved mental health professional (AMHP), the receiving officer should go through the documents and check their accuracy with the AMHP.

Receiving officers should have access to a manager for advice outside office hours, especially at night.'

5.41 The above paragraphs refer to the initial checking which should take place to ensure that the application is one which 'appears to be duly made and to be founded on the necessary medical recommendations', and which therefore entitles the hospital managers to act on it under s 6(3) of the 1983 Act. Scrutiny is dealt with in paras 13.12 and 13.13 of the Department of Health Code:[30]

'Documents should be scrutinised for accuracy and completeness and to check that they do not reveal any failure to comply with the procedural requirements of the Act in respect of applications for detention. Medical recommendations should also be scrutinised by someone with appropriate clinical expertise to check that the reasons given appear sufficient to support the conclusions stated in them.

If admission documents reveal a defect which fundamentally invalidates the application and which cannot, therefore, be rectified under section 15 of the Act, the patient can no longer be detained on the basis of the application. Authority for the patient's detention can be obtained only through a new application (or, in the interim, by the use of the holding powers under section 5 if the patient has already been admitted to the hospital.)'

---

[29]   Ibid, paras 13.7–13.10.
[30]   Ibid, paras 13.12–13.13.

5.42   In *Re S-C (Mental Patient Habeas Corpus)* Neill LJ made the following observations about s 6(3) stating that:[31]

'[T]he hospital managers have a defence in civil proceedings, but s.6(3) is not intended to nor does it have the effect of preventing a court, if satisfied that the original application was not made in accordance with s.3 of the Act, from issuing a writ of habeas corpus or making some other appropriate order. The responsibility for release is that of the court.'

5.43   In *TTM* v *London Borough of Hackney*[32] the claimant had successfully obtained discharge by habeas corpus for detention under s 3 on the grounds that the AMHP's conclusion that the nearest relative was not objecting was an unreasonable one. He subsequently applied for judicial review, seeking (a) a declaration that his admission under s 3 was unlawful, (b) damages under Art 5(5) and 8, (c) leave under s 139(2) to pursue a damages claim, and (d) a declaration of incompatibility in relation to s 139(1) and s 6(3). In the judicial review the claimant sought, unsuccessfully, to establish that there had also been a breach of s 12(2) in that neither of the doctors providing recommendations had previous acquaintance with him. This argument was rejected by Collins J.

5.44   Collins J held that a declaration that the detention was unlawful from the moment Burton J reached his decision to grant habeas corpus was all the relief that the claimant could obtain. However, such a declaration was unnecessary since Burton J's decision had made that clear in any event.[33] His Lordship considered that the protection afforded by s 6(3) depended on what degree of scrutiny the hospital managers are required to carry out when presented with an application for admission, and that the hospital was protected against liability by s 6(3) since it was entitled to rely on the AMHP's assertion that the nearest relative had not objected, and because there had been no breach of s 12(2).[34] In any event the correct defendant was the LSSA which was vicariously liable for any bad faith or negligence on the part of the AMHP.[35]

5.45   As for the action for damages for breach of Art 5(5), Collins J held that the decision to detain had not been unlawful from the beginning. It was lawful until the point when Burton J had granted habeas corpus declaring it prospectively unlawful. Hence:[36]

'the detention was not unlawful in domestic law so that there was no breach of Article 5 and so no claim for compensation under Art 5(5). Thus there can be no claim under s 7 of the Human Rights Act 1998.'

---

[31]   [1996] QB 399.
[32]   [2010] EWHC 1349 (Admin).
[33]   Ibid, para [54].
[34]   Ibid, paras [7], [30] and [34].
[35]   Ibid, para [35].
[36]   Ibid, para [52].

Collins J's decision was reversed by the Court of Appeal.[37] Toulson LJ, delivered the leading judgment, holding that there could be a claim for compensation against the local social services authority because the AMHP had proceeded with the application when she ought reasonably to have concluded that the nearest relative had objected to detention for treatment, that M's rights under Art 5 had been infringed and that he was entitled to compensation.

5.46 The Court of Appeal held that the detention had been unlawful from the beginning and did not only become unlawful when Burton J had granted habeas corpus. Section 6(3) only protected the hospital managers and did not protect the LSSA. The Court of Appeal 'read down' s 139(1) by virtue of s 3 of the Human Rights Act so as to permit a claim by M for compensation from the local authority, even though there had been no negligence or bad faith. Toulson LJ concluded that Collins J had been wrong to dismiss the application for judicial review, and should have given leave under s 139, even though there had been no bad faith and it was not necessary to make a finding that the social worker had been negligent.[38]

Duties to give patients information concerning their rights under the Act and to help from advocates (ss 132, 132A and 130D)

5.47 Section 130D places a duty on the hospital managers to inform patients of their right to advocacy help from IMHAs (see **5.28** above). Under s 132 the managers have a duty to take such steps as are practicable to ensure that the patient understands under which provision of the MHA 1983 he is detained and the effects of that provision, as well as any rights to apply to a Mental Health Tribunal ('MHT'). These steps must be taken as soon as practicable after the commencement of detention. The managers must also take such steps as are practicable to ensure that the patient understands who has the power of discharge under s 23, the restrictions on the nearest relative's power of discharge under s 25, the nearest relative's right to apply to the MHT if the RC bars discharge, the effect of Part IV of the Act relating to medical treatment, the existence of the Code of Practice, his right to complain to the Care Quality Commission under s 120, and, if applicable, his rights in relation to postal packets under s 134. The duty is to give the requisite information both orally and in writing, and the DH and Welsh Assembly Government have produced 'rights leaflets'.

5.48 Section 132A requires the managers of the responsible hospital to take such steps as are practicable to ensure that a community patient understands the effect of the CTO and their right to make an application to a MHT.[39]

---

[37] *TTM v LB Hackney East London NHS Foundation Trust and the Secretary of State for Health* [2011] EWCA Civ 4.
[38] Ibid, para 66.
[39] As inserted by MHA 2007, Sch 3, para 30.

5.49   Sections 130D(5), 132(4) and 132A(3) all provide that, unless the patient otherwise requests, the managers must take such steps as are practicable to a give a copy of any written information to the person appearing to them to be the nearest relative. This must be done when the information is given to the patient or within a reasonable time thereafter, unless the patient objects. If the patient lacks capacity to object to the information being copied to the nearest relative, the information should be provided, unless either the patient has, whilst capable, refused to allow the information to be imparted, or if to do so would be likely to harm the patient.[40]

5.50   The duties under ss 130, 132 and 132A are all delegable to hospital staff, but managers should ensure that staff who carry out the explanation are adequately trained in the Act.

Duty to notify social services when patient admitted on nearest relative application

5.51   Where a patient is detained under ss 2 or 3 on the application of the nearest relative, the managers are under a duty to give notice of that fact to the social services department for the area in which the patient resided immediately prior to admission. This must be done as soon as practicable after admission. The LSSA then has a duty to direct an AMHP to visit and prepare a social circumstances report which is to be forwarded to the managers.[41]

Responsibilities in relation to Supervised Community Treatment

5.52   Where a RC is contemplating a CTO for a patient, the managers should liaise with the relevant authorities to ensure arrangements are put in place for suitable aftercare services.

5.53   The Department of Health Code places responsibility on the managers to ensure that no community patient is detained on recall for longer than 72 hours without having their community treatment order revoked. 'Arrangements should be put in place to ensure that the time of recall is recorded and the length of stay monitored.'[42] The managers also have a duty to ensure a patient is referred to the MHT as soon as is practicable (the Department of Health Code says 'without delay' if their community treatment order is revoked). If a patient's CTO is revoked and the patient is subsequently detained in a hospital other than the responsible hospital, the managers of the detaining hospital must inform the managers of the responsible hospital without delay.

---

[40]   See *R (E) v Bristol City Council* [2005] EWHC 74 (Admin) [2005] MHLR 83 where it was held for the purposes of s 11(4) that it would not be reasonably practicable to consult the nearest relative if it would cause harm to the patient and therefore breach his or her rights under Art 8 of the European Convention on Human Rights.

[41]   MHA 1983, s 14.

[42]   Ibid, para 25.71.

Complaints

5.54 All detained patients have the right to complain to the regulatory authority, the Care Quality Commission ('CQC'). Section 120(4) requires the regulatory authority to 'make arrangements for persons authorised by it to investigate any complaint as to the exercise of the powers or the discharge of the duties conferred or imposed by this Act in respect of a person who is or has been so detained or who is or has been a relevant patient.[43] By virtue of s 120(7) anyone authorised by the regulatory authority may at any reasonable time:

(a)   visit and interview in private any patient in a hospital or regulated establishment,if the authorised person is a registered medical practitioner or approved clinician, examine the patient in private there, and

(b)   require the production of and inspect any records relating to the detention or treatment of any person who is or has been detained under this Act or who is or has been a community patient or a patient subject to guardianship.

It is an offence under s 129 of the MHA 1983 to obstruct any person carrying out functions under s 120.

5.55 Staff have the responsibly of bringing the complaints procedures to the attention of all patients, both orally and in writing, and in the case of detained patients must give equivalent information about the right to complain to the CQC. If a patient is unable to formulate a complaint, he or she should be given reasonable assistance to do so by staff, including assistance in accessing advocacy. Complaint records should be kept separate from medical records.

Patients' correspondence

5.56 Section 134 of the MHA 1983 allows the Hospital Managers to withhold outgoing mail from detained patients provided the addressee has made a written request to the managers, the patient's RC or the Secretary of State. The fact that mail has been withheld must be recorded in writing and the patient must be informed. In the special hospitals managers have wider powers under s 134 to withhold an outgoing postal packet if it is likely:

(i)   to cause distress to the person to whom it is addressed or to any other person (not being a person on the staff of the hospital); or

(ii)   to cause danger to any person.

The managers of a special hospital may also withhold incoming mail if, in their opinion, it is necessary to do so in the interests of the safety of the patient or

---

[43]   MHA 1983, s 120(4).

for the protection of other persons. Managers of special hospitals should have a written policy on the use of this power. Decisions are subject to review by the CQC.

Transfers of detained and community patients

5.57 Section 19 of the MHA 1983, and the regulations made under it allow the Hospital Managers to transfer a detained patient from one hospital to another. Section 19A provides for responsibility for patients on SCT to be assigned to another hospital, in circumstances to be specified in regulations. Section 17F of the Act and the regulations made under it allow the hospital managers to transfer a patient on SCT who has been recalled to hospital from one hospital to another.[44]

5.58 Transfers are a potential interference with a patient's right of respect for family life under Art 8 of the European Convention. For that reason the Department of Health Code emphasises that they should be for valid reasons:[45]

> 'Valid reasons for transfer might be clinical – the need, for example, for the patient to be in a more suitable environment or in a specialist facility. They could also be to move the patient closer to home. In some cases, a transfer may be unavoidable, because the hospital is no longer able to offer the care that the patient needs.'

The Code underlines the importance that, wherever practicable, patients should be involved in the process leading to any decision to transfer them to another hospital, and that the reasons be explained to the patient and where appropriate, family or friends, and recorded. The Code also stresses that 'Only in exceptional circumstances should patients be transferred to another hospital without warning.'[46] For restricted patients, the Hospital Managers' power is subject to the prior agreement of the Secretary of State for Justice.

Duties regarding renewal of detention

5.59 Section 20 of the MHA 1983 provides that the authority to detain a patient under ss 3 or 37 lasts for six months beginning on the day of admission. Within the last two months of the current period of detention, the RC has the power to renew detention. This is done by furnishing a report in the prescribed form to the managers, stating that:

---

[44] The relevant regulations for England are the Mental Health (Hospital, Guardianship and Treatment) (England) Regulations 2008, SI 2008/1184, regs 7–12 and the Mental Health (Hospital, Guardianship, Community Treatment and Consent to Treatment) (Wales) Regulations 2008, SI 2008/2439 (W 212), regs 23–25.

[45] Department of Health *Code of Practice: Mental Health Act 1983* (2008) http://www.doh.gov.uk, para 30.16.

[46] Ibid, para 30.17.

(a)   the patient continues to suffer from mental disorder of a nature or degree which makes it appropriate for him to receive medical treatment in a hospital; *and*

(b)   it is necessary for the health or safety of the patient or for the protection of other persons that he should receive such treatment which cannot be provided unless he continues to be detained; *and*

(c)   appropriate medical treatment is available for him.

5.60   New s 20(5A) requires that before furnishing that report the RC must secure written agreement that the renewal conditions are satisfied from a person who has been professionally concerned with the patient's medical treatment; but who belongs to a profession other than that to which the responsible clinician belongs.[47] The act of furnishing the report has the effect of renewing the detention.[48] When they are duly furnished with the RC's report, the managers must then consider whether to exercise their power of discharge under s 23(2).

The Managers' power of discharge and Managers' Hearings (s 23)

5.61   Section 23 of the MHA 1983 gives hospital managers the power to discharge unrestricted patients from detention or from Supervised Community Treatment ('SCT').

Managers' Panels

5.62   Section 23(6) enables the board of any NHS Trust to authorise three or more people to exercise this power, provided they are neither an executive director of the board nor an employee or officer of the trust. The committee may be made up of non-executive directors of the trust and people appointed from outside the trust. Section 45 amends s 23 to allow Foundation Trusts similar powers to those enjoyed by NHS trusts, to delegate the discharge power to any three or more people 'appointed' by the trust board, provided that those persons are neither executive directors nor employees of the trust. New s 142B provides that:[49]

> 'A NHS foundation trust's constitution may not permit its functions under the 1983 Act to be delegated to executive directors or committees of directors unless that is permitted by or under the 1983 Act itself. But the Constitution may permit delegation to other people, where that is allowed by or under the 1983 Act.'

The persons registered in respect of an independent hospital retain final responsibility in relation to the managers' power of discharge. They too may

---

[47]   Inserted by the MHA 2007, s 9(4)(b).
[48]   *R v Managers of Warlingham Park Hospital, ex parte B* (1994) 22 BMLR 1, CA.
[49]   *Explanatory Notes*, para 181.

delegate their discharge function to a committee or subcommittee. The Department of Health Code says the following about the need for independence and proper training:[50]

> 'In independent hospitals, managers' panels should not include people who are on the staff of the hospital or who have a financial interest in it. In all cases, the board (or the equivalent) of the organisation concerned should ensure that the people it appoints properly understand their role and the working of the Act. It should also ensure that they receive suitable training to equip them to understand the law, work with patients and professionals, reach sound judgements and properly record their decisions. This should include training in how risk is assessed and how to comprehend a risk assessment report.'

5.63 Where a patient is liable to be detained for assessment or for treatment in an independent hospital, or is a community patient whose responsible hospital is an independent one, the Secretary of State has a power of discharge. If the patient is being cared for pursuant to a contract with a NHS body, the managers of that body have the power of discharge.[51] The Department of Health Code suggests that, where detained patients are placed in an independent hospital under a contract with a Trust, the Trust committee which is appointed to undertake Hospital Managers' functions should also monitor the way those functions are performed by the managers of the independent hospital, and both sets of managers should cooperate in exercising their respective discharge functions.[52]

5.64 Chapter 31 of the Department of Health Code of Practice provides detailed guidance on the managers' power of discharge and the managers' duty to ensure that all patients are aware that they may seek discharge by this route, and of the distinction between this and their right to a Mental Health Tribunal ('MHT') hearing.[53]

5.65 Managers may undertake a review at any time at their discretion. The managers must consider holding a review when they receive a request from a patient or when the RC issues a barring certificate opposing a nearest relative's application for the patient's discharge. They might decide that it is inappropriate to hold a review where one has been held recently and there is no evidence that the patient's condition has changed or where a MHT hearing is either due soon or has been held recently.[54] Managers have a statutory duty to decide whether to exercise their discretion to discharge from detention or a CTO when the RC submits a report renewing detention or SCT. Therefore, a review must be held on renewal, whether or not the patient objects.

---

[50] Department of Health *Code of Practice: Mental Health Act 1983* (2008), paras 31.7–31.8.

[51] MHA 1983, s 23(3) and (3A), as inserted by MHA 2007, Sch 3, paras 10(5) and 10(6).

[52] Department of Health *Code of Practice: Mental Health Act 1983* (2008), para 31.47.

[53] The equivalent chapter of the Welsh Code of Practice is Welsh Assembly Government, *Mental Health Act 1983 Code of Practice for Wales* (2008) Chapter 27 http://www.wales.nhs.uk.

[54] Department of Health *Code of Practice: Mental Health Act 1983* (2008), paras 31.11–31.13 http://www.doh.gov.uk.

5.66 The Department of Health Code distinguishes between contested renewal cases where the patient or NR are disputing the need for detention or SCT and uncontested cases where they are not. However, the Code acknowledges that:[55]

> 'It is for hospital managers to decide whether to adopt a different procedure in uncontested cases. Some hospitals, as a matter of policy, do not differentiate between contested and uncontested cases.'

With uncontested cases, where a different procedure is used the Code advises that the patient should be interviewed by a single member of the panel if the patient requests it, or if the panel think it appropriate after reading the renewal report or the other papers. Otherwise managers' panels may consider the case on the papers, but should hold a full hearing if they think there is reason to believe the patient may wish to be discharged, or if there are prima facie grounds for thinking that the decision to renew detention or SCT may not be correct. The mere fact that a patient has not voiced an objection to renewal should not be taken as evidence of agreement that it is the correct decision.[56] If the panel agrees that the patient should not be discharged the review can be concluded and the outcome recorded in the patient's records.

5.67 With contested cases the recommended procedure very much mirrors that of the MHT, with the crucial difference that the managers do not have the benefit of a medical member of the decision-making panel. For this reason managers are advised that members will not, as a rule, be qualified to form clinical assessments of their own, and where there is any divergence of view between the managers and the RC about whether the patient reaches the clinical grounds for continued detention especially in relation to risk assessment, the panel should consider an adjournment for further professional advice.[57] This is intended to encourage the the managers to exercise extreme caution before discharging against medical advice.

5.68 Written reports are to be obtained from the RC, in which an essential element will be full information about any history of violence or self-harm, a full risk assessment, the history of the patient's care and treatment, and details of the care plan. The Code recommends that the patient should receive copies of the reports unless the managers consider the information disclosed would be likely to cause serious harm to the physical or mental health of the patient or any other individual. Relatives and carers should be informed of the review and should be invited to attend and put their views to the panel in person. If the patient objects to this a suitable member of the professional care team should be asked to include the relative's or carer's views in a report to the panel. The panel should have before them a copy of the RC's renewal report supplemented

---

55   Ibid, para 31.40.
56   Ibid, para 31.41–31.42.
57   Ibid, para 31.35.

by a record of the consultation undertaken by the RC under s 20(5) and the written agreement of that other professional under s 20(5A) that the renewal criteria are met.

Principles

5.69 The Act does not define the criteria or the procedure for reviewing detention. Noting this, the Code sets three principles of fairness, reasonableness and lawfulness which must be satisfied in the conduct of managers' reviews.[58] They must adopt and apply a fair and reasonable procedure appropriate to the important issue of deprivation of liberty. They must not behave in a way which is irrational or *Wednesbury* unreasonable, meaning that they must avoid decisions which no reasonable body of Hospital Managers, properly directing themselves as to the law and on the available information, could have made.[59] Finally, they must not act unlawfully. They must interpret and apply the Mental Health Act and any other applicable legislation correctly. They must neither fail to take into account relevant evidence nor take into account material which is irrelevant. As public authorities exercising functions of a public nature, they must act compatibly with Convention rights under the Human Rights Act 1998.

5.70 In relation to continuation of detention it is important to recognise that mental health detention will be unlawful under Art 5 of the European Convention on Human Rights and the HRA 1998 without objective evidence of a true mental disorder which is of a kind or degree warranting confinement. There must also be regular review to ensure that the conditions justifying detention continue to be met.

5.71 Where a patient is subject to a CTO, Art 8 is likely to be engaged which means that interferences with the right must be in accordance with the law and necessary for one of the goals in Art 8(2), such as the patient's health, for the prevention of crime or to protect the rights and freedoms of others.

5.72 The key issue with detention or SCT is whether the statutory grounds justifying compulsion continue to be met. This entails considering, in this order, the following questions:

- is the patient still suffering from mental disorder?

- if so, is the disorder of a nature or degree which makes treatment in a hospital appropriate, or in the case of a patient on SCT, which makes treatment while liable to recall appropriate?

- is detention in hospital still necessary in the interests of the patient's health or safety, or for the protection of other people, or in the case of a

---

[58] Ibid, para 31.23.
[59] *Associated Provincial Picture Houses Ltd v Wednesbury Corpn* [1948] 1 KB 223, CA.

patient on SCT, is liability to recall still necessary in the interest of the patient's health and safety or for the protection of other people?

- in the case of a patient detained under s 3 (or its equivalent) or subject to SCT, is appropriate medical treatment available for the patient?[60]

If, on the evidence, the panel is satisfied that the answer to any of these questions is 'no', the patient should be discharged.

5.73 Where the nearest relative ('NR') has sought to discharge the patient and the RC has issued a barring certificate on grounds that the patient if discharged would be likely to act in a manner dangerous to self or to others, the NR may apply to the Mental Health Tribunal. If the patient does not apply to the MHT but there is a managers' review instead, the managers have to consider whether there is a risk that the patient would act dangerously to self or others. As the Code says, this is a 'more stringent test for continuing detention' since the focus of this question should be 'on the probability of dangerous acts, such as causing serious physical injury rather than on the patient's general need for safety and others' general need for protection.' The Code then suggests that if the managers disagree with the RC and decide the answer to this question is 'no', 'they should *usually* discharge the patient, and in all cases should ensure that a full risk assessment is carried out when considering discharge'.[61]

Hearing procedures

5.74 Various key points for the hearing procedure are covered in paras 31.24–31.34 of the Department of Health Code. They include the requirement that:

- the patient should be given a full opportunity, and any necessary help, to explain why he or she wishes to be discharged;

- the patient should be allowed to be accompanied by a friend or representative of his or her own choosing to help in putting his or her point of view to the panel;

- the RC and other professionals should be asked to give their views on: whether the patient's continued detention or continued SCT order is justified; and the factors on which those views are based;

- the patient and the other parties to the review should, if the patient wishes it, be able to hear each other's statements to the panel and to put questions to each other. However, the patient should always be offered the opportunity of speaking to the panel alone.

---

[60]   Ibid, paras 31.16–31.17.
[61]   Ibid, paras 31.19–31.22.

If the panel concludes that the patient ought to be discharged but arrangements for after-care need to be made, they may adjourn the panel, for a brief period, to enable a full CPA/care planning meeting to take place.

The decision

5.75   The managers have a common law duty to give reasons for their decision. The decision and the reasons for it should be recorded, and communicated immediately, both orally and in writing, to the patient, to the nearest relative with the patient's consent, and to the professionals concerned. At least one of the members of the panel should offer to see the patient to explain in person the reasons for the decision.[62] Copies of the papers relating to the review, and the formal record of the decision, should be placed in the patient's records.

Duties to refer cases to MHTs

5.76   Duties of managers to refer cases to MHTs arise under s 68. Under the MHA 1983 if a patient had not applied to a MHT within the six-month period immediately following admission under s 3, the managers had a duty to refer the case to a MHT. The aim was to ensure that detained patients who lack capacity should not fall below the radar of the system of review. Currently, a period of detention under s 2 does not count when calculating the six-month period. Section 37 of the MHA 2007 amends s 68, and introduces a new requirement to refer six months from 'the applicable day', which is the day on which the patient was first detained, whether that was under s 2 for assessment, s 3 for treatment, or following a transfer from guardianship.[63] The six-month period can be reduced by order made under s 68A by the Secretary of State, in relation to hospitals in England, or the Welsh Ministers, in relation to hospitals in Wales. In England the Tribunals Service Mental health has issued a standard form on which referrals can be made to the English Mental Health Tribunal, which is available on the Mental Health Tribunal website.[64]

5.77   The duty also arose under the MHA 1983 where the authority to detain was renewed and three years (or one year in the case of a child under 16) had elapsed since the patient's case was last considered by a MHT. The amended s 68 breaks the link between renewal and referral. Now there is a duty to refer if a MHT has not considered the patient's case in three years (or one year if the patient is under 18). The order making power under new s 68A can be used to reduce the three-year and one-year periods.

5.78   Patients who are absent without leave at the point at which they should be referred to the MHT must be referred on their return to hospital.[65] Section 68(7) requires the managers to refer the case of a community patient to the MHRT as soon as possible after the community treatment order is revoked.

---

[62]   Ibid, paras 31.43–31.44.
[63]   MHA 1983, s 68(5), as inserted by MHA 2007, s 37(3).
[64]   www.tribunals.gov.uk.
[65]   MHA 1983, s 21(3), as inserted by MHA 2007, s 37(2).

5.79   A managers' referral to the MHT should include a statement containing the information about the patient specified in the *Practice Direction: First-tier Tribunal: Health Education and Social Care Chamber: Mental Health Cases,*[66] or in Sch 1 to the MHRT Rules for Wales.[67] In the case of a restricted patient this information must also be sent to the Ministry of Justice.

5.80   Section 68(8), which entitles a patient to commission an independent report from a doctor in preparation for a MHT hearing, is extended to entitle an AC or a doctor to prepare such a report and for that purpose to visit and examine a detained or a community patient and to inspect records.

5.81   The hospital managers are only under a duty to refer to the MHT in specified circumstances. The Secretary of State for Health has the power under s 67 to refer the case of a Part II patient or an unrestricted Part 3 patient at any time. The Department of Health Code states that: 'Anyone may request such a referral and the Secretary of State will consider each such request on its merits'.[68] The importance of this power is underlined in *R (on the application of MH) v Secretary of State for Health*.[69] MH was severely mentally disabled by Down's Syndrome. She lacked mental capacity to consent to admission. She was admitted under s 2 for assessment when her mother became ill and she became increasingly disturbed. The plan was to assess MH's needs in hospital and then find a suitable residential placement where she could be received into guardianship under s 7 of the MHA 1983. MH's mother was her nearest relative. She objected to guardianship. Objection by a nearest relative cannot block detention under s 2, but it can veto detention under s 3 or guardianship. Steps were taken to displace MH's mother as nearest relative by application to the county court on the grounds of unreasonable objection.

5.82   By virtue of s 29(4), if such an application is made during the currency of detention under s 2, the 28-day period authorised by that section is extended until the county court deals with the case. In MH's case the effect of this was to extend her detention under s 2 from 28 days to over two years, and since she had not applied for a MHT within the first 14 days of her s 2 detention, MH had no right, herself or through a proxy, to seek review of the lawfulness of her detention as required by Art 5(4). Baroness Hale delivered the only speech for a unanimous House of Lords, holding that there was no necessary incompatibility between ss 2 and 29(4) of the MHA 1983 and Art 5(4) as long as either the county court proceedings were determined swiftly or the Secretary of State referred the case to the MHRT under s 67.

5.83   The Department of Health Code of Practice takes the consequences of the House of Lords decision in MH and advises the hospital managers 'always' to consider requesting referral by the Secretary of State where detention is

---

[66]   Available at: www.tribunals.gov.uk/Tribunals/Documents/Rules/Mentalhealthcaseshesc.pdf.
[67]   Mental Health Review Tribunal for Wales Rules 2008, SI 2008/2705 (L 17).
[68]   Department of Health *Code of Practice: Mental Health Act 1983* (2008), para 30.39.
[69]   [2005] UKHL 60.

extended pending a displacement decision and the patient is unable for any reason to make a request. The Code advises that:[70]

'Hospital managers should consider asking the Secretary of State to make a reference in respect of any patients whose rights under Article 5 of the European Convention on Human Rights might otherwise be at risk of being violated because they are unable (for whatever reason) to have their cases considered by the MHRT.'

In particular they should normally seek a reference where the patient has never had a MHT hearing or, if there was one, it was a long time ago.

5.84 The Department of Health Code recognises that the availability of community care facilities and a care plan will often be crucial in determining eligibility for discharge and advises that where a Tribunal hearing has been arranged:[71]

'Primary care trusts and LSSAs should take reasonable steps to identify appropriate after-care services for patients before their actual discharge from hospital if there is a reasonable prospect of the patient being discharged by hospital managers or the MHT. Where a tribunal hearing has been arranged for a patient who might be entitled to after-care under section 117 of the Act, the hospital managers should inform the relevant PCT and LSSA.'

Managers' duties in relation to children

5.85 Section 31 adds new s 131A to the MHA 1983. This places hospital managers under a duty to ensure that patients aged under 18 admitted to hospital for mental disorder are accommodated in an environment that is suitable for their age (subject to their needs). This provision came into force in April 2010 (for more detailed discussion see chapter 11 at **11.15** below) In determining whether the environment is suitable, the managers must consult a person whom they consider to be suitable because of their experience in child and adolescent mental health services cases.[72]

CONCLUSION

5.86 The Nearest Relative and the Hospital Managers continue to occupy a significant role under the MHA 1983 (as amended), and the new role of IMHAs is to be welcomed. The IMHA is not a public authority for the purposes of the Human Rights Act 1998. The hospital managers will clearly be a 'public authority' exercising public functions when making decisions concerning detention or community treatment. More difficult is the situation of

---

[70] Department of Health *Code of Practice: Mental Health Act 1983* (2008), para 30.40 http://www.doh.gov.uk.

[71] Ibid, paras 27.8–27.9.

[72] See C Parker *Young Minds Briefing on the Responsibilities of NHS Trust Boards under Section 131A of the Mental Health Act 1983* (2010) young minds.org.uk.

the Nearest Relative when making an application for detention. Would the NR be exercising functions of a public nature, sufficient to make them a public body and therefore bound to act in a manner consistent with convention rights. Although a NR might be held to be a public authority, the practical significance of this issue is less marked in relation to the NR than in relation to the AMHP, who has procedural obligations such as interviewing the patient in a suitable manner.

Chapter 6

POWERS OF DETENTION UNDER THE MENTAL HEALTH ACT 1983 AND THE MENTAL CAPACITY ACT 2005

OVERVIEW

6.1   Under the MHA 1983 there were two routes whereby an adult needing in-patient treatment of mental disorder could be admitted: informally under s 131; or under the powers of compulsory admission in ss 2, 3, and 4. Now there are three routes:

(a)   informal admission;

(b)   detention under ss 2, 3 or 4; or

(c)   detention under the *'Bournewood'* Deprivation of Liberty ('DoL') procedures in the Mental Capacity Act 2005, Schs 1A and A1.

This chapter outlines what is meant by informal status, and then examines each of the procedures for depriving people of their liberty, explaining the circumstances in which each is appropriate. The chapter also explains the approved clinician's, doctor's, and nurse's holding powers under s 5 to prevent informal patients from leaving hospital.

INFORMAL ADMISSION

6.2   The MHA 1983 is based on the principle that, wherever possible, patients should be admitted to hospital on an informal basis and powers of compulsion should be used as a last resort. In 2009–2010 Approximately 107,765 people were admitted as psychiatric in-patients of whom 42,479 were detained under the 1983 Act. It used to be that ninety per cent of all admissions to mental illness and learning disability hospitals and units were informal – now the figure is just over sixty per cent.[1]

6.3   Informal admission is provided for in s 131 of the MHA 1983 which states that nothing in the Act:

---

[1]   Mithran Samuel 'Sharp Rise in Number Detained under Mental Health Act, Community Care, 11 January 2011 NHS Information Centre Fourth Annual Report on NHS Adult Specialist Mental Health Services and Those Who Use Them'.

'shall be construed as preventing a patient who requires treatment for mental disorder from being admitted to any hospital or registered establishment in pursuance of arrangements made in that behalf and without any application, order or direction rendering him liable to be detained under this Act.'

Informal patients are free to leave hospital at any time (they need not seek permission from their doctor, approved clinician, or anyone else, although it is desirable to inform the hospital staff), unless it is felt necessary in the interests of their health or safety or for the protection of others to prevent them from leaving by invoking the holding power under s 5. The Department of Health Code of Practice states that:[2]

'patients should be made aware of their legal position and rights. Local policies and arrangements about movement around the hospital and its grounds must be clearly explained to the patients concerned. Failure to do so could lead to a patient mistakenly believing that they are not allowed freedom of movement, which could result in an unlawful deprivation of their liberty.'

The least restrictive alternative

6.4   The Department of Health Code of Practice states that:[3] 'Before it is decided that admission to hospital is necessary, consideration must be given to whether there are alternative means of providing the care and treatment which the patient requires.' It is a condition of detention for treatment under s 3(2)(c) that the necessary treatment cannot be provided unless the patient is detained under that section. Hence an application cannot proceed if there are safe and effective ways, other than detention under s 3, in which the necessary treatment may be provided. Those other ways might be informal admission or admission under the Deprivation of Liberty ('DoL') safeguards in the MCA 2005.

Patients who lack capacity to consent to admission

6.5   Until *HL* v *the United Kingdom*[4] informal admission was traditionally seen as being not only for patients who were capable of consenting and agreeing to admission, but also for patients who lacked capacity to consent to admission, as long as they were not resisting or protesting. Compliant incapable patients were admitted informally. Detention was reserved for cases where admission was necessary to prevent risk to self or others, and the patient, whether capable or incapable of consenting, was refusing to go into hospital, or is persistently or purposefully seeking to leave. In *HL* v *United Kingdom* the European Court held that the absence of objection on the part of the patient was not decisive in determining whether there is a deprivation of liberty, and that:[5]

---

[2]   Department of Health *Code of Practice: Mental Health Act 1983* (2008), para 2.45.
[3]   Ibid, para 4.4.
[4]   (2004) 40 EHRR 761.
[5]   (2004) 40 EHRR 761, para 90.

'The right to liberty in a democratic society is too important for a person to lose the benefit of Convention protection simply because he has given himself up to detention, especially when it is not disputed that that person is legally incapable of consenting to, or disagreeing with, the proposed action.'

In *P and Q* v *Surrey County Council* the Court of Appeal considered the relevance of objections on the part of the patient. Wilson LJ concluded that whilst 'a person's happiness, as such, I not relevant to whether she is deprived of her liberty',[6] it was relevant to whether the placement was in her best interests, and it was relevant to a factor which 'overlaps' with happiness, namely 'whether the person **objects** to the confinement which is imposed on her. The Equality and Human Rights Commission had made a written submission (but did not present oral argument) contending that the existence of objections was relevant, not just to the subjective element of deprivation of liberty (absence of consent), but also to the objective element (the existence of confinement). Wilson LJ said this:[7]

'The Commission submits ... that the existence of objections is relevant to the objective element. To that extent I agree with it. Guardedly it then proceeds to submit, however, that it "is not necessarily true" that the absence of objections is relevant to it. To that extent I disagree with it. If a person objects to the confinement, the consequence will be conflict. At the very least there will be arguments and she will suffer the stress of having her objections overruled [The] level of conflict inherent in overruled objections seems to me to be highly relevant to the objective element. Equally, however, the absence of objections generates an absence of conflict and thus a peaceful life, which seems to me to be capable of substantial relevance in the opposite direction.'

His Lordship concluded that lack of objection was a relevant factor in deciding whether there was a deprivation of liberty.[8] This view of the relevance of absence of objection is difficult to square with the statement of the European Court in *HL* v *United Kingdom* that a person should not lose the protection of Article 5 'simply because he has given himself up to detention.'

6.6 In *HL* v *United Kingdom*[9] (for full discussion of the case see **1.32–1.36** above), the European Court of Human rights held that a procedure prescribed by law must be followed where a mentally disordered person is subject to a degree of control over their residence, treatment, and movement which reaches a degree and intensity sufficient to amount to a deprivation of liberty. Section 131 did not provide a procedure prescribed by law, as required by Article 5. Also of importance in relation to deprivation of liberty is Article 14 of the European Convention on the Rights of Persons with Disabilities which provides that:

---

6   [2011] EWCA Civ 190, para 24.
7   Ibid, para 25.
8   Ibid, para 34.
9   (2004) 40 EHRR 761, ECtHR.

'1.   States Parties shall ensure that persons with disabilities, on an equal basis
       with others: (a) Enjoy the right to liberty and security of person; (b) Are not
       deprived of their liberty unlawfully or arbitrarily, and that any deprivation
       of liberty is in conformity with the law, and that the existence of a disability
       shall in no case justify a deprivation of liberty.
2.   States Parties shall ensure that if persons with disabilities are deprived of
       their liberty through any process, they are, on an equal basis with others,
       entitled to guarantees in accordance with international human rights law
       and shall be treated in compliance with the objectives and principles of the
       present Convention, including by provision of reasonable accommodation.'

Although states might argue that Art 14 was intended to prohibit only
detention which is solely based on disability, the UN High Commissioner for
Human Rights has rejected this potential interpretation stating that:[10]

[U]nlawful detention encompasses situations where the deprivation of liberty is
grounded in the combination between a mental or intellectual disability and other
elements such as dangerousness, or care and treatment. Since such measures are
partly justified by the person's disability, they are to be considered discriminatory
and in violation of the prohibition of deprivation of liberty on the grounds of
disability, and the right to liberty on an equal basis with others prescribed by
article 14.

Hence a psychiatric detention which might be lawful for the purposes of
Article 5 of the European Convention on Human Rights is quite likely to be
declared by the UN Committee for the Protection of the Rights of Persons
with Disabilities to be contrary to Art 14 the UNCPRD.

Informal admission post-*HL v United Kingdom*

6.7   Informal admission of adult patients now applies to two groups: first to
those who are capable and consenting to admission; and second, to those who

(a)   lack capacity to consent to admission or treatment; and

(b)   are not resistant to hospitalisation, and

(c)   where the level of control to be exercised over residence, movement, and
       treatment is insufficient in degree and intensity to amount to a deprivation
       of liberty.

---

[10]   *Annual Report of the United Nations High Commissioner for Human Rights and Reports of the
       Office of the High Commissioner and the Secretary-General,* Thematic Study by the Office of
       the United Nations High Commissioner for Human Rights on enhancing awareness and
       understanding of the Convention on the Rights of Persons with Disabilities.
       http://www2.ohchr.org/english/bodies/hrcouncil/docs/10session/A.HRC.10.48.pdf, para 48.

Patients with capacity who consent

6.8   The Department of Health Code says that:[11]

> 'Informal admission to hospital is usually appropriate when a patient who has the capacity to do so consents to admission. But this is not a hard and fast rule.'

Compulsory admission may be justified despite the patient's stated willingness to be admitted voluntarily, especially if detention is necessary because of the danger the patient presents to him or herself or others. The English Code states that:[12]

> 'If this is the case, compulsory admission should be considered if the 'patient's current medical state, together with reliable evidence of past experience, indicates a strong likelihood that he or she will have a change of mind about informal admission either prior to or after admission, with a resulting risk to their health or safety or to the safety of other people.'

Hence, MHA detention may be justified, even when the patient has capacity and is consenting, if <u>both</u>: (a) without detention there would be danger to self or others; <u>and</u> (b) the patient's history or current behaviour suggests that consent will be withdrawn.

Patients who lack capacity to consent to treatment or admission

6.9   Where a patient aged 16 or over lacks mental capacity to consent to admission or treatment, AMHPs and doctors will need to consider whether the patient could instead safely and effectively be treated informally under the MCA 2005. If should be noted that the deprivation of liberty safeguards under the MCA 2005 do not apply to people under 18. If admission to hospital does not involve deprivation of liberty a person lacking capacity may be admitted informally under s 131, as long as the conditions in s 5 of the Mental Capacity Act 2005 are met. These provide a defence in respect of any act done in connection with care or treatment, provided 'D' (the person doing the act):

(a)   has taken reasonable steps to assess the person's capacity;

(b)   reasonably believes that the person lacks capacity; and

(c)   reasonably believes that the action is in the person's best interests.

6.10   Section 5 of the MCA provides a defence for anyone ('D') carrying out an act of care and treatment in respect of a person ('P') if D has taken reasonable steps to assess P's capacity, if D reasonably believes that P lacks capacity, and that D reasonably believes that the act is in D's best interests. For the purposes of the MCA restraint means 'the use or threat of force to secure

---

[11]   Department of Health *Code of Practice: Mental Health Act 1983* (2008), paras 4.9–4.10.
[12]   Ibid, para 4.11.

the doing of an act which P resists, or the placing of any restriction of P's liberty of movement, whether or not P resists.' D can restrain P if the conditions in s 6 of the MCA 2005 are met. These are

(a)   that D reasonably believes that the act is necessary to prevent harm to P; and

(b)   that the act is a proportionate response both to the likelihood of P's suffering harm, and the seriousness of that harm.

6.11   Section 4A of the MCA 2005 provides as follows:

'(1)   This Act does not authorise any person ("D") to deprive any other person ("P") of his liberty.
(2)   But that is subject to –
    (a)   the following provisions of this section, and
    (b)   section 4B.
(3)   D may deprive P of his liberty if, by doing so, D is giving effect to a relevant decision of the court.
(4)   A relevant decision of the court is a decision made by an order under section 16(2)(a) in relation to a matter concerning P's personal welfare.
(5)   D may deprive P of his liberty if the deprivation is authorised by Schedule A1 (hospital and care home residents: deprivation of liberty).'

Hence s 6 cannot be used to authorise a deprivation of liberty.

6.12   Section 4B authorises a deprivation of liberty in limited circumstances. D is authorised to deprive P of his liberty while a decision as respects any relevant issue is sought from the court if:

(1)   There is a question about whether D is authorised to deprive P of his liberty under section 4A; and.

(2)   The deprivation of liberty:

    (a)   is wholly or partly for the purpose of:

        (i)   giving P life-sustaining treatment; or
        (ii)   doing any vital act; or
    (b)   consists wholly or partly of:

        (i)   giving P life-sustaining treatment; or
        (ii)   doing any vital act; and

(3)   The deprivation of liberty is necessary in order to:

    (a)   give the life-sustaining treatment; or
    (b)   do the vital act.

Section 4B (5) defines a 'vital act' as any act which the person doing it reasonably believes to be necessary to prevent a serious deterioration in P's condition.

6.13   Anyone who is to be subject to restrictions amounting to a deprivation of liberty must be subject to a procedure prescribed by law. This will either be by detention under the Mental Health Act 1983, or by Deprivation of Liberty 'DoL' authorisation under the Mental Capacity Act 2005. The answer to the question whether the patient is subject to a deprivation of liberty is the key to deciding whether a person who lacks capacity may be admitted to hospital informally or whether the Deprivation of Liberty safeguards should be used.

Deprivation of liberty

6.14   In *HL v United Kingdom* the court held that the distinction between a deprivation of liberty, which requires authorisation by a procedure prescribed by law, and a restriction of liberty, which does not, was a matter of 'degree and intensity.' The starting point must be the 'concrete situation of the individual' and a whole range of criteria must be taken into account such as the type, duration, effects and manner of implementation of the measure in question.[13]

6.15   In *HL v United Kingdom* the Court found that those having care of HL exercised complete and effective control over his assessment, care, treatment, contacts, movement and residence. He was under constant supervision and control, and was not free to leave the hospital. This amounted to a deprivation of liberty. Since the deprivation of liberty had not been carried out in accordance with a procedure prescribed by law, and HL had not been able to seek speedy review of the lawfulness of his detention, there were breaches of his Convention rights under Art 5(1)(e) and (4).

6.16   The Supplement to the Mental Capacity Act 2005 Code of Practice states that:

> 'There are many ways in which providers and commissioners of care can reduce the risk of taking steps that amount to a deprivation of liberty, by minimising the restrictions imposed and ensuring that decisions are taken with the involvement of the relevant person and their family, friends and carers.'

The Code sets out six processes for staff to follow:[14]

(a)   Make sure that all decisions are taken (and reviewed) in a structured way, and reasons for decisions recorded.

(b)   Follow established good practice for care planning.

---

[13]   *Guzzardi v Italy* (1980) 3 EHRR 333, para 92. *HL v United Kingdom*, para 89.

[14]   Mental Capacity Act 2005: Deprivation of Liberty Safeguards – Code of Practice to supplement the main Mental Capacity Act 2005 Code of Practice (2008) DoH and WAG, para 2.7.

(c) Make a proper capacity assessment in relation to the decision whether or not to accept the care or treatment proposed, following the principles in the MCA 2005.

(d) Before admitting a person to hospital or residential care in circumstances that may amount to a deprivation of liberty, consider whether the person's needs could be met in a less restrictive way. Any restrictions placed on the person while in hospital or in a care home must be kept to the minimum necessary, and should be in place for the shortest possible period.

(e) Take proper steps to help the relevant person retain contact with family, friends and carers. Where local advocacy services are available, their involvement should be encouraged to support the person and their family, friends and carers.

(f) Review the care plan at periodic intervals. The Code advises that 'It may well be helpful to include an independent element, possibly via an advocacy service, in the review.' Following the fifth principle in s 1 of the MCA 2005 (see **2.40** and **2.41** above), before an authorisation is sought for deprivation of liberty, attempts must always be made to identify ways to meet the person's needs in a less restrictive way.

6.17 However, minimising restrictions on freedom within institutions may not be enough to avoid reaching the level of control needed to deprive someone of their liberty, as is indicated by the decision in *JE v DE (by his litigation friend the Official Solicitor), Surrey County Council and EW*.[15] DE lacked mental capacity to decide where he should live, but had made it abundantly clear that he wished to leave the residential care home where he had been placed by the local authority. Munby J (as he then was) accepted that a deprivation of liberty consisted of both an *objective* element – a person's confinement in a particular restricted space for a not negligible length of time – and a *subjective* element – that the person has not validly consented to the confinement in question.[16] The third element is whether the deprivation is such as to engage the responsibility of the state. As far as the objective element is concerned, the judge held that the crucial question was not so much whether (and, if so, to what extent) DE's freedom or liberty was or is curtailed *within* the institutional setting. The fundamental issue was:[17]

> 'whether DE was deprived of his liberty to leave the homes where he was placed not in the sense of leaving for the purpose of some trip or outing approved by those managing the institution, but rather leaving in the sense of removing himself permanently in order to live where and with whom he chooses.'

Because he was not free to leave he had been deprived of his liberty. The starting point should therefore be that it is likely there will be a deprivation of

---

[15] [2006] EWHC 3459 (Fam).
[16] Ibid, at [77], following *Storck v Germany* (2005) 43 EHRR 96, at para 74.
[17] Ibid, at [115].

liberty if it is known that a person is to be prevented from leaving the place where they are being taken to reside. However, not everyone who would be prevented from leaving will necessarily be deprived of liberty. As was emphasised in both *Guzzardi* v *Italy* and *HL* v *United Kingdom*, context is all important. The starting point must be the 'concrete situation of the individual' and a whole range of criteria must be taken into account such as the type, duration, effects and manner of implementation of the measure in question, to see whether the confinement reaches the degree and intensity necessary to cross the boundary between restriction on freedom of movement and deprivation of liberty.[18]

6.18 What is meant by the type of infringement? This potentially refers to the questions of where the confinement takes place, and also by whom it is carried out. There are various 'paradigm' types of deprivation of liberty, such as arrest in the sense of removal from home or from a public place and conveyance under close confinement to another location, and detention is a prison cell or psychiatric hospital. An example of the former would be a patient being taken and conveyed to hospital under the Mental Health Act 1983. The MHA 1983 specifies specifies that any person in respect of whom an application for detention has been made may be taken and conveyed to hospital, and anyone being taken to hospital, or who is in hospital, subject to an application for compulsory admission, is deemed to be in legal custody, and may be 'retaken' by a constable or Approved Mental Health Professional if s/he escapes.[19] There can be little doubt that a person, deemed to be in legal custody, is being deprived of their liberty.

6.19 The Mental Capacity Act (MCA) 2005 and its Deprivation of Liberty safeguards do not carry a similar power to take and convey, and ss 5 and 6 of the MCA will not justify any taking and conveying which amounts to a deprivation of liberty. Richard Jones in his *Mental Capacity Act Manual* (Fourth Edition) lists three circumstances where taking an incapacitated person to a hospital or care home would constitute a deprivation of liberty. They are:[20]

(a) Force, threats or medication being used to overcome the patient's resistance to being taken to the hospital or care home. However, a deprivation of liberty will not occur if the force used constitutes restraint which is authorised by s 6 of the Act.

(b) Subterfuge being used to ensure the patient's co-operation in being taken to the hospital or care home, e.g the patient being misled into believing that he or she will return home the next day.

(c) The decision to admit the patient to the care home being opposed by carers or relatives who either live with the person or are closely involved in caring for the patient.

---

[18] *Guzzardi v Italy* (1980) 3 EHRR 333, para 92. *HL v United Kingdom*, para 89.
[19] MHA 1983 ss 6(1) and 137.
[20] Richard Jones *Mental Capacity Act Manual* (Fourth Edition) (2010), pp 251–252.

Circumstance (a) above raises a number of issues. First of all the second sentence begs the question, since section 6 cannot authorise a deprivation of liberty, so if the type duration, effects, and manner of implementation amount to a deprivation of liberty, s 6 cannot justify it. In *HL* v *United Kingdom,* it is not clear whether HL was sedated in order to overcome resistance to going to the hospital, or in order to calm his disturbed behavior. Whilst still sedated he was taken to the hospital with a nurse on either arm. He was not threatened, and it is not recorded that he offered any resistance. In his speech in the House of Lords decision in *R* v *Bournewood Community and Mental Health NHS Trust ex parte L* Lord Goff of Chievely said that:[21]

> 'There were times during the episode when it might be said that Mr. L was "detained" in the sense that, in the absence of justification, the tort of false imprisonment would have been committed. I have particularly in mind the journey by ambulance from the Day Centre to the Accident and Emergency Unit.'

His Lordship considered that this was justified by the doctrine of necessity. In *P and Q v Surrey County Council*, Wilson LJ expressed the following view about the relevance of sedation:[22]

> 'In my view the administration to a person of medication, at any rate of antipsychotic drugs and other tranquilisers, is always a pointer towards the existence of the objective element: for it suppresses her liberty to express herself as she would otherwise wish. Indeed, if the administration of it is attended by force, its relevance is increased. Furthermore, in that objections may be highly relevant, medication which has the effect of suppressing them may be relevant to an equally high degree. But again, conversely, the absence of medication is a pointer in the other direction.'

It would appear that the use of forcible sedation will be a strong pointer words a deprivation of liberty, but it is submitted that even unforced sedation which has the effect of rendering a person will also be a strong indicator that a deprivation of liberty is taking place, regardless of the motive of the person administering it.

6.20 Detention in an institution may fall within Art 5 whilst similar restrictions imposed in the person's own home might not. In *Mancini* v *Italy*[23] the Court observed that there was an important difference in the nature of the place of detention between a private home and a public institution. Unlike the former, the latter required integration of the individual into an overall organisation and strict supervision by the authorities of the main aspects of his day-to-day life. In *Atanasov* v *Bulgaria*[24] the applicant suffered from schizophrenia and was arrested on suspicion of a number of serious offences. He was initially placed under house arrest and then transferred to a psychiatric hospital where he was detained. The Bulgarian authorities relied on the initial

---

21   [1998] 3 All ER 289 at 301.
22   *P and Q v Surrey County Council and others* [2011] EWCA Civ 190, para 26.
23   European Court of Human Rights App No 44955/98, ECHR 2001-IX, paras 13–26.
24   European Court of Human Rights Judgment of 6 November 2008.

decision to place under house arrest as justifying detention in the psychiatric hospital. The European Court held that there had been a breach of Article 5(1). The court said this:[25]

> '[I]t is evident that despite the fact that his situation in law remained unchanged, in practice the nature and degree of the restrictions on his liberty while in the hospital must have been very different from those associated with house arrest.'

6.21 'Type' may also refer to the issue of who is carrying out the deprivation, and where it is carried out. It will be relevant if the restrictions are imposed in the context of life at home with the patient's family rather than in an institution. *A Local Authority* v *A, B and the Equality and Human Rights Commission: A Local Authority* v *C, D and E and the Equality and Human rights Commission*[26] concerned A and C, who suffered from Smith Magenis Syndrome. The features of the disorder include the following behaviour problems: self injurious behaviour, physical and verbal aggression, temper tantrums, destructive behaviour, hyperactivity, restlessness, excitability, distractibility and severe sleep disturbances, which include frequent and prolonged night waking and early morning waking Both were under 'exemplary' care at home, A from her mother, and C from her mother and father. Both had to be locked in their bedrooms at night to prevent them from wandering and coming to harm. Neither could consent to the restrictions, so there was no doubt that the subjective element had been satisfied. As to the objective element, Munby J said this:[27]

> '115. In neither home does the regime involve a deprivation of liberty. And in saying this I should make clear that I do not see this as being a borderline case or a case which falls to be decided on a fine balance. In my judgment, the loving, caring, regime in each of these family homes – a reasonable, proportionate and entirely appropriate regime implemented by devoted parents in the context of a loving family relationship and with the single view to the welfare, happiness and best interests of A and C respectively – falls significantly short of anything that would engage Article 5.
>
> 150. ... [N]either A nor C is being deprived of her liberty. Their happy family life, in the heart of a caring and loving family, can hardly be further removed from the paradigm case of the prisoner or, indeed the immensely different case of someone subject to control order and curfew. Does the fact that, during the night time, they are locked in their bedrooms, alone make the difference? In my judgment it does not.
>
> 155. ... [W]hat we have here is merely a restriction upon liberty – and, I should add, an entirely appropriate and proportionate restriction upon liberty – rather than a deprivation of liberty. Not the least important and telling of the factors which have to be evaluated, and which in my judgment point towards the conclusion that there is no deprivation of liberty here, are the facts (a) that the

---

[25] Ibid, para 71.
[26] [2010] EWHC 978 (Fam) Munby J.
[27] Ibid, para 115.

regime in question applies only at night time and at a time when, but for their disabling condition, A and C would otherwise be expected to be asleep and (b) that although locked in their bedrooms both A and C are checked at night by their parents who, moreover, respond if their daughter wants to come out.'

In arriving at this conclusion, Munby J followed the earlier case of *Re MIG and MEG*, which has subsequently been ruled upon by the Court of Appeal in *P (otherwise known as MIG) and Q (otherwise known as MEG) by the Official Solicitor* v *Surrey County Council, CA, LA and the Human Rights Commission.*[28] MIG and MEG were sisters with substantial and permanent learning disabilities who suffered abuse at the hands of their stepfather and who had been removed from home. P had been placed with foster parents, and Q in a home where she was one of only four residents. The question was whether they had been deprived of their liberty. Wilson LJ identified the following factors common to both:[29]

(a)   they were not free to leave their respective accommodation;

(b)   they did not object to the arrangements for them and did not seek to leave – and therefore did not have to be restrained from leaving – their accommodation;

(c)   their daily care needs were met by virtue of supervision and control;

(d)   they had their own bedrooms;

(e)   they were not under close confinement within their accommodation;

(f)   they were taken out each day to the unit of further education;

(g)   they were taken on other outings;

(h)   they had good outside contact with family members under elaborate arrangements made by Surrey; although their contact with the mother was not as frequent as she had wished (being, with respect, one of Mr Gordon's thinner points), they had reasonable contact with her and, apparently more importantly for them, reasonable contact with each other, with the half-sister and with the sister; and

(i)   the elements of confinement, supervision and control in their lives were likely to be permanent.

P lived in a family home, was not receiving any medication and her social life was limited. Q was not living in a family home, and although her social life was

---

[28]   [2010] EWHC 785 (Fam) Parker J. See now *P (otherwise known as MIG) and Q (otherwise known as MEG) by the Official Solicitor* v *Surrey County Council, CA, LA and the Human Rights Commission* [2011] EWCA Civ 190.

[29]   [2011] EWCA Civ 190, para 31.

fuller than P's she was receiving sedative medication for anxiety, and she was subject to physical restraint because she suffered outbursts.

6.22 Duration can also be relevant to the issue of whether there is a deprivation of liberty. In *Gillan and Quinton v United Kingdom*, involving stop and search, the European Court observed that:[30]

> 'Although the length of time during which each applicant was stopped and searched did not in either case exceed 30 minutes, during this period the applicants were entirely deprived of any freedom of movement. They were obliged to remain where they were and submit to the search and if they had refused they would have been liable to arrest, detention at a police station and criminal charges. This element of coercion is indicative of a deprivation of liberty within the meaning of Article 5.'

However, the court did not make a formal finding of breach of Art 5, since it decided the case on the basis that the applicants' Art 8 rights had been infringed. In *Novotka v Slovakia*[31] a decision on admissibility, the European Court held that there had been a deprivation of liberty within the meaning of Art 5(1) of the Convention as the applicant was brought to a police station against his will and was held there in a cell. The relatively short duration of the interference (just under one hour) did not affect the position. In the control order case of *JJ v Secretary of State for the Home Department,*[32] the House of Lords held that a control order under the Prevention of Terrorism Act 2005 imposing a curfew of 18 hours in a private home gave rise to a deprivation of liberty. However, in *Secretary of State for the Home Department v AP*[33] Lord Brown said that 'for a control order with a 16-hour curfew (a fortiori one with a 14-hour curfew) to be struck down as involving a deprivation of liberty, the other conditions imposed would have to be unusually destructive of the life the controlee might otherwise have been living.' What these cases show is that duration is relevant, but its importance will vary depending on the context, particularly the setting of the confinement and its effects.

6.23 As for effects, in *Atanasov v Bulgaria* the European Court held that the effects of detention in a psychiatric clinic were sufficiently different in kind from those associated with house arrest to amount to deprivation of liberty and held that:[34]

> '[H]aving regard to its specific nature and potential effect on the physical and psychological well-being of the individual concerned, confinement in a psychiatric clinic must be accompanied by specific procedural and substantive guarantees tailored for this type of deprivation of liberty.'

---

[30] European Court of Human Rights, App No 4158/05 Judgment of 12 January 2010 (2010) 50 EHRR 45, para 57.
[31] European Court of Human Rights, App No 47244/99 Judgment of 4 November 2003.
[32] [2007] UKHL 45.
[33] [2010] UKSC 24, [2010] 3 WLR 51, para 4.
[34] Ibid, para 71.

6.24 Furthermore, the effect of being deprived of association with family and friends was held to be relevant in both *HL* v *United Kingdom*, where HL's carers were stopped from visiting him, and in *Secretary of State for the Home Department v AP*,[35] where the fact that the control order required AP to reside at a considerable distance from his friends and family who found it extremely difficult to visit him was a significant factor in the decision that a 16 hour curfew could amount to a deprivation of liberty. Effects on everyday life were also afforded significant importance in *LLBC v TG*[36] where MacFarlane J held that there was no deprivation of liberty in circumstances where P was in an 'ordinary care home with the ordinary restrictions one would expect in that setting', P's family were free to come and take him on outings, and P had expressed himself to be happy where he was. The fact that the family objected to him being in that setting did not convert it into a deprivation of liberty. In *A Local Authority* v *A* where Munby J held that:[37]

> 'Not the least important and telling of the factors which have to be evaluated, and which in my judgment point towards the conclusion that there is no deprivation of liberty here, are the facts (a) that the regime in question applies only at night time and at a time when, but for their disabling condition, A and C would otherwise be expected to be asleep and (b) that although locked in their bedrooms both A and C are checked at night by their parents who, moreover, respond if their daughter wants to come out.'

In *P and Q v Surrey County Council*[38] Wilson LJ held that whilst the purpose of the placement (in this case rescue of the young women from an abusive situation) was irrelevant to the question whether there was a deprivation of liberty, it was relevant to the question of whether the placement was in their best interests. However, although Parker J had been wrong to attach 'significance to the fact that the purpose of the arrangements for the girls was to further their best interests' in her determination of whether there was a deprivation of liberty, Wilson LJ considered that nevertheless she had highlighted 'a relevant feature', namely the relative normality of the living arrangements under scrutiny:[39]

> 'If the person is living with her parents or other members of his natural family in their home, she is living – in that respect – the most normal life possible. Typically – but sadly not always – there will be no deprivation of liberty in such circumstances ... Not much less normal for this purpose is the life of a child in the home of foster parents or of an adult, such as Mr HL, in the home of carers; ... But, even when the person lives in an institution rather than in a family home, there is a wide spectrum between the small children's home or nursing home, on the one hand, and a hospital designed for compulsory detentions like *Bournewood*; and it is in my view necessary to place each case along it.'

---

35   [2010] UKSC 24, [2010] 3 WLR 51, para 4.
36   [2007] EWHC 2640 (Fam).
37   *A Local Authority v A, B and the Equality and Human Rights Commission: A Local Authority v C, D and E and the Equality and Human Rights Commission* [2010] EWHC 978 (Fam) Munby J.
38   [2011] EWCA Civ 190.
39   Ibid, para 28.

Relevant to the enquiry into 'normality' would be whether the person was allowed to go out to school, college, or a day centre, and the extent to which restrictions were placed on outside social contact.

The consequences of a finding that there has been a deprivation of liberty in a domestic setting or in a residential home which is not a care home would be that the deprivation would have to be authorised by and reviewed by the Court of Protection, it could not be authorized under Sch A1 of the MCA 2005. As Wilson LJ put it in *P and Q v Surrey County Council*, Art 5(4) of the Convention:[40]

> 'would impose a duty on the court itself periodically, again probably at least annually, to review the continued necessity for the arrangements which deprive them of their liberty, albeit perhaps only on paper unless requested otherwise: see *Re BJ (Incapacitated Adult)* [2009] EWHC 3310 (Fam), [2010] 1 FLR 1373, at [26] – [28]. The court's review would probably again require independent representation of them.'

Wilson LJ said that if this appeal were to be allowed, there would be a 'vast, if unquantifiable, number of necessary reviews of such a character' which 'would surely be beyond the present capacity of the Official Solicitor's department and in particular of the Court of Protection.' However, 'To have an eye to that factor would be to raise to it the wrong end of the telescope ... The importance of the right to liberty is paramount ... and the state's positive obligation to provide the facilities necessary for its effective exercise is absolute.'[41] However studiously the judges avoid consideration of these consequences, they make it unlikely that a person who is placed in a domestic setting, which is designed to achieve or simulate normal family life, and which is beyond the reach of the Schedule A1 procedures, will be held to be deprived of liberty.

6.25 'Manner of implementation' may include use of force or locked doors to prevent a person from leaving where the person has persistently indicated a desire to leave, or an indication that a person who has persistently expressed their unwillingness to remain would be prevented from leaving if they attempted to do so, as in *JE v DE and Surrey County Council*.[42] In that case, where DE had repeatedly said that he was being held against his will, Munby J said that the local authority's assertion that DE would not have been prevented from leaving, simply 'would not wash', and that he was being deprived of his liberty. Use of sedative medication which effectively prevents the patient from making any attempt to leave the hospital or care home would amount to a deprivation of liberty, as would restrictions on the patient's movement within a hospital or home which are intended to prevent a patient from attempting to leave.[43] In *Dorset County Council v EH (by her litigation friend the Official*

---

40   Ibid, para 4.
41   Ibid, para 5.
42   [2006] EWHC 3459 (Fam).
43   Richard Jones *Mental Capacity Act Manual* (Fourth Edition) (2010), pp 251–252. See also *DH NHS Foundation Trust v PS* [2010] EWHC 1217 (COP) where Sir Nicholas Wall P held that

Solicitor)[44] EH, an elderly patient, was being placed in a secure residential care home with the intention that she would not be able to leave unaccompanied, and without the agreement of the staff. If EH resisted the move, and there would be a degree of force and coercion, which would also involve deprivation of her liberty. The home carried out risk assessments before admission, and it had a 'Service User's Absconding and Missing policy' stating that if a resident leaves or absconds, enquiries will be made of all who may have information; a thorough search will be made of the premises, twice; the resident's family will be contacted; the local area will be searched; and in the last resort the police will be called and photographs circulated. The home had windows and doors which had been made secure and there had been no incidents over the past five years where a resident had wandered or got lost on unaccompanied excursions. Parker J held that there was no doubt that residence in this home would involve deprivation of EH's liberty. In *BB v AM*,[45] BB was under sedation; staff exercised control over her care, movements, assessments and treatments; staff also exercised control over her residence and the contacts she has with other people; her family were hostile to her placement in the hospital; the court was refusing to sanction her discharge into the care of her parents pending the conclusion of investigations being carried out by the police. Since BB was away from her family, in an institution under sedation in circumstances in which her contact with the outside world was strictly controlled, her capacity to have free access to her family was limited by court order, and her movements were under the strict control and supervision of hospital staff, the cumulative effect was that BB was deprived of her liberty.[46]

6.26   The Department of Health Code of Practice lists the following factors drawn from the Strasbourg case law as 'potentially indicating that a deprivation of liberty is taking place':[47]

'(1)   Restraint is used, including sedation, to admit a person to an institution where that person is resisting admission;

(2)   Staff exercise complete and effective control over the care and movement of a person for a significant period;

(3)   Staff exercise control over assessments, treatment, contacts and residence;

(4)   A decision has been taken by the institution that the person will not be released into the care of others or permitted to live elsewhere, unless the staff in the institution consider it appropriate.;

(5)   A request by carers for the person to be discharged to their care is refused;

(6)   The person is unable to maintain social contacts because of restrictions placed on their access to other people;

---

sedating PS for the purposes of getting her into hospital and preventing her from leaving after a cancer operation would amount to detaining her, but that it was not necessary to invoke the DoLs procedures since the detention was being carried out on the authority of a declaration granted under s 15 of the MCA 2005.

44   [2009] EWHC 784 (Fam), paras 115–117.
45   [2010] EWHC 1916 (Fam).
46   Ibid, paras 29–32.
47   Mental Capacity Act 2005: Deprivation of Liberty Safeguards – Code of Practice to supplement the main Mental Capacity Act 2005 Code of Practice (2008) DoH and WAG, para 2.5.

(7)   The person loses autonomy because they are under continuous supervision and control.'

6.27   For the purposes of the Convention, a deprivation of liberty must be carried out in accordance with a procedure prescribed by law. In England and Wales deprivations of liberty may be authorised by detention under the Mental Health Act, by decision of the Court of Protection under s 16 of the MCA 2005, by authorisation under Sch A1 of the MCA 2005, or where it is necessary to carry out life sustaining treatment or perform a vital act pending a decision of the Court of Protection.[48]

'In Accordance with a Procedure Prescribed by Law'

6.28   In *Winterwerp v Netherlands* the European Court of Human Rights held that the notion underlying the phrase 'in accordance with a procedure prescribed by law' in Art 5 ECHR is:[49]

> 'one of fair and proper procedure, namely that any measure depriving a person of his liberty should issue from and be executed by an appropriate authority and should not be arbitrary.'

6.29   In *HL v United Kingdom* the Court made important statements about what is required by a procedure prescribed by law. A number of key ingredients of a procedure prescribed by law had been missing in HL's case in the court's opinion. These were:[50]

> '(a)   The lack of any formalised admission procedures which indicate who can propose admission, for what reasons and on the basis of what kind of medical and other assessments and conclusions.
>
> (b)   There was no requirement to fix the exact purpose of admission (for example, for assessment or for treatment) and, consistently, no limits in terms of time, treatment or care attach to that admission.
>
> (c)   There was no specific provision requiring a continuing clinical assessment of the persistence of a disorder warranting detention.
>
> (d)   There was no provision for the appointment of a representative of a patient who could make certain objections and applications on his or her behalf, a procedural protection accorded to those committed involuntarily under the 1983 Act and which would be of equal importance for patients who are legally incapacitated and have extremely limited communication abilities.'

The Court found striking 'the lack of any fixed procedural rules by which the admission and detention of compliant incapacitated persons is conducted'. The Deprivation of Liberty authorisations in the MCA 2005 are designed to remedy the failure to provide a procedure prescribed by law.

---

[48]   MCA 2005, ss 4A and 4B.
[49]   (1979) 2 EHRR 387, at para 45.
[50]   (2004) 40 EHRR 761, at para 120.

6.30 The issue of what is required by a procedure prescribed by law was addressed in *Re PS (incapacitated or vulnerable adult)* where Munby J said that where a court was authorising deprivation of liberty, the following minimum requirements must be satisfied in order to comply with Art 5:[51]

'(1) The detention must be authorised by the court on application made by the local authority and *before* the detention commences.

(2) Subject to the exigencies of urgency or emergency the evidence must establish unsoundness of mind of a kind or degree warranting compulsory confinement. In other words, there must be evidence establishing at least a prima facie case that the individual lacks capacity and that confinement of the nature proposed is appropriate.

(3) Any order authorising detention must contain provision for an adequate review at reasonable intervals, in particular with a view to ascertaining whether there still persists unsoundness of mind of a kind or degree warranting compulsory confinement.'

The requirement of authorisation before detention under the MHA 1983 commences is covered by s 6(1) of the 1983 Act which provides that a duly completed application under Part II with medical recommendations is sufficient authority for the AMHP to authorise the patient to be taken and conveyed to hospital (see **4.40** above). The MHA 2007 introduced new s 18(7) into the MHA 1983, which gives a power to take and convey a person to their place of residence under guardianship.[52] No such power is expressly provided in relation to the MCA authorisation procedure. However, in *DCC v KH (by the Official solicitor), PJ, AH, and FCC*.[53] The declaration sought was in terms the patient was in a care home subject to a standard authorisation under Sch A1. Judge O'Regan held that there was no need for a declaration to be granted that it should be lawful for no more than reasonable and proportionate force to be used for the least possible duration and only if necessary in order to facilitate the return of the respondent from a contact session back to the home. The standard authorisation was sufficient protection for the local authority.

6.31 However, in subsequent cases such declarations were granted. In *Dorset County Council v EH (by her litigation friend the Official Solicitor)*[54] Parker J held that it was in EH's best interests to reside in secure residential accommodation provided by the council, and declared that the Council could use reasonable force to restrain and transport EH to the accommodation it provided for her, and that the Council could use reasonable measures to prevent her from leaving the accommodation and return her if she did leave. In *LBH v GP & MP*[55] the court at an earlier hearing had given authority for the removal of an adult lacking capacity from his mother's home – with police assistance. It appeared that the police used considerably more force than anticipated and

---

[51] [2007] EWHC 623 (Fam) at [23].
[52] MHA 1983, s 18(7), as inserted by MHA 2007, Sch 3, para 3(5).
[53] [2009] EWCOP Birmingham County Court 11 September 2009 Case No 1720380.
[54] [2009] EWHC 784 (Fam).
[55] (2010) Family Division No FD08P01058, 8 April 2010.

accordingly Coleridge J gave Guidance (approved by the President of the Family Division) as to how such action should take place in the future:

'In the event that it is expected that the assistance of the Police may be required to effect or assist with the removal of a vulnerable/ incapacitated adult ("P") which the Court is being asked to authorise, the following steps should generally be taken:

(1) the Local Authority/NHS body/other organisation/person (the Applicant) applying to the Court for an authorisation to remove P should, in advance of the hearing of the Application, discuss and, where possible, agree with the Police the way in which it is intended that the removal will be effected, to include, where applicable, the extent to which it is expected that restraint and/or force may be used and the nature of any restraint (for example, handcuffs) that may be used;

(2) the applicant should ensure that information about the way in which it is intended that removal will be effected is provided to the Court and to the litigation friend (in cases where a person has been invited and/or appointed to act as P's litigation friend) before the Court authorises removal. In particular, the Court and the litigation friend should be informed whether there is agreement between the Applicant and the Police and, if there is not, about the nature and extent of any disagreement;

(3) where Applicant and the Police do not agree about how removal should be effected, the Court should give consideration to inviting/directing the Police to attend the hearing of the Application so that the Court can, where appropriate, determine how it considers removal should be effected and/or ensure that any authorisation for removal is given on a fully informed basis.'

6.32 The Government instead placed reliance on the defence in respect of acts done in connection with care and treatment, involving proportionate restraint in ss 5 and 6 of the Mental Capacity Act 2005, but this cannot apply to restrictions which amount to a deprivation of liberty. It is doubtful whether a retrospective defence can amount to a procedure prescribed by law. In *Storck v Germany* the European Court of Human Rights held that states have an obligation to take positive steps to secure the right to liberty under Art 5 and the right to physical and moral integrity under Art 8. This obligation placed them under a duty to exercise supervision and control over private psychiatric institutions. The court noted that in the sphere of interferences with a person's physical integrity, German law provided for strong penal sanctions and for liability in tort, but went on to say that:[56]

'Just as in cases of deprivation of liberty, the Court finds that such retrospective measures alone are not sufficient to provide appropriate protection of the physical integrity of individuals in such a vulnerable position as the applicant.'

Section 6 cannot authorise deprivation of liberty, so authority to take and convey must come from an order under s 16 of the MCA or a standard or an urgent authorisation. An urgent authorisation is form of self certification,

---

[56] *Storck v Germany (App no 61603/00)* (2005) 43 EHRR 96, at para 150.

allowing the detaining institution to authorise detention for up to 7 days without the need for any prior assessments. The Winterwerp criteria for lawful detention on grounds of unsoundness of mind have an exception for emergencies, so this may be lawful, but it is noteworthy that emergency detention under s 4 of the MHA 1983 lasts up to 72 hours and still requires a medical assessment.

Which procedure to use? The interface between the Mental Health Act 1983 and the Mental Capacity Act 2005

6.33 If deprivation of liberty is necessary this will have to be under either the Mental Health Act or the Mental Capacity Act. Which one to use is a matter of professional judgment, and the interface is not always clear cut. Detention under the Mental Health Act will be appropriate if the person needs deprivation of liberty in order to provide some aspect of their treatment for mental disorder and either:

(a)   they are ineligible for *Bournewood* safeguards; or

(b)   their care cannot be safely and effectively provided using those safeguards.

6.34 If AMHPs and doctors are satisfied that a patient can safely and effectively be assessed or treated by relying on the MCA, it is likely to be difficult to demonstrate that the criteria for detaining them under s 3(2)(c) are met, namely that the treatment which the patient needs cannot be provided unless he is detained under this section. However, a person may not be subject to a MCA authorisation if he or she is 'ineligible.' One of the grounds of ineligibility is that the person is already detained under s 2 of the 1983 Act. Most applications for detention under s 3 of the Mental Health Act are made in respect of people who are already detained for assessment under s 2. In such a case the patient would be ineligible for the Deprivation of Liberty safeguards. The decision which framework to use is a judgment for the professionals concerned. A person may not be subject to a MCA authorisation unless they are 'eligible', and the 'no refusals' condition is satisfied.

Eligibility for the *Bournewood* safeguards

6.35 The purpose of the eligibility requirement for the MCA Deprivation of Liberty Safeguards under Sch 1A to the MCA 2005 is to mark the interface between cases which can be dealt with under the *Bournewood* DoL authorisations and 'cases where a person is, or might be made, subject to the 1983 Act'.[57]

---

[57]   *Explanatory Notes*, paras 201–220.

Patients already subject to the Mental Health Act 1983

6.36 The cases where a person is already subject to the MHA 1983 are relatively straightforward. A person is ineligible for MCA detention if he is already subject to a hospital treatment obligation[58] under the MHA 1983 and will continue to be detained in hospital under that regime. In such a case there is authority to detain already, so a further application for detention under either legislation is unnecessary.

6.37 A person on leave of absence from detention, subject to guardianship, supervised community treatment or conditional discharge will also be ineligible if the authorisation would be inconsistent with an obligation placed on the patient under the MHA 1983 to reside somewhere else. The Explanatory Notes state that:[59]

> 'a person who is subject to the 1983 Act but who is not in hospital could be subject to an authorisation under these new provisions. This might be necessary for example if a person subject to guardianship who normally lived at home needed respite care in a care home.'

However, a MCA DoL authorisation would not be available if the person is on leave of absence from detention, or subject to SCT or conditional discharge and the authorisation, if given, would be for deprivation of liberty in a hospital for treatment for mental disorder. This means that an authorisation cannot be used as an alternative to the procedures for recall in the MHA 1983.[60]

Patients not already subject to the Mental Health Act 1983 or the Mental Capacity Act 2005

6.38 More difficult is the situation where a person is subject to neither regime, but is 'within the scope of the Mental Health Act 1983.' A patient ('P') is within the scope of the 1983 Act if an application in respect of P could be made under s 2 or s 3 and P could be detained in hospital if an application were to be made.[61]

6.39 P is within the scope of s 2 if those carrying out the assessment consider that P is suffering from mental disorder of a nature or degree which warrants detention of the patient in a hospital for assessment (or for assessment followed by medical treatment); and that (b) P ought to be so detained in the interests of his own health or safety or with a view to the protection of other persons.

6.40 A patient is within the scope of s 3 if those carrying out the assessment consider that (a) he is suffering from mental disorder of a nature or degree which makes it appropriate for him to receive medical treatment in a hospital;

---

58   That is, detained under ss 2, 3, 4, 35, 36, 37, 38, 44, 45A, 47, 48 or 51.
59   *Explanatory Notes*, para 201.
60   Ibid.
61   MCA 2005, Sch A1, para. 12.

(b) it is necessary for P's health *or* safety *or* for the protection of other persons that P should receive such treatment; and (c) appropriate medical treatment is available for him.

6.41 In determining whether an application under s 2 or s 3 could be made it is to be assumed that the medical recommendations have been given if the grounds for detention in the respective sections are met in the patient's case. In determining whether the criterion in s 3(2)(c) is satisfied, that the necessary treatment 'cannot be provided unless P is detained under this section' it is to be assumed that the treatment cannot be provided under the Mental Capacity Act DoL safeguards.[62]

6.42 A person who is 'within the scope of the Mental Health Act', as explained above, will be ineligible for deprivation of liberty in a hospital under the Mental Capacity Act if the following three conditions are met:

(a)   the proposed order of the Court of Protection or *Bournewood* authorisation will authorise the person to be a mental health patient, meaning 'a person accommodated in a hospital for the purpose of being given medical treatment for mental disorder'; and

(b)   the patient objects:

    (a)   to being a mental health patient: or
    (b)   to being given some or all of the mental health treatment; and

(c)   an attorney or deputy has not made a valid decision to consent to each matter to which P objects.[63]

6.43 In deciding whether the person objects, regard is to be had to all the circumstances (insofar as they are reasonably ascertainable, including the person's behaviour, their wishes and feelings, and their views beliefs and values. Regard is to be had to circumstances from the past only insofar as it is reasonable to have regard to them.[64] In *GJ v The Foundation Trust and others*[65] Charles J had to consider whether GJ was a 'mental health patient' a person accommodated in a hospital for the purpose of being given medical treatment for mental disorder. Charles J held that the regime created by the 2005 Act was that the MHA 1983 was to have primacy when it applies, and medical practitioners ... 'cannot pick and choose between the two statutory regimes as they think fit having regard to general considerations (eg preservation or promotion of a therapeutic relationship) that they consider render one regime preferable.'[66] *GJ* suffered from dementia as a result of which he was failing to manage his diabetes and regularly experienced potentially fatal hypoglycaemic

---

62   Ibid, Sch 1A para 12(3)–(5).
63   MCA 2005, Sch 1A, para 5.
64   Schedule 1A, paras 5(6)–5(7).
65   [2009] EWHC 2972 (Fam) 2 November 2009.
66   Ibid, para 45.

attacks. These attacks arose as a result of his mental illness (because it meant he was unable to appreciate the importance of eating and taking his medication) and also exacerbated his illness. Charles J considered that in such cases it was helpful to adopt a 'but for' approach: but for the diabetes, would this person have been detained for mental disorder treatment. In this case, he considered that the answer was 'no' and accordingly (albeit a borderline case) he was therefore eligible to be detained under the 2005 Act. In *BB* v *AM*[67] Baker J followed the approach of Charles J in *GJ v the Foundation Trust* and held that BB was eligible to be deprived of her liberty under a welfare order made under s 16 of the MCA 2005. BB's consultant psychiatrist had said that:[68]

> 'She is not detainable under the Mental Health Act because she is happy to stay in hospital and take medication. She has made no attempts to leave. She reports being happy. She changes the subject when asked about her home and family but she does so without showing any negative emotion or particular interest... if she said she wished to be discharged or to return home, we would assess her mental state and assess for detention under the Mental Health Act. It might be she would be easily persuaded to stay; it might be she would be detainable'

Baker J held that it was therefore not established that the criteria under s 2 or 3 of the Mental Health Act were made out and it was not proved that BB fell within the scope of that Act. She was therefore eligible to be deprived of her liberty under the MCA 2005.

6.44 It is important to recognise that the patient's objection may be overridden, and they still may be subject to the *Bournewood* procedure if their attorney or deputy validly consents to the placement and treatment. The 'no refusals' requirement means that the attorney or deputy, acting within the scope of their authority, also has the right to block a *Bournewood* authorisation. The only way in which a patient may block a *Bournewood* authorisation is by a valid and applicable advance decision refusing in sufficiently precise terms admission to hospital in circumstances amounting to a deprivation of liberty, or refusing some or all of the treatment proposed to be given. Such an advance directive could only be overridden by detention under the Mental Health Act.

6.45 If deprivation of liberty in hospital is needed to provide necessary care for a patient who lacks capacity to consent to it, the policy intent appears to be that consideration should be given first to whether this may be achieved by a MCA DoL authorisation. However, the Code suggests that preference should be given to detention under the Mental Health Act 1983 in the following cases:[69]

(a) Where the person needs treatment which cannot lawfully be provided under the MCA, because for example because he has made a valid and applicable advance decision refusing it.

---

67   [2010] EWHC 1916 (Fam).
68   Ibid, para.
69   Mental Health Act 1983 Code of Practice (England) 2008 paras 4.20–4.23.

(b)   Where the person is objecting to the deprivation of liberty and that objection has not been overridden by an attorney or deputy acting within the scope of their authority

(c)   Where the patient is being considered for detention under Part 3 of the Act in connection with criminal proceedings.

(d)   A degree of restraint needs to be used which is justified by the risk to other people but which is not permissible under MCA because, exceptionally, it cannot be said to be proportionate to the risk to the patient personally. Sections 6, 11, and 20 of the MCA allow restraint but only as a proportionate response to risk of harm to the patient.

(e)   Where the patient lacks capacity now but that capacity is fluctuating and the patient is not expected to co-operate when they have capacity. This may be particularly relevant to patients suffering acute psychotic, manic or depressive episodes.

Finally, the decision may be made on the basis of risk, if 'there is some other specific identifiable risk that the person might otherwise not receive the treatment they need if the MCA is relied on, and either the person or others might potentially suffer harm as a result.'

THE MENTAL CAPACITY ACT 2005

6.46   In order to understand the DoL safeguards and the interface between the MCA and the MHA it is important to understand the basic concepts and instruments of the Mental Capacity Act 2005. Five principles apply to decision-making under the MCA 2005 (see further **2.40** above). They are:

(a)   a person must be assumed to have capacity unless it is established that they lack capacity;

(b)   a person is not to be treated as unable to make a decision unless all practicable steps to help him to do so have been taken without success;

(c)   a person is not to be treated as unable to make a decision merely because he makes an unwise decision;

(d)   an act done, or decision made, under this Act for or on behalf of a person who lacks capacity must be done, or made, in his best interests;

(e)   before the act is done, or the decision is made, regard must be had to whether the purpose for which it is needed can be as effectively achieved in a way that is less restrictive of the person's rights and freedom of action.[70]

---

[70]   MCA 2005, s 1.

Incapacity

6.47 A patient lacks capacity in relation to a matter if, at the material time he or she is unable to make a decision for him or herself in relation to the matter because of a temporary or permanent impairment of, or disturbance in the functioning of, the mind or brain.[71] Hence stage one of a capacity assessment is the so called 'diagnostic test' – is the person suffering from an impairment of or disturbance in the functioning of the mind or the brain.[72] Note that a person lacks capacity 'in relation to a matter', making capacity task specific. A person may be able to make some decisions but not others. Section 2(3) states that lack of capacity cannot be established merely by reference to a person's age or appearance, or 'a condition of his, or an aspect of his behaviour, which might lead others to make unjustified assumptions about his capacity'. These provisions reinforce the presumption of capacity and emphasise that people are not to be treated as incapable because they have a particular diagnosis. Incapacity is to be established on the balance of probabilities, the standard of proof in civil proceedings.

6.48 Section 2 states that a person lacks capacity if they are unable to make a decision, and s 3(1) sets out the 'stage two functional test' to be met if a person is to be found unable to make the relevant decision.[73] The person must be unable because of a temporary or permanent impairment or disturbance in the functioning of mind or brain:

(a) to understand the information relevant to the decision;

(b) to retain that information;

(c) to use or weigh that information as part of the process of making the decision; or

(d) to communicate his decision (whether by talking, using sign language or any other means).

Relevant treatment information includes information about the reasonably foreseeable consequences of deciding one way or another, or failing to make the decision. A person is not to be regarded as unable to understand the information relevant to a decision if he is able to understand an explanation of it given to him in a way that is appropriate to his circumstances (using simple language, visual aids or any other means). The requirement to be able to retain information is only to retain it long enough to make the relevant decision and the fact that a person is able to retain the information relevant to a decision for a short period only does not prevent him from being regarded as able to make the decision.

---

[71] MCA 2005, s 2(1).
[72] *A Local Authority v Mrs A, by her Litigation Friend, the Official Solicitor and Mr A* [2010] EWHC 1549 (Fam) Bodey J, para 50.
[73] Ibid, para 51.

Best interests

6.49   It is a principle of the MCA 2005 that any act or decision, for or on behalf of a person who lacks capacity, must be done, or made, in his best interests. 'Best interests' was initially to be determined according to the *Bolam* formula.[74] Treatment was in the best interests of a patient if a responsible body of medical opinion (not necessarily the majority) would consider it to be in the patient's best interests.[75] However, the MCA 2005 and subsequent case-law have modified substantially the approach to determining best interests.

A new approach to best interests

6.50   Since *Re A (Male Sterilisation)*[76] a two-stage 'balance sheet' approach has been employed. The first question is whether the treatment is within 'the *Bolam* range? The second is which treatment provides the most 'significant credit' in the balance sheet of probable advantages over disadvantages. As Thorpe LJ put it:

> 'There can be no doubt in my mind that the evaluation of best interests is akin to a welfare appraisal ... Pending the enactment of a checklist or other statutory direction it seems to me that the first instance judge with the responsibility to make an evaluation of the best interests of a claimant lacking capacity should draw up a balance sheet. The first entry should be of any factor or factors of actual benefit. In the present case the instance would be the acquisition of foolproof contraception. Then on the other sheet the judge should write any counterbalancing dis-benefits to the applicant. An obvious instance in this case would be the apprehension, the risk and the discomfort inherent in the operation. Then the judge should enter on each sheet the potential gains and losses in each instance making some estimate of the extent of the possibility that the gain or loss might accrue. At the end of that exercise the judge should be better placed to strike a balance between the sum of the certain and possible gains against the sum of the certain and possible losses. Obviously, only if the account is in relatively significant credit will the judge conclude that the application is likely to advance the best interests of the claimant.'

In *JS v an NHS Trust*[77] the Court insisted on a broader concept of best interests, recognising the interconnectedness of incapacitated people and their carers and families. The duty of the assessor is to consider and assess the best interests of the patients in the widest possible way to include the medical and non-medical benefits and disadvantages, the broader welfare interests of the patient, their abilities, their future with or without treatment, the impact on their families, and the impact of denial of the treatment. Although this case law predates the Mental Capacity Act 2005, these remain the matters which are to be considered. In *Dorset County Council v EH (by her litigation friend the*

---

[74]   *Bolam v Friern Hospital Management Committee* [1957] 2 All ER 118, QBD.
[75]   *Re F (Sterilisation: Mental Patient)* [1990] 2 AC 1.
[76]   [2000] 1 FLR 549, per Thorpe LJ at 560.
[77]   [2002] EWHC 2734 (Fam).

Official Solicitor)[78] Parker J gave an excellent example of how the balance sheet should be applied, with prospective advantages and disadvantages of placement in a secure residential unit laid out on either side. Section 4 of the MCA 2005 does not redefine best interests. Instead it sets out how they are to be determined.

Section 4 of the Mental Capacity Act 2005

6.51　Section 4 of the MCA 2005 sets out the approach to be adopted in assessing best interests. The person making the determination must not make it merely on the basis of the person's age or appearance, or a condition of his, or an aspect of his behaviour, which might lead others to make unjustified assumptions about what might be in his best interests. The assessor must take into account all the circumstances of which he or she is aware and which might reasonably be regarded as relevant. He or she must consider whether it is likely that the person will at some time have capacity in relation to the matter in question, and, if it appears likely that he will, when that is likely to be.

6.52　The person making the best interests determination must, so far as reasonably practicable, permit and encourage the person to participate, or to improve his ability to participate, as fully as possible in any act done for him and any decision affecting him. The decision-maker must take into account the person's past and present wishes and feelings, his beliefs and values which might be likely to influence his decision, and any other factors which he would be likely to consider if able to do so. If practicable and appropriate the decision maker must consider the views of anyone named by the person to be consulted, any carer or person interested in his welfare, any donee of a lasting power of attorney granted by the person, and any deputy appointed by the Court of Protection.

6.53　Where the determination of best interests relates to treatment which those providing health care consider to be necessary to sustain life, the decision-maker must not, in considering whether the treatment is in the best interests of the person concerned, be motivated by a desire to bring about his death. As long as the processes and requirements of s 4 have been fulfilled, and the balance sheet test applied, there is sufficient compliance with the best interests requirement if the decision-maker reasonably believes that what he does or decides is in the best interests of the person concerned.

The defence in relation to acts of care, treatment and restraint done in the best interests of people who lack mental capacity

6.54　Sections 5 and 6 of the Mental Capacity Act 2005 provide a legal defence for anyone who does any act relating to the care or treatment of a person who lacks capacity, provided the act is done in what are reasonably believed to be the patient's best interests. In order for the action to be lawful the person taking

---

[78]　[2009] EWHC 784 (Fam), para 122.

it must have taken reasonable steps to determine whether the person has capacity in relation to the relevant decision, must reasonably believe that the person indeed lacks capacity, and must reasonably believe that what they are doing is in the person's best interests. Section 5 acts may include restraint as long as the conditions in s 6 are met. Restraint may be imposed to prevent harm to the patient as long as it is a proportionate response both to the likelihood of harm *to the patient* and the severity of the harm. The defence is not available if the proposed care or treatment intervention is one which has been refused by a valid and applicable advance decision made by the patient while he or she still retained capacity. Restraint cannot be authorised in the interests of protecting others from harm, although there may be occasions when there is overlap, such as where the person is restrained from rushing into a busy road, potentially harming themselves or other road users. Certain, more serious, treatment decisions require the approval of the Court of Protection unless the person has previously made a Lasting Power of Attorney appointing an attorney to make the decision for them, or they have made a valid advance decision refusing the proposed treatment. The Court of Protection must be asked to make decisions relating to withholding or withdrawal of artificial nutrition and hydration ('ANH') from a patient in a permanent vegetative state ('PVS'), organ or bone marrow donation by a donor who lacks mental capacity, non-therapeutic sterilisation (eg for contraceptive purposes) and cases where there is dispute about whether a treatment will be in a person's best interests.[79] Section 37 of the MCA 2005 applies to decisions about providing, stopping or withholding serious medical treatment where there is no-one other than paid carer to consult, the responsible body must appoint an Independent Mental Capacity Advocate ('IMCA') whose submissions must be taken into account in deciding whether to provide the treatment. The IMCA may consider seeking a second opinion. The requirement to consult an IMCA does not apply to treatment which is urgently needed to save a person's life or prevent a serious deterioration in condition. The IMCA requirement applies if any patient is to be subject to the *Bournewood* deprivation of liberty safeguards, and also to any patient lacking capacity with no-one other than a paid carer to consult is to be placed in hospital for a period likely to exceed 28 days or in a care home for more than eight weeks. The *Bournewood* deprivation of liberty safeguards will be appropriate only when detention is in the patient's own best interests, and necessary detention for the protection of others should take place under the MHA 1983.

Advance decisions

6.55 Sections 24–26 of the MCA 2005 apply to the making of advance decisions refusing treatment. An advance decision is made by an adult to refuse certain defined treatments, to take effect at some time in the future if and when the person loses capacity to make the decision. In order to be valid the decision has to be made while the person still has capacity to make the treatment decision, it must specify clearly the treatment being refused, and must be clear

---

[79]   Ministry of Justice *Mental Capacity Act Code of Practice* (2007), paras 6.18 and 8.18–8.24.

about the circumstances in which it is to apply. For example, if the refusal applies to blood transfusions, is it to apply even if the treatment is necessary to keep the person alive. If so the decision must be in writing. In order to be applicable an advance decision must apply to the circumstances which have currently arisen. A valid and applicable advance decision is binding on the doctors.

6.56 This means that a patient can refuse specified treatment for mental disorder, or to be admitted to hospital for treatment of mental disorder, and if the decision is valid and applicable it will prevent the person being admitted or given the relevant treatment under the Mental Capacity Act. The *Bournewood* deprivation of liberty procedures cannot be applied unless a 'no refusals' requirement is met. If there is a valid advance directive refusing an aspect of the treatment proposed for a patient who is deprived of his liberty, the no-refusals requirement for the DoL procedures is not met, because there is a valid refusal. A person may not be restrained and given treatment for mental disorder under ss 5 and 6 of the Mental Capacity Act 2005, if he or she lacks capacity to consent and has, when capable, made a valid advance decision refusing drug treatment for mental disorder. However, an advance decision refusing admission and medication for mental disorder may be overridden by detention and treatment under the Mental Health Act. Unless it is immediately necessary to save the patient's life or to prevent serious deterioration in her or his condition, ECT may not be given to a patient who has made a valid and applicable advance decision refusing the treatment, even if the patient is detained under the MHA 1983.[80]

Lasting powers of attorney

6.57 Section 9 of the MCA 2005 entitles a person (P), while they still have capacity to grant a lasting power of attorney (LPA), conferring on the attorney authority to make decisions about the P's personal welfare and/or their property and affairs. A lasting power of attorney gives the attorney authority to make decisions in circumstances where P no longer has capacity.[81] The powers of an attorney are subject to the principles in s 1 and the provisions on best interests in s 4. An attorney may act to restrain P if the conditions in s 11(2)–(4) are met. These are that:

- P lacks, or the attorney reasonably believes that P lacks, capacity in relation to the matter in question.

- the attorney reasonably believes that it is necessary to do the act in order to prevent harm to P.

- the act is a proportionate response to:

---

[80]   MHA 1983, ss 58A and 621A.
[81]   The formalities are specified in s 10 and Sch 1 to the MCA 2005.

-    the likelihood of P's suffering harm, and
-    the seriousness of that harm.

The attorney restrains P if he:

'(a)   uses, or threatens to use, force to secure the doing of an act which P resists; or

(b)   restricts P's liberty of movement, whether or not P resists; or

if he authorises another person to do any of those things.'

6.58   The fact that a person is subject to the MHA does not prevent someone from granting a LPA as long as he or she retains capacity to do so, nor does it affect the validity of any existing LPA or the authority of an attorney to make decisions. An attorney acting under a LPA is therefore able to take any decisions in relation to the welfare, property or affairs of a person subject to the MHA that they would otherwise be authorised to take, with two exceptions. The attorney will not be able:

(a)   to consent on the patient's behalf to treatment which is regulated by Part IV of the MHA (including neurosurgery for mental disorder and other treatments under s 57); or

(b)   to take decisions about where a person subject to guardianship is to reside, nor take other decisions which conflict with those of a guardian.[82]

6.59   An attorney's authority to make decisions about P's personal welfare extends to 'giving or refusing consent to the carrying out or continuation of a treatment by a person providing health care for P'. The authority does not come into effect unless the attorney reasonably believes that P lacks capacity to make the decision. The authority is also subject to any valid and applicable advance decision to refuse treatment. The decision to give or refuse consent to treatment is subject to two further limitations. It does not authorise the giving or refusing of consent to the carrying out or continuation of life-sustaining treatment, unless the instrument contains express provision to that effect, and it is subject to any conditions or restrictions in the instrument conferring the LPA.[83] If there is an attorney, the attorney may consent to deprivation of liberty under the MCA even if the patient objects, but no deprivation of liberty may take place if the attorney objects.

The Court of Protection and court appointed deputies

6.60   Where a person (P) is found to lack capacity in relation to decisions about personal welfare or property and affairs, the Court of Protection may itself make an order taking the decision on P's behalf (s 16(2)(a)), or it may appoint a person (a 'deputy') to make decisions on P's behalf (s 16(2)(b)). The

---

[82]   MCA 2005, s 28.
[83]   MCA, s 11(7)–(8).

powers of the court under this section are subject to ss 1 (the principles) and 4 (best interests). The court may not make a welfare order under s 16(2)(a) authorising deprivation of liberty if the person is ineligible under Sch 1A to the MCA 2005.[84]

6.61 When deciding whether it is in P's best interests to appoint a deputy, the court must have regard to P's best interests and to the principles that:

(a)   a decision by the court is to be preferred to the appointment of a deputy to make a decision; and

(b)   the powers conferred on a deputy should be as limited in scope and duration as is reasonably practicable in the circumstances.

6.62 The court may confer powers or impose duties on a deputy as it thinks necessary or expedient in connection with the appointment. Section 17 provides that the Court's powers in relation to P's personal welfare extend in particular to:

(a)   deciding where P is to live;

(b)   deciding what contact, if any, P is to have with any specified persons;

(c)   making an order prohibiting a named person from having contact with P;

(d)   giving or refusing consent to the carrying out or continuation of a treatment by a person providing health care for P;

(e)   giving a direction that a person responsible for P's health care allow a different person to take over that responsibility.

Deputies may be given all of these powers with the exception of (c) and (e).[85]

6.63 A deputy may not refuse life sustaining treatment on P's behalf. Nor may a deputy make a decision which is inconsistent with a decision made by the attorney or the attorneys of a lasting power of attorney conferred by P, acting within the scope of their authority.[86] Deputies exercise their powers subject to s 1 (principles) and s 4 (best interests), and are not authorised to restrain P unless four conditions are met:

(a)   in doing the act, the deputy must be acting within the scope of an authority expressly conferred on him by the court;

(b)   the deputy must reasonably believe that P lacks capacity in relation to the matter in question;

---

[84]   MCA 2005, s 16A, as inserted by MHA 2007, s 50.
[85]   MCA 2005, s 20(2).
[86]   MCA 2005, s 20(4)–(5).

(c)   the deputy must reasonably believe that it is necessary to do the act in order to prevent harm to P;

(d)   the act must be a proportionate response to—

(i)   the likelihood of P's suffering harm; and
(ii)   the seriousness of that harm.[87]

A deputy restrains P if he:

(a)   uses, or threatens to use, force to secure the doing of an act which P resists; or

(b)   restricts P's liberty of movement, whether or not P resists, or if he authorises another person to do any of those things.

Attorneys and deputies have significant powers to consent to or to refuse deprivation of liberty under the *Bournewood* Deprivation of Liberty safeguards in the Mental Capacity Act 2005. They may override the refusal of a patient who lacks capacity to agree to admission to a hospital or care home. They may also exercise a significant role in relation to patients' rights under the Mental Health Act 1983 (see **6.103** below).

THE DEPRIVATION OF LIBERTY SAFEGUARDS

6.64   Section 50 of the MHA 2007 amends the MCA 2005 to add provisions for the lawful deprivation of liberty of a person with a mental disorder, who lacks capacity to consent, if it is in that person's best interests. Section 50(2) inserts two new sections – 4A and 4B – into the MCA 2005. The effect of these will be that deprivation of liberty may only take place under the MCA in one of three situations. These are where:

(a)   the deprivation is authorised by a personal welfare decision of the Court of Protection under s 16(2)(a) of the MCA 2005; or

(b)   the deprivation is authorised in accordance with the deprivation of liberty procedures set out in Sch A1; or

(c)   the deprivation is carried out because it is necessary in order to give life sustaining treatment or to carry out a vital act to prevent serious deterioration in the person's condition 'while a decision as respects any relevant issue is sought from the court'.[88]

6.65   The MCA provisions for authorisation of deprivation of liberty apply to people who are over 18 (Children are dealt with under the MHA 1983 or under

---

[87]   MCA 2005, s 20(8)–(11).
[88]   MCA 2005, s 4B.

s 25 of the Children Act 1989). The person must lack capacity to consent to the arrangements for their care. Receiving care or treatment in circumstances that amount to a deprivation of liberty must be necessary to protect the person from harm and must be in their best interests.

Procedures for authorising deprivation of liberty in Sch A1

6.66 Schedule A1 to the MCA 2005 sets out procedures whereby the managing authority of a hospital or care home may obtain authorisation to deprive someone of their liberty for the purpose of giving them care or treatment. The 'managing authority' of the hospital or care home where the mentally incapacitated person is or is about to be deprived of their liberty will be responsible for requesting authorisation for deprivation of liberty from 'the supervisory body'. If an authorisation is obtained those who carry out the detention are protected against liability in battery or for wrongful imprisonment but not against liability in negligence, or for acting beyond the scope of the authorisation.[89]

The managing authority

6.67 The managing authority is responsible for applying for authorisations. In the case of an NHS hospital, the managing authority will be the NHS body responsible for the running of the hospital in which a person is, or is to be, a resident. In the case of a private hospital or care home, the managing authority will be the person registered, or required to be registered, under the Health and Social Care Act 2008, Part II in respect of the hospital or care home.[90] Managing authorities will require systems to identify when a deprivation of liberty of a mentally incapacitated person may be taking place.

The supervisory body: hospitals

6.68 The supervisory body is responsible for authorising deprivation of liberty. Where the DoLs provisions are applied to a person in a hospital situated in England, the supervisory body will be:

(a) if a PCT commissions the relevant care or treatment, that PCT;

(b) if the National Assembly for Wales or a Local Health Board in Wales commission the relevant care and treatment in England, the National Assembly for Wales;

(c) in any other case, the PCT for the area in which the hospital is situated.[91]

---

[89] MCA 2005, Sch A1, paras 3 and 4.
[90] MCA 2005, Sch A1, paras 167–170.
[91] MCA 2005, Sch A1, para 171.

The supervisory body in a case where the DoLs authorisations are applied to a person in a hospital situated in Wales will be the National Assembly for Wales unless an English PCT commissions the relevant care and treatment in Wales, in which case the PCT will be the supervisory body.[92]

The supervisory body: care homes

6.69   Whether the care home is situated in England or Wales, the supervisory body will be the local authority for the area in which the person is ordinarily resident. However, if the person is not ordinarily resident in the area of a local authority, the supervisory body is the local authority for the area in which the care home is situated.

Standard authorisations

6.70   A managing authority must request a standard authorisation when it appears to them to be likely that, either currently or at some time during the next 28 days, a present or future resident will be accommodated in their hospital or care home in circumstances that amount to a deprivation of liberty.[93] If a person who is subject to a standard authorisation moves to a different hospital or care home, the managing authority of the new hospital or care home must request a standard authorisation.[94] If a personal welfare order granted by the Court of Protection authorising deprivation of liberty is about to expire and the person will continue to be deprived of their liberty, the managing authority should apply in good time before the expiry of the Court of Protection order for a standard authorisation.[95] Standard authorisations are for a maximum period of 12 months and may be renewed. In *A County Council v MB (by the Official Solicitor as her litigation friend) and JB and A Residential Care Home*[96] Charles J held that it is good practice to record the actual time at which an urgent authorisation was given on the form recording its grant and, in any event, a record of that exact time should be kept. However, failure to include the precise time does not render urgent authorisation ineffective. Charles J stated that care needs to be taken in setting out the periods for which urgent and standard authorisations are given, setting out the following guidance on calculating the duration of urgent and standard authorisations:

> 'It would be good practice to record the actual time at which an urgent authorisation and a standard authorisation (which does not run from the expiry of, or a specified time before the expiry of, an existing standard authorisation) was given on the form recording its grant. In any event a record of the exact time on which all authorisations are given should be kept.

---

92   MCA 2005, Sch A1, para 172.
93   MCA 2005, Sch A1, para 24.
94   MCA 2005, Sch A1, para 25–26.
95   MCA 2005, Sch A1, para 27.
96   [2010] EWHC 2508 (COP), paras 35–43.

An approach that (a) includes the whole of the day on which the relevant period starts, and (b) ends at the end of the last day, would produce a result that the maximum period(s) allowed for urgent authorisations and their extension of 7 days, and allowed for standard authorisations, if that is set by a period of days, months or a year, were not exceeded.'

The difficulty in this case had arisen because the best interests assessor had considered that continued deprivation of liberty was not in MB's best interests, and so the standard authorisation could not be extended. Although the judge considered that the reasons for this refusal were flawed (because the BI assessor had not considered whether viable and practically available alternative placements were available) he considered that she could not be criticised – she had performed her role conscientiously and had a difficult, important and independent role to play. The best interests assessor's refusal caused a crisis since there was nowhere safe for Mrs B to be transferred to and so on 30 March 2010 the managing authority issued itself a further urgent authorisation. Pending the case coming before the Court of Protection, Chalres J held that the urgent authorisation was itself unlawful, and the correct approach would have been t make an interim application to the Court of Protection. The managing authority's attempt to rely on s 4B as the basis for continued detention, namely that the deprivation was necessary to administer life sustaining treatment or to carry out a vital act to prevent serious deterioration in MB's condition could not succeed because they had not addressed themselves to those criteria.

Independent persons

6.71 When a person is identified as potentially coming within the scope of the *Bournewood* provisions, the hospital or care home must establish whether there is a suitable independent person to look after their interests. The managing authority must notify the supervisory body if the managing authority concludes that there is nobody, other than a person engaged in providing care and treatment for the relevant person in a professional capacity or for remuneration, whom it would be appropriate to consult in determining the person's best interests. In such a case, the supervisory body must instruct an IMCA to represent the relevant person.[97]

Applications

6.72 Applications are governed by the Mental Capacity (Deprivation of Liberty: Standard Authorisations, Assessments and Ordinary Residence) Regulations 2008.[98] Rule 16(1) specifies the information which must be included in any application for a standard authorisation:

(a) name, gender, address, telephone number and age of the person. If age is not known the managing authority must state whether they believe the person to be over 18;

---

[97] MCA 2005, s 39A.
[98] SI 2008/1858.

(b)   name address and telephone number of the managing authority and of the person dealing with the request;

(c)   the purpose of the authorisation, the date from which it is sought, and information on whether there is an urgent authorisation in force in relation to the patient, and if so when it expires.

6.73   Rule 16(2) requires the managing authority to include in the request for a standard authorisation the following information if it is available or could reasonably be obtained by the authority:

(a)   any medical information relating to the relevant person's health that the managing authority considers to be relevant to the proposed restrictions to the relevant person's liberty;

(b)   the diagnosis of the mental disorder (within the meaning of the Mental Health Act 1983 but disregarding any exclusion for persons with learning disability) that the relevant person is suffering from;

(c)   any relevant care plans and relevant needs assessments;

(d)   the racial, ethnic or national origins of the relevant person;

(e)   whether the relevant person has any special communication needs;

(f)   details of the proposed restrictions on the relevant person's liberty;

(g)   whether section 39A of the Act (person becomes subject to Sch A1) applies;

(h)   where the purpose of the proposed restrictions to the relevant person's liberty is to give treatment, whether the relevant person has made an advance decision that may be valid and applicable to some or all of that treatment;

(i)   whether the relevant person is subject to:

    (i)   the hospital treatment regime,
    (ii)   the community treatment regime, or
    (iii)   the guardianship regime;

(j)   the name, address and telephone number of:

    (i)   anyone named by the relevant person as someone to be consulted about his welfare,
    (ii)   anyone engaged in caring for the person or interested in his welfare,
    (iii)   any donee of a lasting power of attorney granted by the person,
    (iv)   any deputy appointed for the person by the court, and

(v) any independent mental capacity advocate appointed in accordance with ss 37–39D of the Act; and

(k) whether there is an existing authorisation in relation to the detention of the relevant person and, if so, the date of the expiry of that authorisation.

If the request is for renewal of a standard authorisation and any of the information listed at 9(a)–(k) above remains the same as that supplied before, that information need not be supplied again.[99]

Qualifying requirements

6.74 Six qualifying requirements must be met for a standard authorisation to be granted. The supervisory body must carry out assessments of whether each of these requirements is met within 21 days of the request by the managing authority. If an urgent authorisation is already in force, the assessments must be completed during the currency of the urgent authorisation.[100]

6.75 No-one can carry out an assessment unless the supervisory body is satisfied that they have an enhanced criminal record certificate,[101] that they are insured in respect of any liabilities that might arise in connection with carrying out the assessment, and that they have the appropriate skills and experience to carry out the relevant assessment. The appropriate skills include, but are not limited to:[102]

'(a) an applied knowledge of the Mental Capacity Act 2005 and related Code of Practice; and

(b) the ability to keep appropriate records and to provide clear and reasoned reports in accordance with legal requirements and good practice.

(4) The supervisory body must be satisfied that there is in respect of the person–

(a) an enhanced criminal record certificate issued under section 113B of the Police Act 1997; or

(b) if the purpose for which the certificate is required is not one prescribed under subsection (2) of that section, a criminal record certificate issued pursuant to section 113A of that Act.

The qualifying requirements are set out below.

The age requirement

6.76 The person must be 18 or over. A person who is eligible to carry out a best interests assessment (see below) may carry out an age assessment.[103]

---

[99] Ibid, r 16(3).
[100] Ibid, r 13.
[101] Police Act 1997, s 113B.
[102] Mental Capacity (Deprivation of Liberty: Standard Authorisations, Assessments and Ordinary Residence) Regulations 2008, SI 2008/1858, r 3.
[103] Ibid, r 8.

The mental health requirement

6.77   The person must be suffering from mental disorder within the meaning of the Mental Health Act 1983, which will be any disorder or disability of mind. This is subject to the exception that a person with a learning disability can receive *Bournewood* safeguards whether or not the disability is associated with abnormally aggressive or seriously irresponsible conduct.[104] This assessment has to be carried out by a s 12 approved doctor or a registered medical practitioner who the supervisory body is satisfied has at least three years post registration experience in the diagnosis and treatment of mental disorder.[105] The supervisory body must also be satisfied that the assessor has 'successfully completed the Deprivation of Liberty Mental Health Assessors training programme made available by the Royal College of Psychiatrists.'[106] When carrying our a mental health assessment the assessor must consider how (if at all) the person's mental health is likely to be affected by his being a detained resident, and notify the best interests assessor of his conclusions.[107]

The mental capacity requirement

6.78   A person meets the mental capacity requirement if he lacks capacity in relation to the question whether or not he should be accommodated in the relevant hospital or care home for the purpose of being given the relevant care or treatment.[108] This assessment should be done in accordance with ss 1–3 of the Mental Capacity Act 2005, applying the principles in s 1 and starting from a presumption of capacity. The regulations for England specify that the mental capacity assessment can be undertaken by anyone who is eligible to act as a mental health or best interests assessor.[109] The Supplement to the Mental Capacity Act Code of Practice on the Deprivation of Liberty Safeguards states that 'In deciding who to appoint for this assessment, the supervisory body should take account of the need for understanding and practical experience of the nature of the person's condition and its impact on decision-making.'[110] Information relevant to the decision includes information about the consequences of deciding one way or another, and of failing to make a decision.[111] In *RT v LT and a Local Authority*[112] Sir Nicholas Wall P had to resolve the issue of the capacity of a 23-year-old with mild learning disability and significant unspecified disorder of social functioning and interaction to make decisions; (1) about where she should live; and (2) what contact she

---

[104]   Mental Capacity Act 2005, Sch A1, para 14.
[105]   Mental Capacity (Deprivation of Liberty: Standard Authorisations, Assessments and Ordinary Residence) Regulations 2008 SI 2008/1858, r 4.
[106]   Ibid, r 4(3).
[107]   Mental Capacity Act 2005, Sch A1, para 33.
[108]   Ibid, para 15.
[109]   Mental Capacity (Deprivation of Liberty: Standard Authorisations, Assessments and Ordinary Residence) Regulations 2008 SI 2008/1858, r 6.
[110]   Supplement to the Mental Capacity Act Code of Practice on the Deprivation of Liberty Safeguards Ministry of Justice (2008) TSO, para 4.31.
[111]   MCA 2005, s 3(4).
[112]   [2010] EWHC (Fam) 1910.

should have with members of her family. It was agreed between the parties that she met the criteria for impairment of, or disturbance in, the functioning of the mind or brain. As to functional ability LT avoided taking in information she did not want to hear. Sir Nicholas placed great reliance on the evidence of Dr K who felt that whilst this did not amount strictly to a failure to understand, but thought this trait reflected a refusal to receive the relevant information which did impair her ability to understand all relevant information. It was in relation to LT's ability to use information and weigh it in the balance to make a decision where Dr K considered the evidence of LT's incapacity was strongest. His views are summarised at paras 25 and 26 of the judgment:

'**25** As to using the information as part of the decision making process this was where Dr K believed that LT had the greatest difficulty, particularly in areas that were "emotionally laden". In his assessment of LT's capacity he noted particular difficulties in LT making balanced judgments, as she was only able to look at a problem from one perspective. The nature of her social disorder (whether it was an adult form of PDAS or RAD, or autistic spectrum) limited her ability to take in and weigh the relevant information and, in extreme circumstances, communicate it effectively. Thus, he concluded, she demonstrated strong dichotomous (black and white) thinking; for example, social workers were all bad and only lie; parents were all good and never had any problem.

26 Dr K was of the view that this trait would significantly impair LT's ability to weigh information in the balance in coming to a conclusion. Another difficulty was that she held very strong, often pre-formed, views. She was described as stubborn and strong-willed, and also did not like change. Dr K concluded, therefore, that cognitively LT may struggle to take on fresh information and synthesise that into a whole, particularly if it ran counter to her pre-formed views, or did not support her wishes.'

Sir Nicolas Wall P was convinced that 'on any view on Dr K's evidence, which I accept, LT is plainly not capable of using or weighing the information as part of the process of making the decision.' His Lordship went on to say that:[113]

'All this plainly applies to the decision about where she should live. In effect, the only thing she says is: "I want to go home". She cannot either discuss the matter or weigh the advantages and disadvantages of that course. That is the "wall" of which Dr K spoke, and in my judgment it is sufficient to make LT incapable of making the decision about where she should live.'

The best interests requirement

6.79 Four conditions must be met before the person meets the best interests requirement. The first is that the person is, or is to be, a detained resident. The second is that it is in that person's best interests to be a detained resident. The third condition is that it is necessary for him to be a detained resident in order to prevent harm to himself. Finally it must be a proportionate response to (a)

---

[113] Ibid, paras 41–42.

the likelihood of the person suffering harm, and (b) the seriousness of that harm, for him to be a detained resident.[114] In *A County Council* v *MB*[115] Charles J held that in determining best interests the best interests assessor should always have regard to the alternatives that are practically available.

6.80 Rule 5 of the Mental Capacity (Deprivation of Liberty: Standard Authorisations, Assessments and Ordinary Residence) Regulations 2008 provides that the best interests assessor must have at least two years post registration experience in one of the following professions, and not have been struck off the register:

(a)   an approved mental health professional;

(b)   a social worker registered with the General Social Care Council;

(c)   a first level nurse, registered in sub-Part 1 of the Nurses' Part of the Register maintained under art 5 of the Nursing and Midwifery Order 2001;[116]

(d)   an occupational therapist registered in Part 6 of the register maintained under art 5 of the Health Professions Order 2001;[117] or

(e)   a chartered psychologist who is listed in the British Psychological Society's Register of Chartered Psychologists and who holds a relevant practising certificate issued by that Society.

The assessor must also have successfully completed training approved by the Secretary of State for best interests assessors, and the supervisory authority must also be satisfied that the assessor has the skills necessary to obtain, evaluate and analyse complex evidence and differing views and to weigh them appropriately in decision-making.[118]

6.81 The best interests assessor must consult with the managing authority of the hospital or care home and must have regard to any relevant needs assessments and care plans prepared in connection with the relevant person being accommodated in the hospital or care home. The managing authority and supervisory body must provide the best interests assessor with any such needs assessment or care plan that has been undertaken by them, or on their behalf.[119] The best interests assessor must record in writing the name and address of every interested person consulted by him in determining the

---

[114]   Mental Capacity Act 2005, Sch A1, para 16.

[115]   [2010] EWHC 2085.

[116]   SI 2002/253.

[117]   SI 2002/254.

[118]   Mental Capacity (Deprivation of Liberty: Standard Authorisations, Assessments and Ordinary Residence) Regulations 2008 SI 2008/1858, r 5.

[119]   MCA 2005, Sch A1, para 39.

patient's best interests.[120] The best interests assessor must state the maximum recommended authorisation period, which may not exceed one year. The supervising body may not grant an authorisation for longer than the period recommended in the best interests assessment.[121] The best interests assessor may make recommendations about conditions to be attached to the authorisation, and if the supervisory body accepts such conditions the managing authority must ensure that they are complied with.[122]

Patient Representatives

6.82 Paragraph 131 of Sch A1 requires that the supervisory body must appoint a representative for a person in respect of whom a standard authorisation has been issued. Supervisory bodies are only able to appoint representatives who have been selected for that purpose. The role of the representative is to maintain contact with the person and to support and represent them in matters relating to their deprivation of liberty. The best interests assessor is also responsible for making recommendations about who should be appointed as the person's representative, and this process should begin as soon as the best interests assessor is appointed.[123]

The eligibility requirement

6.83 Whether a person is eligible for deprivation of liberty is to be determined in accordance with the new Sch 1A to the Mental Capacity Act. Assessment of eligibility may be undertaken by a section 12 doctor who is qualified to carry out mental health assessments, or an Approved Mental Health Professional who is qualified to carry out best interests assessments If the eligibility assessor and the best interests assessor are not the same person, the eligibility assessor must request that the best interests assessor provide him with any relevant eligibility information that the best interests assessor may have.[124]

6.84 A person is ineligible for *DoL* detention if s/he is subject to a hospital treatment obligation[125] under the MHA 1983 and will continue to be detained in hospital under that regime. A person will also be ineligible if the authorisation would be inconsistent with an obligation under the MHA 1983 to reside somewhere else. This will affect people who are on leave of absence from detention under the Mental Health Act 1983 or who are subject to guardianship, supervised community treatment or conditional discharge. Where a person is subject to neither the MHA nor the MCA regime, but is 'within the scope of the Mental Health Act 1983', they will be ineligible if a

---

[120] MCA 2005, Sch A1, para 40.

[121] MCA 2005, Sch A1, paras 42 and 51.

[122] MCA 2005, Sch A1, paras 43 and 53.

[123] Mental Capacity (Deprivation of Liberty: Appointment of Relevant Person's Representative) Regulations 2008, SI 2008/1315, r 10.

[124] Mental Capacity (Deprivation of Liberty: Standard Authorisations, Assessments and Ordinary Residence) Regulations 2008, SI 2008/1858, r 15.

[125] That is detained under ss 2, 3, 4, 35, 36, 37, 38, 44, 45A, 47, 48 or 51.

patient ('P') is within the scope of the 1983 Act if an application in respect of P could be made under s 2 or s 3 and P could be detained in hospital if an application were to be made.[126] A person who is 'within the scope of the Mental Health Act' will be ineligible for deprivation of liberty in a hospital under the Mental Capacity Act where:

(a) the proposed order of the Court of Protection or *Bournewood* authorisation will authorise the person to be a mental health patient, meaning 'a person accommodated in a hospital for the purpose of being given medical treatment for mental disorder'; and

(b) the patient objects—

    (i)   to being a mental health patient, or
    (ii) to being given some or all of the mental health treatment; and

(3) an attorney or deputy has not made a valid decision to consent to each matter to which P objects.[127] For a full discussion of the case law, see **6.35–6.38** above.

6.85 Refusal by the person himself will not render that person ineligible to be detained in a residential care home under the DoL safeguards. This raises an important issue, since people detained in residential care homes will be subject to the charging regime, whereas those detained in hospital will not.

The no refusals requirement

6.86 The 'no refusals' requirement will be met unless one of two situations appertains. The first is that the person has, when capable, made a valid advance decision refusing some or all of the treatment which would be provided if the authorisation were to be granted. The second is where the proposal to place the person in a hospital or care home in circumstances that amount to deprivation of the person's liberty, or to place them in the hospital or care home at all, would be in conflict with a valid decision of an attorney or a deputy appointed by the court. 'No refusals' assessments may be carried out by anyone eligible to carry out a best interests assessment.[128]

Issuing the standard authorisation

6.87 The supervisory body must give a standard authorisation if all assessments are positive, and they have written copies of all those assessments. If all the assessments are not positive, the supervisory body must not give a

---

[126] MCA 2005, Sch A1, para. 12.
[127] MCA 2005, Sch 1A, para 5.
[128] Mental Capacity (Deprivation of Liberty: Standard Authorisations, Assessments and Ordinary Residence) Regulations 2008 SI 2008/1858, r 9.

standard authorisation.[129] The Supplement to the Mental Capacity Act 2005 Code of Practice on the Deprivation of Liberty Safeguards states that:[130]

> 'If any of the assessments conclude that one of the requirements is not met, then the assessment process should stop immediately and authorisation may not be given. The supervisory body should:
>
> • inform anyone still engaged in carrying out an assessment that they are not required to complete it,
> • notify the managing authority, the relevant person, any IMCA involved and every interested person consulted by the best interests assessor that authorisation has not been given (a standard form is available for this purpose), and
> • provide the managing authority, the relevant person and any IMCA involved with copies of those assessments that have been carried out. This must be done as soon as possible, because in some cases different arrangements will need to be made for the person's care.

If the reason the standard authorisation cannot be given is because the eligibility requirement is not met, but the person needs in-patient treatment for mental disorder, it may be necessary to detain the person under the Mental Health Act 1983. The Code states that:[131]

> 'If this is the case, it may be possible to use the same assessors to make that decision, thereby minimising the assessment processes.'

6.88 A standard authorisation must be in writing and must state the following:

(a)   the name of the relevant person;

(b)   the name of the relevant hospital or care home;

(c)   the period during which the authorisation is to be in force;

(d)   the purpose for which the authorisation is given;

(e)   any conditions subject to which the authorisation is given;

(f)   the reason why each qualifying requirement is met.[132]

---

[129]   Mental Capacity Act 2005, Sch A1, para 50.
[130]   Supplement to the Mental Capacity Act 2005 Code of Practice on the Deprivation of Liberty Safeguards, (2008) para 5.18.
[131]   Ibid, para 5.19.
[132]   MCA 2005, Sch A1, paras 54 and 55.

Urgent authorisations

6.89 Paragraphs 67–83 of Sch A1 provide a procedure for a managing authority to issue an urgent authorisation authorising deprivation of liberty for up to seven days. A managing authority must give an urgent authorisation where it:

(a) is required to make a request to the supervisory body for a standard authorisation but believes that the need for a person to be deprived of liberty is so urgent that it is appropriate to begin the deprivation before the request is made; or

(b) has made a request for a standard authorisation but believes that the need for a person to be deprived of liberty has now become so urgent that it is appropriate to begin the deprivation before the request is dealt with by the supervisory body.[133]

The urgent authorisation must state the name of the person, the name of the hospital or care home, the period during which the authorisation is to be in force and the purpose for which the authorisation has been given.[134]

Extensions

6.90 An urgent authorisation may be extended only once where an application has been made for a standard authorisation and there are exceptional reasons why it has not been possible for the standard authorisation request to be disposed of, and it is essential for the existing detention to continue until the request is disposed of.[135] The Code of Practice gives an example where an extension might be justified if:

• it was not possible to contact a person whom the best interests assessor needed to contact,

• the assessment could not be relied upon without their input, and

• extension for the specified period would enable them to be contacted.[136]

The Code notes that whilst 'It is for the supervisory body to decide what constitutes an exceptional reason, because of the seriousness of the issues involved, the supervisory body's decision must be soundly based and defensible.'[137] The Code rules out using staffing shortages as a reason to extend an urgent authorisation. If an urgent authorisation cannot be extended and it is

---

[133] MCA 2005, Sch A1, para 69.
[134] MCA 2005, Sch A1, para 73.
[135] Ibid, para 77.
[136] Supplement to the Mental Capacity Act 2005 Code of Practice on the Deprivation of Liberty Safeguards, (2008) para 6.23.
[137] Ibid, para 6.24.

not possible to make a standard authorisation, but the managing authority considers that a deprivation of liberty is necessary to provide life sustaining treatment or to carry out a vital act under MCA s 4B, the correct course is to make an interim application to the Court of Protection. Charles J so held in *A County Council* v *MB*,[138] where the best interests assessor had withdrawn her assessment that the DoL was in MB's best interests, and the Local Authority tried to rectify the situation by way of a further urgent authorisation. Charles J held this course to be unlawful, and that if a local authority wishes to avail of s 4B of the MCA they must show that they have addressed their mind to the question whether the DoL is necessary to enable life sustaining treatment or a vital act to be carried out.

6.91 In *Re PS (incapacitated or vulnerable adult)*[139] Munby J said that where a court was authorising deprivation of liberty, the following minimum requirements must be satisfied in order to comply with Art 5:

'(1) The detention must be authorised by the court on application made by the local authority and *before* the detention commences.
(2) Subject to the exigencies of urgency or emergency the evidence must establish unsoundness of mind of a kind or degree warranting compulsory confinement. In other words, there must be evidence establishing at least a prima facie case that the individual lacks capacity and that confinement of the nature proposed is appropriate.
(3) Any order authorising detention must contain provision for an adequate review at reasonable intervals, in particular with a view to ascertaining whether there still persists unsoundness of mind of a kind or degree warranting compulsory confinement.'

Section 4 of the the MHA 1983 allows emergency admission, but requires that an application supported by one medical recommendation be completed prior to admission. This provides authority for the patient to be taken and conveyed to the relevant hospital. There is no procedure here for such emergency applications and there is no provision to take and convey someone to a hospital or care home where they urgently need *Bournewood* detention.

Review by the supervisory body

6.92 Part 8 of Sch A1 (paras 94–118) deal with reviews of standard authorisations. The managing authority is required to monitor each person's case and to request a review if one of the qualifying requirements appears to be reviewable. The person detained may request a review, as may their representative or the managing authority.[140] If such a request is made the supervisory body must carry out a review. They have a discretion themselves to carry out a review at any other time.

---

[138] [2010] EWHC 2085.
[139] [2007] EWHC 623 (Fam) at [23].
[140] MCA 2005, Sch A1, para 95.

6.93   A qualifying requirement may be reviewable on one of three grounds:

(a)   the relevant person does not meet all the qualifying requirements;

(b)   the reason why the relevant person meets a qualifying requirement is not
      the reason stated in the authorisation;

(c)   there has been a change in the relevant person's case and, because of the
      change, it would be appropriate to vary the conditions to which the
      authorisation is subject.

If none of the qualifying requirements appears to the supervisory body to be
reviewable, then it need take no further action. The supervisory body must,
however, carry out a separate review assessment of any requirement that
appears to be reviewable.[141]

Review by the Court of Protection

6.94   Article 5(4) of the European Convention on Human Rights requires that
anybody deprived of his liberty must be able to obtain speedy access to a court
for to review the lawfulness of their detention and order discharge if detention
is not lawful. Paragraph 2 of Sch 8 to the Mental Health Bill inserts a new
s 21A into the MCA 2005, giving the Court of Protection jurisdiction for this
purpose. In *Re GJ, NJ and BJ (Incapacitated Adults)*[142] Munby J said there
should be internal reviews at 8–10 weekly intervals, and court reviews every
twelve months. All reviews must consider the issues of capcity and best
interests, and at all internal reviews the patient must be represented by an
independent person. In *Salford City Council v BJ*,[143] BJ, one of the patients in
the earlier case, was not subject to Sch A1, *but* Munby J said that to comply
with Art 5 there should be the following internal and court reviews:

(a)   internal reviews by the local authority at 6-month intervals;

(b)   an additional internal review, to be called by the local authority and
      inviting BJ's representative, upon finding that there is a need for
      significant changes to the arrangements for BJ;

(c)   a review by the court in November 2010 at which, *inter alia*, the frequency
      of internal reviews thereafter can be reconsidered; and

(d)   reviews by the court every 12 months thereafter.

It would be appropriate for the court reviews to take place on the papers unless
one of the parties seeks an oral hearing, or unless the judge decides that an oral
hearing is appropriate.

---

[141]   MCA 2005, Sch A1, paras 103–104.
[142]   [2008] EWHC 1097 (Fam), [2008] 2 FLR 1295, at para [40].
[143]   [2009] EWHC 3310 (Fam) paras 26–28.

6.95 Where a standard authorisation has been given the Court of Protection may determine any question relating to:

(a) whether the person meets any of the qualifying requirements;

(b) the period for which the standard authorisation is to be in force;

(c) the purpose for which it has been given; or

(d) the conditions subject to which it has been given.

The court may make an order varying or terminating the authorisation or ordering the supervisory body to vary or terminate it.[144]

6.96 Where an urgent authorisation has been given the court may determine any question relating to:

(a) whether the urgent authorisation should have been given;

(b) the period during which the urgent authorisation is to be in force; or

(c) the purpose for which the urgent authorisation is given.

The court may make an order varying or terminating the urgent authorisation, or directing the managing authority of the relevant hospital or care home to vary or terminate the urgent authorisation.[145]

6.97 When making orders under s 21A, the court may make an order about a person's liability for any act done in connection with the standard or urgent authorisation before its variation or termination, and this includes an order excluding a person from liability.[146] In *YA(F)* v *YA(M), A Local Authority, A NHS Trust, and A Primary Care Trust,*[147] Charles J accepted the common ground between the parties that, by virtue of ss 7(1)(b) and 8(1) of the Human Rights Act 1998 and s 15(1)(c) of, Sch 6, para 43 to of the Mental Capacity Act 2005, the Court of Protection has jurisdiction to deal with claims based on Convention rights, and that, in reliance on Convention rights, relief by way of a declaration may be sought.[148] Not only did the court have jurisdiction to make declarations regarding the Convention rights of the incapacitated person, such jurisdiction also extended to making declarations as to the rights of his mother too. Charles J said this:[149]

---

[144] MCA 2005, s 21A(2)–(3).
[145] MCA 2005, s 21A(4)–(5).
[146] MCA 2005, s 21A(6)–(7).
[147] [2010] EWHC 2770 (COP).
[148] Ibid, paras 17–19.
[149] Ibid, para 24.

'Can it therefore be said that Parliament was intending that if a set of events occurs that impact the Article 8 rights of the members of the family of a person who lacks capacity, and those events are properly described as being an act or acts done in relation to the person who lacks capacity (P), the Court of Protection should not have jurisdiction to make declarations as to the lawfulness of such acts by reference to the Convention rights of, and on the application of, those members of the family? To my mind the answer to that question is "No", and that consideration of this question indicates that an ability (and thus a jurisdiction) to deal with such issues is within a secondary purpose of the legislation.'

6.98 His Lordship concluded that the Court of Protection had jurisdiction (a) to hear argument on behalf of the mother that acts done '*in relation to that person (ie the son)*' constitute breaches of her Convention rights, and (b) to make declarations as to the lawfulness of those acts on her application and in respect of breaches of her Convention rights as a result of such acts (ie acts done in relation to the son).[150] As to the issue of the jurisdiction of the Court of protection to award damages under the Human Right s Act 1998, Charles J concluded that there was such jurisdiction:[151]

'[T]he natural reading of section 47(1) in that context is that in exercising its jurisdiction (under the Human Rights Act or indeed the Mental Capacity Act) the Court of Protection has the same powers, rights, privileges and authority as the High Court would have when it is exercising its jurisdiction (under the Human Rights Act and generally) and, therefore, the Court of Protection has an ability to award damages under the Human Rights Act because the High Court can do so under s. 8(2) thereof because of its jurisdiction to award damages in civil claims.'

Hence the Court of Protection has by virtue of ss 15 and 47 of the MCA 2005 jurisdiction not just to make declarations about the Convention rights of incapacitated persons, but also, in an appropriate case in relation to their carers and families, and, again in an appropriate case, to award damages for breaches of Convention Rights.

Monitoring

6.99 Paragraph 153 of Sch A1 confers a regulation making power to enable a monitoring function for the DoL safeguards to be established and for a monitoring body or bodies to be designated as having the responsibility for discharging that function. The Government has conferred the monitoring function on the Care Quality Commission and has issued the Mental Capacity (Deprivation of Liberty: Monitoring and Reporting; and Assessments – Amendment) Regulations 2009 placing a duty on the Care Quality Commission to monitor the operation of the Deprivation of Liberty Safeguards and to report annually to the Secretary of State for Health.[152]

---

[150] Ibid, para 30.
[151] Ibid, paras 40–45.
[152] SI 2009/827, rr 2 and 3.

6.100 For the purpose of monitoring, or reporting on, the operation of Sch A1, the Commission is empowered to:

(a) visit hospitals and care homes;

(b) visit and interview persons accommodated in hospitals and care homes;

(c) require the production of, and inspect, records relating to the care or treatment of persons;

(d) accommodate in hospitals or care homes persons:

    (i) who are the subject of an authorisation under Sch A1; or

    (ii) whom the Commission has reason to consider ought to have been or should be the subject of an assessment under Sch A1.[153]

The Commission may also give the Secretary of State advice on the operation of Sch A1, and must give advice if the Secretary of State requests it.[154] Paragraph 155 of Sch A1 confers a further regulation making power on the monitoring body or bodies to require supervisory bodies and managing authorities of hospitals or care homes to disclose information to the monitoring body or bodies (including data on ethnicity).

6.101 The Care Quality Commission ('CQC') has issued guidance[155] on the MCA 2005 for providers. The CQC has indicated that it can 'set compliance actions and improvement actions, or take enforcement action under the Health and Social Care Act 2008 as a result of breaches of the Mental Capacity Act in certain circumstances, including circumstances where:[156]

> 'People are not being involved in decisions about their care, we can take action in relation to failure to comply with regulation 17 (outcome 1) of the essential standards of quality and safety.

> People are not being properly supported to consent to the care, treatment and support they receive, we can take action in relation to failure to comply with regulation 18 (outcome 2) of the essential standards.'

The CQC can also set 'compliance actions and improvement actions about relevant aspects of people's care, in situations including the following:[157]

> 'If assessments of capacity and decision-making are not being undertaken in a way that complies with the codes of practice, we can consider whether regulation 9 (outcome 4) of the essential standards is being met.

---

[153] Ibid, r 4.
[154] Ibid, r 5.
[155] The Care Quality Commission, *The Mental Capacity Act 2005: Guidance for Providers*, October 2010.
[156] Ibid, p 18.
[157] Ibid, p 19.

If we have concerns about the use of restraint and people's capacity to consent, we can consider whether regulation 11 (outcome 7) of the essential standards is being met.'

The CQC also has power to serve a warning notice about failure to comply with the Mental Capacity Act 2005, which is a 'relevant enactment' for the purposes of the Health and Social Care Act 2008.

6.102 If neither informal admission nor *Bournewood* authorisation is appropriate to authorise in-patient care without consent, consideration should be given to detention under the powers of compulsory admission in ss 2–4 of the MHA 1983. The Code of Practice on the MCA 2005 suggests that professionals 'may need to think about using the MHA to detain and treat somebody who lacks capacity to consent to treatment (rather than use the MCA)', if:

(a) it is not possible to give the person the care or treatment they need without doing something that might deprive them of their liberty;

(b) the person needs treatment that cannot be given under the MCA 2005 (for example, because the person has made a valid and applicable advance decision to refuse an essential part of treatment);

(c) the person may need to be restrained in a way that is not allowed under the MCA 2005;

(d) it is not possible to assess or treat the person safely or effectively without treatment being compulsory (perhaps because the person is expected to regain capacity to consent, but might then refuse to give consent);

(e) the person lacks capacity to decide on some elements of the treatment but has capacity to refuse a vital part of it – and they have done so;

(f) there is some other reason why the person might not get treatment, and they or somebody else might suffer harm as a result.[158]

The MCA Code stresses that before making an application under the MHA, decision-makers should consider whether they could achieve their aims safely and effectively by using the MCA instead. Compulsory treatment under the MHA is not an option if the patient's mental disorder does not justify detention in hospital, or the patient needs treatment only for a physical illness or disability. The order of preference is informal admission, followed by deprivation of liberty under the MCA, with detention under the MHA the last resort, if the powers available under the MCA are insufficient to manage the risk to the patient or others.

---

[158] Department of Constitutional Affairs *Code of Practice on the Mental Capacity Act 2005*, pp 225–226.

The role of attorneys and deputies in relation to patients subject to the Mental Health Act 1983

6.103 Not only may deputies and attorneys consent to or refuse a Deprivation of Liberty authorisation, they also have a significant role under the Mental Health Act 1983. The Code of Practice suggests that it is good practice for clinicians and others acting under the MHA to try and find out if the patient has an attorney or a deputy.[159] An attorney or a deputy may make decisions on behalf of a patient who is subject to detention under the Mental Health Act and may, if they have authority under the LPA or court appointment and the patient lacks capacity to do so, exercise the patient's various rights to apply to a MHT for discharge. A decision of an attorney or a deputy that results in the patient being in breach of conditions attached to guardianship, a CTO, or conditional discharge may result in the patient being recalled to hospital. As the Code of Practice notes, 'Attorneys and deputies may not exercise the rights of nearest relatives, unless they are themselves the nearest relative (because the rights belong to the nearest relative, not the patient).' There may be disagreement between the two, for example about whether the attorney should apply to the MHT or the NR should seek to discharge the patient, but ultimately … 'they have different roles, and each must act as they think best. Specifically, an attorney or deputy must act in accordance with their authority and in the patient's best interests.'[160]

POWERS OF COMPULSORY ADMISSION UNDER PART II

Overview

6.104 There are three powers under Part II which enable a person to be admitted compulsorily from the community, s 2 for assessment for up to 28 days, s 4 emergency admission for assessment for up to 72 hours, and s 3 for treatment for up to six months renewable. In the year 2009–2010, of the total of 30,774 patients admitted under Part II from the community to hospitals in England, 587 were detained under s 4, as against 18,345 admitted under s 2, and 9,545 under s 3. The remaining 2,257 were detained under the Part III offender provisions or under other Acts.[161] A total of 16,293 patients were subject to powers of detention when they were already in-patients.

6.105 In addition to people admitted from the community, over the year 6,009 people who were already psychiatric in-patients were admitted under s 2. Of these, 3,321 went direct from informal in-patient status in NHS hospitals and 70 in private hospitals. A further 2,618 informal NHS patients and 85 private

---

[159] The Mental Health Act 1983 Code of Practice (England) (2008), para 9.7.

[160] Ibid, para 9.10.

[161] National Statistics Information Centre NSIC *In-patients formally detained in hospitals under the Mental Health Act 1983 and subject to Supervised Community Treatment 2009–2010* (2010), Table 1. See http://www.ic.nhs.uk/statistics.

patients were held under s 5 of the Act and subsequently admitted for assessment. This makes a total of 24,354 uses of s 2 over the year 2009–2010.[162]

6.106 Whilst under one third of admissions under s 2 take place in hospital, almost half of admissions under s 3 take place in hospital; 9,545 admissions from the community as against 8,654 of people who were in-patients when the application was made. Of these, 4,521 were informal in-patients in NHS hospitals and 137 in private hospitals. A further 2,408 NHS and 72 private hospital informal patients were made subject to s 5 holding powers (see **6.121–6.131** below) and then detained under s 3. This makes a grand total of 16,683 s 3 detentions.[163]

Admission for assessment

6.107 Section 2 of the Act provides for compulsory admission for assessment for up to 28 days, which is non-renewable. If further detention is necessary, it must take place under s 3 or under the MCA 2005. An application may be made by an AMHP or the patient's nearest relative, supported by two medical recommendations, one of which must come from a doctor approved under s 12 of the MHA 1983 as having expertise in the diagnosis or treatment of mental disorder. The patient must be suffering from mental disorder of a nature or degree which warrants his detention in hospital for assessment or for assessment followed by medical treatment for at least a limited period. In contrast to the position under s 3 admissions, a person with a learning disability who does not exhibit without abnormally aggressive or seriously irresponsible conduct may be detained under s 2 for up to 28 days. This possibility remains following the entry into force of s 2(2) of the MHA 2007.

6.108 It must also be certified that the patient ought to be detained in the interests of his health *or* safety *or* for the protection of other persons. Where the patient meets the 'mental disorder of a nature or degree' criterion, detention may be implemented if necessary in the interests of the patient's own health (including mental health) and it is not necessary to wait until he or she is overtly dangerous to self or others. It is a common misconception that patients need to present some threat to their own safety or that of others before compulsory admission is possible. The MHA 1983 allows detention on 'strong paternalist' grounds, in the sense that a person may be detained in the interests of their own health.

6.109 The nearest relative (NR) of the patient may not block detention under s 2. If it is proposed to detain the patient under s 3 and the NR objects unreasonably, detention under s 2 is extended until the county court displacement proceedings are terminated. A patient detained under s 2 has the right to apply to the MHT for discharge once within the first 14 days following

---

[162] Ibid, Tables 1 and 6a and 6b.
[163] Ibid.

admission (see chapter 9).[164] Treatment for mental disorder of patients detained under s 2 is regulated by Part IV of the MHA 1983, and treatment for physical disorder by the MCA 2005 (see chapter 10).

Emergency admission for assessment

6.110 Section 4 of the MHA 1983 provides a power, to be used only in cases of urgent necessity, to admit compulsorily a patient for assessment for up to 72 hours. An application may be made either by an AMHP or the nearest relative and, although it requires only one medical recommendation, the application must state that it is of urgent necessity that the patient be admitted and detained for assessment, and that compliance with the full s 2 procedure would involve undesirable delay. The doctor giving the recommendation need not be s 12 approved. The form on which the medical recommendation is furnished requires information to be given which clarifies the nature of the emergency. It requires the doctor to estimate the delay which would be involved if the full requirements of s 2 were to be complied with, and to state that, in his or her opinion, such delay might result in harm to the patient, those caring for the patient or to other persons.

6.111 Although when it was introduced in 1959 this power was expected to be used only in exceptional circumstances, the equivalent procedure it was used much more frequently than envisaged, and at one time was the most frequently used power of compulsory admission. To ensure that the procedure is only used in genuine emergencies, new time limits were introduced. The applicant must have seen the patient within the previous 24 hours, and the patient must be admitted to hospital within 24 hours beginning with the time when the application was made or the time when he or she was medically examined, whichever is the earlier.[165] The authority to detain lasts for 72 hours from the time of the admission, unless the second medical recommendation required by s 2 is furnished to the managers within that period. The effect of such a conversion is that the 28 day authority to detain is deemed to have begun to run from the time of admission under s 4. Where s 4 is used, the patient is deprived of a fundamental safeguard at the time of initial detention in the form of an expert medical opinion from a doctor experienced in the diagnosis and treatment of mental disorder. Patients detained under s 4 do not have the right to apply to the MHT, nor do they become subject to the consent to treatment provisions in Part IV[166] unless they become liable to be detained under s 2 by the furnishing of the second medical recommendation.

Admission for treatment

6.112 Section 3 of the MHA 1983 provides for compulsory admission for treatment for up to six months renewable under s 20 for a further six months

---

[164] MHA 1983, s 66(1)(a), (2)(a).
[165] MHA 1983, ss 4(5) and 6(1)(b).
[166] The s 57 second opinion requirement still applies.

and thereafter for periods of 12 months at a time. The renewal procedure is explained in chapter 9. An application may be currently made by either the nearest relative or an AMHP and must be supported by medical recommendations given by two medical practitioners one of which must come from a s 12 approved doctor.

6.113   The criteria which must be met for detention under s 3 are:

(a)   the patient must be suffering from mental disorder of a nature or degree which makes it appropriate for the patient to receive medical treatment in a hospital; and

(b)   it must be necessary in the interests of his health or safety or for the protection of other persons that he should receive such treatment and that it must be the case that the treatment cannot be provided unless he is detained under this section; and

(c)   treatment must be available for the patient which is 'appropriate in his case, taking into account the nature and degree of the mental disorder and all other circumstances of his case'.[167]

The MHA 2007 has dispensed with the subcategories of mental disorder for the purposes of s 3 and replaces them with the definition 'any disorder or disability of mind' which will apply to all uses of compulsory powers under the Act (see chapter 3).

Nature or degree

6.114   In *R v Mental Health Review Tribunal for the South Thames Region, ex parte Smith*[168] Popplewell J held that:

'the word nature refers to the particular mental disorder from which the patient suffers, its chronicity, its prognosis, and the patient's previous response to … treatment. The word degree refers to the current manifestation of the patient's disorder.'

In *Smirek v Williams* Hale LJ said that:[169]

'[W]here there is a chronic condition, where there is evidence that the patient will deteriorate if medicine is not taken, I find it impossible to accept that it is not a mental illness of a nature or degree which makes it appropriate for the patient to be liable to be detained in hospital for medical treatment if the evidence is that, without being detained in hospital, the patient will not take the treatment.'

---

[167]   MHA 1983, s 3(2)(d), as inserted by MHA 2007, s 4.
[168]   [1999] COD 148.
[169]   [2002] MHLR 38 at para 19.

The test may therefore be satisfied if there is a patient with an illness of a serious nature, where the patient is not showing any severe symptoms, but where the patient has ceased taking medication and there is a history of serious relapse when medication is stopped. The illness, although not currently of a degree making detention appropriate, may nevertheless be of a sufficiently serious nature to satisfy the test.

6.115 The mental disorder must be of a nature or degree making it appropriate for the patient to receive treatment *in a hospital*. This means that the intention must be for the patient to receive treatment as an in-patient. In *R v Hallstrom, ex parte W (No 2)*[170] McCullough J said that:

> 'Admission for treatment under s 3 is intended for those whose condition is believed to require treatment as an in-patient.'

Section 3 cannot therefore be used when the intention is that the patient will be detained for a purely nominal period before being sent home on leave under s 17, and where the true purpose of the admission is to provide authority to impose treatment in the community.

Necessary in the interests of the patient's health or safety or for the protection of others and the treatment cannot be provided unless he is detained under this section

6.116 A patient need not be dangerous to him or herself or others in order to be detained. If detention in hospital is necessary in the interests of only one of the goals listed: health (including mental health) *or* safety, *or* the protection of others, this criterion will be met. The requirement to certify that the treatment cannot be provided without detention reflects the European Convention principle of proportionality or the US principle of the least restrictive alternative, namely that treatment should be provided if possible in the setting which imposes the least restrictions on the patient's freedom.

Availability of appropriate treatment

6.117 The so-called 'treatability test' has been abolished to be replaced by the test of availability of appropriate treatment (see chapter 3). Section 7 of the MHA 2007 changed the definition of medical treatment in s 145(1) of the MHA 1983 to state that it includes 'psychological intervention and specialist mental health habilitation, rehabilitation and care'. The addition of psychological interventions makes clear that treatments for personality disorder such as cognitive behaviour therapy are included within medical treatment. Medical treatment for mental disorder must have the purpose of alleviating, or preventing a worsening of, the disorder or one or more of its symptoms or manifestations. As the definition is inclusive, this is not an

---

[170] [1986] 2 All ER 306, QBD.

exhaustive list, and treatment also clearly includes treatments expressly mentioned in Part IV of the MHA 1983 such as medicines and Electro Convulsive Therapy.

6.118 A patient who is detained under s 3 has the right to apply to the MHT for discharge once within the first six months following admission, and once in each period for which the detention is renewed (see chapter 9).[171] Treatment for mental disorder of patients detained under s 2 is regulated by Part IV of the MHA 1983, and treatment for physical disorder by the Mental Capacity Act 2005 (see chapter 10).

When should s 2 be used and when s 3?

6.119 The question of which admission section should be used is a matter for professional judgment guided by the statutory criteria. The only difference in scope of the respective powers relates to learning disability where abnormally aggressive or seriously irresponsible conduct is needed for detention under s 3 but not s 2. The Code of Practice suggests s 2 should be used in the following cases:

- the full extent of the nature and degree of a patient's condition is unclear;

- there is a need to carry out an initial in-patient assessment in order to formulate a treatment plan, or to reach a judgement about whether the patient will accept treatment on a voluntary basis following admission; or

- there is a need to carry out a new in-patient assessment in order to re-formulate a treatment plan, or to reach a judgement about whether the patient will accept treatment on a voluntary basis.

As for s 3, this should be used when the patient is already detained under s 2 and continued detention is necessary, or where 'the nature and current degree of the patient's mental disorder, the essential elements of the treatment plan to be followed and the likelihood of the patient accepting treatment on a voluntary basis are already established.'[172]

APPLICATION FOR DETENTION OF SOMEONE WHO IS ALREADY AN IN-PATIENT

6.120 A patient who initially consents to admission but later seeks to leave hospital may be restrained from doing so using the doctor's, approved clinician's, or nurse's holding power under s 5 of the MHA 1983.

---

[171] MHA 1983, s 66(1)(b), (f), (2)(b), (f).
[172] Code of Practice on the Mental Health Act 1983 (England) (2008), paras 4.26–4.27.

The doctor's (and AC's) holding power

6.121 Section 5(2) confers a holding power on the registered medical practitioner or Approved Clinician ('AC') in charge of the treatment of an in-patient in any hospital, not necessarily a psychiatric one. Section 9 of the MHA 2007 has amended s 5 to extend the power to ACs (see chapter 4). If the doctor or AC considers that an application for compulsory admission needs to be made, s/he should furnish a report to the hospital managers to that effect. Where this happens, the patient may be detained in hospital for a period of 72 hours from the time when the report was furnished.

6.122 In-patient for the purposes of this section does not include anyone who is already liable to be detained or who is a community patient under the 1983 Act. It refers to anyone receiving in-patient care or treatment without being subject to the use of compulsory powers under the Mental Health Act and includes patients who are in hospital by virtue of a Deprivation of Liberty authorisation under the Mental Capacity Act 2005. Section 5 cannot be used for an out-patient attending a hospital's accident and emergency department, and in such cases informal admission procedures should not be implemented with the sole intention of then using s 5(2).[173] The power may be used in the case of a person receiving treatment for a physical condition in a general hospital, provided s/he is an in-patient. The holding power may not be used in respect of a patient who is liable to be detained or is a community patient, so it cannot be used to hold someone in hospital who has been recalled to hospital from a CTO.[174]

6.123 Section 5(3) permits the doctor or AC in charge of the patient's treatment to nominate 'one (but not more than one) other registered medical practitioner or AC on the staff of the hospital to act for him … in his absence.' Only one deputy may be nominated at a time, and it is unlawful for the nominated deputy to delegate the power to someone else.[175]

6.124 The purpose of detention is to enable the assessment necessary for admission under either s 2 or s 3 to take place. Section 5(2) should not therefore be seen as an independent power of short term detention but as a *holding power* to enable a full assessment to be made. This being so, arrangements for such an assessment should be set in train immediately the holding power is implemented. The Code of Practice states that 'Although the holding power lasts for a maximum of 72 hours, it should not be used to continue to detain patients after:

- the doctor or approved clinician decides that, in fact, no assessment for a possible application needs to be carried out; or

- a decision is taken not to make an application for the patient's detention.

---

[173] Ibid, para 12.7.
[174] MHA 1983 s 5(6).
[175] Ibid, para 12.12.

6.125 The Code then emphasises that patients should be informed immediately that they are no longer detained under the holding power and are free to leave the hospital, 'unless the patient is to be detained under some other authority, such as an authorisation under the deprivation of liberty safeguards in the Mental Capacity Act 2005.'[176]

'Detention under section 5(2) will end immediately, where:

(a)   an assessment for admission under s 2 or 3 is made and a decision is taken not to make an application for detention under s 2 or 3;
(b)   the doctor decides that no assessment for possible detention under s 2 or 3 needs to be carried out.[177]

In such a case the Code advises that the patient should be informed that he or she is no longer detained under the holding power, and the decision, the reasons for it, and its time should be recorded. Detention under s 5(2) or 5(4) cannot be renewed, but the Code states that this does not prevent it being used again on a future occasion if necessary.'[178] Patients detained under s 5(2) may not be transferred to another hospital under s 19 (because they are not detained by virtue of an application made under Part 2 of the Act).[179]

The nurse's holding power

6.126 The second power is the nurse's holding power under s 5(4). This enables a nurse 'of the prescribed class' to hold an in-patient in a psychiatric ward or hospital for not more than six hours. During that time the doctor or AC in charge of the patient's treatment or his or her deputy should attend to determine whether the managers should be furnished with a report under s 5(2). A nurse of the prescribed class is currently defined as:

'A nurse registered in sub-part 1 or 2 of the register maintained by the Nursing and Midwifery Council whose entry in the register indicates that their field of practice is either mental health nursing or learning disability nursing.'

The decision to invoke the power is the personal decision of the nurse, who cannot be instructed to exercise the power by anyone else.[180]

6.127 The nurses' holding power can only be used where the patient is receiving treatment for mental disorder as an in-patient. The holding power may not be used in respect of a patient who is liable to be detained or is a community patient, so it cannot be used to hold someone in hospital who has been recalled to hospital from a CTO.[181] The grounds for its use are: (a) that the patient is suffering from mental disorder to such a degree that it is necessary

---

176   Ibid, para 12.19.
177   Ibid, paras 12.19–12.20.
178   Ibid, para 12.36.
179   Mental Health Act Commission Practice Note 3 (March 1994)
180   Department of Health *Code of Practice: Mental Health Act 1983* (2008), para 12.25.
181   MHA 1983 s 5(6).

for his or her health or safety or for the protection of others that s/he be immediately restrained from leaving hospital; and (b) that it is not practicable to secure the immediate attendance of a practitioner (or clinician) for the purpose of furnishing a report under s 5(2). The patient may be detained from the moment the nurse makes the necessary record. The record must then be sent to the hospital managers.[182]

6.128 The nurse must record in writing on a statutory form the fact that the above criteria are satisfied, and must deliver the completed form to the managers or their appointed officer as soon as possible after completion.[183] The reasons for invoking the power must be entered in the patient's nursing and medical notes and that a local incident report form should be sent to the managers. If, following the exercise of the nurse's holding power, the doctor exercises his holding power under s 5(2), s 5(5) provides that the seventy-two hour period runs from the time the nurse furnishes the s 5(4) report to the managers. It is worth noting that this power can be used only where an informal patient is receiving treatment as an in-patient for mental disorder; it cannot, for example be used on a general hospital ward where the patient is receiving treatment for a physical disorder. The Code of Practice on the Mental Health Act 1983 published in 1999 stated explicitly that 'A nurse invoking section 5(4) is entitled to use the minimum force necessary to prevent the patient from leaving hospital.'[184] This passage no longer appears in the 2008 version of the Code, but it must remain correct as a statement of the law.

6.129 The nurse's holding power may only be used to restrain the patient from leaving hospital. Where a patient requires restraint or seclusion but is not showing any inclination to leave the hospital, staff may act in reliance on other statutory and common law powers. Section 3(1) of the Criminal Law Act 1967 allows a person to use 'such force as is reasonably in the circumstances in the prevention of crime'. The common law allows for reasonable force to be used in self-defence, for the defence of others, or to prevent a breach of the peace. Reasonable steps to prevent the breach of the peace can include detaining the person against his will.[185] A breach of the peace can take place in either a public or a private place where a person is in fear of being harmed through an assault, an affray, an unlawful assembly or other disturbance.[186] These powers apply regardless of whether the person has capacity. They can only be used to justify detention or restraint within the hospital insofar as it is reasonably necessary, and only for so long as the risk of breach of the peace or crime subsists. Hence, they would not authorise any restraint or seclusion to continue after the risk had passed.

---

[182] Ibid, para 12.24.
[183] Mental Health (Hospital Guardianship and Treatment) (England) Regulations 2008 SI 2008/1184, reg 4 and Form H2.
[184] Department of Health and Welsh Office *Mental Health Act 1983 Code of Practice* (1999), para 9.6.
[185] *Albert v Lavin* [1982] AC 546, HL.
[186] *R v Howell* [1982] QB 416, CA.

6.130 Sections 5 and 6 of the MCA 2005 provide a legal defence for anyone who takes action that is reasonably believed to be in the best interests of a person who is reasonably believed to lack capacity in relation to the decision to remain in hospital. This includes reasonable restraint where the restraint is imposed to prevent harm to a patient who lacks capacity and is a proportionate response both to the likelihood of harm and the severity of the harm. In order for the action to be lawful the person taking it must have taken reasonable steps to determine whether the person has capacity in relation to the relevant decision, must reasonably believe that the person indeed lacks capacity, and must reasonably believe that what they are doing is in the person's best interests.

CONCLUSION

6.131 The MHA 1983 and the MCA 2005 provide ample powers to deprive mentally disordered people of their liberty. As we have seen, a key issue is the interface between the two Acts and the decision when to use which regime. The MCA Deprivation of Liberty safeguards are complex and voluminous. Schedules A1 and 1A have 205 paras and occupy 53 of the MHA 2007's 168 pages, all for one procedure. The Joint Committee on Human Rights was critical of this complexity:

> 'In *HL v United Kingdom* the Court held (at para 114) that "an important ingredient of lawfulness is that all law must be sufficiently precise to allow the citizen – if need be with appropriate advice – to foresee, to a degree that is reasonable in the circumstances, the consequences which a given action might entail". The proposals to amend the Mental Capacity Act are detailed and complex, and we question whether they will be readily understood.'

This prompts the question whether, and in what circumstances, the simpler and more familiar procedure of guardianship can be used as an alternative to theDoL authorisations. The MHA 2007 introduces a power to take and convey a person to their place of residence under guardianship.[187] Where the Act gives a power to return a person to a place of required residence, a new s 18(7) complements that with a power to take the person there initially – if they have 'yet to comply with a requirement imposed by virtue of this Act to be in a hospital or place'. Guardianship therefore carries the power to require residence at a specified place, to take and convey the person to that place and to bring them back if they abscond. The guardian can also require the person to attend for treatment, work, training or education at specific times and places, and they can demand that a doctor, approved social worker or another relevant person have access to the person wherever they live. It does not, however, give anyone the right to treat the person without their permission or to consent to treatment on their behalf, although the MCA 2005 would apply if the person lacks capacity.

---

[187] MHA 1983, as amended by the MHA 2007, Sch 3, para 3(5).

6.132   The powers of the guardian are discussed in full in chapter 8. It is clear that they are capable of authorising a degree of control over residence, movement and treatment which could amount to deprivation of liberty. There is nothing in the MHA 1983 to say that guardianship cannot authorise deprivation of liberty, but the MCA Code is emphatic that whilst guardianship confers 'the exclusive right to decide where a person should live ... in doing this they cannot deprive the person of their liberty'. The Code goes on to say that: 'Decision-makers must never consider guardianship as a way to avoid applying the MCA.'[188]

6.133   The MCA Code goes on to outline the following possible situations in which guardianship might be considered in relation to a mentally disordered person who lacks capacity to make important decisions about their own welfare:

(a)   where it is thought to be important that decisions about where the person is to live are placed in the hands of a single person or authority over a continuing period – for example where there have been long-running or particularly difficult disputes about where the person should live;

(b)   where the person is thought likely to respond well to the authority and attention of a guardian, and so be more willing to comply with necessary treatment and care for their mental disorder (whether they are able to consent to it, or it is being provided for them under the MCA 2005);

(c)   where there is a particular need to have explicit authority for the person to be returned to the place the person is to live (eg a care home).[189]

6.134   By contrast to the DoL procedures, guardianship has the advantage of clear Convention compliance. If the procedure must be initiated before the patient is removed to hospital or care home, guardianship must be implemented prior to the detention taking place, the DoL procedures need not. Guardianship is familiar to mental health professionals, and is more accessible to patients, carers, and their advisers. It occupies only a few pages of statute and Code of Practice. It could be used to authorise control of a degree and intensity to amount to a deprivation of liberty. The patient or nearest relative may apply for discharge to the managers or to the MHT, which is more likely than the Court of Protection to be in a position to meet the requirements of Art 5(4) that access to such review is speedy, and that legal representation is available.[190] The main limitations on using guardianship as an alternative to the DoL procedures are the exclusion in relation to learning disability without abnormally aggressive or seriously irresponsible conduct, and the right of the nearest relative to block a guardianship application.

---

[188]   Department of Constitutional Affairs *Mental Capacity Act 2005 Code of Practice* (2007), paras 13.16–13.20.
[189]   Ibid, para 13.20.
[190]   *Megyeri v Germany* (1992) 15 EHRR 584, ECtHR.

6.135   The introduction of a power to initiate a deprivation of liberty under the MCA 2005 has added massive complication to the interface with the MHA 1983, mostly for the purpose of ensuring that some groups have their liberty removed under the supposedly more benign MCA without the stigma of a MHA section. It has also generated a voluminous case law where days of argument in the High Court, usually with at least three counsel, have been deployed to the purpose of deciding whether a person has been deprived of his or her liberty, or whether that deprivation is in her or his best interests. Guardianship could provide an effective procedural alternative, with safeguards which do not depend on the finer intricacies of whether the person is deprived of liberty. Without diminishing the importance of vigilance in protecting people against arbitrary detention, there can be a certain sympathy with the argument advanced on behalf of the local authority in *P and Q* v *Surrey County Council* by Barbara Hewson QC that in an era of shrinking resources it was undesirable for the court to be used as a moot or a seminar where interesting issues are discussed which have no practical bearing on the outcome for those subject to the alleged deprivation of liberty.[191] P and Q would stay where they were whatever the outcome of these expensive and lengthy arguments, because everyone agreed that it was in their best interests to be in those placements. Guardianship would apply whether or not the restrictions on the patient amounted to a deprivation of liberty, and a tribunal could decide whether such restrictions as are applied meet the test of proportionality.

---

[191]   [2011] EWCA Civ 190, para 46.

Chapter 7

DETENTION OF MENTALLY DISORDERED OFFENDERS

OUTLINE

7.1 This chapter considers police powers relating to mentally disordered people under ss 135 and 136 of the MHA 1983, the factors determining whether a mentally disordered offender will be prosecuted, the special procedures and defences which apply to mentally disordered and mentally vulnerable suspects and defendants, and finally the sentencing and other disposals available in such cases. The chapter also outlines the powers of the criminal courts to remand mentally disordered defendants to hospital for treatment and for reports, as well as their power to impose hospital orders under s 37 or hospital directions under s 45A of the MHA 1983. The Secretary of State for Justice has assumed the roles formerly occupied by the Home Secretary in relation to the power to transfer mentally disordered prisoners to psychiatric hospital, and the Home Office Mental Health Unit has been transferred to the Ministry of Justice.

7.2 Where a crown court makes a hospital order under MHA 1983, s 37 in respect of a mentally disordered offender it may attach a restriction order under s 41 where it is necessary for the protection of the public from serious harm to impose restrictions on discharge. Where a crown court makes a hospital direction under s 45A, it attaches a restriction direction. Where a prisoner is transferred to hospital, the Minister of Justice may impose a restriction direction. The Ministry of Justice Mental Health Unit supervises the care of offenders who are subject to restriction orders and restriction directions. The MHA 2007 applies the new broad definition of mental disorder to all these powers including the hospital direction which has hitherto only been available for patients with psychopathic disorder. The 2007 Act also removes the possibility for a restriction order to be time limited and provides that all restriction orders shall in future be without limit of time. This provision is already in force. Finally, this chapter considers the MHA 2007 amendments to the rights of victims of crimes committed by mentally disordered offenders under the Domestic Violence, Crime and Victims Act 2004.

BACKGROUND

7.3 Criminal justice policy towards mentally disordered people rests on three basic principles. The first, exemplified in the Police and Criminal Evidence

Act 1984, is that mentally disordered suspects should be subject to special safeguards surrounding their treatment in custody, since they may be particularly prone to make false confessions; the second, elaborated in *Home Office Circular 66/90* is that mentally disordered suspects and offenders should be diverted away from the penal system and into the health and social care system. The policy of diversion was re-emphasised in the Guidance Booklet issued by the Home Office and the Department of Health in 1995 M*entally Disordered Offenders: Inter-Agency Working Produced by the Home Office and the Department of Health*, since reissued by the National Offender Management Service. The 1995 Guidance restates Government policy as being to promote inter-agency working so that:

> '[T]hose suffering from mental disorder who require specialist medical treatment or social support should receive it from the health and social services. Those who are suspected of committing criminal offences should be prosecuted where this is necessary in the public interest. In deciding whether a person should be charged, it is essential that account is taken of the circumstances and gravity of the offence and what is known of the person's previous contacts with the criminal justice system and the psychiatric and social services.'

7.4 More recently the Bradley Report: Lord Bradley's review of people with mental health problems or learning disabilities in the criminal justice system[1] has reaffirmed the policy that mentally disordered suspects and offenders should be diverted away from the penal system and into the health and social care system. Bradley defined 'diversion' as 'a process whereby people are assessed and their needs identified as early as possible in the offender pathway (including prevention and early intervention), thus informing subsequent decisions about where an individual is best placed to receive treatment, taking into account public safety, safety of the individual and punishment of an offence.'[2] Two ideas underpin the policy of diversion: the first is that mental disorder may reduce the person's culpability for their criminal acts; the second that they will be vulnerable to suicide and self harm.

7.5 The third principle, which has come to dominate the discourse of mental health law reform since the early 1990s, is that the public require protection against the risk posed by mentally disordered people.

7.6 It is estimated that a significant proportion of the prison population suffer from mental health problems, with over half of female and three quarters of male prisoners suffering from personality disorders, neurotic disorders being found in 40 per cent of male prisoners and 76 per cent in females. Six per cent of male sentenced prisoners and 13 per cent of all female prisoners were estimated to have a schizophrenic illness, and between 1 and 2 per cent of

---

1   The Bradley Report: Lord Bradley's review of people with mental health problems or learning disabilities in the criminal justice system April 2009. <http://www.dh.gov.uk/en/Publicationsandstatistics/Publications/PublicationsPolicyAndGuidance/DH_098694>.

2   Ibid, p 16.

prisoners have affective psychosis.[3] Given these high levels of psychiatric morbidity in the prison population, and the high risk of suicide and self-harm, it is important to recognise the limits of any policy of diversion of mentally disordered offenders from prison to hospital. Lord Bradley defined 'Offenders with mental health problems' as:[4]

'Those who come into contact with the criminal justice system because they have committed, or are suspected of committing, a criminal offence, and who may be acutely or chronically mentally ill. It also includes those in whom a degree of mental disturbance is recognised, even though it may not be severe enough to bring it within the criteria laid down by the Mental Health Act 1983.'

Hence, despite the broad definition of mental disorder as any disorder or disability of the mind which is of a nature or degree warranting detention in hospital for treatment, not all prisoners with psychiatric problems are viewed as being detainable under the Mental Health Act 1983, and if they were, there would not be enough beds.

7.7 The prison population in England and Wales is over 85,000,[5] and the total number of in-patient beds in psychiatric hospitals is around 30,000. On 31 March 2010 there were 16,622 patients detained in hospital, of whom 12,832 were in NHS hospitals (including the three high security special hospitals Ashworth, Broadmoor and Rampton), and 3,790 in private hospitals. In 2009–2010 there were 30,774 admissions from the community under powers of detention in the Mental Health Act 1983, 2,191 of which occurred under the offender provisions of the Act. Compulsory admissions under both non-offender and offender provisions have been steadily increasing since 2006.[6] Both the prison system and the psychiatric hospital system are running at full stretch, and the capacity of the psychiatric system to cope with treating greater numbers of mentally disordered offenders is strictly limited. Those who are transferred from prison to hospital tend to be people who are exhibiting acute symptoms of mental illness of a psychotic nature, or people with personality disorder who are perceived to pose a risk to the public requiring continued detention, are nearing the end of a determinate sentence, and whose detention can only be continued if they are transferred to hospital under the MHA 1983.

---

[3] C Brooker, J Repper, C Beverley, M Ferriter and N Brewer *Mental Health Services and Prisoners: A Review* (2002), p 8. See http://www.dh.gov.uk/en/Publicationsandstatistics/Publications/PublicationsPolicyAndGuidance/DH_4084149.

[4] Bradley Report, op cit, n 1, p 17.

[5] HM Prison Service, Population Bulletin February 25 2011: http://www.hmprisonservice.gov.uk.

[6] NHS Information Centre, In-Patients Formally Detained under the Mental Health Act 1983 and Patients Subject to Supervised Community Treatment: England 2009–2010, Health and Social Care Information Centre 2010, Table 1.

POLICE POWERS TO REMOVE A MENTALLY DISORDERED PERSON TO A PLACE OF SAFETY: MENTAL HEALTH ACT 1983, SS 135–136

7.8 This section considers police powers to remove to a 'place of safety' a person who is reasonably believed to be suffering from mental disorder, either by an AMHP and a police officer with a warrant, from private premises (s 135) or by a police officer from a public place (s 136). The purpose of removal to a place of safety is to enable the person to be assessed by an AMHP and a doctor. The exercise of this power is covered in Chapter 10 of the Department of Health *Code of Practice on the Mental Health Act 1983*, and Chapter 7 of the Welsh Assembly Government *Mental Health Act 1983 Code of Practice for Wales*.

Power to obtain a warrant to enter premises

7.9 Section 135(1) of the MHA 1983 confers a power on a magistrate to issue a warrant authorising a police officer to enter private premises, using force if necessary, and, 'if thought fit', to remove a person to a place of safety with a view to the making of an application under Part II, or of other arrangements for his treatment or care. A warrant may only be granted where an information has been laid on oath by an AMHP stating reasonable cause to suspect that a person believed to be suffering from mental disorder has been or is being ill-treated, neglected or kept otherwise than under proper control, or is living alone and unable to care for himself. The Department of Health Code of Practice suggests that local authorities should issue guidance to AMHPs on how and when to use the power to apply for a warrant.[7]

7.10 Section 135(2) confers a similar power on magistrates, to grant a warrant authorising entry by any constable, if need be by force, onto premises to remove a patient who is 'liable to be taken or retaken' under English or Scottish mental health legislation. Police constables are among those listed in s 18(1) and 18(3) of the 1983 Act as having the power to retake patients who are absent from a hospital where they are liable to be detained, or from the place where they are required to live by their guardian. They are also empowered to retake patients who escape from a place of safety or any place where they are in lawful custody, or who escape whilst being taken and conveyed.[8] The Department of Health Code of Practice says that patients are considered to be absent without leave for the purposes of s 18 when they:[9]

'• have left the hospital in which they are detained without their absence being agreed (under section 17 of the Act) by their responsible clinician;
• have failed to return to the hospital at the time required to do so by the conditions of leave under section 17;

---

[7] Department of Health *Code of Practice: Mental Health Act 1983* (2008), para 10.7.
[8] MHA 1983, s 138.
[9] Department of Health *Code of Practice: Mental Health Act 1983* (2008), para 22.2.

- are absent without permission from a place where they are required to reside as a condition of leave under section 17;
- have failed to return to the hospital when their leave under section 17 has been revoked;
- are supervised community treatment (SCT) patients who have failed to attend hospital when recalled;
- are SCT patients who have absconded from hospital after being recalled there;
- are conditionally discharged restricted patients whom the Secretary of State for Justice has recalled to hospital; or
- are guardianship patients who are absent without permission from the place where they are required to live by their guardian.'

Where a person who has escaped is on private premises there is a power to seek a warrant under s 135(2), but in limited circumstances the police may have authority to enter premises forcibly without a warrant. In *D'Souza v Director of Public Prosecutions*[10] the House of Lords held that a patient who is absent without leave and liable to be retaken is 'unlawfully at large' within the meaning of s 17(1)(d) of the Police and Criminal Evidence Act 1984, which authorises forcible entry for the purpose of recapturing persons who are 'unlawfully at large, and whom the police are pursuing. In *D'Souza* police officers entered the premises of a patient who was absent without leave. The Law Lords held that a police constable cannot exercise the power of entry and search of the premises under s 17(1) (d) of the 1984 Act for the purposes of retaking a person who is unlawfully at large and whom he is pursuing, unless the pursuit is almost contemporaneous with the entry into the premises. Thus there has to be a pursuit or chase however short in time or distance, before the power of forcible entry may be used.

7.11 The Department of Health Code of Practice states that hospital managers and local authority social services departments should have policies, agreed with the police, which cover the following:[11]

- the immediate action to be taken by any member of staff who becomes aware that a patient has gone missing, including a requirement that they immediately inform the professional in charge of the patient's ward (where applicable), who should in turn ensure that the patient's responsible clinician is informed;

- the circumstances in which a search of a hospital and its grounds should be made;

- the circumstances in which other local agencies with an interest, including the LSSA, should be notified;

---

[10] [1992] 1 WLR 1073.
[11] Department of Health *Code of Practice: Mental Health Act 1983* (2008), paras 22.10–22.12.

- the circumstances in which the police should be informed, who is responsible for informing the police and the information they should be given (this should be in line with local arrangements agreed with the police);

- how and when other people, including the patient's nearest relative, should be informed (this should include guidance on informing people if there is good reason to think that they might be at risk as a result of the patient's absence);

- when and how an application should be made for a warrant under section 135(2) of the Act to allow the police to enter premises in order to remove a patient who is missing; and

- how and by whom patients are to be returned to the place where they ought to be, and who is responsible for organising any necessary transport.

7.12 The Code suggests that the police should be asked to assist in returning a patient to hospital only if necessary.[12] However, the police should always be informed immediately if a patient is missing who is:[13]

- considered to be particularly vulnerable;

- considered to be dangerous; or

- subject to restrictions under Part III of the Act.

Finally, the Code says 'there may also be other cases where, although the help of the police is not needed, a patient's history makes it desirable to inform the police that they are AWOL in the area.'

7.13 To obtain a warrant under s 135(2), an information must have been laid by a constable, AMHP or other person authorised to take or retake the patient, to the effect that:

(a) there is reasonable cause to believe that the patient is to be found on premises within the jurisdiction of the justice; and

(b) that admission to the premises has been refused or that a refusal of such admission is apprehended.

The Department of Health Code suggests that when a warrant under s 135(2) is used to gain access it is good practice for the police officer to be accompanied by a person authorised by the hospital, and for patients on supervised

---

[12] Ibid. para 22.13. see also *Dunn v South Tyneside Health Care NHS Trust* [2003] EWCA Civ 878; [2004] MHLR 74.
[13] Ibid, para 22.14

community treatment, if practicable, this should be a member of the multi-disciplinary team. Good planning should mean that it is 'almost never' necessary to use a police station as a place of safety under s 135.[14] During 2009–2010 there were 262 admissions to hospitals under s 135, 150 men and 112 women.[15]

7.14 In executing a warrant under s 135(1) the police officer must be accompanied by an AMHP and a doctor. The Department of Health Code says that 'It may be helpful if the doctor who accompanies the police officer is approved for the purposes of section 12(2) of the Act.'[16] The Department of Health Code of Practice also states that local social services authorities (LSSAs) and hospital managers should ensure that there are procedures for obtaining warrants, both during and outside court hours, which should describe the necessary processes, the evidence which individuals may be reasonably expected to produce, and the documents that should be prepared to help the process run smoothly. The Code also places responsibility on the AMHP, the hospital managers or the local authority '(as appropriate)' to ensure that an ambulance or other transport is available to take the person to the place of safety or to the place where they ought to be, in accordance with a locally agreed policy on the transport of patients under the Act.[17]

Police power to remove from a public place to a place of safety

7.15 Section 136 of the MHA 1983 empowers a constable who finds a person in 'a place to which the public have access' who appears to be mentally disordered and to require immediate care and control, if the constable thinks it is necessary in that person's interests or for the protection of others, to take that person to a place of safety. The person need not be diagnosed by a doctor as mentally disordered; the constable need only have a reasonable belief that the patient suffers from 'any disorder or disability of mind'. The purpose of removal is to enable the person to be examined by a doctor and interviewed by an AMHP and for any necessary arrangements for his treatment or care to be made. The authority for detention under s 136 and s 135 expires when these arrangements have been made or after 72 hours, whichever is the earlier.

7.16 The s 136 power may be exercised in a public place, defined as a place to which the public have access '(by payment or otherwise)' as the English Code of Practice puts it.[18] In *Carter v Metropolitan Police Comr*[19] the Court of Appeal held that the communal balcony of a block of flats was a place to which the public have access. Police powers to enter private premises to prevent a breach

---

[14] Ibid, paras 106 and 10.11.
[15] NHS Information Centre, In-Patients Formally Detained under the Mental Health Act 1983 and Patients Subject to Supervised Community Treatment: England 2009–2010, Health and Social Care Information Centre 2010, Table 5.
[16] Department of Health *Code of Practice: Mental Health Act 1983* (2008), para 10.3.
[17] Ibid, paras 10.8–10.9.
[18] Ibid, para 10.12.
[19] [1975] 1 WLR 507, CA.

of the peace are preserved by s 17(6) of the Police and Criminal Evidence Act 1984, provided any police action is a proportionate response in all the circumstances.[20] There is also, of course, the power to enter pursuant to a warrant granted under s 135 of the MHA 1983.

7.17 In *Seal v Chief Constable of South Wales Police*[21] the claimant had been arrested in his mother's house for breach of the peace and then removed to the street, where he was then detained under s 136 'as a result of what happened in the street.' The majority of their Lordships decided that the claim was statute barred, as the claimant was out of time and he had neglected to obtain High Court leave to bring proceedings as required by s 139 of the MHA 1983. Baroness Hale dissented. However, her obiter remarks about the use of s 136 in this way carry great weight. She said this:[22]

> 'The police may well have an answer to Mr Seal's claim. But their case is not without difficulty. If he was 'removed' under section 136 of the Mental Health Act from his mother's home, he cannot have been "found in a place to which the public have access". If he was arrested in her home for a breach of the peace, and then "removed" under section 136 after they had taken him outside, can it be said that they "found" him there? (To say otherwise would deprive section 136 of much of its usefulness when an arrested person is later discovered to have a mental disorder.) These are questions which deserve to be addressed at the trial of the claim. By no stretch of the imagination is this vexatious. It may not be worth a great deal of money but that is not the point.'

The Mental Health Act Commission (MHAC) consider Baroness Hale's comment to suggest that a future challenge to such an action would at least receive a hearing'.[23] A subsequent High Court decision in *McMillan v Crown Prosecution Service*[24] concerning a person who was drunk and disorderly and who was physically helped from her doorstep down steep steps into the street because the policemen feared she might fall. Once she had reached the street, she was arrested for being drunk and disorderly in a public place. Whether this can be read across into the context of s 136 decision-making is open to doubt. The MHAC has twice expressed concern in its Biennial Reports, citing evidence from an audit of s 136 by a 'London-based social services authority' which apparently shows that '30 per cent of arrests under s 136 are made at the person's home or outside.'[25]

---

20   *McLeod v United Kingdom* (1998) 27 EHRR 493, ECtHR.
21   [2007] UKHL 31.
22   Ibid, para [60].
23   Mental Health Act Commission, *Risks, Rights, Recovery: Twelfth Biennial Report* 2005–2007, para 4.64.
24   [2008] EWHC 1457 (Admin).
25   Mental Health Act Commission, *Risks, Rights, Recovery: Twelfth Biennial Report* 2005–2007, para 4.63; Mental Health Act Commission, *Coercion and Consent: Thirteenth Biennial Report* 2007–2009, (2009), para 2.138–9.

Place of safety

7.18 A place of safety is defined in s 135(6) as residential accommodation provided by a local social services authority, a hospital, a police station, independent hospital or care home for mentally disordered persons, or any other suitable place the occupier of which is willing temporarily to receive the patient. The English Code of Practice and Home Office Circular 007/2008 *Police Stations as Places of Safety* contain the same guidance to the effect that:[26]

> 'A police station should be used as a place of safety only on an exceptional basis. It may be necessary to do so because the person's behaviour would pose an unmanageably high risk to other patients, staff or users of a healthcare setting. It is preferable for a person thought to be suffering from a mental disorder to be detained in a hospital or other healthcare setting where mental health services are provided (subject, of course, to any urgent physical healthcare needs they may have). In formulating local policy, regard is to be had to the impact different types of place of safety may have on the person and on the outcome of the assessment.'

7.19 The Independent Police Complaints Commission ('IPCC') published research showing that, in 2005–2006, 60 per cent of s 136 detentions took place at police stations rather than health care settings.[27]. The Health and Social Care Information Centre statistics for England suggest that a significant shift may be taking place between the use of police stations and hospitals as places of safety, reporting that during 2009-2010:[28]

> 'The number of Place of Safety Orders (where the place of safety was a hospital) rose to 12,300, an increase of 40.4 per cent since 2008/09 and over double the number reported in 2005/06 (when there were 5,877).'

The changes introduced by the MHA 2007 which allow a person to be moved from one place of safety to another without the need for fresh authority to detain could be having an impact here in that people initially taken to a police station are then being transferred on to hospital under s 136 (see **7.22** below).

7.20 The English Code of Practice states that LSSAs, hospitals, NHS commissioners, police forces and ambulance services should ensure that they have a clear and jointly agreed policy for use of the powers under sections 135 and 136, as well as the operation of agreed places of safety within their localities, and where staff in each agency are properly trained and understand their responsibilities to provide prompt assessment and if appropriate

---

[26] Department of Health *Code of Practice: Mental Health Act 1983* (2008), para 10.21, Home Office Circular 007/2008 *Police Stations as Places of Safety (2008)* para 2.2 see also Welsh Assembly Government, *Mental Health Act 1983 Code of Practice for Wales* paras 7.18–7.20.

[27] Docking M, Grace, K, and Burke T, *Police Custody as a Place of Safety: Examining the Use of Section 136 of the Mental Health Act 1983* Independent Police Complaints Commission Research and Statistics Series: Paper 11.

[28] NHS Information Centre, In-Patients Formally Detained under the Mental Health Act 1983 and Patients Subject to Supervised Community Treatment: England 2009–2010, Health and Social Care Information Centre 2010, p 4.

admission to hospital.[29] The Royal College of Psychiatrists has produced standards on the use of s 136, which the Mental Health Act Commission recommends should 'inform local policies.'[30]

7.21 The LSSA, hospitals and the Chief Constable should establish a clear policy for using the power and identifying appropriate facilities for the safe containment and rapid assessment of the person removed. The Codes go into some detail about the contents of s 136 policies. The English Code says that the policy should define responsibilities for:[31]

'• commissioning and providing secure places of safety in healthcare settings;
  • identifying and agreeing the most appropriate place of safety in individual cases;
  • providing prompt assessment and, where appropriate, admission to hospital for further assessment or treatment;
  • securing the attendance of police officers, where appropriate for the patient's health or safety or the protection of others;
  • the safe, timely and appropriate conveyance of the person to and between places of safety (bearing in mind that hospital or ambulance transport will generally be preferable to police transport, which should be used exceptionally, such as in cases of extreme urgency or where there is a risk of violence);
  • deciding whether it is appropriate to transfer the person from the place of safety to which they have been taken to another place of safety;
  • dealing with people who are also under the effects of alcohol or drugs;
  • dealing with people who are behaving, or have behaved, violently;
  • arranging access to a hospital accident and emergency department for assessment, where necessary;
  • record keeping, monitoring and audit of practice against policy; and
  • the release, transport and follow-up of people assessed under section 135 or 136 who are not then admitted to hospital or immediately accommodated elsewhere.'

The policy should include provisions for the use of s 136 to be monitored so that a check can be made of how and in what circumstances it is being used, including its use in relation to black and minority ethnic communities and children. If the person removed to a place of safety is already subject to supervised community treatment ('SCT'), conditional discharge or, on leave of absence and recall to hospital may need to be considered. The patient's clinical supervisor should be contacted as soon as possible. The Welsh Code contains similar provisions.[32]

---

[29] Department of Health *Code of Practice Mental Health Act 1983* (2008), para 10.16.
[30] Royal College of Psychiatrists, Standards on the Use of Section 136 of the Mental Health Act 1983, College Report CRI49, September 2008; Mental Health Act Commission, *Coercion and Consent: Thirteenth Biennial Report 2007–2009*, (2009), para 2.131.
[31] Department of Health *Code of Practice Mental Health Act 1983* (2008), para 10.18 and 10.40–10.44; Welsh Assembly Government, *Mental Health Act 1983 Code of Practice for Wales*, paras 7.11–7.16.
[32] Department of Health *Code of Practice Mental Health Act 1983* (2008), para 10.4; Welsh Assembly Government, *Mental Health Act 1983 Code of Practice for Wales*, paras 7.18–7.20.

7.22 Section 44 of the MHA 2007 amends ss 135 and 136 to provide that a person who has been removed to one place of safety may be transferred to another one within the 72-hour time limit. This provision will come into force in April 2008. This will mean that a person could initially be detained in a police cell but be removed to a hospital for further assessment, still within the authority of s 136, without need for fresh authority to detain from some other provision of the Act. This power was welcomed by the Mental Health Act Commission, who stated that they expected it to be used 'primarily to avoid unnecessarily long detention in a police cell.'[33] The 72-hour period runs from arrival at the first place of safety. There were attempts in the House of Lords to reduce the maximum period to 24 hours, but the Minister of State rejected these on the basis of 'emerging evidence' collected by the Independent Police Complaints Commission suggesting that whilst the average period spent in police custody under s 136 was 10 hours, and most people were released after 18 hours, 'some people need to be detained for longer than 24 hours'.[34]

7.23 The Police and Criminal Evidence Act (PACE) 1984 preserves the power to remove under s 136(1) as a power of arrest, which allows s 32 of PACE to apply empowering a police officer to search a person at a place other than a police station.[35] The custody officer may also identify what items the person has in their possession. The Mental Health Act Commission has drawn attention to an alleged difference between the two Codes and has advised personnel in England to 'note the Welsh Code's reassurance' that these powers of search are available.[36] The Mental Health Act Commission commends the Welsh guidance to English practitioners since they had 'heard of a number of instances where nursing staff in hospital-based places of safety have found that the person delivered to them by police has not been searched and has concealed about their person a knife or other potential weapon.[37] In actual fact the English Code does also contain clear guidance to the effect that these powers are available.[38]

7.24 The Mental Health Act Commission Twelfth Biennial Report 2005–2007 points to evidence that the use of s 136 may be disclosed through enhanced Criminal Record Bureau checks, and has expressed the view that the recording of s 136 incidents for the purposes of Criminal Records Bureau records is 'unnecessary and discriminating.'[39]

7.25 PACE Code C emphasises the 'imperative' requirement that a mentally disordered or otherwise mentally vulnerable person detained under s 136 be

[33] Mental Health Act Commission, *Coercion and Consent: Thirteenth Biennial Report 2007–2009*, (2009), para 2.132.

[34] *Hansard,* HL Deb, vol 689, cols 1468–1469.

[35] Police and Criminal Evidence Act 1984, s 26 and Sch 2, and s 32.

[36] Welsh Assembly Government, *Mental Health Act 1983 Code of Practice for Wales*, para 7.23.

[37] Mental Health Act Commission, *Coercion and Consent: Thirteenth Biennial Report 2007–2009*, (2009), para 2.136.

[38] Department of Health *Code of Practice: Mental Health Act 1983* (2008), para 10.45.

[39] Mental Health Act Commission, *Risks, Rights, Recovery: Twelfth Biennial Report 2005–2007*, para 2.147.

assessed as soon as possible. If that assessment is to take place at the police station, an AMHP and a doctor must be called to the station as soon as possible in order to interview and examine the detainee. Once the detainee has been interviewed, examined and suitable arrangements made for their treatment or care, they can no longer be detained under s 136. PACE Code C states that a detainee must be immediately discharged from detention under s 136 if the examining doctor concludes they are not mentally disordered within the meaning of the Act.[40] The English Mental Health Act Code advises that 'In no case may the person continue to be detained at the police station under section 136 once a custody officer deems that detention is no longer appropriate.'[41] The Mental Health Act Commission say that whilst this in law correct since the custody officer has a statutory duty under the Police and Criminal Evidence Act to determine who shall or shall not be detained in police custody, they support the Royal College of Psychiatrists recommendation that before reaching a decision that custody is no longer appropriate, the custody officer should first discuss the case with a doctor or an Approved Mental Health Professional.

7.26 In *R (on the application of Anderson) v Inner North Greater London Coroner*, Collins J held that:[42]

> 'The powers contained in s 136 of the 1983 Act to remove to a place of safety inevitably require that the person concerned can be kept safe in the sense that harm to himself or others is prevented until he can be seen by a doctor and, if necessary, given some form of sedation ... A police officer in exercising his powers under s 136 is entitled to use reasonable force. If someone is violent, he can be restrained.'

7.27 Part IV of the Act does not apply to persons detained under ss 135 or 136. In *R (Munjaz) v Mersey Care NHS Trust* Hale LJ (as she then was) said this:[43]

> 'There is a general power to take such steps as are reasonably necessary and proportionate to protect others from the immediate risk of significant harm. This applies whether or not the patient lacks the capacity to make decisions for himself. But where the patient does lack capacity, there is also the power to provide him with whatever treatment or care is necessary in his own best interests.'

A person aged 16 or over can be given necessary treatment using proportionate restraint if they lack capacity to consent and the treatment is administered in accordance with ss 5 and 6 of the MCA 2005.

7.28 During 2009–2010 there were 12,038 admissions under s 136 where the place of safety was a hospital, 6,778 men and 5,260 women. Of the patients taken to hospital under s 136 for whom outcome figures were available 9,211

---

40   Police and Criminal Evidence Act Code of Practice C, para 3.16.
41   Department of Health *Code of Practice: Mental Health Act 1983* (2008), para 10.32.
42   [2004] EWHC 2729 (Admin).
43   [2003] EWCA Civ 1036 at [46].

became informal patients after assessment, 1,555 were detained under s 2, and 367 were detained under s 3.[44] There are no figures relating to the use of police stations as places of safety. Lord Bradley said that 'Accessing data on the numbers of people who are detained under this power again proved difficult', and pointed to the Independent Police Complaints Commission survey as the best available study which estimated that 11,500 people were detained under this power in 2005/06, the average amount of time spent in custody was 10 hours, and that 41 of the 43 constabularies confirmed the continued use of a police station as a place of safety.[45]

7.29 Where an individual has been arrested by the police under s 136 he is entitled to have another person informed of his arrest and whereabouts, and where he is detained in a police station as the place of safety he has a right of access to legal advice.[46] Code of Practice C issued under the Police and Criminal Evidence Act 1984 ('PACE Code C') governs the detention, treatment and questioning of persons by police officers, and applies to people removed to a police station under s 136.

7.30 PACE Code C emphasises the 'imperative' requirement that a mentally disordered or otherwise mentally vulnerable person detained under s 136 be assessed as soon as possible. If that assessment is to take place at the police station, an AMHP and a doctor must be called to the station as soon as possible in order to interview and examine the detainee. Once the detainee has been interviewed, examined and suitable arrangements made for their treatment or care, they can no longer be detained under s 136. The Code also states that a detainee must be immediately discharged from detention under s 136 if the examining doctor concludes they are not mentally disordered within the meaning of the Act.[47]

7.31 Whether or not the person has been detained under s 136, if he or she appears to be suffering from a mental disorder the custody officer must make sure the person receives appropriate clinical attention as soon as reasonably practicable. Where an assessment under s 136 is taking place at a police station the custody officer must consider whether an appropriate health care professional should be called to conduct an initial clinical check on the detainee. This applies particularly when there is likely to be any significant delay in the arrival of a suitably qualified medical practitioner. If a detainee requests a clinical examination, an appropriate health care professional must be called as soon as practicable to assess the detainee's clinical needs.[48] Section 136 may be used for purely paternalistic reasons because the person is at risk of

---

44 NHS Information Centre, *In-Patients Formally Detained under the Mental Health Act 1983 and Patients Subject to Supervised Community Treatment: England 2009–2010*, Health and Social Care Information Centre 2010, Table 6a.

45 *The Bradley Report: Lord Bradley's review of people with mental health problems or learning disabilities in the criminal justice system* April 2009, 45–46.

46 Police and Criminal Evidence Act 1984, ss 56, 58; *Department of Health Code of Practice Mental Health Act*, para 10.47.

47 Police and Criminal Evidence Act Code of Practice C, para 3.16.

48 Ibid, paras 9.3–9.8.

harm in a public place. If the person has committed a criminal offence, the police may decide to assemble a case for prosecution.

THE DECISION TO PROSECUTE

7.32 The decision to proceed with a criminal investigation in respect of a mentally disordered suspect will be taken by the police in the first instance in the light of the public interest as defined in the *Code for Crown Prosecutors*.[49] The decision to prosecute a mentally disordered suspect triggers the use of special interview procedures, may lead to the use of special procedures at trial, may involve decisions about criminal responsibility, and may culminate in the use of a hospital rather than a penal disposal. In most cases, the Crown Prosecution Service ('CPS') are responsible for deciding whether a person should be charged with a criminal offence, and if so, what that offence should be, and the decision is made in accordance with the *Code for Crown Prosecutors* and the Director of Public Prosecutions *Guidance on Charging*. The CPS applies a two-stage test. The first question is evidentiary and asks whether there is a 'realistic prospect of conviction' or in other words whether a jury or bench of magistrates or judge hearing a case alone, properly directed in accordance with the law, is more likely than not to convict the defendant of the charge alleged. The second question is whether a prosecution is needed in the public interest. The general principle here is that:[50]

> 'A prosecution will usually take place unless there are public interest factors tending against prosecution which clearly outweigh those tending in favour, or it appears more appropriate in all the circumstances of the case to divert the person from prosecution.'

7.33 The *Code for Crown Prosecutors* states that factors weighing against proceeding to trial could include where:[51]

'(1)　prosecution is likely to have a bad effect on the victim's physical or mental health, always bearing in mind the seriousness of the offence; or

(2)　the defendant is elderly or is, or was at the time of the offence, suffering from significant mental or physical ill health, unless the offence is serious or there is real possibility that it may be repeated ... Crown Prosecutors must balance the desirability of diverting a defendant who is suffering from significant mental or physical ill health with the need to safeguard the general public.'

So if the offence is not serious and is unlikely to be repeated the public could be adequately safeguarded by a decision to admit as a voluntary patient or under Part II of the MHA 1983 rather than proceed to prosecution. *The Code for Crown Prosecutors* states that alternatives to prosecution should be considered when deciding whether a case should be prosecuted. Alternatives to

---

[49]　Crown Prosecution Service *Code for Crown Prosecutors* (2004) (available at http://www.cps.gov.uk/publications/prosecution/index.html).

[50]　Ibid, para 5.1.

[51]　Police and Criminal Evidence Act Code of Practice C, para 5.10f–5.10g.

prosecution for adult offenders include a simple caution or conditional caution. However, Lord Bradley noted that the National Standards for Conditional Cautioning state that a caution or conditional caution will be inappropriate if there is any doubt about the reliability of admissions made or if the individual's level of understanding prevents them from understanding the significance of the caution and from giving informed consent to it. Lord Bradley observes that:

> 'prosecutors are advised not to assume that all mentally disordered offenders are ineligible for cautioning or conditional cautioning, but there is no definition of or restriction on the particular form of mental condition or disorder that may make an admission unreliable.'

To attempt such a definition might risk adopting a status approach to reliability and capacity, whereby someone with a particular diagnosis or label is at risk of being presumed to lack credibility or capacity to accept a caution.[52]

7.34 The decision to investigate a criminal offence will be made by the police in the light of the CPS guidance. The weightiest factor in the decision to prosecute a mentally disordered suspect rather than divert them from the criminal justice system will be the seriousness of the alleged offence. If the police decide to proceed to interview a mentally disordered or mentally vulnerable suspect in relation to a criminal offence, an 'appropriate adult' must be present.

THE APPROPRIATE ADULT

7.35 If a detainee in a police station is mentally disordered or otherwise mentally vulnerable, the custody officer must, as soon as practicable, inform an 'appropriate adult' of the grounds for their detention and their whereabouts, and ask the adult to come to the police station to see the detainee.[53] PACE Code C recognises the vulnerability of mentally disordered suspects, observing that whilst they:[54]

> 'are often capable of providing reliable evidence, they may, without knowing or wishing to do so, be particularly prone to provide information which is unreliable, misleading or self-incriminating. Special care should therefore be exercised in questioning such a person and the appropriate adult should always be involved if there is any doubt about a person's mental state or capacity.'

PACE Code C refers to appropriate adults being necessary for mentally vulnerable detainees who, because of mental state or capacity, may not understand the significance of what is said, of questions and their replies, as well as for those suffering from mental disorder meaning 'mental illness,

---

[52] *The Bradley Report: Lord Bradley's review of people with mental health problems or learning disabilities in the criminal justice system* April 2009.
[53] Ibid, para 3.15.
[54] Ibid, *Notes for Guidance*, para 11C.

arrested or incomplete development of mind, psychopathic disorder and any other disorder or disability of mind'. The Code states that when the custody officer has any doubt about the mental state or capacity of a detainee, that detainee should be treated as mentally vulnerable and an appropriate adult called.

7.36 The primary role of the appropriate adult is to ensure that no undue pressure is put on the suspect. The appropriate adult is not to act simply as an observer and this is to be explained to him or her. The Code states that the role has three aspects:

(a)   to advise the person being questioned;

(b)   to observe whether or not the interview is being conducted properly and fairly; and

(c)   to facilitate communication with the person being interviewed.[55]

7.37 An appropriate adult in the case of someone who is mentally disordered or mentally vulnerable can be:

(a)   a relative, guardian or other person responsible for their care or custody;

(b)   someone experienced in dealing with mentally disordered or mentally vulnerable people but who is not a police officer or employed by the police; or

(c)   failing these, some other responsible adult aged 18 or over who is not a police officer or employed by the police.[56]

Explanatory Note 1D of PACE Code C states that it may be appropriate if the appropriate adult is someone with qualifications in looking after mentally disordered people, but that if the suspect prefers a relative to a better qualified stranger, that wish should 'if practicable' be respected. A person should not be the appropriate adult if they are suspected of involvement in the offence, a victim, a witness or otherwise involved in the investigation. Nor should someone be an appropriate adult if they have received admissions in relation to the offence from the suspect, as appropriate adults are not covered by legal professional privilege. A solicitor or independent custody visitor may not be an appropriate adult if they are present in the police station in either of those capacities.[57]

7.38 Unless an urgent interview can be authorised by a superintendent or higher rank, a mentally disordered person must not be interviewed or asked to

---

[55]   Ibid, para 11.17.
[56]   Ibid, para 1.7(b).
[57]   Police and Criminal Evidence Act Code of Practice C, Explanatory Notes 1B–1E.

sign a statement without an appropriate adult attending.[58] The only exception is where an officer of at least the rank of superintendent certifies that delay will involve a serious risk of interference with evidence, harm to persons or serious loss or serious damage to property. Even then questioning may not continue in the absence of the appropriate adult once sufficient information to avert the risk has been received. A record must be made of the grounds for any decision to begin an interview in such circumstances.[59]

CONSEQUENCES OF FAILURE TO HAVE AN APPROPRIATE ADULT PRESENT AT INTERVIEW

7.39 Three sections of the Police and Criminal Evidence Act 1984 relate to the admissibility of confession evidence. Only s 77 refers directly to any form of mental disorder. Although the PACE Code refers to mental vulnerability and mental disorder in general, s 77 of the Police and Criminal Evidence Act 1984 refers to the narrower concept of mental handicap ('arrested or incomplete development of mind which includes significant impairment of intelligence and social functioning'), stating that where the case against a defendant depends wholly or substantially on a confession by him and the judge is satisfied (a) that he is mentally handicapped; and (b) that the confession was not made in the presence of an independent person the judge must warn the jury that there is a special need for caution before convicting the accused in reliance on the confession. The decision as to whether a suspect is mentally handicapped is to be based on medical evidence.[60] Although a solicitor cannot be an appropriate adult, a solicitor was held to be an independent person for the purposes of this section in *R v Lewis*.[61] Section 77 of the Police and Criminal Evidence Act 1984 merely requires the judge to warn the jury of the need for caution before relying on a confession, and the warning is only required where the suspect was mentally handicapped and an appropriate adult was not present.

7.40 Sections 76 and 78 allow for confessions to be excluded entirely, and one of the grounds on which they may be excluded is failure to provide an appropriate adult. Section 76(2) provides that where it is represented to the court that a confession may have been (a) obtained by oppression of the person who made it; or (b) in consequence of anything said or done which was likely, in the circumstances existing at the time, to render the confession unreliable, the burden is on the prosecution to show beyond reasonable doubt that the confession was not improperly obtained (notwithstanding that it may be true). Failure to secure the presence of an appropriate adult is unlikely to amount to oppression, unless there is a strong degree of hectoring of a mentally vulnerable suspect. However, it may amount to something said or done which was likely to render the confession unreliable under s 76(2)(b).[62]

---

58 Police and Criminal Evidence Act Code of Practice C, para 11.15.
59 Police and Criminal Evidence Act Code of Practice C, paras 11.1(a), 11.18–11.20.
60 *R v Ham* (1995) 36 BMLR 169, CA.
61 [1996] Crim LR 260, CA.
62 See *R v Everett* [1988] Crim LR 826, CA; and *R v Moss* (1990) 91 Cr App R 371, CA.

7.41 Under s 78(1) the court may refuse to allow evidence on which the prosecution proposes to rely to be given if it appears to the court that, having regard to all the circumstances, including the circumstances in which the evidence was obtained, the admission of the evidence would have such an adverse effect on the fairness of the proceedings that the court ought not to admit it. The attitude of the courts to the effect of failure to provide an appropriate adult on fairness has varied. In some cases it has led to exclusion,[63] in others not.[64]

ASSESSMENT OF MENTALLY DISORDERED OFFENDERS

7.42 The Mental Health Act Code of Practice asserts that:[65]

> 'People subject to criminal proceedings have the same right to psychiatric assessment and treatment as other citizens. Any person who is in police or prison custody, or who is before the courts charged with a criminal offence, and who is in need of medical treatment for mental disorder should be considered for admission to hospital. Such people may be at greatest risk of self-harm while in custody.'

Moreover, the Code makes it clear that a prison health care centre is not a hospital within the meaning of the MHA 1983. As it is not a hospital and as prisoners are not detained under the MHA 1983 they may not be given treatment for mental disorder without consent using the powers and second opinion safeguards in Part IV of the 1983 Act.[66]

7.43 But there is convergence in the regimes in terms of legal powers to treat without consent. Treatment for mental disorder may be given to prisoners using restraint and force under ss 5 and 6 of the Mental Capacity Act 2005 if the person lacks capacity and restraint and treatment are necessary and proportionate responses to prevent harm to the patient. Although ss 5 and 6 are said to codify the common law doctrine of necessity, the statute and supporting Code of Practice show clearly that treatment necessary to prevent harm to the patient may be given without consent outside hospital settings, using force or the threat of force if necessary, where the patient lacks capacity. Under common law, treatment which is immediately necessary and a proportionate response to prevent the patient from harming others may be given using restraint, whether or not the person retains capacity.[67]

7.44 Even after a decision has been made to proceed to trial for a criminal offence there are still ample opportunities for mentally disordered offenders to be diverted away from the prison system to psychiatric hospital (be that high,

---

63   See *R v Aspinall* (1999) 2 Cr App R 115, CA.
64   See *R v Law-Thompson* [1997] Crim LR 674, CA.
65   Department of Health *Code of Practice: Mental Health Act 1983* (2008), para 33.2.
66   Ibid, para 33.2.
67   *R (on the application of Munjaz) v Mersey Care NHS Trust; R (on the application of S) v Airedale NHS Trust* [2003] EWCA Civ 1036, CA.

medium, or low security) or to psychiatric supervision in the community. The MHA 1983 also provides remand powers to enable psychiatric assessment to take place in hospital rather than prison.

REMAND TO HOSPITAL

7.45 The MHA 1983 introduced three remand powers for mentally disordered offenders: the power to remand an accused person for reports on his mental condition under s 35, which was used 80 times in 2009–2010; the power to remand for psychiatric treatment under s 36, used 27 times in 2009–2010; and the power to impose an interim hospital order under s 38, used an unknown number of times in 2009–2010. As Bartlett and Sandland have noted:[68]

> 'When the numbers remanded under both sections [35 and 36] are compared to the thousands of mentally disordered people remanded to prison for medical assessments, the underuse of the power to remand to hospital is truly shocking.'

Since they wrote those words, the use of s 35 remands for reports has steadily declined, although the use of s 36 remands for treatment has increased very slightly.[69]

7.46 There are certain common features to the remand powers. No court can make a remand order unless it is satisfied, on the evidence of the doctor or approved clinician ('AC') who would be responsible for making the report[70] (or who would be in charge of his case,[71] or some other person representing the hospital managers, that arrangements have been made for the patient's admission to hospital within a period of 7 days after the remand order has been made. Remand is for 28 days in the first instance, but the accused may be further remanded for two further 28-day periods up to a maximum of 12 weeks in all. The court can extend the remand of someone remanded under s 35 in his absence (as long as he is represented in court) if it is satisfied on the evidence of the doctor or the 'approved clinician' ('AC') preparing the report, that a further remand is necessary in order to complete the psychiatric assessment.[72]

7.47 In the case of someone remanded for reports under s 35 or for treatment under s 36, remand may be extended if the court is satisfied on the report of the AC who would be in charge of treatment that further remand is necessary to complete the assessment (s 35), of further rmand is 'warranted' (s 36). A person remanded for reports or for treatment is entitled to commission at his own expense an independent report from a doctor or any other AC, and to apply to

---

[68]   P Bartlett and R Sandland *Mental Health Law Policy and Practice* (OUP, 3rd edn, 2007), p 220.
[69]   NHS Information Centre, In-Patients Formally Detained under the Mental Health Act 1983 and Patients Subject to Supervised Community Treatment: England 2009–2010, Health and Social Care Information Centre 2010. Table 2a.
[70]   MHA 1983, s 35(4).
[71]   MHA 1983, s 36(7).
[72]   MHA 1983, s 35(5), (6).

the court for his remand to be terminated.[73] However, remand patients have no right to apply for discharge to a Mental Health Tribunal ('MHT').

REMAND FOR A PSYCHIATRIC REPORT UNDER S 35

7.48 In recognition of the fact that remand to prison may lead to a high risk of suicide in mentally vulnerable people, s 35 of the Act provides for remand to hospital for reports where the court is satisfied that:

(a) there is reason to suspect that the accused is suffering from mental disorder; and

(b) it would be impracticable for a report to be made on his mental condition if he were remanded on bail.

7.49 A Crown Court may remand an accused person awaiting trial or who has been arraigned for an offence punishable by imprisonment and has not yet been sentenced. In relation to the magistrates, 'accused person' has two meanings. First, it includes anyone who has been convicted by the court of an offence punishable with imprisonment. Second, it includes any person charged with such an offence if the court is satisfied that either:

(a) he did the act or made the omission charged; or

(b) he has consented to the making of the remand.

7.50 Evidence is required from one doctor, who must be approved by the Secretary of State under s 12(2) of the MHA 1983 as having special experience in the diagnosis or treatment of mental disorder.[74] The diagnostic threshold for remand is not high. There need only be reason to suspect that the accused is suffering from mental disorder, meaning 'any disorder or disability of mind'. A remand cannot be made unless the court is satisfied on the written or oral evicence of the AC who would be responsible for making the report or some other person representing the managers of the hospital, arrangements have been made for the accused person's admission to hospital within seven days, and, if so satisfied, the court may, pending admission give directions for the person's conveyance to and detention in a place of safety.[75] A 'place of safety' for the purposes of Part III in relation to an adult means 'any police station, prison or remand centre, or any hospital the managers of which are temporarily willing to receive him.' in relation to a child it has the same meaning as in s 107 of the Children and Young Persons Act 1933, namely a community home provided by a local authority or a controlled community

---

[73] MHA 1983, ss 35(8) and 36(7).
[74] MHA 1983, ss 35(3)(a) and 54(1).
[75] Ibid, s 35(4).

home, any police station, or any hospital, surgery or other suitable place, the occupier of which is willing to receive temporarily the child or young person.'[76]

7.51 A report prepared under s 35 should contain a statement of whether a patient is suffering from mental disorder identifying its relevance to the alleged offence. The report should not comment on guilt or innocence, but should include relevant social factors and any recommendations on care and treatment including where and when it should take place and who should be responsible. Section 10(2) of the MHA 2007 has amended s 35 to allow reports to be prepared not just by doctors but also by approved clinicians who might be nurses, psychologists, social workers or occupational therapists.

7.52 A person remanded under s 35 is not subject to the consent to treatment provisions in Part IV of the Act and therefore retains the common law right to refuse treatment.[77] The Code of Practice advises that where a patient remanded under s 35 is thought to be in need of medical treatment for mental disorder under Part IV of the Act, consideration ought to be given to referring the patient back to court with an appropriate recommendation, and with an assessment of whether the patient is in a fit state to attend court. It goes on to suggest that if there is delay in securing a court date, and depending on the patient's mental condition, consideration should be given to whether the patient meets the criteria of s 3. There are various legal issues in relation to detaining a remanded person under civil powers in order to acquire a right to treat compulsorily, most notably that Parliament clearly provided a separate power to remand for treatment which is subject to stricter criteria, and a patient could appeal successfully against detention under the civil powers, but still remain detained under the remand power.[78]

7.53 The MCA 2005 introduces the possibility that a person remanded for reports could be given treatment without consent for mental disorder. Under s 5 a defence is available, in relation to any action based on treatment without consent, to anyone who has taken reasonable steps to carry out an assessment of a patient's capacity, reasonably believes that the person lacks capacity, and reasonably believes that the treatment is in the person's best interests. Restraint (use or threat of force) can also be justified if necessary and proportionate to prevent harm to the incapacitated person under s 6 of the MCA 2005. Under s 3 of the MCA 2005 a person's capacity is to be assessed by asking whether there is any mental disability (disturbance or disability of mind or brain) which renders him unable to communicate a decision, unable to understand and retain relevant treatment information, or unable to use and weigh that information in the balance as part of the process of arriving at a decision. This definition may mean that a person who retains cognitive function and can communicate and understand and retain treatment information long enough to

---

[76] MHA 1983, s 55(1).
[77] MHA 1983, s 56(1)(b).
[78] Department of Health *Code of Practice: Mental Health Act 1983* (2008), para 33.28. For a critical view see P Fennell 'Double detention under the Mental Health Act 1983: a case of extra Parliamentary legislation' (1991) *Journal of Social Welfare and Family Law* 194.

make a decision may still lack capacity if some emotional disturbance of mental functioning, such as depression, renders them unable to weigh the information in the balance to make a decision. Intervention under the MCA may only be carried out where in the patient's best interests, although the definition of best interests, which includes social and psychological interests is capable of being interpreted so as to protect others. It can be argued that it is in X's best interests and necessary to prevent harm to him that X be prevented from assaulting others or provoking them to assault him.

REMAND FOR TREATMENT UNDER S 36

7.54 Remand for treatment may be used to provide treatment before trial and hence potentially avoid an accused person being found unfit to plead. The definition of accused person for this power is any person who is in custody awaiting trial for an offence punishable with imprisonment (other than murder), or who at any time before sentence is in custody in the course of a Crown Court trial. A remand order for treatment may only be made by the Crown Court on the evidence of two doctors, one of whom must be approved by the Secretary of State as having special experience in the diagnosis or treatment of mental disorder. The court must be satisfied that the accused is suffering from mental disorder ('any disorder or disability of mind') of a nature or degree which makes it appropriate for him to be detained in hospital for medical treatment. The MHA 2007 has broadened the definition of mental disorder which applies to remands for treatment, which used to be available only for mental illness or severe mental impairment. The test now is that:

(a) the patient is suffering from mental disorder of a nature or degree which makes it appropriate for him to be detained in a hospital for medical treatment; and

(b) appropriate medical treatment is available to him.

Section 36 was only used 27 times in 2009–2010. For each of the previous two years it had been used 16 times per year. The broader definition of mental disorder has not led to a massive increase in its use.

7.55 Because the sentence is fixed by law, a person accused of murder cannot be remanded for treatment under s 36 (see s 36(2)). However, s 3(6A) of the Bail Act 1976 allows the court to impose the following conditions of bail:

(a) that the accused must undergo examination by two doctors for psychiatric reports to be prepared; and

(b) that he must attend an institution or place as the court directs for that purpose and comply with any other directions from the doctors.

A person remanded for treatment is subject to Part IV of the MHA 1983 and so may be given medicine for mental disorder or Electro Convulsive Therapy ('ECT'), subject to the statutory second opinion procedure in ss 58 and 58A (see **10.36–10.44** below). An accused person remanded for treatment has no right to apply for discharge to a Mental Health Tribunal ('MHT').

INTERIM HOSPITAL ORDER UNDER S 38

7.56 Either the Crown Court or a magistrate's court may make an interim hospital order on the evidence of two doctors (one of whom must be approved under s 12) that the relevant criteria are met. Currently the court must be satisfied that the diagnostic criterion is met, that the offender is suffering from mental illness, psychopathic disorder, severe mental impairment or mental impairment. The court must also be satisfied that there is reason to suppose that the mental disorder is such that it may be appropriate for a hospital order to be made. The MHA 2007 has opened the possibility for patients suffering from any disorder or disability of mind to be subject to interim orders, but since there are no accurate figures on the use of this section it is impossible to tell whether the provision is much used. The statistics merely record that there are between 130 and 140 admissions each year under 'other provisions, including s 38, s 44 committals by a magistrates court, and s 46 admission of members of the armed forces.[79]

7.57 The court must be satisfied on the evidence of the 'responsible clinician' ('RC') who would have overall responsibility for his case' or the hospital managers that arrangements have been made for the patient's admission to hospital within 28 days.[80] An interim hospital order is for an initial period of twelve weeks which may be renewed at 28 day intervals thereafter up to a maximum of twelve months on the written or oral evidence of the 'responsible clinician'. The court may terminate the order if, having considered the evidence of the responsible clinician, it decides to deal with the offender in some other way. The court can renew the interim order or make a full hospital order in the absence of the patient, provided he is represented in court.[81]

7.58 A patient on an interim hospital order is subject to the consent to treatment provisions in Part IV of the Act, and so may be given medicine for mental disorder or Electro Convulsive Therapy, subject to the statutory second opinion procedure in ss 58 and 58A. Patients on interim hospital orders are not entitled to apply to a MHT for discharge.

---

[79] NHS Information Centre, In-Patients Formally Detained under the Mental Health Act 1983 and Patients Subject to Supervised Community Treatment: England 2009–2010, Health and Social Care Information Centre 2010. Table 2a.

[80] MHA 1983, s 38(4).

[81] MHA 1983, s 38(2), (6).

MENTAL CONDITION AT THE TIME OF THE OFFENCE

7.59 The offender's mental condition at the time of the offence can have a bearing on disposal of a mentally disordered offender. Mentally disordered offenders have traditionally been exempt from ordinary penal measures on the grounds that they are not criminally responsible for their behaviour (not guilty by reason of insanity), that their responsibility for doing or being a party to a homicide is diminished by abnormality of mental functioning (diminished responsibility), or that they are unable to understand the course of the proceedings at their trial and contribute to their defence (unfit to plead). Each of these may lead to a psychiatric rather than a penal disposal.

THE INSANITY DEFENCE

7.60 Section 2 of the Trial of Lunatics Act 1883 provides for a special verdict of not guilty by reason of insanity to be returned where a person who was insane at the time the offence was committed.[82] The definition of insanity remains the *McNaghten* rules laid down by Tindal CJ in the decision of the House of Lords in *McNaghten's Case*. For the defence to be made out:[83]

> 'It must be clearly proved that, at the time of committing the act, the accused was labouring under such a defect of reason from disease of the mind that he did not know the nature and quality of the act, or so as not to know that what he was doing was wrong.'

A person must be labouring under a very severe defect of reason to be entitled to the defence not to know the nature and quality of their act (the example often given is chopping someone with an axe believing them to be a block of wood). Similarly, there must be a severe defect of reason if someone knows the nature and quality of their act (for example, killing someone), but does not know that it is wrong. Professor Mackay succeeded in persuading the Royal Court of Jersey in *Attorney-General v Prior*[84] to adopt a definition of insanity more in keeping with modern medical thinking. A person would be entitled to the insanity defence if:

> 'at the time of the offence, his unsoundness of mind affected his criminal responsibility to such a degree that jury consider that he ought not to be found criminally responsible.'

The insanity defence is used between 10 and 15 times per year, and is most often used with serious offences against the person. If the offence is homicide, the defence is more likely to plead guilty to manslaughter on grounds of diminished responsibility rather than rely on the insanity defence.

---

[82] For an excellent review of the insanity defence and the defence of diminished responsibility, see
       Mackay, R D 'Mental Disability at the Time of the Offence', Gostin, L; Bartlett, P; Fennell, P;
       Mackay, R and McHale, J, *Principles of Mental Health Law*, OUP 2010, Chapter 20, 720–756.
[83] *McNaghten's Case* [1843–60] All ER Rep 229, HL.
[84] *A-G v Prior* 2001 JLR 146, Jersey RC.

7.61 Concerns were raised by cases where the insanity defence was imposed when the defendant suffered from epilepsy[85] or hypoglycaemia[86] rather than what psychiatrists would accept as a true mental disorder in accordance with modern principles of medicine. Section 1 of the Criminal Procedure (Insanity and Unfitness to Plead) Act 1991 provides that a jury shall not return a special verdict except on the written or oral evidence of two medical practitioners, one of whom must be approved under s 12. This effectively means that unless a psychiatrist certifies that the person is suffering from a true mental disorder there will not be a special verdict.

7.62 Since the Criminal Procedure (Insanity and Unfitness to Plead) Act 1991 a Crown Court which finds a defendant not guilty by reason of insanity is no longer bound to impose a restriction order without limit of time. The Domestic Violence, Crime and Victims Act 2004 inserts a new s 5 into the Criminal Procedure (Insanity) Act 1964 setting out the three disposal options available to the court:

(a) a hospital order under s 37 of the MHA 1983, which can be accompanied by a restriction order under s 41;

(b) a supervision order; or

(c) absolute discharge of the accused.[87]

7.63 The Home Office Circular's suggests use of absolute discharge 'where the alleged offence was trivial and the accused does not require treatment and supervision in the community'.[88] Where the sentence for the offence is fixed by law the 1991 Act provides that there must be a restriction order without limit of time if the Mental Health Act criteria for making a restriction order are met.[89] If those criteria are not met, the court may only make a supervision order or discharge the defendant absolutely. Absolute discharge is most likely to apply in a case where the defendant is found unfit to plead because of a physical disorder rather than a case where the defendant is found on psychiatric evidence to be not guilty by reason of insanity. The Domestic Violence Crime and Victims Act 2004[90] made it a requirement that there must be medical evidence of mental disorder justifying detention in hospital for specialist mental health treatment. This applies equally to murder charges. If the conditions for making a hospital order are not met then neither a restriction order nor a hospital order can be made. In such cases the court's options are limited to one of the two remaining forms of disposal. The intention here is to

---

[85] See *R v Sullivan* [1983] 2 All ER 673, HL.

[86] As in *R v Hennessy* [1989] 2 All ER 9, CA.

[87] Domestic Violence, Crime and Victims Act 2004, s 24.

[88] Home Office Circular 20/2005 Guidance on the Domestic Violence Crime and Victims Act 2004, para 18.

[89] Criminal Procedure (Insanity and Unfitness to Plead) Act 1991, Sch 1, para 2(2).

[90] The Domestic Violence, Crime and Victims Act 2004, s 24 inserts a new s 5 into the Criminal Procedure (Insanity) Act 1964.

safeguard those who receive an insanity verdict, but are not mentally disordered within the meaning of the Mental Health Act, against detention in a psychiatric hospital which would serve no therapeutic purpose. The Secretary of State no longer has any role in deciding whether or not such defendants who are found 'not guilty by reason of insanity' are admitted to hospital. This is now a matter for the court based on the relevant medical evidence. A court that has made a hospital order in respect of a patient who has been given an insanity verdict or found unfit to plead has the power to require a hospital to accept the patient, unlike the position of the patient has been given a hospital order following a finding of guilt or a finding in the magistrates court that the patient had done the act charged as an offence. However, In addition, admission to the designated hospital must take place within the mandatory 28 day period specified in s 37(4) of the MHA 1983, and if this does not happen the hospital order ceases to have effect.[91] Patients who receive an insanity verdict and are made subject to a hospital order are entitled to a Mental Health Tribunal hearing within the first six months of detention, unlike those who have been sentenced to a hospital order without an insanity verdict or a finding of unfitness to plead. The Secretary of State retains the power to grant leave and discharge to patients who are subject to a restriction order following an insanity verdict.

Supervision order

7.64 A supervision order requires the supervised person to be under the supervision of a supervising officer (social worker or probation officer) for a specified period of not more than two years. A supervision order may require the supervised person to submit to treatment by or under the direction of a registered medical practitioner. The court may only make a supervision order if satisfied that, having regard to all the circumstances of the case, the making of such an order is the most suitable means of dealing with the accused, that the supervising officer is willing to supervise, and that arrangements have been made for the treatment which will be specified in the order.

7.65 The court must be satisfied on the evidence of two doctors, one of them s 12 approved, that the mental condition of the supervised person requires and may be susceptible to treatment; but is not such as to warrant the making of a hospital order under s 37 of the MHA 1983. A supervision order may include a condition that the supervised person shall submit to medical treatment aimed at improving his mental condition. This may be either treatment as a non-resident patient at a specified institution or treatment under the direction of a specified doctor.

7.66 A supervision order may also include a condition that the supervised person submit to medical treatment designed to improve his medical condition other than his mental condition. This may be either treatment as a non-resident patient at a specified institution or treatment under the direction of a specified

---

[91]   *R (DB) v Nottinghamshire Healthcare NHS Trust* [2008] EWCA Civ 1354.

doctor. This option is only available where the court is satisfied on the written or oral evidence of two or more doctors that because of his medical condition, other than his mental condition, the supervised person is likely to pose a risk to himself or others; and the condition may be susceptible to treatment.

7.67 If the doctor in charge of mental or other medical treatment considers that the treatment may be more conveniently given in or at an institution or place which is not specified in the original order where the person will receive treatment under the direction of a doctor, he may, with the consent of the supervised person, make arrangements for that treatment to take place. This may include treatment as a resident patient. Notice must be given to the supervising officer. The supervised person's consent is required for the change of arrangement, but once the change is made, the treatment provided for by the arrangements shall be deemed to be treatment to which he is required to submit in pursuance of the supervision order. A supervision order may also include requirements as to residence but before imposing a residence requirement, the court must consider the home surroundings of the supervised person.

7.68 The insanity defence is available in respect of any offence. The legislation on the special verdict applies to Crown Court trials. Stephen White has argued that the insanity defence is also available in the Magistrates' Court and that a defendant who establishes it there is entitled to an acquittal.[92] Magistrates have jurisdiction if they think fit, to make a hospital order under s 37(3) without convicting the offender if the court is satisfied that the accused meets the criteria for a hospital order, and that he 'did the act or made the omission.'

7.69 In *R (Singh) v Stratford Magistrates' Court*[93] it was stated that s 37(3) empowered the magistrates 'both in cases of alleged insanity at the time of the offence and of apparent unfitness to stand trial, ... to abstain from either conviction or acquittal but rather to make a hospital order or guardianship order, if such is justified medically'.[94] The Court of Appeal considered that in such a case the court could either try and resolve the issue of insanity, or if satisfied that there would be no purpose in doing so, could proceed to make a hospital order if the criteria in s 37(1) and s 37(3) were met.[95] The process was outlined by Hughes LJ in *Singh* as follows:[96]

> '[W]here a s 37(3) order is a possibility, the court should first determine the fact finding exercise. This may be concluded, as here, on admissions, or it may involve hearing evidence. If the court is not satisfied that the act/omission was done, an unqualified acquittal must follow, whatever the anxieties about the accused's state of health.'

---

[92] S White 'Insanity Defences and Magistrates' Courts' [1991] Crim LR 501.
[93] [2007] EWHC 1582 (Admin).
[94] Ibid, para 38.
[95] Ibid, para 39.
[96] Ibid, para 33.

If no section 37(3) hospital order is possible then the suggestion was that the court must normally proceed to trial 'so that if the accused was insane, he is acquitted, and if he was not, he is convicted'.[97]

7.70   Ronnie Mackay offers the following comment:[98]

'While, therefore, it is made abundantly clear in *R v Stratford Magistrates' Court* that there is a common law defence of insanity operating in the magistrates' courts which, if it proceeds to trial and no s 37(3) order can be made, can only result in an unqualified acquittal, its nature and scope remain problematical. First, if the McNaghten Rules do not apply, one must presumably go to the pre-1843 common law to find the appropriate test. In essence this would seem to be the so-called 'wild beast' test, which requires the defendant to be 'totally deprived of his understanding and memory, and doth not know what he is doing no more than an infant, a brute, or a wild beast.'[99]

7.71   The Law Commission has noted the criticisms of the current position and identified the following problems with the insanity defence:[100]

'First, it is not clear whether the defence of insanity is even available in all cases. Secondly, the law lags behind psychiatric understanding, and this partly explains why in practice medical professionals do not apply the correct legal test. Thirdly, the label of "insane" is outdated as a description of those with mental illness, and simply wrong as regards those who have learning disabilities, learning difficulties or those with epilepsy. Lastly, there are potential problems of compliance with the European Convention on Human Rights.'

The Commission has embarked on a review and will publish a consultation paper in 2011.

THE PLEA OF DIMINISHED RESPONSIBILITY

7.72   Section 2 of the Homicide Act 1957 provides for the plea of diminished responsibility to a charge of murder. Section 2 has been extensively amended by s 52 of the Coroners and Justice Act 2009. This provides as follows:

'(1)   A person ("D") who kills or is a party to the killing of another is not to be convicted of murder if D was suffering from an abnormality of mental functioning which –
(a)   arose from a recognised medical condition,
(b)   substantially impaired D's ability to do one or more of the things mentioned in subsection (1A), and

---

[97]   Ibid, para 40.
[98]   Mackay, R D 'Mental Disability at the Time of the Offence', Gostin, L; Bartlett, P; Fennell, P; Mackay, R and McHale, J, *Principles of Mental Health Law*, OUP 2010, Chapter 20, 720–756 at 733.
[99]   The 'wild beast' test comes from *Arnold's Case* (1724) 16 St Tr 695.
[100]   http://www.lawcom.gov.uk.

(c)   provides an explanation for D's acts and omissions in doing or being a
       party to the killing.
(1A) Those things are—

       (a) to understand the nature of D's conduct;
       (b) to form a rational judgment;
       (c) to exercise self-control.
(1B) For the purposes of subsection (1)(c), an abnormality of mental functioning
      provides an explanation for D's conduct if it causes, or is a significant
      contributory factor in causing, D to carry out that conduct.'

7.73   The burden of proof to establish diminished responsibility is on the
defence. Section 2(2) provides that 'On a charge of murder it shall be for the
defence to prove that the person charged is by virtue of this section not liable to
be convicted of murder.' The effect of a successful plea is that a homicide
conviction is reduced from murder with a mandatory life sentence, to
manslaughter where the sentence is within the judge's discretion. However, this
does not necessarily mean that a hospital order will be imposed. The jury must
be satisfied on the balance of probabilities that the accused is suffering from an
abnormality of mental functioning which:

(a)   arose from a recognised medical condition, and

(b)   substantially impaired his ability to do one or more of:

       (i)   understand the nature of his own conduct;
       (ii)   form a rational judgment;
       (iii)   exercise self-control; and

(c)   provides an explanation for D's acts in doing or being a party to the
       killing.

The abnormality of mental functioning will provide an explanation for D's
conduct if it causes or is a significant contributory factor in causing D to carry
out the conduct.

7.74   The first question is whether there is an abnormality of mental
functioning. The previous test was whether there is an abnormality of mind.
This is a question for the jury to decide on the balance of probabilities, based
on medical evidence.[101] In *R v Byrne* Lord Parker CJ contrasted 'abnormality
of mind' with 'defect of reason' in the *McNaghten* rules stating that
abnormality of mind means:[102]

> '[A] state of mind so different from that of ordinary human beings that the
> reasonable man would term it abnormal. It appears to us to be wide enough to
> cover the mind's activities in all its aspects, not only the perception of physical acts

---

[101]   (1979) 69 Cr App R 104, CA.
[102]   *R v Byrne* [1960] 3 All ER 1 at 5, CA.

and matters and the ability to form a rational judgment whether an act is right or wrong, but also the ability to exercise will-power to control physical acts in accordance with that rational judgment.'

The Court in *Byrne* held that a man with a personality disorder could be suffering from an abnormality of mind. It is likely that these same principles would apply following the 2009 Act reforms and that a personality disorder could produce an abnormality of mental functioning resulting from a recognised medical condition.

7.75 The second question is whether the abnormality of mental functioning arises from a recognised medical condition This could include abnormalities of mental functioning arising from learning disability, physical causes such as a toxic confusional state, a stroke, or a brain injury, personality disorders, psychotic illnesses with strong delusions and hallucinations, depressive illness, reactive depression mental disorder brought on by head injury.

7.76 The third issue is whether the defendant's ability to understand the nature of his own conduct, to form a rational judgment or to exercise self control. In *R v Dietschmann*[103] the House of Lords considered the old test that the abnormality of mind had substantially impaired the defendant's responsibility and concluded that a defendant who had an abnormality of mind and was under the influence of drink or drugs did not have to establish that even if he had not had any drink or drugs he would still have killed as he did. Section 2(1) referred to 'substantial impairment' which did not require the abnormality of mental functioning to be the sole cause of the defendant's acts in doing the killing. The abnormality of mind does not have to be the sole cause of the impaired responsibility. The new test is that the abnormality of mental functioning must have substantially impaired D's ability to:

(a) understand the nature of his own conduct;

(b) form a rational judgment;

(c) exercise self-control;

Although the functional dimensions of responsibility are spelt out in more detail, the test remains that of substantial impairment. The abnormality of mental functioning does not have to be the sole cause. Furthermore, the abnormality of mental functioning does not have to be the sole cause of the homicidal conduct. It will be enough if it is a significant contributory factor in causing D to carry out the conduct.

---

[103] *R v Dietschmann* [2003] UKHL 10, [2003] 1 All ER 897, HL.

7.77 In *R v Byrne* Lord Parker CJ considered the issue which would now arise under s 2(1A)(c) (substantial impairment of ability to exercise self-control) and held that a person's responsibility could be diminished as a result of this characteristic alone:[104]

'[T]he expression 'mental responsibility for his acts' points to a consideration of the extent to which the accused's mind is answerable for his physical acts which must include a consideration of the extent of his ability to exercise will-power to control his physical acts.'

This meant that the defence was available to someone with a personality disorder.

7.78 On the question of 'substantially', in *R v Lloyd*, Edmund Davies J said this:[105]

'Substantial does not mean total, that is to say, the mental responsibility need not be totally impaired, so to speak, destroyed altogether. At the other end of the scale substantial does not mean trivial or minimal. It is something in between and Parliament has left it to you and other juries to say, on the evidence, was the mental responsibility impaired, and, if so, was it substantially impaired?

The fourth issue is whether the abnormality of mental functioning provides an explanation for D's acts in doing or being a party to the killing. The abnormality of mental functioning will provide an explanation for D's conduct if it causes or is a significant contributory factor in causing D to carry out the conduct. Again the abnormality of mental functioning does not have to be the sole cause, as long as it is a significant contributory factor.'

7.79 The court will accept pleas of guilty to manslaughter except in cases where medical opinion is divided or is open to challenge.[106] The Mental Health Act Commission ('MHAC') report that 'the number of diminished responsibility verdicts peaked about 25 years ago and has been tailing away ever since'. The MHAC also report that of the 515 diminished responsibility verdicts between 1992 and 2002–2003, 182 (35 per cent) resulted in prison sentences rather than hospital. After 1999–2000 'other' manslaughter verdicts (most likely provocation) account for over 80 per cent of hospital orders.[107]

THE PLEA OF INFANTICIDE

7.80 Infanticide is defined in s 1(1) of the Infanticide Act 1938 as:

---

[104] [1960] 3 All ER 1 at 5.
[105] *R v Lloyd* [1967] 1 QB 175 at 178.
[106] *R v Cox* (1968) 52 Cr App R 130, CA; *R v Vinagre* (1979) 69 Cr App R 104, CA.
[107] Mental Health Act Commission *In Place of Fear* (Eleventh Biennial Report 2003–2005, TSO, 2005), p 369; Mental Health Act Commission *Placed Among Strangers* (Thirteenth Biennial Report 2005–2007, TSO, 2007), pp 375–376.

'Where a woman by any willful act or omission causes the death of her child being a child under the age of twelve months, but at the time of the act or omission the balance of her mind was disturbed by her not having fully recovered from the effect of giving birth to the child or by reason of the effect of lactation consequent upon the birth of the child, then … she shall be guilty … of infanticide, and may for such offence be dealt with and punished as if she had been guilty of the offence of manslaughter of the child.'

This replaced the definition in the Infanticide Act 1922 which only applied to a 'newly born' child. It enables women charged with child killing when in the throes of post-natal depression or any other severe mental illness to escape conviction for murder.

UNFITNESS TO PLEAD

7.81 A defendant in a Crown Court will be under disability in relation to his or her trial ('unfit to plead') if unable to plead to the indictment, to understand the proceedings so as to be able to challenge jurors, to understand and give evidence, and to make a proper defence.[108] In *Pritchard*, Alderson B said this:[109]

'There are three points to be inquired into—first, whether the prisoner is mute of malice or not; secondly, whether he can plead to the indictment or not; thirdly, whether he is of sufficient intellect to comprehend the course of proceedings on the trial, so as to make a proper defence—to know that he might challenge any of you to whom he may object—and to comprehend the details of the evidence, which in a case of this nature must constitute a minute investigation. Upon this issue, therefore, if you think that there is no certain mode of communicating the details of the trial to the prisoner, so that he can clearly understand them, and be able properly to make his defence to the charge; you ought to find that he is not of sane mind. It is not enough, that he may have a general capacity of communicating on ordinary matters.'

This test has been approved and applied in many cases since.[110]

7.82 If the defendant raises the issue, the burden is on him or her to satisfy the judge on the balance of probabilities. If the issue is raised by the prosecution, the prosecution must satisfy the judge beyond reasonable doubt that the defendant is under disability.[111] If the issue of unfitness is raised in the magistrates court the issue should be dealt with under s 37(3) whereby the court may make a hospital order without convicting the offender if satisfied that the

---

[108] *R v Pritchard* (1836) 7 C & P 303. For an excellent analysis of unfitness to plead and the human rights implications of the trial of the facts, see Mackay, R D 'Mental Disability at the Time of the Offence', Gostin, L; Bartlett, P; Fennell, P; Mackay, R and McHale, J, *Principles of Mental Health Law*, OUP 2010, Chapter 21, 757–777.

[109] Ibid, 304.

[110] See most recently *R v M* [2003] EWCA Crim 3452, *R v Diamond* [2008] EWCA Crim 923 at para 43.

[111] Criminal Procedure (Insanity) Act 1964, s 4, as amended by Domestic Violence, Crime and Victims Act 2004, s 22.

accused meets the criteria for a hospital order, and that he 'did the act or made the omission.' Section 11(1) of the Powers of Criminal Courts (Sentencing) Act 2000 provides that:

'If, on a trial by a magistrates court, of an offence punishable on summary conviction with imprisonment, the court (a) is satisfied that the accused did the act or made the omission charged but (b) is of opinion that inquiry ought to be made into his physical or mental condition before the method of dealing with him is determined the court shall adjourn the case to enable a medical examination and report to be made and shall remand him.'

7.83 Section 4A(2)(b) of the Criminal Procedure (Insanity and Unfitness to Plead) Act 1991 provides for 'a trial of the facts' to take place where a defendant is found to be unfit to plead. A full trial will not take place, but a jury will be required to determine whether they are satisfied beyond reasonable doubt that the defendant did the act or made the omission charged against him as an offence regardless of the existence of any necessary mens rea. In *R v Antoine*,[112] the issue was whether the section 4A hearing, in requiring a jury to decide whether the defendant 'did the act or made the omission charged against him' requires proof of all the elements of the offence. The House of Lords held that it did not, and the jury was not to consider the mental elements of the offence, only the actus reus. On an application to the European Court of Human Rights alleging breach of the right to a fair trial in determination of a criminal charge, the Strasbourg Court held that:[113]

'While it is true that the section 4A hearing has strong similarities with procedures at a criminal trial, the Court notes that the proceedings were principally concerned with the *actus reus*, namely whether the applicant had carried out an act or made an omission which would have constituted a crime if done or made with the requisite *mens rea*.'

The Court went on to say that:

'On a finding of unfitness to plead, no conviction was possible. The Court considers that these proceedings did not therefore concern the determination of a criminal charge. The applicant was no longer under any threat of conviction. The applicant argued that the possibility of an acquittal brought the proceedings within the scope of Article 6, since, to that extent, a final decision could be taken regarding a criminal charge. The Court is not persuaded however that this renders the proceedings criminal for the purposes of Article 6 §1. It may be regarded as a mechanism protecting an applicant, wrongly accused of participation in a purported offence, from the making of any preventative orders under section 5(2) of the 1964 Act. The lack of a possibility of a conviction and the absence of any punitive sanctions are more decisive. Though hospital orders may be imposed on defendants in criminal trials and involve the loss of liberty, it cannot be argued that such an order is a measure of retribution or deterrence in the sense of the imposition of a sentence of imprisonment.'

---

[112] [2001] 1 AC 340.
[113] *Antoine* v *United Kingdom* Application No 62960/00 Decision on Admissibility 13 May 2003.

Although the European Court of Human Rights is free to go behind appearances and decide whether a measure is 'in substance' a penalty, here the Strasbourg Court surprisingly concluded that a hospital order with restrictions entailing potentially indeterminate detention lacks the characteristics of a penal sanction.

7.84 If the jury are satisfied that the defendant did the act or made the omission charged, they must make a finding to that effect; if they are not so satisfied, they are obliged to return a verdict of acquittal. Where the defendant is found guilty 'on the facts', the powers of sentence are the same as for a special verdict of not guilty by reason of insanity.

7.85 Paragraph 13 of *Home Office Circular 93/91* states:

> 'Where an accused person is found unfit to be tried he should always be legally represented during the trial of the facts. There may be cases where the accused, because of his mental disorder, repudiates his legal representative prior to, or during the trial of the facts.'

The court should appoint a lawyer to put the case for the accused who may properly be entrusted to pursue his or her interests. This could include someone who has previously represented the accused or any other person whom the court considers appropriate, for example a solicitor known to the court to have experience in such matters. The Official Solicitor has let it be known that he is prepared to act as the legal representative of an accused person who lacks capacity during a trial of the facts.

7.86 The Domestic Violence, Crime and Victims Act 2004 has made a number of changes. First, as we have seen it reduces to three the disposal options available to the court:

(a)   hospital order under s 37 with or without restrictions;

(b)   a supervision order; or

(c)   an absolute discharge.

Second, it clarifies that for a hospital order to be made the criteria in s 37 need to be satisfied. If a restriction order is to be imposed it must be necessary for the protection of the public from serious harm. Third, the court can direct admission, and does not have to rely on the Secretary of State to do so. Fourth, in appropriate cases remand powers under ss 35, 36 and interim orders under s 38 are available to the court. Finally, the Home Secretary is empowered to remit for trial a patient detained under ss 37 or 41 following a finding of unfitness to plead, if satisfied that they can now properly be tried. The Law Commission has identifed numerous problems with the existing law on unfitness to plead:[114]

> 'The current test for determining fitness to plead dates from 1836 when the science of psychiatry was in its infancy. The law developed in a piecemeal way and independently of developments under the European Convention on Human Rights on "effective participation" as part of the right to a fair trial.
>
> The legal test for fitness to plead needs to be reconsidered and should be contrasted with the much wider test contained in the Mental Capacity Act 2005.
>
> Other important questions to be answered include: what is the exact scope of a trial of the facts following a finding of unfitness to plead? What issues can be raised by the defendant, in particular "defences" of accident, mistake and self-defence?'

The Law Commission has proposed a number of reforms to bring the test applied in relation to unfitness more into line with the test under the Mental Capacity Act 2005, and to reform the procedure for trials of the facts.[115]

MENTAL CONDITION AT TIME OF SENTENCING

7.87 The effect of mental disorder on criminal responsibility or fitness for trial is confined to small numbers of cases. Its effect on sentencing disposal is manifest in many thousands of cases. In some of these the result will be that an offender is not imprisoned but is instead admitted to hospital under Part III of the MHA 1983. In others, especially where there is a personality disorder, the result may be an enhanced prison sentence under the Criminal Justice Act 2003. Once a defendant is convicted or has been found to have committed the act constituting the offence, they may be given a community disposal, a prison sentence or a hospital order. A patient may be diverted to the psychiatric system at the sentencing stage. This may be done under the MHA 1983 by a hospital or a guardianship order or by using a community order under the Criminal Justice Act 2003.

7.88 Since the MHA 1959, hospital orders have been a key method of disposal of mentally disordered offenders. Department of Health figures show a long-term decline in unrestricted hospital orders over the lifetime of the MHA 1983. In 1995–1996, 536 such orders were made, but since then the annual figure has steadily declined, the number for 2009–2010 being 245, with a further 329 hospital orders with restrictions on discharge being imposed.[116]

---

[114] Law Commission, Unfitness to Plead: A Consultation Paper Law Com Consultation Paper No 197.

[115] Ibid, para 9.1.

[116] NHS Information Centre, In-Patients Formally Detained under the Mental Health Act 1983 and Patients Subject to Supervised Community Treatment: England 2009–2010, Health and Social Care Information Centre 2010. Table 2a.

7.89 The key question in the decision to impose a hospital order is whether the offender is suffering from mental disorder *at the time of sentencing*, not whether his mental disorder had any bearing on the offending behaviour. Indeed in *R* v *Smith*, Keene LJ said that the wording of s 37 indicated that 'it seems that a hospital order may be made even though the mental disorder suffered by the defendant has developed since the date of the offence.[117] In making a hospital order the court is not concerned with criminal responsibility or the defendant's fitness to participate in the trial; the person has usually already been tried and convicted. The only relevant considerations are his mental condition and the need for psychiatric treatment in hospital at the time of sentencing. The MHA 1983 also provides for the transfer of mentally disordered prisoners (whether on remand or serving a sentence) from prison to hospital on the authority of a Home Secretary's warrant. In 2009–2010, 615 prisoners were transferred from prison to hospital.[118]

7.90 The Criminal Justice Act 2003 now provides a general framework for sentencing offenders, with disposals ranging from community sentences to provisions for sentencing dangerous offenders. Hospital orders and transfers to psychiatric hospital from prison continue to be governed by the MHA 1983. Section 142(1) of the Criminal Justice Act 2003 requires any court dealing with an offender to have regard to five purposes of sentencing. These are:

(a) punishment of offenders;

(b) reduction of crime (including its reduction by deterrence);

(c) reform and rehabilitation of offenders;

(d) protection of the public; and

(d) making reparation by offenders to persons affected by their offences.

This section does not apply to offenders under 18, to offenders convicted of murder, of certain firearms offences or offences requiring a custodial sentence, who are subject to the dangerous offender provisions in ss 225–228 of the Act, or where the court makes a hospital order, an interim hospital order or a hospital direction under Part III of the MHA 1983.

The hierarchy of sentencing severity

7.91 The least serious offences should be dealt with by a fine or a discharge. Those where the purposes of sentencing would not be met by such leniency, are to be dealt with by a community sentence. A community sentence may only be imposed if the court considers that the offence, or the combination of the

---

117   [2001] EWCA Crim 743, para 9.
118   NHS Information Centre, In-Patients Formally Detained under the Mental Health Act 1983 and Patients Subject to Supervised Community Treatment: England 2009–2010, Health and Social Care Information Centre 2010. Table 2a.

offence and one or more offences associated with it, is serious enough to warrant such a sentence.[119] A further threshold is s 151, which requires that a community order must be in the interests of justice and the offender must, since the age of 16, have been fined on three or more occasions, even though their offence may not be serious enough to justify a community sentence and their previous convictions would not justify such a sentence. The Sentencing Guidelines Council advises 'great care ... in assessing whether a community sentence is appropriate, since failure to comply with conditions could result in a custodial sentence'.[120] A court may only impose a prison sentence if it considers a community sentence would be insufficient, and the offence is so serious that neither a fine alone nor a community sentence can be justified for the offence or the offences associated with it.

The community order

7.92 Section 177 sets out 12 forms of community order which a court may attach to a community sentence for an offender over the age of 18. These include:

(i)   an unpaid work requirement (s 199);

(ii)   an activity requirement (s 201);

(iii) a programme requirement (s 202);

(iv)   a prohibited activity requirement (s 203);

(v)   a curfew requirement (s 204);

(vi)   an exclusion requirement (s 205);

(vii) a residence requirement (s 206);

(viii) a mental health treatment requirement (s 207);

(ix)   a drug rehabilitation requirement (s 209);

(x)   an alcohol treatment requirement (s 212);

(xi)   a supervision requirement (s 213); and

(xii) in a case where the offender is aged under 25, an attendance centre requirement (s 214).

---

[119] CJA 2003, s 148(1).
[120] Sentencing Guidelines Council *New Sentences: Criminal Justice Act 2003 Guideline*. See http://www.sentencing-guidelines.gov.uk/docs/New_sentences_guideline1.pdf.

Of greatest interest here is the 'mental health treatment requirement'.[121] A court may not impose a mental health treatment requirement unless satisfied on the evidence of a s 12 doctor that the offender's mental condition requires and may be susceptible to medical treatment but not so as to warrant a hospital or guardianship order. The court must be satisfied that arrangements have or can be made for the treatment intended to be specified in the order, and the offender must have expressed willingness to comply with the requirement.

Powers under a mental health treatment requirement

7.93 A mental health treatment requirement requires the offender to submit, during a period specified in the order, to treatment by or under the supervision of a doctor or a chartered psychologist (or both) 'with a view to the improvement of the offender's mental condition'. A community order can require treatment as an out-patient where the offender must accept treatment as a non-resident patient at any institution specified in the order, or treatment by or under the direction of such registered medical practitioner or chartered psychologist as may be specified. Treatment may be required as a resident patient in an independent nursing home or care home within the meaning of the Health and Social Care Act 2008 or a hospital, but not in a high security hospital. Beyond the above listed specifications, the court may not specify in the order the nature of the treatment to be given.

7.94 Section 208 empowers the doctor or psychologist in charge of treating an offender's mental condition under a mental health treatment requirement to arrange transfer where the offender consents and where the clinician is of the opinion that part of the treatment given by or under the direction of a doctor or a psychologist can be better or more conveniently given in or at an institution or place which is not specified in the relevant order. The requirement to accept treatment at the new location applies as if it had been part of the original order. Interestingly, the arrangements to transfer may provide for the offender to receive part of his treatment as a resident patient in an institution or place 'notwithstanding that the institution or place is not one which could have been specified for that purpose in the relevant order'. It is not clear whether this is intended to authorise admission to a high security hospital, which is not a power available to the court on making the initial order.

Breach

7.95 Section 179 and Sch 8 deal with breach. Schedule 8 provides that where the responsible officer considers that an offender has failed to comply with a community order without reasonable excuse, he must issue a warning specifying the breach, stating that it is unacceptable, and that if there is a further breach within 12 months the offender will be liable to be brought before a court. If, within that period, the responsible officer considers there has been a further breach without reasonable excuse, he must lay an information before

---

[121] CJA 2003, s 207.

the magistrates or bring the matter before a Crown Court. The court may then deal with the offender as if for the original offence by attaching more onerous requirements to the community sentence, or by imprisoning the offender if the original offence was punishable by imprisonment. If an offender over 18 has willfully and persistently failed to comply with the requirements of the order, the magistrates or the Crown Court may impose a sentence for the original offence of up to 51 weeks even though that offence was not punishable by imprisonment. In deciding what to do in the event of persistent and willful non-compliance, the court must take into account the extent to which the offender has complied with the requirements of the community order.

The requirement of a medical report prior to imprisonment

7.96 Section 157 requires any court to obtain and consider a medical report before passing a custodial sentence on an offender who is or who appears to be mentally disordered within the meaning of the MHA 1983. The medical report may be made orally or in writing by a doctor approved under s 12 of the MHA 1983 by the Secretary of State as having special experience in the diagnosis or treatment of mental disorder. However, the obligation is not absolute and does not apply if, in the circumstances of the case, the court is of the opinion that it is unnecessary to obtain a medical report, or in any case where the sentence is fixed by law.

7.97 Where the offender appears to be mentally disordered, unless the sentence is fixed by law, the court must consider any information (whether or not it is in a report) relating to the offender's mental condition and the likely effect of a custodial sentence on the person's mental condition and on any treatment which may be available for it. Failure to obtain and consider a report does not invalidate any custodial sentence, but any court considering an appeal against sentence must obtain a medical report if none was obtained by the court below, and must consider any report obtained by it or by the court below.

7.98 Sections 224–236 of the Criminal Justice Act 2003 contain provisions relating to allowing dangerous offenders guilty of specified serious offences to be sentenced to life imprisonment, imprisonment for public protection or an extended sentence. Schedule 15 specifies the sexual and violent offences which render an offender eligible for dangerous offender sentencing. Section 37(1A) of the Mental Health Act 1983 provides that nothing in ss 225–228 of the Criminal Justice Act 2003 shall prevent a court from making a hospital order under s 37(1) of the MHA 1983. So if the court is satisfied that the criteria for making a hospital order are met, an offender need not be dealt with under the dangerousness sentencing provisions of the 2003 Act.

7.99 If an offender has committed a specified offence and meets the criterion of dangerousness, the court must impose a life sentence, imprisonment for public protection or an extended sentence. An offender is dangerous where the court is 'of the opinion that there is a significant risk to the public of serious harm occasioned by the commission by him of serious offences'. 'Serious harm' means death or serious personal injury, whether physical or psychological. Section 229 governs the way in which the courts are to assess dangerousness. In all cases the court must take into account any available information before it about the offences, about any pattern of behaviour of which it may form part, and about the offender. Section 229(3) creates a presumption of dangerousness where an offender over 18 has previously been convicted of a relevant offence. The court must assume risk of serious harm to the public unless the court considers, after considering the information outlined above that it would be unreasonable to conclude that there is such a risk. The dangerous offender provisions are beyond the scope of this book. Suffice to say that offenders with personality disorders are more likely than their mentally ill counterparts to receive a dangerous offender sentence.

7.100 As noted above, nothing in ss 225–228 of the Criminal Justice Act 2003 prevents a court from making a hospital order under s 37(1) of the MHA 1983. So if the court is satisfied that the criteria for making a hospital order are met, an offender need not be dealt with under the dangerousness sentencing provisions of the 2003 Act and may be given a hospital order instead.

THE HOSPITAL ORDER (MHA 1983, S 37)

7.101 A hospital order sentences a mentally disordered person to detention in hospital for treatment rather than in prison. A hospital order may be imposed without restrictions in which case the patient's responsible clinician ('RC') may discharge the patient without recourse to higher authority, and the detention is renewed in the same way as detention under s 3. If a restriction order is imposed by a Crown Court (see **7.109–7.116** below) this will automatically be without limit of time, and there is no need for the RC to renew detention. The patient may not be discharged by the RC. Only the Home Secretary or the MHT may direct discharge. In 1995–1996, 536 hospital orders without restrictions on discharge were made. This figure has declined to 245 in 2009–2010. At the same time the number of restriction orders was 321 in 1995–1996, declined to 235 in 2003–2004 and has since risen to 329 in 2009–2010. Since 2005–2006 (the first year ever when this happened) the annual number of hospital orders with restrictions has consistently exceeded the numbers of hospital orders without restrictions.[122]

7.102 If sent to prison a mentally disordered person can only be treated without consent under the terms of ss 5 and 6 of the Mental Capacity Act 2005 which authorise treatment without consent of a person who lacks capacity and who needs treatment in his own best interests, and authorise restraint of a mentally incapacitated person where necessary and a proportionate response to prevent harm to the person. A person, whether or not they lack capacity, may also be treated without consent under common law, where restraint and

---

[122] NHS Information Centre, In-Patients Formally Detained under the Mental Health Act 1983 and Patients Subject to Supervised Community Treatment: England 2009–2010, Health and Social Care Information Centre 2010. Table 2a.

treatment may be authorised where they represent the minimum force necessary to prevent that person from harming others. People who are detained under the MHA 1983 may be given treatment without consent subject to the second opinion safeguards in Part IV.

7.103 A hospital order may be made by magistrates or by the Crown Court. The Crown Court can make an order if the person is convicted of an offence punishable with imprisonment, except in the case of murder (for which the sentence is fixed by law). A magistrates' court can make a hospital order without recording a conviction if the person is suffering from mental illness or severe mental impairment, and the court is satisfied that he committed the act with which he is charged.[123] One of the two doctors giving evidence must be approved under s 12 of the MHA 1983. An order authorises detention for up to six months in the first instance, renewable for a further six months, and then for periods of one year at a time. Under the MHA 2007 the old categories of mental disorder will cease to be relevant and the court will be required to be satisfied that:

(a)   the offender is suffering from mental disorder ('any disorder or disability of mind') of a nature or degree making it appropriate for him to be detained in hospital for medical treatment; and

(b)   that appropriate treatment is available for him.

The court must also be of the opinion, having regard to all the circumstances, including the nature of the offence and the character and antecedents of the offender, and to other methods of dealing with him, that the most suitable method of disposing of the case is by means of a hospital order.

7.104 Even if the criteria for making a hospital order are met, the court still has considerable discretion to consider other alternatives such as a dangerous offender sentence. Guidance was given by the Court of Appeal in *R v Birch* on the circumstances where prison might be chosen as an alternative for a patient found to be suffering from mental disorder.[124] The first is where the offender is dangerous and there is no suitable secure hospital bed. The second is where there was an element of culpability for the offence which merited punishment. This might happen where there is no connection between the mental disorder and the offence, or where the offender's responsibility for the offence 'is diminished but not extinguished'. In *R v Drew*[125] the House of Lords held that under both national law and the European Convention case-law a sentence of imprisonment could be imposed on a mentally disordered defendant who was criminally responsible and fit to be tried.

7.105 Appropriate treatment can include psychological treatment, care, habilitation and rehabilitation and is defined as treatment which is intended to

---

[123]   MHA 1983, s 37(3).
[124]   (1989) 11 Cr App R (S) 202 at 215, CA.
[125]   [2003] UKHL 25.

alleviate or prevent deterioration in the patient's condition. The new definition of mental disorder means that people with learning disability, people with mental illness and people with personality disorders (who are thought to benefit most from psychological interventions such as cognitive behaviour therapy) may be detained if their disorder is of a nature or degree making it appropriate for them to be detained for treatment.

7.106   A hospital order cannot be made unless the court is satisfied, on the evidence of the approved clinician who would have overall responsibility for his case or the hospital managers, that arrangements have been made for the patient's admission to hospital within 28 days. Admission to the designated hospital must take place within the mandatory 28 day period specified in s 37(4) of the MHA 1983, and if this does not happen the hospital order ceases to have effect.[126] Hospitals have discretion to decide whether to admit an offender under a hospital order, unless the patient has been found not guilty by reason of insanity or unfit to plead.

7.107   In some cases under the MHA 1959, mentally disordered people were sentenced to imprisonment because hospitals refused to accept them. Section 39 of the MHA 1983 therefore, empowers a court considering making a hospital order, an interim hospital order, or a hospital direction with a restriction direction to request the Primary Care Trust or Health Authority where the person resides or last resided or any other Health Authority or PCT which appears to be appropriate to furnish the court with such information as they can reasonably obtain with respect to the hospital or hospitals in their area or elsewhere where arrangements could be made for the admission of the offender. The Trust or Authority approached by the Court must comply with any such request. In relation to a person who is under 18 the duty to provide information arises in relation not only to hospital orders but also to remands under ss 35 or36 and to committals under s 44 of the MHA 1983. It also requires that information be provided as to the availability of information about accommodation or facilities deigned to be specifically suitable for patients under 18.[127]

7.108   The effect of a hospital order is similar to that of an admission for treatment as a non-offender under s 3. Detention is renewed under s 20, and the patient has the right to apply for discharge to the MHRT on the same basis as a patient detained under s 3, except that no application is allowed within the first six months following the making of the order, and treatment for mental disorder is subject to Part IV of the MHA 1983. The most important difference is that a hospital order patient cannot be discharged by his nearest relative. A hospital order can be made with or without a s 41 'restriction order' imposing restrictions on discharge.

---

[126]   *R (DB) v Nottinghamshire Healthcare NHS Trust* [2008] EWCA Civ 1354.
[127]   MHA 1983, s 39(1A)–(1B).

RESTRICTION ORDER (MHA 1983, S 41)

7.109 Where a hospital order has been made, a Crown Court may make a restriction order. A magistrates' court has no power to make a restriction order, but if the criteria are met, it may commit an offender over fourteen years of age to the Crown Court where a restriction order can be made. The evidence of one of the two doctors supporting the hospital order must have been given orally. In 2009–2010 Department of Health figures indicate that 329 hospital orders with restriction orders were made by courts. Home Office data show that in 1995, 1,548 patients subject to restriction orders were resident in hospitals under detention, including 264 women. By 2005 that figure had risen to 2,344, 411 of whom were women. By the end of 2008 that figure had risen to 3,937, 477 of whom were women.[128]

7.110 The grounds for making a restriction order are that it appears to the court, having regard to the nature of the offence, the antecedents of the offender, and the risk of his committing further offences if set at large, that a restriction order is necessary for the protection of the public from serious harm. The Court of Appeal in *R v Birch*[129] held that the sentencing court is required to assess the seriousness of the risk not that he will re-offend, but the risk that if he does, the public will suffer serious harm. The harm in question need not be limited to personal injury, nor need it relate to the public in general, but the potential harm must be serious, and a high possibility of the recurrence of minor offences will not be sufficient. In *R v Osker*[130] Ms Osker suffered from a borderline personality disorder. She pleaded guilty to causing a public nuisance and she was given a hospital order with a restriction order without limit of time. She had caused roads to be closed in October 2008 when she mounted the roof of a shopping centre, slashed her arms with a razor blade and threatened to throw herself off the building. It was argued she was wrongly sentenced, as she posed little danger to the public, only a risk of self-harm. The Court of Appeal held that the evidence before the crown court did not substantiate sufficient risk to the public to justify a restriction order, and the restriction order was quashed.

7.111 Where the medical opinion is unanimous that a restriction order should be imposed and there is a secure bed, a decision not to impose a hospital order should not be made because of concerns about risk to the public should the offender be released.[131] However, if the doctors giving medical evidence are not unanimous about a hospital disposal, the sentencing decision is for the judge to resolve in the light of all the evidence and the circumstances of the case.[132]

---

[128] Ministry of Justice *Statistics of Mentally Disordered Offenders 2008 England and Wales* 2010 Ministry of Justice, p 4.
[129] (1989) 11 Cr App R (S) 202.
[130] [2010] EWCA Crim 955.
[131] *R v Howell* (1985) 7 Cr App R (S) 360, CA.
[132] *R v Reid* [2005] EWCA Crim 392, CA.

7.112　The MHA 1983 provided for restriction order to be made for either a specified period or without limit of time. The possibility of a time limited restriction order has been removed by s 40(1) of the Mental Health Act 2007.

7.113　The effect of a restriction order is that a patient does not have to have his or her detention renewed by the hospital managers. Detention carries on, subject to a requirement on the responsible clinician to submit a report at least once a year 'on that person'. The patient cannot be granted leave of absence, transferred or discharged by the responsible clinician or hospital managers without the consent of the Secretary of State for Justice. This is dealt with by the Mental Health Unit in the Ministry of Justice. If the patient is discharged with Home Office permission this may be absolutely or subject to conditions. Except in rare cases (such as extreme age) where the offender is assessed as posing no risk, conditional discharge will be the route chosen.

7.114　Restriction order patients used to have only limited rights to challenge detention. A patient detained for treatment under the civil power (s 3) or by a criminal court under a hospital order (s 37), has the right to apply to a Mental Health Tribunal ('MHT') to seek discharge. The MHT must order discharge if not satisfied that the patient is suffering from mental disorder of a nature or degree warranting detention. Under the MHA 1959 restriction order patients did not have this right. They could only ask the Home Secretary to refer their case to a MHT, and the tribunal did not have the power to order release, only to advise the Home Secretary to exercise his power of discharge.

7.115　The tribunal's lack of power to order discharge was held in *X v United Kingdom*[133] to breach the requirement in Art 5(4) that a person detained because of unsoundness of mind must be able, at intervals, to seek review of the lawfulness of their detention before a court or tribunal *with the power to order release*. The MHA 1983 now authorises a MHT to order the absolute or conditional discharge of a restriction order patient if not satisfied that the conditions of detention are met (mental disorder of a nature or degree warranting confinement). This introduced the possibility that an offender patient might persuade a tribunal to discharge him when the Home Office (now the Ministry of Justice) Mental Health Unit still considered discharge to pose too great a risk, hence removing the absolute control exercised by the Ministry of Justice over the duration of detention of offenders sentenced to restriction orders without limit of time.

7.116　In *R v A*[134] the Court of Appeal held that the risk that an offender might be released prematurely by a MHT is not a ground for a court to pass a life sentence rather than making a restriction order, since the composition and powers of the MHRT and the Parole Board panels are 'closely analogous'. Each consists of a legally qualified president who has experience in the criminal courts, a psychiatrist and a lay member. The figures show that since 1990 the

---

[133]　(1981) 4 EHRR 188, ECtHR.
[134]　[2005] EWCA Crim 2077, CA.

tribunal gives many more conditional discharges than the Home secretary. In 2008, of the 407 conditional discharges of restricted patients 333 were by the MHT and 74 were by the Ministry of Justice Mental Health Unit.

Conditional discharge

7.117 The restriction order with its conditional discharge option is seen as an effective means of risk management. Re-offending rates in terms of serious sexual offences or violent offences of the 1,500 patients conditionally discharged between 1999 and 2006 are assessed by the Home Office as averaging 1 per cent for grave offences and 7 per cent for all offences.[135]

7.118 A restriction order patient can be discharged by the Secretary of State for Justice or a MHT either absolutely or subject to conditions. If the patient is given an absolute discharge, both the hospital and restriction orders cease to have effect, and he cannot be recalled to hospital. A conditionally discharged restricted patient may, for example, be directed to live in a specified place, to attend for treatment, and to accept treatment by or under the direction of the responsible clinician. Because it may be a condition of discharge that the patient must accept treatment for mental disorder, a conditionally discharged restricted patient is not eligible to seek review of treatment by a second opinion doctor under Part IV of the MHA 1983.

GUARDIANSHIP ORDER (MHA 1983, S 37)

7.119 As Jones points out, 'Little use has been made of guardianship orders by the courts', with figures running at under 30 cases per year.[136] The diagnostic criteria for making an order are that the offender must be sixteen or over, and suffering from any disorder or disability of mind warranting reception into guardianship. The court has wide discretion to decide whether guardianship is 'suitable', since it must be of the opinion, having regard to all the circumstances, including the nature of the offence and the character and antecedents of the offender and to other methods of dealing with him, that the most suitable method of disposing of the case is by means of a guardianship order.

7.120 The medical evidentiary requirements for making a guardianship order are virtually the same as for making a hospital order. The court enjoys similar powers to request information to those available for hospital order cases request. Under s 39A, a court considering making a guardianship order will be empowered to request the local social services authority (or any other social services authority considered by the court to be appropriate):

---

[135] Ministry of Justice *Statistics of Mentally Disordered Offenders England and Wales 2008* Ministry of Justice 2010, Table 7.
[136] Ibid, p 230.

(a) to inform the court whether it or any person authorised by it is prepared to receive the patient into guardianship; and

(b) if so, to give such information as it reasonably can about how it or the other person could be expected to exercise guardianship powers.

TRANSFER TO HOSPITAL OF SENTENCED PRISONERS (SS 47 AND 49)

7.121 Section 47 allows for the transfer of a sentenced prisoner to hospital by Home Secretary's direction. Section 49 empowers the Home Secretary to attach a restriction direction, imposing restrictions on discharge. By far the majority of transfers are subject to restrictions. In 1995–1996, 222 patients were transferred under ss 47 and 49. In 2005–2006 the figure was 273. The equivalent figures for s 47 transfers without restrictions were 31 for 1995–1996 and 56 for 2005–2006.[137] In 1995, 402 prisoners were resident in hospital having been transferred under ss 47 and 49 restrictions. After 2003 the numbers of in-patients detained following s 47 transfer directions with restrictions began to rise significantly, the total for 2005 being 561, and at the end of 2008 the total was 703.[138]

7.122 If no restriction direction is made, detention lasts for up to six months, renewable for six months and then for periods of one year at a time. If a restriction direction is made, the restrictions expire on the earliest date on which the offender would have been released from prison (the earliest release date); thereafter, the patient is detained as if he were a patient under a s 37 hospital order without restrictions, and may be discharged by the clinical supervisor or the Mental Health Tribunal without recourse to the Ministry of Justice.

7.123 Before issuing a transfer direction the Secretary of State for Justice must be satisfied that the prisoner is:

(a) suffering from mental disorder (any disorder or disability of mind); and

(b) the mental disorder is of a nature or degree which makes it appropriate for him to be detained in hospital for medical treatment; and

(c) that appropriate medical treatment is available for him; and

(d) having regard to the public interest and to all the other circumstances, a transfer is expedient.

---

[137] NHS Information Centre, In-Patients Formally Detained under the Mental Health Act 1983 and Patients Subject to Supervised Community Treatment: England 2009–2010, Health and Social Care Information Centre 2010. Table 2a.

[138] Ministry of Justice *Statistics of Mentally Disordered Offenders 2008* Ministry of Justice 2010 Table 2.

The direction must be based on two medical reports, one from a doctor approved under s 12.

7.124 The initial version of the Mental Health Act Code of Practice (1993) stated that the need for in-patient treatment of a prisoner must be identified and acted on swiftly, and contact made urgently between the prison doctor and the hospital doctor. It also emphasises that the transfer of a prisoner to hospital should not be delayed until close to his release date, since a transfer in such circumstances may well be seen by the prisoner as being primarily intended to extend his detention.[139] These paragraphs no longer appear in the Code, but have been replaced by a short statement that:[140]

'The need for in-patient treatment for a prisoner should be identified and acted upon quickly and contact made immediately with the responsible PCT by Prison Health Care staff.'

7.125 The Mental Health Act Commission have expressed their continuing concern that transfers late in the sentence are distorting mental health law by using it for primarily public protection purposes, and that transfer should take place as soon as is therapeutically indicated rather than being delayed until risk is the primary factor.[141] When a patient is transferred to hospital near the end of their sentence the hospital authorities must carefully scrutinise the medical reports to ensure that they provide a sound basis for transfer. In *R (SP)* v *Secretary of State for Justice*[142] the Secretary of State used a pre-2007 Act form where reference was to the likelihood that treatment would alleviate or prevent deterioration in the patient's condition rather than the availability of appropriate treatment. The decision was made by an official in the Mental Health Unit who applied the availability of appropriate treatment test. The court considered that the question was whether the medical reports provided a sound basis for the view that appropriate treatment was available, and the answer was 'Yes' since a bed was available at Rampton high security hospital.

Restriction direction

7.126 Where the Secretary of State for Justice thinks fit, he may attach to a transfer direction a restriction direction. If a restriction direction is not given, or once it expires because the prisoner's earliest release date has passed, the offender is detained 'as if' under a hospital order without restrictions, sometimes known as 'a notional s 37'. Patients transferred from prison to hospital are entitled to make applications to have their cases referred to MHRTs. If the Secretary of State for Justice is notified by the clinical supervisor, another clinician or the MHRT that the offender no longer requires

---

[139] Department of Health and Welsh Office *Mental Health Act 1983 Code of Practice*, paras 3.12–3.13.

[140] Department of Health *Code of Practice Mental Health Act 1983* (2008), para 33.31.

[141] Mental Health Act Commission *Placed Among Strangers* (Thirteenth Biennial Report 2005–2007, TSO, 2007), pp 382–383.

[142] [2010] EWHC 1124 (Admin).

treatment in hospital, he has two options: he can either discharge an offender who would have been eligible for release on parole had he remained in prison, or he can direct that he be returned to prison to serve the remainder of his sentence. This means that the Secretary of State for Justice retains greater control over the duration of detention of a transferred prisoner with a restriction direction than he does over a restriction order patient. To comply with Art 5 of the European Convention a tribunal must have the power to discharge a restriction order patient, but because a transferred person is a prisoner, the Secretary of State for Justice may remit them to prison to serve out their term. This fact was undoubtedly one of the inspirations behind the introduction of the hybrid order under s 45A (discussed below).

TRANSFER OF UN-SENTENCED PRISONERS TO HOSPITAL (S 48)

7.127 Section 48 provides the same power of transfer from prison to psychiatric hospital of civil prisoners, remand prisoners and prisoners detained under Immigration legislation. Under the MHA 2007 the Secretary of State for Justice will have to be satisfied:

(a) that the person is suffering from mental disorder (again the new braod definition of any disorder or disability of mind) of a nature or degree which makes it appropriate for him to be detained in hospital for medical treatment; and

(b) he is in urgent need of such treatment; and

(c) appropriate medical treatment is available for him.

The same requirements for medical reports apply to s 48 as apply to a transfer direction under s 47. The main difference between ss 47 and 48 is that for the latter the need for treatment must be urgent.

7.128 In 1995–1996 there were 359 transfers of un-sentenced prisoners with restriction directions, and 51 without. In 2009–2010 there were 266 with restrictions and 2 without.[143] In 1995, 183 prisoners were resident in hospital having been transferred under s 48 with s 49 restrictions. The total population for 2008 was 236.[144] Under the MHA 1983 the power was confined to people with mental illness or severe mental impairment. The MHA 2007 extends it to patients with any form of disorder or disability of mind. Transfer of remand prisoners is an important power to rescue people who may be at risk of suicide or self harm due to mental illness such as depression but who equally might

---

[143] NHS Information Centre, In-Patients Formally Detained under the Mental Health Act 1983 and Patients Subject to Supervised Community Treatment: England 2009–2010, Health and Social Care Information Centre 2010. Table 2a.

[144] Ministry of Justice *Statistics of Mentally Disordered Offenders 2008* Ministry of Justice 2010 Table 2.

need urgent treatment to prevent risk to self or others brought on by personality problems. Patients transferred under s 48 may be given treatment under the regime of powers and second opinions in Part IV of the MHA 1983.

HOSPITAL DIRECTIONS AND RESTRICTION DIRECTIONS (S 45A)

7.129 Section 45A, introduced into the MHA 1983 by the Crime (Sentences) Act 1997 provides for a 'hybrid order' whereby a mentally disordered offender may be given a sentence of imprisonment coupled with an immediate direction to hospital. Initially confined to people with a personality disorder diagnosis, the MHA 2007 extends this to people with any disorder or disability of mind. The conditions which must be met before a court may impose a hospital and restriction direction are that there must be written or oral evidence from two doctors:

(a)   that the offender is suffering from mental disorder;

(b)   that the mental disorder from which the offender is suffering is of a nature or degree which makes it appropriate for him to be detained in a hospital for medical treatment; and

(c)   that appropriate medical treatment is available for him.

The result of this is that, although directed initially to hospital, the offender has the legal status of prisoner rather than patient. This means that in the event of the mental disorder being successfully treated before the expiry of the prison sentence the offender can be returned to prison to serve the remainder of the tariff sentence. The offender is given a prison sentence which is calculated in accordance with normal sentencing principles, but is directed to hospital in the first instance. If he recovers prior to the expiry of the sentence, he will be remitted to prison to serve the remaining sentence. This avoids the problem of the MHRTs discharging patients 'early', because if the offender is no longer mentally disordered, the Home Secretary has the ultimate say in whether he returns to prison. The hybrid order was initially confined to patients with psychopathic disorder, but the MHA 2007 extends it to anyone suffering from mental disorder in the broad sense of 'any disorder or disability of mind'.

7.130   The MHAC have criticised of the Home Office for its suggestion that hybrid orders 'could provide a punitive element in the disposal ... to reflect the offenders whole or partial responsibility'.[145] They adopt Bartlett and Sandland's argument that it is purportedly the aim of mental health disposals to divert the mentally disordered from punitive sanctions and the hybrid orders

---

[145]   Mental Health Act Commission *In Place of Fear* (Eleventh Biennial Report 2003–2005, TSO, 2006), pp 389–394.

require clinicians to become involved in determining levels of criminal responsibility and to engage in the process of deciding what is a suitable punishment.[146]

7.131 Home Office Guidance has dropped reference to criminal responsibility, preferring instead to stress that the power should be used in two situations. First is where the alternative would be a mandatory life sentence under the 'two strikes and you're out' provision in s 109 of the Powers of Criminal Courts (Sentencing) Act 2000 which provides, absent exceptional circumstances, for a mandatory life sentence on conviction of a second serious offence. Mental disorder is not an exceptional circumstance. The second situation is where it would be the most effective way to protect the public from further harm.[147] If the Home Office entertained hopes that this provision would be widely used, they have been disappointed. The courts have not used the power extensively. Only two such orders were made in 2009–2010, and at the end of 2008 there were only 13 section 45A patients resident in hospitals.[148]

7.132 The MHAC remained concerned that hybrid orders if they are to be used at all should not become the normal disposal for any mentally disordered offender whom the court views as criminally responsible to some degree. They were also worried about imposition of punishment alongside medical treatment may undermine treatment compliance and foster a sense of 'doing time'. Moreover, since mental illness may be relapsing and episodic a return to prison might trigger relapse and result in a form of 'ping pong' between prison and hospital throughout the tariff period.[149]

VICTIMS

7.133 In keeping with the general move to increase the legal rights of victims of crime to make representations in relation to disposal and release, ss 36–38 of the Domestic Violence, (Crime and Victims) Act 2004 provide that where a person convicted of a violent or sexual offence defined in s 45 of the 2004 Act is given a hospital order with restrictions or a hospital and limitation direction the local probation board must take all reasonable steps to ascertain whether the person who appears to be the victim of the offence or who appears to act for the victim wishes to make representations about whether the offender should be subject to any conditions if discharged or wishes to receive information about any conditions which may be imposed. If the person makes representations, the local probation board must forward them to the body making the decision on discharge.

---

[146] P Bartlett and R Sandland *Mental Health Law Policy and Practice* (OUP, 3rd edn, 2007).

[147] Home Office *Guidance on the Crime Sentences Act 1997*, para 3.

[148] NHS Information Centre, In-Patients Formally Detained under the Mental Health Act 1983 and Patients Subject to Supervised Community Treatment: England 2009–2010, Health and Social Care Information Centre 2010. Table 2a; Ministry of Justice *Statistics of Mentally Disordered Offenders 2008* Ministry of Justice 2010 Table 2.

[149] Mental Health Act Commission *In Place of Fear* (Eleventh Biennial Report 2003–2005, TSO, 2006), pp 392–393.

7.134   The Mental Health Act 2007 significantly amends Chapter 2 of Part III of the Domestic Violence, Crime and Victims Act 2004. These provisions entitle a victim or any person acting for a victim of a sexual or violent offence where the offender is subject to a restriction order or and restriction direction, to be notified of their right to make representations to the local probation board about whether the patient should be subject to any conditions in the event of his conditional discharge from hospital and if so what those conditions should be. Section 48 and Sch 6 to the MHA 2007 extend this right to victims of sexual or violent offences where the offender is sentenced to a hospital order without restrictions, or is given a transfer direction without restrictions.

7.135   In such cases the victim or representative is entitled to make representations as to what conditions the patient should be subject to in the event of his discharge from hospital under a community treatment order.[150] The victim or representative is entitled to receive information about any conditions that are imposed on discharge.[151] Furthermore, where the offender is subject to a hospital order without restrictions, the victim may ask to make representations or to receive information, and if they do so the probation board must notify the victim of the hospital's name and address and the hospital must be notified of the victim's address.[152] The probation board is required to forward any representations made to the person or body responsible for determining matters to do with discharge, ending of restrictions, conditional discharge or discharge subject to a community treatment order.

7.136   The changes to the Domestic Violence, Crime and Victims Act 2004 require responsible clinicians, Mental Health Review Tribunals, and the Secretary of State (in the case of a restricted patient) when considering whether to discharge to notify the hospital managers who must notify the local probation board, and give victims the chance to make representations and information about discharge and conditions. Since the 2004 Act came into force MHRTs have been granting rights to victims to make representations in relation to discharge and conditions of discharge. The changes to the Domestic Violence, Crime and Victims Act 2004 are significant in that they require responsible clinicians of all offender patients who have committed sexual or violent offences to consider the victim's representations before discharging either conditionally or under a community treatment order. Tribunals too must consider the victim's representations.

CONCLUSION

7.137   The Department of Health's *Offender Mental Health Care Pathway (2005)* provides a best practice template and aims to meet two targets: first, no one with acute severe mental illness should be in prison; and, second, prisons

---

[150]   Domestic Violence, Crime and Victims Act 2004, s 36(5).
[151]   Ibid, s 36(6).
[152]   Ibid, s 36A.

should be safe places for other people with mental health problems, with a particular focus on the creation of in-reach services and suicide prevention. With a prison population now over 85,000, limited capacity in the psychiatric services, and overcrowding rife in British jails, these goals are far from realisation. The small numbers transferred from prison of around 800 per year represents less than one per cent of the prison population. The 3,900 restricted patients equal just over four per cent of the prison population. It cannot seriously be doubted that there are many people in the prison system who are in need of hospital treatment for mental disorder.

7.138 This chapter has examined the mechanisms for diverting mentally disordered offenders from the penal system to the mental health system, and has revealed a certain convergence between the powers of detention under the respective regimes. Mental health law and penal law each provide a range of options for indeterminate detention with closely supervised discharge either via MHA 1983 restriction orders or CTOs, or CJA dangerousness sentences followed by release on licence subject to close supervision. The advantage of indeterminate detention has been transplanted from the psychiatric system to the penal system. Before a prisoner assessed as high risk for causing serious harm emerges from prison following a determinate sentence, he may be transferred to hospital under s 47. If he falls through the net and is released, he or she will be subject to the Multi-Agency Public Protection Arrangements ('MAPPA') system established by the Criminal Justice and Court Services Act 2000, and now re-enacted and reinforced in ss 325–327 of the Criminal Justice Act 2003. These are joint committees including police, probation, health, social services and housing to assess and manage risks posed by violent or sexual offenders. These are intended to identify people who may require admission to hospital under civil powers on grounds of risk before they commit an offence. Throughout England and Wales police, prison and probation authorities are to form responsible authorities to establish arrangements for assessing and managing the risks posed by sexual and violent offenders, to review and monitor these arrangements and to prepare and publish an annual report on their activities. Local authorities and NHS bodies have a duty to co-operate under s 325 of the Criminal Justice Act 2003.[153]

7.139 Mental health and penal law each have a network of community powers with the capacity to impose significant limits on freedom of movement, to choose residence, and to refuse treatment for mental disorder alcoholism or drug addiction. In addition any condition may be attached to a patient's community treatment order which is either necessary or appropriate to secure that the patient receives medical treatment or to prevent risk to self or others. This could include the power to impose a curfew or restrictions of movement on an individual. Here we see strong cross-fertilisation between conditional discharged restricted patient status, community orders under the Criminal Justice Act 2003, and community treatment orders under the Mental Health

---

[153] Department of Health, LASSL (2004): The Multi-Agency Public Protection Arrangements (the MAPPA) and the 'duty to co-operate'.

Act. Obligations under a community treatment order may only include such limits on behaviour as are necessary to ensure that the patient receives treatment for mental disorder and to manage risk to self or to others, not exactly an onerous restriction of the range of conditions which may be applied. The range of controls available under all of these measures has effectively meant that anyone subject to them is broadly in a similar position to a conditionally discharged restricted patient. Compulsory community powers are considered in chapter 8.

Chapter 8

COMPULSORY POWERS IN THE COMMUNITY

OVERVIEW

8.1   Under the Mental Health Act 1983 there are three compulsory powers over patients in the community:

(a)   guardianship under ss 7 or 37;

(b)   extended leave under s 17;

(c)   'Community treatment orders' ('CTOs') under ss 17A–17G also referred to in the MHA 2007 as supervised community treatment ('SCT').

Neither guardianship nor after-care under supervision (under the now repealed ss 25A–25J) was much used (see note to **2.24** above). Section 17 leave was the most frequently used vehicle for imposing control over patients in the community. The main reason for its attractiveness is its simplicity. It is granted and may be revoked on the authority of a single clinician. The ultimate sanction for non-compliance is detention, if the clinician considers continued non-compliance will make it necessary to recall the patient for the patient's health or safety or for the protection of others. The difficulty is that, in order for recall to be an effective sanction, there must be a bed available for the patient to be recalled to.

8.2   The most relevant Convention case law on compulsion in the community is the 1988 Commission decision in *L v Sweden,* where a decision provisionally to release someone who had been detained in a psychiatric hospital was held to constitute a potential interference with his right to respect for private life. However, the Commission declared the application manifestly ill-founded, that the measure was justified in the interests of the person's health under Art 8(2) and that the applicant could not be said to have an 'arguable claim' of a violation of Art 8.[1] If compulsory powers are necessary on grounds of health, to prevent crime, or to protect the rights and freedoms of others, the interference can be justified provided it is necessary in a democratic society and is done in accordance with law.

---

[1]   *(Application 10801/84)* Decisions and Reports of the European Commission of Human Rights, vol 45, pp 181–189 (Decision of 20 January 1986 on admissibility). Report of the Commission (adopted on 3 October 1988), para 93.

8.3 This chapter considers guardianship and guardianship orders under ss 7 and 37, extended leave under s 17, supervised community treatment ('SCT') under ss 17A–17G, and conditional discharge of restricted patients under Part III of the MHA 1983. Before discussing these powers it is important to understand the policy and legal framework of community care services for mentally disordered people and their carers.

THE LEGAL AND POLICY FRAMEWORK OF COMMUNITY CARE

8.4 Before the decision is taken to discharge or grant leave to a patient, or place a patient under SCT, the RC is responsible for ensuring, in consultation with the other professionals concerned, that the patient's needs for health and social care are fully assessed and the care plan addresses them. The original Illustrative Draft of the Code of Practice on the Mental Health Act stated that the RC is also responsible for ensuring that:

(a) a proper assessment is made of risks to the patient or other people and that plans, services and support are available to manage any risks;

(b) in the case of offender patients, the circumstances of any victim and their families are taken into account; and

(c) consideration is given to whether the patient meets the criteria for guardianship or supervised community treatment.[2]

This paragraph does not appear in the final Code. The administrative framework within which care is to be provided is the Care Programme Approach ('CPA'), based on United States models of care management.

Care programme approach

8.5 All service users, whether or not they have been detained, who have been in contact with the specialist psychiatric service are entitled to be dealt with under the CPA. The CPA requires a risk assessment, a needs assessment, a written care plan which will be regularly reviewed and a key worker (now known as a care co-ordinator). In 1996 the CPA was extended to all patients receiving care from the specialist psychiatric services.[3] Under Guidance issued in 2003 *Modernising the Care Programme Approach*.[4] there were two levels of CPA, standard and enhanced. Standard CPA is for people whose mental illness is less severe or who have low risk factors or have an active informal support network. Some social services authorities tried to limit services to both patients

---

2　　Draft Illustrative Code, paras 27.5–27.6.

3　　NHS Executive *Audit Pack for Monitoring the Care Programme Approach: Background and Explanatory Notes* (NHS Executive, 1996, HSG 96(6)).

4　　Care Programme Approach Association The Care Programme Approach Handbook (Chesterfield, 2003).

to those who are on CPA. In *R (HP) v London Borough of Islington* it was held to be unlawful to rule out providing services under s 47 of the National Health Service and Community Care Act 1990 because someone was not eligible for CPA.[5] People were on enhanced CPA if their mental disorder is assessed as posing a potential risk to their own safety or to that of other people and their needs required involvement of multiple agencies.

8.6 From October 2008 new guidance has applied in England whereby the two tiers have been abolished and 'New CPA' will be available to manage complex and serious cases who according to the DoH guidance should not be significantly different from those currently needing the support of enhanced CPA . The Guidance states that:[6]

> 'New CPA is a process for managing complex and serious cases – it should not be used as a badge of entitlement to receive any other services and benefits. Eligibility for services continues to be in accordance with statutory definitions and based upon assessment of individual need.'

The Guidance stresses that services should continue to use current local eligibility criteria to make decisions about an individual's need for secondary mental health services. The Guidance then provides a list to decide if the person needs new CPA. This is the list of characteristics to consider:[7]

- severe mental disorder including mental disorder with a high degree of clinical complexity;

- current or potential risks including suicide self harm or harm to others;

- relapse history requiring urgent response;

- self neglect non compliance with treatment;

- vulnerable adult eg financial or sexual exploitation, dis-inhibition, physical or emotional abuse cognitive impairment;

- current or significant history of severe distress instability or disengagement;

- presence of non physical co-morbidity eg substance alcohol or drug misuse or learning disability;

- multiple service provision from different agencies including housing physical care employment criminal justice voluntary agencies;

---

[5] *R (on the application of HP) v London Borough of Islington* [2004] EWHC 7 (Admin).
[6] *Refocusing the Care Programme Approach* Department of Health, March 2008, p 13.
[7] Ibid, pp 13–14.

- currently/recently detained under MHGA or referred to crisis or home treatment team significant reliance on carers or has own caring responsibilities;

- experiencing disadvantage as a result of parenting responsibilities, physical health problems or disability, unsettled accommodation, employment issues when mentally ill, significant impairment of function due to mental disorder, ethnicity sexuality or gender issues.

All services users on supervised community treatment or Guardianship should be supported by New CPA.

Section 117 of the Mental Health Act 1983

8.7   Section 117 of the MHA 1983 places a duty jointly on Primary Care Trusts and social services authorities, in co-operation with relevant voluntary agencies, to provide after-care services for patients who have been detained in hospital for treatment under s 3, under a s 37 hospital order with or without restrictions, under a s 45A hospital direction, or following transfer from prison under s 47 or 48 with or without restrictions. The duty applies when the patient ceases to be detained and leaves hospital, whether or not immediately after so ceasing. The duty continues until the health and local social services authorities are satisfied that the person concerned is no longer in need of such services, 'but they shall not be so satisfied in the case of a community patient while he remains such a patient'.[8] Hence patients on SCT remain entitled to s 117 after-care services throughout the duration of their community treatment order ('CTO').

8.8   Section 117 services are community care services under s 46 of the National Health Service and Community Care Act 1990. Section 47 provides that where it appears to a local authority that any person for whom they may provide or arrange to provide community care services may be in need of any such services, the authority:

(a)   shall carry out an assessment of his needs for those services; and

(b)   having regard to the results of that assessment, shall then decide whether his needs call for the provision by them of any such services.[9]

There is a two stage process of needs assessment followed by a care provision decision. A person for whom the LSSA is responsible, who is being considered for discharge, extended leave or a CTO will be someone who appears to the local authority to be in potential need of community care services. Local

---

8   MHA 1983, s 117(2).
9   National Health Service and Community Care Act 1990, s 47.

authorities may lawfully employ eligibility criteria.[10] Unlike other community care services, for which the service user may be charged, it is unlawful to charge for s 117 after-care.[11]

8.9 In *R (on the application of H) v Secretary of State for the Home Department*[12] the House of Lords ruled on the nature of the health authority's duty when a MHRT defers a patient's conditional discharge, pending the provision of community care services, which in this case included supervision by a psychiatrist. The House of Lords held that:

> 'The duty of the health authority, was not absolute, whether it arose under s 117 of the 1983 Act or in response to the tribunal's order. The authorities had to use their best endeavours to procure compliance with the conditions laid down by the tribunal. This they had done.'

The authorities were not under an absolute duty to secure compliance with a tribunal's order for deferred discharge. They had not been able to find a psychiatrist who considered that IH could be safely supervised in the community. The House left open the question whether a clinician who declines to supervise a community patient could be a hybrid public authority for the purposes of the Human Rights Act 1998.

Relevant authorities

8.10 In *R v Mental Health Review Tribunal, ex parte Hall* Scott Baker LJ held that:[13]

> 'For the purposes of s 117 of the 1983 Act, the relevant health and social services authorities were those for the area where the patient was ordinarily resident at the time of his detention, unless he had no place of residence. In the latter case, the relevant authorities would be those of the area where the patient was sent on discharge, but the placing authority where the patient resided did not cease to be the appropriate local social services authority by virtue of the fact that he was sent to a different authority on discharge.'

8.11 In *R (M) v Hammersmith & Fulham LBC and others*[14] at issue was the identity of the authority which was responsible for the s 117 accommodation costs of a patient who had been discharged from a hospital in Sutton. He had been initially provided with social care support by and in Hammersmith under s 21 of the National Assistance Act 1948. The patient was then admitted to hospital after a road traffic accident, and on discharge went into a care home funded by Hammersmith but situated in Sutton. Since he was funded by Hammersmith, the deeming provisions under s 24 of the National Assistance Act 1948 meant that he was still 'ordinarily resident' in that authority, although

---

[10] *R v Gloucestershire County Council, ex parte Barry* [1997] 2 All ER 1, HL.
[11] *R v Manchester City Council, ex parte Stennett* [2002] UKHL 34, [2002] 4 All ER 124, HL.
[12] [2003] UKHL 59.
[13] [1999] 3 All ER 132, QBD.
[14] (2010) QBD 3 March 2010.

accommodated elsewhere. Subsequently he was admitted to a psychiatric unit in Sutton for assessment under s 2 of the MHA 1983 and then returned to the care home where Hammersmith continued to fund him under s 21 NAA 1948.

8.12 However shortly afterwards he was again admitted to the same psychiatric unit, but this time under s 3. Henceforth his community care needs ceased to be governed by s 21 and now derived from s 117 of the 1983 Act. On discharge a dispute arose as to which local authority was responsible. Hammersmith contended that s 117 was now engaged and responsibility lay with the council in whose area he was 'resident' in prior to admission – and this was Sutton. Mitting J held that there was little or no difference in meaning between 'resident' and 'ordinarily resident', since both connoted settled presence in a particular place other than under compulsion. He further held that the deeming provision in s 24(5) of the National Assistance Act 1948 had no application for s 117 purposes. Hence Sutton was the responsible authority for the purposes of s 117.

Carers' rights

8.13 Many mentally disordered service users depend on the support of carers to enable them to survive in the community without need for frequent admission to hospital. The National Service Frameworks for Mental Health for England and Wales emphasise service user and carer involvement in the planning and delivery of services and ideals of equity and empowerment.[15]

8.14 A carer is someone who provides or intends to provide a substantial amount of care to a disabled person (including someone disabled by mental disorder) on a regular (not necessarily frequent) basis. Caring for someone with a mental illness may not involve hands-on physical or practical care on a regular basis, but it does require constant vigilance, and if relapse seems imminent or actually occurs, intense support of an emotional and a practical nature. The physical and psychological impact on carers can be significant. The final requirement to be a carer is that the person must not be a paid professional carer, and must indicate the wish to be a carer of the patient. The Practice Guidance states that 'willingness'[16] to care 'should not be assumed', and that carers should have the 'freedom to choose the nature of the tasks they will perform and how much time they will give to their caring role'.

---

[15] Department of Health *National Service Framework for Mental Health England* (1999) at http://www.dh.gov.uk/PolicyAndGuidance/HealthAndSocialCareTopics/ HealthAndSocialCareArticle/fs/en?CONTENT_ID=4070951&chk=W3ar/W; Welsh Assembly Government *National Framework for Adult Mental Health Services in Wales* (2001) at http://www.wales.nhs.uk/sites3/docmetadata.cfm?orgid=438&id=48286&pid=11071; Welsh Assembly Government *Mental Health Policy Guidance: The Care Programme Approach for Mental Health Service Users* (2003) at http://www.wales.nhs.uk/sites3/Documents/438/mental% 2Dhealth%2Dpolicy%2Dimple%2Dguide%2De%2Epdf; Welsh Assembly Government *Revised National Service Framework for Adult Mental Health Services Wales* (2005) at http://www.wales.nhs.uk/sites3/page.cfm?orgid=438&pid=11071.

[16] Department of Health *Practice Guidance under the Carers and Disabled Children Act 2000* (2000), para 68. See www.carers.gov.uk/pdfs/practiceguidecarersparents.pdf.

8.15 The Carers (Recognition and Services) Act 1995 provides that during a community care needs assessment local authorities must consider whether there are any carers, and, where they think it appropriate, must consult those carers. Section 1(2) of the 1995 Act provides that the carer may request the local authority, before they make a service provision decision, to carry out an assessment of the carer's ability to provide and continue to provide care.

8.16 The Carers and Disabled Children Act 2000 entitles the carer to an assessment of their own need for support services to enable them to carry on caring for the person, a move towards recognising the carer as a separate entity from the cared for person. A carer's assessment may be requested even if the disabled person refuses a community care assessment for themselves. Where a carer asks for an assessment, the local authority must carry one out, deciding first whether the carer has needs in relation to the care being provided, secondly whether those needs could be wholly or partly satisfied by local authority services, and thirdly whether to provide services to the carer. The right to a separate assessment can be particularly important where the care recipient has mental disorder and may refuse a community care assessment. The Act recognises that often the best way of supporting the carer is to provide breaks from the caring role, through 'respite care', which may involve providing services to the cared for person. Section 2(3) provides that although a service is provided to the carer, it may take the form of a service delivered to the person cared for, as long as it does not include anything 'of an intimate nature'.

8.17 The Carers (Equal Opportunities) Act 2004 introduced an obligation on social services to inform carers of their right to an assessment, thereby obliging authorities to be proactive in their work practices. The Act also seeks to combat social exclusion by requiring carers' assessments to consider whether the carer works or wishes to work and is undertaking, or wishes to undertake, education, training or any leisure activity. The 2004 Act is designed to provide state support to enable the carer to work.

COMPULSORY POWERS IN THE COMMUNITY

Guardianship

8.18 Guardianship applications in respect of non-offender patients are made under s 7. Either the nearest relative or an AMHP may apply. Two medical recommendations are necessary. The nearest relative may block a guardianship application but unreasonable objection will be grounds for displacement by the county court under s 29. The patient must be 16 or over and suffering from mental disorder of a nature or degree warranting reception into guardianship. In addition, guardianship must be necessary in the interests of the patient's welfare or for the protection of others. Section 8 of the Act sets out the three powers conferred on the guardian:

(a)   to require the patient to live at a place specified by the guardian. The
      person may be taken and conveyed to the place of residence and may be
      returned there if she or he absconds;

(b)   to require the patient to attend at specified places for medical treatment,
      occupation, education or training. If the patient refuses to attend, the
      guardian is not authorised to use force to secure attendance, nor does the
      Act enable medical treatment to be administered in the absence of the
      patient's consent (although it may be under ss 5 and 6 of the Mental
      Capacity Act 2005 if the patient lacks capacity to consent); or

(c)   to require access to the patient to be given at the place where he or she is
      living to persons detailed in the Act. A refusal without reasonable cause to
      permit an authorised person to have access to the patient is an offence
      under s 129 but no force may be used to secure entry.

Although guardianship was the flagship community power of both the MHA
1959 and the MHA 1983 in terms of providing the underpinning of
compulsion necessary to enforce community care, it has never been much used.

8.19   Over the past five years there has been a steady decline in the use of
guardianship. In England on 31 March 2010 there were 836 patients subject to
guardianship (in 831 cases the local authority was the guardian). In the year to
31 March 2010, 420 new cases were initiated, and 433 cases were closed during
the year, 57% of which had lasted less than 12 months.[17] At 31 March 2010 in
England there were 800 people under s 7 guardianship, and 36 under
guardianship orders made by a criminal court under s 37.

Guardianship orders

8.20   As Jones points out, 'Little use has been made of guardianship orders by
the courts', with figures running at under 30 cases per year.[18] The diagnostic
criteria for making an order are that the offender must be sixteen or over, and
suffering from any disorder or disability of mind warranting reception into
guardianship. The court has wide discretion to decide whether guardianship is
'suitable', since it must be of the opinion, having regard to all the
circumstances, including the nature of the offence and the character and
antecedents of the offender and to other methods of dealing with him, that the
most suitable method of disposing of the case is by means of a guardianship
order.

8.21   The guardian under a guardianship order has the same powers as a
guardian under Part II.[19] The medical evidence required for a guardianship
order is the same as for making a hospital order. The court enjoys similar

---

[17]   National Statistics Information Centre *Guardianship under the Mental Health Act 1983* (2010)
       at http://www.ic.nhs.uk.
[18]   Ibid, p 230.
[19]   MHA 1983, s 40(2).

powers to request information to those available for hospital order cases. Under s 39A, a court considering making a guardianship order is empowered to request the local social services authority (or any other social services authority considered by the court to be appropriate):

(a)   to inform the court whether it or any person authorised by it is prepared to receive the patient into guardianship; and

(b)   if so, to give such information as it reasonably can about how it or the other person could be expected to exercise the powers of guardian in relation to the offender.

8.22   The small numbers under guardianship have declined even though the MHA 2007 extended guardianship to anyone who suffers from 'any disorder or disability of mind'. The exclusion in relation to learning disability without abnormally aggressive or seriously irresponsible conduct remains. Schedule 3, para 3(5) broadens the powers of the guardian by introducing a new power to take and convey a person to their required place of residence under guardianship alongside the power which already exists to return a guardianship patient who has absconded to their place of residence. Although these changes might have been expected to bring about an increase in the use of guardianship, this has not happened.

Section 17 leave

8.23   Under s 17 the RC may grant either indefinite leave or leave for a specified period, subject to such conditions as he or she considers necessary in the interests of the patient or for the protection of others. Where it appears to the RC to be necessary in the interests of the patient's health *or* safety *or* for the protection of others, the patient may be recalled from leave by the RC giving notice in writing to the patient or person in charge of him or her. The MHA 2007 amendments preserved the RC's power to send on leave under s 17, but it was clearly intended that its role in relation to long term leave would be reduced and supplanted by the CTO under s 17A. To reinforce this policy, a RC considering granting leave for more than seven days must first consider whether the patient should be 'dealt with' under s 17A by a community treatment order ('CTO') instead.[20]

8.24   The 1990s saw increasing legal recognition of the problem of the 'revolving door' patient, who gets well on medication but, once discharged, ceases to take it and relapses. Instead of using mental health guardianship to provide a framework for compulsion in the community, the psychiatric profession's preferred solution was s 17 leave. A patient could be required to accept medication as a condition of leave and recalled to hospital in the event of non-compliance. Detention must be renewed at intervals, and a problem came if the patient was in the community when the time came to renew

---

[20]   MHA 1983, s 17(2A) and (2B), inserted by MHA 2007, s 33(2).

detention. To overcome this, patients would be recalled from the community to hospital for one night to have their detention renewed, and would then be sent on leave for a further six or twelve months until the detention next required renewal. By this ingenious device, a long-term community treatment order was fashioned out of the power to grant leave from detention. However, the obligation to accept treatment whilst resident in the community could only be imposed on someone who has already been detained, since only a detained patient can be granted leave.

8.25 In *R v Hallstrom, ex parte W (No 2)*[21] McCullough J declared unlawful two widely used practices in psychiatry. The first was that of compulsorily admitting patients for treatment under s 3 of the Mental Health Act 1983 when there was no intention that they should receive in-patient treatment for mental disorder. Such patients would be sent on leave under s 17 of the Act shortly after admission, subject to the condition that they took their medication. This was declared unlawful on the grounds that one of the conditions of admission is that the patient must need treatment in hospital for their mental disorder and that the treatment cannot be provided unless they are detained. It remains unlawful to detain a patient in the first place when there is no intention to provide any in-patient treatment.

8.26 The second practice at issue in *Hallstrom* was that of returning patients on leave under s 17 to hospital for one night, renewing their detention and discharging them the next day subject to the condition that they continued to take their medication. The judge held that a patient's detention could not be renewed unless it was intended that they should receive treatment in hospital as an in-patient. The implication of this was a limit on the duration of a patient's subjection to compulsory powers in the community. The amendments to the 1983 Act (ss 25A–25H now repealed) introduced by the Mental Health (Patients in the Community) Act 1995 providing for supervised discharge, introduced to overcome the effect of *Hallstrom*, were little used.

8.27 Subsequent case-law almost completely reversed the effect of *Hallstrom*. It provides that a patient's detention can be renewed as long as a patient needs some treatment at a hospital, not necessarily as an in-patient. In *B v Barking Havering and Brentwood Community Healthcare NHS Trust*[22] the Court of Appeal held that it was lawful to renew detention of a patient even though she spent only two nights a week in hospital, Lord Woolf holding that:[23]

> 'As long as treatment viewed as a whole involves treatment as an in-patient the requirements of the section can be met.'

Then in *R (on the application of DR) v Mersey Care NHS Trust*[24] the patient was receiving no in-patient treatment whilst on leave, but was receiving

---

21   [1986] 2 All ER 306.
22   [1999] 1 FLR 106, CA.
23   Ibid, para 113.
24   *R (on the application of DR) v Mersey Care NHS Trust* [2002] EWHC 1810 (Admin).

treatment in hospital as an out-patient. Wilson J held that the only relevant question to renewal was whether a significant component of the treatment of the plan for the claimant was for treatment in hospital. That treatment did not have to be as an in-patient.

8.28 In *R (on the application of S) v Mental Health Review Tribunal*[25] the patient was residing at her home on s 17 leave on condition that she attend weekly sessions with her psychologist and attended ward rounds once per month. The purpose of the ward round requirement was to give the patient the necessary motivation and encouragement to progress in the community. Pitchford J held that the MHRT had acted lawfully in declining to discharge on the grounds that some treatment in hospital was still required

8.29 By the time these later cases were decided, supervised discharge had already been introduced by the Mental Health (Patients in the Community) Act 1995 inserting into the MHA 1983 new ss 25A–25H, following the exposure of failures of community care in cases such as that of Christopher Clunis. Supervised discharge has been little used. In *R (on the application of DR) v Mersey Care NHS Trust*, which so markedly increased the scope of extended leave, the argument was put that supervised discharge should have been at least considered, if not used in preference to extended leave. The judge rejected this argument, stating that it was a[26]

> '[C]entral feature, regarded by many as a central deficiency, of the provisions for after-care under supervision that, although under section 25D (3)(b) and (4) a patient can be required to attend the place where he is due to receive the treatment and to allow himself to be conveyed there, he cannot be required to actually take the medication. If he refuses to take it, the power to administer it compulsorily arises only when he has again been made liable to be detained by the properly cumbersome procedures set by s 3 of the Act.'

The Mental Health Act 2007 repealed ss 25A–25J of the MHA 1983 and replaces them with a new regime of powers (ss 17A–17G) to impose supervised community treatment ('SCT').

SUPERVISED COMMUNITY TREATMENT ('SCT')

8.30 The new provisions on SCT have been in force since 2008. To be eligible for SCT the patient must be liable to be detained in hospital under s 3 or, if a Part III patient, be subject to a hospital order, a hospital direction, or a transfer direction without restrictions. SCT is also available for patients treated as being subject to s 3 or subject to an unrestricted hospital order or transfer direction, following transfer from Northern Ireland, Scotland, the Isle of Man, or the Channel Islands.[27] A patient who is subject to SCT is known as a 'community

---

25   [2004] EWHC 2958 (Admin), [2004] MHLR 355.
26   [2002] EWHC 1810 (Admin) at [33].
27   Department of Health *Code of Practice: Mental Health Act 1983* (2008), para 25.4.

patient'. A person with a learning disability cannot be detained under s 3 or s 37 unless the learning disability results in abnormally aggressive or seriously irresponsible conduct on her or his part. Such patients, being ineligible for detention under s 3 or s 37 are also ineligible for SCT. Such a person could be given treatment without consent in the community under the Mental Capacity Act 2005, ss 5 and 6, if they lack capacity and treatment is in their best interests.

8.31   Section 17A(1) gives the RC the power, 'by order in writing' to 'discharge a detained patient from hospital subject to his being liable to recall in accordance with section 17E'. This is called a 'community treatment order' ('CTO').[28] The RC must be of the opinion that:

(a)   the patient is suffering from mental disorder (any disorder or disability of mind) of a nature or degree which makes it appropriate for him to receive medical treatment;

(b)   it is necessary for his health or safety or for the protection of other persons that he should receive such treatment;

(c)   subject to his being liable to be recalled, such treatment can be provided without his continuing to be detained in a hospital;

(d)   it is necessary that the responsible clinician should be able to exercise the power to recall the patient to hospital (the Bill said necessary for the patient's health or safety or for the protection of others – the Act simply says necessary); and

(e)   appropriate medical treatment is available for him.

All of the above criteria must be satisfied for a patient to be eligible for SCT.

8.32   The order will be made by the patient's Responsible Clinician ('RC'). The RC may not make a CTO without a written statement from an AMHP agreeing with the RC's opinion and that it is appropriate to make the order. When considering an order the RC must give priority to the risk of deterioration, and the risk of non-compliance with medication if the patient were not to remain in detention. When considering whether a person should be liable to recall under s 17E, the RC must:[29]

> '*in particular*, consider, having regard to the patient's history of mental disorder and any other relevant factors, what risk there would be of a deterioration of the patient's condition if he were not detained in a hospital (as a result, for example, of his refusing or neglecting to receive the medical treatment he requires for his mental disorder).'

---

[28]   MHA 1983, s 17A(3).
[29]   MHA 1983, s 17A(6). [Emphasis added].

Conditions

8.33 The Mental Health Bill 2006 listed specific types of condition which might be imposed in a CTO, as follows:

(a) that the patient reside at a particular place;

(b) that the patient make himself available at particular times and places for the purposes of medical treatment;

(c) that the patient receive medical treatment in accordance with the responsible clinician's directions;

(d) that the patient makes himself available for examination;

(e) that the patient abstain from particular conduct.

Most noteworthy on the list of conditions was the obligation to receive medical treatment, rather than as before to attend a specified place for the purpose of medical treatment, and the obligation to desist from specified conduct, a condition which led to the contention that this amounts to the psychiatric equivalent of the anti-social behaviour orders ('ASBOs') introduced by s 1 of the Crime and Disorder Act 1998. New s 17B of the Mental Health Act 1983 does not list the types of condition which may be applied.

8.34 Without listing all the types of condition, s 17B of the MHA 1983 requires that a community treatment order must 'specify conditions to which the patient is to be subject'. There are two 'mandatory conditions', which are set out in s 17B(3). They are:

(a) a condition that the patient make himself available for examination under section 20A below; and

(b) a condition that, if it is proposed to give a certificate under Part IVA of this Act in his case, he make himself available for examination so as to enable the certificate to be given.

Any other conditions must be agreed between the RC and the AMHP. The only limitation on the scope of the discretionary conditions is that the RC and AMHP must agree that they are 'necessary or appropriate' for:

(a) ensuring that the patient receives medical treatment;

(b) preventing risk of harm to the patient's health or safety;

(c) protecting other persons.[30]

---

[30] MHA 1983, s 17B introduced by MHA 2007, s 32.

8.35 Although the abandonment of the list approach to powers was heralded as a major concession by the Government, the new provisions confer wide discretionary power. The Code of Practice says that conditions should:[31]

> '[B]e kept to a minimum number consistent with achieving their purpose; restrict the patient's liberty as little as possible while being consistent with achieving their purpose; have a clear rationale, linked to one or more of the purposes listed above; and be clearly and precisely expressed, so that the patient can readily understand what is expected. Conditions can cover avoidance of known risk factors or high-risk situations relevant to the patient's mental disorder.

There is still wide discretionary power, but the conditions are subject to the constraint that they must be realistically enforceable, and should not be such that they set the patient up to fail. The RC may vary the conditions by order in writing, and may suspend any condition.[32] If a community patient fails to comply with one of the discretionary conditions, that fact may be taken into account for the purposes of exercising the RC's power of recall under s 17E.[33]

8.36 There are several disturbing factors of this power from a human rights point of view. First, the scope of the conditions and limitations on personal freedom is left to the discretion of health care professionals, subject only to loose requirements as to purpose which would allow conditions that the patient must desist from specified conduct. This was supposedly one of the Government's concessions during the debates on the 2006 Bill. The MHA 2007, allows just as much scope for expansion of the powers, as long as they can be necessary or appropriate for treatment or to prevent risk to self or others. The 'necessary or appropriate' test is lax indeed. 'Necessary and appropriate' would have required the professionals to address their minds to whether the conditions were necessary and whether they are appropriate. As it is one may question what sort of condition might not be necessary but would be appropriate and vice versa. The main constraints here are the professionalism and common sense of AMHPs and RCs.

8.37 There is no power to seek review before the MHT of the need for specified conditions, although the patient may apply to the MHT on the grounds that one or more of the conditions for making an order are not met. The MHT must direct discharge on an application by the patient or a reference if it is not satisfied that:

(a) the patient is then suffering from mental disorder or mental disorder of a nature or degree which makes it appropriate for him to receive medical treatment; or

(b) that it is necessary for his health or safety or for the protection of other persons that he should receive such treatment; or

---

[31] Department of Health *Code of Practice: Mental Health Act 1983* (2008), paras 25.33–25.34.
[32] MHA 1983, s 17B(4)–(5).
[33] Ibid, s 17B(6).

(c)   that it is necessary that the responsible clinician should be able to exercise the power to recall the patient to hospital; or

(d)   that appropriate medical treatment is available for him.[34]

The tribunal is also under a duty to discharge on an application by the nearest relative if not satisfied that the patient if discharged would be likely to act in a manner dangerous to self or to others.[35]

8.38   In deciding whether it is satisfied that the power of recall is necessary the tribunal must *in particular* consider having regard to the patient's history of mental disorder and any other relevant factors, what risk there would be of a deterioration of the patient's condition if he were to continue not to be detained in a hospital (as a result, for example, of his refusing or neglecting to receive the medical treatment he requires for his mental disorder).[36]

8.39   Failure to comply with conditions will not lead to automatic recall, but a patient who fails to comply with any of the conditions may be recalled to hospital and held there for up to 72 hours. If they do not agree to comply within that period, and the conditions for detention under s 3 are met, the community treatment order may be revoked and they will resume status as a detained patient. If that happens, the six month maximum period of detention will begin on the day that the CTO is revoked.[37]

8.40   CTOs potentially engage the right of respect for privacy under Art 8. Interferences with Art 8 rights may be justified if carried out in the interests of the patient's health or to protect the rights and freedoms of others. There will be no breach of Art 8 if the CTO is made in accordance with the law and is necessary in a democratic society for one of the purposes listed in Art 8(2).[38] A patient subject to SCT is known as a 'community patient'.[39]

Power to recall to hospital from s 17 leave or from a CTO (ss 17 and 17E)

8.41   Patients on s 17 leave from a hospital may have their leave revoked and be recalled only to the hospital where they were detained if the RC considers it necessary in the interests of the patient's health or safety or for the protection of other persons. Revocation and recall are by the RC giving notice in writing 'to the patient or to the person for the time being in charge of the patient'.[40]

---

[34]   MHA 1983, s 72(1)(c) inserted by MHA 2007, Sch 3, para 21.
[35]   Ibid, s 72(1)(c)(5).
[36]   Ibid, s 72(1A).
[37]   Ibid, s 17G.
[38]   *(Application 10801/84)*, Decisions and Reports of the European Commission of Human Rights, vol 45, pp 181–189 (Decision of 20 January 1986 on admissibility). Report of the Commission (adopted on 3 October 1988).
[39]   MHA 1983, s 17A(3).
[40]   MHA 1983, s 17(4).

8.42 A community patient subject to a CTO may be recalled to any hospital (not necessarily the responsible hospital)[41] if in the RC's opinion:

(a) the patient requires medical treatment in hospital for his mental disorder; and

(b) there would be a risk of harm to the health or safety of the patient or to other persons if the patient were not recalled to hospital for that purpose.

A patient may also be recalled for breach of a condition of a CTO, although if the above criteria are met breach of condition is not a necessary condition of recall.

8.43 The RC may also recall a community patient to hospital if the patient fails to comply with a condition of the CTO. Section 17B requires that CTOs specify conditions to which a community patient will be subject. A CTO must contain conditions that the patient must make himself available for medical examination to determine whether the CTO should be extended, and secondly to allow a Second Opinion Approved Doctor ('SOAD') to issue a certificate authorising treatment under Part IVA. Apart from these mandatory conditions any other conditions may be imposed, provided an AMHP agrees they are necessary or appropriate to ensure that the patient receives medical treatment, to prevent harm to the patient's health or safety, or to protect others.

8.44 The Explanatory Notes on the MHA 2007 state that:[42]

> 'Other than the conditions about availability for examination, the conditions specified under section 17B are not in themselves enforceable but, if a patient fails to comply with any condition, the RC may take that into account when considering if it is necessary to use the recall power.'

However, provided the recall criteria are met, the patient may still be recalled even if he or she is complying with the conditions.[43] A community patient can be recalled to a hospital even though he is already in the hospital at the time when the power of recall is exercised.[44]

8.45 The power of recall is exercisable by notice in writing to the patient, which is sufficient authority for the managers of that hospital to detain the patient. A patient who has been recalled under ss 17(4) or 17E can be taken and conveyed to hospital by any AMHP, officer on the staff of the hospital, any constable or by any person authorised in writing by the responsible clinician or the hospital managers. The RC is responsible for co-ordinating the recall, which is designed to provide a means to respond to evidence of relapse or high risk

---

[41] MHA 1983, s 17E(3) provides that: 'The hospital to which a patient is recalled need not be the responsible hospital'.

[42] MHA 1983, s 17B(6) and *Explanatory Notes*, para 113.

[43] MHA 1983, s 17B(7).

[44] MHA 1983, s 17E(4).

behaviour before it becomes critical and leads to the patient or other people being put at risk. The Department of Health Code states that:[45]

> 'Particular attention should be paid to carers and relatives when they raise a concern that the patient is not complying with the conditions or their mental health appears to be deteriorating. The community team needs to give due weight to those concerns and any requests made by the carers or relatives in deciding what action to take. Carers and relatives are typically in much more constant contact with the patient than professionals, even under well-run care plans.'

Power to revoke a community treatment order (s 17F)

8.46 Recalling a patient from extended leave under s 17(4) automatically revokes the leave and the patient resumes detained patient status in the hospital from which they were granted leave. By contrast, recalling a community patient means that the patient may be detained in a hospital for up to 72 hours immediately following return to hospital, but the CTO is not automatically revoked. A separate decision under s 17F is necessary to revoke a CTO. The RC may revoke a CTO by order in writing if of the opinion that the conditions for detention under s 3(2) are satisfied in respect of the patient. An AMHP must agree with that opinion and that it is appropriate to revoke the order. If a CTO is revoked, the patient reverts to detained patient status and is treated for the purposes of renewal of detention as if they had been admitted for treatment on the date of the order being revoked.[46]

8.47 The RC may 'release' the patient at any time during the 72 hours in which case the patient remains subject to the CTO.[47] If the CTO has not been revoked by the end of the 72-hour period and the patient is still in hospital, he must be released. Again, the patient remains subject to the CTO.[48] 'Released' means 'released from that detention (and accordingly from being recalled to hospital)',[49] it does not mean that the patient is discharged from the CTO. The patient remains liable to s 17E recall. If a recalled patient, whose CTO has not been revoked, remains in hospital as an informal patient, s/he may not be prevented from leaving by using the holding power under s 5 of the MHA 1983. This is prohibited by s 5(6) which provides that references to in-patients in s 5 do not include in-patients who are already liable to be detained or community patients. Since a recalled community patient whose CTO has not been revoked remains a community patient, s/he is not eligible to be detained under s 5. If the patient in such a case is to be prevented from leaving hospital, this must be done by recall. A community patient can be recalled to a hospital even though he is already in the hospital at the time when the power of recall is exercised.[50]

---

[45] Department of Health *Code of Practice: Mental Health Act 1983* (2008), para 25.46.
[46] MHA 1983, s 17G.
[47] MHA 1983, s 17F(5) and (7).
[48] MHA 1983, s 17F(6) and (7).
[49] MHA 1983, s 17F(8)(b).
[50] MHA 1983, s 17E(4).

Power to renew a community treatment order (s 20A)

8.48 Within the last two months of a community treatment order the RC must:

(a)   examine the patient; and

(b)   consult 'one or more other persons who have been professionally concerned with the patient's medical treatment';

(c)   if there is a written statement from an AMHP agreeing that the renewal conditions are met and it is appropriate to do so submit to the hospital managers a report renewing the CTO.

The renewal conditions are:

(a)   the patient is suffering from mental disorder of a nature or degree which makes it appropriate for him to receive medical treatment;

(b)   it is necessary for his health or safety or for the protection of other persons that he should receive such treatment;

(c)   subject to his continuing to be liable to be recalled, such treatment can be provided without his being detained in a hospital;

(d)   it is necessary that the responsible clinician should continue to be able to exercise the power of recall; and

(e)   appropriate medical treatment is available for him.

Furnishing the report has the effect of renewing the CTO for six months if it is the first renewal, and for 12 months in the case of the second or subsequent renewals.[51]

Authority to treat community patients

8.49 Section 35 of the MHA 2007 introduces a new Part IVA into the Mental Health Act 1983 providing authority to treat community patients without their consent. New ss 64A–64K authorise 'relevant treatment' (medicines for mental disorder or Electro Convulsive Therapy ('ECT')) to be given to a community patient who has not been recalled to hospital. Medicine may be given in the community, not necessarily in a hospital or clinic. ECT can only safely be given in hospital. Part IVA applies aspects of the decision-making framework of the Mental Capacity Act 2005 to treatment under the Mental Health Act and permits treatment in the community of a community patient if:

---

[51]   MHA 1983, s 20A, as inserted by MHA 2007, s 34(3).

(a)   if the treatment is immediately necessary and the patient is capable and consents to the treatment;

(b)   if the treatment is immediately necessary and there is consent from someone authorised under the Mental Capacity Act to make decisions on the patient's behalf;

(c)   if the patient lacks capacity and force is not necessary to secure compliance; or

(d)   if emergency treatment needs to be given, using force if necessary, to a patient who lacks capacity.

8.50   The effect of these changes is explained in chapter 10. Safeguards are provided in the shape of a 'certificate requirement' from a second opinion doctor appointed for the purposes of Part IVA. If the treatment is medicines for mental disorder, a certificate is not required until the expiry of one month from the date the community treatment order was made.[52] However, if the CTO is made before the patient has been receiving medicine as a detained patient for three months, the certificate must be provided before the expiry of that three month period. The certificate requirement only applies to 's 58 type treatment', namely, treatment to which 's 58 would have applied at the time it was given' Since s 58 would only apply to medicines after three months had elapsed since the first time medicines were given in that period of detention. A certificate is not required where the treatment is 'immediately necessary' and the patient has capacity and consents. Nor is one required if the treatment is 'immediately necessary' and there is consent from a person exercising a lasting power of attorney or from a Deputy appointed by the Court of Protection. The test of 'immediate necessity' depends on the treatment. In a case where the treatment is section 58 type treatment (medicines for mental disorder), treatment is immediately necessary if:[53]

(a)   it is immediately necessary to save the patient's life; or

(b)   it is immediately necessary to prevent a serious deterioration of the patient's condition and is not irreversible; or

(c)   it is immediately necessary to alleviate serious suffering by the patient and is not irreversible or hazardous; or

(d)   it is immediately necessary, represents the minimum interference necessary to prevent the patient from behaving violently or being a danger to himself or others and is not irreversible or hazardous.

---

[52]   MHA 1983, s 64B(4).
[53]   Ibid, s 64C(5).

If the treatment is a s 58A type treatment, (ECT) treatment is immediately necessary if:[54]

(a)   it is immediately necessary to save the patient's life; or

(b)   it is immediately necessary to prevent a serious deterioration of the patient's condition and is not irreversible.

8.51   Finally, no certificate is required where emergency treatment is given under s 64G.[55] The conditions for giving emergency treatment under s 64G are as follows:

*   First, when giving the treatment, the person giving it must reasonably believe that the person lacks capacity, or if under 16 lacks competence to consent to it.

*   Second, the treatment must be immediately necessary according to the criteria set out above in relation to medicine and ECT respectively.

*   Third, if it is necessary to use force to give the treatment, the treatment must be given in order to prevent harm to the patient *and* the use of force must be proportionate to the likelihood of harm and the seriousness of harm.

Although the Department of Health Code emphasises that s 64G does not authorise forcible treatment aimed at preventing harm to others,[56] treatment which prevents harm to others might be given on the basis that it could have the effect of preventing harm to the patient, either through the other person retaliating, or through criminal proceedings in relation to the harm to others being brought against the patient.

8.52   The certificate requirement is met where a Second Opinion Appointed Doctor ('SOAD') appointed to act under Parts IV and IVA has certified that it is appropriate for the medicines to be given subject to conditions specified in the certificate.

CONDITIONALLY DISCHARGED RESTRICTED PATIENTS

8.53   The restriction order and restriction direction with their conditional discharge option are seen as effective means of risk management. Re-offending rates in terms of grave offences (indictable offences carrying a maximum

---

54   Ibid, s 64C(6).
55   MHA 1983, s 64B(3).
56   Department of Health *Code of Practice: Mental Health Act 1983* (2008), para 23.17.

sentence of life imprisonment, also including arson) of the 1,500 patients conditionally discharged between 1999 and 2008 are assessed by the Ministry of Justice as averaging 1 per cent.[57]

8.54 A patient subject to Ministry of Justice restrictions on discharge can be discharged by the Minister of Justice or a tribunal either absolutely or subject to conditions. If the patient is given an absolute discharge, both the hospital and restriction orders cease to have effect, and he cannot be recalled to hospital. If a patient's discharge is conditional, he may, for example, be directed to live in a specified place, to attend for treatment, and to accept treatment by or under the direction of the responsible clinician. Because it may be a condition of discharge that the patient must accept treatment for mental disorder, a conditionally discharged restricted patient is not eligible to seek review of treatment by a second opinion doctor under Part IV of the MHA 1983. The patient may apply to the tribunal for absolute discharge.

8.55 The Ministry of Justice say that they should be notified by the responsible clinician in the case of a conditionally discharged patient where:

(a)   there appears to be a risk to the public;

(b)   contact with the patient is lost;

(c)   the patient is unwilling to co-operate with supervision;

(d)   the patient needs further in-patient treatment; or

(e)   the patient is charged with an offence.

A conditionally discharged restricted patient may be recalled to hospital by the Minister of Justice or by the RC at any time whilst the restriction order is in force but, unless it is an emergency recall, there must be medical evidence of mental disorder warranting confinement *Kay v United Kingdom*.[58] The patient must be informed that he or she is being recalled to hospital at the time, and a further explanation of reasons for recall must be given as soon as is reasonably practicable.[59] The case of a conditionally discharged restricted patient who is recalled to hospital must be referred by the Minister of Justice to a MIIT within a month of his return to hospital.

CONCLUSION

8.56 The Government's intention is clearly that the new CTO power will replace s 17 leave for any compulsion in the community lasting longer than

---

[57]   Ministry of Justice, *Statistics of Mentally Disordered Offenders 2008* September 2010.
[58]   (1994) 40 BMLR 20, EComHR.
[59]   Ministry of Justice, 'Recall of Conditionally Discharged Restricted Patients' February 4 2009.
      See RM Jones *Mental Health Act Manual* (Sweet and Maxwell, 13th edn, 2010), pp 268–269.

seven days. The NHS Information Centre Annual figures for CTOs for England 2009/2010 note that there have been 6,237 orders made since the introduction of SCT in November 2008 and the data show that just 1,965 (31.5 per cent) of these orders had ended (either via a revocation or a discharge) by 31 March 2010, suggesting to the authors that 'some people are being kept on SCT for long periods of time.'[60] Patients subject to each of these powers are entitled to apply for discharge to a Mental Health Tribunal (see chapter 9). Their treatment without consent is regulated by Part IV in the case of s 17 patients and Part IVA in the case of CTO patients (see chapter 10).

8.57 Detention as an in-patient is governed by Art 5. Compulsory community treatment falls under Art 8. Article 8 contains no explicit procedural requirement, but the decision-making process leading to interference must be fair and such as to afford due respect to the interests safeguarded by Art 8. Where guardianship or other community compulsion includes a duty to reside at a specified place enforceable by a power to take and convey, a requirement to grant access to professionals, and any requirement connected with medical treatment or the management of risk, there is a question whether civil rights and obligations are engaged.[61]

8.58 The Joint Committee on Human Rights noted that there is no procedure on the face of the statute requiring objective medical evidence to be presented to a competent authority. The CTO should be signed by the responsible clinician and the AMHP and sent to the Hospital Managers. Regulation 6 of the Draft Mental Health (Hospital, Guardianship and Treatment) Regulations 2008 provide that a CTO must be on prescribed documentation and that the RC must, as soon as reasonably practicable, furnish the managers of the responsible hospital with a copy of the order. The CTO will be effective from the date on which the patient is discharged from detention. The Department of Health Code of Practice states that:[62]

> 'There are no provisions in the Act for community treatment orders and related documents to be rectified once made. Hospital managers should nonetheless ensure that arrangements are in place to check that documents have been properly completed. Significant errors or inadequacies in community treatment orders themselves may render patients' supervised community treatment (SCT) invalid, and errors in recall notices or revocations may invalidate hospital managers' authority to detain.

---

60   The NHS Information Centre In-patients formally detained in hospitals under the Mental Health Act 1983 and patients subject to supervised community treatment, Annual figures, England 2009/10, p 4.

61   As has been held in relation to public law issues in family law such as placement of children in care or placing them for adoption or fostering: *Olsson v Sweden* (1988) 11 EHRR 259; *Keegan v Ireland* (1994) 18 EHRR 342; and *Eriksson v Sweden* (1989) 12 EHRR 183. See N Mole *Council of Europe Guide to Article 6*. See http://hrls.echr.coe.int/uhtbin/cgisirsi.exe/x/0/0/5?searchdata1=human+rights+handbooks%7b440%7d.

62   Department of Health *Code of Practice: Mental Health Act 1983* (2008), paras 13.16–13.17.

To avoid errors being made, hospital managers should ensure that responsible clinicians have access to advice about how the relevant forms should be completed and the opportunity (where practicable) to have them checked in advance by someone else familiar with what the Act requires.'

The Joint Committee considered that a procedure should be on the face of the statute. Furthermore, the potential breadth of conditions may well mean that a civil right could be infringed engaging the protection under Art 6 of speedy access to an independent court in determination of civil rights and obligations, or at the very least that the procedural obligation under Art 8 might be engaged.[63]

---

[63] House of Lords, House of Commons, Joint Committee on Human Rights *Legislative Scrutiny: Mental Health Bill: Fourth Report of Session 2006–2007* (HL Paper 40, HC Paper 288, 4 February 2007), paras 48–51.

Chapter 9

DISCHARGE AND REVIEW OF THE LAWFULNESS OF DETENTION BY MENTAL HEALTH TRIBUNALS AND THE COURTS

OVERVIEW

9.1   An unrestricted patient detained under the MHA 1983 may be discharged by the Responsible Clinician ('RC') (see **4.75** above), by the nearest relative (NR) (see **5.6** above), by the Hospital Managers (see **5.65–5.69** above), or by a Mental Health Tribunal ('MHT'). Only the Secretary of State for Justice or a MHT may discharge a restriction order patient. The Secretary of State for Justice has the final say on discharge of restriction direction, or hospital direction patients. Patients detained for longer than 72 hours under the 1983 Act have the right to apply to a MHT to seek review of the lawfulness of detention. If the patient does not apply within specified periods the case must be automatically referred to the MHT. Article 5(4) of the European Convention on Human Rights states that everyone deprived of liberty:

> 'by arrest or detention shall be entitled to take proceedings by which the lawfulness of his detention shall be decided speedily by a court and his release ordered if the detention is not lawful.'

The Strasbourg Court has recognised, in light of 'the gravity of detention in a psychiatric hospital'[1], that Art 5(4) also requires that the patient must have an effective remedy, and it must be possible to maintain a challenge to the lawfulness of detention even if it has already terminated. This chapter considers the power of discharge, and the respective roles of MHTs and the courts in reviewing the lawfulness of psychiatric detention.

Mental Health Tribunals ('MHTs')

9.2   Mental Health Review Tribunals (MHRTs) were established under the Mental Health Act 1959 with the task of reviewing the continued need for the detention of the patient, and were empowered to direct discharge. MHRTs have been radically reformed by the Tribunals, Courts and Enforcement Act 2007 (TCEA) 2007, which creates two new tribunals in England: the (FTT) and the Upper Tribunal. The FTT is divided into chambers which deal with cases at

---

[1]   *Herz v Germany (Application 44672/98)* Judgment of 12 June 2003, ECtHR.

first instance. The jurisdiction of the MHRT in England has been transferred by the Transfer of Tribunal Functions Order 2008 to the Health, Education and Social Care Chamber whose procedure will be governed by the First-Tier Tribunal (Health Education and Social Care Chamber) Rules 2008, and the tribunal is now known as the Mental Health Tribunal ('MHT').[2] The tribunal judiciary and members are appointed by the Lord Chancellor. There are two Regional Tribunal Judges for England, currently based in London and Preston. There is a separate Mental Health Review Tribunal for Wales, which is administered from and based in Cardiff. The tribunal's duties in hearing cases may be performed by three or more of its members. At least one must be a 'legal member', one a 'medical member', and one a member who is neither a legal nor a medical member.[3] The legal members are called judge (England) or president (Wales) and are appointed by the Lord Chancellor from persons whom he considers to have suitable legal experience. The FTT (Mental Health) website states that in practice, he will normally consider only persons who hold a seven year general qualification within the meaning of s 71 of the Courts and Legal Services Act 1990 (namely a right of audience in any class of proceedings in the county courts or Magistrates' courts).[4] Where a tribunal is appointed to hear a particular case, the legal member/judge is the chairman (in Wales the President) of that tribunal and has wide discretion in the conduct of the proceedings, subject always to the Tribunal Rules. In the case of a restricted patient, the legal member has to be chosen from a panel of legal members who have been approved by the Lord Chancellor to hear such cases. The intention of this provision was to ensure that persons presiding over tribunals in cases of patients who have been convicted of serious offences have 'substantial judicial experience in the criminal courts.' In July 2010 the Lord Chancellor, Kenneth Clarke announced that 'salaried judges who are not judges or recorders, but who have the necessary experience can chair restricted patient cases. Although circuit judges and recorder QCs would continue to deal with the majority of cases, authorising some of the salaried mental health judges with the necessary experience increases the pool of available chairs to hear the cases, and it is hoped will reduce delays in bringing these cases to a hearing.[5] Each tribunal hearing is conducted by a panel of three. In England the tribunal service has issued a Practice Statement on the Composition of the Health, Education and Social Care Chamber which states that:

> 'A decision that disposes of proceedings or determines a preliminary issue made at, or following, a hearing must be made by one judge who is the presiding member; one doctor; and one other member who has substantial experience of health or social care matters.'[6]

---

2   SI 2008/2699.
3   Mental Health Act 1983, s 65(3) and Sch 2, para 4.
4   <www.mhrt.org.uk>.
5   Hansard HC Debs 26 July 2010.
6   Practice Statement on the Composition of the Health, Education and Social Care Chamber (<www.tribunals.gov.uk/Tribunals/Documents/Rules/HESC.pdf>).

The judge presides over the hearing, is responsible for ensuring that the proceedings are conducted fairly in accordance with the 1983 Act and the Tribunal Rules, and advises on any points of law. The judge also takes responsibility for drafting the reasons for the decision, following discussion with the other members. The medical member performs two roles. Prior to the hearing he or she must 'examine the patient and take such other steps as he or she considers necessary to form an opinion of the patient's mental condition'. At the hearing the medical member shares judicial responsibility with the other members and must decide whether or not the patient should remain in detention. The medical member advises the tribunal on medical matters. The third category of member is 'lay members', although this term does not appear in the 1983 Act, which refers to 'members who are neither legal nor medical members'. These are persons 'having such experience in administration, such knowledge of social services or such other qualifications or experience as the Lord Chancellor considers suitable'. The lay member is there to provide balance by representing the social view rather than bringing to bear legal or medical professional expertise.

9.3   Since the Mental Health Act 1983, there has been a remarkable development of case law in relation to tribunals, resulting from judicial review applications not only from patients, but also from hospital authorities, the Secretary of State and victims, all seeking to assert their rights and prerogatives. One result has been that tribunals may have many parties appearing before them, each offering different perspectives on whether the patient is fit for discharge. The tribunal has been affected by the MHA 2007 and the Tribunals, Courts and Enforcement Act 2007 in six main ways. First, its organization has been changed so that Wales has its own MHRT with its own Chairman. In England the MHT has been subsumed into the Health Education and Social Care Chamber of the First Tier Tribunal established under the Tribunals Courts and Enforcement Act 2007. There is a National President and the panel for each hearing is presided over by a tribunal judge. Second, new provisions for automatic referrals are introduced (see **9.42–9.43** below). Third, the discharge criteria are altered by the new broad definition of mental disorder, the removal of the exclusion for sexual deviancy, and the condition that appropriate treatment must be available. Fourth, the jurisdiction to reclassify as suffering from a different form of disorder is abolished. Fifth, a new jurisdiction over CTO patients is introduced. Sixth, changes to the Domestic Violence, Crime and Victims Act 2004 mean that victims of certain crimes committed by mentally disordered offenders are entitled to make representations to MHTs.

The role of the Tribunal

9.4   In *R v Canons Park Mental Health Review Tribunal, ex parte A*, Sedley J said that the MHRT is:[7]

---

7   [1994] 1 All ER 481 at 490.

'a body charged with reviewing the operative decisions of the responsible authorities to detain the patient, and its functions are to reappraise the patient's condition at the time of the hearing and in the light of its findings do one of three things – to direct discharge as of right, to direct discharge in the exercise of its discretion, or to do neither.'

In essence the tribunal's task is to determine whether at the time of the hearing, the criteria justifying detention continue to be met. It was envisaged that the lawfulness of initial admission and renewal of detention would continue to be a matter to be dealt with in the High Court by way of judicial review or habeas corpus.[8]

Article 5(1) and discharge powers

9.5 In *Winterwerp v Netherlands* the Strasbourg Court held that the lawfulness of continued psychiatric detention under Art 5(1)(e) depends on the persistence of unsoundness of mind of a nature or degree warranting confinement. This means that all those with a power of discharge, particularly the RC, must keep under review the continued need for detention, and if the criteria for detention are not met, must discharge the patient. However, before doing so the RC must carry out a full risk assessment, must formulate a care plan (see **5.68** above), and must give victims of certain offender patients the right to make representations (see **7.133–7.136** above).

Article 5(4) and review of the lawfulness of detention

9.6 Whilst *Winterwerp* is the classic case on Art 5(1)(e), *X v United Kingdom*[9] has equivalent status in relation to the right to take proceedings to challenge the lawfulness of detention under Art 5(4). If the detention was ordered by a court, the requirement of speedy review does not apply during the initial stages of detention, but there must be periodic opportunities for the detained person to assert, before a court with the power of discharge, that the conditions of detention no longer apply. In *X v United Kingdom* this was held to mean that:[10]

'A person of unsound mind compulsorily confined in a psychiatric institution for an indefinite or lengthy period is in principle entitled, at any rate where there is no automatic review of a judicial character, to take proceedings before a court at reasonable intervals to put in issue the lawfulness ... of his detention, whether that detention was ordered by a civil or criminal court, or by some other authority.'

The expectation here is that the norm will be automatic review of a judicial character, but that where that is not present the patient must have the right to take proceedings at reasonable intervals. Under the MHA 1959 there was no automatic review of a judicial character. Referrals were introduced by the

---

8   *R v Hallstrom and another, ex parte W* (1985) 2 BMLR 54, [1985] 3 All ER 775; and *R v North West Thames Mental Health Review Tribunal, ex p Cooper* (1990) 5 BMLR 7, QBD.
9   (1981) 4 EHRR 188.
10   (1981) 4 EHRR 188, at para 52.

MHA 1983, in recognition that some patients might lack the necessary capacity or motivation to apply themselves due to their disorder.

Scope of the review

9.7   The review must be able to consider whether, on the facts, the *Winterwerp* criteria for lawful detention are still met. In *X v United Kingdom*, the Court held that:[11]

> 'The right guaranteed by Article 5(4) to test the lawfulness of detention does not incorporate a right for the court to substitute its discretion for that of the decision-making authority; but the scope of the judicial review must be sufficient to enable enquiry to be made whether, in the case of detention of a mental patient, the reasons which initially justified the detention continue thereafter to subsist.'

This means that the court must be able to rule on the applicability of the *Winterwerp* criteria in the patient's case. Is there, at the time of the hearing, a true mental disorder which is of a kind or degree warranting detention?

9.8   The applicant in *X v United Kingdom* was a restricted patient. Under the MHA 1959, the only judicial body which could look at the substantive justification for detention was the MHRT, but the MHRT had no power to direct discharge if the criteria were found not to be met. They could only give advice to the Home Secretary. This was held to be a breach of Art 5(4). Although the High Court could have discharged the patient by way of habeas corpus or judicial review, these avenues considered the formal legality rather than the substantive factual and diagnostic justification for detention. In its implementation of the ruling in *X v United Kingdom*, the MHA 1983 extended the right to apply to the tribunal for discharge to restricted patients, and also to non-offender patients detained for up to 28 days under s 2.

9.9   In order to be a competent court for the purposes of reviewing the lawfulness of detention, the review must be sufficient in scope to address the *Winterwerp* criteria and the court or tribunal must have the power to direct discharge. *X v United Kingdom* meant that the Home Office lost the final word in the discharge of restriction order patients. The decision as to discharge was now for the judicial body, the MHRT, and was no longer an administrative decision within the sole province of the Secretary of State (then the Home Secretary, now the Secretary of State for Justice). Instead of having the final word, the Secretary of State, through the Mental Health Unit is now a party to tribunal proceedings relating to restricted patients, and the Secretary of State's rights as party have been asserted with vigour before Tribunals and in judicial review. With restriction direction patients transferred from prison or on a hospital direction, the Secretary of State retains the final say on discharge. As a safeguard for the public interest, tribunals in restricted cases are chaired by a judge rather than a solicitor or barrister. These developments have inevitably made the proceedings more formal, and potentially more adversarial.

---

[11]   (1981) 4 EHRR 188, at para 53.

9.10 In *Reid v United Kingdom*[12] the ECHR elaborated further on the features of a competent court. For the purposes of Art 5(4), the body does not necessarily have to be a court of law of the classic kind integrated within the standard judicial machinery of the country. Tribunals are courts for the purposes of this provision. The most important feature is independence from the executive and the parties to the case. Secondly, the safeguards must be 'appropriate to the kind of deprivation of liberty in question.' This means there must be a 'judicial procedure', the forms of which may vary but which must include the competence to 'decide' the lawfulness of the detention and to order release if the detention is not lawful.[13] Finally, review of the 'lawfulness' of detention must be carried out in light not only of domestic law requirements but also of the text of the Convention, the general principles embodied therein (including proportionality) and the aim of the restrictions permitted by para (1)(e).[14] This task is shared by the MHT which reviews the current need for continued detention, and the courts which have jurisdiction to review the lawfulness of the initial decision to detain, by habeas corpus, judicial review or civil action for the tort of false imprisonment. Damages may be obtained if a person is imprisoned (the Convention equivalent is deprived of liberty) and there is no lawful authority to justify it.[15]

Habeas corpus

9.11 The writ of habeas corpus requires the detaining body to show lawful justification for a detention, and the detainee is entitled to release if such justification is lacking. The scope of the court's inquiry in habeas corpus applications is to review the facial validity of the application and medical recommendations, and to consider any irregularities which go to the jurisdiction of the detaining body. Reviewing whether the documents show sufficient authority is carried out in the context that if any of the statutory documents is incorrect or defective it may be amended within the first 14 days following admission.[16] Examples of irregularities going to jurisdiction are where a key jurisdictional fact is missing as, for example, if a magistrates' court made a hospital order in a case of an offender convicted of a non-imprisonable offence. In *R v Board of Control, ex parte Rutty*[17] habeas corpus was granted because the power to detain could only be used on someone who was 'found neglected' and Kathleen Rutty had been living at all times in institutional care. A key jurisdictional fact was missing. In *Re S-C (mental patient: habeas corpus)*,[18] the ASW, knowing that the father, who was the nearest relative, objected to s 3 admission, had consulted the mother, who did not. Since an objection by the NR deprives the managers of jurisdiction to detain, habeas

---

12   (2003) 37 EHRR 9, ECtHR.
13   *Weeks v United Kingdom (Application 9787/82)* (1987) 10 EHRR 293, at para 61.
14   *Brogan v United Kingdom* (1988) 11 EHRR 117, ECtHR.
15   *R v Deputy Governor of Parkhurst Prison, ex parte Hague* [1991] 3 WLR 340.
16   MHA 1983, s 15.
17   [1956] 2 QB 109.
18   [1996] 1 All ER 532, CA.

corpus was granted on the basis of want of jurisdictional fact. Sir Thomas Bingham held that habeas corpus was appropriate since:

> 'There was no attempt being made to overturn an administrative decision. The object is simply to show that there was never jurisdiction to detain the appellant in the first place.'

On the evidence this was plainly made out. More recently in *M v East London NHS Foundation Trust*[19] habeas corpus was granted because the AMHP had telephoned the nearest relative 'NR' prior to making an application under s 3 and the NR had objected. The AMHP had called back just prior to making the application, and although the NR had not reiterated the objection he had not withdrawn it. The AMHP proceeded with the application. The Court granted habeas corpus, holding that it had not been reasonable for the AMHP to believe that there was no objection from the NR, and that the application was therefore unlawful.

9.12 Although an application for habeas corpus takes priority over any other High Court business, the scope of the review which it allows means that it cannot examine whether the person is still suffering from a true mental disorder of a kind or degree warranting detention for the purposes of Art 5(4). In *X v United Kingdom* a duly completed recall warrant was held sufficient to defeat a habeas corpus application. The Strasbourg Court held that although habeas corpus carried a power of discharge as required by Art 5(4), the limited scope of review which it permitted was insufficient for the purposes of that Article.

Judicial review

9.13 The purpose and limits of judicial review were described as follows by Lord Hailsham in *Chief Constable of North Wales Police v Evans*:[20]

> '[T]o ensure that the individual is given fair treatment by the authority to which he has been subjected … it is no part of that purpose to substitute the opinion of the judiciary or individual judges for that of the authority constituted by law to decide the matter in question.'

Judicial review does *not* challenge the merits of the decision, since the doctrine of the separation of powers requires them to avoid usurping functions given to the decision-maker by statute. The process is governed by s 31 of the Senior Courts Act 1981 and Parts 8 and 54 of the Civil Procedure Rules which govern the way that courts exercise supervisory jurisdiction over the proceedings and decisions of bodies performing public law duties or functions.

9.14 There are six basic grounds for judicial review:

(a) Illegality / Error of Law

---

[19] CO/1065/2009.
[20] [1982] 1 WLR 1155 at 1160, HL.

The decision maker must understand correctly the law that regulates his decision-making power and must give effect to it.

(b) Procedural Impropriety
This means more than failure to observe basic rules of natural justice (audi alteram partem, nemo judex in causa sua) or failure to act with procedural fairness towards the person affected. It also includes failure by an administrative tribunal to observe procedural rules.

(c) Irrationality / *Wednesbury* unreasonableness[21]
Where the decision is so outrageous in its defiance of logic or accepted moral standards that no sensible person who had applied his mind to the question to be decided could have arrived at it.

(d) Abuse of Power
This includes failing to have regard to relevant considerations, taking account of irrelevant considerations, acting for an improper purpose, or following a policy unduly rigidly without allowing for exceptional circumstances.

(e) Human Rights Act 1998
Challenges may be brought by way of judicial review alleging that actions of public bodies have violated a person's Convention rights.

(f) EC Law
EC Law challenges based on the infringement of enforceable Community rights under the European Communities Act 1972.

9.15 The tribunal's jurisdiction is confined to reviewing the patient's condition at the time of the hearing and determining whether detention is still necessary. If a person wishes to challenge the validity of the decision to detain in the first place or the renewal of detention the correct avenue will be judicial review. Although there was a procedure for appeal by cased stated from the tribunal to the High Court it was much more common for parties aggrieved by a tribunal decision to seek judicial review. Judicial review in the High Court is now used to challenge the lawfulness of the initial decision to detain or a subsequent decision to renew detention. The Upper Tribunal now deals with appeals from tribunals and judicial review of their decisions. The Upper Tribunal is a newly created court of record with jurisdiction throughout the United Kingdom, established under the Tribunals, Courts and Enforcement Act 2007. The Upper Tribunal consists of High Court judges and other specialist judges. The Upper Tribunal is divided into three chambers. The Administrative Appeals Chamber hears appeals and exercises judicial review over the decisions of the First Tier Mental Health Tribunal (FTT) and the MHRT Wales. The High Court in England and Wales, the Court of Session in Scotland, and the High Court in Northern Ireland all have power to transfer judicial review applications to the

---

21 *Associated Provincial Picture Houses Ltd v Wednesbury Corpn* [1948] 1 KB 223, CA.

Upper Tribunal. For England and Wales the Lord Chief Justice, has the power to issue directions transferring classes of judicial review to the Upper Tribunal. The main functions of the Upper Tribunal are to hear appeals from the decisions of First Tier Tribunals;[22] to exercise powers of judicial review in certain circumstances;[23] and to deal with enforcement of decisions, directions and orders made by tribunals.[24] The procedure of the Upper Tribunal is regulated by the Tribunal Procedure (Upper Tribunal) Rules 2008.[25] Any party to a case in the FTT has the right to appeal (with the leave of the FTT or the Upper Tribunal), on a point of law arising from the decision to the Upper Tribunal.[26] It is important to note that before granting leave to appeal one of its decisions, the FTT may, on its own initiative or on application by anyone with a right of appeal, review a decision made by it on a matter in a case.[27] Applications for leave to appeal must identify the decision of the Tribunal, the error of law alleged and the result the party is seeking.[28] The FTT must then decide whether to review the decision itself. This may only happen if the Tribunal is satisfied that there was an error of law.[29] If the FTT reviews the decision itself it can set a decision aside and must then either re-decide the case, or refer the case to the Upper Tribunal for the re-decision.[30] The Explanatory Notes to the TCEA 2007 describe in the following terms the purpose of the FTT's jurisdiction to review its own decisions:[31]

> 'Sections 9 and 10 provide powers for the First-Tier and Upper Tribunals to review their own decisions without the need for a full onward appeal and, where the tribunal concludes that an error was made, to re-decide the matter. This is intended to capture decisions that are clearly wrong, so avoiding the need for an appeal. The power has been provided in the form of a discretionary power for the Tribunal so that only appropriate decisions are reviewed. This contrasts with cases where an appeal on a point of law is made, because, for instance, it is important to have an authoritative ruling.'

9.16 Important rulings on points of law are referred to the Upper Tribunal, which, as a court of record, can lay down authoritative precedents. Section 12 of the Tribunals, Courts and Enforcement Act 2007 deals with the powers of the Upper Tribunal on hearing appeals. The Upper Tribunal may (but need not) set aside the decision of the FTT, and if it does, must either (i) remit the case to the FTT with directions for its reconsideration, or (ii) re-make the decision. If the case is remitted, the Upper Tribunal may direct that the

---

22   Tribunals Courts and Enforcement Act 2007, s 11.
23   Ibid, s 15.
24   Ibid, s 25.
25   SI 2008/2698.
26   Tribunals, Courts and Enforcement Act 2007, s 11.
27   Tribunals, Courts and Enforcement Act 2007, s 9 and First-tier Tribunal (Health Education and Social Care Chamber) Rules 2008, SI 2008/2699, rr 46 and 47.
28   First-tier Tribunal (Health Education and Social Care Chamber) Rules 2008 SI 2008/2699, r 46(5).
29   Ibid, r 49(1).
30   Tribunals, Courts and Enforcement Act 2007, s 9(4) and (5).
31   Tribunals, Courts and Enforcement Act 2007, Explanatory Notes, para 100. <www.opsi.gov. uk/acts/acts2007/en/ukpgaen_20070015_en_2#cpt1-ch2-pb3-l1g9_IDAEX2WB>.

members of the FTT who are chosen to reconsider the case are not to be the same as those who made the decision that has been set aside and may give procedural directions in connection with the reconsideration of the case by the FTT. If the Upper Tribunal remakes the decision it may make any decision which the FTT could make if the FTT were re-making the decision, and may make any findings of fact considered appropriate.

9.17 The powers of the Upper Tribunal in relation to judicial review are set out in ss 15–17 of the TCEA 2007 and Part 4 of the Tribunal Procedure (Upper Tribunal) Rules 2008.[32] Section 15 empowers the Upper Tribunal to grant (a) a mandatory order; (b) a prohibiting order; (c) a quashing order; (d) a declaration; or (e) an injunction. In exercising this jurisdiction any relief granted by the Upper Tribunal has the same effect as the corresponding relief granted by the High Court on an application for judicial review, and is enforceable as if it were relief granted by the High Court on an application for judicial review. In deciding whether to grant relief, the Upper Tribunal must apply the principles that the High Court would apply in deciding whether to grant that relief on an application for judicial review. The tribunal may award damages, restitution or the recovery of a sum due if the application includes a damages claim and the tribunal is satisfied that such an award would have been made by the High Court if the claim had been made in an action begun in the High Court by the applicant at the time of making the application.[33] If the Upper Tribunal grants a quashing order it may (a) remit the matter concerned to the court, tribunal or authority that made the decision, with a direction to reconsider the matter and reach a decision in accordance with the findings of the Upper Tribunal, or (b) substitute its own decision for the decision in question.[34]

9.18 Section 25 provides the Upper Tribunal with the powers of the High Court or Court of Session to require the attendance and examination of witnesses and the production and inspection of documents, and all other matters incidental to the Upper Tribunal's functions. Rule 7(3) of the First-tier Tribunal (Health Education and Social Care Chamber) Rules 2008 permits the Tribunal to refer to the Upper Tribunal any failure to comply with a requirement in relation to six types of direction listed, including non-compliance with a subpoena.

9.19 Wales retains a separate Mental Health Review Tribunal subject to the Mental Health Review Tribunal for Wales Rules 2008.[35] Section 32 of the TCEA 2007 allows the Lord Chancellor by order to provide for an appeal against a decision of a scheduled tribunal to be made to the Upper Tribunal, instead of to the court to which an appeal would otherwise fall to be made,

---

[32]   SI 2008/2698.
[33]   Tribunal Courts and Enforcement Act 2007, s 16(6).
[34]   Ibid s 17(1).
[35]   SI 2008/2705.

where the decision is made by the tribunal in exercising a function in relation to Wales. Hence appeals from the MHRT Wales and judicial review can be heard by the Upper Tribunal.

Speedy review of the lawfulness of detention

9.20   Article 5(4) entitles anyone detained on grounds of unsoundness of mind to take proceedings by which the lawfulness of their detention shall be decided speedily by a court and their release ordered if their detention is not lawful. If the initial decision was ordered by administrative procedure, the review must be available 'speedily' following the detention.

9.21   In *Reid v the United Kingdom*[36] the Court found a breach of the speediness requirement in Art 5(4). Reid applied for release in April 1994, and the House of Lords finally determined his appeal almost four years later. The speediness requirement in Art 5(4) applies to appellate instances as well as the initial review, so time continues to run until all appeals or judicial review proceedings are determined. The Strasbourg Court does not rule on speediness by stating that a particular time delay (three months for example) is or is not compatible with Art 5(4). Instead it asks whether, on the facts of the individual case, there was a failure to proceed with reasonable dispatch having regard to all the material circumstances.

9.22   In *R (on the application of C) v Mental Health Review Tribunal*[37] C's case was listed for a date precisely eight weeks after his application. The tribunal Chairs had adopted a policy of seeking to bring all cases on within eight weeks. The tribunal administration had translated this into a practice of giving all applicants a hearing date precisely eight weeks from the date of the application. The Court of Appeal held this was incompatible with Art 5(4), unless this was the only practicable way of ensuring that individual cases are determined as speedily as their individual circumstances reasonably permit. In *R (on the application of K) v Mental Health Review Tribunal*[38] Stanley Burnton J held that the right of seven applicants to a speedy hearing under Art 5(4) had been breached and that the evidence before him indicated the basic responsibility for the delays experienced by patients was that of central government rather than the tribunal chairmen or their staff.

9.23   Following the friendly settlement in *Roux v United Kingdom*[39] the UK Government agreed that a new r 29(cc) should be introduced for cases of recall of conditionally discharged restricted patients, whereby the tribunal would be required to fix a date between five and eight weeks from the date of reference. *R (on the application of B) v Mental Health Review Tribunal*[40] concerned delay of eight months in the hearing of a recalled restricted patient. Scott Baker J held

---

[36]   (2003) 37 EHRR 9, ECtHR.
[37]   [2002] 1 WLR 176, CA.
[38]   [2002] EWHC 639 (Admin).
[39]   *(Application 25601/94)* Decision of 4 September 1996, ECtHR.
[40]   [2002] EWHC 1553 (Admin).

that there had been a breach of Art 5(4), and that the underlying problem was a lack of case management on the tribunal's part. At each stage the tribunal ought to have had in mind the delay which had accrued and given directions against that background. The longer the delay, the more aggressive the directions would have to be in order to ensure an early disposal of the case. There would come a time where the convenience of expert witnesses had to cede to the need for the tribunal to conclude a substantive hearing. No adequate explanation had been given for the delays.

BURDEN OF PROOF

9.24   For the first 40 years of its existence the tribunal operated under a reverse of the normal common law presumption that it is for those carrying out the detention to justify it, rather than for the detainee to justify his or her freedom. A patient would only be entitled to discharge if he or she could satisfy the tribunal that he or she was no longer suffering from mental disorder of a nature or degree warranting confinement. This faced patients with the considerable burden of establishing a negative, the absence of mental disorder of a nature or degree making detention for medical treatment appropriate. In a series of cases decided prior to the coming into force of the Human Rights Act 1998 the courts emphasised the importance of this reverse burden of proof. In *R v Canons Park Mental Health Review Tribunal, ex parte A* the majority in the Court of Appeal held that a tribunal was only required to direct discharge:[41]

> 'if it is satisfied of a negative, because the tribunal is not intended to duplicate the role of the medical officer, whose diagnosis stands until the tribunal is satisfied that it is wrong.'

9.25   The Strasbourg case law contained suggestions that the burden of proof might be incompatible with Convention rights. The stipulation in *X v United Kingdom* that an Art 5 court must conduct an inquiry whether the reasons which initially justify detention continue to subsist implies that the court ought to be satisfied they are met. In *James Kay v United Kingdom*, the European Commission on Human Rights declared admissible a complaint where one of the applicant's contentions was that the tribunal could not provide an effective remedy 'because it does not have to find positive evidence that the patient is suffering from mental disorder'.[42] One of the first declarations of incompatibility granted under the Human Rights Act 1998 was *R (H) v London North and East Region Mental Health Review Tribunal (Secretary of State for Health intervening)*[43] where the Court of Appeal held that the

---

41   [1994] 2 All ER 659, CA. The reverse burden was also emphasised in *Perkins v Bath District Health Authority; R v Wessex Mental Health Review Tribunal, ex parte Wiltshire County Council* (1989) 4 BMLR 145, CA; and *R v Merseyside Mental Health Review Tribunal, ex parte K* [1990] 1 All ER 694, (1989) 4 BMLR 60, CA.

42   *(Application 17821/91)* Decision of 7 July 1993, ECtHR.

43   [2001] 3 WLR 512, CA. See also *Lyons v The Scottish Ministers* (unreported) 17 January 2002, First Division of Scottish Court of Session.

positioning of the burden of proof under ss 72 and 73 on the applicant to satisfy the tribunal of the absence of detainable mental disorder was incompatible with Art 5 of the ECHR.

9.26 The Government introduced a remedial order to rectify the incompatibility. Under the amended s 72(1)(b) a patient is entitled to discharge if the tribunal is not satisfied:[44]

'(i) that the patient is then suffering from mental disorder of a *nature or degree* which makes it appropriate for him to be *liable to be detained* in hospital for medical treatment; or

(ii) that it is necessary for the health or safety of the patient or for the protection of other persons that he should receive such treatment; or

(iia) that appropriate medical treatment is available for him; or

(iii) in the case of an application by the nearest relative following the barring of a discharge order, that the patient if released would be likely to act in a manner dangerous to himself or to other persons.'

The tribunal must discharge if not satisfied that any one of conditions (i)–(ii) or (iia) is met or, in the case of a nearest relative application, if not satisfied that condition (iii) is met.

Standard of proof

9.27 In *R (on the application of N) v Mental Health Review Tribunal (Northern Region)*[45] the Court of Appeal affirmed that the standard of proof was the balance of probabilities and considered this to be 'compliant with the ECHR case-law requiring it to be "reliably shown" that detention was justified.' The court recognised that standard of proof had a potential part to play in the decision-making process, 'even in relation to issues that were the subject of judgment and evaluation.' 'Standard of proof' and 'balance of probabilities' are words which go naturally with the concept of evidence relating to fact, but in the Court's view were less than perfect with evaluative assessments where it was best to speak of the 'burden of persuasion'. Tribunals should approach the entire range of issues by reference to the standard of proof on the balance of probabilities, whilst recognising that in practice the standard of proof will have a much more important part to play in the determination of disputed issues of fact than it will generally have in matters of judgment as to appropriateness and necessity.

Congruence between admission and discharge criteria

9.28 The Court of Appeal decision in *R (on the application of H) v London North and East Region Mental Health Review Tribunal (Secretary of State for Health intervening)* is not only important because the burden of proof was held

---

[44] MHA 1983, ss 72 and 73, as amended by Mental Health Act 1983 (Remedial) Order 2001 (SI 2001/3712), and MHA 2007, Sch 1, para 14 and s 4(8)(a).

[45] [2005] EWCA Civ 1605, 88 BMLR 59, CA.

to be incompatible with Art 5(4), but also because the Court held that Art 5(4) required congruence between the criteria for admission and discharge (per Lord Phillips MR):[46]

> 'So far as Article 5(4) is concerned, it seems to us axiomatic that if the function of the tribunal is to consider whether the detention of the patient is lawful, it must apply the same test that the law required to be applied as a precondition to admission unless it be the case that the patient can lawfully be detained provided some other test is satisfied.'

There is one area of incongruence between the admission and discharge criteria for s 3, where patients may only be detained if:

(a) they are suffering from mental disorder of a nature or degree which makes it appropriate for them to receive medical treatment in a hospital treatment; and

(b) treatment is necessary for their own health or safety or for the protection of other persons and it cannot be provided unless they are detained.

9.29 The tribunal only comes under a duty to discharge if not satisfied that the patient is then suffering from mental disorder of a nature or degree which makes it appropriate for him to be *liable to be detained* in hospital for medical treatment. This means that the MHT does not come under a duty to discharge where it is not satisfied that actual detention is still necessary. That duty only applies where it is not satisfied that it is necessary for the patient to be liable to be detained. Hence, the MHT is not under a duty to discharge a patient who is on extended leave in the community if it is satisfied that the patient still needs the discipline of liability to recall under s 17. The Mental Health (Amendment) Bill 1981 would have entitled a patient to discharge if their mental disorder was not of a nature or degree requiring *detention*. The phrase 'liable to be detained' was retained from the MHA 1959 and introduced in the MHA 1983 as a result of the intervention before the Special Standing Committee of the late James Cooke, then Chairman of the South East Thames MHRT, who argued that the tribunal should not be obliged to discharge someone who was on s 17 leave. This point is less likely to arise in practice since RC's are now required before sending someone on s 17 leave for more than 7 days to consider making a community treatment order.[47]

9.30 Despite the incongruence between admission and discharge criteria the criteria for renewal of detention by the RC are congruent with the criteria for admission. For renewal it must be necessary for the health or safety of the patient or for the protection of others that he receives treatment and it must be the case that it cannot be provided unless he is detained.[48] However, in *B v*

---

46   [2001] 3 WLR 512 at [31].
47   MHA 1983, s 17(2A).
48   MHA 1983, s 20(4)(c).

Barking Havering and Brentwood Community Healthcare NHS Trust[49] the Court of Appeal held that the words 'unless he continues to be detained' mean 'unless he continues to be liable to be detained' rather than 'unless he continues to be actually detained.' Accordingly, the conditions of renewal can be satisfied even in relation to a patient who is no longer actually detained but has been granted leave of absence under s 17. This point is less likely to arise in practice since RC's are now required before sending someone on s 17 leave for more than 7 days to consider making a community treatment order.[50]

Organisation of the MHT

9.31 The jurisdiction of the MHRT in England has been transferred by the Transfer of Tribunal Functions Order 2008 to the Health, Education and Social Care Chamber whose procedure will be governed by the First-Tier Tribunal (Health Education and Social Care Chamber) Rules 2008, and the tribunal is now known as the Mental Health Tribunal ('MHT').[51] The tribunal judiciary and members are appointed by the Lord Chancellor. There are two Regional Tribunal Judges for England, currently based in London and Preston. There is a separate Mental Health Review Tribunal for Wales, which is administered from and based in Cardiff.

9.32 The purpose of the tribunals is set out in s 65(1A) 'to deal with applications and references by and in respect of patients under ... this Act'. The tribunal's duties may be performed by three or more of its members. At least one must be a 'legal member', one a 'medical member' and one a member who is neither a legal nor a medical member.[52] The legal member is known as the tribunal judge in England or President in Wales (see **9.2** above). The judge presides over the hearing, is responsible for ensuring that the proceedings are conducted fairly in accordance with the 1983 Act and the Tribunal Rules, and advises on any points of law. The judge also takes responsibility for drafting the reasons for the decision, following discussion with the other members.

The panel for a hearing

9.33 The President (in Wales the Chairman) or another member of the tribunal appointed by the President, appoints the members of the panel for each hearing, which must include a legal member, a medical member and a lay member.[53] In practice the tribunal office staff carry out the task of assembling the panel for a hearing. Delegation of functions to staff is expressly provided for in r 4 of the First Tier Tribunal Health Education and Social Care Rules 2008 whereby the Senior Tribunal president can issue approval for general classes of tribunal staff to carry out specified classes of 'function of a judicial nature permitted or required to be done by the Tribunal.' The MHRT

---

49   [1999] 1 FLR 106, CA.
50   MHA 1983, s 17(2A).
51   SI 2008/2699.
52   MHA 1983, s 65(3) and Sch 2, para 4.
53   Ibid, Sch 2, paras 3 and 4.

Wales Rules 2008 contain no equivalent express power to delegate, perhaps in the belief that there is an implied power to delegate to staff such functions as choosing the panel for the hearing. Under the MHRT Wales Rules in Wales the Chairman of the Tribunal is empowered to issue directions dealing with any matter which is preliminary or incidental to the hearing.[54] Where a tribunal is appointed to hear a particular case, the judge is the chairman of that tribunal and has wide discretion in the conduct of the proceedings. In the case of a restricted patient, it used to be the case that the legal member had to be chosen from a panel of legal members who approved by the Lord Chancellor to hear such cases.[55] The intention of this provision was to ensure that persons presiding over tribunals in cases of patients who have been convicted of serious offences have 'substantial judicial experience in the criminal courts'. In July 2010 the Lord Chancellor, Kenneth Clarke announced that 'salaried judges with the necessary experience can chair restricted patient cases'. Although circuit judges and recorder QCs would continue to deal with the majority of cases, authorising some of the salaried mental health judges with the necessary experience would increase the pool of available chairs to hear the cases.[56]

9.34 The medical members are psychiatrists who are nominated by the Secretary of State for Health on recommendation by the health authorities. Applicants must be either a Member or a Fellow of the Royal College of Psychiatrists and have held either a full or a part-time appointment as a consultant psychiatrist for at least three years. They should also be participants in the Royal College of Psychiatrists continuing professional development programme.[57] The medical member has a duty to examine the patient prior to the proceedings and to form an opinion about the patient's mental condition.[58] The medical member performs two roles. Prior to the hearing he or she must, so far as practicable 'examine the patient and take such other steps as he or she considers necessary to form an opinion of the patient's mental condition'. At the hearing the medical member shares judicial responsibility with the other members and must decide whether or not the patient should remain in detention. The medical member advises the tribunal on medical matters.

9.35 The other tribunal members are neither legal members nor medical members. They are appointed by the Lord Chancellor after consultation with the Secretary of State for Health and are persons having experience in administration or social services, or who are persons with other experience or qualifications which are considered suitable.

---

54 Mental Health Review Tribunal Wales Rules 2008, SI 2008/2705, r 4.
55 Mental Health Review Tribunal Rules 1983, SI 1983/942, r 8(3).
56 Hansard HC Debs 26 July 2010.
57 <www.mhrt.org.uk/>.
58 First-tier Tribunal (Health Education and Social Care Chamber) Rules 2008, SI 2008/2699, r 34, the Mental Health Review Tribunal for Wales Rules 2008, SI 2008/2705, r 20.

Disqualifications

9.36 Rule 8(2) of the MHRT Rules 1983 precluded a tribunal member from serving on a particular case if he or she is a member or an officer of the responsible authority or if he or she has recently treated the patient or has some other close acquaintance or connection with him.[59] The First Tier HESC Rules 2008 are silent on the question of disqualification, but r 11 of the MHRT Wales Rules deals with people who are disqualified from sitting in certain cases, and gives an indication of who should be disqualified. Rule 11 provides that 'A person shall not be qualified to serve as a member of a Tribunal in Wales for the purpose of any proceedings where – (a) that person is a member, director or registered person (as the case may be) of the responsible authority concerned in the proceedings; or (b) that person is a member or director of a local health board or National Health Service Trust which has the right to discharge the patient under s 23(3) of the Act; or (c) the chairman or, as the case may be, president of the Tribunal considers that that person appears to have a conflict of interest or bias of opinion in respect of the patient, or any other member of that Tribunal or party to the proceedings, or has recently been involved with the medical treatment of the patient in a professional capacity. This gives the Chairman of the MHRT Wales or the President of the Tribunal panel for the hearing the power to decide that a member is disqualified. A member is not disqualified by virtue of having heard a previous tribunal application by the same patient.[60] In *R (on the application of M) v Mental Health Review Tribunal* the court held that in the circumstances, a fair-minded and informed observer, having taken account of all the facts of the case, would not have said that there was a real possibility of bias on the part of the judge President of the tribunal, who had just over a year previously sentenced the patient to a hospital order with restrictions under the MHA 1983.[61] In *R (on the application of D) v West Midlands and North West Mental Health Review Tribunal*[62] the issue was whether the medical member of the Tribunal was sufficiently independent as he was employed as a Consultant Psychiatrist by Mersey Care NHS Trust ('Mersey Care'), which was the 'mega' Trust that was responsible for detaining the claimant. The doctor had never worked in the hospital in which the claimant was detained and he did not know the claimant or any of the medically qualified or other witnesses at the hearing. It was not suggested that there was any actual bias on the part of the medical member. The Court of Appeal held that the wording of r 8 did not lead to the conclusion that the doctor was disqualified from sitting on the tribunal. He was not a member of the trust, and the meaning of the word 'officer' would depend on the context. In the present context it was natural to exclude those who managed the affairs of the authority in question. Moreover, no appearance of bias arose simply from the fact that the doctor was employed by the trust. Indeed, Lord Phillips MR, delivering the judgment of the court, described the

---

[59] Mental Health Review Tribunal Rules 1983, SI 1983/942, r 8(2).
[60] *R v Oxford Regional Mental Health Review, ex parte Mackman* (1986) *The Times*, 2 June.
[61] [2005] EWHC 2791 (Admin).
[62] *R (on the application of D) v West Midlands and North West Mental Health Review Tribunal* [2004] EWCA Civ 311, CA.

contention that the doctor might have been biased as absurd, and expressed the court's wonderment that the proceedings had ever been brought.[63] Appended to the Court of Appeal's decision is the Guidance issued by the MHRT on conflict of interest.

Tribunal clerks and tribunal assistants

9.37 Tribunal clerks are responsible for the administration of the tribunals, and advise on matters such as the appointment of tribunal members and administrative issues. The clerk exercises some administrative powers on behalf of the tribunal: he or she receives the application from the patient; sends out the necessary notices; obtains the responsible authority's statement and sends copies to the applicant, the applicant's representative and any other person who is entitled to receive it; arranges the time and place of the hearing; pays expenses and informs the applicant and other interested persons of the tribunal's decision. In Wales tribunal clerks perform the role of usher and note taker, but in England this role is performed by tribunal assistants where they are available.

Entitlement to apply for a Tribunal hearing

9.38 Under the MHA 1959, only patients detained following admission for treatment (now s 3) or under a hospital order (now s 37) were eligible to apply for discharge to a tribunal. Restricted patients could ask the Secretary of State for their case to be referred to the tribunal, but the jurisdiction of the tribunal in these cases was purely advisory. In *X v the United Kingdom*,[64] the European Court held that this advisory role breached Art 5(4) of the Convention. Following that ruling the UK Government empowered tribunals to direct the discharge of restriction order patients.[65] The MHA 1983 also introduced new rights for patients detained for up to 28 days' assessment, and for restricted patients to apply to a tribunal, as well as automatic referrals where patients had not applied.[66]

Part II patients

9.39 A patient admitted for assessment under s 2 may apply once within the first 14 days of detention.[67] In *R v South Thames Mental Health Review Tribunal, ex parte M*[68] Collins J explained a patient's tribunal entitlement where he or she is initially detained under s 2, but then detained under s 3 before the tribunal has heard the application for discharge from s 2. The tribunal hears the appeal as if it were an appeal against detention under s 3, and the patient's right to apply for a tribunal under s 66(1)(b) in the first period of detention after his

63 [2004] EWCA Civ 311 at [46].
64 (1981) 4 EHRR 178, 1 BMLR 98, ECtHR.
65 MHA 1983, s 73.
66 MHA 1983, s 66(1)(a), (2)(a), 68 and 70.
67 MHA 1983, s 66(1)(a) and (2)(a).
68 (unreported) 3 September 1997 (CO/2700/97), QBD.

change of status is unaffected. A patient admitted for treatment under s 3 may apply once in the first six months, and thereafter once in every period for which the detention is renewed.[69] Patients subject to guardianship may apply once in the first six months, and thereafter once in every period for which the guardianship is renewed.[70] Patients who are transferred from guardianship to hospital may apply within six months of the transfer, and once during each period where detention is renewed. In such cases the renewal date is six months from the date of acceptance or the original guardianship application.[71] Patients who are subject to SCT (a CTO) may apply once within six months of the making or revocation of a CTO and once within every period for which the CTO is renewed.[72] Where a detained patient absents her or himself without leave, and a report under s 21B is furnished by the RC to the managers extending or renewing detention or a CTO, the patient may apply once within the period for which the detention or CTO is extended or renewed.[73]

9.40 If a patient applies for a tribunal whilst detained under s 3, but before the hearing takes place is made subject to a CTO, the tribunal hears the application as if it were for discharge from the CTO. In *AA v Chester and Wirral Foundation NHS Trust* Judge Rowland said this:[74]

> 'In my judgment, there are no reasons for giving section 72(1) of the 1983 Act anything other than a literal construction. A tribunal has the power – or, if the conditions of section 72(1)(c) are satisfied, a duty – to direct that a person subject to a community treatment order be discharged notwithstanding that that person made the application to the tribunal while liable to be detained under section 2 or 3. Therefore, an application to the First-tier Tribunal made by or on behalf of a person detained under section 2 or 3 of the 1983 Act does not lapse if a community treatment order is made in respect of that person before the application is determined.'

Judge Rowland went on to say that:[75]

> '[P]arties need to co-operate sensibly with each other and the First-tier Tribunal if a patient is made the subject of a community treatment order while an application to the tribunal is pending. In particular, it will clearly be incumbent on any representative of the applicant to inform the tribunal as soon as possible whether or not the application is being withdrawn and it is also clearly incumbent on all parties to inform the tribunal whether or not a postponement of any hearing that has already been fixed will be required in the light of the change of circumstances.

---

69   MHA 1983, ss 66(1)(b), (2)(b), (1)(f), (2)(f) and 20(2).
70   MHA 1983, ss 66(1)(c), (2)(c), (1)(f), (2)(f), and 20(2).
71   MHA 1983, ss 66(1)(e), (2)(e) and 19(2)(d).
72   MHA 1983, ss 66(1)(ca), (1)(cb), (1)(fza), (2)(ca), (2)(cb), and (2)(fza).
73   MHA 1983, ss 66(1)(fa), (1)(faa), (2)(f) and (2)(fza).
74   [2009] UKUT 195 (AAC), para 59.
75   Ibid, para 61.

Rights of Nearest Relatives ('NRs') or patients detained under Part II

9.41 Where the NR has sought to discharge the patient from detention or a CTO and the RC has issued a barring certificate, the NR may apply for a tribunal hearing within 28 days.[76] Where the NR has been displaced by order of the county court on grounds of unreasonable objection to admission for treatment or guardianship or exercising the power of discharge without regard to the welfare of the patient or the public interest, he or she may apply to the tribunal once within every 12-month period during which the order remains in force.[77] A NR displaced on grounds of unsuitability, or being too ill to act as NR, will not have the right to apply to the tribunal.

Automatic references

9.42 Section 37 of the MHA 2007 amends s 68 to introduce a requirement on the hospital managers to refer to the tribunal the case of any patient who has not applied for a hearing within six months from 'the applicable day', which is the day on which the patient was first detained, whether that was under s 2 for assessment, s 3 for treatment, or following a transfer from guardianship.[78] The requirement to make referrals also applies to community patients.[79] The duty to refer also arose under the MHA 1983 where the authority to detain was renewed and three years had elapsed since the patient's case was last considered by a tribunal. The amended s 68 breaks the link between renewal and referral. Now there is a duty to refer if a tribunal has not considered a detained or community patient's case in three years (or one year if the patient is under 18). The six-month, three-year and one-year periods can be reduced by order made under s 68A by the Secretary of State, in relation to hospitals in England, or the Welsh Ministers, in relation to hospitals in Wales. If there is an undetermined reference to the tribunal and the patient has changed status from s 3 to a CTO, the validity of the reference is not affected by the change of status. In *KF v Birmingham and Solihull Mental Health NHS Foundation Trust,* the Upper Tribunal held that:[80]

> '[A]ny movement from section 2 to section 3 or to community patient status does not affect the continuing validity of an extant and undetermined application or reference to the First-tier Tribunal. The application or reference still falls to be determined by the tribunal in accordance with the patient's status at the time of the actual hearing and subject to the relevant criteria under section 72(1)(a)–(c).'

9.43 There is also a duty on the managers to refer the case of a community patient whose CTO is revoked to the tribunal as soon as possible after the order

---

76 MHA 1983, ss 66(1)(g) and (2)(d).
77 MHA 1983, ss 66(1)(h) and (2)(g).
78 MHA 1983, s 68(5), as inserted by MHA 2007, s 37(3).
79 Ibid., s 68(1)(c).
80 [2010] UKUT 185 (AAC).

is revoked.'[81] In 2010 the Deputy Chamber President, Mark Hinchliffe, issued guidance on s 68(7) references to deal with the situation where a person's CTO is revoked, but they are then shortly afterwards placed on a new CTO. The Guidance states that:[82]

> 'After careful consideration of the overriding objective, and to enable the tribunal to deal with its cases proportionately, I have decided that following a reference under section 68(7), if the patient is subsequently placed on a new CTO, the 68(7) reference will be treated as having lapsed, and no further action will be taken by the tribunal in relation to it ... Accordingly, if a CTO patient is recalled and the CTO is revoked under section 17F, Hospital Managers must continue to refer cases to the tribunal pursuant to section 68(7) – but *must then notify the tribunal immediately if the patient is placed on a new CTO*. Following such notification the referral will be treated as having lapsed, the parties should be notified, and the file will be closed unless there are other outstanding references or applications.'

A managers' referral to the tribunal should include a statement containing the information about the patient required to be provided for a tribunal hearing, and in the case of a restricted patient, this information must also be sent to the Ministry of Justice. Section 68(8), which entitles a patient to commission an independent report from a doctor in preparation for a tribunal hearing, is extended to entitle an AC or a doctor to prepare such a report and for that purpose to visit and examine a detained or a community patient and to inspect records.

Reference by the Secretary of State for Health

9.44 The case of a patient who is liable to be detained, subject to guardianship or is a community patient under Part II or a non-restricted patient subject to a hospital or guardianship order may be referred by the Secretary of State for Health, or in Wales the Welsh Ministers under s 67. The Secretary of State for Health has the power under s 67 to refer the case of a Part II patient or an unrestricted Part 3 patient at any time. The Department of Health Code states that: 'Anyone may request such a referral and the Secretary of State will consider each such request on its merits.'[83] Any letter requesting a reference by the Secretary of State or Welsh Ministers should state the reasons for the request, the length of time since the patient's case was last considered by a tribunal, the length of time before a fresh application or referral can be made, and whether any decision sought falls within the tribunal's jurisdiction. In *MH v Secretary of State for the Department of Health and others*[84] MH was severely mentally disabled by Down's Syndrome. She lacked mental capacity to consent to admission. She was admitted under s 2 for assessment when her mother became ill and she became increasingly disturbed. The plan was to assess MH's needs in hospital and then find a suitable residential placement where she could be received into guardianship under s 7 of the 1983 Act. MH's mother was her

---

[81]   Ibid, s 68(7).
[82]   http://www.mhrt.org.uk/Documents/News/68_7_Guidance_CTO_22July10.pdf.
[83]   Department of Health *Code of Practice: Mental Health Act 1983* (2008), para 30.39
[84]   [2005] UKHL 60.

nearest relative. She objected to guardianship. Objection by a nearest relative cannot block detention under s 2, but it can veto detention under s 3 or guardianship. Steps were taken to displace MH's mother as nearest relative by application to the county court on the grounds of unreasonable objection.

9.45 By virtue of s 29(4), if such an application is made during the currency of detention under s 2, the 28 day period authorised by that section is extended until the county court deals with the case. In MH's case the effect of this was to extend her detention under s 2 from 28 days to over two years, and since she had not applied for a MHRT within the first 14 days of her s 2, MH had no right, herself or through a proxy, to seek review of the lawfulness of her detention as required by Art 5(4). Baroness Hale delivered the only speech for a unanimous House of Lords, holding that there was no necessary incompatibility between ss 2 and 29(4) of the 1983 Act and Art 5(4) as long as either the county court proceedings were determined swiftly or the Secretary of State referred the case to the tribunal under s 67.

9.46 The Code of Practice takes the consequences of the House of Lords decision in MH and advises the hospital managers 'always' to consider requesting referral by the Secretary of State where detention is extended pending a displacement decision and the patient is unable for any reason to make a request. The Code advises that managers should normally seek a reference where:

- a patient's detention under s 2 has been extended under s 29 of the Act pending the outcome of an application to the county court for the displacement of their nearest relative;

- the patient lacks the capacity to request a reference; and

- either the patient's case has never been considered by the Tribunal, or a significant period has passed since it was last considered.[85]

The Code also advises hospital managers to 'consider asking the Secretary of State to make a reference in respect of any patients whose rights under Article 5(4) of the European Convention on Human Rights might otherwise be at risk of being violated because they are unable (for whatever reason) to have their cases considered by the Tribunal speedily following their initial detention or at reasonable intervals afterwards.[86] Anyone making a request should append the relevant tribunal application form.[87]

---

[85] Department of Health *Code of Practice: Mental Health Act 1983* (2008), para 30.41.
[86] Ibid, para 30.40.
[87] http://www.mhrt.org.uk/FormsGuidance/forms.htm.

Part III patients

9.47 Hospital order patients and their NRs may apply to the tribunal within the second six-month period, and thereafter once in every 12-month period.[88] Guardianship order patients and their NRs may apply once within the first six months of the guardianship order, and once in every period for which it is renewed.[89] Restriction order, restriction direction and hospital direction patients may apply once within the second six-month period following the restriction order, and thereafter once in every 12-month period.[90] Transfer direction patients detained under ss 47, 48 or 47 and 49, may apply to the tribunal within six months of the making of the direction, and thereafter at the same intervals as restriction order patients.[91] Their nearest relative may only apply if they are subject to a transfer direction without restrictions. Patients who have been conditionally discharged are entitled to apply for absolute discharge once in the period between 12 months and two years following conditional discharge, and thereafter once in every two-year period.[92] The date on which a patient is considered conditionally discharged is the date of actual release from detention in hospital.[93]

References by the Secretary of State for Justice

9.48 The Secretary of State for Justice may at any time refer the case of a restricted patient to a tribunal and has a duty to do so if the patient's case has not been considered by a tribunal, whether on his own application or otherwise, within the last three years. The Secretary of State must refer the case of a recalled conditionally discharged patient to a tribunal within one month of recall. Following the friendly settlement in *Roux v United Kingdom*[94] the UK Government agreed that a new r 29(cc) should be introduced to the MHRT Rules for cases of recall of conditionally discharged restricted patients, whereby the tribunal would be required to fix a date between five and eight weeks from the date of reference. *R (on the application of B) v Mental Health Review Tribunal*[95] concerned delay of eight months in the hearing of a recalled restricted patient. Scott Baker J held that there had been a breach of Art 5(4), and that the underlying problem was a lack of case management on the tribunal's part. At each stage the tribunal ought to have had in mind the delay which had accrued and given directions against that background. The longer the delay, the more aggressive the directions would have to be in order to ensure an early disposal of the case. There would come a time where the convenience

---

[88] MHA 1983, ss 66(1)(f), (2)(f), 40(4), Sch 1, Pt 1, paras 2, 6 and 9, and MHA 1983, s 69.
[89] MHA 1983, ss 69(1)(b) and 66(1)(f), (2)(f), 40(4), Sch 1, Pt 1, paras 2, 6 and 9 and MHA 1983, s 69.
[90] MHA 1983, s 70.
[91] MHA 1983, s 69(2)(b).
[92] MHA 1983, s 75(2).
[93] *R v Cannons Park Mental Health Review Tribunal, ex parte Martins* (1995) 26 BMLR 134, QBD.
[94] *(Application 25601/94)* Decision of 4 September 1996, ECtHR.
[95] [2002] EWHC 1553 (Admin).

of expert witnesses had to cede to the need for the tribunal to conclude a substantive hearing. No adequate explanation had been given for the delays.

9.49 It should be noted that the practice which has been widely employed of bringing restricted patients back to hospital under ss 2 or 3 of the Act has been accepted as an appropriate alternative to recall in certain circumstances. In *R v North West London Mental Health NHS Trust, ex p S*,[96] the Court of Appeal held that the power to admit under s 3 was not excluded by the provisions of Part 3, and the rights of a patient detained under that power exist, including those of access to the tribunal under s 66, whether or not he happened also to be a conditionally discharged restricted patient. If he were discharged by the tribunal, it would be a discharge in relation to his liability to detention under s 3 which would in no way affect the Minister of Justice's power to recall him as a restricted patient. The independent operability of Parts 2 and 3 has important consequences for patients remanded by a criminal court for reports under s 35 of the MHA 1983. Section 56 of the Act provides that people remanded under s 35 are not subject to the provisions of Part 4 which authorise treatment without consent. In order to circumvent this, some psychiatrists have arranged for the admission of the patient under s 3 of the Act which does authorise treatment without consent under Part 4.[97] In *Dlodlo v Mental Health Review Tribunal for South Thames Region*[98] the patient had been conditionally discharged and re-admitted to hospital under s 3 of the MHA 1983. The Home Secretary recalled him to the hospital where he was already detained under s 3. The Court of Appeal held that the wider power of the Secretary of State may be exercised even if the person is already present and under detention at the hospital to which he is being recalled.

Legal aid

9.50 The rights of patients to put forward their cases for discharge in tribunalproceedings were enhanced by the introduction in 1983 of new tribunal rules, and by the extension of legal aid in the form of assistance by way of controlled representation (formerly called ABWOR) to MHRT proceedings. The means test in respect of controlled legal representation for tribunals has been abolished.[99]

POWERS AND DUTIES IN RELATION TO DISCHARGE OF UNRESTRICTED PATIENTS

9.51 In respect of non-restricted patients, the tribunal has a general discretion to discharge a patient from liability to detention or guardianship in any case.[100]

---

96   [1997] 4 All ER 871, (1997) 39 BMLR 105, CA.
97   See also *R (on the application of Wirral Health Authority) v Finnegan* [2001] All ER (D) 52 (Mar); confirmed by the Court of Appeal at [2001] EWCA Civ 1901.
98   (1996) 36 BMLR 145, CA.
99   Legal Advice and Assistance (Amendment) Regulations 1994, SI 1994/805.
100 MHA 1983, s 72(1).

Section 72(2) which specified factors which must be considered by the MHRT in exercising the discretion, including the likelihood of medical treatment alleviating or preventing deterioration of the patient's condition, was repealed by s 4(8) of the MHA 2007. Nevertheless the discretion remains, and the tribunal must give reasons for exercising it. Where there has been risk to self or to others, the tribunal will still have to consider and spell out what treatment is considered necessary and satisfy itself that this would be available without the need for the patient to remain liable to be detained.[101] The circumstances in which a tribunal comes under a duty to discharge an unrestricted patient are set out in s 72(1). Paragraph 23(4) of Sch 3 to the MHA 2007 introduces a new subs (3A) which provides that nothing in s 72(1) requires a tribunal to direct the discharge of a patient just because they think it might be appropriate for the patient to be discharged (subject to the possibility of recall) under a CTO. If they think that, the tribunal may recommend that the RC consider a CTO, and may (but need not) further consider the patient's case if the responsible clinician does not make an order.

Duty to discharge s 2 patients

9.52 The tribunal must discharge a patient admitted under s 2 if they are not satisfied *either*:

(a)   that he is then suffering from mental disorder or from mental disorder of a nature or degree which warrants detention in hospital for assessment; or

(b)   that his detention is justified in the interests of his health or safety or the protection of others.[102]

The criteria for discharge correspond with the criteria for admission. The tribunal *must* discharge a patient if they are not satisfied that he is then suffering from mental disorder of a nature or degree warranting detention for assessment. In criterion (2), 'interests of his own health or safety' is an alternative to 'the protection of other persons'. The tribunal may continue to detain the patient if only one of the grounds – own health *or* safety *or* the protection of others – is fulfilled.

Patients detained under ss 3 or 37

9.53 The tribunal has a duty to discharge a patient detained under ss 3 or 37 if it is *not* satisfied:

(i)   that he is then suffering from mental disorder or from mental disorder of a nature or degree which makes it appropriate for him to be liable to be detained in a hospital for medical treatment; or

---

[101]   *R (on the application of East London and the City Mental Health NHS Trust) v Mental Health Review Tribunal* [2005] EWHC 2329 (Admin), per Collins J at [19]–[20].

[102]   MHA 1983, s 72(1)(a).

(ii)   that it is necessary for the health of safety of the patient or for the protection of other persons that he should receive such treatment; or

(iia) that appropriate medical treatment is available for him; or

(iii) in the case of an application by the nearest relative following the barring of a discharge order, that the patient, if released, would be likely to act in a manner dangerous to other persons or to himself.[103]

If the tribunal is not satisfied that any one of these grounds applies, they are under a duty to discharge. The terms 'nature or degree' in relation to mental disorder are disjunctive. In other words a person can have a detainable mental disorder which although not currently exhibiting symptoms of a degree justifying detention, nevertheless is of such a serious nature that detention is warranted.[104] The tribunal must discharge if it is not satisfied that the treatment is necessary for the health *or* safety of the patient *or* for the protection of other persons. If it is necessary for one of these reasons, that will be enough to justify continued detention, provided the availability of appropriate treatment test has been met. Cases like *R v Canons Park Mental Health Review Tribunal, ex parte A*,[105] *Reid v Secretary of State for Scotland*,[106] and *Reid v United Kingdom*[107] show a trend towards requiring tribunals to apply discharge criteria which mirror the admission criteria. Note here that the mental disorder must be of a nature or degree which makes it appropriate for the patient to be *liable to be detained* in hospital, not of a nature or degree making detention appropriate. The discharge criteria do not mirror the admission criteria in this respect.

Patients subject to community treatment orders

9.54   The tribunal must direct the discharge of a community patient if they are not satisfied:

(a)   that he is then suffering from a mental disorder or mental disorder of a nature or degree which makes it appropriate for him to receive medical treatment; or

(b)   that it is necessary for his health or safety or for the protection of other persons that he should receive such treatment; or

(c)   that it is necessary that the responsible clinician should be able to exercise the power under s 17E(1) to recall the patient to hospital; or

---

[103]   MHA 1983, s 72(1)(b).
[104]   *R v Mental Health Review Tribunal for the South Thames Region, ex parte Smith* (1998) 47 BMLR 104.
[105]   [1995] QB 60, CA.
[106]   [1999] 2 WLR 28, HL.
[107]   (2003) 37 EHRR 9, ECtHR.

(d)   that appropriate medical treatment is available for him; or

(e)   in the case of an application by the nearest relative following barring of a discharge order, that the patient, if discharged, would be likely to act in a manner dangerous to other persons or to himself.

It is difficult for a community patient to challenge (i), (ii) and (iv). Anecdotal experience reported by individual advocates to the author suggests that a patient is most likely to achieve discharge own his own application by relying on ground (iii), that it is not necessary for the RC to have the power of recall. This argument is more likely to find favour if the patient has been complying with medication in the community for a substantial period without need for recall.

9.55   When determining whether it is necessary that the RC should have the power of recall, the tribunal must:[108]

> 'in particular, consider, having regard to the patient's history of mental disorder and any other relevant factors, what risk there would be of a deterioration of the patient's condition if he were to continue not to be detained in a hospital (as a result, for example, of his refusing or neglecting to receive the medical treatment he requires for his mental disorder).'

A patient is not entitled to seek review of specific conditions before the tribunal. That will only be possible by judicial review. Nor does the tribunal have the power to vary, set aside or discharge conditions unlike a tribunal considering the case of a conditionally discharged restriction order patient.

Guardianship patients

9.56   Tribunals have a general discretion to discharge a guardianship patient in any case, and must so direct if satisfied:

(a)   that the patient is not then suffering from mental disorder; or

(b)   that it is not necessary in the interests of the welfare of the patient, or for the protection of other persons, that the patient should remain under such guardianship.

Unlike patients detained in hospital there is no specification as to the nature or degree of the disorder. In criterion (b), 'the interests of the welfare of the patient' is wider than the corresponding term 'for the health or safety of the patient' which is applicable to detained patients. It should be noted that the burden of proof in relation to guardianship remains as before on the patient. There will be an issue of compatibility with Art 5(4) if the new possibilities to take and convey a person to a place of required residence and to return them there are used to amount in effect to a deprivation of liberty. In relation to

---

[108]   MHA 1983, s 72(1A), as inserted by MHA 2007, Sch 3, para 21(3).

people under guardianship who are not subject to sufficient control to be deprived of their liberty, there are equally compelling arguments for removing the reverse burden of proof. In *R (on the application of SC) v Mental Health Review Tribunal* Munby J said that when concerned with the exercise by State authorities of compulsory powers in relation to persons suffering from mental disorder, increased vigilance is called for in reviewing whether the Convention has been complied with.[109] The judge accepted that tribunal decisions in relation to conditionally discharged restricted patient could engage Art 8 and Art 6 as the patient could be required to reside at a specified place, was required to comply with the directions of the RC and could be recalled to hospital. If civil rights and obligations under Art 8 are engaged, any interference with private life upheld by the tribunal must be in accordance with law, which must be foreseeable in its effects, and the tribunal is acting as an independent and impartial tribunal for the purposes of Art 6. In such a situation where the State is interfering with private life, it is submitted that it should be for the State to bear the burden of justifying the interference.

Nearest Relative applications

9.57 Where the nearest relative of a patient applies for discharge, the tribunal must discharge if it is satisfied that the patient would not, if discharged, be likely to act in a manner dangerous to self or to others. This is based on the principle that the family is permitted to take responsibility for the health needs of their loved one, but they are not entitled to take over the role of protecting society and the patient from dangerous conduct: this is the function of the State. *In R v Mental Health Review Tribunal for North Thames Region, ex p Pierce* the patient lost her application for discharge since detention for treatment was necessary for her health, but her mother was successful in obtaining discharge on the grounds that the patient was not likely to act dangerously to self or to others.[110]

Discharge on a future date

9.58 Section 72(3) empowers the tribunal to direct the discharge of a patient on a future date specified in the direction. The power is not available for restricted patients.[111] In *R v Mental Health Review Tribunal for North Thames Region, ex parte Pierce* Harrison J held that that s 72 operates in the following way:[112]

> 'The tribunal deals first with the principle whether or not to direct discharge. If (i), the patient is not suffering from mental disorder of a nature or degree making treatment in hospital appropriate, or (ii), detention is not necessary in the interests of his health or safety or for the protection of others, applies, they are obliged to

---

[109]　[2005] EWHC 17 (Admin) at [54].
[110]　*R v Mental Health Review Tribunal for North Thames Region, ex parte Pierce* (1996) 36 BMLR 137.
[111]　*Grant v Mental Health Review Tribunal* (1986) *The Times*, 28 April, QBD.
[112]　(1996) 36 BMLR 137.

direct discharge. If not, they have to decide whether to direct discharge in the exercise of their discretion. Having decided whether or not to direct discharge, the tribunal has to decide whether that discharge should be immediate or should be delayed under s 72(3).'

Reasons for directing discharge on a future date would include setting up community support. Discharge on a future date means that the discharge takes place on that date, whether or not the services are in place. In *R (on the Application of H) v Ashworth Hospital Authority and others* the Court of Appeal held that the tribunal must give careful consideration to the likelihood that the services will be available within that time:[113]

> 'If the tribunal is in doubt as to whether suitable after-care arrangements will be made available, it is difficult to see how they can specify a specific date on which to discharge. In cases of doubt, the safer course is to adjourn. On the facts of the case, the tribunal could not reasonably have assumed that the services would be provided as soon as H was discharged into the community.'

For that reason alone the Court of Appeal held the tribunal's decision to be *Wednesbury* unreasonable.

Recommendations with the power to reconvene

9.59 The tribunal has power to recommend leave of absence, transfer to another hospital or into guardianship and to reconsider the case in the event of the recommendation not being complied with.[114] The First Tier HESC Rules 2008 (rr 42 and 45) state that a decision with recommendations is a decision which disposes of the proceedings and therefore like any other decision disposing of proceedings may be set aside if it is in the interests of justice to do so and one of the following conditions applies:

(a)   a document relating to the proceedings was not sent to, or was not received at an appropriate time by, a party or a party's representative;

(b)   a document relating to the proceedings was not sent to the Tribunal at an appropriate time;

(c)   a party, or a party's representative, was not present at a hearing related to the proceedings; or

(d)   there has been some other procedural irregularity in the proceedings.[115]

9.60   In *Mental Health Review Tribunal v Hempstock* Kay J held that tribunals have all the powers at the time of further consideration that they had originally. They can order immediate discharge, or future discharge. Although the

---

[113]   [2002] EWCA Civ 923.
[114]   MHA 1983, s 72(3)(a) and (b).
[115]   First Tier HESC Rules 2008, SI 2008/2699, rr 42 and 45.

circumstances in which they might exercise the power might be rare, the powers were available for consideration.[116] The tribunal may also recommend that the RC consider a CTO may (but need not) further consider the patient's case if the RC does not make an order.[117] It should be noted that these are the only express powers to make recommendations which the tribunal has been granted under the Act. There is no power to make other recommendations, such as changes of medication, and these can be confusing and dangerous for those who have to implement tribunals' findings. Tribunals should therefore exercise extreme caution, and a self-denying ordinance may be the preferred course.[118]

POWERS WITH REGARD TO RESTRICTION ORDER PATIENTS

General

9.61 In cases involving restricted patients, tribunals have no overriding discretion to discharge. They may only do so when they are satisfied that the relevant statutory criteria are met. One of the circumstances where a restricted patient's case must be referred to a tribunal is following recall to hospital by the Home Secretary. Here the tribunal's function is to consider the justification for detention at the time of the hearing, not whether the recall was justified. But events prior to recall might be relevant to the decision as to whether the patient currently meets the criteria for continued detention. In *R v Merseyside Mental Health Review Tribunal, ex parte Kelly*, the patient had been recalled after a number of criminal allegations were made against him. Proceedings were not taken in relation to these allegations and he denied them. The medical evidence of his RMO assumed that he was guilty and concluded that it was difficult to assess the risk presented by the patient, given his denials. Keene J concluded that it was:[119]

> 'unfair procedurally for the tribunal to prevent cross-examination of the RMO about the factual basis for his conclusions and to prevent evidence being led by the applicant on the same topic. If that factual basis could not be tested in that way, one can only wonder how it was that the applicant would be able to conduct his case in a proper manner with any prospect at all of success.'

The only statutory powers available to a tribunal in relation to restricted patients are to direct either absolute discharge or conditional discharge. A tribunal may make non-statutory recommendations in relation to leave of absence or transfer to another hospital, often at a lower level of security, and the Secretary of State for Justice has indicated that these will be considered, but it is for the Secretary of State to decide whether to act upon those

---

[116] (1997) 39 BMLR 123.
[117] MHA 1983, s 78(3A), as inserted by MHA 2007, Sch 3, para 21(4).
[118] Blom-Cooper, Grounds et al *The Case of Jason Mitchell: Report of the Independent Inquiry* (Duckworth, 1996), chap 9.
[119] (1997) 39 BMLR 114.

recommendations. It is unlawful for the tribunal to adjourn solely for the purpose of the exercise of this non-statutory advisory role.[120]

Absolute discharge

9.62   Section 73(1) requires the tribunal to direct the absolute discharge of the patient if they are not satisfied:

(a)   –

   (i)   that he is then suffering from mental disorder or from mental disorder of a nature or degree which makes it appropriate for him to be liable to be detained in a hospital for medical treatment; *or*
   (ii)   that it is necessary for the health of safety of the patient or for the protection of other persons that he should receive such treatment; *or*
   (iia) that appropriate medical treatment is available for him; *and*

(b)   that it is appropriate for the patient to remain liable to be recalled to hospital for further treatment.

9.63   Even if a tribunal is not satisfied that a patient is mentally disordered at the time of the hearing, it must direct conditional discharge unless satisfied that it is not appropriate for the patient to remain liable to recall.[121] In *R (on the application for the Secretary of State for the Home Department) v Mental Health Tribunal* Moses J said that:

'It might very well be in such a case that, whilst a Tribunal would not be satisfied at one particular moment that someone was suffering from a psychopathic disorder, later on symptoms might emerge which would make it highly appropriate and indeed necessary for such a patient to be recalled to hospital'.

9.64   There must be an express finding that it is not appropriate for the patient to remain subject to recall for further treatment. In *R (on the application for the Secretary of State for the Home Department) v Mental Health Tribunal* Pill LJ said:[122]

'The possible consequences for the safety of members of the public and the patient, when an order for absolute discharge is made, are such that the question of liability to be recalled must be dealt with expressly. A failure to deal with the requirement of s 73(1)(b) is a fatal flaw to the tribunal's decision.'

Reasons for preferring absolute discharge to conditional discharge should be given, and such decisions are open to challenge by the Secretary of State by

---

[120]   *R (Secretary of State for the Home Department) v Mental Health Review Tribunal* [2000] MHLR 209.
[121]   *R v Merseyside Mental Health Review Tribunal, ex parte K* [1990] 1 All ER 694, (1989) 4 BMLR 60, CA.
[122]   [2001] EWHC Admin 849.

way of judicial review.[123] The effect of an absolute discharge is that both the hospital order and the restriction order are discharged.[124]

Conditional discharge

9.65 Section 72(2) requires the tribunal to direct conditional discharge where it is satisfied that the patient needs to be subject to recall but is not satisfied that the patient has mental disorder of the requisite nature or degree, that detention is necessary for health safety or the protection of others, or that appropriate treatment is available. In *Secretary of State for the Home Department v Mental Health Review Tribunal for Wales*,[125] it was held that a tribunal must be satisfied that the patient should be released from hospital before directing conditional discharge. In *R (Secretary of State for the Home Department) v Mental Health Review Tribunal*[126] the tribunal had decided to direct a conditional discharge of the patient, PH, subject to suitable accommodation being identified. The Secretary of State sought judicial review arguing that there could be no "discharge" in law without release from detention, and the tribunal should have held that the effect of the conditions was that PH remained detained. The Court of Appeal proceeded on the basis that this proposition of law was correct, but declined to reverse the tribunal's conclusion of that PH would not be deprived of his liberty. Since the PH ruling there have been three first instance decisions on the issue of whether a patient's conditional discharge is unlawful because they are being discharged to conditions amounting to a deprivation of liberty. In *R (on the application of Secretary of State for the Home Department) v Mental Health Review Tribunal*[127] Collins J upheld a challenge by the Home Office to a decision to discharge a patient to a 24-hour staffed hostel which he would only be able to leave under escort. Collins J held that the fact of the patients consent made no difference to the conclusion that he was deprived of his liberty. Since this would amount to a deprivation of liberty rather than a discharge, the tribunal had no jurisdiction to make such an order. In *R (on the application of G) v Mental Health Review Tribunal* it was held that a condition of residence in a rehabilitation flat within the hospital grounds could be a deprivation of liberty. Collins J held that the lack of any changes in regime or accommodation led inexorably to the conclusion that there was a deprivation of liberty.[128] In *IT v Secretary of State for Justice*, Bean J considered the effect of the Court of Appeal's decision, and said:[129]

> 'This is a curious area of human rights jurisprudence, in which the Secretary of State prays Article 5 of the ECHR in aid of an argument that a patient should be detained in hospital. The ratio of the *PH* case, in my view, is that the MHRT acts

---

[123] *R (on the application of the Secretary of State for the Home Department) v Mental Health Review Tribunal* [2005] EWCA Civ 1616.

[124] MHA 1983, s 73(3).

[125] [1986] 1 WLR 1170, [1986] 3 All ER 233.

[126] [2002] EWCA Civ 1868; [2003] MHLR 202.

[127] [2004] EWHC 219 (Admin).

[128] [2004] EWHC 2193 (Admin).

[129] [2008] EWHC 1707 (Admin) at paras 17–18.

ultra vires if it imposes conditions which amount to a transfer from one state of detention to another. Restrictions on liberty of movement do not amount to deprivation of liberty; the distinction between the two is one of fact and degree; and among other matters the duration of the measures in question is relevant...'

On the facts of the case Bean J held that the transfer was not to conditions amounting to 'detention under another name'.

9.66 In *Secretary of State for Justice v RB*[130] the Upper Tribunal considered the effect of this case law, and concluded that, although it should exercise caution, it was not bound by the Court of Appeal decision in *PH*, 'because it did not purport to decide the relevant point. We are not formally bound by the successive decisions of the High Court, because we are exercising a jurisdiction of equivalent status for these purposes.' The Tribunal concluded that:[131]

'In conclusion on this point, we do not think that we are bound by the Court of Appeal decision in *PH* or the High Court cases which followed it, to hold (contrary to our clear view as to the effect of section 73) that the validity of the conditions proposed by the First-tier Tribunal depended solely on whether or not they amounted to detention. A tribunal's finding that a care home, not being a hospital, is an appropriate place for a patient's accommodation, subject to conditions, is enough to give them jurisdiction (and indeed require them) to direct conditional discharge.

On the other hand, a qualified PH principle holds good. A tribunal cannot conditionally discharge a person with conditions that amount to detention in a hospital for treatment. That is not because the detention would be an assault on the patient's human rights but because a finding that such conditions are necessary would be inconsistent with the premise upon which any conditional discharge under s 73 must be based which is that the tribunal is not satisfied as to the matters mentioned in s 72(b)(i), (ii) or (iia).'

9.67 The Upper Tribunal concluded that the patient could lawfully be discharged to a care home, but not a hospital under the conditions that:

'[1] he resides at a care home
[2] he abides by the rules of that institution
[3] he does not leave the grounds of [the care home] except when supervised
[4] he accepts his prescribed medication
[5] he engages with social supervision
[6] he engages with medical supervision.'

These conditions are clearly capable of reaching a degree and intensity to amount to a deprivation of liberty, but in comparison with remaining in hospital they would represent clear progress for the patient to a less restrictive setting.

---

[130] [2010] UKUT 454 (AAC), para 47.
[131] Ibid., paras 54 and 55.

Conditions

9.68 The patient must abide by any conditions laid down by the tribunal or subsequently imposed by the Secretary of State for Justice. A patient who is conditionally discharged may be recalled to hospital by the Secretary of State. The Secretary of State may also vary any condition which either he or the tribunal has imposed.[132] It should be noted that the tribunal is not obliged to lay down specific conditions when it makes its order for conditional discharge. However, in practice it is unlikely that a patient will be conditionally discharged without conditions being imposed either by the tribunal or by the Secretary of State. The rationale of the power of recall rests on the opportunity to detect any deterioration in the patient's condition and to intervene before any further offence is committed.

Power to defer conditional discharge

9.69 The power to defer a conditional discharge differs significantly from the power to delay a discharge in the case of a non-restricted patient (see **9.58** above). Where a tribunal delays the discharge of an unrestricted patient, it makes an order for discharge which is to take effect at a specified date in the future; discharge must be effected on or before that date, irrespective of whether arrangements for the patient's care have been completed. On the other hand, where a tribunal considering the case of a patient subject to a restriction order defers a direction for his conditional discharge, it postpones the coming into effect of the discharge direction until arrangements are made to its satisfaction. In *Secretary of State for the Home Department v Mental Health Review Tribunal for the Mersey Regional Health Authority* it was held that the tribunal cannot defer a conditional discharge until arrangements are made for admission to another hospital.[133]

9.70 The difficulty with the power of deferred conditional discharge is that it can result in an impasse where the tribunal suggests conditions which for one reason or another are not met by the relevant authorities. The classic Convention case on this is *Johnson v United Kingdom*.[134] Johnson was found by three tribunals (1989, 1990 and 1991) not to be suffering from mental disorder, but his conditional discharge was deferred until a suitable hostel could be found. However, no hostel was found, and he was finally released following a tribunal hearing in 1993. The European Court held that there had been a breach of Art 5(1). The court rejected the argument that a finding by an expert authority that a person is no longer suffering from the form of mental illness which led to his confinement must inevitably lead to his immediate and unconditional release into the community. This would be an unfortunate curtailment of the expert authority's discretion to assess, part of the 'margin of appreciation' left to the national authorities. Nevertheless, discharge must not

---

[132]   MHA 1983, s 73(4), (5).
[133]   [1986] 1 WLR 1170, [1986] 3 All ER 233.
[134]   (1997) 27 EHRR 296.

be unreasonably delayed, and there must be safeguards, including remedies of a judicial nature to ensure that discharge is not unduly delayed.

9.71   The classic British case on this issue is now the decision of the House of Lords in *R (on the application of H) v Secretary of State for the Home Department*[135] which concerned a patient with a diagnosis of paranoid psychosis. He had a tribunal hearing in June which was adjourned until December 1999 at the latest for a full care plan to be drawn up for the patient's conditional discharge. The consultant forensic psychiatrist of the North London Forensic Service, which provided psychiatric services on behalf of the authority, took the view, shared by all his colleagues, that 'a proposed conditional discharge ... direct into the community was clinically inappropriate, and unsafe'. He was willing to admit the appellant to his medium secure unit, but he and his colleagues declined to supervise the appellant as named forensic psychiatrist on conditional discharge. Transfer to the regional secure unit in question was precluded by the Home Secretary withholding consent. The tribunal reconvened on 3 February 2000, and directed the applicant's deferred conditional discharge. The tribunal expressed itself satisfied that the patient was not then suffering from mental disorder of a nature or degree which made it appropriate for the patient to be liable to be detained in a hospital for medical treatment. The tribunal was also satisfied that, if suitable after-care arrangements could be put in place, it would not be necessary in the interests of the patient's health or safety or for the protection of others that he should receive such treatment. They considered that the patient should remain liable to recall. However, because of the risk factors involved, the tribunal deferred the discharge until suitable arrangements could be made for after-care supervision in the community.

9.72   Further unsuccessful attempts were made by the health authority to find a psychiatrist willing to supervise the appellant but without success and his detention continued. The House of Lords held that in order to ensure compatibility with Art 5(4) a decision to defer conditional discharge should be treated as a provisional decision, and the tribunal should monitor progress towards implementing it so as to ensure that the patient is not left 'in limbo for an unreasonable length of time'. The tribunal should meet after an appropriate interval to monitor progress in making these arrangements if they have not been put in place. Once the arrangements have been made, the tribunal can direct a conditional discharge without a further hearing. If problems arise with making arrangements to meet the conditions, the tribunal may:

(a)   defer for a further period;

(b)   amend or vary the proposed conditions;

(c)   order conditional discharge without specific conditions, thereby making patient subject to recall;

---

[135]   [2003] UKHL 59.

(d)   decide that patient remain detained in hospital for treatment.

9.73   The House of Lords went on to hold that the duty of the health authority, whether under s 117 of the MHA 1983 or in response to the tribunal's order of deferred conditional discharge, was to use its best endeavours to procure compliance with the conditions laid down by the tribunal. This it had done. It was not subject to an absolute obligation to procure compliance and was not at fault in failing to do so. It had no power to require any psychiatrist to act in a way which conflicted with the conscientious professional judgment of that psychiatrist. Thus, the appellant could base no claim on the fact that the tribunal's conditions were not met. This conclusion made it unnecessary to address the question on which the House heard argument, but which was not considered below, whether in a context such as this psychiatrists were or could be a hybrid public authority under s 6 of the Human Rights Act 1998. Determination of that question was best left to a case in which it is necessary to the decision. It is suggested that even if a clinician in such a situation is a public authority, a decision not to act as a responsible clinician would not be held to breach Art 5 if it were taken in a genuine and bona fide exercise of clinical judgment.

Recommendations

9.74   Section 72(3), which gives tribunals power to make recommendations and reconvene if these are not complied with, does not apply to restricted patients.[136] Although the Home Office has indicated that it will be happy to receive recommendations in restriction order cases, the tribunal has no power to reconvene in the event of their not being complied with. Nor may the tribunal adjourn a restricted patient hearing *solely* to gather information relating to making a recommendation, although there is nothing to stop it gathering such information if it adjourns to obtain further information on a matter within its jurisdiction (discharge).[137] Rule 25(2) of the previous 1983 Tribunal Rules was amended to make it clear that it was not intended for MHRTs to be able to reconvene to consider recommendations.[138] As for the duties of health and social services under s 117, in *R (on the application of W) v Doncaster Metropolitan Borough Council*[139] Stanley Burnton J held that the authority's duty was, before actual discharge, to endeavour to put in place the arrangements required by the tribunal as conditions of a conditional discharge, or which the tribunal required to be satisfied before a deferred discharge took effect, or which the tribunal provisionally decided should be put in place.

9.75   In *R (on the application of H) v Mental Health Review Tribunal*[140] Stanley Burnton J held that the power to make recommendations is expressly

---

[136]   *Grant v Mental Health Review Tribunal* (1986) *The Times*, 28 April, QBD.
[137]   *R (on the application of the Secretary of State for the Home Department) v Mental Health Review Tribunal* (unreported) 2000 (CO/1928/2000).
[138]   MHRT (Amendment) Rules 1998, SI 1998/1189, r 2(3).
[139]   [2003] EWHC 192 (Admin).
[140]   [2002] EWHC 1522 (Admin).

qualified. There is no power to make recommendations with a view to anything else than facilitating future discharge. Where discharge is not in contemplation, the Convention does not require the MHRT to give reasons for not making recommendations. The applicant was detained under s 3 in an institution remote from his mother's home. The tribunal found that the patient continued to require detention and that this could only be provided in conditions of high security. The applicant argued that the tribunal had breached Art 8 of the Convention because it had failed to make a recommendation in relation to the patient that she live at home, and had failed to give reasons for that failure. Stanley Burnton J held that there was no evidence to justify making a recommendation of transfer. In those circumstances the absence of any reasons was wholly explicable.

9.76   In *R v Secretary of State for the Home Department, ex parte Harry*[141] the MHRT recommended transfer from a special hospital to a regional secure unit. The patient's RMO subsequently made a proposal for the patient to be granted a period of trial leave. The Home Office submitted the proposal to the Advisory Board on Restricted Patients (known as the Aarvold Board after Sir Carl Aarvold, chair of the committee which recommended its establishment following the *Graham Young* case in the 1970s). After considering a report from a non-medical member of the board that Harry was still as dangerous as ever, the Home Office did not approve the leave. The applicant sought judicial review of the Home Secretary's decisions:

(a)   to refer the proposal to the board; and

(b)   to act on its recommendations.

The court held that the MHA 1983 entrusted the Home Secretary with the task of deciding whether to consent, and he could not deprive himself of further information if he considered it to be required; the only limitation on his freedom to consult and act on the board's recommendation was his obligation to act in a procedurally fair manner. The patient should be furnished with the report, given the gist of its contents, and invited to make representations on it to the Board. He should also have been furnished with the advice note and invited to make representations to the Secretary of Home Secretary.

Status of recommendations

9.77   The fact that a tribunal has made a recommendation with funding implications does not mean that the NHS commissioning bodies are obliged under the Human Rights Act 1998 to fund it. In *R (on the application of F) v Oxfordshire Mental Healthcare NHS Trust*[142] the tribunal recommended transfer to a RSU, and recommended that the patient go to a unit in Manchester where her parents lived and where she wanted to go, rather than

---

[141]   [1998] 3 All ER 360, QBD.
[142]   [2001] EWHC Admin 535.

the Oxford unit with which the Trust contracted for its secure psychiatric provision, and which was in the area of her index offence, described as horrific. The Manchester placement would necessitate a costly extra-contractual referral. The Trust set up a forum to decide on funding declined to fund the Manchester placement. The applicant sought judicial review arguing that her rights to family life under Art 8 were engaged by the denial of an extra-contractual referral, and this meant that the forum had to attach sufficient weight to the opinion of her current RMO who was in favour of Manchester. Sullivan J held that the forum was not obliged, either as a matter of proportionality or rationality, to accept the RMO's view. Fairness required that the claimant should have the opportunity to tell the forum in writing why it was contended that resources should be allocated to her. If Art 8 was engaged a balancing Act had to be carried out under Art 8(2):

> 'in a world where the funds available for medical treatment are limited and where granting a patient's request will inevitably mean that other patients will be disappointed. They will have to wait longer or be denied pain-killing drugs.'

The judge went on to say that:[143]

> 'Decisions on funding affect lives, not just liberty. That is a good reason not to judicialise them. They are agonisingly difficult decisions, and they will not be made any easier or better by being encumbered with legalistic procedures.'

The courts have traditionally been unwilling to involve themselves in decisions about the allocation of resources in health care generally. This case applies that principle in the mental health context.

PATIENTS SUBJECT TO A RESTRICTION DIRECTION (INCLUDING HOSPITAL DIRECTIONS WITH LIMITATION DIRECTIONS)

Role of the MHT

9.78 Patients transferred from prison to hospital, including those transferred under s 48, have the right to apply to the tribunal. Where a patient has been transferred from prison to a hospital under a restriction direction, or is detained under a hospital direction, the tribunal is not empowered to order his discharge. This is because, technically, the patient is still subject to his sentence and thus any decision regarding his discharge must be taken by the Minister of Justice. The legislation gives the final decision to the Secretary of State for Justice as to whether the patient is discharged or remitted to prison. Under the MHA 1983 the tribunal's role is limited to notifying the Secretary of State whether the patient would be entitled to be absolutely or conditionally

---

[143] [2001] EWHC Admin 535 at [76]–[80].

discharged had he been subject to a restriction order. Thus, the tribunal must consider the same statutory criteria that apply to a patient subject to a restriction order.[144]

Notification of entitlement to absolute discharge

9.79 If the Secretary of State for Justice is notified that the patient would be entitled to be absolutely discharged, he may, within 90 days, consent to the discharge and the tribunal must accordingly discharge the patient. If, at the end of the 90-day period, the Secretary of State has not given his consent, the hospital managers must transfer the patient back to prison or to the other institution from where he came; the patient would then serve the remainder of his sentence or be dealt with as if he had not been transferred to hospital. The logic of this provision is that if the person is entitled to an absolute discharge, there is no case for continuing to detain him in a hospital. The issue becomes whether the person is dangerous and requires further detention in prison to complete his sentence or whether he can be released. Section 74 makes this a matter for the Secretary of State.

Notification of entitlement to conditional discharge

9.80 Where the tribunal notifies the Secretary of State for Justice that the patient would be entitled to be conditionally discharged it may add a recommendation that the patient should remain in hospital if his discharge is not approved. As with absolute discharge, if, within 90 days, the Secretary of State gives his consent, the tribunal must conditionally discharge the patient; it may defer the direction for conditional discharge in the same way as for patients subject to a restriction order.[145] Section 74(3) provides that if the Secretary of State does not give his consent and the tribunal has not recommended that the patient should remain in hospital, then the hospital managers must return him to the prison or other institution from which he came. If the tribunal has recommended that the patient should remain in hospital if not discharged, then he cannot be returned to prison. The logic of this is that for the patient who is entitled to conditional discharge but is not so discharged there is a choice to be made: whether he would benefit from further hospital care as opposed to prison confinement. The tribunal assists the Secretary of State in this choice by making appropriate recommendations.

9.81 This means that the patient who is declared suitable for discharge from mental health detention can have that discharge blocked and be returned to prison unless the Secretary of State consents to the implementation of the tribunal's decision of entitlement to discharge. Hence, a patient could be remitted to prison in such a case, and have to seek review of the continued need for their detention via the Parole Board which has the power to release them. If the tribunal has recommended the patient should remain in hospital if not

---

[144] MHA 1983, s 74(1).
[145] MHA 1983, s 74(1)(b), (2), (6) and (7).

discharged, they remain in hospital and are still entitled to review by the Parole Board by virtue of s 74(5A), introduced following a declaration of incompatibility in *R (on the application of D) v Secretary of State for the Home Department*.[146] Stanley Burnton J held s 74(3) to be incompatible with Art 5 of the ECHR in relation to discretionary lifers where the tribunal recommended that they remain in hospital if not discharged, on the grounds that it deprived them of their right to Art 5(4) review. Section 74(5A) is intended to rectify this incompatibility, by providing that if the Parole Board make a direction or recommendation by virtue of which the patient would become entitled to be released, any restriction or limitation direction ceases to have effect 'at the time when he would become entitled to be so released'.

CONDITIONALLY DISCHARGED PATIENTS

9.82 Section 75 of the MHA 1983 gives the right to conditionally discharged patients to apply to tribunals; such patients did not have a right to a tribunal hearing under the MHA 1959. The tribunal has the power to change the conditions, or to discharge absolutely. The tribunal may vary any condition by which the patient must abide or impose a new condition.[147] Thus, the tribunal may change a condition in accordance with a change in the patient's circumstances or remove a condition if it is no longer necessary. In *R (on the application of SC) v Mental Health Review Tribunal* Munby J agreed that decisions under s 75 could engage Arts 6 and 8. This means that any interference with private life authorised by the MHRT must be in accordance with law, which must be foreseeable in its effects, and that the MHRT is acting as an independent and impartial tribunal for the purposes of Art 6. Whilst Munby J accepted that Arts 6 and 8 were engaged, he dismissed the application on the grounds that, whilst s 75(3) lays down no criteria for the exercise of the discretion it bestows, it was sufficiently foreseeable in it effects. Munby J said that tribunals exercising the s 75(3) power:[148]

> '[W]ill need to consider such matters as the nature, gravity and circumstances of the patient's offence, the nature and gravity of his mental disorder, past, present and future, the risk and likelihood of the patient re-offending, the degree of harm to which the public may be exposed if he re-offends, the risk and likelihood of a recurrence or exacerbation of any mental disorder, and the risk and likelihood of his needing to be recalled in the future for further treatment in hospital. The Tribunal will also need to consider the nature of any conditions previously imposed, whether by the Tribunal or by the Secretary of State, the reasons why they were imposed and the extent to which it is desirable to continue, vary or add to them.'

The tribunal's general statutory role is to review the justification for detaining the patient or for otherwise restricting his liberty. Only in the most exceptional

---

146 [2002] EWHC 2805 (Admin), [2003] MHLR 193. See also *Benjamin v United Kingdom* (2003) 36 EHRR 1, ECtHR. Section 74(5A) was introduced by the Criminal Justice Act 2003, s 295.
147 MHA 1983, s 75(3)(a).
148 [2005] EWHC 17 (Admin) at [57].

circumstances will the tribunal be likely to conclude that its duty is to impose upon the patient conditions more restrictive than those already imposed by the Secretary of State for Justice or by a previous tribunal. The tribunal may direct that the restriction order, restriction direction, or limitation is lifted. The patient will then cease to be liable to be detained under the hospital order or transfer direction and will not be subject to recall to hospital.[149]

9.83 In *RH v South London and Maudsley NHS Foundation Trust*[150] Judge Mark Rowland followed Munby J's approach in *SC* holding that:

> '26. [E]vidence of current mental disorder is not actually required in all cases. Nonetheless, I would accept that the mere existence of current, or possible future, mental disorder is not enough to justify the continuation of a restriction order. The First-tier Tribunal must also have regard to the seriousness of any risk of harm to others.
>
> 27. However, manslaughter may, and murder must, be punished by a sentence of life imprisonment. It therefore cannot be regarded as surprising that a restriction order imposed in a case of manslaughter arising out of a deliberate killing – in this case, two deliberate killings – should remain in force for as long as that person continues to be subject to what the First-tier Tribunal here called "vulnerabilities", even if that has the effect that, in some cases, it will remain in force for life. In this case, the First-tier Tribunal regarded the risk of harm to others to be sufficiently serious to justify the continuation of the restriction order. Reading its decision as a whole against the background of the evidence before it and a proper understanding of the law, there can be no doubt as to why it reached that conclusion or that the decision was one it was entitled to reach. Accordingly, I dismiss this appeal.'

The tribunal's general statutory role is to review the justification for detaining the patient or for otherwise restricting his liberty. Only in the most exceptional circumstances will the tribunal be likely to conclude that its duty is to impose upon the patient conditions more restrictive than those already imposed by the Minister of Justice or by a previous tribunal. The tribunal may direct that the restriction order, restriction direction, or limitation is lifted. The patient will then cease to be liable to be detained under the hospital order or transfer direction and will not be subject to recall to hospital.[151]

PROCEDURES

9.84 Following the Mental Health Act 2007 and the Tribunals, Courts and Enforcement Act 2007, mental health tribunal procedure in England and Wales is governed by broadly similar but separate procedural regimes. Proceedings in the Mental Health Chamber of the First Tier Health Education and Social

---

[149] The power to lift a limitation direction or restriction direction is added to s 75(3) by s 41 of the MHA 2007.

[150] [2010] UKUT 32 (AAC).

[151] The power to lift a limitation direction or restriction direction is added to s 75(3) by s 41 of the MHA 2007.

Care Tribunal in England are regulated by the First-Tier Tribunal (Health Education and Social Care Chamber) Rules 2008[152] (hereafter the 'FTTHESC Rules 2008') and by Practice Directions issued by the Chamber President. MHRT proceedings in Wales are regulated by the Mental Health Review Tribunal for Wales Rules 2008 (hereafter 'the MHRT Wales Rules').[153] The content of the statements required to be provided for the tribunal prior to the hearing by the responsible authority and the Secretary of State for the tribunal is regulated in England by the 2008 Practice Direction[154] whilst in Wales it is in the Schedule to the MHRT Wales Regulations 2008.[155]

The Overriding Objective

9.85   Both the English First Tier HESC Tribunal and the MHRT Wales are required to seek to give effect to the overriding objective in exercising any power or interpreting any rule (or Practice Direction in England). The First Tier HESC Tribunal Rules states that the overriding objective is to deal with cases 'fairly and justly', the MHRT Wales Rules say fairly, justly, efficiently and expeditiously.'[156] Each set of rules provides an non-exclusive list of what dealing with a case in accordance with the overriding objective which includes:

(a)   avoiding unnecessary formality and seeking flexibility in the proceedings;

(b)   ensuring, so far as practicable, that the parties are able to participate fully in the proceedings;

(c)   using any special expertise of the Tribunal effectively; and

(d)   avoiding delay, so far as compatible with proper consideration of the issues.

Note that the MHRT Wales Rules leave out a fifth element which the First Tier HESC Rules place at the top of the list, namely dealing with the case in ways which are proportionate to the importance of the case, the complexity of the issues, the anticipated costs and the resources of the parties. Since the list of what is entailed by the overriding objective is inclusive rather than exclusive, MHRTs in Wales may consider that this fifth element is part and parcel of dealing with cases fairly, justly and expeditiously.[157] The Welsh rules do not include an equivalent to r 2(4) of the HESC Rules which puts an obligation on the parties (a) to help the tribunal to further the overriding objective; and (b)

---

[152]   SI 2008/2699.
[153]   SI 2008/2705, r 14.
[154]   Tribunals Judiciary, *Practice Direction Health Education and Social Care Chamber Mental Health Cases: Content of Statements by the Responsible Authority and the Secretary of State.* <www.mhrt.org.uk/Documents/3nov08/ TribunalJudiciaryPracticeDirectionHealthEducationandSocialCareChamberMentalHealthCases.pdf>.
[155]   Schedule to the Mental Health Review Tribunal for Wales Rules 2008, SI 2008/2705.
[156]   FTTHESC Rules 2008, r 2(1), MHRT Wales Rules 2008, r 3(1).
[157]   FTTHESC Rules 2008, r 2(1), MHRT Wales Rules 2008, r 3(1).

co-operate with the tribunal generally. The reason for leaving this out was that it was felt that placing an obligation on a detained patient to co-operate with the tribunal was undesirable.

9.86   In *Dorset Healthcare NHS Foundation Trust v MH*[158] the Upper Tribunal held that the overriding objective provisions in the English Rules:[159]

> '[I]mpose an express obligation upon the parties to assist in the furtherance of the objective of dealing with cases fairly and justly, which includes the avoidance of unnecessary applications and unnecessary delay. That requires parties to cooperate and liaise with each other concerning procedural matters, with a view to agreeing a procedural course promptly where they are able to do so, before making any application to the tribunal.'

The effect of this ruling in Wales is uncertain since the Welsh Rules impose no obligation on the parties, whether or not they are represented.

Applications and notice of the Application

9.87   An application must be made to the tribunal in writing, signed by the applicant or any person authorised by him to do so on his behalf. And sent to the tribunal within the time specified for making applications. Where possible it should contain specified information, including the patient's name and address and the address of the hospital, but if any of this information is not included, it must, so far as is practicable, be provided by the responsible authority or the Minister of Justice if requested by the MHT.[160] Notice must be given to the patient (if not the applicant), to the responsible authority, and to the Home Secretary in the case of a restricted patient. Failure to give notice to the Home Secretary in a restricted case invalidates the proceedings. In *R (on the application of the Secretary of State for the Home Department) v Mental Health Review Tribunal* Owen J quashed the decision of a MHRT where the Home Office had not had notice because the effect of failure to notify is to undermine the statutory scheme and remove the essential mechanism for safeguarding the public interest.[161]

The responsible authority's statement

9.88   The 'responsible authority' is (a) the hospital managers if the patient is detained under the Act in a NHS or independent hospital, (b) the managers of the responsible hospital if the patient is a community patient, or (c) the responsible local social services authority if the patient is subject to guardianship. The first impression which the members of the tribunal panel

---

158   [2009] UKUT 4 (AAC). <www.osscsc.gov.uk/Aspx/view.aspx?id=2607>.
159   Ibid, para 11.
160   First-Tier Tribunal (Health Education and Social Care Chamber) Rules 2008 SI 2008/2699, r 32; Mental Health Review Tribunal for Wales Rules 2008, SI 2008/2705, r 14.
161   [2004] EWHC 650 (Admin), applying the House of Lords ruling in *Secretary of State for the Home Department v Oxford Regional Mental Health Review Tribunal* [1987] 3 All ER 8, HL.

will have of the patient will come from the responsible authority's report, which provides the tribunal with a case history, including up to date clinical and social circumstances reports. In England the provision of information by the responsible authority and the Secretary of State for Justice is governed by First-tier Tribunal HESC Rules 2008 and a Practice Direction issued by the Tribunal.[162] In Wales the matter is governed by the MHRT Wales Rules 2008 and the Schedule to the Regulations.[163] These require that the responsible authority's statement, including biographical information, an up-to-date clinical report, and, insofar as is reasonably practicable to provide it, an up-to-date social circumstances report, must be sent within three weeks, or two weeks if the patient is a recalled conditionally discharged patient. If the hearing concerns a section 2 patient, the hearing must be within seven days of receipt of the application and duty of the responsible authority is to provide a copy of the application and the medical recommendations supporting detention and such of the above information as can reasonably be provided in the time available.[164]

9.89 Under the Practice Direction for a patient detained otherwise than under s 2, the statement to the Tribunal must contain the information, documents and reports specified at (a)–(d) below:

(a) The biographical information about the patient set out in para 11 of the Practice Direction.[165]

(b) An up to date clinical report which, unless it is not reasonably practicable must be written or countersigned by the patient's responsible clinician, and must describe the patient's relevant medical history, to include:

   (i) full details of the patient's mental state, behaviour and treatment for mental disorder;
   (ii) in so far as it is within the knowledge of the person writing the report a statement as to whether the patient has ever neglected or harmed himself, or has ever harmed other persons or threatened them with harm, at a time when he was mentally disordered, together with details of any neglect, harm or threats of harm;
   (iii) an assessment of the extent to which the patient or other persons would be likely to be at risk if the patient is discharged by the Tribunal, and how any such risks could best be managed;
   (iv) an assessment of the patient's strengths and any other positive factors that the Tribunal should be aware of in coming to a view on whether he should be discharged; and

---

[162] First-tier Tribunal (Health Education and Social Care Chamber) Rules 2008 SI 2008/699, r 32(5) and Practice Direction Health Education and Social Care Chamber Mental Health Cases; Contents of Statements from the Responsible Authority and the Secretary of State. <www.tribunals.gov.uk/Tribunals/Documents/Rules/Mentalhealthcaseshesc.pdf>.
[163] Mental Health Review Tribunal for Wales Rules 2008, SI 2008/2705, r 15 and Schedule.
[164] FTTHESC Rules 2008 r 32(5), MHRT Wales Rules 2008, r 15(3).
[165] HESC Mental Health Cases Practice Direction 2008, paras 5, 8 and 11.

(v)   if appropriate, the reasons why the patient might be treated in the community without continued detention in hospital, but should remain subject to recall on supervised community treatment.[166]

(c)   An up to date social circumstances report, which must include

(i)   the patient's home and family circumstances;

(ii)   in so far as it is practicable, and except in restricted cases, a summary of the views of the patient's nearest relative, unless (having consulted the patient) the person compiling the report thinks it would be inappropriate to consult the nearest relative;

(iii)   in so far as it is practicable, the views of any person who plays a substantial part in the care of the patient but is not professionally concerned with it;

(iv)   the views of the patient, including his concerns, hopes and beliefs in relation to the Tribunal proceedings and their outcome;

(v)   the opportunities for employment and the housing facilities available to the patient;

(vi)   what (if any) community support is or will be made available to the patient and its effectiveness, if the patient is discharged from hospital;

(vii) the patient's financial circumstances (including his entitlement to benefits);

(viii) an assessment of the patient's strengths and any other positive factors that the Tribunal should be aware of in coming to a view on whether he should be discharged; and

(ix)   an assessment of the extent to which the patient or other persons would be likely to be at risk if the patient is discharged by the Tribunal, and how any such risks could best be managed.[167]

(d)   If the patient is an in-patient, a nursing report which must include in relation to the patient's current in-patient episode, full details of the following:

(i)   the patient's understanding of and willingness to accept the current treatment for mental disorder provided or offered;

(ii)   the level of observation to which the patient is subject;

(iii)   any occasions on which the patient has been secluded or restrained, including the reasons why seclusion or restraint was considered to be necessary;

(iv)   any occasions on which the patient has been absent without leave whilst liable to be detained, or occasions when he has failed to return when required, after being granted leave of absence; and

(v)   any incidents where the patient has harmed himself or others, or has threatened other persons with violence.

---

[166]   Ibid, paras 5, 8 and 13–15.
[167]   HESC Mental Health Cases Practice Direction 2008, paras 5, 8 and 16–17.

A copy of the patient's current nursing plan must be appended to the report.[168]

9.90 If the tribunal so directs the responsible authority's statement must include:

(a) the application, order or direction that constitutes the original authority for the patient's detention or guardianship under the Mental Health Act 1983, together with all supporting recommendations, reports and records made in relation to it under the Mental Health (Hospital, Guardianship and Treatment) Regulations 2008;

(b) a copy of every Tribunal decision, and the reasons given, since the application, order or direction being reviewed was made or accepted; and

(c) where the patient is liable to be detained for treatment under section 3 of the Mental Health Act 1983, a copy of any application for admission for assessment that was in force immediately prior to the making of the section 3 application.[169]

9.91 In Wales the responsible authority's statement must contain 'an up-to-date clinical report including the relevant clinical history and a full report on the patient's mental condition.[170] Other reports are to be provided as long as it is reasonably practicable to provide them. They include:

(a) An up-to-date social circumstances report prepared for the tribunal including reports on the following:

    (i)   the patient's home and family circumstances, including the views of the patient's nearest relative or the person so acting;

    (ii) the opportunities for employment or occupation and the housing facilities which would be available to the patient if discharged;

    (iii) the availability of community support and relevant medical facilities;

    (iv) the financial circumstances of the patient.

(b) The views of the responsible authority on the suitability of the patient for discharge.

(c) Where the provisions of section 117 of the Act may apply to the patient, a proposed after care plan in respect of the patient.

(d) Any other information or observations on the application which the responsible authority wishes to make.[171]

---

[168] Ibid, paras 5, 8 and 18–19.
[169] Ibid, paras 5, 8 and 12.
[170] MHRT Wales Rules 2008, r 15(5) and Schedule, Pt B, para 1.
[171] Ibid, r 15(5) and Schedule, Pt B, paras 2–5.

Note that no nursing report is required for in-patients in Wales, and the up-to-date social circumstances report need not be provided if it is not reasonably practicable to do so. Given the vital importance of the social circumstances report to the patient's chances of discharge, it is submitted that cases where it is not reasonably practicable to provide one should be extremely rare. Indeed it would be difficult to square non-provision of a social circumstances report with the overriding objective to deal with cases fairly, justly, expeditiously, and efficiently under r 2 of the MHRT Wales Rules 2008. It is also arguable that there is a positive obligation on bodies exercising a review function under Article 5(4) to seek information about the community support available to ensure that detention is a proportionate response to the patient's needs.

9.92   Even in England, where social circumstances reports are obligatory, the Mental Health Act Commission has referred to the 'considerable number of Tribunal postponements appearing to be caused by the unavailability of these reports, or by reports containing insufficient information.'[172] The MHAC recommended following the guidance on content produced by Curran and Golightly who warn that 'where SCRs fail to comply with the new 2008 PD (i.e. providing insufficient information to reach an informed decision) the Tribunal may be compelled to adjourn the case (with all that that involves) and 'direct' the responsible authority to furnish a supplementary SCR.'[173] According to the authors, the most common fault being the 'simply that the writer was obviously unaware of the required content of such reports.' They offer Guidance on the recommended content of a Social Circumstances Report under the 2008 Practice Direction.

9.93   Clearly the obligations to provide information to the tribunal in England are more detailed and extensive than in Wales, but, given the overriding objective it is hard to see circumstances where a social circumstances report is not a mandatory requirement, even if the patient's discharge is not likely to be ordered.

Disclosure of information to the applicant, the patient, the responsible authority and the Secretary of State

9.94   Under the 1959 Act, patients laboured under many disadvantages. Responsible authorities' reports, making the case for continued detention, including a case history, were widely withheld on grounds that disclosure would 'injure the doctor/patient relationship.' They could be disclosed to the patient's representative, but representation was the exception rather than the rule. This meant that inaccuracies in this influential documentary evidence might go unchallenged. In 1978 an Inter-Departmental Committee reported on MHRT procedures, recommending various changes. New rules were introduced to

---

[172]   Mental Health Act Commission *Coercion and Consent Thirteenth Biennial Report 2007–2009*, (2009) paras 2.102–2.103.

[173]   C Curran, M Golightly and J Horne 'Social circumstances reports for Mental Health Review Tribunals under 2008 Practice Direction Section E' *Open Mind* 156 March/April 2009, 24–25.

accompany the 1983 Act, requiring tribunals to give written reasons for their decisions, which must explain why the tribunal reached its decision and must be more than mere rehearsals of the statutory criteria.[174] They also increased patient access to reports, by creating a presumption in favour of disclosure unless the tribunal concludes that it would adversely affect the health or welfare of the patient or of other persons.[175] If a party considers that the tribunal should make a direction prohibiting disclosure of part or all of a document or any information to another party, the party must exclude the document or information from the material it provides to the other party and must provide the tribunal with a copy of the excluded information and reasons for non disclosure so that the tribunal may decide whether it ought to be withheld. The final decision as to whether the patient should see these is for the tribunal. In practice, there has been much more disclosure since the MHA 1983.

9.95 The test of non-disclosure has since been changed again in both the FTTHESC Rules 2008 and the MHRT Wales Rules 2008. The presumption is still in favour of disclosure unless the Tribunal is (a) satisfied that such disclosure would be likely to cause that person or some other person serious harm; and (b) having regard to the interests of justice, that it is proportionate to give such a direction. In England the Tribunal has a discretion to order non-disclosure if the tests are met. In Wales it has a duty.[176] The FTTHESC Rules 2008 make the power to direct non-disclosure discretionary the 'Tribunal may give a direction prohibiting the disclosure of a document or information to a person if (a) the Tribunal is satisfied that such disclosure would be likely to cause that person or some other person serious harm; and (b) the Tribunal is satisfied, having regard to the interests of justice, that it is proportionate to give such a direction.'[177] The MHRT Wales Rules use the same test of serious harm and proportionality, but place a duty on the tribunal to direct non-disclosure if it is satisfied that the tests are met.[178] The document to be withheld must be kept separate so that the tribunal may decide whether to direct non-disclosure, and reasons have to be given by the responsible authority. The tribunal must then consider if disclosure would have adverse effect claimed and, if satisfied that it would, must record in writing its decision not to disclose. The tribunal must conduct proceedings so as to avoid undermining the effect of a direction to withhold information.[179]

9.96 In *Dorset Healthcare NHS Foundation Trust v MH* the Upper Tribunal held that 'the starting point is that full disclosure of all relevant material should generally be given.'[180] Under the Data Protection (Subject Access

---

174   Mental Health Review Tribunal Rules 1983, SI 1983/942, r 23. In *Bone v Mental Health Review Tribunal* [1985] 3 All ER 330, and *R v Mental Health Review Tribunal ex p Clatworthy* [1985] 3 All ER 699 it was held that these must enable the patient to know why the case he had presented had not been accepted.

175   Ibid, r 12.

176   FTTHESC Rules 2008, r 14, MHRT Wales Rules 2008, r 17.

177   FTTHESC Rules 2008, r 14(2).

178   MHRT Wales Rules 2008, r 17(1).

179   FTTHESC Rules 2008, r 14, MHRT Wales Rules 2008, r 17.

180   [2009] UKUT 4 (AAC), para 20. <www.osscsc.gov.uk/Aspx/view.aspx?id=2607>.

Modification) (Health) Order 2000,[181] materials are exempt from disclosure if they would be 'likely to cause serious harm to the physical or mental health or condition of the data subject or any other person.' In *Roberts v Nottinghamshire Healthcare NHS Trust*[182] Cranston J adopted Munby J's definition of likely as a 'degree of probability where there is a very significant and weighty chance of prejudice to the identified public interests; the degree of risk must be such that there 'may very well' be prejudice to those interests, even if the risk falls short of being more probable than not'.[183] Cranston J went on to hold that:

> 'The question is whether there may very well be a risk of harm to health even if the risk falls short of being more probably than not. Harm to health could arise in various ways. In the context of mental health, it could be self harm or harm to others. The issue demands a factual inquiry: taking all matters into account such as the personality of the applicant, his past history, the care regime to which he is subject and so on, might there very well be a risk of harm to health on release of the data?'[184]

9.97 In *RM v St Andrews Healthcare*,[185] the issue was whether the tribunal judge had been right to order non-disclosure of the fact that the applicant had been covertly medicated. Judge Jacobs followed the House of Lords decision in *Secretary of State for the Home Department v AF (No 3)*[186] and held as follows:

> '31. The overriding objective in rule 2 requires that the rules of procedure be applied so that cases are dealt with fairly and justly. This includes ensuring full participation, so far as practicable. Rule 14(2) requires the tribunal to have regard to the interests of justice. Justice and fairness generally require openness. Sometimes, they are not compatible and a compromise is possible. It may, for example, be possible and necessary to conduct proceedings while concealing that the true prognosis is worse than the patient realises. In this case, I have set out the full implications of the tribunal's order. They involve more than a compromise between justice and openness. They involve the sacrifice of the patient's right to challenge his detention effectively.
>
> 32. The judgment of proportionality under rule 14(2) must, expressly, involve regard to the interests of justice. The effect of the order in this case would be a series of further non-disclosure orders. In total, they would exclude the claimant completely from knowing of the real process that was being followed and allow him to participate only in a pretence of a process. They would severely hamper his legal team in participating effectively in that process.'

Judge Jacobs went on to say that non-disclosure orders should not be limited to documents but should specify information and offered the following suggested form of words:

---

[181] SI 2000/413, art 5.
[182] [2008] EWHC 1934 (QB), para [9].
[183] *R (Lord) v Secretary of State for the Home Department* [2003] EWHC 2073 (Admin).
[184] [2008] EWHC 1934 QB para [10].
[185] [2010] UKUT 119 (AAC).
[186] [2009] 3 WLR 74.

'36. The tribunal prohibits disclosure to the patient of:

(a)   information relating to ... ;
(b)   any document containing or referring to that information, in particular-
    (i)   the reports of ... ;
    (ii)   any other report prepared in connection with these proceedings; and
    (iii) this order.'

Paragraph (a) deals with the key issue of the information that must not be disclosed. It needs to be precise, clear and exhaustive. Paragraph (b) deals with the means by which disclosure might be made, directly or indirectly. It is supportive of paragraph (a) and need not be exhaustive.

9.98 Subject to the rules on withholding information where necessary to prevent harm, the rules require the tribunal to disclose in full every document it receives to each other party. 'Party' includes the applicant, the patient if he or she is not the applicant, the responsible authority and the Secretary of State in a restricted patient case. Each has the right to submit written comments on any document released to them.[187]

9.99 If any document is withheld from a party it may be disclosed to their representative. The Tribunal may give a direction that the documents or information be disclosed to that representative if the Tribunal is satisfied that (a) disclosure to the representative would be in the interests of the party; and (b) the representative will not disclose the information either directly or indirectly to any other person without the Tribunal's consent. In Wales the tribunal must also be satisfied that the information will not be used otherwise than in connection with the proceedings. In a case involving a restricted patient, the Secretary of State is entitled to all relevant documents received by the tribunal. Breach of this requirement will invalidate the proceedings.[188]

Parties

9.100 The following are parties to the proceedings: the patient, the responsible authority, the Secretary of State (or in Wales the Welsh Ministers) (if the patient is a restricted patient or in a reference seeking approval for removal of an 'alien' patient from the jurisdiction under s 86 of the Mental Health Act 1983)), and any other person who starts a mental health case by making an application.[189] The HESC Rules refer only to parties, but allow the FTT to give a direction adding a person to the proceedings as a 'respondent'.[190] The rules governing jurisdictions other than mental health in the FTT refer to 'respondents'. It is not clear who might be added as a respondent to the proceedings in a mental health case. The equivalent provision in the MHRT

---

[187]   FTTHESC Rules 2008, r 32(3) and of the MHRT Wales Rules 2008, r 15(1).
[188]   FTTHESC Rules 2008, r 14(5), (6), MHRT Wales Rules 2008, r 17 (4), (5). *Campbell v Secretary of State for the Home Department* [1988] 1 AC 120, HL.
[189]   FTTHESC Rules 2008, r 1, MHRT Wales Rules 2008, r 2.
[190]   Ibid, r 9(2).

Wales Rules allows the MHRT to give a direction adding a person not as a respondent but as an 'interested party'.[191] The 2008 Rules have a more restrictive definition of parties, who have extensive rights. Subject to the rules on non-disclosure where serious harm is likely to result, parties have the right to receive all documents received by the tribunal; interested parties or respondents do not. Subject to the rules on excluding disruptive parties,[192] each party is entitled to attend a hearing.[193]

Notice to other persons interested

9.101   Rule 7 of the MHRT Rules 1983 provided that people such as the guardian or the nearest relative, once notified, became parties. Under the 2008 Rules they no longer enjoy the entitlements of parties. The 2008 Rules require the tribunal, once the reports from the responsible authority and the Secretary of State are in, to give notice of the proceedings to a list of 'interested persons' (England) or 'interested parties' (Wales). These are: (a) to the private guardian of a guardianship patient; (b) to the Court of Protection, where there is an extant order relating to the patient; (c) subject to a patient with capacity to do so requesting otherwise, the nearest relative; (d) any body which has a right to discharge the patient under s 23(3) of the Mental Health Act 1983; and (e) to any other person who, in the opinion of the Tribunal, should have an opportunity of being heard.[194] Interested persons (England) or interested parties (Wales) may either attend and take part in a hearing to such extent as the Tribunal considers proper or provide written submissions to the Tribunal.[195] In *R (on the application of T) v Mental Health Review Tribunal* Scott Baker J dismissed an application for judicial review of a decision not to make a victim a party by giving her notice of the proceedings under r 7 of the 1983 Rules.[196] The Domestic Violence, Crime and Victims Act 2004 provides that victims of violent or serious sexual offences are entitled to be notified of any tribunal hearing held in respect of an offender who has received a hospital order with or without a restriction order and to make representations on certain matters. It will be open to a tribunal to consider whether they are someone who ought to be joined as a respondent or interested party on the grounds that they should have an opportunity of being heard, and this might include an Independent Mental Health Advocate.[197]

9.102   The Domestic Violence, Crime and Victims Act 2004 procedures apply to offences after July 2005, but the MHRT has determined that similar rights will also be conferred on victims of offences occurring prior to that date. The Act applies to violent or sexual offences where the offender is subject to;

---

[191]   MHRT Wales Rules 2008, r 12(2).
[192]   FTTHESC Rules 2008, r 38(4); MHRT Wales Rules 2008, r 25(4).
[193]   FTTHESC Rules 2008, r 36(1).
[194]   FTTHESC Rules 2008, r 33; MHRT Wales Rules 2008, r 16.
[195]   FTTHESC Rules 2008, r 36(2).
[196]   [2001] EWHC Admin 602.
[197]   FTTHESC Rules 2008, r 33(e); MHRT Wales Rules 2008, r 16(e).

(a)   a hospital order with or without restrictions following conviction, finding of not guilty by reason of insanity or finding of unfitness to plead;

(b)   a hospital direction with or without a limitation direction; or

(c)   those sentenced to 12 months or more imprisonment for sexual or violent offence and made subject of a transfer direction with or without a restriction direction under ss 47 and 49.

Victims are entitled to make representations as to conditions to be attached to conditional discharge or a CTO if the patient is to be discharged into the community. Conditions relevant to victims would include 'no contact' conditions or exclusion zones.

Notice of the hearing

9.103   Rule 24(1) provides that section 2 cases must start within 7 days after the date on which the Tribunal received the application notice (the original draft said listed to start – now they must actually start).[198] The Tribunal must give the parties reasonable notice, and in any event no less than 14 days' notice, of the date, time and place of any hearing (including any adjourned or postponed hearing) and any changes to the time and place of any hearing, except that in a section 2 case the Tribunal must give at least 3 days' notice.[199] As was the case under the old rules,[200] the 2008 Rules require notice of the hearing to be given to a list of interested persons including:[201]

(a)   where there is a private guardian, to the guardian;

(b)   where there is an extant order of the Court of Protection, to that court;

(c)   subject to a patient with capacity to do so requesting otherwise,[202] where any person other than the applicant is named by the authority as exercising the functions of the nearest relative, to that person;

(d)   where a health authority, local health board, Primary Care Trust, National Health Service trust, NHS foundation trust, Strategic Health Authority, or the Secretary of State or the Welsh Ministers has a right to discharge the patient under s 23(3) of the Mental Health Act 1983, to that authority, trust or minister; and

(e)   to any other person who, in the opinion of the Tribunal, should have an opportunity of being heard.

---

[198]   FTTHESC Rules 2008, r 37; MHRT Wales Rules 2008, r 24(1).
[199]   FTTHESC Rules 2008, r 37; MHRT Wales Rules 2008, r 24.
[200]   Mental Health Review Tribunal Rules 1983, SI 1983/942, rr 10(4) and 20.
[201]   FTTHESC Rules 2008 r 33; MHRT Wales Rules 2008 r 16.
[202]   See *R (E) v Bristol City Council* [2005] EWHC 74 (Admin), [2005] MHLR 83.

Any person given notice of the hearing has the right to (a) attend and take part in a hearing to such extent as the Tribunal considers proper; or (b) provide written submissions to the Tribunal.[203] In *Campbell v Secretary of State for the Home Department*, the tribunal proceedings were declared invalid because the Home Secretary had not been informed in advance of the date of the tribunal hearing and had received the independent psychiatric report only on the very day of the hearing.[204]

Representation

9.104 The European Commission and Court of Human Rights have repeatedly emphasised the need for effective legal representation as part of the 'special procedural guarantees' required in mental health cases.[205] In 1982, as a result of *Collins v the United Kingdom*,[206] the British Government extended legal aid to applicants to MHRTs where the applicant has insufficient means to pay for his own lawyer. Legal aid also allowed funding for the patient to commission his own psychiatric report. The Law Society operates a specialist panel for MHRT advocates, to guarantee the existence of a pool of suitably qualified representatives. In 1994 the Lord Chancellor abolished the means test, so that all detained patients are eligible for free legal assistance regardless of means.[207] Where there is representation, it is usually the patient who is legally represented, although in restricted cases the Minister of Justice may engage a lawyer to put the case for continued detention. Any party may appoint a representative (whether legally qualified or not) to represent them in the proceedings, as long as that person is (a) not liable to be detained (b) subject to guardianship (c) subject to after-care under supervision (d) subject to a community treatment order under the Act, or (e) a person receiving treatment for mental disorder at the same hospital or registered establishment as the patient.[208]

9.105 Either the party or the representative must send or deliver to the Tribunal written notice of the representative's name and address. Once a representative has been appointed 'Anything permitted or required to be done by or provided to a party under these Rules or a direction, other than signing a witness statement, may be done by or provided to the representative of that party.' Once a representative has been duly appointed the Tribunal and other parties may assume that the representative is and remains authorised until receiving written notification to the contrary from the representative or the represented party; and the Tribunal must provide to the representative any

---

203 FTTHESC Rules 2008, r 36; MHRT Wales Rules 2008, r 16.
204 [2003] EWHC 1182 (Admin).
205 See for example *Winterwerp v the Netherlands* 4 EHRR 288, paras 60–61, 101–2, and more recently in *Megyeri v Germany* (63/1991/315/386) Judgment of 12 May 1992 (1992) BMLR.
206 Application 9729/82. Collins argued that the failure to grant him legal aid for his MHRT hearing was a breach of Art 5(4). The case was declared admissible by the Commission, but withdrawn when legal aid was introduced for MHRT hearings.
207 Legal Advice and Assistance (Amendment) Regulations 1994. SI 1994/805.
208 FTTHESC Rules 2008 r 11; MHRT Wales Rules 2008 r 13.

document which is required to be sent to the represented party, and need not provide that document to the represented party.

9.106   The Tribunal may appoint a legal representative for the patient if the patient has not appointed a representative; and either (a) the patient has stated that they do not wish to conduct their own case or that they wish to be represented; or (b) the patient lacks the capacity to appoint a representative but the Tribunal believes that it is in the patient's best interests for the patient to be represented.

9.107   The First Tier HESC Rules provide that 'At a hearing a party may be accompanied by another person whose name and address has not been notified under paragraph (2) but who, with the permission of the Tribunal, may act as a representative or otherwise assist in presenting the party's case at the hearing'. No one may act as a representative if they are liable to be detained, a community treatment order patient, subject to guardianship or after-care under supervision, or receiving treatment for mental disorder at the same hospital as the patient.[209] Although the English Rules allow the accompanying person to represent, the MHRT Wales Rules provide that 'Unless the Tribunal otherwise directs, a patient or any other party may be accompanied by such other person as the patient or party wishes, in addition to any representative that may have been appointed under this Rule, provided that such person does not act as the representative of the patient or other party.'[210] Given the overriding objective, and given that the Welsh Rule allows the Tribunal to 'direct otherwise' there may be little difference in practice between the position in England and that in Wales, despite the apparent presumption in Wales against allowing the accompanying person to represent. Both sets of Rules state that: 'If a party appoints a representative, that party (or the representative if the representative is a legal representative) must send or deliver to the Tribunal and to each other party written notice of the representative's name and address.'[211]

9.108   Often the responsible authority's views are represented at the hearing by the RC, but and although the responsible authority is entitled to put questions to anyone appearing before the tribunal, the RC is not the responsible authority. However, if the RC wishes to be able to question and cross-examine witnesses and represent in that sense, then the tribunal must be notified to that effect. In *R (on the application of Mersey Care NHS Trust) v Mental Health Review Tribunal*[212] Sullivan J held that the RMO (now the RC) is entitled to put questions to other witnesses, but only if he or she has notified the tribunal that he or she has been authorised by the responsible authority to represent them.

---

[209]   Tribunal Procedure (First-tier Tribunal) (Health, Education and Social Care Chamber) Rules 2008, SI 2008/2699, r 11(8).
[210]   MHRT Wales Rules 2008 r 13(6).
[211]   FTTHESC Rules 2008, SI 2008/2699, r 11(2), the Mental Health Review Tribunal for Wales Rules 2008, SI 2008/2705, r 13(2).
[212]   [2003] EWHC 1182 (Admin).

Medical examination of the patient

9.109 Rule 34(1) of the FTTHESC Rules and Rule 20 of the MHRT Rules Wales are cross headed 'medical examination of the patient' and state that before a hearing to consider the disposal of a mental health case, an appropriate member of the Tribunal (England) the medical member (Wales) must, so far as practicable (a) examine the patient; and (b) take such other steps as that member considers necessary to form an opinion of the patient's mental condition. Those steps may include (a) examining the patient in private; (b) examining records relating to the detention or treatment of the patient and any after-care services; (c) taking notes and copies of records for use in connection with the proceedings.[213] In England there is a practice statement stating that the appropriate member means the medical member.[214] The medical member examines the patient before the hearing and presents his opinion to the other two members when they convene. He or she may provide a written report or, more commonly, will discuss her or his opinion with them during their deliberations. The medical member may also make notes from the medical records and copies of them. Where the notes or copies of the records are submitted to the tribunal, the authorized representative is entitled to receive copies of them. They must also be disclosed to the applicant unless withheld by the tribunal on grounds of potential serious harm. At the initial meeting with the patient to receive instructions the patient's representative should obtain the written authority of the patient to apply for access to the patient's health records.

9.110 In *R (on the application of S) v Mental Health Review Tribunal*[215] Stanley Burnton J rejected an application for judicial review on grounds of incompatibility between the old rule 11 of the 1983 Rules which provided for medical examinations and Art 5(4) of the Convention. The claimant believed that all psychiatrists viewed him unfavourably. He instructed his solicitors to inform the regional chairman that he objected to being seen before the hearing by the medical member and requested that the rule not be applied. The chairman replied that the rule was mandatory. The claimant sought judicial review of the decision, contending that the mandatory requirement of medical examination was incompatible with his rights under Art 5(4) to an independent and impartial judicial determination of the lawfulness of his detention. Stanley Burnton J held that as a matter of domestic law there could be no objection to the expression of a provisional opinion by a medical member of a tribunal to his colleagues, provided that the other members were aware that it was a provisional opinion and treated it as such, and provided they knew that they were free to disagree with it if the evidence and submissions before them led to a different conclusion.

---

[213] FTTHESC Rules 2008 SI 2008/2699, r 34, the Mental Health Review Tribunal for Wales Rules 2008 SI 2008/2705, r 20.

[214] <www.tribunals.gov.uk/Tribunals/Documents/Rules/HESC.pdf>.

[215] [2002] EWHC 2522 (Admin).

9.111   Moreover, on the proper interpretation of the relevant Strasbourg jurisprudence,[216] the old r 11 was not inconsistent with Art 5(4). Impartiality in the present context required a member of a tribunal not to have a preconceived concluded opinion on the merits of the claimant's case. A provisional view formed before the commencement of the hearing was not necessarily objectionable, unless an otherwise impartial and independent member of a tribunal has a preconceived opinion or expresses himself in such a way as to give rise to a reasonable apprehension that he had a preconceived concluded opinion.

9.112   In *R (on the application of RD) v Mental Health Review Tribunal*[217] the medical member examined the patient and, at the outset of the hearing, the President gave an account of the medical member's interview with RD reporting a 'preliminary view' that:[218]

> '[RD] appeared to be ready for transfer to medium security, but because of the length of time at Broadmoor, the lack of testing in the community, and concern about how he would manage in the community, he would appear to need the regime of a secure unit rather than community living.'

The President said that this was 'a very preliminary view, subject to anything we hear today'. RD argued that whilst it was legitimate for the medical member to communicate an opinion about the patient's mental state, it was not legitimate for her to communicate an opinion as to whether he should be discharged. Munby J rejected this argument stating that:[219]

> 'The communication by the medical member of her 'very preliminary' view was manifestly lawful, notwithstanding that it went to the ultimate issue and not merely to the question of RD's mental condition. There is nothing in r 11 to disable the medical member from doing what she (like the other members of the Tribunal) would otherwise plainly be entitled to do, namely to discuss all aspects of the case with the other members of the Tribunal before the hearing and to express to them her preliminary views either on the case as a whole or on any particular aspect of the case, just as there is nothing in rule 11 to disable the medical member (like the other members of the Tribunal) from expressing to the parties at the outset of the hearing her preliminary views either on the case as a whole or on any particular aspect of the case. The contrary, in my judgment, is simply unarguable.'

This means that a 'preliminary view' may be expressed not only on the patient's mental state and also, as long as it is made very clear that it is a preliminary view, on the question of whether the patient should be discharged.

9.113   In a case where a tribunal makes its decision on the basis of some point in the opinion of its own medical member on which evidence has not been put

---

[216]   *DN v Switzerland (Application 27154/95)* Decision of 29 March 2001, ECtHR.
[217]   [2007] EWHC 781 (Admin).
[218]   [2007] EWHC 781 (Admin) at [13].
[219]   [2007] EWHC 781 (Admin) at [19].

before it, it must make the applicant or his representative aware of the views of the medical member and give the patient the opportunity to address them. If material evidence is contained in the medical member's report which is not apparent in any document made available to the parties, the report or its substance should be disclosed.[220] In *R (H) v MHRT for North and East London* Crane J held that, provided the patient and his or her representatives were alerted to the evidence of the medical member and his or her expert views in sufficient detail and sufficiently early in the proceedings to enable them to deal with them, there would be no breach of Article 5(4). This is now standard practice in tribunals.[221]

Independent psychiatric report

9.114 The applicant may engage a psychiatrist or AC to provide an independent report on his medical condition. A copy of each independent report should be sent to the tribunal no later than seven days before the hearing, since late submission may lead to the need for an adjournment. A psychiatrist or AC who provides such a report owes a duty of confidence to the patient. However, this confidential duty is subject to the exception described by Sir Stephen Brown P in *W v Egdell*:[222]

> 'A consultant psychiatrist who becomes aware, even in the course of a confidential relationship, of information which leads him, in the exercise of what the court considers a sound professional judgment, to fear that such decisions may be made on the basis of inadequate information and with a real risk of consequent danger to the public, is entitled to take such steps as are reasonable in all the circumstances to communicate the grounds of his concern to the responsible authorities.'

The doctor or AC may disclose the information to the responsible authorities even where the patient has withdrawn his application.

The power to issue directions

9.115 Rule 13 of the 1983 MHRT Rules empowered the tribunal to give such directions as it thinks fit to ensure the speedy and just determination of the application, hence providing the MHRT with broad powers of case management. These have been significantly extended by both the First Tier HESC Rules 2008, and MHRT Wales Rules 2008.[223] Rule 5(1) of the HESC Rules gives the tribunal wide power to regulate its own procedure (subject to the Tribunal Courts and Enforcement Act 2007), any other enactment, and, of course, the overriding objective. This express statement is not replicated in the

---

[220]   *R v Mental Health Review Tribunal, ex parte Clatworthy* [1985] 3 All ER 699, QBD. See also *R v Mental Health Review Tribunal (Mersey Region), ex parte Davies* (unreported) 21 April 1986, QBD.

[221]   (CO 2120/2000) High Court per Crane J. The decision of the Court of Appeal can be found at [2001] EWCA Civ 415. I am indebted to John Horne for this point.

[222]   *W v Egdell* [1990] Ch 359, [1989] 1 All ER 1089, ChD; [1990] 1 All ER 835, CA.

[223]   FTTHESC Rules 2008, rr 5–6; MHRT Wales Rules, rr 5, 6.

MHRT Wales Rules. Both English and Welsh Rules permit the giving of directions at any time.[224] Directions may be used for any of the purposes in the non-exclusive list in r 5, for example, to extend or shorten the time for complying with any rule or direction, permitting or requiring a party to amend any document, stay execution of its own decision pending an appeal, or staying proceedings generally. Rule 6 makes it clear that the Tribunal may make a direction on the application of a party *or* on its own initiative. Any application for a direction must be made in accordance with the procedure in r 6 and must include the reasons for making that application.[225] The application can be made prior to the hearing or orally during the course of the hearing.[226] According to r 6(5), a direction may be challenged by applying for a fresh direction which amends, suspends, or sets aside the first direction.

Evidence

9.116   Under r 15 of the HESC Rules the Tribunal may give directions as to (a) issues on which it requires evidence or submissions; (b) the nature of the evidence or submissions it requires; (c) whether the parties are permitted or required to provide expert evidence, and if so whether the parties must jointly appoint a single expert to provide such evidence; (d) any limit on the number of witnesses whose evidence a party may put forward, whether in relation to a particular issue or generally. Rule 15(1)(e) allows a direction for evidence or submissions to be given either (i) orally at a hearing; or (ii) by written submissions or witness statement; and to specify the time at which any evidence or submissions are to be provided.

9.117   Rule 15(2) empowers the tribunal to receive any document or information in evidence, notwithstanding that it would be inadmissible in a civil trial, or it had been available to a previous decision-maker. This has been held to include the power to receive a written statement from victims in cases involving offender patients. Victims may make a statement in writing which can be received under r 15.[227] In *R (on the application of N) v Mental Health Review Tribunal (Northern Region)* Munby J sounded a note of caution in relation to hearsay evidence:[228]

> 'In relation to past incidents which are centrally important to the decision it has to take, the tribunal must bear in mind the need for proof to the civil standard of proof; it must bear in mind the potential difficulties of relying on second or third hand hearsay; and if the incident is really fundamental to its decision it must bear in mind fairness may require the patient to be given the opportunity to cross examine the relevant witness if their evidence is to be relied upon.'

---

[224]   FTTHESC Rules 2008, r 5(2); MHRT Wales Rules, r 5(1).
[225]   FTTHESC Rules 2008, r 6(3); MHRT Wales Rules, r 6(3).
[226]   FTTHESC Rules 2008, r 6(2); MHRT Wales Rules, r 6(2).
[227]   *R (on the application of T) v Mental Health Review Tribunal* [2001] EWHC 602 (Admin).
[228]   [2005] EWHC 587 (Admin) at [129].

Under r 15(2)(b) the Tribunal may issue a direction excluding evidence if it was not provided in time or in a manner complying with a direction or practice direction, or if 'it would otherwise be unfair to admit the evidence.[229] Both rules allow the tribunal to require evidence to be given under oath, In Wales evidence may be given on oath or affirmation.[230] In both England and Wales there is provision for summonsing witnesses to attend.[231] The tribunal may issue a summons on application by a party or of its own motion and must give 14 days' notice (England) reasonable notice (Wales). No-one may be compelled to give any evidence or produce any document that they could not be compelled to give or produce on a trial of an action in a court of law. The summons must state that the person summonsed may apply to the Tribunal to vary or set it aside, if they have not had an opportunity to object to it, and in England must state the consequences of failure to comply.

HEARING PROCEDURE

9.118 'Hearing' is defined in the 2008 Rules as 'an oral hearing and includes a hearing conducted in whole or in part by video link, telephone or other means of instantaneous two-way electronic communication.'[232] Rule 35 of the FTTHESC Rules 2008 states that the Tribunal must not dispose of proceedings without a hearing, unless the issue arises under Part 5 of the HESC Rules, which deals with correcting, setting aside, reviewing and appealing Tribunal decisions. The MHRT Wales Rules contain no such express requirement.

9.119 In relation to public and private hearings the English and Welsh Rules differ. In both jurisdictions hearings must be held in private unless the tribunal directs otherwise.[233] Under the English Rules all hearings must be held in private unless the Tribunal considers that it is *in the interests of justice* for the hearing to be held in public. Under the MHRT Wales Rules a public hearing can only take place following a request from the patient, and the Tribunal may only allow a public hearing if satisfied that that would be in the *interests of the patient*.[234] The Tribunal in either jurisdiction may direct that a hearing begun in public shall continue in private, and in Wales if it does this it must record its reasons in writing and inform the patient of those reasons.

9.120 Where a hearing is held in private, the Tribunal may determine who is permitted to attend the hearing or part of it – although English and Welsh

---

[229] FTTHESC Rules 2008, r 15(2)(b); MHRT Wales Rules, r 18.
[230] FTTHESC Rules 2008, r 15(3); MHRT Wales Rules 2008, r 18(3).
[231] FTTHESC Rules 2008, r 16; MHRT Wales Rules 2008, r 19.
[232] FTTHESC Rules 2008, r 1; MHRT Wales Rules 2008, r 2.
[233] FTTHESC Rules 2008, r 38(1); MHRT Wales Rules 2008, r 25(1).
[234] This was the test under the Mental Health Review Tribunal Rules 1983, SI 1983/942, r 21(1) and was ruled on in *Pickering v Liverpool Daily Post and Echo Newspapers plc* [1991] 1 All ER 622, (1991) 6 BMLR 108, HL.

rules are in different terms their effect is the same.[235] The Tribunal may give a direction excluding from any hearing, or part of it, any person (including the patient):

(a)   whose conduct is, in the opinion of the Tribunal, is disrupting or is likely to disrupt the hearing;

(b)   whose presence the Tribunal considers is likely to prevent another person from giving evidence or making submissions freely; or

(c)   who the Tribunal considers should be excluded in order to give effect to a direction withholding information likely to cause harm.

The English Rules add a fourth category not present in the Welsh equivalent, namely 'any person where the purpose of the hearing would be defeated by the attendance of that person.'[236] Finally the Tribunal may give a direction excluding a witness from a hearing until that witness gives evidence.[237]

9.121   Rule 38(1) of the Tribunal Procedure (First-tier Tribunal) (Health, Education and Social Care Chamber) Rules 2008 provides that all hearings must be held in private unless the Tribunal considers that it is in the interests of justice for the hearing to be held in public. In *AH v West London Mental Health Trust and Secretary of State for Justice*[238] the Upper Tribunal held that the r 38 presumption was not of itself incompatible with Art 6 of the European Convention on Human Rights but that the following factors must be considered in any application for a public hearing:[239]

(a)   whether it is consistent with the subjective and informed wishes of the patient (assuming that he is competent to make an informed choice;

(b)   whether it will have an adverse effect on his mental health in the sort or long term, taking account of the views of those treating him and any other expert views;

(c)   whether there are any other special factors for or against a public hearing;

(d)   whether practical arrangements can be made for an open hearing without disproportionate burden on the hospital or relevant authority.

9.122   The Upper Tribunal set aside the FTT's decision to refuse a public hearing and directed that there be a further hearing (at which the Department of Health was invited to appear) to consider further evidence as to:[240]

---

[235]   FTTHESC Rules 2008, r 38(3); MHRT Wales Rules 2008, r 25(3).
[236]   FTTHESC Rules 2008, r 38(4); MHRT Wales Rules 2008, r 25(4).
[237]   FTTHESC Rules 2008, r 38(5); MHRT Wales Rules 2008, r 25(5).
[238]   [2010] UKUT 264 (AAC).
[239]   Ibid, para 44.
[240]   Ibid, para 53.

(a) the practicalities and potential cost of providing a public hearing (including by use of video facilities);

(b) how often public hearings have been applied for in the last five years, the number of occasions on which they have in practice been held and how they have been managed; and

(c) (so far as readily available) practices elsewhere in the United Kingdom, in Europe and in other common law countries.

9.123 The Clinical Director of Broadmoor had argued that to grant a public hearing would require the hearing to be held off site due to security if the press were to be present, and would set a precedent which could prove disproportionately costly for Broadmoor. In *AH v West London Mental Health Trust and Secretary of State for Justice*[241] the Upper Tribunal heard evidence from the parties and the Department of Health and took into consideration Arts 13 and 14 of the UN Convention on the Rights of Persons with Disabilities. Under Art 13(1) a ratifying state agrees to ensure 'effective access to justice for persons with disabilities on an equal basis with others.' Under Art 14 a ratifying state also agrees to ensure that if persons with disabilities are deprived of liberty through any process 'they shall be treated in compliance with the objectives and principles of the present Convention, including by provision of reasonable accommodation.'

9.124 Lord Justice Carnworth held that once the threshold tests outlined above for establishing a right to a public hearing had been satisfied:[242]

> 'Article 6 of the European Convention on Human Rights (re-enforced by article 13 of the CRPD) requires that a patient should have the same or substantially equivalent right of access to a public hearing as a non-disabled person who has been deprived of his or her liberty, if this article 6 right to a public hearing is to be given proper effect. Such a right can only be denied a patient if enabling that right imposes a truly disproportionate burden on the state.'

His Lordship also referred to the principle enunciated by the European Court of Human Rights, most recently in *Kiss v Hungary* emphasising the need for special consideration to be given to the rights of particularly vulnerable groups such as the mentally disabled.[243] In the interests of avoiding further delay, the UT ordered a public hearing at an off-site location for this case, but said this about future cases:[244]

> 'How the right to a public hearing can practically and proportionately be achieved will depend on the facts of each individual case, including the facilities available in the hospital in question. On the evidence provided to us by the Broadmoor Hospital Clinical Director, it seems likely that if similar cases arise in the future, it

---

[241] [2011] UKUT 74 (AAC).
[242] Ibid, para 22.
[243] Application No 38832/06, Judgment of 20 May 2010, para 42.
[244] [2011] UKUT 74 (AAC), para 23.

should be possible for arrangements to be made between the hospital and the Tribunals Service for a hearing at the hospital with a video-link to suitable premises off-site where any interested members of the press or public can view the proceedings.'

The interview with the patient

9.125 Under the MHRT Rules 1983 the Tribunal had a duty to interview the patient if he so requested and without the presence of any other person, again if requested. Under the MHRT Wales Rules 2008 the Tribunal is now afforded discretion as to whether a private interview is granted. Rule 20(3) of the MHRT Wales Rules provides that 'At any time before the Tribunal makes the final determination, the Tribunal or any one or more of its members may interview the patient, which interview may take place in the absence of any other person.' Hence in Wales the private interview is now at the discretion of the tribunal, and the HESC Rules 2008 contain no equivalent provision for private interviews with the patient. Tribunals in both jurisdictions, when considering requests for a private interview, will need to be mindful of the 'overriding objective', as well as what the European Court of Human Rights has referred to in *Herczegfalvy v Austria*[245] as 'the situation of vulnerability and powerlessness' of detained patients which requires special vigilance on the part of the authorities'.

Rights of the Parties

9.126 The following are parties to the proceedings: the patient, the responsible authority, the Secretary of State (or in Wales the Welsh Ministers) (if the patient is a restricted patient or in a reference seeking approval for removal of an 'alien' patient from the jurisdiction under s 86 of the Mental Health Act 1983), and any other person who starts a mental health case by making an application.[246] The 2008 Rules have a more restrictive definition of parties, who have extensive rights. Subject to the rules on non-disclosure where serious harm is likely to result, parties have the right to receive all documents received by the tribunal; interested parties or respondents do not. Subject to the rules on excluding disruptive parties,[247] each party is entitled to attend a hearing.[248] Both the English and the Welsh Rules provide that, subject to the provisions on withholding evidence likely to cause harm, when the Tribunal receives a document from any party it must send a copy of that document to each other party.[249] 'Document' is defined under both sets of Rules identically to mean anything in which information is recorded in any form. The definition goes on to state that 'An obligation under these Rules or any practice direction or

---

[245] (1992) 15 EHRR 437. See also *Kiss v Hungary* Application no 38832/06, Judgment of 20 May 2010, para 42.
[246] FTTHESC Rules 2008, r 1; MHRT Wales Rules 2008, r 2.
[247] FTTHESC Rules 2008, r 38(4); MHRT Wales Rules 2008, r 25(4).
[248] FTTHESC Rules 2008, r 36(1).
[249] FTTHESC Chamber Rules 2008, SI 2008/2699, rr 32(3) and 14(2); MHRT Wales Rules 2008, SI 2008/2705, rr 15 and 17.

direction to provide or allow access to a document or a copy of a document for any purpose means, unless the Tribunal directs otherwise, an obligation to provide or allow access to such document or copy in a legible form or in a form which can be readily made into a legible form.'[250]

9.127 Unless they are excluded from the proceedings, the English rules expressly entitle each party to attend the hearing.[251] The MHRT Wales Rules contain no equivalent provision entitling parties to attend the hearing. The Rules in both England and Wales allow hearings to be conducted in the absence of one of the parties if the Tribunal is satisfied that the party has been notified of the hearing or that reasonable steps have been taken to notify the party of the hearing. In such a case a Tribunal in England may proceed with the hearing if it considers that it is *in the interests of justice* to do so.[252] In Wales the test is that the Tribunal is satisfied that the party has been notified or that reasonable steps have been taken to notify *and the Tribunal is not aware of any good reason for the failure to attend.*[253] The Wales Rules provide that it is an alternative ground for proceeding in the absence of a party, whether or not they have been informed, steps have been taken to inform them, or they have an excuse, if 'the Tribunal otherwise considers that it is *in the interests of the patient* to do so.'[254]

9.128 If the absent party is the patient, under the FTTHESC Rules the Tribunal may not proceed with a hearing unless the requirements of the rule requiring the medical member to form an opinion of the patient's condition have been met, and the Tribunal is satisfied that either the patient has decided not to attend the hearing; or the patient is unable to attend the hearing for reasons of ill health.[255] The MHRT Wales Rules 2008 do not make express provision for the situation where the patient is the absent party.

9.129 After all the evidence has been given, the applicant and, where s/he is not the applicant, the patient, have the opportunity to address the tribunal. This allows the applicant, the patient or the representative to sum up the case and to add any final points.

Rights of other parties or persons

9.130 Mental Health Review Tribunal Wales Rules 2008, SI 2008 705 rr 3, 12, 16 and 26. The HESC Rules refer only to parties, but allow the FTT to give a direction adding a person to the proceedings as a 'respondent'.[256] The rules governing jurisdictions other than mental health in the FTT refer to 'respondents'. The equivalent provision in the MHRT Wales Rules allows the MHRT to give a direction adding a person not as a respondent but as an

---

[250] FTTHESC Chamber Rules 2008, SI 2008/2699, r 1; MHRT Wales Rules 2008, r 2.
[251] FTTHESC Rules 2008, r 36.
[252] First Tier Tribunals HESC Rules 2008, r 39.
[253] MHRT Wales Rules 2008, r 27.
[254] Ibid.
[255] FTTHESC Rules 2008 r 39(2).
[256] Ibid, r 9(2).

'interested party'.[257] Under the English Rules, anyone who is an interested party or an interested person may attend and take part in the hearing to such extent as the tribunal considers proper, or provide written submissions to the tribunal.[258] The MHRT Wales Rules 2008 contain no equivalent provision but they do confer discretion on the Tribunal to give a direction permitting or requesting any person to attend and take part in a hearing to such extent as the Tribunal considers appropriate; or make written submissions in relation to a particular issue. In exercising this discretion in relation to an interested party, the Tribunal in Wales would need to have regard to the overriding objective.[259]

Subpoenas and Summons

9.131 The Tribunal, on the application of any party or on its own initiative, may summon witnesses to attend and order them to answer questions or produce any document in their possession or control which relate to the proceedings.[260] No-one can be compelled to give evidence or produce any document that they could not be compelled to give or produce on a trial of a civil action in a court of law.[261] In England any summons must give 14 days notice (or such shorter period as the Tribunal may direct) and in Wales 'reasonable notice' of the hearing must be given. Where the person summoned is not a party the summons must state that their reasonable expenses of attendance will be paid and by whom. The summons must also state that the person summoned may apply to the Tribunal to have the summons varied or set aside. The English rules (but not their Welsh equivalent) require that the summons state the consequence of non-compliance. In England FTTHESC r 7(3) states the consequences of non-compliance with a summons to give evidence, refusal to swear an oath, failure to provide a document or to allow inspection of a document or premises. In such a case the Tribunal may refer the matter to the Upper Tribunal, and ask the Upper Tribunal to exercise its power under s 25 of the Tribunals, Courts and Enforcement Act 2007 which gives the Upper Tribunal the same powers as the High Court in relation to contempt of court.

Adjournment

9.132 A Tribunal may adjourn a hearing at any time. Under the English Rules the power to adjourn is part of the general power to issue directions.[262] Under the Welsh Rules there is a specific rule[263] dedicated to adjournment which is in similar terms to the old provision under the MHRT Rules 1983.[264] This confers a discretion on the Tribunal to adjourn in order to obtain further information

---

257 MHRT Wales Rules 2008, r 12(2).
258 FTTHESC Rules 2008, rr 33 and 36(2).
259 Mental Health Review Tribunal Wales Rules 2008, SI 2008/2705, rr 3, 16 and 26.
260 FTTHESC Rules 2008, r 16; MHRT Wales Rules 2008, r 19.
261 FTTHESC Rules 2008, r 16(3); MHRT Wales Rules 2008, r 19(4).
262 FTTHESC Rules 2008, r 5(3)(h).
263 MHRT Wales Rules 2008, r 21.
264 Mental Health Review Tribunal Rules 1983, SI 1983/942, r 16.

or for such other reason as it thinks appropriate, and the MHRT Wales will normally grant a request for adjournment by a representative if there are reasonable grounds for it. Although the second limb of r 21 of the Welsh Rules allows an adjournment for such other purposes as the tribunal may think necessary, the tribunal has no power to adjourn to give the patient's condition an opportunity to improve or to see whether an improvement already made is sustained. The purpose of the power to adjourn is primarily to obtain information about the patient's current condition. Where the tribunal is satisfied that the criteria for discharge are not met at the time of the hearing, it has no power to adjourn to give the patient's condition an opportunity to improve.[265]

9.133   In *R (on the application of B) v Mental Health Review Tribunal*[266] Scott Baker J held that where there is an adjournment the tribunal should fix a time-limit within which the reconvened hearing will take place, with clear direction to ensure that relevant expert evidence is obtained in time. He also held that experts should meet to narrow any differences of opinion and that adjournments should not be granted without giving the patient's representative an opportunity to be heard. An adjournment which is not requested by the patient may interfere with the patient's right to a speedy determination of the case. Brief reasons should also be given for any decision to adjourn.

9.134   In *R (on the application of X) v Mental Health Review Tribunal*[267] Collins J held that whilst the MHRT has the power of its own motion to adjourn to obtain information, it should not do so unless it regards it as necessary to do justice and reach the right result in the case. This required a balance to be struck between the need for any information and any delay which will occur in the determination of the case.

9.135   The tribunal may only adjourn to obtain information for a purpose which is within its jurisdiction. Hence the tribunal may not adjourn a restricted patient hearing *solely* to gather information relating to making a recommendation, although there is nothing to stop it gathering such information if it adjourns to obtain further information on a matter within its jurisdiction (discharge).[268] Rule 25(2) of the old MHRT Rules was amended to make it clear that it was not intended for MHRTs to be able to reconvene to consider recommendations in restricted cases.[269] Compare this with the power to defer conditional discharge under s 73 until such arrangements as appear to be necessary for that purpose have been made to the tribunal's satisfaction.

---

[265]   *R v Nottingham Mental Health Review Tribunal, ex p Secretary of State for the Home Department, The Times*, 12 October 1988, CA.

[266]   [2002] EWHC 1553 (Admin).

[267]   [2003] All ER (D) 160 (May).

[268]   *R (on the application of the Secretary of State for the Home Department) v Mental Health Review Tribunal* (2000) 63 BMLR 181, QBD.

[269]   MHRT (Amendment) Rules 1998, SI 1998/1189, r 2(3).

THE MHT DECISION

9.136 The Tribunal may give its decision orally at the hearing or it may reserve its decision.[270] The rules then proceed to outline the requirement to give written notice of their decision and their reasons to each party in any case where the Tribunal has made a 'decision which finally disposes of all issues' (England) or in Wales has made a 'final determination'. 'Decision which disposes of all the issues' and 'final determination' each include decisions with recommendations and deferred directions for conditional discharge, but do not include decisions about permission to appeal.[271] Subject to the rules on withholding information likely to cause serious harm, the Tribunal must, as soon as reasonably practicable (and in any event within three *working* days after the hearing in s 2 cases, and in all other cases within seven days) provide a decision notice stating the tribunal's decision, and stating written reasons for the decision.[272] In England the decision notice must also contain notification of any right of appeal against the decision the manner of exercise of the appeal right, and the time limits within which an appeal may be lodged.[273] The MHRT Wales Rules 2008 do not contain this last requirement to notify about rights of appeal, but the overriding objective would appear to require it.

9.137 An exception to the duty to provide written reasons may be made in cases where the tribunal considers that full disclosure would be likely to cause serious harm to the patient or others. In such cases the tribunal may communicate its decision to the patient in any other appropriate manner. The Tribunal may decide to disclose to the patient's representative subject to a duty not to disclose any one or all of those reasons to the patient (see above). In a decision to discharge the tribunal must give reasons why they are or are not satisfied that the patient is suffering from mental disorder of the relevant nature or degree for detention, guardianship or a CTO, or why they are or are not satisfied that detention, guardianship, or a CTOis justified. Similarly, they must give reasons in a restriction order case why they are or are not directing absolute or conditional discharge.[274] As Jack Beatson QC summed it up in *R (on the application of Warren) v Mental Health Review Tribunal (London and North East Region)*:[275]

> 'the tribunal's reasons must address the diagnostic question of whether there is mental disorder and the policy question of whether it is safe to discharge.'

9.138 The early case-law on the 1983 Act – *Bone v Mental Health Review Tribunal*,[276] *R v Mental Health Review Tribunal, ex parte Clatworthy*[277] and *R v*

---

[270] FTTHESC Rules 2008, r 41(1); MHRT Wales Rules 2008, r 28(1).

[271] FTTHESC Rules 2008, r 41(1); MHRT Wales Rules 2008, r 28(1).

[272] Mental Health Review Tribunal Rules 1983, SI 1983/942, r 23(3), FTTHESC Rules 2008, r 41(2), MHRT Wales Rules 2008, r 28(2).

[273] FTTHESC Rules 2008, r 41(2)(c).

[274] Mental Health Review Tribunal Rules 1983, SI 1983/942, r 23(2).

[275] *R (on the application of Warren) v Mental Health Review Tribunal (London and North East Region)* [2002] EWHC 811 (Admin).

[276] *Bone v Mental Health Review Tribunal* [1985] 3 All ER 330, per Nolan J.

Mental Health Review Tribunal, ex parte Pickering[278] – held that reasons must not be mere rehearsals of the statutory criteria, must be adequate and intelligible, and must reasonably be said to deal with the substantial points that have been raised. It has to be possible to read from the reasons the issue to which they are directed. Where there is a conflict of evidence the reasons have to reveal why the tribunal had accepted the evidence of one party and not the other. The overriding question was:

'Is the tribunal providing both parties with the materials which will enable them to know that the tribunal has made no error of law in reaching its finding of fact?'

9.139 In *R (on the application of Ashworth Hospital Authority) v Mental Health Review Tribunal for West Midlands and Northwest Region,*[279] the Court of Appeal upheld Stanley Burnton J's decision to quash as *Wednesbury* irrational the tribunal's direction to discharge the patient immediately where the preponderance of the medical evidence was against it, and the tribunal's reasons showed that they had not give adequate attention to the need for and availability of after-care support. The court held that reasons must deal with the entirety of its decision and not merely whether there is mental disorder of the relevant nature or degree and whether it is safe to discharge. Hence reasons would have to be given for not adjourning to see if adequate after-care could be arranged. Dyson LJ held that where the tribunal is required to resolve a difference of opinion between experts as to whether the patient should be discharged it is important that the tribunal should state which, if any of the expert evidence it accepts and which it rejects, giving reasons. The reasons must at least indicate the reasoning process by which they have decided to accept some and reject other evidence. The reasons given for deciding to accept the evidence of one doctor and reject that of the other experts were 'wholly inadequate'. Moreover, the tribunal was required to give reasons for not adjourning to see whether adequate after-care arrangements could be made, or not making an order for deferred discharge.

9.140 In *MD v Nottinghamshire Healthcare Trust*[280] Judge Jacobs considered the availability of appropriate treatment test and rejected the contention made on behalf of the patient that detention without the possibility of reduction of the risk posed by the patient was containment. Judge Jacobs said this:[281]

'The treatment has to be appropriate, but it need not reduce the risk. Section 145(4) provides that it is sufficient if the treatment is for the purpose of preventing a worsening of the symptoms or manifestations. That envisages that

---

[277] *R v Mental Health Review Tribunal, ex parte Clatworthy* [1985] 3 All ER 699 at 703, per Mann J.

[278] *R v Mental Health Review Tribunal, ex parte Pickering* [1986] 1 All ER 99 at 104, per Forbes J.

[279] *R (on the application of Ashworth Hospital Authority) v Mental Health Review Tribunal for West Midlands and Northwest Region* [2002] EWCA Civ 923.

[280] [2010] UKUT 59 (AAC).

[281] Ibid, para 34.

the treatment required may not reduce risk. It is also sufficient if it will alleviate but one of the symptoms or manifestations, regardless of the impact on the risk posed by the patient.'

9.141 In *DH-L v Devon Partnership NHS Trust*[282] Judge Jacobs returned to the issue of availability of appropriate treatment. Here he had to consider the reasons given by the tribunal for finding that appropriate treatment was available to the patient, who had a personality disorder and was not engaging with the nursing staff, who were offering anger management, among other interventions. The tribunal's reasons were:[283]

> 'We accept the opinion of Dr Parker that continued treatment in hospital provides alleviation or prevention of a deterioration in his condition. Appropriate medical treatment is available on C Ward with the hope that he will begin to engage in treatment.'

Judge Jacobs held that the tribunal's reason were inadequate, as they were too general to deal with the issue and ignored evidence to the contrary. He identified the danger that the availability of appropriate treatment test might 'produce the danger that a patient for whom no appropriate treatment is available may be contained for public safety rather than detained for treatment. In his view this could be resolved by adopting the following approach:[284]

> 'The solution lies in the tribunal's duty to ensure that the conditions for continued detention are satisfied. The tribunal must investigate behind assertions, generalisations and standard phrases. By focusing on specific questions, it will ensure that it makes an individualised assessment for the particular patient.
>
> • What precisely is the treatment that can be provided?
> • What discernible benefit may it have on this patient?
> • Is that benefit related to the patient's mental disorder or to some unrelated problem?
> • Is the patient truly resistant to engagement?
>
> The tribunal's reasons then need only reflect what it did in the inquisitorial and decision-making stages.'

Although he found the tribunal's reasons inadequate, Jacobs J, exercised his discretion under not to set its decision aside under s 12(2)(a) of the Tribunals, Courts and Enforcement Act 2007). The patient's circumstances had changed significantly. He had been transferred to a different hospital elsewhere in the country and was back on anti-psychotic medication. His diagnosis was now likely to be one of mental illness rather than a personality disorder. Second, the

---

[282] [2010] UKUT 102 (AAC).
[283] Ibid, para 34.
[284] Ibid, para 33.

patient had a right to apply again to the First-tier Tribunal to consider his discharge. He should be left to do so, if he thought his new circumstances justified it.[285]

9.142 It is important to remember that the decision and reasons will be studied closely by the parties to the tribunal, the patient and/or the representative, the hospital, and, in the case of a restricted patient, the Ministry of Justice. Those dissatisfied with the decision may well be seeking grounds for appeal or judicial review. Each member has a vital contribution to make to the formulation of the decision and the reasons. It is essential, therefore, that the decision is taken by the three members of the tribunal either unanimously or, in extremis by a majority, and that each participate and accept responsibility for it. It is also crucial that the process of agreeing its wording is not delegated to or reserved to the legal chairman.

Effects of a MHT decision

9.143 Although the decision of a tribunal to terminate detention makes further detention under that authority unlawful, it does not necessarily prevent a fresh application being made for detention or guardianship.[286] In *R (on the application of Von Brandenburg (aka Hanley)) v East London and the City Mental Health NHS Trust*[287] the House of Lords rejected the argument that the test for compulsory admission following discharge by a tribunal had to be based on a 'material change of circumstances'. Instead what was necessary was that the social worker had to have information which had not been available to the tribunal. Lord Bingham of Cornhill said that:[288]

> 'An [AMHP] may not lawfully apply for the admission of a patient whose discharge has been ordered by the decision of a MHRT of which the [AMHP] is aware unless the [AMHP] has formed the reasonable and bona fide opinion that he has information not known to the tribunal which puts a significantly different complexion on the case as compared with that which was before the tribunal.'

In such a case the AMHP may properly apply for the admission of a patient, subject of course to obtaining the required medical support, notwithstanding a tribunal decision directing discharge. The position of the patient's nearest relative, in those cases where he or she makes the application with knowledge of the tribunal decision, does not differ in principle from that of the AMHP, although the NR could not in many cases be expected to be familiar with the evidence or appreciate the grounds on which the tribunal had based its decision.

---

[285] Ibid, para 35.
[286] *Bath and North East Somerset Council v Crowsley* (unreported) 8 December 1999 (CO/3384/99).
[287] [2003] UKHL 58.
[288] [2003] UKHL 58 at [10].

Applying for a stay of a MHT decision

9.144 Where the hospital authorities consider that a tribunal decision may have been arrived at due to an error of law, the appropriate course will usually be to apply for a stay of the tribunal decision, rather than to encourage re-sectioning. In *R (on the application of Ashworth Hospital Authority) v Mental Health Review Tribunal for West Midlands and Northwest Region* Dyson LJ held that since the tribunal is a court for the purposes of Art 5(4), the fact that the professionals have been advised that there are substantial grounds for saying that the tribunal's decision is arguably unlawful is not a sufficient ground for sanctioning as lawful a decision to resection a patient in the absence of material circumstances of which the tribunal was not aware when it made the decision.[289] An application to the High Court for a stay was the correct course in such a case. Now the rules allow a party to apply to the Tribunal itself to stay proceedings or to suspend the effect of its own decision pending the determination by the Tribunal or the Upper Tribunal of an application for permission to appeal against, and any appeal or review of, that decision.[290] In Wales the MHRT may issue a direction staying execution of its own decision pending an appeal of such decision or it may stay proceedings.[291]

CONCLUSION

9.145 The new separate arrangements for Mental Health (Review) Tribunals in England and Wales have now been brought fully into operation. Clearly the intent behind the Tribunals Courts and Enforcement Act 2007 was to make the tribunals more court like in their functioning, and to introduce the benefits of a full time judiciary and case management. This has been achieved, but at the cost of increased formalism and complexity. Although tribunals strive to make the hearing as unintimidating as possible for the patient, the vision of informality promulgated by the Franks Committee in 1957 would seem more and more difficult to achieve in the case of Mental Health Tribunals.[292] After an initial period when the First-tier Tribunal appeared to be correcting errors without cases going to appeal or judicial review, this phase seems to have come to an end and a significant body of Upper Tribunal case law is now emerging, alongside the substantial pre-existing jurisprudence on Mental Health Review Tribunals developed by way of judicial review following the passage of the MHA 1983.

---

[289] *R (on the application of Ashworth Hospital Authority) v Mental Health Review Tribunal for West Midlands and Northwest Region* [2002] EWCA Civ 923.

[290] FTTHESC Rules 2008, r 5(3)(j), (l).

[291] MHRT Wales Rules 2008, r 5(2)(g), (h).

[292] Report of the Committee on Administrative Tribunals and Enquiries 1957 Cmnd, 218.

Chapter 10

CONSENT TO TREATMENT FOR MENTAL DISORDER

OVERVIEW

10.1 Part IV of the MHA 1983 introduced a framework of powers to administer treatment for mental disorder without consent, subject to a system of second opinion safeguards. Those imposing treatment without consent and the Second Opinion Appointed Doctors ('SOADs') who act under Part IV of the Act are public authorities for the purposes of the Human Rights Act 1998 and must act compatibly with Convention rights. Section 57 specifies the treatments, psychosurgery and surgical hormone implants for the reduction of male sex drive, which cannot be given without both the patient's valid consent and a second opinion that the treatment is appropriate. This procedure must be observed whether or not the patient is detained. Section 58 authorises treatment without consent. Section 58 applies only to patients who are liable to be detained under powers authorising detention for more than 72 hours, and who are not conditionally discharged restricted patients, or remand patients subject to s 35. Section 58 treatments were medicines for mental disorder (specified in s 58(1)(b)) and Electro Convulsive Therapy ('ECT' – added by regulations under s 52(1)(a)). Section 58 treatments require either the patient's consent or a certificate from a second opinion appointed doctor stating that the patient is either (a) incapable of consenting, or (b) capable and refusing, but that the treatment ought to be given. Previously, in deciding whether the treatment ought to be given the SOAD under the MHA 1983 had to have regard to the likelihood that it will 'alleviate or prevent deterioration in the patient's condition'. The MHA 2007 replaces this test with the test that 'it is appropriate for the treatment to be given'.[1] Another important change to Part IV relates to the removal of ECT from s 58 and its subjection to a separate procedure under s 58A. This provides that, except in an emergency threatening life or serious deterioration in the patient's condition, ECT may not be given to a capable patient who is refusing the treatment.

ECT

10.2 During the debates on the 1982 Bill there was some lobbying to make ECT subject to the s 57 procedure, hence requiring consent before it could be given. The Government responded by making ECT subject to s 58 by regulation rather than on the face of the Act thus leaving themselves the option

---

[1]   MHA 1983, ss 57(2)(b), 58(3)(b), 58A(5)(b), as inserted by MHA 2007 s 6(2).

to move it to the s 57 category, without resort to amending legislation, if experience showed the need.[2] Instead of making ECT subject to s 57 where it could only be given with the consent of a capable patient, the MHA 2007 creates a third procedure under s 58A whereby ECT can be given if the patient lacks capacity, but cannot be given where the patient has capacity and is refusing it. The MHA 2007 removes ECT from s 58 and creates a new second opinion regime under s 58A whereby ECT may not be given to a patient who has capacity and is refusing, although it may be given to a person who lacks capacity if it is appropriate for the treatment to be given. Like s 58, s 58A applies to patients who are liable to be detained under powers authorising detention for more than 72 hours, and who are not conditionally discharged restricted patients or subject to remand under s 35. Unlike s 58, s 58A also applies to informal (non-sectioned) patients who are under 18. The MHA 2007 means that there are three second opinion regimes under Part IV, with the capacity to move specified treatments from one group to another by regulations.

Treatment without a prior second opinion

10.3   Part IV also provides for emergency treatment without prior second opinion (s 62), and for treatments other than those specified in ss 57 and 58, to be administered without consent (s 63). Under the 1983 Act this power only applied if the treatment was given by or under the direction of the Responsible Medical Officer (s 63). Under s 63 as amended by the 2007 Act, these powers pass to the Approved Clinician ('AC') in charge of treatment. Section 62(1A) authorises emergency ECT without compliance with the second opinion procedures in s 58A if the treatment is immediately necessary to save the patient's life; or is not irreversible and is immediately necessary to prevent a serious deterioration of his condition.[3]

Part IVA

10.4   Patients who have been on a CTO, but have been recalled to hospital and had their CTO revoked are treated for mental disorder under ss 58 and 58A.[4] The treatment of non-recalled community patients who remain in the community is governed by new Part IVA of the MHA 1983. Part IVA regulates treatment for mental disorder of mentally capable, mentally incapable and child patients who are subject to CTOs and who have not been recalled to hospital. The basic principle is that a patient with capacity (or competence if a child) may only be given treatment in the form of medicine for mental disorder if they consent and there is a certificate authorising the treatment from a SOAD. If the patient is capable and refusing, treatment may only be given without consent by recalling the patient. For the purposes of Part IV capacity means capacity to understand the nature purpose and likely effects of the treatment. Part IVA

---

2   Speech of Kenneth Clarke, *Hansard*, HC Deb, vol 29, ser 6, col 87 (18 October 1982).
3   Inserted by MHA 2007, s 28(6).
4   MHA 1983, s 56(4), as inserted by MHA 2007, s 34.

employs the concept of capacity in ss 2 and 3 of the MCA 2005, and authorises attorneys or deputies to consent to treatment in the community on a community patient's behalf.

The Interface between Parts IV and IVA and the Mental Capacity Act 2005

10.5 Section 28 of the MCA 2005 states that nothing in the MCA authorises anyone to give a patient medical treatment for mental disorder, or to consent to a patient being given medical treatment for mental disorder, if, at the time when it is proposed to treat the patient, his treatment is regulated by Part IV of the Mental Health Act 1983. This means that the power under s 5 of the MCA 2005 to administer treatment in the best interests of an incapacitated patient does not apply in relation to treatment for mental disorder regulated by Part IV. Treatment regulated by Part IV includes treatments under s 57 requiring the consent of a capable patient and a favourable second opinion. By definition a patient who lacks capacity may not be given these treatments, and no-one other than the patient can consent to them, so only s 57 of the MHA 1983 can apply. Treatment may be given under the second opinion procedures in ss 58 and 58A to detained patients without their consent. The effect of s 28 is that only patients already detained under the MHA 1983 who fall within the scope of s 56 (see **10.13** below) may not be given treatment for mental disorder under s 5 of the MCA 2005. Nor may an attorney, deputy or the Court of Protection consent to such treatment on their behalf. Treatment for physical disorder is not regulated by Part IV, and so detained patients who lack capacity may be given treatment for physical ailments under the provisions of the MCA 2005 (see **6.54** above).

10.6 The MHA 2007 has amended s 28 of the MCA 2005 to take account of the new provisions on ECT in s 58A, and the new rules on treatment in the community in Part IVA. New s 28 (1A) of the MCA 2005 states that the exclusion of the MCA does not apply in relation to s 58A treatments if the patient comes within s 58A(7). Section 58A(7) provides that:

> 'This section shall not by itself confer sufficient authority [for an informal patient under 18 to be given ECT] if he is not capable of understanding the nature, purpose and likely effects of the treatment (and cannot therefore consent to it).'

It is necessary to have a SOAD certify that a child patient is capable of consenting to ECT and that it is appropriate for the treatment to be given. If the child is informal and lacks capacity, some other additional authority will be required to give the treatment without consent. Section 5 of the Mental Capacity Act cannot authorise treatment of a person under 16.[5] The Department of Health Code of Practice states that:[6]

---

[5]   MCA 2005, s 2(5).
[6]   Department of Health *Code of Practice: Mental Health Act 1983* (2008), paras 36.58–36.60.

'No child or young person under the age of 18 may be given ECT without the approval of a second opinion appointed doctor (SOAD), unless it is an emergency, even if they consent to it.

There is nothing in the Act itself to prevent a person with parental responsibility consenting to ECT on behalf of a child or young person who lacks the ability to consent for themselves and who is neither detained nor an SCT patient.

However, although there is no case law at present directly on this point, it would not be prudent to rely on such consent, because it is likely to lie outside the parental zone of control. Therefore, if a child under 16 who is not detained or an SCT patient needs ECT, court authorisation should be sought, unless it is an emergency. This should be done before a SOAD is asked to approve the treatment. In practice, the issues the court is likely to address will mirror those that the SOAD is required to consider.'

As for 16 or 17-year-olds who are not detained or on a CTO, and who lack capacity to consent for themselves, the Department of Health Code advises that the approval of a SOAD would be needed and it would not be prudent to rely on parental consent, 'except where the MCA could be used to provide the necessary authority.' The Code advises that MCA can be used for this only where it is not necessary to deprive the young person of liberty.[7] A SOAD certificate will be needed in all these cases, unless it is an emergency covered by s 62(1A). If it is not prudent to rely on parental consent, it may also be questioned whether it is prudent to rely on s 5 of the MCA 2005 to provide authority to treat, especially if the young person who lacks capacity is resisting. The relevance of the patient being deprived of liberty to the authority to provide ECT under s 5 of the MCA is also open to question.

Children and young people who are not detained under the Act but may require ECT are eligible for access to independent mental health advocates.[8]

10.7 Where treatment for mental disorder is given to a community patient under s 64B of Part IVA, new s 28(1B) prohibits treatment from being given under s 5 of the MCA 2005, which does not apply.[9] Section 28 defines where each Act applies in relation to patients who are detained or subject to SCT. It does not give guidance on what to do where a mentally disordered person lacks mental capacity and is not already subject to compulsory powers. Guidance on this issue is found in the Mental Capacity Act Code of Practice.[10]

---

[7]   Ibid, para 36.61.
[8]   Ibid, para 36.62.
[9]   MCA 2005, s 28(1B), as inserted by MHA 2007, s 35(4) and (5).
[10] Ministry of Justice, *Mental Capacity Act 2005 Code of Practice*, chap 13 http://www.dca.gov. uk/legal-policy/mental-capacity/mca-cp.pdf.

HUMAN RIGHTS AND TREATMENT WITHOUT CONSENT

10.8 Approved clinicians in charge of treatment, and SOADs providing second opinions for the purposes of Parts IV and IVA are performing functions of a public nature, and are public authorities for the purposes of the Human Rights Act 1998. They must therefore act compatibly with Convention rights. Treatment without consent potentially engages Arts 3 and 8 of the European Convention on Human Rights. Remedies are available for infringement of these rights under English law. In *R (on the application of Wilkinson) v Responsible Medical Officer Broadmoor Hospital* Hale LJ (as she then was) said that proceedings in respect of forcible treatment of detained patients may be brought by way of an ordinary action in tort, an action under s 7(1) of the Human Rights Act 1998, or by judicial review. ACs, whether proposing treatment for the purposes of ss 57, 58 and 58A, or administering treatment under ss 62 or 63, owe a duty of care to patients.[11]

Article 3

10.9 Article 3 provides that:

'No-one shall be subjected to torture or to inhuman or degrading treatment or punishment.'

This is an absolute right. In *Herczegfalvy v Austria*, the applicant complained of breaches of Arts 3 and 8, in that he had been tied to a bed, given strong anti-psychotic medication and forcibly fed, all without his consent and contrary to his wishes. The European Court held that the position of inferiority and powerlessness typical of patients confined in psychiatric hospitals called for increased vigilance in reviewing compliance with Convention rights, and that the protection of Art 3 extended to 'therapeutic methods to be used, if necessary by force, to preserve the physical and mental health of patients who are entirely incapable of deciding for themselves'. However, the Court admitted that:[12]

'The established principles of medicine are in principle decisive in such cases; as a general rule, a measure which is a therapeutic necessity cannot be regarded as inhuman or degrading. The Court must nevertheless satisfy itself that the medical necessity has been convincingly shown to exist.'

In *R (on the application of Wilkinson) v Responsible Medical Officer Broadmoor Hospital*, Hale LJ concluded from *Herczegfalvy* that:[13]

---

[11]   *R (on the application of Wilkinson) v Responsible Medical Officer Broadmoor Hospital* [2001] EWCA Civ 1545, per Hale LJ at [68].
[12]   (1992) 15 EHRR 437, at para 82.
[13]   [2001] EWCA Civ 1545 at [79].

'forcible measures inflicted upon an incapacitated patient which are *not* a medical necessity may indeed be inhuman or degrading. The same must apply to forcible measures inflicted upon a capacitated patient.'

10.10 For treatment to breach Art 3 its effects must reach a minimum level of severity entailing physical injury or recognised psychiatric injury. In *R (on the application of N) v Dr M and others* the Court of Appeal held that the key questions in determining whether treatment is a 'therapeutic necessity' include:

(a) how certain is it that the person suffers from a treatable mental disorder;

(b) how serious the disorder is;

(c) how serious a risk is presented to others;

(d) how likely is it that, if the patient does suffer from such a disorder, the proposed treatment will alleviate the condition;

(e) how much alleviation there is likely to be;

(f) how likely it is that the treatment will have adverse consequences for the patient; and

(g) how severe may they be.[14]

Article 8

10.11 Article 8 protects the right to respect for private life, which includes the right to physical integrity. This right is not absolute and may be interfered with by the state if justified under Art 8(2). In *Storck v Germany* the European Court held that:[15]

'even a minor interference with the physical integrity of an individual must be regarded as an interference with the right of respect for private life under Article 8, if it is carried out against the individual's will.'

The Court went on to say that states had an obligation to secure to their citizens the right to physical and moral integrity, and this meant a duty to exercise effective supervision and control over treatment in private psychiatric institutions.[16] This positive duty under Art 8 applies equally to supervision and control over state institutions. Retrospective regulation by tort action or criminal prosecution is not enough.[17] Regulation must be directed at Convention compliance, and the issue of whether any treatment without consent has been given in compliance with Art 8(2).

---

[14] *R (on the application of N) v Dr M and others* [2002] EWCA Civ 1789.
[15] (2005) 43 EHRR 96, at para 143.
[16] (2005) 43 EHRR 96, at para 150.
[17] (2005) 43 EHRR 96.

10.12 Article 8(2) allows public authorities to interfere with the rights guaranteed in Art 8(1) if the interference is in accordance with the law and is necessary in a democratic society in the interests of national security, public safety or the economic well-being of the country, for the prevention of disorder or crime, for the protection of health or morals, or for the protection of the rights and freedoms of others. In *Herczegfalvy* the court applied the same test of therapeutic necessity to Art 8 and again concluded that 'according to the psychiatric principles generally accepted at the time, medical necessity justified the treatment in issue', attaching 'decisive weight to the lack of specific information capable of disproving the Government's opinion that the hospital authorities were entitled to regard the applicant's psychiatric illness as rendering him entirely incapable of taking decisions for himself.'[18] Medical interferences with the right of respect for physical integrity must be in accordance with law and *therapeutically necessary* in a democratic society (ie proportionate) for protection of public safety, prevention of disorder and crime, the protection of health or the rights and freedoms of others. In accordance with law under Art 8(2) is not as stringent as in accordance with a procedure prescribed by law under Art 5(1), but there must be effective supervision and review, and to be in accordance with law any powers should be transparent and predictable in their effects.

PART IV

Application

10.13 New s 56 of the MHA 1983 sets out the categories of patient to whom Part IV applies. Section 57 applies to all patients, whether detained, deprived of their liberty under the *Bournewood* safeguards, or informal. Sections 58 and 58A apply to patients who are liable to be detained, with the exception of the following patients, listed in s 56:

(a) admitted under s 4 of the Act, where a second medical recommendation has not been issued to convert to a s 2 detention;

(b) liable to be detained under the AC's (s 5(2)) or the nurse's (s 5(4)) holding power;

(c) remanded to hospital for assessment by a criminal court under s 35 of the MHA 1983;

(d) detained in a place of safety under ss 135 or 136;

(e) detained in a place of safety (ss 37(4) or 45A(4)) pending admission to hospital under a hospital order or a hospital direction; and

---

[18] *Herczegfalvy v Austria (Application 10533/83)* (1992) 15 EHRR 437, at paras 83, 86.

(f)   conditionally discharged restricted patients for whom acceptance of treatment may be a condition of discharge.[19]

A community patient is not subject to the provisions of Part IV of the MHA 1983 (except s 57 which applies to any patient) unless recalled to hospital for treatment under s 17E.[20] The s 58A procedure for ECT applies to patients under 18 whether they are detained or informal.[21]

Medical treatment for mental disorder

10.14   Parts IV and IVA apply to treatment for mental disorder. Treatment without consent for physical disorder is governed by the Mental Capacity Act 2005. Section 145(1) of the 1983 Act provides an inclusive definition of 'medical treatment for mental disorder' which 'includes nursing, psychological intervention and specialist mental health habilation, rehabilitation and care.'[22] These interventions are included, but others not listed, such as medicines or ECT, are not excluded. New s 145(4) states that:[23]

> 'Any reference in this Act to medical treatment, in relation to mental disorder, shall be construed as a reference to medical treatment the purpose of which is to alleviate, or prevent a worsening of, the disorder or one or more of its symptoms or manifestations.'

This provision acknowledges the Court of Appeal decision in *B v Croydon Health Authority*[24] that treatment for mental disorder includes treatment designed to address the symptoms and sequelae as well as the 'core disorder'. Section 145(4) also requires that treatment have the 'purpose', rather than, as before, the likely effect, of alleviating or preventing deterioration in the patient's condition.

10.15   The Explanatory Notes list among practical examples of psychological interventions 'cognitive therapy, behaviour therapy and counselling'. 'Habilitation' and 'rehabilitation' refer to interventions designed to improve or modify patients' physical and mental abilities and social functioning. The distinction between habilitation and rehabilitation depends in practice on the extent of patients' existing abilities – 'rehabilitation' is appropriate only where the patients are relearning skills or abilities they have had before.[25]

---

[19]   As inserted by MHA 2007, s 34.
[20]   MHA 1983 s 56(4), as inserted by MHA 2007, s 34.
[21]   MHA 1983 s 56(5), as inserted by MHA 2007, s 34(2).
[22]   As amended by MHA 2007, s 7(2).
[23]   MHA 1983 s 145(4), as inserted by MHA 2007, s 7(3).
[24]   [1995] 1 All ER 683, CA.
[25]   *MHA 2007 Explanatory Notes*, para 39.

The concept of authority to treat in Part IV

10.16 The Scheme of Part IV is as follows. There must be 'authority to treat' a patient. The most obvious 'authority to treat' is the valid consent of an adult or child patient who has capacity (or competence). For treatments subject to s 57, the authority to treat comes from the patient's consent and the second opinion doctor's certificate that the treatment is appropriate, and the s 57 procedures set the procedural and other conditions required to act on that authority. For informal child patients under 18 who lack capacity to consent to ECT the authority comes from the MCA 2005 if they are between 16 and 18 (see **10.6** above), or from parental or court consent if they are under 16 and lack *Gillick* competence, and the procedures in s 58A set conditions on the exercise of that authority.[26] For detained patients the authority to treat comes from s 63 unless the treatment is covered by the procedures in s 57, 58 or 58A.

It is appropriate for the treatment to be given

10.17 The new test for deciding under ss 57, 58 and 58A whether treatment may lawfully be given is 'that it is appropriate for the treatment to be given.'[27] The test employed under the MHA 1983 was that 'the treatment ought to be given having regard to the likelihood that it will alleviate or prevent deterioration in the patient's condition.' Section 57 treatments may not be carried out unless the patient consents and a SOAD states that it is appropriate for the treatment to be given. Treatment without consent may not be authorised under ss 58 or 58A unless it is appropriate for the treatment to be given. The policy intention appears to be that there will not be much difference in practice between the two tests in relation to treatment without consent. 'Medical treatment for mental disorder' under the MHA 1983 has been held to include not merely treatment directed at the core disorder, but also treatment of the 'symptoms and sequelae' of the disorder.[28] For the purposes of Part IV it is appropriate for treatment to be given to a patient 'if the treatment is appropriate in his case, taking into account the nature and degree of the mental disorder from which he is suffering and all other circumstances of his case'.[29] The English Code of Practice states that:[30]

> 'Medical treatment which aims merely to prevent deterioration is unlikely in general to be appropriate in cases where normal treatment approaches would aim (and be expected to) alleviate the patient's condition significantly. For some patients with persistent mental disorders however, management of the undesirable effects of their disorder may be all that can realistically be hoped for.'

---

26   MHA 1983, s 58(7).
27   MHA 2007, s 12(2).
28   *B v Croydon Health Authority* [1995] 1 All ER 683, CA.
29   MHA 1983 s 64(3), as inserted by MHA 2007, s 6(3).
30   Department of Health *Code of Practice: Mental Health Act 1983* (2008), para 6.15.

10.18 In *R (on the application of PS) v Responsible Medical Officer*[31] Silber J held that Art 3 would only be contravened by the administration of medicine against a patient's will where:

(a) the proposed treatment reached the minimum level of severity for ill-treatment, taking into account all the circumstances, including positive and adverse physical and mental consequences, the nature and context of the treatment, the manner and method if its execution, its duration, and if relevant the age sex and health of the patient; and

(b) medical and therapeutic necessity for the treatment had not been convincingly shown to exist.

In determining whether treatment is appropriate, the AC or SOAD must consider whether it is medically and therapeutically necessary and in the patient's best interests.

Capacity under Part IV

10.19 Capacity is relevant to all the second opinion procedures, but of central importance to ss 57 and 58A. The assessment of a patient's capacity to make a decision about medical treatment is a matter for clinical judgment, guided by current professional practice and subject to legal requirements. It is the personal responsibility of any doctor or other professional proposing to treat a patient to determine whether the patient has capacity to give a valid consent. Any assessment of capacity has to be made in relation to a particular treatment, that capacity in an individual with a mental disorder can be variable over time and should be assessed at the time the treatment is proposed, and all assessments of an individual's capacity should be fully recorded in the patient's medical notes. The explanation of the treatment given by the AC should be appropriate to the level of the patient's assessed ability. Although refusal of ECT by a detained patient with capacity operates as a bar to ECT under s 58A, the same is not true in relation to medicines for mental disorder. With medicines under s 58, a capable patient's refusal is not a bar, but is an important factor to be taken into account in deciding whether the treatment is appropriate, clinically necessary and in the patient's best interests.[32]

10.20 The concept of capacity employed in Part IV remains as it was under the MHA 1983, 'that the patient is capable of understanding the nature, purpose and likely effects of the treatment'. Under ss 2 and 3 of the MCA 2005 a person lacks capacity if unable to make a decision for her/himself because of an impairment of, or disturbance in the functioning of, the mind or brain. A person is unable to make a decision if he or she is unable:

(a) to understand the information relevant to the decision;

---

31 [2003] EWHC 2335 (Admin). See also Mental Health Act Commission *Guidance for RMOs following the PS Case* (available at www.mhac.org.uk).

32 *R (on the application of PS) v Responsible Medical Officer* [2003] EWHC 2335 (Admin).

(b)   to retain the information;

(c)   to weigh the information in the balance as part of the process of arriving at a decision; or

(d)   to communicate the decision either by talking using sign language or any other means.

Section 64K(2) provides that for the purposes of Part IVA references to a patient who lacks capacity are to a patient who lacks capacity within the meaning of the MCA 2005. Part IV uses its own definition of capacity, 'capable of understanding the nature, purpose and likely effects of the treatment'.

Although the concepts of capacity employed in Parts IV and IVA are different in wording, the Department of Health Code of Practice states that where the Act requires healthcare professionals to determine whether a patient has capacity to consent 'the rules for answering these questions are the same as for any other patients'[33], that is, for patients over 16, the test in the Mental Capacity Act ss 2 and 3.

10.21   The Code of Practice on the MHA 1983 advised that to be capable for Part IV purposes an individual must have the ability to:

- understand what medical treatment is and that somebody has said that he needs it and why the treatment is being proposed;

- understand in broad terms[34] the nature of the proposed treatment;

- understand its principal benefits and risks;

- understand what will be the consequences of not receiving the proposed treatment; and

- possess the capacity to make a choice.[35]

10.22   In *R v Mental Health Commission, ex parte X* Stuart Smith LJ noted (obiter) that:[36]

'the words are "capable of understanding", and not "understands". Thus the question is capacity and not actual understanding.'

Despite this literal approach, the advice from the Mental Health Act Commission ('MHAC') now the Care Quality Commission (CQC) to SOADs remains that in assessing validity of consent they should look not just at

---

[33]   Department of Health *Code of Practice: Mental Health Act 1983* (2008), para 23.27.
[34]   *Chatterton v Gerson* [1981] 1 QB 432, (1980) 1 BMLR 80, QBD.
[35]   *Mental Health Act 1983 Code of Practice* (1993), para 15.10.
[36]   (1988) 9 BMLR 77 at 85.

capacity to understand in the abstract, but at actual understanding of the treatment proposal in question. The CQC's approach is correct.[37] In *Re R (a minor)* Lord Donaldson said that capacity entails:[38]

> '[N]ot merely an ability to understand the nature of the proposed treatment – in this case compulsory medication – but a full understanding and appreciation both of the treatment in terms of intended and possible side effects and, equally important, the anticipated consequences of failure to treat.'

It is not necessary 'to understand the precise physiological process involved before he can be said to understand the nature and likely effects'.[39] Although the Mental Health Act threshold of capacity does not expressly include the issue of weighing the information in the balance as part of the process of making a decision, the Code clearly expects that, despite the clear difference in wording, inability to weigh will be taken into account. There are also indications that the courts will expect similar factors to be considered.

10.23 A convergence between the MHA and MCA concepts of capacity seems likely from the statement of Hale LJ (as she then was) in *R (on the application of Wilkinson) v Responsible Medical Officer Broadmoor Hospital*[40] when her Ladyship referred to the common law test of capacity in *Re MB (an adult: medical treatment)* and commented that: 'It would be equally suitable for assessing capacity for the purpose of s 58(3)(b) of the Mental Health Act 1983.'[41] The test in *Re MB* was:[42]

> 'A person lacks capacity if some impairment or disturbance of mental functioning renders the person unable to make a decision whether to consent to or refuse treatment. The inability to make a decision will occur when:
>
> (a)   the patient is unable to comprehend and retain the information which is material to the decision, especially as to the likely consequences of having or not having the treatment in question;
> (b)   the patient is unable to use the information and weigh it in the balance as part of the process of arriving at a decision ...'

10.24 The *Re MB* test forms the basis of the statutory test in ss 2 and 3 of the MCA 2005. If Baroness Hale's approach is followed, the courts will apply similar criteria to assessing capacity under the MHA, despite the differences in wording. In the same judgment Hale LJ recognised that:[43]

---

37   P Fennell 'Sexual Suppressants and the Mental Health Act 1983' [1988] Crim LR 660.
38   [1991] 4 All ER 177 at 187, CA.
39   Ibid, per Stuart Smith LJ.
40   [2001] EWCA Civ 1545, [2002] 1 WLR 419, CA.
41   [2001] EWCA Civ 1545 at [65]–[66].
42   [1997] 2 FLR 426 at 437. This was closely modeled on the test proposed by the report of the investigation headed by Baroness Hale when she was at the Law Commission: *Mental Incapacity*, Law Com No 231 (TSO, 1995), paras 3.2–3.19.
43   [2001] EWCA Civ 1545 at [80].

'Our threshold of capacity is rightly a low one. It is better to keep it that way and allow some non-consensual treatment of those who have capacity than to set such a high threshold for capacity that many would never qualify.'

It is not clear from the context of this statement whether her Ladyship was referring to the MHA test, the common law test, or both. On the face of it the MHA concept of incapacity presents a lower threshold than the MCA test. The issue is only likely to be of great practical significance in relation to s 58A where ECT may not be given in the face of a refusal by a patient who can understand the nature purpose and likely effects of the treatment, the argument being that the MHA standard of capacity applies to the right to refuse ECT rather than the potentially more exacting MCA test which would find someone incapable who cannot weight the information.

10.25　The English Code reminds those assessing capacity that the presence of mental disorder does not mean that the patient lacks capacity to give or refuse consent, that assessment is in relation to the particular decision being made, that capacity of a person with mental disorder may vary over time and should be assessed when the decision needs to be taken, that in a case of fluctuating capacity consideration should be given to delaying the decision until the patient has capacity again, and finally, that all assessments of capacity should be fully recorded in the patient's notes.[44]

10.26　In relation to adults it is for the AC or a SOAD to certify that the patient is capable and consenting to ECT. For children under 18 only a SOAD can certify capacity and consent, and the test for children under 16 is whether the child has sufficient maturity intelligence and understanding to enable them to be capable as set out in *Gillick v West Norfolk and Wisbech Health Authority*[45] (see **11.32–11.34** below).

Refusal of a patient with capacity not a bar to treatment under s 58

10.27　Although refusal of ECT by a capable patient is a bar to treatment under s 58A, under s 58, medication can be given to a refusing patient who is capable of understanding its nature purpose and likely effects, if it is 'appropriate to give it'. The European Committee for the Prevention of Torture and Inhuman or Degrading Treatment ('CPT') exists to police compliance with Art 3 by Council of Europe Member States. The Committee has issued a set of Standards, the CPT standards, which establish the principle that even though a person is detained, they must still be placed in a position to give or withhold consent to treatment:[46]

---

[44]　Department of Health *Code of Practice: Mental Health Act 1983* (2008), para 23.29.

[45]　*Gillick v West Norfolk and Wisbech* Area Health Authority [1986] AC 112.

[46]　The European Committee for the Prevention of Torture and Inhuman or Degrading Treatment *The CPT Standards* Chap Vl, para 41.

'Patients should as a matter of principle be placed in a position to give their free and informed consent to treatment to treatment. The admission of a person to a psychiatric establishment on a involuntary basis should not be construed as authorising treatment without his consent. It follows that every competent patient, whether voluntary or involuntary, should be given the opportunity to refuse treatment or other medical intervention. Any derogation for this fundamental principle should be based upon law and only relate to clearly defined exceptional circumstances.'

To escape criticism by the CPT a Member State has to ensure that treatment without consent is based on law and only relates to strictly defined exceptional circumstances.

10.28 Article 12 of Council of Europe Recommendation (2004) concerning the protection of the human rights and dignity of persons with mental disorder (not ratified by the United Kingdom), provides that treatment of a mentally disordered person must be with consent if the patient is capable, and must be authorised by a representative, authority, person or body provided for by law. Treatment in emergencies may be carried out without such authority only when medically necessary to avoid serious harm to the health of the individual concerned, or to protect the safety of others. It was argued in *R (on the application of B) v Dr SS RMO Broadmoor Hospital, and others*[47] that s 58 was incompatible with Arts 3 and 8 in that it authorised treatment without consent of a capable person and did not define without sufficient precision the circumstances in which treatment may be given without consent. The test under s 58 was that the treatment was likely to alleviate or prevent deterioration. The Court of Appeal held that capacity is not the critical factor in determining whether treatment can lawfully be administered without consent under Arts 3 or 8. It was contended for the applicant that instruments such as the CPT Standards and the Council of Europe Recommendation showed a developing international consensus that the threshold criteria for overriding competent refusal should be that the treatment is necessary to protect other persons from serious harm, or where without such treatment, serious harm is likely to result to the patient's health. This argument was rejected by the court, which refused a declaration of incompatibility.

The Approved Clinician ('AC') or other person in charge of treatment

10.29 Under the MHA 1983 the RMO was responsible for deciding whether the patient had capacity to consent to treatment and was consenting to it, and for setting in motion the second opinion process. Section 12 transfers these powers to the AC, or (in the case of s 57 treatments) 'other person', in charge of the treatment in question. Even if treatment may lawfully be given without consent to a detained or SCT patient, consent should always be sought. The Code of Practice states that:[48]

---

[47] [2005] EWHC 1936 (Admin); [2006] EWCA Civ 28.
[48] Department of Health *Code of Practice: Mental Health Act 1983* (2008), para 24.69

'The fact that the SOAD has authorised a particular treatment does not mean that it will always be appropriate to administer it on any given occasion, or even at all. People administering the treatment (or directing its administration) must still satisfy themselves that it is an appropriate treatment in the circumstances.'

The Explanatory Notes to the MHA 2007 Act state that:[49]

'In the majority of cases the AC in charge of the treatment will be the patient's RC, but where, for example, the RC is not qualified to make decisions about a particular treatment (e.g. medication if the RC is not a doctor or a nurse prescriber) then another appropriately qualified professional will be in charge of that treatment, with the RC continuing to retain overall responsibility for the patient's case.'

Where the person in charge of a particular treatment is not the patient's RC, they should ensure that the RC is kept informed about the treatment and that treatment decisions are discussed with the RC.

10.30 The person in charge of a treatment must be an AC where treatment is given:

(a) under s 58;

(b) under s 58A to a person other than an under 18-year-old who is an informal patient; or

(c) to a patient subject to Part IVA who lacks capacity.

The person in charge of treatment may be an appropriately qualified professional who need not be an AC where the treatment is given:

(a) under s 57;

(b) under s 58A to an informal patient who is under 18 years old; or

(c) under Part IVA to a patient with capacity.

To ensure that there is an independent assessment of whether treatment should be given, s 12 also amends Part IV of the MHA 1983 so that the patient's RC and the person in charge of their treatment are excluded from being the registered medical practitioner to give the second opinion required by ss 57, 58, and 58A (the SOAD).[50] These professionals are also prevented from being one of the persons the SOAD has a statutory duty to consult.[51]

---

[49] *Explanatory Notes to the MHA 2007*, para 57.
[50] MHA 1983, ss 57(2)(a), 58(3)(b) and 58A(5).
[51] MHA 1983, ss 57(3)(b), 58(4) and 58A(6)(b).

10.31 Where the treatment is medicine under s 58, in addition to certifying that the patient is capable and has consented, the AC must give a brief description of the treatment consented to. The Code of Practice requires the AC to indicate on Form T2 (Wales CO2) the drugs prescribed by the classes described in the British National Formulary ('BNF'), the method of their administration, and the dose range, indicating the dosages if they are above the BNF limit.[52] The BNF is not the only prescribing guide available to doctors, but it has played an important part in the second opinion process. Not only do ACs describe the drugs consented to in terms of BNF categories, so too do the SOADs when they authorise treatment without consent. The BNF is published jointly by the British Medical Association and the Royal Pharmaceutical Society and updated biannually. It describes the effects and side effects of each drug, specifying recommended maximum dosage levels, determined on the advice of medical advisers working mainly from the manufacturer's data sheet, and produced after the available information has been considered by the Committee for the Safety of Medicines in the process of deciding to give the drug a product licence. Some of the less sedative anti-psychotics have no BNF recommended maximum. The BNF is intended for the guidance of doctors, pharmacists and others who have the necessary training to interpret the information it provides. Each category (for example 4.2.1 anti-psychotic drugs, or 4.2.2 depot anti-psychotics) includes a large number of different drugs, so this method of describing treatment consented to confers considerable scope for the RMO to change medication within categories, or to give more than one drug within the same category at the same time. The Royal College of Psychiatrists has issued guidance on high dose anti-psychotics.[53]

10.32 The AC is the gatekeeper of the system, since where a patient agrees to treatment the decision about capacity will determine whether there will be a second opinion, and where the patient disagrees a second opinion will only be needed if the AC decides to persist with the treatment. It scarcely upholds the principle of self-determination if an AC accepts the consent of a patient who does not understand the decision being made, or who has not been given information about the treatment's nature, purpose, and effects. Here the Commissioners who visit and interview detained patients in hospital play a potentially important role. If they come across someone who is described as capable and consenting by the AC in charge of treatment, but who is in their view incapable, they may ask the RMO to refer the case for a second opinion. If a second opinion is required because the patient cannot consent or is refusing, it is the personal responsibility of the AC in charge of treatment to ensure that a second opinion visit is requested. Requests for a second opinion are made to the Care Quality Commission ('CQC'), who administer and monitor the system.

---

52   Department of Health *Code of Practice: Mental Health Act 1983* (2008), para 24.17.
53   See http://www.rcpsych.ac.uk/files/pdfversion/CR138.pdf.

SECOND OPINION PROCEDURES

10.33 There are now three categories of second opinion treatment under Part IV:

(1) Section 57 treatments which cannot be given unless a patient certified to be capable has consented and a SOAD has certified that it is appropriate for the treatment to be given (England Form T1, Wales Form CO1);

(2) Section 58A treatments (currently ECT) which may not be given if a capable patient has refused them. ECT, however, may be given subject to a second opinion where the patient lacks capacity, it is appropriate to give the treatment, and giving it does not conflict with a valid and applicable advance decision refusing it, or a refusal by an attorney or a deputy with power to do so; (England Form T6, Wales Form CO6); and

(3) Section 58 treatments where, whether the patient is:

    (a) incapable of consenting; or
    (b) capable and refusing,
    medicines for mental disorder may be given without consent if appropriate (England Form T3, Wales Form CO3).[54]

Section 57

10.34 The 'special treatments', so called because of their potential long-term effects and the ethical issues they raise, require true consent and a second opinion. They are psychosurgery or surgical implants of hormones to reduce male sex drive. The Government's interpretation of how this section works is that the patient's consent provides authority to treat, with s 57 providing additional safeguards (subject to s 62) before the treatment can lawfully be given. The procedure applies to all patients, whatever their legal status. The decision as to the patient's capacity and the existence of valid consent is made by a team of three people, a psychiatrist and two others, appointed by the Care Quality Commission ('CQC'). They must certify that the patient is capable of understanding the nature, purpose and likely effects of the treatment and has consented to it. Even if the patient has given valid consent, the treatment may not proceed unless the medical member of the team certifies that it is appropriate for the treatment to be given.[55] The non-medical members of the appointed panel have no involvement in the second part of the decision.

---

[54] References to forms are to the forms in the Mental Health (Hospital Guardianship and Treatment) (England) Regulations SI 2008/1184, Sch 1 and the Mental Health (Hospital, Guardianship Community Treatment and Consent to Treatment) (Wales) Regulations, SI 2008 2349 (W 212), Sch 1.

[55] MHA 1983, s 57(2)(b). The certificate authorising treatment to proceed in England is Form T1 of Sch 1 to the Mental Health (Hospital, Guardianship and Treatment) (England) Regulations 2008, SI 2008/1184, reg 27(1)(b) and Sch 1. In Wales it is Form CO1 of Sch 1 to the Mental Health (Hospital, Guardianship Community Treatment and Consent to Treatment) (Wales) Regulations 2008, SI 2008 2349 (W 212).

However, before deciding that the treatment is appropriate, the SOAD must consult two other people who have been professionally concerned with the patient's medical treatment, one of whom must be a nurse, and the other neither a nurse nor a doctor. Neither may be the responsible clinician ('RC') or the person in charge of the treatment in question.[56]

Interface with the Mental Capacity Act 2005

10.35   As the Code of Practice on the Mental Capacity Act 2005 emphasises, the combined effect of s 57 of the MHA 1983 and s 28 of the MCA 2005, is:[57]

> 'effectively that a person who lacks capacity to consent to s 57 treatment may not be given it. Healthcare staff cannot use the MCA as an alternative way of giving these kinds of treatment.'

Section 58

10.36   Section 58 applies to medicines for mental disorder, but the patient only becomes eligible for a second opinion if:[58]

> 'three months or more have elapsed from the first occasion in that period [of detention] when medicine was administered to him by any means for his mental disorder.'

Medication does not necessarily have to be administered continuously throughout the three months. This is the so-called 'stabilising period', a result of lobbying by the Royal College of Psychiatrists, during which medicine may be given at the direction of the AC in charge of treatment without consent or a second opinion. The Secretary of State, Kenneth Clarke, described its rationale in these terms:[59]

> 'The danger against which everyone wished to protect patients was the continuing course of heavy drug therapy, which has to be resorted to and can be beneficial in some cases. There are different views about that sort of treatment and it was felt that some safeguards were required. If we start applying safeguards from the moment any drug treatment is embarked upon there will be difficulties. There will be no time to see whether the treatment is working and the patient may object bitterly, because he does not understand that it will do him good.'

The Joint Committee on Human Rights considered that:[60]

---

56   MHA 1983, s 57(3).
57   Ministry of Justice, *Mental Capacity Act 2005 Code of Practice*, para 13.51.
58   MHA 1983, s 58(1)(b).
59   Kenneth Clarke, *Hansard*, HC Deb, vol 29, ser 6, col 86 (18 October 1982).
60   House of Lords, House of Commons Joint Committee on Human Rights *Legislative Scrutiny: Mental Health: Bill Fourth Report of Session 2006–2007* (HL Paper 40, HC Paper 288, 4 February 2007), para 66.

'Three months is a long time to be in receipt of compulsory psychiatric treatment without the opportunity for review and supervision of the responsible clinician's decision to impose that treatment, and we consider it doubtful whether the Government's obligation under Article 8 to provide effective supervision and review of treatment without consent is discharged by such a long waiting time.'

10.37 It should not be assumed that a patient subject to the Act lacks capacity to consent to any or all of their treatment. For detained and SCT patients, the patient's consent should be sought for all proposed treatments, even if they may lawfully be given under the Act without consent. It is the personal responsibility of the person in charge of the treatment to ensure that valid consent has been sought. The interview at which such consent was sought should be properly recorded in the patient's notes.[61] This complies with the principle in the CPT standards that even though a person is detained, they must still be placed in a position to give or withhold consent to treatment.[62] So, even though medicines may be given without consent during the first three months, the Draft Code of Practice advised that the AC in charge of medication should ensure that the patient's valid consent is sought before it is administered. Moreover, refusal or withdrawal of consent should be taken into account when deciding whether to proceed with treatment:[63]

'The patient's consent or refusal should be recorded in the case notes. If such consent is not forthcoming or is withdrawn during this period, the approved clinician in charge of the medication must consider whether to proceed in the absence of consent, to give alternative treatment or no further treatment.'

This provision has not been incorporated into the final version of the Mental Health Act Code, but it is suggested that this practice should be observed in order to ensure compliance with the CPT Standards. Capacity and consent to treatment under s 58 may be certified either by the AC in charge of treatment or a SOAD on Statutory Form T2 (England) CO2 (Wales).[64] The Department of Health Code states that:[65]

'Certificates under this section must clearly set out the specific forms of treatment to which they apply. All the relevant drugs should be listed, including medication to be given "as required" (prn), either by name or, ensuring that the number of drugs authorised in each class is indicated, by the classes described in the British National Formulary (BNF). The maximum dosage and route of administration should be clearly indicated for each drug or category of drugs proposed. This can exceed the dosages listed in the BNF but particular care is required in these cases.'

---

[61] Department of Health *Code of Practice: Mental Health Act 1983* (2008), para 23.37.
[62] The European Committee for the Prevention of Torture and Inhuman or Degrading Treatment *The CPT Standards* Chap VI, para 41.
[63] Department of Health *Mental Health Act 1983 Draft Revised Code of Practice* (2007), para 25.48. See http://www.dh.gov.uk/en/Consultations.
[64] Mental Health (Hospital, Guardianship and Consent to Treatment) Regulations 1983, SI 1983/893, reg 16(2)(b) and Sch 1.
[65] Department of Health *Code of Practice: Mental Health Act 1983* (2008), para 24.17.

Role of the Second Opinion Appointed Doctor ('SOAD') under s 58

10.38 The position of the CQC appointed SOAD is different from that of the AC in charge of treatment. The SOAD does not carry out the treatment or order others to carry it out. As Hale LJ (as she then was) put it in *R (on the application of Wilkinson) v Responsible Medical Officer Broadmoor Hospital*:[66]

> 'the SOAD performs a statutory watchdog function on behalf of the public, to protect detained patients who are in an especially vulnerable position. This is a function which must be subject to judicial review.'

The SOAD's role under the s 58 procedure is to safeguard the patient's rights under Arts 3 and 8, to interview the patient and determine whether he or she is capable of giving valid consent. If the patient is refusing treatment or is not capable of giving consent, the SOAD has to determine whether the proposed treatment is appropriate and should be given. The English Code of Practice reiterates the principle from *R (on the application of Wilkinson) v Responsible Medical Officer Broadmoor Hospital*[67] that the SOAD acts as an individual and must reach his or her own judgment as to whether the proposed treatment is appropriate in the light of the general consensus about treatment for the condition in question. In reaching this judgment the SOAD should consider not only the therapeutic efficacy of the proposed treatment but also, where a patient is objecting to treatment or expressing a preference for an alternative, the reasons for such an objection or preference, which should be given their due weight.[68] This reflects the ruling in *R (on the application of PS) v Responsible Medical Officer*[69] that refusal on the part of a capable patient was not a bar to treatment under s 58 but was a very important factor to be taken into account, in deciding the questions of medical necessity and best interests, which must be addressed by ACs and SOADs in deciding that treatment is appropriate.

10.39 Before making the decision the SOAD must consult two other people who have been professionally concerned with the patient's medical treatment, one of whom must be a nurse, and the other neither a nurse nor a doctor. Neither may be the RC or a doctor. The Department of Health Code suggests that 'People who may be particularly well placed to act as statutory consultees include the patient's care co-ordinator (if they have one) and, where medication is concerned, a mental health pharmacist who has been involved in any recent review of the patient's medication.'[70] The Code advises that issues which the consultees should consider commenting upon include:

- the proposed treatment and the patient's ability to consent to it;

---

66   [2001] EWCA Civ 1545, [2002] 1 WLR 419. See also *R v Mental Health Commission, ex parte X* (1988) 9 BMLR 77, QBD.

67   [2001] EWCA Civ 1545, [2002] 1 WLR 419.

68   Department of Health *Code of Practice: Mental Health Act 1983* (2008), para 24.58.

69   [2003] EWHC 2335 (Admin). See also Mental Health Act Commission *Guidance for RMOs following the PS Case* (available at wwwcqcc.org.uk).

70   Department of Health *Code of Practice: Mental Health Act 1983* (2008), para 24.50.

- their understanding of the past and present views and wishes of the patient;

- other treatment options and the way in which the decision on the treatment proposal was arrived at;

- the patient's progress and the views of the patient's carers; and

- where relevant, the implications of imposing treatment on a patient who does not want it and the reasons why the patient is refusing treatment.

If the SOAD wants to speak to the consultees face to face the hospital managers should arrange this. The consultees should record the consultation with the SOAD in the patient's notes. The SOAD should take into account any previous experience of comparable treatment of a similar episode of disorder. The SOAD certifies that it is appropriate for the treatment to be given on Form T3 (England) or Form CO3 (Wales).[71]

Reasons

10.40 In *R (on the application of Wooder) v Feggetter*, the Court of Appeal held that fairness requires the SOAD to give in writing the reasons for his opinion when certifying under s 58 that a detained patient should be given medication against his will, and that these reasons should be disclosed to the patient unless the SOAD or the RMO considers that such disclosure would be likely to cause serious harm to the physical or mental health of the patient or any other person.[72] Brooke LJ said that the law would not require a SOAD to 'dot every "i" and cross every "t" when giving reasons'. It would suffice if clear reasons are given on the substantive points on which the clinical judgment was made that the treatment is appropriate. Judicial review would only be available if a patient could show a real prospect of establishing that a SOAD has not addressed any substantive point which he should have addressed, or that there is some material error underlying the reasons given.[73] The SOAD must therefore give reasons which address the substantive points upon which the SOAD reached the decision, and the CQC has produced useful guidance for SOADs on the issues to be addressed in a statement of reasons.[74] The reasons must be given as soon as practicable to the RC or the AC in charge of treatment, not direct to the patient, and must state whether the SOAD considers disclosure of those reasons to the patient would be likely to cause serious harm to the physical or mental health of the patient or any other

---

[71] Mental Health (Hospital, Guardianship and Treatment) (England) Regulations 2008, SI 2008/1184, reg 27(1)(b), Sch 1; the Mental Health (Hospital, Guardianship Community Treatment and Consent to Treatment) (Wales) Regulations, SI 2008 2349 (W 212), Sch 1.

[72] [2002] EWCA Civ 554, per Brooke LJ at [34]. Sedley LJ (at para [49]) considered that the duty to give reasons could equally be founded on Art 8 of the ECHR.

[73] Ibid at [34].

[74] Mental Health Act Commission *Guidance to SOADs following the Wooder Case*, paras 9 and 10 (accessible at www.mhac.org.uk).

person. The duty to provide reasons applies equally to treatment without consent under s 58A or under Part IVA.

Interface with the Mental Capacity Act 2005

10.41 If the patient is not capable of consenting but has made a valid and applicable advance refusal of s 58 treatment, this is not binding, but must be taken into account in determining appropriateness of the treatment and whether it is in the patient's best interests. The English Code of Practice states that 'Even where clinicians may lawfully treat a patient compulsorily under the Mental Health Act, they should, where practicable try to comply with the patient's wishes as expressed in an advance decision. They should for example consider whether it is possible to use a form of treatment not refused by the advance decision.'[75] The Code states that a patient's advance statement about what treatment they should be given is relevant as a statement of the patient's wishes and feelings which should be given the same consideration as wishes expressed at any other time.[76] The MCA Code of Practice says that staff should consider whether they could use a different type of treatment which the patient has not refused in advance. If health care staff do not follow an advance decision, they should record in the patient's notes why they have chosen not to follow it.[77] Even if a patient is being treated without their consent for mental disorder under Part IV, an advance decision to refuse other forms of treatment may still be valid.

Section 58A

10.42 New s 58A provides that ECT and any other treatment provided for by regulations made under subs (1)(b), can only be given when the patient either gives consent, or is incapable of giving consent. Section 58A states that, subject to the possibility of emergency treatment under s 62, ECT may not be given unless one of three circumstances applies:

(1)   where the patient is over 18, has consented, and either the AC in charge of treatment or a SOAD certifies that the patient is capable of understanding the nature purpose and likely effects of the treatment;

(2)   where the patient is under 18, has consented, and a SOAD has certified both:

(a)   that the patient is capable of understanding the nature purpose and likely effects and has consented; and
(b)   that it is appropriate for the treatment to be given;

---

[75]   Department of Health *Code of Practice: Mental Health Act 1983* (2008), para 17.8.
[76]   Department of Health *Code of Practice: Mental Health Act 1983* (2008), para 17.13.
[77]   Department of Constitutional Affairs *Mental Capacity Act 2005 Code of Practice*, para 13.37.

(3) where a SOAD has certified that the patient is not capable of understanding the nature purpose and likely effects of ECT but it is appropriate for the treatment to be given, and giving it would not conflict with a valid and applicable advance decision refusing it or a decision by someone holding a lasting power of attorney, a deputy or the Court of Protection.

As with medicines, the AC in charge of treatment certifies that an adult patient is capable and has consented.[78] If the patient is under 18 the certificate of capacity and consent must come from a SOAD, who must go on to certify that it is appropriate for the treatment to be given.[79] ECT may no longer be given without consent to an adult patient with capacity or a competent child patient who is refusing the treatment, unless it is an emergency covered by s 62(1A).

Treatment without consent of patients lacking capacity or competence

10.43 The threshold of capacity assumes great importance under s 58A. If capable a patient is entitled to refuse ECT; if incapable, ECT can be given subject to a second opinion. If a patient understands in broad terms the nature, purpose and likely effects of ECT and is refusing it, thereby passing the MHA 1983 capacity test, will he or she nevertheless be deemed incapable if he or she is so depressed that he or she wants to die and does not care if ECT is thought necessary to save his or her life? Under the common law test s/he might be said to be incapable by virtue of a disorder or disability of the mind or brain of using the information to weigh it in the balance to arrive at a decision. Whichever is the appropriate test, if found incapable, the patient could be given ECT subject to a second opinion under s 58A(5). If a patient is incapable of understanding the nature, purpose and likely effects of ECT, and there is no valid and applicable advance decision refusing it, it may nevertheless be authorised by a SOAD if it is appropriate for ECT to be given. Before issuing the certificate the SOAD must consult with two persons who have been professionally concerned with the patient's medical treatment; one must be a nurse and the other shall be neither a nurse nor a doctor nor the patient's RC or the AC in charge of the treatment.[80]

Emergency treatment under s 62

10.44 Section 62 applies to ensure that a patient, including one who is not consenting, can still receive treatment in the urgent circumstances set out in s 62(1)(a) and (b) if there is insufficient time to apply the 58A procedure. As Jones notes, since ss 57, 58 or 58A do not apply to treatments given under s 62,

---

[78] Mental Health (Hospital, Guardianship and Treatment) (England) Regulations 2008, SI 2008/1184, reg 27(1)(b), Sch 1, Form T4; the Mental Health (Hospital, Guardianship Community Treatment and Consent to Treatment) (Wales) Regulations, SI 2008 2349 (W 212), Sch 1, Form CO4.

[79] Ibid, Form T5 (England), Form CO5 (Wales).

[80] MHA 1983, s 58A(6).

there is no requirement to certify capacity, but it is good practice to record issues relating to capacity and the patient's attitude to treatment in the clinical notes.[81] Whether or not the patient is capable s 62(2) applies to authorise ECT in an emergency where immediately necessary to save life or prevent serious deterioration in the patient's condition.[82] It is difficult to envisage an emergency where the patient immediately needs ECT for one of these reasons yet retains decision-making capacity.

Interface with the Mental Capacity Act 2005

10.45 A certificate may not be given if it would conflict with a valid and applicable advance decision made by the patient when capable, a decision by a health care attorney, by a deputy, or by the Court of Protection. Section 58A protects refusal by valid and applicable advance decisions, proxy decision-makers, and the Court of Protection. The Code makes it clear that before issuing a certificate under s 58A that ECT may be given to a patient who is not capable of consenting, the SOAD must certify that the treatment is appropriate, that there is no valid and applicable advance decision refusing ECT, that there is no refusal from an attorney or a deputy appointed under the MCA 2005 with authority to refuse, and that the treatment would not conflict with a valid order of the Court of Protection that treatment with ECT should not be given to the patient.[83] It is for the SOAD to confirm whether the advance decision is valid and applicable. In order to be valid the patient has to have been capable when the advance decision was made. An advance decision is not valid if the person 'P':[84]

(a) has withdrawn the decision at a time when he had capacity to do so,

(b) has, under a lasting power of attorney created after the advance decision was made, conferred authority on the donee (or, if more than one, any of them) to give or refuse consent to the treatment to which the advance decision relates, or

(c) has done anything else clearly inconsistent with the advance decision remaining his fixed decision.

In order to be applicable the advance decision has to refuse ECT in the circumstances which have now arisen. Section 25(3) of the MCA 2005 provides that an advance decision is not applicable to the treatment in question if at the material time P has capacity to give or refuse consent to it. It is also not applicable if the proposed treatment is not the treatment specified in the advance decision, any circumstances specified in the advance decision are absent, or there are reasonable grounds for believing that circumstances exist which P did not anticipate at the time of the advance decision and which would

---

[81] RM Jones *Mental Health Act Manual* (Sweet and Maxwell, 13th edn, 2010), p 344.
[82] MHA 1983, s 62(2), as amended by MHA 2007, s 28(6).
[83] Department of Health *Code of Practice: Mental Health Act 1983* (2008), para 24.21.
[84] MCA 2005, s 25(2).

have affected his decision had he anticipated them.[85] If ECT is necessary to sustain life, the advance decision must be in writing, and must clearly specify that it is intended to refuse ECT even if given as a life-sustaining treatment.

10.46   Section 58A(7) states that:

> 'this section shall not by itself confer sufficient authority for a patient who falls within s 56(5) above to be given a form of treatment to which this section applies if he is not capable of understanding the nature, purpose and likely effects of the treatment (and cannot therefore consent to it).'

Section 56(5) extends the protection of s 58A to informal child patients who are neither detained nor subject to a CTO. The intention here is that the authority to treat an informal child patient must come from somewhere other than s 58A itself. This means that where a patient is between 16 and 18 and lacks competence, treatment may be given under ss 5 or 6 of the MCA 2005, or the Court of Protection. The Department of Health Code of Practice suggests that ECT could not be given on the basis of parental consent.[86] The MCA provides the authority to treat a patient between 16 and 18, and ss 58A and 62, which are intended to apply additionally, lay down the procedures and criteria for exercising that authority to treat without consent. Similarly, if a patient is under 16 and being treated with parental consent, the parental consent provides the authority to treat, and ss 58A and 62(1A) apply additional safeguards to the exercise of that authority (see **10.6** above).

Consent and withdrawal of consent to a plan of treatment

10.47   Section 59 provides that the patient's consent or a second opinion under ss 57, 58 or 58A may authorise a plan of treatment under which one or more of the forms of treatment mentioned in the relevant section may be given. Section 60 allows a patient to withdraw consent at any time before the completion of the plan of treatment consented to. If this happens, subject to the emergency provisions of s 62, a second opinion will be required before the treatment can be resumed. Section 29 of the 2007 Act introduces new subss (1A)–(1D) into s 60. Subsections (1A) and (1B) apply where the patient has given consent, but before completion of the treatment ceases to be capable of understanding its nature, purpose and likely effects. Subject to the possibility of emergency treatment under s 62, the patient is treated as having withdrawn consent and the relevant second opinion procedure must be undertaken afresh. Subsections (1C) and 1D) apply where a certificate has been given under ss 58 or 58A that the patient is not capable of understanding the nature, purpose and likely effects of the treatment to which the certificate applies, but before the completion of the treatment, the patient becomes capable. In such a case, again subject to the possibility of emergency treatment under s 62, the certificate

---

[85]   Ibid, s 25(4).
[86]   Department of Health *Code of Practice: Mental Health Act 1983* (2008), para 36.14.

ceases to apply to the treatment and the relevant second opinion procedure must be undertaken afresh as if the remainder of the treatment were a separate form of treatment.

Section 61: reports on condition of patients who have had treatment following a second opinion

10.48 A prime concern behind the enactment of s 61 was to ensure that patients were not subject to heavy drug regimes for prolonged periods. Section 61 requires the AC or other person in charge of the treatment to report to the CQC on the treatment and condition of anyone given treatment following a second opinion under ss 57, 58 or 58A or, following recall from SCT, under s 62A in accordance with a Part IVA certificate. A report must be given on subsequent occasion when the authority for the patient's detention or SCT is renewed. If the patient is subject to a restriction order, restriction direction or limitation direction and the treatment is within the first six months following the order or direction, a report must be furnished at the end of that six-month period. If the treatment takes place later than six months from the date of the order or direction the report is due the next time the RC submits a twelve-monthly report to the Secretary of State. A report may also be required at any other time if directed by the CQC.

Section 62: Emergency Treatment

10.49 Section 62 is intended to allow treatment to be given if a second opinion cannot be arranged sufficiently speedily to cope with an emergency, whilst at the same time protecting patients against hazardous or irreversible treatments. The application of s 62 is not limited by any requirement that the patient must lack decision-making capacity. It applies whether or not the patient is capable in the terms of Part IV. It applies to informal patients where ss 57 or 58A is applicable. Treatment which would in normal circumstances require a second opinion may be given in emergencies defined in s 62 without prior compliance with the second opinion procedures. Section 62(1) states that ss 57 and 58 do not apply to any treatment which is:

'(a) immediately necessary to save the patient's life; or
(b) which (not being irreversible) is immediately necessary to prevent a serious deterioration in his condition; or
(c) which (not being irreversible or hazardous) is immediately necessary to alleviate serious suffering by the patient; or
(d) which (not being irreversible or hazardous) is immediately necessary and represents the minimum interference necessary to prevent the patient behaving violently or being a danger to himself or others.'

Section 62(1A) provides that ECT may be given without compliance with s 58A if immediately necessary on grounds (a) or (b) to save life, or, not being irreversible, immediately necessary to prevent serious deterioration in the patient's condition. ECT is not regarded as an irreversible treatment. Section 62 applies whether or not the patient retains capacity. Any treatments made subject to s 58A in the future by regulations under s 58A(1)(b) may be given in an emergency on the full range of grounds specified in (a)–(d) above. Section 62(2) provides that withdrawal of consent by the patient or withdrawal by the CQC of a certificate authorising treatment does not preclude the continuation of any treatment or of treatment under any plan pending compliance with ss 57, 58 or 58A above if the AC in charge of the treatment considers that the discontinuance of the treatment or of treatment under the plan would cause serious suffering to the patient.

10.50 The Department of Health Code of Practice stresses that s 62 treatment must be given by or under the direction of the AC or person in charge of the treatment, who must be an AC if the patient is detained. Treatment must be immediately necessary to achieve one of the objects specified in the section. These are strict tests. The Code emphasises that:[87]

> 'It is not enough that there is an urgent need for treatment, or for the clinicians involved to believe it is necessary or beneficial.'

The CQC consistently maintains that where s 62 is invoked, 'a request should simultaneously be made for a second opinion, so that repeated use does not arise,' having noted a case where no fewer than 12 ECT treatments were given to a patient under s 62.[88] The Code provides that urgent treatment given under s 62 can only continue for as long as it is immediately necessary to achieve the statutory objective, and if it is no longer immediately necessary the normal certificate requirements apply.[89] A treatment is deemed irreversible if it has unfavourable irreversible physical or psychological consequences, and hazardous if it entails 'significant physical hazard'.[90] The person in charge of the treatment, or other appropriately qualified person, is responsible for judging whether treatment falls into either of these categories, and whether therefore the Act allows it to be given, having regard to generally accepted medical opinion. The Code urges hospital managers to monitor the use of s 62 in their hospital, including requiring completion of a form giving details of the treatment, why it is of urgent necessity to give the treatment, the duration of the treatment and the subheading of s 62 under which treatment was given.[91] The National Institute of Clinical Excellence produced a recommended list of medications to achieve 'rapid tranquilisation' which includes Lorazepam, a strong sedative, Haloperidol an old-style antipsychotic, and Olanzapine, a more modern 'a-typical antispychotic' designed to have fewer Parkinsonian side-effects that the old style anti-psychotics.[92]

---

[87] Ibid, para 24.34.
[88] Mental Health Act Commission *First Biennial Report 1983–1985* (HMSO, 1985), p 40; *Second Biennial Report 1985–1987* (HMSO, 1987), p 23.
[89] Department of Health *Code of Practice: Mental Health Act 1983* (2008), para 24.35.
[90] MHA 1983, s 62(3).
[91] Department of Health *Code of Practice: Mental Health Act 1983* (2008), para 24.37.
[92] National Institute for Clinical Excellence *Violence: The Short Term Management of Disturbed/Violent Behaviour in In-Patient Psychiatric Settings* (Clinical Guideline 25, February 2005), pp 47–59.

Section 62A: treatment of CTO Patients on recall or revocation

10.51 Section 62A applies where a community patient is recalled under s 17E, or where the CTO is revoked under s 17F. For the purposes of s 58 the patient is to be treated as if he had remained liable to be detained since the making of the CTO. This means that if there was a certificate covering s 58 treatment before the CTO was made which covers the patient's current treatment, there is no need for a new s 58 certificate on recall. If the period from the time the patient first received medication during that period of detention is less than three months then a new s 58 certificate will not be required until that three-month period has elapsed. On recall to hospital, a patient may be given treatment which would otherwise require a certificate under ss 58 or 58A (medicines or ECT) on the basis of a certificate given by a SOAD under the new Part IVA of the MHA 1983. However, that certificate must specify the treatment as being appropriate to be given on recall, and giving the treatment would not be contrary to any condition in the certificate. If a patient's CTO is revoked, so that the patient is once again detained in hospital for treatment, treatment can be given on the basis of a Part IVA certificate only until a s 58 or s 58A certificate can be arranged. If the Part IVA certificate does not specify any such treatment, then ECT or medicines cannot be given on recall unless or until their administration is permitted under Part IV.

10.52 A Part IVA certificate will not provide authority to give s 58A type treatment to a patient who has capacity or competence to consent but who refuses consent when recalled or when the community treatment order is revoked.[93] A s 58 or s 58A certificate is not required in circumstances where discontinuing the treatment or the plan of treatment at that point would cause serious suffering to the patient.[94] Nor is a certificate required if the treatment is immediately necessary under s 62, or, if the treatment is medicine, the patient is still within the period before which a certificate is required, that is either one month has not elapsed from the time when the CTO was made or the three-month period from when medication was first given to the patient during that period of detention has not elapsed. If a CTO is made before expiry of the three month period during which medicine may be given to a patient detained under s 3 or equivalent, the patient does not require a certificate under Part IVA until expiry of that three month period if that comes later than the expiry of one month following the making of the CTO.

Section 63: general power to treat detained patients without consent

10.53 An important concern behind Part IV was to clarify the powers of staff to treat without consent. Section 63 provides that any medical treatment for mental disorder not specifically identified under ss 57, s 58 or s 58A as requiring a second opinion may be given to a detained patient without consent

---

[93]   See MHA 1983, s 62A(4) and Department of Health *Explanatory Notes to the MHA 2007*, para 128.

[94]   MHA 1983, s 62A(6).

by or under the direction of the AC in charge of treatment. In *R (on the application of B) v Ashworth Hospital Authority* Baroness Hale said that the MHA 1983:[95]

> 'enacted the general power in s 63, defined in s 56 the patients to whom it applied, and provided safeguards for the most controversial treatments specified in or under ss 57 and 58.'

Hence s 63 provides a general power to treat detained patients without consent for mental disorder, s 58 and s 58A provide procedures and safeguards attending the administration of medicines or ECT without consent, and s 62 provides for emergency treatment without a prior second opinion. 'Medical treatment for mental disorder' is defined broadly and extends beyond those treatments which require a second opinion. In Lord Elton's words, spoken in the Lords debate in 1982, s 63 was included 'to put the legal position beyond doubt ... for the sake of the psychiatrists, nurses and other staff who care for these very troubled patients.' When faced with the criticism that this provision might authorise a disturbingly wide range of interventions, Lord Elton emphasised that this provision was not intended to apply to 'borderline' or 'experimental' treatments but:[96]

> 'things which a person in hospital for treatment ought to undergo for his own good and for the good of the running of the hospital and for the good of other patients ... perfectly routine, sensible treatment.'

10.54 Subsequent case-law has made it clear that force-feeding patients suffering from anorexia nervosa or other eating disorders can be treatment for mental disorder covered by s 63. Anorexia nervosa is viewed as a mental illness, and therefore force feeding could be seen as a treatment of that disorder. In *Re KB (adult) (mental patient: medical treatment)*, Ewbank J said that 'relieving symptoms was just as much part of treatment as relieving the underlying cause'.[97] *B v Croydon Health Authority* differed from *Re KB* in that the patient suffered from a borderline personality disorder rather than anorexia, but the Court of Appeal held that s 63 applied to treatment directed at the symptoms or sequelae of mental disorder just as much as to treatment directed to remedying B's underlying personality disorder which caused her compulsion to harm herself by not eating.[98] The self-harm by starvation was a symptom of the underlying disorder. In *R v Collins and Ashworth Hospital Authority, ex parte Brady*[99] the court held that it would be lawful under s 63 to feed forcibly a patient on hunger strike. The pursuit of the hunger strike was held to be a manifestation of his histrionic personality disorder which led him to embark on dramatic conflicts with authority.

---

[95] *R (on the application of B) v Ashworth Hospital Authority* [2005] UKHL 20 at [26].
[96] *Hansard*, HL Deb, vol 426, ser 5, cols 1064–1065 and 1071 (1 February 1982).
[97] *Re KB (adult) (mental patient: medical treatment)* (1994) 19 BMLR 144 at 146.
[98] [1995] 1 All ER 683, CA.
[99] [2000] Lloyd's Rep Med 355.

10.55 In *Tameside and Glossop Acute Services Trust v CH*,[100] s 63 was held to authorise use of reasonable force to secure delivery of a baby by Caesarean section as a treatment for mental disorder, where the mother was detained under s 3. The doctors feared placental failure. Administering a Caesarean was held to be a treatment for mental disorder for the following reasons. CH's schizophrenia could only be treated by tranquillisers rather than anti-psychotic drugs, because the latter would cross the placental barrier and might damage the foetus. It was therefore in the interests of her mental health that her pregnancy be brought to a swift conclusion to enable the new drug regime to start. It was also in CH's interests that the baby be born alive, since if it were not she would blame herself and the doctors and this would exacerbate her schizophrenic illness. This case stretched the concept of treatment for mental disorder to the very limit. *St George's Healthcare NHS Trust v S*[101] represented a step back from the *CH* position. Here the Court of Appeal held that a person who is detained under the Act cannot be forced to undergo medical procedures unconnected with her mental condition unless she is deprived of capacity to decide for herself, in which case the treatment could be authorised under common law now superseded by the MCA 2005. If the treatment is needed to cope with a physical cause or symptom or consequence of the disorder, it can be a treatment for mental disorder.[102]

10.56 Section 63 was not intended to apply to controversial treatments like force-feeding or Caesarean sections, but the Department of Health has resisted extending the second opinion procedures in s 58 by regulation to include force feeding. The Department has been content to leave the position as it is.[103] Forcible feeding is potentially a breach of Arts 3 and 8.[104] The Joint Committee on Human Rights asked the Government whether it considered it necessary to provide more effective supervision and review of decisions to forcibly feed a patient than is currently provided by s 63. The Government response was that:[105]

> 'While s 58 provides an additional safeguard of a SOAD (Second Opinion Approved Doctor) in relation to certain treatments, there is no requirement in the Convention for a second opinion. With respect to the Committee, the key question is whether the provisions of the Act which provide for the forcible feeding of patients without consent, with or without a second opinion, are compatible with the Convention. The Department considers that they are.'

---

[100]   [1996] 1 FLR 762, FD. See also *Norfolk and Norwich Healthcare (NHS) Trust v W* [1996] 2 FLR 613; and *Rochdale Healthcare (NHS) Trust v C* [1997] 1 FCR 274, where force was authorised at common law to administer a Caesarean. These cases are discussed in E Fegan and P Fennell 'Feminist Perspectives on Mental Health Law' in S Sheldon and M Thomson (eds) *Feminist Perspectives on Health Care Law* (Cavendish, 1998), at pp 87–94.

[101]   [1998] 3 All ER 673, CA.

[102]   DoH and Welsh Office *Code of Practice on the Mental Health Act 1983* (TSO, 1998), para 16.5.

[103]   (1995) 145 NLJ 319–320.

[104]   *Nevmerzhitsky v Ukraine (Application 54825/00)* Judgment of 5 April 2005, ECtHR.

[105]   House of Lords, House of Commons Joint Committee on Human Rights *Legislative Scrutiny: Mental Health Bill Fourth Report of Session 2006–2007* (HL Paper 40, HC Paper 288, 4 February 2007), para 80 and App 3, para 67.

It seems anomalous and arbitrary that similar safeguards are not applicable to forcible feeding by naso-gastric tube given its invasiveness by comparison with other treatments covered by second opinion procedures under Part IV.

Seclusion

10.57 Although there have at various points in recent history been calls to ban seclusion, it has retained its place as an accepted psychiatric practice, to the extent that the present day Code of Practice on the Mental Health Act 1983, whilst not regarding it as 'a treatment technique', describes it as falling within the broad legal definition of 'medical treatment', a position confirmed by the Court of Appeal and the House of Lords in *R (on the application of Munjaz) v Mersey Care NHS Trust* where Lord Bingham said that:[106]

> 'medical treatment is in my opinion an expression wide enough to cover nursing and caring for a patient in seclusion, even though seclusion cannot properly form part of a treatment programme.'

The NICE Guidance on the management of violence in psychiatric settings states that:[107]

> 'These interventions are *management strategies* and are *not* regarded as *primary treatment techniques*.'

Although legally these are 'treatments for mental disorder', in reality they are legally sanctioned treatments *of mentally disordered people*. The courts have been willing to accept that treatment designed to prevent harm to others can be in the best interests of the patient.

10.58 The Code of Practice on the Mental Health Act 1983 defines seclusion as:

> 'the supervised confinement of a patient in a room, which may be locked to protect others from significant harm. Its sole aim is to contain severely disturbed behaviour which is likely to cause harm to others.'

The Code further prescribes a number of principles that seclusion should only be used as a last resort and for the shortest period possible, a reflection of principles of both common law (necessity) and of the European Convention case-law (proportionality). The Code states that seclusion should never be used as a punishment or threat, as part of a treatment programme, because of shortage of staff or where there is a risk of suicide or self-harm.[108]

10.59 *R (on the application of Munjaz) v Mersey Care NHS Trust* was a challenge to Ashworth's seclusion policy, which provided for one daily medical

---

[106] [2003] EWCA Civ 1036; [2005] UKHL 58 at [20].
[107] Emphasis added.
[108] Department of Health *Code of Practice: Mental Health Act 1983* (2008), para 15.43 et seq.

review after the third day, in contrast to the Code of Practice recommendation of four-hourly review by a doctor. Furthermore, the Ashworth policy did not meet the requirement of the Code that a patient should have a review after two hours, and that one of the nurses reviewing the seclusion must not have been involved in the original decision to seclude. The 'independent' nurse requirement under the Code applies 'where practicable'. The House of Lords by a majority held that the Code was not mandatory and could be departed from if there was a cogent reason for doing so. Lord Hope considered that Ashworth's status as a high security special hospital justified the departure from the Code:[109]

> 'If good reasons are required for departing from the system that the Code sets out for the monitoring and review of the use of seclusion, there are ample grounds for thinking that they have been well demonstrated at Ashworth. There is no doubt that the situation there differs from that in the generality of institutions in which mental patients who are severely disturbed may find themselves. As the introduction to Ashworth's Policy states, special considerations need to be applied to the use of seclusion in a high security hospital, bearing in mind that the very reason why patients are there is because they cannot be dealt with by mental health services elsewhere in a way that will protect others from harm. The Code does not address this problem. Nor is it designed to do so.'

Lord Bingham in *Munjaz* accepted that improper use of seclusion might breach the right of respect for private life under Art 8, but refused to accept that there would be any breach if it were 'properly used', 'as the only means of protecting others from violence or intimidation and it is used for the shortest time possible':[110]

> 'A detained patient, when in his right mind or during lucid intervals, would not wish to be free to act in such a way and would appreciate that his best interests were served by his being prevented from doing so.'

On the assumption that Art 8 might be engaged, Lord Bingham then considered seclusion could be necessary to meet one of the legitimate grounds for interference in Art 8(2), whether it would be a proportionate response, and whether it would be in accordance with law:[111]

> 'Seclusion under the policy is plainly necessary for the protection of health or morals, or for the protection of the rights and freedoms of others, properly used the seclusion will not be disproportionate because it will match the necessity giving rise to it. The procedure adopted by the Trust does not permit arbitrary or random decision-making. The rules are accessible, foreseeable and predictable. It cannot be said ... that they are not in accordance with or prescribed by law.'

The majority in the House of Lords accepted that Ashworth had considered the issues carefully before adopting its own seclusion policy which was at

---

[109] [2005] UKHL 58 at [70].
[110] [2005] UKHL 58 at [32].
[111] [2005] UKHL 58 at [33]–[34].

variance with the Code, that the Code could be departed from if there was a cogent reason to do so, and that Ashworth's policy complied with Arts 3 and 8.[112]

PART IVA: AUTHORITY TO TREAT IN THE COMMUNITY

10.60   New Part IVA (ss 64A–64K) regulates the giving of 'relevant treatment' (ie treatments not governed by s 57) of community patients whilst they are in the community, in other words 'when they are not recalled to hospital'.[113] Treatment of community patients recalled to hospital is governed by s 62A (see **10.51** and **10.52** above). The basic principle is that a patient with capacity (or competence if a child) may only be given treatment in the form of medicine for mental disorder or ECT if they consent and there is a certificate authorising the treatment from a SOAD. If the patient is capable and refusing treatment may only be given without consent by recalling the patient and treating under s 62A. Sections 64A–64K authorise 'relevant treatment' to be given to a community patient who has not been recalled to hospital. Sections 64A–64K set out the circumstances in which treatment for mental disorder (other than treatments covered by s 57) may be given to an adult or child community patient in the community (not necessarily in a hospital or clinic). They apply parts of the decision-making framework of the MCA 2005 to treatment under the MHA 1983 and authorise treatment in the community without the consent of an incapable patient:

(a)   if there is consent from someone authorised under the MCA 2005 to make decisions on the patient's behalf;

(b)   if the patient lacks capacity and force is not necessary to secure compliance; or

(c)   if emergency treatment needs to be given, using force if necessary, to a patient who lacks capacity.

Relevant treatment

10.61   Relevant treatment for the purposes of Part IVA is any treatment for mental disorder which is not covered by s 57 (ie is not psychosurgery or surgical hormone implants to reduce male sex drive).[114] In practice 'relevant treatment' will probably be most frequently applied to the administration of medicines for mental disorder, although ECT can be a relevant treatment too. Relevant treatment may be given by or under the direction of the responsible clinician to an adult patient (ie one over 16) under s 64B, or to a child under

---

[112]   In *Ramirez Sanchez v France (App no 59450/00)* Judgment of the European Court of Human Rights of 27 January 2005, the Court held that in certain cases prisoners were entitled to a remedy to enable applicant to contest decision to place in solitary confinement.

[113]   *Explanatory Notes to the MHA 2007*, para 129.

[114]   MHA 1983, s 64A, introduced by MHA 2007, s 35.

s 64E. There must be authority to give the treatment. In addition, for s 58 or s 58A type treatments, unless one of the exceptions applies, the 'certificate requirement' must be met. Treatment is a s 58 or s 58A type treatment if ss 58 or 58A would have applied to it if the patient had remained liable to be detained instead of being on a CTO.[115]

Authority to treat under Part IVA

10.62   Before treatment may be given under Part IVA there must be 'authority to treat'. There is authority to give treatment to a patient over 16 if:

(a)   the patient has capacity and consents to it being given; or

(b)   a donee of a lasting power of attorney, or a deputy appointed by the Court of Protection, or the Court of Protection itself, consents to it on his behalf; or

(c)   Section 64D (treatment for adult patients lacking capacity) or s 64G (emergency treatment for patients lacking capacity) applies.[116]

For a child under 16 there is authority to treat if:

(a)   the patient is competent and consents to it being given; or

(b)   it is authorised by s 64F (treatment for child patients lacking competence); or

(c)   the treatment is emergency treatment under s 64G.[117]

No one can consent or refuse on the patient's behalf if they are under 16, since they are ineligible to appoint an attorney and there is no jurisdiction to appoint a deputy for them. The test of capacity for both adult and child patients is that set out in ss 2 and 3 of the MCA 2005, not the test used in relation to Part IV (see **10.19–10.23** above). Treatment of child community patients under Part IVA is dealt with in chapter 11 below at **11.56–11.64**.

The certificate requirement

10.63   The certificate requirement must be met if the treatment is medicines for mental disorder or ECT, unless one of the exceptions applies. The certificate requirement is met where a SOAD under Part IVA of the MHA 1983 has certified that it is appropriate for the medicines to be given subject to such conditions as may be specified in the certificate. The conditions in the certificate must be satisfied before the certificate requirement can be met in

---

[115]   MHA 1983, s 64C(3).
[116]   MHA 1983, s 64C(2).
[117]   MHA 1983, s 64E.

respect of a treatment.[118] The certificate may relate to a plan of treatment where a patient is to be given one or more treatments covered by s 58. The Explanatory Notes state that:[119]

'For medication, a certificate is not required immediately, but must be in place within one month from when a patient leaves hospital under a CTO, or three months from when the medication was first given to the patient during that period of detention (whether that medication was given in the community or in hospital), whichever is later.'

The SOAD must certify in writing that it is appropriate for the treatment to be given. On the certificate the SOAD may specify that certain treatment can be given to the patient only if certain conditions are satisfied. The Explanatory Notes give the example that:[120]

'[T]he SOAD could specify that a particular antipsychotic and dosage can only be given in the community if the patient retains capacity to consent to it. The SOAD can also specify whether and if so what treatments can be given to the patient on recall to hospital and the circumstances in which the treatment can be given. For example, the SOAD can specify, if appropriate, that an antipsychotic can be given to the patient on recall without the patient's consent.'

If the certificate specifies conditions the treatment may only be given in accordance with those conditions.

10.64 The exceptions where the certificate requirement need not be met are as follows:

(a) it need not be met until the expiry of one month from the date the community treatment order was made or three months from the day when medicine was first given during the period of detention immediately preceding the CTO;[121] or

(b) if the treatment is emergency treatment given under s 64G (see **10.68** below); or

(c) if treatment is immediately necessary and the patient is capable (or if a child under 16 is 'competent') and consents to it; or

(d) if treatment is immediately necessary and a donee of a lasting power of attorney or a deputy appointed by the Court of Protection has consented to it.[122]

---

[118] MHA 1983, s 64C(4).
[119] *Explanatory Notes to the MHA 2007*, para 133.
[120] Ibid, para 134.
[121] MHA 1983, s 64B(4).
[122] MHA 1983, s 64B(3).

10.65 The full s 62 criteria apply in determining whether s 58 treatment (medicine for mental disorder) is 'immediately necessary':

(a)   to save the patient's life; or

(b)   to prevent a serious deterioration in the patient's condition and is not irreversible; or

(c)   to prevent serious suffering by the patient and is not irreversible or hazardous; or

(d)   to prevent the patient from behaving violently or being a danger to himself or others, as long as the treatment is the minimum interference necessary, and is neither irreversible nor hazardous.[123]

Irreversible means having unfavourable irreversible physical or psychological consequences, and hazardous means entailing significant physical hazard.[124] If the treatment is ECT it is 'immediately necessary' if it falls within (a) or (b) above; if it is any s 58A treatment by virtue of regulations under s 58A(1)(b) criteria (a)–(d) apply in determining whether it is immediately necessary.[125]

Treatment without force of adult patients who lack capacity

10.66   Section 64D authorises the approved clinician in charge of the patient's treatment to give or direct the giving of relevant treatment, subject to the following conditions. First, the AC must follow the steps outlined in s 5(1)(a) and (b)(i) of the MCA 2005, namely:

(a)   take reasonable steps to establish whether the patient lacks capacity to consent to the treatment; and

(b)   when giving the treatment, must reasonably believe that the patient lacks capacity to consent to it.

Second, giving the treatment must not conflict with a valid and applicable advance decision,[126] or a decision of an attorney or deputy or the Court of Protection. Third, the AC must either have no reason to believe that the patient objects to the treatment being given, or if he does have reason to believe that the patient objects, it must not be necessary to use force in order to give the treatment. Section 64J states that in deciding whether there is reason to believe that a patient objects, the relevant person must consider all the circumstances so far as they are reasonably ascertainable. This includes the patient's behaviour, wishes, feelings, views beliefs and values. Circumstances from the past are to be considered only so far as it is still appropriate to consider them.

---

[123]   MHA 1983, s 64C(5).
[124]   MHA 1983, s 62(3).
[125]   MHA 1983, s 64C(6).
[126]   MCA 2005, s 25.

Paragraph 1 of the Explanatory Notes note that force cannot be used under s 64D to administer treatment if the patient objects to that treatment, but state that:[127]

> 'If the patient does not object to treatment, force is permitted and that may be in cases where, for example, the patient is suffering from tremor and physical force is needed as a practical measure to administer the treatment.'

10.67 Adult patients have greater protection than children since it is a condition under s 64D that treatment must not conflict with an advance decision which the person giving the treatment is satisfied is valid and applicable. Equally, for adults, but not for children treatment may not be given if it conflicts with a decision of a donee, a deputy or of the Court of Protection. It is important to remember that the conditions of using s 64D only prohibit the use of force, undefined, whereas s 6 of the MCA 2005 prohibits restraint, which includes the use or threat of physical force, unless the restraint is a proportionate response to the likelihood of the person suffering harm and the seriousness of the harm. So a situation might arise where a patient objects to the treatment, and is told that if he or she does not agree to have it, he or she may be recalled to hospital. No force is used within the meaning of Part IVA to secure compliance, but the threat of forcible recall would amount to restraint under s 6 of the MCA 2005.

Emergency treatment, using force if necessary, of adult and child patients

10.68 Force may only be used to give treatment to patients who lack capacity or to children who lack competence against their objections if the emergency conditions in s 64G are met. Section 64G authorises emergency treatment of patients over 16 who are reasonably believed to lack capacity, or children under 16 reasonably believed to lack competence to consent. Treatment is emergency treatment where it is immediately necessary:

(a) to save the patient's life; or

(b) to prevent a serious deterioration in the patient's condition and is not irreversible; or

(c) to prevent serious suffering by the patient and is not irreversible or hazardous; or

(d) to prevent the patient from behaving violently or being a danger to himself or others, as long as the treatment is the minimum interference necessary, and is neither irreversible nor hazardous.[128]

---

[127] *Explanatory Notes to the MHA 2007*, para 130.
[128] MHA 1983, s 64C(5).

If the treatment is ECT it may only be given under paras (a) or (b) above, not paras (c) or (d). Irreversible means having unfavourable irreversible physical or psychological consequences, and hazardous means entailing significant physical hazard.[129] Section 64G authorises force to be used, but only where emergency treatment needs to be given to prevent harm to the patient and the use of force is proportionate to the likelihood of the patient's suffering harm and to the seriousness of that harm. It is possible that force could be used to prevent harm to others if harm to the patient could also thereby be prevented. For example if a patient is stopped from verbally abusing others or assaulting them, he or she will not suffer harm from retaliation.

CONCLUSION

10.69 There are two parallel regimes authorising treatment without consent, under the MCA 2005 where the patient lacks capacity and the treatment is necessary in the patient's best interests, or under Parts IV or IVA of the MHA 1983. Following the MHA 2007 there are now four second opinion procedures under the MHA 1983 – under ss 57, 58, 58A and 64C. Part IV employs the MHA concept of capacity. Part IVA employs the MCA concept of capacity, but whilst the MCA places limits on the use of 'restraint' (the use or threat of force) under s 6, Part IVA places limits only on the use of force. Each must operate within the requirements of Arts 3 and 8 of the Convention. A particular issue is the interface between the two statutes. Section 28 only prohibits the use of the MCA decision-making framework where the patient is already subject to Parts IV or IVA. It does not answer the question whether s 58 or s 58A type treatment for mental disorder may be given under the MCA if the patient is not already subject to the MHA regimes for treatment without consent.

10.70 What would the position be of an informal adult patient who lacks capacity and is deemed to require ECT or anti-psychotic medication? Richard Jones argues that the '1983 Act should be invoked in respect of a mentally incapacitated person who needs to be hospitalised for treatment for mental disorder in two circumstances' (assuming the criteria for compulsion are met):

(a)   where there is a deprivation of liberty; and

(b)   where it is considered that the provisions of a valid and applicable advance decision refusing a particular treatment for the patient's mental disorder should be overridden.[130]

It has been argued elsewhere in this work that:[131]

---

[129]   MHA 1983, s 62(3).
[130]   RM Jones *Mental Capacity Act Manual* (Sweet and Maxwell, 2nd edn, 2007), p 96.
[131]   P Fennell 'The Mental Capacity Act 2005, the Mental Health Act 1983 and the Common Law' (2005) *Journal of Mental Health Law* 167.

'if a person lacks capacity and the decision-maker is assuming complete control over treatment to the extent that they are making decisions about the administration of strong psychotropic medication or even ECT to a patient, then that is assuming complete control over treatment and would be a factor tipping the balance firmly towards there being a deprivation of liberty requiring use of the MHA 1983.'

Jones disagrees, contending that:[132]

'As the provision of any medical treatment to a mentally incapacitated patient involves a clinician assuming complete control over that patient's treatment ... the provision of treatments mentioned by Fennell in the absence of other factors confirming that professionals treating and managing the patient exercised complete and effective control over his movements would not lead to a finding that there has been a deprivation of liberty ... a whole range of factors must be taken into account.'

10.71 Peter Bartlett agrees with Richard Jones that ECT can be given to an informal patient lacking capacity 'provided that procedures in the MCA 2005 are followed', although this view was expressed before the passage of s 58A.[133] The MCA 2005, ss 5 and 6 do not provide procedures, they provide a defence to proceedings for battery if certain steps have been taken. If ECT is a treatment which can be given under the MCA 2005, it is likely to be deemed a 'serious treatment' for the purposes of s 37 of the MCA 2005. If there is nobody other than a paid carer to consult in determining what would be in P's best interests, there would be a requirement on the relevant NHS body to appoint and consult an Independent Mental Capacity Advocate ('IMCA') and the submissions made by the IMCA must be taken into account in deciding whether to provide the treatment. Section 37 does not apply to any treatment regulated by Part IV of the Mental Health Act. Treatment is only regulated by Part IV if the patient is detained or liable to be detained.

10.72 It is important to bear in mind the statement of the scope of the positive obligation under Art 8, as outlined in *Storck v Germany*:[134]

'The Court ... considers that on account of its obligation to secure to its citizens the right to physical and moral integrity, *the state remained under a duty to exercise supervision and control over private psychiatric institutions.* [emphasis added – The court noted that in the sphere of interferences with a person's physical integrity, German law provided for strong penal sanctions and for liability in tort and went on to say that]. Just as in cases of deprivation of liberty, the Court finds that such retrospective measures alone are not sufficient to provide appropriate protection of the physical integrity of individuals in such a vulnerable position as the applicant. The above findings as to the lack of effective state control over private psychiatric institutions at the relevant time are equally applicable as far as the protection of individuals against infringements of their personal integrity is concerned. The Court therefore concludes that the respondent state failed to

[132] RM Jones *Mental Capacity Act Manual* (Sweet and Maxwell, 2nd edn, 2007), p 99.
[133] P Bartlett *Blackstones Guide to the Mental Capacity Act 2005* (OUP, 2005), para 3.43.
[134] *Storck v Germany* (2005) 43 EHRR 96, at para 150.

comply with its positive obligation to protect the applicant against interferences with her private life as guaranteed by Article 8(1).'

Section 58A provides safeguards in relation to ECT without consent to incapacitated detained patients, and to informal patients who are under 18. In the case of informal child patients the treatment is authorised under parental authority or the MCA, but the s 58A safeguards apply as well. Informal patients who are children will have superior safeguards in relation to ECT compared with their counterparts who are over 18. This may be argued to be a discrimination on grounds of age in the protection of Art 8 rights to physical integrity, contrary to Art 14 of the Convention. It may well also be that, despite the views of Jones, Bartlett and others, to administer a course of ECT without consent to an informal patient who lacks capacity lifts the level of control over treatment and movement above the threshold for deprivation of liberty.

Chapter 11

CHILDREN[1]

OVERVIEW

11.1 A 'child' is anyone under 18 years old.[2] There is no age limit to the powers of detention or supervised community treatment under the Mental Health Act, although guardianship may not be used where the patient is under 16.[3] Children may be admitted to a psychiatric institution in one of three ways:

(a) informally with their own consent;

(b) informally with the consent of a parent or someone with parental responsibility;

(c) under the compulsory powers in Part II or Part III of the 1983 Act.
   In addition to these routes of admission to psychiatric hospital a child may also be detained in secure accommodation under s 25 of the Children Act 1989.

Patients detained under the Mental Health Act 1983 have the same rights to review of detention by Mental Health Tribunals ('MHTs') as their adult counterparts (see chapter 9).

11.2 Treatment of a child patient who is detained under the MHA 1983 is governed by Part IV of the MHA 1983. Treatment of child community patients who remain in the community is governed by Part IVA. Authority to treat an informal capable child patient is based on the consent of the child her or himself. Authority to treat an informal patient admitted on parental consent who lacks capacity in relation to the treatment decision is based either on the MCA 2005 if the child is 16 or 17, or on parental consent if the patient is under 16. Guidance on the care and treatment of children under the Mental Health Act 1983, the Children Act 1989 and the Mental Capacity Act 2005 is found in the Mental Health Act Codes of Practice for England and Wales,[4] and the

---

[1]   The revisions of this chapter in the second edition owe a considerable debt to my discussions of this subject with Camilla Parker, to whom my sincere thanks.

[2]   Children Act 1989, s 105(1).

[3]   MHA 1983, s 7(1).

[4]   Department of Health *Code of Practice: Mental Health Act 1983* (2008), Chapter 36, see http://www.dh.gov.uk/prod_consum_dh/groups/dh_digitalassets/@dh/@en/documents/digitalasset/dh_0870 Welsh Assembly Government, Mental Health Act 1983 Code of Practice for Wales (2008),

Code of Practice on the Mental Capacity Act 2005.[5] The Department of
Health and the National Institute for Mental Health in England (NIMHE)
have also published an extremely useful guide for professionals entitled *The
Legal Aspects of the Care and Treatment of Children and Young People with
Mental Disorder*.[6]

11.3 Section 2(5) of the MCA 2005 provides that no power which a person
may possess in relation to a person who lacks capacity or is reasonably believed
to lack capacity is exercisable in relation to a person under 16. This means that
the power to carry out acts of care or treatment and to restrain people who lack
capacity under ss 5 and 6 of the MCA 2005 is not available in relation to under
16-year-olds. Acts of care and treatment and restraint would be carried out
under common law or under the Children Act 1989 if relevant. Neither the
power to make an advance decision refusing treatment, nor to grant a lasting
power of attorney in relation to care and treatment or property and affairs is
exercisable by a person under the age of 18. The MCA provisions for
deprivation of liberty (see **6.45–6.103** above) do not apply to people under 18.
If a 16 or 17-year-old child who lacks capacity requires admission to a
psychiatric hospital, as long as the circumstances do not amount to a
deprivation of liberty, ss 5 and 6 of the MCA 2005 may be used.

Mental health services for children

11.4 Best Practice Guidance issued by the DfES and DoH states that:[7]

> 'All children and young people, from birth to their eighteenth birthday, who have
> mental health problems and disorders, should have access to timely, integrated,
> high quality, multi-disciplinary mental health services to ensure effective
> assessment, treatment and support, for them and their families.'

Specialist Child and Adolescent Mental Health Services ('CAMHS') are
designed to treat children and young people suffering from mental disorder.
The Code of Practice emphasises that 'Where possible, those responsible for
the care and treatment of children and young people should be child specialists.
Where this is not possible, it is good practice for the clinical staff to have
regular access to and make use of a CAMHS specialist for advice and
consultation.'[8]

Chapter 33, see
http://www.wales.nhs.uk/sites3/Documents/816/Mental%20Health%20Act%201983%20Code%
20of%20Practice%20for%20Wales.pdf.

[5]   Ministry of Justice, *Mental Capacity Act 2005 Code of Practice*, chap 12 http://www.dca.gov.
      uk/legal-policy/mental-capacity/mca-cp.pdf.

[6]   NIHME/Department of Health *The Legal Aspects of the Care and Treatment of Children and
      Young People with Mental Disorder: A Guide for Professionals* (January 2009).

[7]   Department for Education and Department of Health *The Mental Health and Psychological
      Well-being of Children and Young People* (October 2004, Standard 9).

[8]   Department of Health *Code of Practice: Mental Health Act 1983* (2008), para para 36.75.

The Mental Health Act 2007

11.5 Section 31 of the MHA 2007 has amended the MHA 1983 to introduce new duties in relation to providing suitable accommodation for children, and to amend the existing rules about informal admission of 16 and 17-year-olds to make clear that those with parental responsibility cannot admit the patient informally by parental consent. New s 58A provides additional safeguards in relation to Electro Convulsive Therapy ('ECT') given to children (discussed in full above at **10.42–10.46** and **10.69–10.72**), and new ss 64E, 64F and 64G set out the rules for treating child patients in the community.

Human rights

11.6 The UK Government has ratified the UN Convention on the Rights of the Child 1989 ('CRC'), thereby undertaking to respect, protect and promote the rights in the Convention. Article 3 of the CRC states that the best interests of the child shall be the primary consideration in all actions concerning children. Article 12 of the CRC requires states parties to:

> 'assure to the child who is capable of forming his or her own views the right to express those views freely in all matters affecting the child, the views of the child being given due weight in accordance with the age and maturity of the child.'

In *R (on the application of Williamson) v Secretary of State for Education and Employment* Baroness Hale of Richmond said that:[9]

> 'the State is entitled to give children the protection they are given by an international instrument to which the United Kingdom is a party, the United Nations Convention on the Rights of a Child.'

11.7 Article 19 of the CRC entitles children to protection from all forms of physical or mental violence, injury or abuse, neglect or negligent treatment, maltreatment or exploitation including sexual abuse. The Art 19 right under the CRC reflects the positive obligation on states under Art 3 of the European Convention on Human Rights to protect all citizens against torture or inhuman or degrading treatment. Article 37(c) of the Convention on the Rights of the Child states that 'every child deprived of his liberty shall be separated from adults unless it is considered in the child's best interests not to do so'. This provision potentially offers wider protection than the duty under new s 131A of the MHA 1983.

11.8 In *Nielsen v Denmark* the European Court of Human Rights considered the lawfulness of admitting a twelve-and-a-half-year-old for over five months by a decision of his mother who was the sole holder of parental rights. Because he was admitted in this way he had no rights to challenge his detention and claimed breach of Art 5(1) and (4) of the European Convention on Human Rights ('ECHR'). The court held that his admission did not amount to a

---

[9]   [2005] UKHL 15 at [80].

deprivation of liberty within Art 5, but was a responsible exercise by the mother of her custodial rights in the interests of the child.[10] Those rights include 'a broad range of parental rights and responsibilities in regard to the care and custody of minor children' and were incorporated in the right to respect for family life in Art 8. The court accepted however that parental rights could not be unlimited and it was incumbent on states to provide safeguards against abuse.

11.9 Article 12 of the Convention on the Rights of the Child requires consideration of children's views in deciding issues affecting them, 'taking into account the age and maturity of the child'. This, coupled with the European Court's 2005 ruling in *Storck v Germany*[11] that there had been breaches of Arts 5 and 8 of the ECHR, suggests that the scope of parental authority is narrower today than it was in *Nielsen*, and is certainly not sufficient to oust the protection of the child's right to liberty under Art 5 and to physical integrity under Art 8. Ms Storck was 15-year-old (almost three years older than Nielsen) when she was admitted at the behest of her father and against her wishes to a private clinic in Germany, where she was detained and forcibly treated. The Court held that States have a positive obligation under Arts 5 and 8 to ensure that there is effective supervision and review of decisions to detain or to treat without consent. In this case parental responsibility and rights comprised in the right to respect for family life under Art 8 did not operate to exclude the protection of the child's right to liberty and physical integrity under Arts 5 and 8. The Court held that states are under an obligation to provide effective supervision and review of deprivations of liberty and interferences with the physical integrity of a young person.

THE CHILD'S RIGHT TO SUITABLE ACCOMMODATION AND CARE

11.10 There was considerable debate during the passage of the MHA 2007 about the practice of placing children on adult psychiatric wards, and the risks of abuse to which they may thereby be exposed, highlighted in the Children's Commissioner's report *Pushed into the Shadows: Young People's Experience of Adult Mental Health Facilities*. This provided evidence from young people's experiences that their health or safety may be seriously compromised by such placements.[12] The Parliamentary Joint Committee on Human Rights considered that the positive obligation under Art 3 was potentially engaged by a placement on an adult ward, if a child is not effectively protected from abuse. The Committee recommended adoption of an amendment to ensure that

---

[10]   (1988) 11 EHRR 175, at paras 61, 72, 73.
[11]   (2005) 43 EHRR 96, ECtHR.
[12]   The Children's Commissioner for England (January 2007).

young people receive age appropriate assessment and placement, but avoids rendering illegal the placement of a child on an adult ward when this is the only way that their needs can be met.[13]

11.11 The Government accepted amendments designed to promote the care of children in age appropriate environments. Section 31 of the MHA 2007:

(a) introduces a new s 131A to the MHA 1983, placing a limited duty on hospital managers to ensure that the hospital environment of a child patient is 'suitable having regard to his age (subject to his needs)';

(b) inserts new subss (1A) and (1B) into s 39 of the MHA 1983 to empower a sentencing court to request information about the availability of accommodation designed to be specially suitable for child patients; and

(c) amends s 140 of the MHA 1983 to require relevant health bodies to notify local social services authorities within their area of their arrangements for providing accommodation or facilities designed to be specially suitable for child patients.

These stand alongside the duties to visit and exercise parental responsibility where a child in care is admitted to hospital under s 116 of the MHA 1983, and the duty under ss 85 and 86 of the Children Act 1989 of health bodies and managers of private institutions where a child is accommodated for more than three months to notify the appropriate social services.

The section 131A duty to provide an age suitable environment

11.12 Section 131A came into force in England and Wales in April 2010.[14] It applies to detained and informal child patients, and requires the managers of a NHS or private hospital to ensure that the patient's environment in the hospital is suitable having regard to his age (subject to his needs). The duty is not absolute, since if the patient's needs for mental health care and treatment cannot be met in an environment which suitable for his age, it will be acceptable for them to be met elsewhere. However, the duty is reinforced by the fact that in England Government Policy is that no child is to be placed on an adult ward, such admissions to be treated as serious untoward incidents and reported to the Strategic Health Authority.[15] In deciding how to carry out their duty managers must consult 'a person who appears to them to have knowledge or experience

---

[13] House of Lords, House of Commons Joint Committee on Human Rights *Legislative Scrutiny: Seventh Progress Report: Fifteenth Report of Session 2006–2007* (HL Paper 555, HC Paper 112), para 1.17.

[14] Mental Health Act 2007 (Commencement No 11 Order) 2010, SI 2010/143.

[15] Department of Health, letter to SHA Chief Executives, 29 June 2007 (Gateway Number 8390) quoted in Young Minds *Briefing on the Responsibilities of NHS Trust Boards under Section 131A of the Mental Health Act 1983*
http://www.youngminds.org.uk/professionals/policy-and-knowledge/key-topics/
YM_AgeAppropriate_flyer-finaluse.pdf.

of cases involving patients who have not attained the age of 18 years which makes him suitable to be consulted'. The English MHA Code stresses that:[16]

> 'At least one of the people involved in the assessment of a person who is less than 18 years old, that is one of the two medical practitioners or the AMHP should be a clinician specialising in CAMHS. Where this is not possible, a CAMHS clinician should be consulted as soon as possible.'

11.13 This means that at least one of the two doctors or the AMHP involved in any Mental Health Act assessment of a child should be a clinician specialising in CAMHS. Where this is not possible a CAMHS clinician should be consulted as soon as possible. Where possible those responsible for the care and treatment of children should be CAMHS specialists. Where this is not possible, it is good practice for the clinical staff to have access to a CAMHS specialist for advice and consultation. The English MHA Code says that:[17]

> Children and young people should have
>
> • appropriate physical facilities;
> • staff with the right training skills and knowledge to understand and address their specific needs as children and young people;
> • a hospital routine that will allow their personal, social and educational development to continue as normally as possible;
> • equal access to educational opportunities as their peers, in so far as that is consistent with their ability to make use of them, considering their mental state.

Hospital managers are to 'ensure that the environment is suitable, and in reaching their determination they must consult a person whom they consider to be suitable because they are experienced in CAMHS cases'.[18] Hospital managers should also be mindful of the duty under the UN Convention on the Rights of the Child, Article 37(c) of which states that: '... every child deprived of liberty shall be separated from adults unless it is considered in the child's best interests not to do so ...'.

Finally, in relation to education the Code stresses that:[19]

> 'No child or young person below the school leaving age should be denied access to learning merely because they are receiving medical treatment for a mental disorder. Young people over school leaving age should be encouraged to continue learning.'

11.14 The duty is to ensure that the environment is suitable 'having regard to the patient's needs'. There may be exceptional circumstances therefore where a child's need to be accommodated in a safe environment will take precedence

---

[16]   Department of Health *Code of Practice: Mental Health Act 1983* (2008), para 36.45.
[17]   Ibid, para 36.68.
[18]   Ibid, para. 36.69.
[19]   Ibid, para 36.77.

over their entitlement to a suitable environment. So, if accommodation dedicated to children is not available and a child needs in-patient treatment, the Code advises that:[20]

> 'Discrete accommodation in an adult ward, with facilities, security and staffing appropriate to the needs of the child, might provide the most satisfactory solution, eg young female patients should be placed in single-sex accommodation. Where possible, all those involved in the care and treatment of children and young people should be child specialists. Anyone who looks after them must always have enhanced disclosure clearance from the Criminal Records Bureau and that clearance must be kept up to date.'

The Code stresses that 'There is a clear difference between what is a suitable environment for a child or young person in an emergency and what is acceptable on a long-term basis. The Code advises that once an emergency situation is over hospital managers, in determining whether an environment continues to be suitable, 'would need to consider issues such as whether the patient can mix with individuals of their own age, receive visitors of all ages, and have access to education.' Hospital managers have a duty under s 131A to consider whether a patient should be transferred to more appropriate accommodation and, if so, for this to be arranged as soon as possible.[21]

The section 39 duty to provide information about age suitable hospital provision for child offenders

11.15 Section 39 empowers a criminal court deciding whether to make a hospital order or interim hospital order in respect of any person to request from the relevant PCT or Health Authority information about hospitals in their area where the person could be admitted if an order were to be made. The relevant PCT or Health Authority is either the one for the area where the person resides or last resided or any other PCT or Health Authority that appears to the court to be appropriate. The PCT or Health Authority must comply with the court's request.

11.16 Section 31 adds new subss (1A) and (1B) to s 39. Section 39(1A) extends the s 39 power in the case of children so that it may be exercised where the court is considering remand to hospital for reports (s 35) or treatment (s 36) or committal by the magistrates under s 44. The purpose of this provision is to ensure that courts do not place a child in a prison setting when a suitable hospital bed would be more appropriate.[22] Section 39(1B) specifies that in the case of a child, the information which may be requested includes 'in particular, information about the availability of accommodation or facilities designed so as to be specially suitable for patients who have not attained the age of 18 years'.

---

[20] Ibid, para 36.70
[21] Ibid, para 36.71.
[22] *Explanatory Notes to the Mental Health Act 2007*, para 105.

The section 140 duty on NHS bodies to notify social services about hospital accommodation suitable for children

11.17 Section 140 of the MHA 1983 places a duty on PCTs and Health Authorities to notify the local social services authorities in their area of the hospitals administered by them or otherwise available to them where:[23]

'arrangements are from time to time in force –

(a)   for the reception of cases of special urgency, and
(b)   for the provision of accommodation or facilities designed so as to be specially suitable for patients who have not attained the age of 18 years.'

The section 116 duty to visit and exercise parental responsibility

11.18 Section 116 of the MHA 1983 places a duty on each local authority, where a child who is in their care under a care order is admitted to a hospital, independent hospital or care home, to arrange for visits to be made to the patient on their behalf. This duty applies whether the admission 'is for treatment for mental disorder or for any other reason'. The local authority is also required to take such other steps in relation to the patient while they are in the hospital or home, as would be expected to be taken by his parents.

Sections 85 and 86 of the Children Act 1989: the duty to notify social services about child in-patients

11.19 These provisions require that when a child is provided with accommodation for a period of three months by any Health Authority, NHS Trust, local education authority, independent hospital or residential care home, the body or the proprietors of the relevant private hospital or home must notify the appropriate local authority. That local authority is then under a duty to take steps to ensure that the child's welfare is safeguarded.

Section 11 of the Children Act 2004: the duty to safeguard and promote the child's welfare

11.20 All NHS bodies and the services they contract for have a duty under the Children Act 2004, s 11, to carry out their functions having regard to the need to safeguard and promote the welfare of children.[24]

---

23   MHA 1983, s 140, as amended by MHA 2007, s 31(4).
24   HM Government *Statutory guidance on making arrangements to safeguard and promote the welfare of children under section 11 of the Children Act 2004* (available at http://www.everychildmatters.gov.uk/_files/9204C14C73ACCA279701DDF9731B16F6.pdf).

THE DECISION TO ADMIT A CHILD TO HOSPITAL

11.21 With children, as with other groups of mentally disordered people perceived as vulnerable (such as elderly and learning disabled people) there is often a reluctance to use the compulsory powers in the MHA 1983, justified on the grounds that it will be 'less stigmatising' to rely on informal admission by parental consent or powers under the Children Act 1989. The counter argument is that patients who are detained under mental health legislation are entitled to the statutory safeguards in the shape of the statutory admission procedures, the right of appeal against detention to a Mental Health Tribunal, and the right to a second opinion in relation to treatment without consent.

11.22 A child may consent to treatment if they are 16 or 17 and have capacity,[25] or are under 16 and are *Gillick* competent.[26] As with adults, children may be admitted informally if they have capacity and consent to admission. A difficult question arises over the circumstances in which a child may be admitted informally with consent from someone with parental responsibilities. The Children Act 1989 defines parental responsibility as all the rights, duties, powers, responsibilities and authority which by law a parent of a child has in relation to the child and his property.[27] There are four categories of child patient requiring consideration:

(a)   children aged 16 or 17 with capacity;

(b)   children aged 16 and 17 who lack capacity;

(c)   children under 16 who are '*Gillick* competent';

(d)   children under 16 who are not '*Gillick* competent'.

Each will be discussed in turn.

16- and 17-year-olds with capacity

11.23 Section 8(1) of the Family Law Reform Act 1969 provides that the consent of a young person of 16 years:

> 'to any surgical, medical or dental treatment which, in the absence of consent, would constitute a trespass to his person, [and the consent] shall be as effective as it would be if he were of full age; and where a minor has by virtue of this section given an effective consent to any treatment, it shall not be necessary to obtain any consent for it from his parent or guardian.'

---

[25]   Family Law Reform Act 1969, s 8(1): 'the consent of a minor who has attained the age of sixteen ... shall be as effective as it would be if he were of full age; and where a minor has ... given an effective consent to any treatment it shall not be necessary to obtain any consent for it from his parent or guardian'.

[26]   *Gillick v West Norfolk and Wisbech Area Health Authority* [1986] AC 112, HL.

[27]   Children Act 1989, s 3(1).

The Family Law Reform Act 1969 was enacted in response to the Latey Committee Report which recommended lowering the age of majority from 21 to 18.[28] The Latey Committee recommended that 'without prejudice to any consent that may otherwise be lawful, the consent of young persons 16 and over to medical or dental treatment shall be as valid as the consent of a person of full age.'[29] As we shall see, in *Re W (a minor) (medical treatment)* [30] the Court of Appeal held that this provision entitled a 16 or a 17-year-old to consent to treatment but did not entitle such a person to refuse treatment where either the High Court or someone with parental responsibility consented to that treatment. A refusal by the child would be a very important consideration in the clinical judgment of the doctors and for parents and the court in deciding whether themselves to give consent, and its importance would increase with the age and maturity of the minor.[31]

11.24 Section 43 of the MHA 2007 inserts four new subss into s 131 of the MHA 1983 dealing with informal admission of 16 and 17-year-olds. A patient aged 16 or 17 who has capacity within the terms of ss 2 and 3 of the MCA 2005 may consent to informal admission even though there may be one or more persons who have parental responsibility for him. In such a case the child should be treated as an informal patient even if a person with parental responsibility is refusing consent.

11.25 Conversely, if the patient has capacity but does not consent, he or she may not be admitted by the consent of anyone with parental responsibility.[32] In *Re W (a minor) (medical treatment)*,[33] W was 16, suffering from anorexia, and subject to a care order. The local authority made an application to the High Court for authority under the inherent jurisdiction to act in the welfare and best interests of a child, and admit her, against her wishes, to a specialist unit for treating eating disorders. Lord Donaldson MR said that s 8 of the Family Law Reform Act 1969 did not empower a child to veto treatment:[34]

> 'No minor of whatever age has power by refusing consent to treatment to override a consent to treatment by someone who has parental responsibility for the minor, and a fortiori a consent by the Court. Nevertheless such a refusal is a very important consideration in making clinical judgments and for parents and the court in deciding whether themselves to give consent. Its importance increases with the age and maturity of the child.'

Although *Re W (a minor) (medical treatment)*[35] may be authority for the proposition that a capable 16 or 17-year-old's decision to consent to or refuse treatment in general may be over-ridden by a person with parental

---

28   Report of the Committee on the Age of Majority (Cmnd 3342 (1967)).
29   Ibid, para 484.
30   [1992] 4 All ER 627, CA.
31   Ibid, p 640 per Lord Donaldson MR.
32   MHA 1983, s 131(2)–(5), as inserted by MHA 2007, s 43.
33   [1992] 4 All ER 627, CA.
34   [1992] 4 All ER 627 at 639–640.
35   [1992] 4 All ER 627, CA.

responsibility, by virtue of ss 131(2)–(5) of the MHA 1983 this does not apply in relation to detention for treatment of mental disorder. If admission to hospital for treatment for mental disorder is necessary in the case of refusal, it will have to be carried out under Part II of the MHA 1983, assuming the criteria for detention are met.

11.26 If the primary issue is not the provision of medical treatment for mental disorder but the deprivation of the young person's liberty, it may be appropriate to use s 25 of the Children Act 1989. If a child or young person is seriously mentally ill they may require treatment under the Mental Health Act, whereas if they are behaviourally disturbed and there is no need for them to be hospitalised their need to be detained to protect them from harm might be more appropriately met within secure accommodation under the Children Act 1989.[36]

16- and 17-year-olds without capacity

11.27 Where a 16 or 17-year-old is regarded as unable to make a decision for himself in relation to a matter because of an impairment of, or a disturbance in, the functioning of the mind or brain, the provisions of the Mental Capacity Act apply (see **6.46–6.55** above and the Mental Capacity Act 2005 Code of Practice). The MCA provisions for deprivation of liberty do not apply to people under 18, so the choice of powers of detention should deprivation of liberty be needed, is between Part II of the MHA or s 25 of the Children Act 1989. If the primary purpose is treatment of the mental disorder, as long as the conditions of detention are met, the MHA 1983 should be used (see chapter 6 above). If the primary purpose is to deprive the child of liberty for their own safety or the safety of others, then s 25 of the Children Act 1989 should be used.

11.28 Section 25 of the Children Act 1989 provides criteria for a child to be placed in secure accommodation, meaning any accommodation used for the restriction of liberty. Local authorities are under a duty to take reasonable steps to avoid a child being placed in secure accommodation.[37] The maximum aggregate period for which a child can be placed in secure accommodation without a court order under s 25 is 72 hours in any 28 days.[38] If a court order is required the grounds in s 25 must be met. They are either:

(a) the child has a history of absconding and is likely to abscond from any other description of accommodation; and if he absconds he is likely to suffer significant harm; or

(b) if the child is kept in any other kind of accommodation he is likely to injure himself or other persons.

---

[36] Department of Health *Code of Practice: Mental Health Act 1983* (2008), para 36.18.
[37] Children Act 1989, Sch 2, para 7(c).
[38] SI 1991/1505, reg 10.

The maximum permissible period of detention of a child who has been remanded by a criminal court to secure accommodation is the period of the remand. For others it is three months, which may be extended for periods of up to six months at a time.[39] Children detained under the MHA 1983 may be placed in secure accommodation without a court order, as there is already authority to detain them.

16- or 17-year-olds lacking capacity

11.29   Section 2(5) of the Mental Capacity Act 2005 provides that no power which a person may possess in relation to a person who lacks capacity or is reasonably believed to lack capacity is exercisable in relation to a person under 16. This leaves open the possibility that under 16 year olds are entitled to the presumption of capacity in s 1 of the MCA. The *Bournewood* provisions for deprivation of liberty do not apply to people under 18.[40] The effect is that if a 16 or 17-year-old child who lacks capacity requires admission to a psychiatric hospital in circumstances not amounting to a deprivation of liberty, ss 5 and 6 of the MCA 2005 may be used. In such a case, if appropriate, the parents would have to be consulted about whether admission is in the child's best interests as required by s 4 of the MCA 2005.

11.30   If a 16 or 17-year-old lacks capacity and their primary need is treatment for mental disorder in conditions amounting to a deprivation of liberty, Part 2 of the MHA 1983 should be used to authorise detention. If the primary need is containment for their own safety or that of others, then s 25 of the Children Act 1989 should be used. Section 131(2) and (4) provide that if a patient *who has capacity* within ss 2 and 3 of the MCA 2005 does not consent to arrangements for informal admission, they may not be made or carried out on the basis of the consent of a person who has parental responsibility for him. This does not rule out the possibility that parental responsibilities might encompass the right to admit an incapacitated 16 or 17-year-old informally, even if they object, but the guidance in the Code and the developing case-law on the balance between parental responsibility and the child's right of self-determination (discussed at **11.44–11.47** below) suggest that this should occur only in the most exceptional circumstances.

Children under 16 who are *Gillick* competent

11.31   Children under 16 who are capable of consenting to treatment are described as '*Gillick* competent'. It is a matter for the treating doctor to determine whether a child is '*Gillick* competent' in the sense that she/he has the capacity to make the decision to have the proposed treatment and has sufficient maturity and understanding to be capable of making up her or his own mind.[41]

---

[39]   SI 1991/1505, regs 11–13.
[40]   Mental Capacity Act 2005, Sch A1, para 13, as inserted by MHA 2007, Sch 7.
[41]   *Gillick v West Norfolk and Wisbech Area Health Authority* [1986] AC 112, HL.

Gillick competence

11.32   In *Re R (a minor)* Lord Donaldson said that what *Gillick* competence involves is a full understanding and appreciation not only of the nature of the proposed treatment, but also of the intended effects of the treatment and its possible side effects, and 'equally important, of the consequences of a failure to treat'.[42]

11.33   Although the test of capacity in ss 2 and 3 of the MCA 2005 does not apply to children under the age of 16, the issue of *Gillick* competence is whether the child has the maturity and understanding to be capable for the purposes of the MCA 2005. This involves asking whether the child has the necessary maturity and understanding to be able to understand and retain relevant treatment information, to weigh it in the balance as part of the process of arriving at a decision, and to communicate that decision. The test for competence for adults is whether the adult has sufficient understanding, intelligence, memory and ability to communicate to be able to understand treatment information about what is proposed, to hold it in their head, to weigh it in the balance to arrive at a decision, and to communicate that decision. Support for the view that, in terms of these functional components, *Gillick* competence is to be judged against the adult standard is found in *Re C (Detention: Medical Treatment)*,[43] where Wall J applied the common law test of capacity[44] for adults in the case of a child under 16.

11.34   In a sense it is misleading to refer to *Gillick* competence, since what a *Gillick* competent child achieves is the competence to make the relevant decision which an adult would have. The difference for children under 16 is that doctors must ask themselves whether the child has the maturity and understanding to be competent in relation to that treatment proposal.[45] The only ground on which an adult may be found to lack capacity is that the functional deficit leading to a finding of incapacity must arise from an impairment of or disturbance in the functioning of the mind or the brain. Whilst an adult may only lack capacity because of an impairment of or disturbance in the functioning of the mind or the brain, a child under 16 may lack capacity for that reason or because s/he lacks the maturity and intelligence to be able to understand and appreciate the issues involved. The Code of Practice for England notes that, just as with adults, a child's capacity may fluctuate due to mental disorder:[46]

'In some cases, for example because of a mental disorder, a child's mental state may fluctuate significantly, so that on some occasions the child appears to be *Gillick* competent in respect of a particular decision and on other occasions does

---

[42]   [1991] 4 All ER 177 at 187e.

[43]   [1997] 2 FLR 180, FD.

[44]   *Re MB (an adult: medical treatment)* [1997] 2 FLR 426, CA.

[45]   P Fennell 'Informal Compulsion: The Informal Treatment of Juveniles at Common Law' (1992) *Journal of Social Welfare and Family Law* 311–333.

[46]   Department of Health *Code of Practice: Mental Health Act 1983* (2008), para 36.40.

not. In cases such as these, careful consideration should be given to whether the child is truly *Gillick* competent at any time to take a relevant decision.'

It is submitted that the same functional characteristics apply to adult capacity and *Gillick* competence. The difference is that with adults, the functional incapacity must arise from an impairment of or disturbance in the functioning of the mind or the brain. In the case of children it may arise from such a cause, but it could equally arise from immaturity or lack of intelligence.

11.35 A *Gillick* competent child can consent to informal admission. The Draft Code stated that:[47]

> 'For children who are *Gillick* competent the assumption is that they are able to make their own decisions and clinicians are advised not to rely on the consent of a person with parental responsibility. As a result, children who are *Gillick* competent (and have the capacity to make a decision on their health care) should be treated in the same way as adults. To put it simply, their decisions to consent or refuse admission to hospital for treatment or to the treatment itself should not be over-ridden by a person with parental responsibility.'

This strong statement of the rights of *Gillick* competent children has disappeared from subsequent drafts of the Code, perhaps because it runs counter to the case-law from the 1990s. Although it is clear that a *Gillick* competent child can consent to treatment where there is a doctor willing to offer it, there is a line of Court of Appeal decisions from the 1990s to the effect that even a *Gillick* competent child's refusal can be overridden by the High Court, by those with parental responsibility, or by the local authority if the child is in care.[48] These cases have been described as reflecting 'a retreat from *Gillick,* in that they allow a *Gillick* competent child to consent to treatment but not to refuse it.'[49]

11.36 In *Re R (a minor)* R was under 16 and the issue was whether the court could authorise treatment by antipsychotic medication against her wishes. R was not regarded as being *Gillick* competent, but the Court of Appeal held that, even if she had been competent her wishes could have been overridden by the Court or her parents.[50] In *R v Kirklees Metropolitan Borough Council, ex parte C (a minor)* C was not *Gillick* competent. The Court of Appeal held she could be admitted on parental consent, and since C was in care parental consent could be given by the authority in whose care the child is. In this case the council's action was held to be a responsible exercise of parental authority.[51] Whatever the legal position about overriding refusal by a child,

---

[47] Department of Health *Mental Health Act 1983 Draft Illustrative Code of Practice* (2006), para 35.17.

[48] See *Re R (a minor)* [1992] Fam 11, CA; *R v Kirklees Metropolitan Borough Council, ex parte C (a minor)* [1993] 2 FLR 187, CA; *Re W (a minor) (medical treatment)* [1992] 4 All ER 627, CA.

[49] G Douglas 'The Retreat from Gillick' (1992) 55 MLR 569.

[50] [1992] Fam 11.

[51] [1993] 2 FLR 187, CA.

refusal by a *Gillick* competent child would clearly be a strong countervailing factor in a clinician's decision whether to effect informal admission by parental consent.

11.37 Jones argues that whilst Lord Donaldson's statement in *Re W* 'may be regarded as the authoritative statement of the law on this issue' the child's refusal 'would clearly influence the doctors decision whether to admit him or her informally'[52] by parental or local authority consent. Despite the disappearance in the final version of the Code of the strong statement of the rights of *Gillick* competent children, that their right to consent to or refuse admission to hospital or treatment should not be overridden by those with parental responsibility, it is submitted that this is correct and that in such cases if the patient is to be detained for treatment the powers under Part II of the MHA 1983 should be used.

11.38 The MHA Code of Practice for England advises that where a child or young person cannot be admitted by parental consent or with their own valid consent, 'consideration should be given to alternative ways to treat them.'[53]

11.39 The MHA Code of Practice for England goes on to say this:[54]

'Where a child who is *Gillick* competent refuses to be admitted for treatment, in the past the courts have held that a person with parental responsibility can overrule their refusal. However, there is no post-Human Rights Act decision on this. The trend in recent cases is to reflect greater autonomy for competent under 18s, so it may be unwise to rely on the consent of a person with parental responsibility.

Consideration should be given to whether the child meets all the criteria for detention under the Mental Health Act. If they do not, it may be appropriate to seek authorisation from the court, except in cases where the child's refusal would be likely to lead to their death or to severe permanent injury, in which case the child could be admitted to hospital and treated without consent.'

It is hard to imagine a situation where a child suffering from mental disorder ('any disorder or disability of the mind') would fail to meet the criteria for detention in circumstances where failure to admit would lead to death or severe permanent injury. The MHA detention criteria are that the child must be suffering or appearing to suffer from mental disorder of a nature or degree warranting compulsory admission, treatment is necessary for the patient's health or safety or for the protection of others, and in the case of admission for treatment that appropriate treatment is available which cannot be provided unless the person is detained. This does not mean that there will not be applications to court, but these should be few in number, and the circumstances where emergency treatment without recourse to the Mental Health Act or the courts would be justified will surely be extremely exceptional.

---

52   RM Jones *Mental Health Act Manual* (Sweet and Maxwell, 10th edn, 2006), para 1.1182.
53   Department of Health *Code of Practice: Mental Health Act 1983* (2008), para 36.15.
54   Ibid, paras 36.43–36.44.

11.40 Support for the view that it is unwise to admit a refusing *Gillick* competent under 16-year-old on parental consent is found in the decision of the European Court of Human Rights in *Storck v Germany*[55] that parental responsibility does not extinguish the protection of Arts 5 and 8 ECHR, as well as from *R (on the application of Axon) v Secretary of State for Health (Family Planning Association intervening)* where Silber J said:[56]

> 'As a matter of principle, it is difficult to see why a parent should still retain an Article 8 right to parental authority relating to a medical decision where the young person concerned *understands* the advice provided by the medical professional and its implications ...'

Children under 16 lacking competence

11.41 Where a child is not *Gillick* competent the English Code suggests that:[57]

> 'it will usually be possible for a person with parental responsibility to consent on their behalf to their informal admission.'

However the Code also cautions that:[58]

> 'Before relying on parental consent in relation to a child under 16 and who is not *Gillick* competent, an assessment should be made of whether the matter is within the zone of parental control.'

'The zone of parental control'

11.42 If a child under 18 lacks capacity or competence, a decision to admit on parental consent may be made if it is within the zone of parental control The 'zone of parental control' is not a legal concept. The idea has been through several incarnations. In the initial drafts of the 2008 Code of Practice it was referred to as the 'zone of parental responsibility.' In the final version it is renamed the zone of parental control. An earlier Draft of the English MHA Code of Practice tired to encapsulate the idea in the following terms:[59]

> 'A decision is likely to be within the parental zone of responsibility if it is the sort of decision that a parent would be expected to make, having regard to what is considered to be normal practice in our society having regard to any relevant decisions in relation to Human Rights by the courts.'

---

55   (2005) 43 EHRR 96, ECtHR.
56   [2006] 2 FLR 206, [2006] 2 WLR 1130 at [130]. *Axon* has been described by Taylor as potentially marking a reversal of the retreat from *Gillick*: see Taylor 'Reversing the Retreat from *Gillick*?' (2007) 17 *Child and Family Law Quarterly* 81–97.
57   Department of Health *Code of Practice: Mental Health Act 1983* (2008), para 36.45.
58   Ibid, para 36.46.
59   Department of Health *Mental Health Act 1983 Draft Revised Code of Practice* (2007), para 39.43. See http://www.dh.gov.uk/en/Consultations.

As Lord Fraser of Tullybelton put it in his speech in *Gillick*, 'In times gone by the father had almost absolute authority over his children until they attained majority'. In essence the zone of parental control is an attempt to encapsulate the idea enunciated in 1969 by Lord Denning in *Hewer* v *Bryant*[60] where he said that:

> 'The common law can, and should, keep pace with the times. It should declare, ... that the legal right of a parent to the custody of a child ends at the eighteenth birthday and even up till then, it is a dwindling right which the courts will hesitate to enforce against the wishes of the child, the older he is. It starts with a right of control and ends with little more than advice.'

Although parental responsibility is a well-known concept, 'the zone of parental control' is not a term used in family law. It is intended to assist in identifying the circumstances when parental consent may be relied upon as authority to admit or treat without consent where the patient is under 16, or is 16 or 17 and lacks capacity to consent.

Parental responsibilities

11.43 'Parental responsibilities' is a broad concept consisting of 'a collection of rights and duties that concerns the taking care of the child's person and property'.[61] In domestic legal terms, s 3 of the Children Act 1989 defines 'parental responsibility' as 'all the rights, duties, powers, responsibilities and authority which by law a parent of a child has in relation to the child and his property.' Parental responsibilities include the duty to seek medical assistance for a child under the age of 16. Those with parental responsibilities risk prosecution for child neglect if they do not seek necessary treatment for the child, and it can be established that they knew that medical treatment was required, but decided not to secure it or did not care whether the child needed medical assistance.[62] A prosecution under s 127 of the MHA 1983 for willful neglect might also be possible. Whilst Art 5 of the UN Convention on the Rights of the Child requires states to respect the responsibilities rights and duties of parents, it also, in Art 12, requires them to assure to the child who is capable of forming his or her own views the right to express those views freely in all matters affecting the child, the views of the child being given due weight in accordance with the age and maturity of the child. Parental control may be seen as part of parental responsibilities.

---

[60]   (1970) 1 QB 357 at 369.

[61]   K Boele-Woelki, F Ferrand, C Gonzalez Beilfuss, M Jantera-Jareborg, N Lowe, D Martiny, W Pintens *Commission on European Family Law Principles of European Family Law Regarding Parental Responsibilities* (Intersentia Antwerpen, 2007), p 14.

[62]   *R v Sheppard* [1981] AC 394, HL.

Balancing children's rights to autonomy and physical integrity and parental control

11.44 There is a need to achieve a delicate balance between the child's right to autonomy and need for protection. As Boele-Woelki et al put it in their important study *Principles of European Family Law Regarding Parental Responsibilities*:[63]

'Almost every right in the convention includes elements of participation in the decision-making process. The child's autonomy should be respected in accordance with the developing ability and need for the child to act independently.'

They go on to say that: 'Medical treatment for the child is part and parcel of the right and duty to care for the child.' The authors urge a 'careful approach' to resolving:[64]

'the tension between the right and duty of the holders of parental responsibility to take all necessary steps concerning medical treatment in order to safeguard the physical and mental well-being of the child, and ... his or her right of self-determination ... If the child is sufficiently mature, his or her consent should be required.'

11.45 Parental controls are to be exercised for the benefit of the child and they are justified only in so far as they enable the parent to perform his duties towards the child and towards other children in the family.[65] In *Mabon v Mabon*[66] Thorpe LJ referred to the need for judges in deciding whether there was compliance with Art 12 of the Convention on the Rights of the Child:

'correctly to focus on the sufficiency of the child's understanding and, in measuring that sufficiency, reflect the extent to which, in the 21st century, there is a keener appreciation of the autonomy of the child and the child's consequential right to participate in decision-making processes that fundamentally affect his family life.'

11.46 The Code states that there are two key questions when deciding whether a particular decision is in the zone of parental control:[67]

'• firstly, is the decision one that a parent would be expected to make, having regard both to what is considered to be normal practice in our society and to any relevant human rights decisions made by the courts?; and
• secondly, are there no indications that the parent might not act in the best interests of the child or young person?'

---

[63] K Boele-Woelki, F Ferrand, C Gonzalez Beilfuss, M Jantera-Jareborg, N Lowe, D Martiny, W Pintens *Commission on European Family Law Principles of European Family Law Regarding Parental Responsibilities* (Intersentia Antwerpen, 2007), p 39.
[64] Ibid, p 129.
[65] *Gillick v West Norfolk and Wisbech Area Health Authority* [1986] 1 AC 112, per Lord Frazer at 170D.
[66] [2005] 3 WLR 460, CA.
[67] Department of Health *Code of Practice: Mental Health Act 1983* (2008), para 36.10.

The Code states that the parameters of what was then called 'the zone of parental responsibility' depend on a number of factors, all of which required consideration by the doctor or approved clinician. They are:[68]

- the nature and invasiveness of what is to be done to the child (including the extent to which the child's liberty will be curtailed) – the more extreme the intervention, the more likely it will be that it falls outside the zone;

- whether the child is resisting – treating a child that is resisting needs more justification;

- general social standards in force at the time as to the sorts of decisions it is acceptable for parents to make – anything that goes beyond the kind of decisions parents routinely make will be more suspect;

- the age and maturity of the child – the greater this is, the more likely it will be that it should be the child who is taking the decision; and

- the extent to which a parent's interest may conflict with those of the child – this may suggest the parent will not act in the child or young person's best interests.

The zone of parental responsibility applies not only to decisions to admit to hospital, it also applies to parental consent to treatment.

Treatment of children admitted informally by parental consent

11.47 The Draft Code gave the example that it might be within the zone of parental responsibility for a parent to consent to treatment of a 15-year-old child against his will for an eating disorder (where the nature of the illness makes the child unable to consent for himself). However, if force-feeding was required by means of invasive treatment in the form of a gastric tube, it might be considered that the extremity of the treatment took it outside the kind of treatment to which a parent could give consent. In such a case the child might need to be detained under the MHA 1983 rather than treated as an informal patient.[69] It may be observed that detaining a patient who requires forcible feeding by naso-gastric tube will not provide extra procedural safeguards, since forcible feeding may be given under s 63 of the MHA 1983 without consent or a second opinion if it is given by or under the authority of the Responsible Clinician or Approved Clinician in charge of treatment.[70] The Parliamentary Joint Committee on Human Rights ('JCHR') considered that, given the potential for forcible feeding to breach Arts 3 and 8 of the ECHR,[71] it should be subject to regulation by statutory second opinion under s 58 of the MHA 1983. The JCHR considered that the positive obligation under Art 8 as

---

[68] Ibid, para 36.12.
[69] Ibid, para 39.45.
[70] *Re C (a minor) (detention for medical treatment)* [1997] 2 FLR 180, FD.
[71] *Nevmerzhitsky v Ukraine (Application 54825/00)* Judgment of 5 April 2005, ECtHR.

elaborated in *Storck v Germany*[72] requires effective supervision and review of decisions to treat against an individual's will, and that the direction of the responsible clinician, even if that person is a medical practitioner, is not sufficient to provide such supervision and review.[73] The MHA Code of Practice for England clearly envisages that the nature of treatment proposed may take the decision to consent to it outside the zone of parental control, 'eg where, like electroconvulsive therapy (ECT), it could be considered particularly invasive or controversial.'[74]

11.48 The idea of the 'zone of parental control' is that parental consent will not provide authority for treatments which are invasive or controversial, because of the need to recognise a mature minor's objection under Art 12 of the CRC, and the positive obligation under Arts 5 and 8 of the ECHR to provide effective supervision and review of decisions to detain and treat without consent.

11.49 The child's views should be taken into account, even if they are not *Gillick* competent, but how much weight should be attached to them depends on the maturity and understanding of the child. If the decision regarding the treatment of a child (including how the child is to be kept safely in one place) is within the zone of parental control and consent is given by a person with parental responsibility, then the clinician may rely on that consent and treat on that basis as an informal patient. If it is within the zone of parental responsibility, reliance can be placed on the person with parental responsibility to act in the best interests of the child.

11.50 The Draft Code emphasised that those responsible for the care and treatment of the child must be 'clear about who has parental responsibility and always request copies of any court orders for reference on the hospital ward.' These orders may include care orders, residence orders, contact orders, evidence of appointment as the child's guardian, parental responsibility agreements or orders, and any order under wardship.[75] This guidance does not appear in the final version of the Code but it is good advice nevertheless.

11.51 Informal admission under parental responsibility does not mean that there is automatic consent to all components of a treatment programme regarded as 'necessary'. The Code emphasises that:[76]

> 'Consent must be sought for each aspect of the child's care and treatment as it arises, and "blanket" consent forms should not be used.'

---

72 (2005) 43 EHRR 96, ECtHR.
73 House of Lords, House of Commons Joint Committee on Human Rights *Legislative Scrutiny: Seventh Progress Report: Fifteenth Report of Session 2006–2007* (HL Paper 555, HC Paper 112), paras 67–69.
74 Department of Health *Code of Practice: Mental Health Act 1983* (2008), para 36.14.
75 Children Act 1989, ss 4 and 8.
76 Department of Health *Code of Practice: Mental Health Act 1983* (2008), para 36.49.

11.52 Treatment which is subject to the s 57 second opinion procedure (psychosurgery and the surgical implantation of hormones to reduce male sex drive) may only be given with the consent of a patient who is capable of understanding the nature purpose and likely effects of the treatment and has consented to it. Under s 58A a child informal patient may only be given ECT when they are not capable of consenting if a SOAD has certified that it is appropriate for the treatment to be given.

11.53 Where a child is under 16, the English MHA Code recommends that an application to the Family Division of the High Court should be considered, particularly in one of the following four situations where the child is not *Gillick* competent:[77]

'• and where the person with parental responsibility cannot be identified or is incapacitated;
• and where one person with parental responsibility consents but another strongly disagrees and is likely to take the matter to court themselves;
• and where there is concern that the person with parental responsibility may not be acting in the best interests of the child in making treatment decisions on behalf of the child, e g where hostility between parents is a factor in any decision making or where there are concerns as to whether a person with parental responsibility is capable of making a decision in the best interests of the child;
• and where a person with parental responsibility consents but the decision is not within the zone of parental control, e g where the treatment in question is ECT.'

A court application should also be made if the child is *Gillick* competent or is a young person who is capable of making a decision on their treatment and is refusing treatment.

It is possible to treat a child on the basis of an order made by the court under its inherent jurisdiction or by way of a specific issue order made under s 8 of the Children Act 1989, but this is not likely to be used if there is a statutory alternative of treating under the MHA 1983. In relation to forcible feeding it may be advisable to seek the authority of a s 8 specific issue order.

Treatment of 16- or 17-year-olds admitted under the Mental Capacity Act 2005

11.54 If a child aged 16 or 17 lacks capacity and is admitted to hospital in circumstances not amounting to a deprivation of liberty under the MCA 2005, they may be given treatment which is necessary in their best interests for physical or mental disorder under ss 5 and 6 of the MCA 2005. If the treatment is ECT it may only be given with the approval of a Second Opinion Appointed Doctor ('SOAD') under s 58A (see **10.6** above).

---

[77] Department of Health *Code of Practice: Mental Health Act 1983* (2008), para 36.66.

Treatment of patients subject to Part IV of the Mental Health Act 1983

11.55 If a child patient is liable to be detained and, according to s 56, subject to Part IV (see **10.14** above), treatment will be authorised by s 63, subject to the safeguards in ss 57, 58 and 58A. Patients may be given emergency treatment subject to s 62. The second opinion safeguards apply. A child patient who lacks capacity may not be given a s 57 treatment. A child patient may not be given ECT if he or she is capable (over 16) or competent (under 16) and refusing it. However, ECT may be given it if a SOAD deems the patient to be incapable of understanding its nature purpose and likely effects, and the SOAD considers it appropriate for the treatment to be given. Medicines for mental disorder may be given subject to a second opinion under s 58 without consent whether a child patient is incapable or refusing treatment (see **10.14–10.59** above).

Treatment of 16- and 17-year-old community patients under Part IVA

11.56 Supervised community treatment ('SCT') may be applied to a patient who is under 18 (see **8.20–8.49** above). Treatment in the community without recall to hospital may be administered to a community patient if there is:

(a) authority to give it; and

(b) if it is medicine or ECT for mental disorder, where the certificate requirement is met.

Authority to treat

11.57 There is authority to give treatment in the community if the patient consents. As long as force is not necessary, there is authority to give treatment in the community without consent if:

(a) the patient lacks capacity;

(b) the treatment is 'immediately necessary'; and

(c) it is not in conflict with a valid and applicable advance decision, the decision of a health care attorney, a deputy, or the Court of Protection.

Force may be used to administer treatment if the emergency conditions in s 63G are met. Children under 18 may not make advance decisions or take out lasting powers of attorney, and a deputy may not be appointed by the Court of Protection if the patient is under 16.

Scope of Part IVA

11.58 Part IVA applies to 16 or 17-year-olds as if to an adult (see **10.60–10.68** above), and to child community patients under 16 with the substitution of competence for capacity wherever it appears. The principal difference between children under 18 and adults is that treatment in the community may not be given to an incapable adult in a non-emergency situation if it is contrary to a valid and effective advance decision, or is contrary to the decision of a health care attorney, a deputy or the Court of Protection. Children under 18 may not make an advance decision, nor may they appoint a deputy, so the right to make arrangements in advance is not open to them.

11.59 The difference between 16 and 17 year-olds and children under 16 is that the test of 'competence' rather than 'capacity' applies to their decision-making, although (as suggested at **11.32–11.33** above) in practice there may be little difference between the two tests. The main difference is not in relation to the functional deficits necessary to be found to lack capacity, but as a result of the fact that a person over 16 may only lack capacity as the result of an impairment of or disturbance in the functioning of the mind or the brain. A person under 16 may lack capacity either because of such a mental disability, or because they lack the maturity to be able to make the decision.

Treatment of community patients under 16 under Part IVA

11.60 Part IVA makes special provision for 'child community patients' defined as those who are under 16 and have not been recalled to hospital.[78] Section 64E provides that treatment may not be given to a child community patient unless there is authority to give it.

Authority to treat

11.61 There is authority to give treatment to a child community patient under 16 if:

(a) the patient is competent and consents to it being given; or

(b) it is authorised by s 64F (treatment for child patients lacking competence); or

(c) the treatment is emergency treatment under s 64G.[79]

If the treatment is a s 58 or s 58A type treatment (currently medicines or ECT) the certificate requirement must be met unless one of the exceptions applies. These are:

(a) the treatment is emergency treatment authorised under s 64G; or

---

[78]   MHA 1983, s 64E(1).
[79]   MHA 1983, s 64E.

(b)   in a case where the patient is competent to consent to the treatment and does consent to it, the treatment is immediately necessary; or

(c)   where the treatment is medicines and one month has not elapsed since the CTO was made.[80]

If none of these exceptions applies the SOAD must have authorised treatment by medication or ECT, and treatment will only be authorised in the circumstances specified by the SOAD.

Treatment without force of child community patients who lack competence

11.62   Section 64F sets out the conditions that must be satisfied before ECT or medicines for mental disorder can be provided to a community patient who is under 16 and who lacks the competence to consent. The treatment cannot be given if force would have to be used to ensure that an objecting patient received the treatment. Force can be used in an emergency if the conditions in s 64G are met. Section 64F authorises the approved clinician in charge of a child community patient's treatment to give or direct the giving of relevant treatment, subject to the following conditions. First, the AC must follow the steps outlined in s 5(1)(a) and (b)(i) of the MCA 2005, namely:

(a)   take reasonable steps to establish whether the patient lacks competence to consent to the treatment; and

(b)   when giving the treatment, must reasonably believe that the patient lacks competence to consent to it.

Second, the AC must have no reason to believe that the patient objects to being given the treatment; or if the AC does have reason to believe that the patient objects, it must not be necessary to use force against the patient in order to give the treatment. Adult patients have greater protection than children since it is a condition under s 64D but not s 64F that treatment must not conflict with an advance decision which the person giving the treatment is satisfied is valid and applicable. Equally, for adults, but not for children treatment may not be given if it conflicts with a decision of a donee under a LPA, a deputy or of the Court of Protection.

Emergency treatment, using force if necessary, of child patients

11.63   Force may only be used to give treatment to patients who lack capacity or to children under 16 who lack competence against their objections if the emergency conditions in s 64G are met. Section 64G authorises emergency treatment of patients over 16 who are reasonably believed to lack capacity, or

---

80   MHA 1983, s 64E(3)–(4).

children under 16 reasonably believed to lack competence to consent. Treatment is emergency treatment where it is immediately necessary:

(a)   to save the patient's life; or

(b)   to prevent a serious deterioration in the patient's condition and is not irreversible; or

(c)   to prevent serious suffering by the patient and is not irreversible or hazardous; or

(d)   to prevent the patient from behaving violently or being a danger to himself or others, as long as the treatment is the minimum interference necessary, and is neither irreversible nor hazardous.[81]

If the treatment is ECT it may only be given under paras (a) or (b) above, not paras (c) or (d). Irreversible means having unfavourable irreversible physical or psychological consequences, and hazardous means entailing significant physical hazard.[82] Section 64G authorises force to be used, but only where emergency treatment needs to be given to prevent harm to the patient and the use of force is proportionate to the likelihood of the patient's suffering harm and to the seriousness of that harm.

REVIEWING DETENTION

11.64   If a child patient is admitted informally on their own consent they may seek to leave hospital at anytime subject to the AC's or the nurse's power under s 5 of the MHA 1983 to hold them in hospital. A child patient admitted on parental consent may challenge that decision by invoking the inherent jurisdiction of the High Court on the basis that the intervention is not in their best interests, by seeking a specific issue order under s 8 of the Children Act 1989, or by seeking judicial review on the grounds that their detention infringes a Convention right. A child patient who is detained or subject to SCT under the MHA 1983 (as amended) has the same rights to seek review of detention or a CTO before a Mental Health Tribunal as if they were an adult (see chapter 9 above).

CONCLUSION

11.65   Admission of children to psychiatric hospital brings difficult ethical and legal issues into play, including the need for a safe and appropriate treatment environment, the need to provide safeguards in relation to controversial treatments, and the tension between the package of powers and rights attached to parental responsibilities, which diminish as the child matures,

---

[81]   MHA 1983, s 64C(5).
[82]   MHA 1983, s 62(3).

and the right of the child to self determination. Complexity is added to the law by the distinction between adult capacity and *Gillick* competence.

11.66 As with other aspects of mental health law there is a choice of legal regimes under which admission to hospital may take place. Anthony Harbour has argued that during the 1990s there has been an increase in use of MHA powers to detain children, despite the law's retreat from *Gillick* with statements that parental rights or the court could override the refusal of even a competent child to authorise informal admission at common law. Harbour ascribes this to a number of factors, including a desire to ensure that child patients have rights themselves to challenge detention and compulsory treatment, but perhaps most notably because many specialist child and adolescent units had for the first time obtained registration to allow them to receive patients detained under the MHA 1983.[83] The 1983 Act as amended now provides a complete (and elaborate) statutory framework for treating children whether they are in hospital or the community. There are gaps in the protection afforded to children, and the extent to which the procedural obligation under Art 8 ECHR is met, such as in relation to forcible feeding by naso-gastric tube.

11.67 The Code of Practice introduces the novel concept of the 'zone of parental control' which as we have seen is an attempt to reflect Art 12 of the UN Convention on the Rights of the Child, and the need to provide effective supervision and review of decisions to detain and treat without consent following *Storck v Germany*.[84] The key factors in identifying whether an issue is within 'the zone' are the age and maturity of the child, the nature and invasiveness of the procedure and the extent to which it restricts liberty, whether the child is refusing, and whether the relationship between the parent and the child has broken down and there is concern that the parent may not act in the best interests of the child. In this sense 'the zone' is intended to offer greater protection for the autonomy rights of the child than the case-law,[85] but it is important to realise that detention under the MHA 1983 will not necessarily bring increased protection for Art 8 rights, as in relation to naso-gastric feeding.

---

[83] A Harbour 'Young People and Psychiatric Treatment' Paper delivered at the Seminar: 'Children, Mental Health and Human Rights' held at Northumbria University on 22 June 2007.

[84] (2005) 43 EHRR 96, ECtHR.

[85] *Re R (a minor)* [1992] Fam 11, CA; *R v Kirklees Metropolitan Borough Council, ex parte C (a minor)* [1993] 2 FLR 187, CA; *Re W (a minor)* [1992] 4 All ER 627, CA.

Chapter 12

CRIMINAL OFFENCES AND TRANSFER OF PATIENTS BETWEEN JURISDICTIONS

OVERVIEW

12.1 The positive duty under Art 2 of the European Convention on Human Rights requires states to take positive steps to protect of the right to life.[1] The positive duty under Art 3 requires states to take steps to provide effective protection of vulnerable people against torture or inhuman or degrading treatment.[2] The positive duty under Art 8 requires states to take positive steps to protect the right to physical integrity, including protection against sexual abuse.[3] Ill-treatment of mentally disordered people and sexual abuse amount to inhuman and degrading treatment, as well as infringements of the right to physical integrity and States have a duty to provide effective protection via the criminal law.

12.2 The positive duty under Art 3 was at issue in *R (B) v DPP and the Equality and Human Rights Commission*[4] where the applicant, B, suffered from schizoaffective disorder, and was the victim of an assault in which part of his ear was bitten off. The prosecutor declined to prosecute for assault causing grievous bodily harm, and decided to offer no evidence on the basis of a psychiatric report which concluded that at all material times B suffered from a mental condition which *might* affect his perception and recollection of events so as to make his account unreliable. The report did not go so far as to suggest that B was incapable of giving reliable evidence. Prosecuting Counsel formed the view that the conclusion set out in the report precluded him from putting B before the jury as a reliable witness in the absence of any other evidence to confirm the identity of the ear biter. Not only did the Court hold that the prosecutor's decision was irrational, it was also held to breach B's Convention Rights under Art 3. Toulson LJ held it to be 'established law that Article 3 carries with it a positive obligation on a state to provide protection through its legal system against a person suffering such ill-treatment at the hands of others. One aspect of the duty is the provision of a legal system for bringing to justice those who commit serious acts of violence against others.'[5] The court awarded £8,000 in compensation for B being deprived of the opportunity of the

---

[1] *Osman v United Kingdom* [1998] 29 EHRR 245.
[2] *A v United Kingdom (Human Rights: Punishment of Child) (Application 25599/94)* (1998) 27 EHRR 611, ECtHR.
[3] *X and Y v the Netherlands,* Judgment of 26 March 1985, Series A no 91, para 22.
[4] [2009] EWHC 106 (Admin).
[5] Ibid, para 65.

proceedings running their proper course and the damage to his self respect 'from being made to feel that he was beyond the effective protection of the law.'[6] Toulson LJ condemned the breach of Art 3 in the following terms:[7]

> 'In this case B suffered a serious assault. The decision to terminate the prosecution on the eve of the trial, on the ground that it was not thought that B could be put before the jury as a credible witness, was to add insult to injury. It was a humiliation for him and understandably caused him to feel that he was being treated as a second class citizen. Looking at the proceedings as a whole, far from them serving the State's positive obligation to provide protection against serious assaults through the criminal justice system, the nature and manner of their abandonment increased the victim's sense of vulnerability and of being beyond the protection of the law. It was not reasonably defensible and ... there was a violation of his rights under Article 3.'

This case emphasises the need to avoid what the Law Commission called a 'status-based' approach to capacity. The status approach excludes all people with a particular characteristic, illness or condition from a particular decision, irrespective of their actual capacity to make it at the time.[8] It was assumed that Mr B's evidence would not be credible because he had a mental condition which *might* affect his perception and recollection of events so as to make his account unreliable. The question to ask was whether the mental disorder did actually affect his perception and recollection so as to make his evidence unreliable. One of the ways in which existing criminal procedure can be modified to increase access to criminal justice for mentally disordered people is exemplified in the Youth Justice and Criminal Evidence Act 1999 provides for special measures directions in case of vulnerable and intimidated witnesses.

12.3 The MHA 1983 (as amended) contains a number of offences. Some are designed to protect mentally disordered people against wilful neglect and abuse. Others are designed to protect the integrity of the system of compulsory powers, such as the prohibition on forgery of statutory documents or obstruction of people carrying out statutory functions. Yet others are designed to proscribe harbouring or offering assistance to patients who have escaped or absented themselves without leave. Protection of mentally disordered people against inhuman or degrading treatment in the form of sexual abuse is provided under the Sexual Offences Act 2003 where the victim suffers from a mental disorder.

12.4 This chapter also deals with the arrangements in Part VI of the MHA 1983 for transfer of patients from England and Wales to other jurisdictions and vice versa. These provisions have been substantially amended by the MHA 2007 to provide, inter alia, for the transfer of patients who are subject to CTOs to other jurisdictions. Such transfers have to be in the patient's interests, and since the right to respect for family life is potentially engaged, there should be

---

6   Ibid, para 71.
7   Ibid, para 70.
8   The Law Commission, *Mental Incapacity* Law Com 231 (1995), para 3.3.

consultation with the nearest relative unless the patient has objected. Finally, the chapter deals with the provisions of s 86, cross-titled 'Removal of Aliens'.

OFFENCES UNDER THE MENTAL HEALTH ACT 1983

12.5 Part IX of the MHA 1983 makes provision for a number of criminal offences in connection with the operation of the Act and for the protection of people suffering from mental disorder. The maximum penalty on imprisonment on summary conviction for offences under ss 126, 127 or 128 will increase from six months to one year on the commencement of ss 154 and 282 of the Criminal Justice Act 2003. The offences under Part IX of the MHA 1983 may be prosecuted by local authorities, although proceedings under s 127 for ill-treatment or wilful neglect of a patient require the consent of the Director of Public Prosecutions. As Jones notes, local authority staff charged with the duty of investigating offences under Part IX must refer to the relevant provisions of the Police and Criminal Evidence Act 1984 Codes of Practice, and must administer the following caution to a suspect before questioning:[9]

> 'You do not have to say anything. But it may harm your defence if you do not mention when questioned something which you later rely on in court. Anything you do say may be given in evidence.'

Section 126: forgery and false statements

12.6 There are four offences under s 126:

(a)   it is an offence for anyone, without lawful authority or excuse, to have in his custody or control any document which he knows or believes to be false, and which purports to be an application under Part II, a medical recommendation or other report, or 'any other document required or authorised to be made for any of the purposes of this Act';

(b)   it is an offence for anyone, without lawful authority or excuse, to make, or have in his custody or under his control, any document so closely resembling a document mentioned in (a) above as to be calculated to deceive;

(c)   it is an offence for anyone wilfully to make a false entry or statement in any application, recommendation, report, record or other document required or authorised to be made for any of the purposes of the MHA 1983;

(d)   it is an offence for anyone, with intent to deceive, to make use of any entry or statement in any such document which he knows to be false.

---

[9]   Police and Criminal Evidence Act Code of Practice C, para 10.5.

Offences under s 126 are triable either summarily (where a fine or maximum prison term of six months[10] may be imposed) or in the Crown Court (where a fine or maximum prison term of two years may be imposed).

Section 127: ill-treatment of patients

12.7   At common law those who have care or control of mentally disordered patients or are responsible for their treatment owe a duty of care.[11] Section 127 creates two separate offences of ill-treatment or wilful neglect of patients:

(a)   it is an offence for anyone who is an officer on the staff of or otherwise employed in, or who is one of the managers of, a hospital, independent hospital or care home to ill-treat or wilfully to neglect a patient who is receiving treatment for mental disorder as an in-patient in that hospital or home. This offence also applies to ill-treatment or wilful neglect on the premises of the hospital or home of a person who is receiving treatment there as an out-patient;

(b)   it is an offence for any individual to ill-treat or wilfully to neglect a mentally disordered patient who is for the time being subject to his guardianship under this Act or otherwise in his custody or care (whether by virtue of any legal or moral obligation or otherwise).[12]

To be guilty of an offence under s 127(2) the individual must have the patient in their custody or care by virtue of any legal or moral obligation, so a carer who is looking after a CTO patient could be guilty of either offence by virtue of a moral obligation.

12.8   In *R v Newington*[13] the Court of Appeal advised the Crown Prosecution Service that ill-treatment and wilful neglect are separate offences. Section 139 does not apply to prosecutions brought under this section, so there is no defence of lack of bad faith or negligence.[14] A single act of ill-treatment can be sufficient to constitute an offence under this section.[15] To secure a conviction for ill-treatment the prosecution must prove:

(a)   deliberate conduct by the accused which could properly be described as ill-treatment irrespective of whether it damaged or threatened to damage the patient's health;

---

[10]   To be increased to 12 months when the Criminal Justice Act 2003, ss 154 and 282 are introduced. These provisions are not yet in force.

[11]   *R (on the application of Munjaz) v Mersey Care NHS Trust* [2005] UKHL 58 at [4].

[12]   Schedule 5, para 11 of the MHA 2007 repeals s 127(2A) which created the offence of ill-treatment and neglect of a person who is subject to after-care under supervision.

[13]   (1990) 91 Cr App R 247, CA.

[14]   MHA 1983, s 139(3).

[15]   *R v Holmes* [1979] Crim LR 52.

(b)   a guilty mind involving either an appreciation by the defendant that s/he was inexcusably ill-treating a patient, or recklessness at to whether she was inexcusably committing acts of ill-treatment;

(c)   that the victim is a mentally disordered person.[16]

12.9   'Neglect' was defined by Sir Thomas Bingham MR in the following terms in *R v Humberside and Scunthorpe Coroner ex p Jamieson*:[17]

> '[A] gross failure to provide adequate nourishment or liquid, or provide basic medical attention or shelter or warmth for someone in a dependent position (because of youth, age or incarceration) who cannot provide it for himself. Failure to provide medical attention for a dependent person whose physical condition is such as to show that he obviously needs it may amount to neglect. So may it be if it is the dependent person's mental condition that obviously calls for attention.'

Section 44 of the Mental Capacity Act 2005 provides that if a person (D), (a) has the care of a person (P) who lacks or whom D reasonably believes to lack capacity; or (b) is the donee of a lasting power of attorney or an enduring power of attorney ... created by P; or (c) is a deputy appointed by the court for P; it is an offence for D to ill-treat or wilfully neglect P. Wilful neglect, according to the MCA Code 'usually means that a person has deliberately failed to carry out an act they knew they had a duty to do.'[18]

12.10   In 2000 the Department of Health issued guidance entitled *No Secrets*: *Developing and Implementing Multi Agency Policies and Procedures to Protect Vulnerable Adults from Abuse* under s 7 of the Local Authority Social Services Act 1970.[19] In the same year the National Assembly for Wales issued equivalent s 7 guidance entitled *In Safe Hands*: *Implementing Adult Protection Procedures in Wales*.[20] Each provides the same starting point for a definition of abuse: 'Abuse is a violation of an individual's human and civil rights by any other person or persons.'[21] Each has been subject to review.[22]

---

[16]   *R v Newington* (1990) 91 Cr App R 247, CA.

[17]   [1994] 3 All ER 972 at 990–991.

[18]   Department of Constitutional Affairs, *Mental Capacity Act 2005 Code of Practice* TSO 2007, para 14.26.

[19]   Department of Health (2000), *No Secrets: Guidance on Developing and Implementing Multi Agency Policies and Procedures to Protect Vulnerable Adults from Abuse*. Guidance Issued by the Secretary of State for Health and the Home Secretary under s 7 of the Local Authority Social Services Act 1970.

[20]   National Assembly for Wales (2000) *In Safe Hands: Implementing Adult Protection Procedures in Wales* Guidance Issued by the National Assembly for Wales under s 7 of the Local Authority Social Services Act 1970.

[21]   'No Secrets' para 2.5; *In Safe Hands* para 7.4.

[22]   Department of Health, Home Office and the Ministry of Justice, Safeguarding Adults: A Consultation on the Review of the No Secrets Guidance (2008); Julia Magill, Vicky Yeates and Marcus Longley, *Review of In Safe Hands A Review of the Welsh Assembly Government's Guidance on the Protection of Vulnerable Adults in Wales 193 pp* Feb 2010 Welsh Institute for Health and Social Care.

12.11 Although a local authority may institute proceedings under this section the consent of the Director of Public Prosecutions is required for a prosecution to proceed.[23] This offence is triable either summarily (where a fine or maximum prison term of six months[24] may be imposed) or in the Crown Court (where a fine or maximum prison term of 5 years may be imposed). The maximum Crown Court sentence was increased from two to five years by s 42 of the MHA 2007.

Section 128: assisting patients to absent themselves without leave

12.12 Although it is not an offence for a patient to absent her or himself without leave or escape from legal custody under s 137, it is an offence to assist such a person to do so. It is also an offence knowingly to 'harbour', or assist a patient who has escaped or is absent without leave to avoid being retaken.

12.13 There are four offences under s 128:

(a) it is an offence to induce or knowingly assist anyone who is liable to be detained, or is subject to guardianship or a CTO to absent himself without leave. This might include assisting someone to absent her or himself from the place where they are required to reside as a condition of guardianship or a CTO;

(b) it is an offence to induce or knowingly to assist another person to escape from legal custody within the meaning of s 137;

(c) it is an offence knowingly to harbour a patient who is absent without leave or is otherwise at large and liable to be retaken under the MHA 1983;

(d) it is an offence knowingly to assist a patient who is absent without leave or is otherwise at large and liable to be retaken with intent to prevent, hinder or interfere with his being taken into custody or returned to the hospital or other place where he ought to be.

The phrase 'other place where he ought to be' is sufficiently wide to cover required places of residence under guardianship or a CTO. The maximum period of imprisonment which may be imposed on summary conviction is six months[25] or two years following conviction on indictment in the Crown Court.

Section 129: Obstruction

12.14 The offence of obstruction under s 129 is committed by any person who, without reasonable cause:

---

[23] MHA 1983, ss 127(4) and 130.
[24] To be increased to 12 months when the Criminal Justice Act 2003, ss 154 and 282 are introduced.
[25] To be increased to 12 months when the Criminal Justice Act 2003, ss 154 and 282 are introduced. They have not yet been introduced.

(a) refuses to allow the inspection of any premises; or

(b) refuses to allow the visiting, interviewing or examination of any person by a person authorised in that behalf by or under this Act or to give access to any person to a person so authorised; or

(c) refuses to produce for the inspection of any person so authorised any document or record the production of which is duly required by him; or

(ca) fails to comply with a request under s 120C (provision to the regulatory authority of such information as it may reasonably request in the course of an investigation); or

(d) otherwise obstructs any such person in the exercise of his functions.

A separate offence under s 129(2) is committed by anyone who insists on being present when required to withdraw by a person authorised under the Act to interview or examine a person in private. The offence under s 129(1)(d) would be committed by anyone who obstructs an AMHP or a doctor in carrying out their functions in relation to assessment prior to compulsory admission.

12.15 The maximum penalty on summary conviction is three months' imprisonment. The Committee of Inquiry into Complaints at Ashworth Hospital 'inclined to the view' that s 129 abrogates the right of silence by making it an 'offence for anyone, without reasonable excuse, to obstruct an authorised investigation'.[26]

OFFENCES UNDER PART 1 OF THE SEXUAL OFFENCES ACT 2003

12.16 Part 1 of the Sexual Offences Act 2003 ('SOA 2003') creates a number of sexual offences against persons with what the cross-headings but not the sections themselves call 'a mental disorder impeding choice'. The Home Office has issued a circular giving Guidance on the 2003 Act.[27] There are three groups of offences. Sections 30–33 apply in cases where the victim is unable to agree to the sexual activity because of a mental disorder which impedes their choice. Sections 34–37 deal with cases it might appear that the victim had agreed to the sexual activity but, because of a mental disorder which makes her or him vulnerable to inducements, threats or deceptions, their consent was not or could be deemed not to have been freely given. Finally, ss 38–41 deal with offences where the victim has a mental disorder and, because they are in a relationship of care, their consent was not or could be deemed not to have been freely given. However, as the Home Office Circular notes:[28]

---

[26] *The Committee of Inquiry into Complaints at Ashworth Hospital*, Cm 2028 (1992), vol 1, chap XIII, para 126.
[27] Home Office (2004), Guidance on Sexual Offences Act 2003 HO Circular 21/2004.
[28] Ibid, paras 129–130.

'It is important to appreciate that where a person with a mental disorder is able to consent freely to sexual activity, they have the same rights to engage in consensual sexual activity as anyone else, and ... that where a person with a mental disorder did not consent to the sexual activity, there are other offences such as rape, sexual assault etc., which apply just as much them as to anyone else.'

'Mental disorder' has the wide meaning given in s 1 of the Mental Health Act 1983, namely 'any disorder or disability of the mind.'[29]

Mental disorder impeding choice

12.17 To be guilty the offender must have known or be reasonably be expected to have known that the person has a mental disorder and that because of it or for a reason related to it is likely to be unable to refuse. A person is unable to refuse if:

(a)   he or she lacks the capacity to choose whether to agree to the touching (whether because he or she lacks sufficient understanding of the nature or reasonably foreseeable consequences of what is being done, or for any other reason); or

(b)   he or she is unable to communicate such a choice to the defendant.

12.18 Hence a mental disorder impeding choice is a mental disorder which causes the person to lack capacity to choose whether to agree to the touching or to communicate such a choice. The key case on mental disorder impeding choice is *R v C*,[30] where the complainant, X, was a 28-year-old woman diagnosed with schizo-affective disorder and an emotionally unstable personality disorder. The effects and manifestations of the disorders were intermittent. X had met C while she was suffering from a relapse. She was in a distressed, agitated state, and told C that she wanted to leave the area in which she was living for her own safety. X alleged that C offered to help her and took her to his friend's house, where she was given crack cocaine and asked by C to engage in a sexual activity. X stated that she had been 'really panicky and afraid' and had wanted to leave the premises, but that, through fear of death, she had stayed and complied with C's request. The defendant was charged with intentionally touching the complainant by penetrating her mouth with his penis in circumstances where the touching was sexual, the complainant was unable to refuse because of or for a reason related to a mental disorder and the defendant knew or could reasonably have been expected to know that she had a mental disorder and that because of it or for a reason related to it she would be likely to be unable to refuse. Section 30(2)(b), read together with s 30(2)(a), provides that a complainant is unable to refuse if she is unable to communicate to the defendant a choice whether to agree to the touching, whether because she lacks sufficient understanding of the nature or reasonably foreseeable consequences of what is being done, or for any other reason.

---

[29]   Sexual Offences Act 2003, s 79(1).
[30]   [2009] UKHL 42.

12.19   The trial judge in his summing up had stated that X would have been:[31]

> '[U]nable to refuse if she lacked the capacity to choose whether to agree to the touching, in other words the sexual activity, for any reason, for example, an irrational fear arising from her mental disorder or such confusion of mind arising from her mental disorder, that she felt that she was unable to refuse any request the defendants made for sex. Alternatively, [she] would be unable to refuse if through her mental disorder she was unable to communicate such a choice to the defendants even though she was physically able to communicate with them.'

The Court of Appeal set aside C's conviction, finding the trial judge's summing up to be inadequate and the conviction to be unsafe. It decided that an irrational fear resulting from a mental disorder could not be equated with a lack of capacity to choose, and that there was no evidence that X was physically unable to communicate any choice that she had made. The Court of Appeal further ruled that a lack of capacity to choose to agree to sexual activity could not be person-specific or situation-specific. The House of lords was asked to consider whether the Court of Appeal's decision had unduly limited the scope of s 30(1) beyond that which Parliament intended, by holding that (a) a lack of capacity to choose could not be person or situation-specific; (b) an irrational fear that prevented the exercise of choice could not be equated with a lack of capacity to choose; and (c) to fall within s 30(2)(b) of the Act, a complainant had to be physically unable to communicate by reason of their mental disorder. The House of Lords held unanimously that the Court of Appeal had unduly limited the scope of s 30(1), and restored the conviction.

12.20   Delivering the leading speech, Baroness Hale dismissed the Court of Appeal's view that a lack of capacity to choose cannot be person or situation specific:[32]

> 'Any particular choice to engage in sexual activity is, of course, both person-specific and occasion-specific: with you here and now, or not with you, (although possibly with some-one else), or not here, or not now.'

12.21   The key here is that capacity under s 30(2)(a) is more than the cognitive capacity in the sense of having 'sufficient understanding of the nature or reasonably foreseeable consequences of what is being done.' It also includes inability to choose whether to agree to the touching 'for any other reason', which may include the evaluative capacity to weigh in the balance as part of the process of arriving at a decision. To quote Baroness Hale again:[33]

> 'The words "for any other reason" are clearly capable of encompassing a wide range of circumstances in which a person's mental disorder may rob them of the ability to make an autonomous choice, even though they may have sufficient understanding of the information relevant to making it. These could include the kind of compulsion which drives a person with anorexia to refuse food, the

---

[31]   Ibid, speech of Baroness Hale of Richmond, para 21.
[32]   Ibid, para 15.
[33]   Ibid, para 26.

delusions which drive a person with schizophrenia to believe that she must do
something, or the phobia (or irrational fear) which drives a person to refuse a
life-saving injection or a blood transfusion.'

Hence contrary to the view adopted by the Court of Appeal, an irrational fear
brought on by mental disorder could give rise to inability to exercise choice to
agree to the touching: 'Provided that the inability to refuse is 'because of or for
a reason related to a mental disorder', and the other ingredients of the offence
are made out, the perpetrator is guilty.'[34] Inability to communicate a choice was
not limited to physical inability to communicate a choice.

12.22   There are four offences where an ingredient of the offence is that the
victim must suffer from a mental disorder impeding choice. Two carry a
maximum sentence of 14 years or life imprisonment. They are the offences
under ss 30 and 31 of engaging in sexual activity (intentional touching of a
sexual nature) with a person who is unable to refuse because of, or for a reason
related to, mental disorder, or intentionally causing or inciting such a person to
engage in sexual activity.

12.23   The maximum sentence for sexual activity or incitement generally on
summary conviction is six months,[35] and following conviction on indictment 14
years. The offender is liable, on conviction on indictment, to imprisonment for
life if the sexual activity involves penetrative sex with insertion of any part of
the offender's body or any other object into the anus or vagina of the victim, or
if it involves fellatio by or on either party.

12.24   The other two offences are engaging in sexual activity in the presence of
a person with mental disorder impeding choice, and causing a person with a
mental disorder impeding choice to watch a sexual act.[36] They carry a
maximum sentence of 10 years' imprisonment following conviction on
indictment or six months following summary conviction.[37]

12.25   Sections 34–38 of the SOA 2003 create the offences where the victim
suffers from mental disorder, but there is no requirement that the mental
disorder must impede choice. The offences under ss 34 and 35 carry the same
penalties as offences under ss 30 and 31 (see **12.23** above). They are:

- offering an inducement or making a threat or deception in order to
  procure sexual activity. Sexual activity must have taken place, and the

---

[34]   Ibid, para 25.
[35]   To be increased to 12 months on the commencement of ss 154 and 282 of the Criminal Justice
       Act 2003.
[36]   Sexual Offences Act 2007, ss 32–33.
[37]   To be increased to 12 months on the commencement of ss 154 and 282 of the Criminal Justice
       Act 2003.

mentally disordered victim's participation must have been secured by an inducement offered, a threat made or a deception practised by the offender;[38]

- causing a person with a mental disorder to engage in or agree to engage in sexual activity by inducement, threat or deception.

For both offences the offender must have known or be reasonably expected to have known that the victim had a mental disorder.[39]

12.26 The offences under ss 36 and 37 are:

- engaging in sexual activity in the presence, procured by inducement, threat or deception, of a person with a mental disorder;

- causing a person with a mental disorder to watch a sexual act by inducement, threat or deception.

These offences carry the same maximum penalties as offences under ss 33 and 34 (see **12.24** above).

Offences by carers

12.27 As Jones notes:[40]

'the 2003 Act also introduces a number of specific offences in relation to care workers [which] elevate the position of trust and responsibility enjoyed by a care worker from a simple aggravating feature of an offence to an offence in its own right.'

Sections 38–41 of the SOA 2003 introduce four offences which may be committed by what the cross heading calls 'care workers', or more accurately 'persons involved in the care of another person in a way which falls within s 42 of that Act'. Section 42 applies to three groups:

(a) anyone whose work in the course of their employment brings or is likely to bring them into regular face to face contact with the mentally disordered person in a care home, community home, children's home, or voluntary home;

(b) anyone whose work in the course of their employment brings or is likely to bring them into regular face-to-face contact with a mentally disordered person for whom services are provided by a NHS body or an independent medical agency, or in an independent clinic or an independent hospital;

---

[38] Sexual Offences Act 2003, s 34.
[39] Sexual Offences Act 2003, s 35.
[40] RM Jones *Mental Health Act Manual* (Sweet and Maxwell, 13th edn, 2010), para 1–1115.

(c)   anyone who is, whether or not in the course of employment, a provider of
       care, assistance or services to a mentally disordered person in connection
       with their mental disorder, and as such, has had or is likely to have regular
       face-to-face contact with B.

Hence these offences may be committed not only by 'care workers' who provide
care in the course of their employment, but also by unpaid carers, family
members, or friends who provide care, assistance, or services in connection with
the mental disorder.

12.28   With all four offences a defendant can only be found guilty if he or she
knew or ought reasonably to have known that the alleged victim was suffering
from mentally disorder, but once it is proved that the person has a mental
disorder the burden shifts to the defendant to adduce sufficient evidence to
'raise an issue as to whether he knew or could reasonably have been expected to
know it.'[41]

Engaging in, or causing or inciting, sexual activity with a person with a mental disorder

12.29   Under ss 38 and 39 a carer commits an offence if he or she engages in
sexual activity (intentional touching of a sexual nature) with a person whom he
or she knew or ought reasonably to have known was suffering from mentally
disorder, or causes or incites such activity to take place. The maximum sentence
for sexual activity or incitement generally on summary conviction is six
months,[42] and following conviction on indictment 10 years. The offender is
liable, on conviction on indictment, to imprisonment for up to 14 years if the
sexual activity involves penetrative sex with insertion of any part of the
offender's body or any other object into the anus or vagina of the victim, or if it
involves fellatio by or on either party.

12.30   The offences under ss 40 and 41 are sexual activity in the presence of a
person with a mental disorder, and causing a person with a mental disorder to
watch a sexual act. Anyone convicted summarily of these offences faces a
maximum sentence of six months, or seven years following trial on indictment.

CROSS-BORDER ARRANGEMENTS

12.31   Part VI of the MHA 1983 deals with the transfer of patients subject to
compulsory powers between United Kingdom jurisdictions and the Channel
Islands or the Isle of Man, by ensuring that they remain in legal custody whilst
in transit and on arrival at their destination are liable to equivalent compulsory
powers in the receiving jurisdiction. Part VI applies to people who are detained
(other than those detained under ss 35, 36 or 38), who are conditionally

---

[41]   Sexual Offences Act 2003, ss 38(2), 39(2), 40(2) and 41(2).
[42]   To be increased to 12 months on the commencement of ss 154 and 282 of the Criminal Justice
        Act 2003.

discharged restricted patients, or who are subject to guardianship or to a community treatment order or equivalent. Part VI also provides, in s 86 for the removal of patients suffering from mental disorder who are neither British citizens nor Commonwealth citizens with the right of abode here to other jurisdictions. Since the right to respect for family life under Article 8 is engaged, there should be consultation with the nearest relative, unless the patient has objected.

12.32 Section 39(1) of the MHA 2007 has introduced new subss (6) and (7) into s 17 of the MHA 1983, dealing with cross-border leave and transfer between jurisdictions. These provisions apply to patients from Scotland, Northern Ireland, the Isle of Man and the Channel Islands who are given leave of absence to visit England and Wales and where the clinician has determined that it is necessary in the patient's own interests, or for the protection of others that he or she remain in custody during the leave of absence. Subsections (6) and (7) of s 17 are designed to authorise patients from these jurisdictions who visit England and Wales on escorted leave to be conveyed, be kept in custody or detained by their escort while in England and Wales, and be re-taken in the event that they escape. In terms of short term leave *to* Scotland, in March 2008 the Mental Health Unit at the Ministry of Justice issued Guidance for Responsible Clinicians on *Leave of absence for patients subject to restrictions* which makes it clear that restricted patients will not be granted short term leave to Scotland:[43]

> 'We can no longer grant permission for short-term leave to Scotland for restricted patients. This applies to both escorted and unescorted leave. Section 17 leave cannot be used for this purpose as there is no power to keep patients in legal custody once they enter Scotland, and no power to re-take them if they abscond in Scotland. We have previously given effect to leave requests through short-term transfers but, following a change in the Scottish regulations regarding cross-border transfers, the Scottish Executive will not accept requests for a patient to remain in Scotland for less than 21 days before being transferred back to England or Wales'.

12.33 Section 39(2) of the MHA 2007 gives effect to Sch 5. The amendments in Sch 5 to the MHA 2007 provide for community patients to be transferred between jurisdictions. They also provide for detained patients to be transferred from Scotland to England. The various provisions also specify what date the detention or community compulsion in the receiving jurisdiction is to run from, which is important in terms of the renewal requirement and entitlement to apply for or have a case referred to a Mental Health Tribunal.

Scotland

12.34 Under the MHA 1983 removal of detained (other than those detained under ss 35, 36 or 38) and guardianship patients to Scotland is dealt with by s 80. Schedule, 5 para 2 removes the provision in s 80 for transfer of patients

---

[43]   Ministry of Justice Mental Health Unit, *Leave of absence for patients subject to restrictions*: *Guidance for Responsible Clinicians* 18 March 2008, para 17.

under guardianship in England and Wales to Scotland as Scotland no longer has the equivalent of mental health guardianship. It then introduces four new sections, ss 80ZA and 80B–80D. The Secretary of State for Health (England) or the National Assembly for Wales may authorise the transfer of a non-restricted patient if it is in the interests of the patient to remove him to Scotland, and that arrangements have been made for admitting him to hospital there. If the patient is subject to restrictions or to a limitation direction the decision-maker is the Minister of Justice. Before transfer takes place the views of the nearest relative should be ascertained and reported to the decision-making authority.

12.35 New s 80ZA empowers the Secretary of State or the Welsh Ministers to authorise the transfer of a community patient to Scotland if a transfer under this section is in the patient's interests; and 'arrangements have been made for dealing with him under enactments in force in Scotland corresponding or similar to those relating to community patients in this Act'. The relevant national authority may not act if the patient has been recalled to hospital.[44]

12.36 Section 80A empowers the Minister of Justice, with the consent of the relevant Scottish Minister, to authorise the transfer of a conditionally discharged restriction order patient to Scotland if it appears to be in the interests of the patient.

12.37 Schedule 5, para 4(1) to the Mental Health Act 2007 introduces new ss 80B–80D in relation to transfers from Scotland to England and Wales, providing for transfer of detained patients, CTO patients, and conditionally discharged restricted patients respectively. Section 290 of the Mental Health (Care and Treatment) (Scotland) Act 2003 ('the 2003 Act') and the Mental Health (Cross-border Transfer: Patients Subject to Detention Requirement or otherwise in Hospital) (Scotland) Regulations 2005,[45] provide for transfer of in-patients to and from Scotland. Section 289 of the 2003 Act deals with the transfer of patients subject to a requirement other than detention to a place outside Scotland and for patients subject to corresponding requirements in England, Wales, Northern Ireland, the Isle of Man or the Channel Islands to be received in Scotland. The process for such transfers is dealt with in the Mental Health (England and Wales Cross-border Transfer: Patients Subject to Requirements other than Detention) (Scotland) Regulations 2008.[46]

12.38 New s 80C applies to a patient who is subject to compulsion in the community in Scotland and is transferred to England or Wales. On arrival at the required place of residence in England or Wales, the patient will be treated as if admitted to a hospital in England or Wales on that date under ss 3 or 37 and a CTO had been made discharging him from that hospital. The Explanatory Notes to the MHA 2007 say that:[47]

---

44 MHA 1983, s 80ZA(3).
45 SSI 2005/467 <http://www.opsi.gov.uk/legislation/scotland/ssi2005/20050467.htm>.
46 SSI 2008/356 <http://www.opsi.gov.uk/legislation/scotland/ssi2008/ssi_20080356_en_1>.
47 *Explanatory Notes to the MHA 2007*, para 164.

'As soon as practicable after the arrival of a community patient in England and Wales a CTO should be made and deemed to be dated from the day of the patient's arrival. A community patient transferred from Scotland will not be detained in hospital following their transfer prior to becoming a community patient in England and Wales.'

As soon as practicable after the patient's arrival, the RC must specify the conditions that the patient will be subject to under the CTO.

12.39 New s 80D provides for transfer of a conditionally discharged patient from Scotland to England or Wales. On his arrival in England or Wales the patient will be treated as a restricted patient who had been granted a conditional discharge under either s 42 or s 73.

Northern Ireland

12.40 Under the MHA 1983, removal of detained and guardianship patients to Northern Ireland is dealt with by s 81. The Secretary of State for Health (England) or the Welsh Ministers may authorise the transfer of a non-restricted patient or guardianship if it is in the interests of the patient to remove him to Northern Ireland, and that arrangements have been made for admission to hospital or reception into guardianship there. If the patient is subject to restrictions or to a limitation direction the decision-maker is the Minister of Justice. Before transfer takes place the views of the nearest relative should be ascertained and reported to the decision-making authority. A patient who is transferred to Northern Ireland shall be treated as if on the day of admission he or she had been admitted in pursuance of an application made under the corresponding enactment in Northern Ireland, and the English authority to detain will cease to have effect.

12.41 New s 81ZA applies the removal arrangements to Northern Ireland for detained and guardianship patients.[48] No provision is made in the Act for the transfer of community patients from Northern Ireland as there is currently no provision for community patients in Northern Ireland.

12.42 Section 81A empowers the Minister of Justice, with the consent of the Minister exercising corresponding functions in Northern Ireland to arrange for the transfer of responsibility for a conditionally discharged restricted patient, where it appears that to do so would be in the interests of the patient. The patient is treated as if he or she had been conditionally discharged on the date of the transfer and as if subject to a restriction order or restriction direction under the corresponding enactment in force in Northern Ireland. Although since the MHA 2007 came into force all subsequent restriction orders have been be without limit of time, time limited orders made prior to the 2007 Act, or orders made outside England and Wales having the same effect, expire on the date when they would have expired had the patient not been transferred.

---

[48] Introduced by MHA 2007, Sch 5, para 6.

12.43 Section 82 empowers the Department of Health and Social Services for Northern Ireland in Northern Ireland to authorise removal to England or Wales of a patient who is detained (other than under the equivalents of ss 35, 36 or 38) or subject to guardianship under the (Northern Ireland) Order 1986. It must appear to the relevant authority that it is in the interests of the patient to remove him to England and Wales, and that arrangements have been made for the patient's admission to hospital or reception into guardianship. Detention or guardianship under the corresponding provision of the MHA 1983 will commence on the date of admission to hospital or arrival at the required place of residence in England or Wales.

12.44 Section 82A empowers the Minister in Northern Ireland exercising functions corresponding to those of the Minister of Justice, acting with the consent of the Minister of Justice, to authorise the transfer of a conditionally discharged restricted patient subject to the Mental Health (Northern Ireland) Order 1986 if it appears to be in the interests of the patient to do so. The patient is then treated as if he or she had been conditionally discharged under ss 42 or 73 of the MHA 1983 on the date of the transfer. If the patient was in Northern Ireland subject to a time limited restriction order or restriction direction, the English restriction order or direction shall expire on the date when it would have expired had the transfer not been made.

12.45 Schedule 5 also amends s 88 of the MHA 1983, which provides for patients absent from hospitals in England and Wales to be taken into custody and returned to England and Wales, to apply to Northern Ireland only. The Channel Islands and the Isle of Man have powers of their own, which they can use to return patients from England and Wales. In Scotland regulations have been made on such matters under s 309 (patients from other jurisdictions) of the Mental Health (Care and Treatment) (Scotland) Act 2003 (see **12.37** above).

The Channel Islands and the Isle of Man

12.46 Schedule 5 to the MHA 2007 amends the provisions in ss 83 and 85 of the MHA 1983 providing for detained (other than those detained under ss 35, 36 or 38), guardianship and conditionally discharged restricted patients to be transferred from England and Wales to the Channel Islands and the Isle of Man and vice versa. These provisions are similar to those authorising transfer to and from Scotland and Northern Ireland in terms of the criteria (in the patient's interests and arrangements must exist for reception of the patient), and in terms of the 'deeming provisions' whereby detention guardianship and CTOs are deemed to commence on the date of transfer or arrival at the place of residence or receiving hospital.

12.47 New ss 83ZA and 85ZA provide for community patients to be transferred from England and Wales to the Channel Islands and the Isle of Man and vice versa. Section 83ZA applies to community patients s 83 of the MHA 1983 which authorises transfer of guardianship or detained patients to the Channel Islands or the Isle of Man. Section 85ZA, which authorises transfer from the Channel Islands or the Isle of Man, comes into effect only if there are in force in the relevant jurisdictions 'relevant enactments' corresponding or similar to those relating to community patients in this Act. The Explanatory Notes say that:[49]

> 'At present the Channel Islands and the Isle of Man do not have legislation enabling patients to be treated in the community under arrangements similar to Supervised Community Treatment so [these sections] would not, as things stand, have any effect in relation to the Channel Islands or the Isle of Man.'

Curiously, although Northern Ireland also currently has no provision for community patients, the 2007 Act amendments provide only for transfer to Northern Ireland of CTO patients, and no anticipatory provision equivalent to s 85ZA has been introduced.

Removal of aliens

12.48 Section 86 empowers the Secretary of State for Health to issue a warrant authorising removal from the place where he or she is receiving treatment in England and Wales or Northern Ireland of any in-patient detained under an application for admission for treatment, who is neither a British citizen nor a Commonwealth citizen having the right of abode in the United Kingdom. A similar power in relation to patients subject to a hospital order or equivalent is conferred on the Secretary of State for Justice. Whereas previously the section applied only to people with mental illness, it now applies to all mental disorders. The conditions for issuing a warrant are that it must appear to the Secretary of State:

(a)   that proper arrangements have been made for the removal of the patient to a country or territory outside the United Kingdom, the Isle of Man and the Channel Islands and for his care or treatment there; and

(b)   that it is in the interests of the patient to remove her or him.

The Secretary of State may give such directions as he or she thinks fit for the conveyance of the patient to his destination in that country or territory and for his detention in any place or on board any ship or aircraft until his arrival at any specified port or place in any such country or territory.

12.49 The Secretary of State's powers under this section may only be exercised with the approval of a Mental Health Tribunal for England, Wales or Northern Ireland. However in *R (on the application of X) v Secretary of State for the Home Department* the Court of Appeal held that a parallel power existed where the patient had no basis to remain under the Immigration Act 1971. Hence, the Secretary of State was entitled to remove him using powers under the parallel regime of the Immigration Act and was not confined by the power in s 86 with its requirement for approval by the MHT. Schiemann LJ said that clearly if the

---

[49]   *Explanatory Notes to the MHA 2007*, para 166.

Secretary of State wishes to use Immigration Act powers in relation to a mentally disordered person, the mental disorder would be a factor which he must take into account.[50] The Court of Appeal in *X* held that, whatever power was used, there would be no breach of the prohibition of inhuman or degrading treatment in Art 3 under the principle in *D v United Kingdom*[51] if X was returned to Malta to receive in-patient treatment there.

CONCLUSION

12.50 The offences under the MHA 1983 are virtually untouched by the MHA 2007 with the exception of the increased penalty for ill-treatment or wilful neglect. Reform of the antiquated sexual offences with their unfortunate terminology in relation to mentally disordered people had already been achieved by the Sexual Offences Act 2003. The Human Rights Act 1998 has meant that the courts and the Government are much more conscious of the positive obligation to extend the protection of the criminal law to mentally vulnerable people. Moreover, the new criminal offences under the Sexual Offences Act 2003 are designed to recognise that the presence of certain mental disorders does not necessarily mean that a person is incapable of consenting to sexual relations, hence seeking to enhance the rights of mentally disordered people to sexual expression. Nevertheless, the ruling in *R v C*[52] shows that the courts are still astute to protect the vulnerable against sexual exploitation, whilst demonstrating a strong move away from the status approach to capacity in relation to consent to sexual activity. The case of *R (B) v DPP and the Equality and Human Rights Commission*[53] shows how the fact that a person suffers from a severe mental disorder should not be taken as disqualifying them from giving evidence. Both cases, together with the Protection of Vulnerable Adults Guidance, show an increased willingness of the courts and the Government to extend the protection of the criminal law to mentally disordered people.

12.51 The changes in relation to transfers between jurisdictions are significant. The MHA 2007 achieves a complete system of rules for detention and compulsory treatment in the community of adult and child patients. The provisions in relation to transfer replace a somewhat haphazard system with an attempt at a comprehensive code for the transfer in custody of patients subject to compulsion in hospital or the community between all jurisdictions. They create the possibility to move patients in custody from one jurisdiction to another with a seamless transition between the patient being subject to the powers of detention or community compulsion in one country and becoming subject to those in the receiving jurisdiction.

---

50 [2000] MHLR 67 at [28].
51 (1997) 24 EHRR 423, ECtHR.
52 [2009] UKHL 42.
53 [2009] EWHC 106 (Admin).

Appendix

MENTAL HEALTH ACT 1983 (1983 C 20) (AS AMENDED BY THE MENTAL HEALTH ACT 2007)

ARRANGEMENT OF SECTIONS

PART I
APPLICATION OF ACT

PART II
COMPULSORY ADMISSION TO HOSPITAL AND GUARDIANSHIP

Procedure for hospital admission

General provisions as to applications and recommendations

Community Treatment Orders

PART III
PATIENTS CONCERNED IN CRIMINAL PROCEEDINGS OR UNDER SENTENCE

PART VI
REMOVAL AND RETURN OF PATIENTS WITHIN UNITED KINGDOM, ETC
Removal to and from Scotland

PART VII (*REPEALED*)

PART VIII
MISCELLANEOUS FUNCTIONS OF LOCAL AUTHORITIES AND THE SECRETARY OF STATE

PART IX
OFFENCES

PART I
APPLICATION OF ACT

1 Application of Act: 'mental disorder'

(1) The provisions of this Act shall have effect with respect to the reception, care and treatment of mentally disordered patients, the management of their property and other related matters.

(2) In this Act –

'mental disorder' means any disorder or disability of the mind; and
'mentally disordered' shall be construed accordingly;

and other expressions shall have the meanings assigned to them in section 145 below.

(2A) But a person with learning disability shall not be considered by reason of that disability to be –

    (a)   suffering from mental disorder for the purposes of the provisions mentioned in subsection (2B) below; or

    (b)   requiring treatment in hospital for mental disorder for the purposes of sections 17E and 50 to 53 below,

unless that disability is associated with abnormally aggressive or seriously irresponsible conduct on his part.

(2B) The provisions are –

    (a)   sections 3, 7, 17A, 20 and 20A below;

    (b)   sections 35 to 38, 45A, 47, 48 and 51 below; and

    (c)   section 72(1)(b) and (c) and (4) below.

(3) Dependence on alcohol or drugs is not considered to be a disorder or disability of the mind for the purposes of subsection (2) above.

(4) In subsection (2A) above, 'learning disability' means a state of arrested or incomplete development of the mind which includes significant impairment of intelligence and social functioning.'

Amendments. Definitions in subs (2) repealed and substituted: MHA 2007, s 1(1), (2). Subss (2A), (2B) inserted: MHA 2007, s 2(1), (2). Subs (3) substituted: MHA 2007, s 3. Subs (4) inserted: MHA 2007, s 2(1), (3). For transitional provisions and savings see MHA 2007, s 53, Sch 10, paras 1, 2.

PART II
COMPULSORY ADMISSION TO HOSPITAL AND GUARDIANSHIP

Procedure for hospital admission

2 Admission for assessment

(1) A patient may be admitted to a hospital and detained there for the period allowed by subsection (4) below in pursuance of an application (in this Act

referred to as 'an application for admission for assessment') made in accordance with subsections (2) and (3) below.

(2) An application for admission for assessment may be made in respect of a patient on the grounds that –

(a) he is suffering from mental disorder of a nature or degree which warrants the detention of the patient in a hospital for assessment (or for assessment followed by medical treatment) for at least a limited period; and

(b) he ought to be so detained in the interests of his own health or safety or with a view to the protection of other persons.

(3) An application for admission for assessment shall be founded on the written recommendations in the prescribed form of two registered medical practitioners, including in each case a statement that in the opinion of the practitioner the conditions set out in subsection (2) above are complied with.

(4) Subject to the provisions of section 29(4) below, a patient admitted to hospital in pursuance of an application for admission for assessment may be detained for a period not exceeding 28 days beginning with the day on which he is admitted, but shall not be detained after the expiration of that period unless before it has expired he has become liable to be detained by virtue of a subsequent application, order or direction under the following provisions of this Act.

3 Admission for treatment

(1) A patient may be admitted to a hospital and detained there for the period allowed by the following provisions of this Act in pursuance of an application (in this Act referred to as 'an application for admission for treatment') made in accordance with this section.

(2) An application for admission for treatment may be made in respect of a patient on the grounds that –

(a) he is suffering from mental disorder of a nature or degree which makes it appropriate for him to receive medical treatment in a hospital; and

(b) (*repealed*)

(c) it is necessary for the health or safety of the patient or for the protection of other persons that he should receive such treatment and it cannot be provided unless he is detained under this section; and

(d) appropriate medical treatment is available for him.

(3) An application for admission for treatment shall be founded on the written recommendations in the prescribed form of two registered medical practitioners, including in each case a statement that in the opinion of the practitioner the conditions set out in subsection (2) above are complied with; and each such recommendation shall include –

(a) such particulars as may be prescribed of the grounds for that opinion so far as it relates to the conditions set out in paragraphs (a) and (d) of that subsection; and

(b)   a statement of the reasons for that opinion so far as it relates to the conditions set out in paragraph (c) of that subsection, specifying whether other methods of dealing with the patient are available and, if so, why they are not appropriate.

(4) In this Act, references to appropriate medical treatment, in relation to a person suffering from mental disorder, are references to medical treatment which is appropriate in his case, taking into account the nature and degree of the mental disorder and all other circumstances of his case.

Amendments. Words in subs (2)(a) substituted: MHA 2007, s 1(4), Sch 1, Pt 1, paras 1, 2. Subs 2(b) repealed, subs (2)(d) inserted and words in subs (3)(a) substituted: MHA 2007, s 4(1), (2)(a)–(c) Subs (4) inserted: MHA 2007, s 4(1), (3).

4 Admission for assessment in cases of emergency

(1) In any case of urgent necessity, an application for admission for assessment may be made in respect of a patient in accordance with the following provisions of this section, and any application so made is in this Act referred to as 'an emergency application'.

(2) An emergency application may be made either by an approved mental health professional or by the nearest relative of the patient; and every such application shall include a statement that it is of urgent necessity for the patient to be admitted and detained under section 2 above, and that compliance with the provisions of this Part of this Act relating to applications under that section would involve undesirable delay.

(3) An emergency application shall be sufficient in the first instance if founded on one of the medical recommendations required by section 2 above, given, if practicable, by a practitioner who has previous acquaintance with the patient and otherwise complying with the requirements of section 12 below so far as applicable to a single recommendation, and verifying the statement referred to in subsection (2) above.

(4) An emergency application shall cease to have effect on the expiration of a period of 72 hours from the time when the patient is admitted to the hospital unless –

(a)   the second medical recommendation required by section 2 above is given and received by the managers within that period; and
(b)   that recommendation and the recommendation referred to in subsection (3) above together comply with all the requirements of section 12 below (other than the requirement as to the time of signature of the second recommendation).

(5) In relation to an emergency application, section 11 below shall have effect as if in subsection (5) of that section for the words 'the period of 14 days ending with the date of the application' there were substituted the words 'the previous 24 hours'.

Amendments. Words in subs (2) substituted: MHA 2007, s 21, Sch 2, para 2(a).

5 Application in respect of patient already in hospital

(1) An application for the admission of a patient to a hospital may be made under this Part of this Act notwithstanding that the patient is already an in-patient in that hospital or, in the case of an application for admission for treatment, that the patient is for the time being liable to be detained in the hospital in pursuance of an application for admission for assessment; and where an application is so made the patient shall be treated for the purposes of this Part of this Act as if he had been admitted to the hospital at the time when that application was received by the managers.

(2) If, in the case of a patient who is an in-patient in a hospital, it appears to the registered medical practitioner or approved clinician in charge of the treatment of the patient that an application ought to be made under this Part of this Act for the admission of the patient to hospital, he may furnish to the managers a report in writing to that effect; and in any such case the patient may be detained in the hospital for a period of 72 hours from the time when the report is so furnished.

(3) The registered medical practitioner or approved clinician in charge of the treatment of a patient in a hospital may nominate one (but not more than one) person to act for him under subsection (2) above in his absence.

(3A) For the purposes of subsection (3) above –

- (a) the registered medical practitioner may nominate another registered medical practitioner, or an approved clinician, on the staff of the hospital; and
- (b) the approved clinician may nominate another approved clinician, or a registered medical practitioner, on the staff of the hospital.

(4) If, in the case of a patient who is receiving treatment for mental disorder as an in-patient in a hospital, it appears to a nurse of the prescribed class –

- (a) that the patient is suffering from mental disorder to such a degree that it is necessary for his health or safety or for the protection of others for him to be immediately restrained from leaving the hospital; and
- (b) that it is not practicable to secure the immediate attendance of a practitioner or clinician for the purpose of furnishing a report under subsection (2) above,

the nurse may record that fact in writing; and in that event the patient may be detained in the hospital for a period of six hours from the time when that fact is so recorded or until the earlier arrival at the place where the patient is detained of a practitioner or clinician having power to furnish a report under that subsection.

(5) A record made under subsection (4) above shall be delivered by the nurse (or by a person authorised by the nurse in that behalf) to the managers of the hospital as soon as possible after it is made; and where a record is made under that subsection the period mentioned in subsection (2) above shall begin at the time when it is made.

(6) The reference in subsection (1) above to an in-patient does not include an in patient who is liable to be detained in pursuance of an application under this Part of this Act or a community patient and the references in subsections (2) and (4) above do not include an in-patient who is liable to be detained in a hospital under this Part of this Act or a community patient.

(7) In subsection (4) above 'prescribed' means prescribed by an order made by the Secretary of State.

Amendments. Words in subss (2) and (4) inserted, and subss (3) and (3A) substituted for previous subs (3): MHA 2007, s 9(1), (2). Words in subs (6) inserted: MHA 2007, s 32(4), Sch 3, paras 1, 2.

Note. Previous subs (3) allows nomination only of a person on the staff of the hospital, but see prospectively inserted subs (3A). The following orders have been made under subs (7). The Mental Health (Nurses) (England) Order 2008 SI 2008 No. 1208; The Mental Health (Nurses) (Wales) Order 2008 SI 2008 No. 2441 (W.214).

6 Effect of application for admission

(1) An application for the admission of a patient to a hospital under this Part of this Act, duly completed in accordance with the provisions of this Part of this Act, shall be sufficient authority for the applicant, or any person authorised by the applicant, to take the patient and convey him to the hospital at any time within the following period, that is to say –

(a) in the case of an application other than an emergency application, the period of 14 days beginning with the date on which the patient was last examined by a registered medical practitioner before giving a medical recommendation for the purposes of the application;

(b) in the case of an emergency application, the period of 24 hours beginning at the time when the patient was examined by the practitioner giving the medical recommendation which is referred to in section 4(3) above, or at the time when the application is made, whichever is the earlier.

(2) Where a patient is admitted within the said period to the hospital specified in such an application as is mentioned in subsection (1) above, or, being within that hospital, is treated by virtue of section 5 above as if he had been so admitted, the application shall be sufficient authority for the managers to detain the patient in the hospital in accordance with the provisions of this Act.

(3) Any application for the admission of a patient under this Part of this Act which appears to be duly made and to be founded on the necessary medical recommendations may be acted upon without further proof of the signature or qualification of the person by whom the application or any such medical recommendation is made or given or of any matter of fact or opinion stated in it.

(4) Where a patient is admitted to a hospital in pursuance of an application for admission for treatment, any previous application under this Part of this Act by virtue of which he was liable to be detained in a hospital or subject to guardianship shall cease to have effect.

7 Application for guardianship

(1) A patient who has attained the age of 16 years may be received into guardianship, for the period allowed by the following provisions of this Act, in pursuance of an application (in this Act referred to as 'a guardianship application') made in accordance with this section.

(2) A guardianship application may be made in respect of a patient on the grounds that –

   (a)   he is suffering from mental disorder of a nature or degree which warrants his reception into guardianship under this section; and

   (b)   it is necessary in the interests of the welfare of the patient or for the protection of other persons that the patient should be so received.

(3) A guardianship application shall be founded on the written recommendations in the prescribed form of two registered medical practitioners, including in each case a statement that in the opinion of the practitioner the conditions set out in subsection (2) above are complied with; and each such recommendation shall include –

   (a)   such particulars as may be prescribed of the grounds for that opinion so far as it relates to the conditions set out in paragraph (a) of that subsection; and

   (b)   a statement of the reasons for that opinion so far as it relates to the conditions set out in paragraph (b) of that subsection.

(4) A guardianship application shall state the age of the patient or, if his exact age is not known to the applicant, shall state (if it be the fact) that the patient is believed to have attained the age of 16 years.

(5) The person named as guardian in a guardianship application may be either a local social services authority or any other person (including the applicant himself); but a guardianship application in which a person other than a local social services authority is named as guardian shall be of no effect unless it is accepted on behalf of that person by the local social services authority for the area in which he resides, and shall be accompanied by a statement in writing by that person that he is willing to act as guardian.

Amendments. Words in subs (2)(a) repealed: MHA 2007, ss 1(4), 55, Sch 1, paras 1, 3, Sch 11, Pt 1.

8 Effect of guardianship application, etc

(1) Where a guardianship application, duly made under the provisions of this Part of this Act and forwarded to the local social services authority within the period allowed by subsection (2) below is accepted by that authority, the application shall, subject to regulations made by the Secretary of State, confer on the authority or person named in the application as guardian, to the exclusion of any other person –

   (a)   the power to require the patient to reside at a place specified by the authority or person named as guardian;

(b)   the power to require the patient to attend at places and times so specified for the purpose of medical treatment, occupation, education or training;

(c)   the power to require access to the patient to be given, at any place where the patient is residing, to any registered medical practitioner,approved mental health professional or other person so specified.

(2) The period within which a guardianship application is required for the purposes of this section to be forwarded to the local social services authority is the period of 14 days beginning with the date on which the patient was last examined by a registered medical practitioner before giving a medical recommendation for the purposes of the application.

(3) A guardianship application which appears to be duly made and to be founded on the necessary medical recommendations may be acted upon without further proof of the signature or qualification of the person by whom the application or any such medical recommendation is made or given, or of any matter of fact or opinion stated in the application.

(4) If within the period of 14 days beginning with the day on which a guardianship application has been accepted by the local social services authority the application, or any medical recommendation given for the purposes of the application, is found to be in any respect incorrect or defective, the application or recommendation may, within that period and with the consent of that authority, be amended by the person by whom it was signed; and upon such amendment being made the application or recommendation shall have effect and shall be deemed to have had effect as if it had been originally made as so amended.

(5) Where a patient is received into guardianship in pursuance of a guardianship application, any previous application under this Part of this Act by virtue of which he was subject to guardianship or liable to be detained in a hospital shall cease to have effect.

Amendments. Words in subs (1)(c) substituted: MHA 2007, s 21, Sch 2, paras 1, 2(b).

9 Regulations as to guardianship

(1) Subject to the provisions of this Part of this Act, the Secretary of State may make regulations

(a)   for regulating the exercise by the guardians of patients received into guardianship under this Part of this Act of their powers as such; and

(b)   for imposing on such guardians, and upon local social services authorities in the case of patients under the guardianship of persons other than local social services authorities, such duties as he considers necessary or expedient in the interests of the patients.

(2) Regulations under this section may in particular make provision for requiring the patients to be visited, on such occasions or at such intervals as may be prescribed by the regulations, on behalf of such local social services authorities as may be so prescribed, and shall provide for the appointment, in

the case of every patient subject to the guardianship of a person other than a local social services authority, of a registered medical practitioner to act as the nominated medical attendant of the patient.

Notes. The following regulations have been made under this section The Mental Health (Hospital, Guardianship and Treatment) (England) Regulations 2008 SI 2008 No. 1184; The Mental Health (Hospital, Guardianship, Community Treatment and Consent to Treatment) (Wales) Regulations 2008 SI 2008 No. 2439 (W.212).

10 Transfer of guardianship in case of death, incapacity, etc of guardian

(1) If any person (other than a local social services authority) who is the guardian of a patient received into guardianship under this Part of this Act –

(a) dies; or

(b) gives notice in writing to the local social services authority that he desires to relinquish the functions of guardian,

the guardianship of the patient shall thereupon vest in the local social services authority, but without prejudice to any power to transfer the patient into the guardianship of another person in pursuance of regulations under section 19 below.

(2) If any such person, not having given notice under subsection (1)(b) above, is incapacitated by illness or any other cause from performing the functions of guardian of the patient, those functions may, during his incapacity, be performed on his behalf by the local social services authority or by any other person approved for the purposes by that authority.

(3) If it appears to the county court, upon application made by an approved mental health professional acting on behalf of the local social services authority, that any person other than a local social services authority having the guardianship of a patient received into guardianship under this Part of this Act has performed his functions negligently or in a manner contrary to the interests of the welfare of the patient, the court may order that the guardianship of the patient be transferred to the local social services authority or to any other person approved for the purpose by that authority.

(4) Where the guardianship of a patient is transferred to a local social services authority or other person by or under this section, subsection (2)(c) of section 19 below shall apply as if the patient had been transferred into the guardianship of that authority or person in pursuance of regulations under that section.

(5) In this section 'the local social services authority', in relation to a person (other than a local social services authority) who is the guardian of a patient, means the local social services authority for the area in which that person resides (or resided immediately before his death).

Amendments. Words in subs (3) substituted, and subs (5) inserted: MHA 2007, s 21, Sch 2, paras 1, 3.

General provisions as to applications and recommendations

11 General provisions as to applications

(1) Subject to the provisions of this section, an application for admission for assessment, an application for admission for treatment and a guardianship application may be made either by the nearest relative of the patient or by an approved mental health professional; and every such application shall specify the qualification of the applicant to make the application.

(1A) No application mentioned in subsection (1) above shall be made by an approved mental health professional if the circumstances are such that there would be a potential conflict of interest for the purposes of regulations under section 12A below.

(2) Every application for admission shall be addressed to the managers of the hospital to which admission is sought and every guardianship application shall be forwarded to the local social services authority named in the application as guardian, or, as the case may be, to the local social services authority for the area in which the person so named resides.

(3) Before or within a reasonable time after an application for the admission of a patient for assessment is made by an approved mental health professional, that professional shall take such steps as are practicable to inform the person (if any) appearing to be the nearest relative of the patient that the application is to be or has been made and of the power of the nearest relative under section 23(2)(a) below.

(4) An approved mental health professional may not make an application for admission for treatment or a guardianship application in respect of a patient in either of the following cases –

   (a)   the nearest relative of the patient has notified that professional, or the local social services authority on whose behalf the professional is acting, that he objects to the application being made; or

   (b)   that professional has not consulted the person (if any) appearing to be the nearest relative of the patient, but the requirement to consult that person does not apply if it appears to the professional that in the circumstances such consultation is not reasonably practicable or would involve unreasonable delay.

(5) None of the applications mentioned in subsection (1) above shall be made by any person in respect of a patient unless that person has personally seen the patient within the period of 14 days ending with the date of the application. Subsection 6 is deleted. It related to the subcategories of mental disorder and required each medical recommendation to describe the patient as suffering from at least one subcategory of mental disorder in common.

(6) (*repealed*)

(7) Each of the applications mentioned in subsection (1) above shall be sufficient if the recommendations on which it is founded are given either as

separate recommendations, each signed by a registered medical practitioner, or as a joint recommendation signed by two such practitioners.

Amendments. Words in subss (1) and (3) substituted, and subs (4) substituted: MHA 2007, s 21, Sch 2, paras 1, 4. Subs (6) repealed: MHA 2007, s 55, Sch 11, Pt 1.

12 General provisions as to medical recommendations

(1) The recommendations required for the purposes of an application for the admission of a patient under this Part of this Act or a guardianship application (in this Act referred to as 'medical recommendations') shall be signed on or before the date of the application, and shall be given by practitioners who have personally examined the patient either together or separately, but where they have examined the patient separately not more than five days must have elapsed between the days on which the separate examinations took place.

(2) Of the medical recommendations given for the purposes of any such application, one shall be given by a practitioner approved for the purposes of this section by the Secretary of State as having special experience in the diagnosis or treatment of mental disorder; and unless that practitioner has previous acquaintance with the patient, the other such recommendation shall, if practicable, be given by a registered medical practitioner who has such previous acquaintance.

(2A) A registered medical practitioner who is an approved clinician shall be treated as also approved for the purposes of this section under subsection (2) above as having special experience as mentioned there.

(3) No medical recommendation shall be given for the purposes of an application mentioned in subsection (1) above if the circumstances are such that there would be a potential conflict of interest for the purposes of regulations under section 12A below.

Amendments. Words in sub s (1) inserted: MHA 2007, s 22(1), (3). Subs (2A) inserted: MHA 2007, s 16. Subs (3) substituted for previous subss (3)–(7): MHA 2007, s 22(1), (4).

12A Conflicts of interest

(1) The appropriate national authority may make regulations as to the circumstances in which there would be a potential conflict of interest such that –

(a)   an approved mental health professional shall not make an application mentioned in section 11(1) above;

(b)   a registered medical practitioner shall not give a recommendation for the purposes of an application mentioned in section 12(1) above.

(2) Regulations under subsection (1) above may make –

(a)   provision for the prohibitions in paragraphs (a) and (b) of that subsection to be subject to specified exceptions;

(b)   different provision for different cases; and

(c)   transitional, consequential, incidental or supplemental provision.

(3) In subsection (1) above, 'the appropriate national authority' means –

(a)   in relation to applications in which admission is sought to a hospital in England or to guardianship applications in respect of which the area of the relevant local social services authority is in England, the Secretary of State;

(b)   in relation to applications in which admission is sought to a hospital in Wales or to guardianship applications in respect of which the area of the relevant local social services authority is in Wales, the Welsh Ministers.

(4) References in this section to the relevant local social services authority, in relation to a guardianship application, are references to the local social services authority named in the application as guardian or (as the case may be) the local social services authority for the area in which the person so named resides.'

Amendments. Section inserted: MHA 2007, s 22(1), (5).

Note. The following regulations have been made under this section: The Mental Health (Conflicts of Interest) (England) Regulations 2008 SI 2008 No. 1205; The Mental Health (Conflicts of Interest) (Wales) Regulations 2008 SI 2008 No. 2440.

13 Duty of approved mental health professionals to make applications for admission or guardianship

(1) If a local social services authority have reason to think that an application for admission to hospital or a guardianship application may need to be made in respect of a patient within their area, they shall make arrangements for an approved mental health professional to consider the patient's case on their behalf.

(1A) If that professional is –

(a)   satisfied that such an application ought to be made in respect of the patient; and

(b)   of the opinion, having regard to any wishes expressed by relatives of the patient or any other relevant circumstances, that it is necessary or proper for the application to be made by him,

he shall make the application.

(1B) Subsection (1C) below applies where –

(a)   a local social services authority makes arrangements under subsection (1) above in respect of a patient;

(b)   an application for admission for assessment is made under subsection (1A) above in respect of the patient;

(c)   while the patient is liable to be detained in pursuance of that application, the authority have reason to think that an application for admission for treatment may need to be made in respect of the patient; and

(d)   the patient is not within the area of the authority.

(1C) Where this subsection applies, subsection (1) above shall be construed as requiring the authority to make arrangements under that subsection in place of the authority mentioned there.

(2) Before making an application for the admission of a patient to hospital an approved mental health professional shall interview the patient in a suitable manner and satisfy himself that detention in a hospital is in all the circumstances of the case the most appropriate way of providing the care and medical treatment of which the patient stands in need.

(3) An application under subsection (1A) above may be made outside the area of the local social services authority on whose behalf the approved mental health professional is considering the patient's case.

(4) It shall be the duty of a local social services authority, if so required by the nearest relative of a patient residing in their area, make arrangements under subsection (1) above for an approved mental health professional to consider the patient's case with a view to making an application for his admission to hospital; and if in any such case that approved social worker that professional decides not to make an application he shall inform the nearest relative of his reasons in writing.

(5) Nothing in this section shall be construed as authorising or requiring an application to be made by an approved mental health professional in contravention of the provisions of section 11(4) above or of regulations under section 12A above, or as restricting the power of a local social services authority to make arrangements with an approved mental health professional to consider a patient's case or of an approved mental health professional to make any application under this Act.

Amendments. Section heading substituted, subss (1)–(1C) substituted for previous subs (1), words in subss (2), (4), (5) substituted, subs (3) substituted, and words in subs (5) inserted: MHA 2007, s 21, Sch 2, paras 1, 5. Words in subs (5) inserted: MHA 2007, s 22(1), (6).

14 Social reports

Where a patient is admitted to a hospital in pursuance of an application (other than an emergency application) made under this Part of this Act by his nearest relative, the managers of the hospital shall as soon as practicable give notice of that fact to the local social services authority for the area in which the patient resided immediately before his admission; and that authority shall as soon as practicable arrange for an approved mental health professional to interview the patient and provide the managers with a report on his social circumstances.

Amendments. Words repealed: Children Act 2004, s 64, Sch 5, Words substituted: MHA 2007, s 21, Sch 2, paras 1, 6.

15 Rectification of applications and recommendations

(1) If within the period of 14 days beginning with the day on which a patient has been admitted to a hospital in pursuance of an application for admission for assessment or for treatment the application, or any medical recommendation given for the purposes of the application, is found to be in any respect

incorrect or defective, the application or recommendation may, within that period and with the consent of the managers of the hospital, be amended by the person by whom it was signed; and upon such amendment being made the application or recommendation shall have effect and shall be deemed to have had effect as if it had been originally made as so amended.

(2) Without prejudice to subsection (1) above, if within the period mentioned in that subsection it appears to the managers of the hospital that one of the two medical recommendations on which an application for the admission of a patient is founded is insufficient to warrant the detention of the patient in pursuance of the application, they may, within that period, give notice in writing to that effect to the applicant; and where any such notice is given in respect of a medical recommendation, that recommendation shall be disregarded, but the application shall be, and shall be deemed always to have been, sufficient if –

(a) a fresh medical recommendation complying with the relevant provisions of this Part of this Act (other than the provisions relating to the time of signature and the interval between examinations) is furnished to the managers within that period; and

(b) that recommendation, and the other recommendation on which the application is founded, together comply with those provisions.

(3) Where the medical recommendations upon which an application for admission is founded are, taken together, insufficient to warrant the detention of the patient in pursuance of the application, a notice under subsection (2) above may be given in respect of either of those recommendations.

(4) Nothing in this section shall be construed as authorising the giving of notice in respect of an application made as an emergency application, or the detention of a patient admitted in pursuance of such an application, after the period of 72 hours referred to in section 4(4) above, unless the conditions set out in paragraphs (a) and (b) of that section are complied with or would be complied with apart from any error or defect to which this section applies.

Amendments. Words in subs (3) repealed: MHA 2007, s 55, Sch 11, Pt 1.

16 (*repealed*)

Amendment. Section repealed: MHA 2007, s 55, Sch 11, Pt 1.

Note. Section 16, which governed reclassification of patients, is repealed consequent upon the abolition of the sub-categories of mental disorder.

17 Leave of absence from hospital

(1) The responsible clinician may grant to any patient who is for the time being liable to be detained in a hospital under this Part of this Act leave to be absent from the hospital subject to such conditions (if any) as that clinician considers necessary in the interests of the patient or for the protection of other persons.

(2) Leave of absence may be granted to a patient under this section either indefinitely or on specified occasions or for any specified period; and where

leave is so granted for a specified period, that period may be extended by further leave granted in the absence of the patient.

(2A) But longer-term leave of absence may not be granted to a patient unless the responsible clinician first considers whether the patient should be dealt with under section 17A instead.

(2B) For these purposes, longer-term leave is granted to a patient if –

   (a)   leave of absence is granted to him under this section either indefinitely or for a specified period of more than seven consecutive days; or
   (b)   a specified period is extended under this section such that the total period for which leave of absence will have been granted to him under this section exceeds seven consecutive days.

(3) Where it appears to the responsible clinician that it is necessary so to do in the interests of the patient or for the protection of other persons, he may, upon granting leave of absence under this section, direct that the patient remain in custody during his absence; and where leave of absence is so granted the patient may be kept in the custody of any officer on the staff of the hospital, or of any other person authorised in writing by the managers of the hospital or, if the patient is required in accordance with conditions imposed on the grant of leave of absence to reside in another hospital, of any officer on the staff of that other hospital.

(4) In any case where a patient is absent from a hospital in pursuance of leave of absence granted under this section, and it appears to the responsible clinician that it is necessary so to do in the interests of the patient's health or safety or for the protection of other persons, that clinician may, subject to subsection (5) below, by notice in writing given to the patient or to the person for the time being in charge of the patient, revoke the leave of absence and recall the patient to the hospital.

(5) A patient to whom leave of absence is granted under this section shall not be recalled under subsection (4) above after he has ceased to be liable to be detained under this Part of this Act.

(6) Subs (7) below applies to a person who is granted leave: or: virtue of a provision –

   (a)   in force in Scotland, Northern Ireland, any of the Channel Islands or the Isle of Man; and
   (b)   corresponding to subs (1) above.

(7) For the purpose of giving effect to a direction or condition imposed: virtue of a provision corresponding to subs (3) above, the person may be conveyed to a place in, or kept in custody or detained at a place of safety in, England and Wales: a person authorised in that behalf: the direction or condition.

Amendments. Words 'responsible clinician' and 'that clinician' in subss (1), (3), (4) substituted: MHA 2007, s 9(1), (3). Subss (2A) and (2B) inserted: MHA 2007, s 33(1), (2), in subs 5, words repealed: Mental Health (Patients in the Community) Act 1995, s 3(1), (3). Subss (6), (7) inserted: MHA 2007, s 39(1).

Community Treatment Orders

17A Community treatment orders

(1) The responsible clinician may by order in writing discharge a detained patient from hospital subject to his being liable to recall in accordance with section 17E below.

(2) A detained patient is a patient who is liable to be detained in a hospital in pursuance of an application for admission for treatment.

(3) An order under subsection (1) above is referred to in this Act as a 'community treatment order'.

(4) The responsible clinician may not make a community treatment order unless –

  (a)   in his opinion, the relevant criteria are met; and
  (b)   an approved mental health professional states in writing –
      (i)   that he agrees with that opinion; and
      (ii)   that it is appropriate to make the order.

(5) The relevant criteria are –

  (a)   the patient is suffering from mental disorder of a nature or degree which makes it appropriate for him to receive medical treatment;
  (b)   it is necessary for his health or safety or for the protection of other persons that he should receive such treatment;
  (c)   subject to his being liable to be recalled as mentioned in paragraph (d) below, such treatment can be provided without his continuing to be detained in a hospital;
  (d)   it is necessary that the responsible clinician should be able to exercise the power under section 17E(1) below to recall the patient to hospital; and
  (e)   appropriate medical treatment is available for him.

(6) In determining whether the criterion in subsection (5)(d) above is met, the responsible clinician shall, in particular, consider, having regard to the patient's history of mental disorder and any other relevant factors, what risk there would be of a deterioration of the patient's condition if he were not detained in a hospital (as a result, for example, of his refusing or neglecting to receive the medical treatment he requires for his mental disorder).

(7) In this Act –

  'community patient' means a patient in respect of whom a community treatment order is in force;
  'the community treatment order', in relation to such a patient, means the community treatment order in force in respect of him; and
  'the responsible hospital', in relation to such a patient, means the hospital in which he was liable to be detained immediately before the community treatment order was made, subject to section 19A below.

Amendments. Section inserted: MHA 2007, s 32(1), (2). For transitional provisions and savings, see MHA 2007, s 53, Sch 10, paras 1, 5.

17B Conditions

(1) A community treatment order shall specify conditions to which the patient is to be subject while the order remains in force.

(2) But, subject to subsection (3) below, the order may specify conditions only if the responsible clinician, with the agreement of the approved mental health professional mentioned in section 17A(4)(b) above, thinks them necessary or appropriate for one or more of the following purposes –

> (a)   ensuring that the patient receives medical treatment;
> (b)   preventing risk of harm to the patient's health or safety;
> (c)   protecting other persons.

(3) The order shall specify –

> (a)   a condition that the patient make himself available for examination under section 20A below; and
> (b)   a condition that, if it is proposed to give a certificate under Part 4A of this Act in his case, he make himself available for examination so as to enable the certificate to be given.

(4) The responsible clinician may from time to time by order in writing vary the conditions specified in a community treatment order.

(5) He may also suspend any conditions specified in a community treatment order.

(6) If a community patient fails to comply with a condition specified in the community treatment order by virtue of subsection (2) above, that fact may be taken into account for the purposes of exercising the power of recall under section 17E(1) below.

(7) But nothing in this section restricts the exercise of that power to cases where there is such a failure.

Amendments. Section inserted: MHA 2007, s 32(1), (2). For transitional provisions and savings, see MHA 2007, s 53, Sch 10, paras 1, 5.

17C Duration of community treatment order

A community treatment order shall remain in force until –

> (a)   the period mentioned in section 20A(1) below (as extended under any provision of this Act) expires, but this is subject to sections 21 and 22 below;
> (b)   the patient is discharged in pursuance of an order under section 23 below or a direction under section 72 below;
> (c)   the application for admission for treatment in respect of the patient otherwise ceases to have effect; or
> (d)   the order is revoked under section 17F below, whichever occurs first.

Amendments. Section inserted: MHA 2007, s 32(1), (2). For transitional provisions and savings, see MHA 2007, s 53, Sch 10, paras 1, 5.

17D Effect of community treatment order

(1) The application for admission for treatment in respect of a patient shall not cease to have effect by virtue of his becoming a community patient.

(2) But while he remains a community patient –

(a) the authority of the managers to detain him under section 6(2) above in pursuance of that application shall be suspended; and

(b) reference (however expressed) in this or any other Act, or in any subordinate legislation (within the meaning of the Interpretation Act 1978), to patients liable to be detained, or detained, under this Act shall not include him.

(3) And section 20 below shall not apply to him while he remains a community patient.

(4) Accordingly, authority for his detention shall not expire during any period in which that authority is suspended by virtue of subsection (2)(a) above.

Amendments. Section inserted: MHA 2007, s 32(1), (2). For transitional provisions and savings, see MHA 2007, s 53, Sch 10, paras 1, 5.

17E Power to recall to hospital

(1) The responsible clinician may recall a community patient to hospital if in his opinion –

(a) the patient requires medical treatment in hospital for his mental disorder; and

(b) there would be a risk of harm to the health or safety of the patient or to other persons if the patient were not recalled to hospital for that purpose.

(2) The responsible clinician may also recall a community patient to hospital if the patient fails to comply with a condition specified under section 17B(3) above.

(3) The hospital to which a patient is recalled need not be the responsible hospital.

(4) Nothing in this section prevents a patient from being recalled to a hospital even though he is already in the hospital at the time when the power of recall is exercised; references to recalling him shall be construed accordingly.

(5) The power of recall under subsections (1) and (2) above shall be exercisable by notice in writing to the patient.

(6) A notice under this section recalling a patient to hospital shall be sufficient authority for the managers of that hospital to detain the patient there in accordance with the provisions of this Act.

Amendments. Section inserted: MHA 2007, s 32(1), (2). For transitional provisions and savings, see MHA 2007, s 53, Sch 10, paras 1, 5.

17F Powers in respect of recalled patients

(1) This section applies to a community patient who is detained in a hospital by virtue of a notice recalling him there under section 17E above.

(2) The patient may be transferred to another hospital in such circumstances and subject to such conditions as may be prescribed in regulations made by the Secretary of State (if the hospital in which the patient is detained is in England) or the Welsh Ministers (if that hospital is in Wales).

(3) If he is so transferred to another hospital, he shall be treated for the purposes of this section (and section 17E above) as if the notice under that section were a notice recalling him to that other hospital and as if he had been detained there from the time when his detention in hospital by virtue of the notice first began.

(4) The responsible clinician may by order in writing revoke the community treatment order if –

(a)   in his opinion, the conditions mentioned in section 3(2) above are satisfied in respect of the patient; and

(b)   an approved mental health professional states in writing –

(i)   that he agrees with that opinion; and

(ii)   that it is appropriate to revoke the order.

(5) The responsible clinician may at any time release the patient under this section, but not after the community treatment order has been revoked.

(6) If the patient has not been released, nor the community treatment order revoked, by the end of the period of 72 hours, he shall then be released.

(7) But a patient who is released under this section remains subject to the community treatment order.

(8) In this section –

(a)   'the period of 72 hours' means the period of 72 hours beginning with the time when the patient's detention in hospital by virtue of the notice under section 17E above begins; and

(b)   references to being released shall be construed as references to being released from that detention (and accordingly from being recalled to hospital).

Amendments. Section inserted: MHA 2007, s 32(1), (2). For transitional provisions and savings, see MHA 2007, s 53, Sch 10, paras 1, 5.

17G Effect of revoking community treatment order

(1) This section applies if a community treatment order is revoked under section 17F above in respect of a patient.

(2) Section 6(2) above shall have effect as if the patient had never been discharged from hospital by virtue of the community treatment order.

(3) The provisions of this or any other Act relating to patients liable to be detained (or detained) in pursuance of an application for admission for treatment shall apply to the patient as they did before the community treatment order was made, unless otherwise provided.

(4) If, when the order is revoked, the patient is being detained in a hospital other than the responsible hospital, the provisions of this Part of this Act shall have effect as if –

    (a)   the application for admission for treatment in respect of him were an application for admission to that other hospital; and

    (b)   he had been admitted to that other hospital at the time when he was originally admitted in pursuance of the application.

(5) But, in any case, section 20 below shall have effect as if the patient had been admitted to hospital in pursuance of the application for admission for treatment on the day on which the order is revoked.'

Amendments. Section inserted: MHA 2007, s 32(1), (2). For transitional provisions and savings, see MHA 2007, s 53, Sch 10, paras 1, 5.

18 Return and readmission of patients absent without leave

(1) Where a patient who is for the time being liable to be detained under this Part of this Act in a hospital –

    (a)   absents himself from the hospital without leave granted under section 17 above; or

    (b)   fails to return to the hospital on any occasion on which, or at the expiration of any period for which, leave of absence was granted to him under that section, or upon being recalled under that section; or

    (c)   absents himself without permission from any place where he is required to reside in accordance with conditions imposed on the grant of leave of absence under that section,

he may, subject to the provisions of this section, be taken into custody and returned to the hospital or place by any approved mental health professional, by any officer on the staff of the hospital, by any constable, or by any person authorised in writing by the managers of the hospital.

(2) Where the place referred to in paragraph (c) of subsection (1) above is a hospital other than the one in which the patient is for the time being liable to be detained, the references in that subsection to an officer on the staff of the hospital and the managers of the hospital shall respectively include references to an officer on the staff of the first-mentioned hospital and the managers of that hospital.

(2A) Where a community patient is at any time absent from a hospital to which he is recalled under section 17E above, he may, subject to the provisions of this section, be taken into custody and returned to the hospital by any approved mental health professional, by any officer on the staff of the hospital, by any constable, or by any person authorised in writing by the responsible clinician or the managers of the hospital.

(3) Where a patient who is for the time being subject to guardianship under this Part of this Act absents himself without the leave of the guardian from the place at which he is required by the guardian to reside, he may, subject to the provisions of this section, be taken into custody and returned to that place by any officer on the staff of a local social services authority, by any constable, or by any person authorised in writing by the guardian or a local social services authority.

(4) A patient shall not be taken into custody under this section after the later of –

   (a)   the end of the period of six months beginning with the first day of his absence without leave; and
   (b)   the end of the period for which (apart from section 21 below) he is liable to be detained or subject to guardianship or, in the case of a community patient, the community treatment order is in force

and, in determining for the purposes of paragraph (b) above or any other provision of this Act whether a person who is or has been absent without leave is at any time liable to be detained or subject to guardianship, a report furnished under section 20 or 21B below before the first day of his absence without leave shall not be taken to have renewed the authority for his detention or guardianship unless the period of renewal began before that day.

(4A) In determining for the purposes of subsection (4)(b) above or any other provision of this Act whether a person who is or has been absent without leave is at any time liable to be detained or subject to guardianship, a report furnished under section 20 or 21B below before the first day of his absence without leave shall not be taken to have renewed the authority for his detention or guardianship unless the period of renewal began before that day.

(4B) Similarly, in determining for those purposes whether a community treatment order is at any time in force in respect of a person who is or has been absent without leave, a report furnished under section 20A or 21B below before the first day of his absence without leave shall not be taken to have extended the community treatment period unless the extension began before that day.

(5) A patient shall not be taken into custody under this section if the period for which he is liable to be detained is that specified in section 2(4), 4(4) or 5(2) or (4) above and that period has expired.

(6) In this Act 'absent without leave' means absent from any hospital or other place and liable to be taken into custody and returned under this section, and related expressions shall be construed accordingly.

(7) In relation to a patient who has yet to comply with a requirement imposed by virtue of this Act to be in a hospital or place, references in this Act to his

liability to be returned to the hospital or place shall include his liability to be taken to that hospital or place; and related expressions shall be construed accordingly.

Amendments. Words in subs (1) substituted: MHA 2007, s 21, Sch 2, para 7(a). Subss (2A), (4A), (4B) and (7), and words in subs (4), inserted: MHA 2007, s 32(4), Sch 3, paras 1, 3(1), (2), (4), (5). Words in subs (4) repealed: MHA 2007, s 32(4), (55), Sch 3, paras 1, 3(1), (3)(b), Sch 11, Pt 5.

19 Regulations as to transfer of patients

(1) In such circumstances and subject to such conditions as may be prescribed by regulations made by the Secretary of State –

(a) a patient who is for the time being liable to be detained in a hospital by virtue of an application under this Part of this Act may be transferred to another hospital or into the guardianship of a local social services authority or of any person approved by such an authority;

(b) a patient who is for the time being subject to the guardianship of a local social services authority or other person by virtue of an application under this Part of this Act may be transferred into the guardianship of another local social services authority or person, or be transferred to a hospital.

(2) Where a patient is transferred in pursuance of regulations under this section, the provisions of this Part of this Act (including this subsection) shall apply to him as follows, that is to say –

(a) in the case of a patient who is liable to be detained in a hospital by virtue of an application for admission for assessment or for treatment and is transferred to another hospital, as if the application were an application for admission to that other hospital and as if the patient had been admitted to that other hospital at the time when he was originally admitted in pursuance of the application;

(b) in the case of a patient who is liable to be detained in a hospital by virtue of such an application and is transferred into guardianship, as if the application were a guardianship application duly accepted at the said time;

(c) in the case of a patient who is subject to guardianship by virtue of a guardianship application and is transferred into the guardianship of another authority or person, as if the application were for his reception into the guardianship of that authority or person and had been accepted at the time when it was originally accepted;

(d) in the case of a patient who is subject to guardianship by virtue of a guardianship application and is transferred to a hospital, as if the guardianship application were an application for admission to that hospital for treatment and as if the patient had been admitted to the hospital at the time when the application was originally accepted.

(3) Without prejudice to subsections (1) and (2) above, any patient who is for the time being liable to be detained under this Part of this Act in a hospital vested in the Secretary of State for the purposes of his functions under the

National Health Service Act 2006, in a hospital vested in the Welsh Ministers for the purposes of their functions under the National Health Service (Wales) Act 2006, in any accommodation used under either of those Acts, by the managers of such a hospital or in a hospital vested in a National Health Service trust, NHS foundation trust, Local Health Board or Primary Care Trust, may at any time be removed to any other such hospital or accommodation which is managed by the managers of, or is vested in the National Health Service trust, NHS foundation trust, Local Health Board or Primary Care Trust for, the first mentioned hospital; and paragraph (a) of subsection (2) above shall apply in relation to a patient so removed as it applies in relation to a patient transferred in pursuance of regulations made under this section.

(4) Regulations made under this section may make provision for regulating the conveyance to their destination of patients authorised to be transferred or removed in pursuance of the regulations or under subsection (3) above.

Amendments. Words in subs (3): inserted and substituted: National Health Service and Community Care Act 1990, s 66(1), Sch 9, para 24(2); Health Act 1999 (Supplementary, Consequential etc Provisions) Order 2000, SI 2000 No. 90, arts 1, 3(1), Sch 1, para 16(1), (3); inserted: Health and Social Care (Community Health and Standards) Act 2003, s 34, Sch 4, paras 50, 52; inserted: National Health Service (Consequential Provisions) Act 2006, s 2, Sch 1, paras 63, 64; inserted: MHA 2007, s 46(1), (2).

Note. The following regulations have been made under this section: The Mental Health (Hospital, Guardianship and Treatment) (England) Regulations 2008, SI 2008 No. 1184; The Mental Health (Hospital, Guardianship, Community Treatment and Consent to Treatment) (Wales) Regulations 2008, SI 2008 No. 2439 (W.212).

19A Regulations as to assignment of responsibility for community patients

(1) Responsibility for a community patient may be assigned to another hospital in such circumstances and subject to such conditions as may be prescribed by regulations made by the Secretary of State (if the responsible hospital is in England) or the Welsh Ministers (if that hospital is in Wales).

(2) If responsibility for a community patient is assigned to another hospital –

    (a)   the application for admission for treatment in respect of the patient shall have effect (subject to section 17D above) as if it had always specified that other hospital;

    (b)   the patient shall be treated as if he had been admitted to that other hospital at the time when he was originally admitted in pursuance of the application (and as if he had subsequently been discharged under section 17A above from there); and

    (c)   that other hospital shall become 'the responsible hospital' in relation to the patient for the purposes of this Act.

Amendments. Section inserted: MHA 2007, s 32(4), Sch 3, paras 1, 4. See: Mental Health (Hospital, Guardianship and Treatment) (England) Regulations 2008, SI 2008 No. 1184, r 17; The Mental Health (Hospital, Guardianship, Community Treatment and Consent to Treatment) (Wales) Regulations 2008, SI 2008 No. 2439 (W.212), r 25.

Duration of authority and discharge

Amendments. Word in cross-heading substituted: MHA 2007, s 32(1), (3).

20 Duration of authority

(1) Subject to the following provisions of this Part of this Act, a patient admitted to hospital in pursuance of an application for admission for treatment, and a patient placed under guardianship in pursuance of a guardianship application, may be detained in a hospital or kept under guardianship for a period not exceeding six months beginning with the day on which he was so admitted, or the day on which the guardianship application was accepted, as the case may be, but shall not be so detained or kept for any longer period unless the authority for his detention or guardianship is renewed under this section.

(2) Authority for the detention or guardianship of a patient may, unless the patient has previously been discharged under section 23 below, be renewed –

(a) from the expiration of the period referred to in subsection (1) above, for a further period of six months;

(b) from the expiration of any period of renewal under paragraph (a) above, for a further period of one year,

and so on for periods of one year at a time.

(3) Within the period of two months ending on the day on which a patient who is liable to be detained in pursuance of an application for admission for treatment would cease under this section to be so liable in default of the renewal of the authority for his detention, it shall be the duty of the responsible clinician –

(a) to examine the patient; and

(b) if it appears to him that the conditions set out in subsection (4) below are satisfied, to furnish to the managers of the hospital where the patient is detained a report to that effect in the prescribed form;

and where such a report is furnished in respect of a patient the managers shall, unless they discharge the patient under section 23 below, cause him to be informed.

(4) The conditions referred to in subsection (3) above are that –

(a) the patient is suffering from mental disorder of a nature or degree which makes it appropriate for him to receive medical treatment in a hospital; and

(c) it is necessary for the health or safety of the patient or for the protection of other persons that he should receive such treatment and that it cannot be provided unless he continues to be detained; and

(d) appropriate medical treatment is available for him.

(5) Before furnishing a report under subsection (3) above the responsible clinician shall consult one or more other persons who have been professionally concerned with the patient's medical treatment.

(5A) But the responsible clinician may not furnish a report under subsection (3) above unless a person –

(a) who has been professionally concerned with the patient's medical treatment; but

(b) who belongs to a profession other than that to which the responsible clinician belongs, states in writing that he agrees that the conditions set out in subsection (4) above are satisfied.'

(6) Within the period of two months ending with the day on which a patient who is subject to guardianship under this Part of this Act would cease under this section to be so liable in default of the renewal of the authority for his guardianship, it shall be the duty of the appropriate practitioner –

(a) to examine the patient; and

(b) if it appears to him that the conditions set out in subsection (7) below are satisfied, to furnish to the guardian and, where the guardian is a person other than a local social services authority, to the responsible local social services authority a report to that effect in the prescribed form; and where such a report is furnished in respect of a patient, the local social services authority shall, unless they discharge the patient under section 23 below, cause him to be informed.

(7) The conditions referred to in subsection (6) above are that –

(a) the patient is suffering from mental disorder of a nature or degree which warrants his reception into guardianship; and

(b) it is necessary in the interests of the welfare of the patient or for the protection of other persons that the patient should remain under guardianship.

(8) Where a report is duly furnished under subsection (3) or (6) above, the authority for the detention or guardianship of the patient shall be thereby renewed for the period prescribed in that case by subsection (2) above.

Amendments. Words in subss (2), (3) and (6) inserted: MHA 2007, s 32(4), Sch 3, para 5. Words in subss (3), (5) substituted: MHA 2007, s 9(1), (4)(a). Words in sub (4)(a) and (7)(a) substituted: MHA 2007, s 1(4), Sch 1, paras 4(a), (b). Subs (4)(b) repealed: MHA 2007, ss 4(1), (4)(a), 55, Sch 11, Pt 2. Subs (4)(d) and preceding word inserted: MHA 2007, s 4(1), (4)(b). Words in subs (4) repealed: MHA 2007, ss 4(1), (4)(c), 55, Sch 11, Pt 2. Subs 5A inserted: MHA 2007, s 9(1), (4)(b). Words in subs (6) substituted: MHA 2007, s 9(1), (4)(c). Subs (9) repealed: MHA 2007, s 55, Sch 11, Pt 1. Subs (10) repealed: MHA 2007, ss 9(1), (4)(d), 55, Sch 11, Pt 3.

20A Community treatment period

(1) Subject to the provisions of this Part of this Act, a community treatment order shall cease to be in force on expiry of the period of six months beginning with the day on which it was made.

(2) That period is referred to in this Act as 'the community treatment period'.

(3) The community treatment period may, unless the order has previously ceased to be in force, be extended –

(a) from its expiration for a period of six months;

(b) from the expiration of any period of extension under paragraph (a) above for a further period of one year, and so on for periods of one year at a time.

(4) Within the period of two months ending on the day on which the order would cease to be in force in default of an extension under this section, it shall be the duty of the responsible clinician –

(a) to examine the patient; and

(b) if it appears to him that the conditions set out in subsection (6) below are satisfied and if a statement under subsection (8) below is made, to furnish to the managers of the responsible hospital a report to that effect in the prescribed form.

(5) Where such a report is furnished in respect of the patient, the managers shall, unless they discharge him under section 23 below, cause him to be informed.

(6) The conditions referred to in subsection (4) above are that –

(a) the patient is suffering from mental disorder of a nature or degree which makes it appropriate for him to receive medical treatment;

(b) it is necessary for his health or safety or for the protection of other persons that he should receive such treatment;

(c) subject to his continuing to be liable to be recalled as mentioned in paragraph (d) below, such treatment can be provided without his being detained in a hospital;

(d) it is necessary that the responsible clinician should continue to be able to exercise the power under section 17E(1) above to recall the patient to hospital; and

(e) appropriate medical treatment is available for him.

(7) In determining whether the criterion in subsection (6)(d) above is met, the responsible clinician shall, in particular, consider, having regard to the patient's history of mental disorder and any other relevant factors, what risk there would be of a deterioration of the patient's condition if he were to continue not to be detained in a hospital (as a result, for example, of his refusing or neglecting to receive the medical treatment he requires for his mental disorder).

(8) The statement referred to in subsection (4) above is a statement in writing by an approved mental health professional –

(a) that it appears to him that the conditions set out in subsection (6) above are satisfied; and

(b) that it is appropriate to extend the community treatment period.

(9) Before furnishing a report under subsection (4) above the responsible clinician shall consult one or more other persons who have been professionally concerned with the patient's medical treatment.

(10) Where a report is duly furnished under subsection (4) above, the community treatment period shall be thereby extended for the period prescribed in that case by subsection (3) above.

Amendments. Section inserted: MHA 2007, s 32(1), (3).

20B Effect of expiry of community treatment order

(1) A community patient shall be deemed to be discharged absolutely from liability to recall under this Part of this Act, and the application for admission for treatment cease to have effect, on expiry of the community treatment order, if the order has not previously ceased to be in force.

(2) For the purposes of subsection (1) above, a community treatment order expires on expiry of the community treatment period as extended under this Part of this Act, but this is subject to sections 21 and 22 below.

Amendments. Section inserted: MHA 2007, s 32(1), (3).

21 Special provisions as to patients absent without leave

(1) Where a patient is absent without leave –

(a) on the day on which (apart from this section) he would cease to be liable to be detained or subject to guardianship under this Part of this Act or, in the case of a community patient, the community treatment order would cease to be in force; or

(b) within the period of one week ending with that day,

he shall not cease to be so liable or subject, or the order shall not cease to be in force, until the relevant time.

(2) For the purposes of subsection (1) above the relevant time –

(a) where the patient is taken into custody under section 18 above, is the end of the period of one week beginning with the day on which he is returned to the hospital or place where he ought to be;

(b) where the patient returns himself to the hospital or place where he ought to be within the period during which he can be taken into custody under section 18 above, is the end of the period of one week beginning with the day on which he so returns himself; and

(c) otherwise, is the end of the period during which he can be taken into custody under section 18 above.

(3) Where a patient is absent without leave on the day on which (apart from this section) the managers would be required under section 68 below to refer the patient's case to the appropriate tribunal, that requirement shall not apply unless and until –

(a) the patient is taken into custody under section 18 above and returned to the hospital where he ought to be; or

(b) the patient returns himself to the hospital where he ought to be within the period during which he can be taken into custody under section 18 above.

(4) Where a community patient is absent without leave on the day on which (apart from this section) the 72-hour period mentioned in section 17F above would expire, that period shall not expire until the end of the period of 72 hours beginning with the time when –

    (a)   the patient is taken into custody under section 18 above and returned to the hospital where he ought to be; or

    (b)   the patient returns himself to the hospital where he ought to be within the period during which he can be taken into custody under section 18 above.

(5) Any reference in this section, or in sections 21A to 22 below, to the time when a community treatment order would cease, or would have ceased, to be in force shall be construed as a reference to the time when it would cease, or would have ceased, to be in force by reason only of the passage of time.

Amendments. Section Substituted, together with ss 21A, 21B, for s 21 as originally enacted: Mental Health (Patients in the Community) Act 1995, s 2(2), words in subss (1) inserted, and subss (4) and (5) inserted: MHA 2007, s 32(4), Sch 3, paras 1, 6(1)–(3). Subs (3) inserted: MHA 2007, s 37(1), (2). Words in Subs (3) substituted: Transfer of Tribunal Functions Order 2008, SI 2008 No. 2833, arts 1(1), 9(1), Sch 3, paras 39, 40.

21A Patients who are taken into custody or return within 28 days

(1) This section applies where a patient who is absent without leave is taken into custody under section 18 above, or returns himself to the hospital or place where he ought to be, not later than the end of the period of 28 days beginning with the first day of his absence without leave.

(2) Where the period for which the patient is liable to be detained or subject to guardianship is extended by section 21 above, any examination and report to be made and furnished in respect of the patient under section 20(3) or (6) above may be made and furnished within the period as so extended.

(3) Where the authority for the detention or guardianship of the patient is renewed by virtue of subsection (2) above after the day on which (apart from section 21 above) that authority would have expired, the renewal shall take effect as from that day.

(4) In the case of a community patient, where the period for which the community treatment order is in force is extended by section 21 above, any examination and report to be made and furnished in respect of the patient under section 20A(4) above may be made and furnished within the period as so extended.

(5) Where the community treatment period is extended by virtue of subsection (4) above after the day on which (apart from section 21 above) the order would have ceased to be in force, the extension shall take effect as from that day.

Amendments. Section Substituted, together with ss 21, 21B, for s 21 as originally enacted: Mental Health (Patients in the Community) Act 1995, s 2(2), Subss (4), (5) inserted: MHA 2007, s 32(4), Sch 3, para 7.

21B Patients who are taken into custody or return after more than 28 days

(1) This section applies where a patient who is absent without leave is taken into custody under section 18 above, or returns himself to the hospital or place where he ought to be, later than the end of the period of 28 days beginning with the first day of his absence without leave.

(2) It shall be the duty of the appropriate practitioner, within the period of one week beginning with the day on which the patient is returned or returns himself to the hospital or place where he ought to be (his 'return day') –

    (a)   to examine the patient; and
    (b)   if it appears to him that the relevant conditions are satisfied, to furnish to the appropriate body a report to that effect in the prescribed form; and where such a report is furnished in respect of the patient the appropriate body shall cause him to be informed.

(3) Where the patient is liable to be detained or is a community patient (as opposed to subject to guardianship) the appropriate practitioner shall, before furnishing a report under subsection (2) above, consult –

    (a)   one or more other persons who have been professionally concerned with the patient's medical treatment; and
    (b)   approved mental health professional.

(4) Where –

    (a)   the patient would (apart from any renewal of the authority for his detention or guardianship on or after his return day) be liable to be detained or subject to guardianship after the end of the period of one week beginning with that day; or
    (b)   in the case of a community patient, the community treatment order would (apart from any extension of the community treatment period on or after that day) be in force after the end of that period, he shall cease to be so liable or subject, or the community treatment period shall be deemed to expire, at the end of that period unless a report is duly furnished in respect of him under subsection (2) above.

(4A) If, in the case of a community patient, the community treatment order is revoked under section 17F above during the period of one week beginning with his return day –

    (a)   subsections (2) and (4) above shall not apply; and
    (b)   any report already furnished in respect of him under subsection (2) above shall be of no effect.

(5) Where the patient would (apart from section 21 above) have ceased to be liable to be detained or subject to guardianship on or before the day on which a report is duly furnished in respect of him under subsection (2) above, the report shall renew the authority for his detention or guardianship for the period prescribed in that case by section 20(2) above.

(6) Where the authority for the detention or guardianship of the patient is renewed by virtue of subsection (5) above –

    (a)   the renewal shall take effect as from the day on which (apart from section 21 above and that subsection) the authority would have expired; and

    (b)   if (apart from this paragraph) the renewed authority would expire on or before the day on which the report is furnished, the report shall further renew the authority, as from the day on which it would expire, for the period prescribed in that case by section 20(2) above.

(6A) In the case of a community patient, where the community treatment order would (apart from section 21 above) have ceased to be in force on or before the day on which a report is duly furnished in respect of him under subsection (2) above, the report shall extend the community treatment period for the period prescribed in that case by section 20A(3) above.

(6B) Where the community treatment period is extended by virtue of subsection (6A) above –

    (a)   the extension shall take effect as from the day on which (apart from section 21 above and that subsection) the order would have ceased to be in force; and

    (b)   if (apart from this paragraph) the period as so extended would expire on or before the day on which the report is furnished, the report shall further extend that period, as from the day on which it would expire, for the period prescribed in that case by section 20A(3) above.

(7) Where the authority for the detention or guardianship of the patient would expire within the period of two months beginning with the day on which a report is duly furnished in respect of him under subsection (2) above, the report shall, if it so provides, have effect also as a report duly furnished under section 20(3) or (6) above; and the reference in this subsection to authority includes any authority renewed under subsection (5) above by the report.

(7A) In the case of a community patient, where the community treatment order would (taking account of any extension under subsection (6A) above) cease to be in force within the period of two months beginning with the day on which a report is duly furnished in respect of him under subsection (2) above, the report shall, if it so provides, have effect also as a report duly furnished under section 20A(4) above.

(8), (9) (*repealed*)

(10) In this section –

    'the appropriate body' means –

        (a)   in relation to a patient who is liable to be detained in a hospital, the managers of the hospital;

        (b)   in relation to a patient who is subject to guardianship, the responsible local social services authority;

        (c)   in relation to a community patient, the managers of the responsible hospital; and

    'the relevant conditions' means –

    (a)   in relation to a patient who is liable to be detained in a hospital, the conditions set out in subsection (4) of section 20 above;

    (b)   in relation to a patient who is subject to guardianship, the conditions set out in subsection (7) of that section;

    (c)   in relation to a community patient, the conditions set out in section 20A(6) above.

Amendments. Section Substituted, together with ss 21, 21A, for s 21 as originally enacted: Mental Health (Patients in the Community) Act 1995, s 2(2), words in subss (2) and (3) substituted: MHA 2007, s 9(1), (5)(a). Words in subss (2), (3) inserted: MHA 2007, s 32(4), Sch 3, para 8. Words in subs (3)(b) substituted: MHA 2007, s 21, Sch 2, paras 1, 7(b). Subs (4) substituted, and subss (4A), 6(A), 6(B) and (7A) inserted: MHA 2007, s 32(4), Sch 3, paras 8(1), (4)–(7). Subss (8) and (9) repealed: MHA 2007, s 55, Sch 11, Pt 1. Definition in subs (10) repealed: MHA 2007, s 9(1), (5)(b), 55, Sch 11, Pt 3. Definitions in subs (10) substituted: MHA 2007, s 32(4), Sch 3, paras 1, 8(1), (8).

22 Special provisions as to patients sentenced to imprisonment, etc

(1) If –

    (a)   a qualifying patient is detained in custody in pursuance of any sentence or order passed or made by a court in the United Kingdom (including an order committing or remanding him in custody); and

    (b)   he is so detained for a period exceeding, or for successive periods exceeding in the aggregate, six months, the relevant application shall cease to have effect on expiry of that period.

(2) A patient is a qualifying patient for the purposes of this section if –

    (a)   he is liable to be detained by virtue of an application for admission for treatment;

    (b)   he is subject to guardianship by virtue of a guardianship application; or

    (c)   he is a community patient.

(3) 'The relevant application', in relation to a qualifying patient, means –

    (a)   in the case of a patient who is subject to guardianship, the guardianship application in respect of him;

    (b)   in any other case, the application for admission for treatment in respect of him.

(4) The remaining subsections of this section shall apply if a qualifying patient is detained in custody as mentioned in subsection (1)(a) above but for a period not exceeding, or for successive periods not exceeding in the aggregate, six months.

(5) If apart from this subsection –

    (a)   the patient would have ceased to be liable to be detained or subject to guardianship by virtue of the relevant application on or before the day on which he is discharged from custody; or

    (b)   in the case of a community patient, the community treatment order would have ceased to be in force on or before that day, he shall not cease and shall be deemed not to have ceased to be so liable or subject, or the order shall not cease and shall be deemed not to have ceased to be in force, until the end of that day.

(6) In any case (except as provided in subsection (8) below), sections 18, 21 and 21A above shall apply in relation to the patient as if he had absented himself without leave on that day.

(7) In its application by virtue of subsection (6) above section 18 shall have effect as if –

(a)   in subsection (4) for the words from 'later of' to the end there were substituted 'end of the period of 28 days beginning with the first day of his absence without leave'; and

(b)   subsections (4A) and (4B) were omitted.

(8) In relation to a community patient who was not recalled to hospital under section 17E above at the time when his detention in custody began –

(a)   section 18 above shall not apply; but

(b)   sections 21 and 21A above shall apply as if he had absented himself without leave on the day on which he is discharged from custody and had returned himself as provided in those sections on the last day of the period of 28 days beginning with that day.

Amendments. Section substituted: MHA 2007, s 32(4), Sch 3, paras 1, 9.

23 Discharge of patients

(1) Subject to the provisions of this section and section 25 below, a patient who is for the time being liable to be detained or subject to guardianship under this Part of this Act shall cease to be so liable or subject if an order in writing discharging him absolutely from detention or guardianship is made in accordance with this section.

(1A) Subject to the provisions of this section and section 25 below, a community patient shall cease to be liable to recall under this Part of this Act, and the application for admission for treatment cease to have effect, if an order in writing discharging him from such liability is made in accordance with this section.

(1B) An order under subsection (1) or (1A) above shall be referred to in this Act as 'an order for discharge'.

(2) An order for discharge may be made in respect of a patient –

(a)   where the patient is liable to be detained in a hospital in pursuance of an application for admission for assessment or for treatment by the responsible clinician, by the managers or by the nearest relative of the patient;

(b)   where the patient is subject to guardianship, by the responsible clinician, by the responsible local social services authority or by the nearest relative of the patient;

(c)   where the patient is a community patient, by the responsible clinician, by the managers of the responsible hospital or by the nearest relative of the patient.

(3) Where the patient falls within subsection (3A) below, an order for his discharge may, without prejudice to subsection (2) above, be made by the Secretary of State and, if arrangements have been made in respect of the patient under a contract with a National Health Service trust, NHS foundation trust, Local Health Board, Special Health Authority or Primary Care Trust, by that National Health Service trust, NHS foundation trust, Local Health Board, Special Health Authority or Primary Care Trust.

(3A) A patient falls within this subsection if –

(a)   he is liable to be detained in a registered establishment in pursuance of an application for admission for assessment or for treatment; or

(b)   he is a community patient and the responsible hospital is a registered establishment.

(4) The powers conferred by this section on any authority trust, board (other than an NHS foundation trust),board or body of persons may be exercised subject to subsection (3) below by any three or more members of that authority, trust, board or body authorised by them in that behalf or by three or more members of a committee or subcommittee of that authority, trust, board or body which has been authorised by them in that behalf.

(5) The reference in subsection (4) above to the members of an authority, trust, board or body or the members of a committee or sub-committee of an authority, trust, board or body, –

(a)   in the case of a Local Health Board, Special Health Authority or Primary Care Trust or a committee or sub-committee of a Local Health Board, Special Health Authority or Primary Care Trust, is a reference only to the chairman of the authority or trust or board and such members (of the authority, trust, board, committee or sub-committee, as the case may be) as are not also officers of the authority or trust or board within the meaning of the National Health Service Act 2006 or the National Health Service (Wales) Act 2006; and

(b)   in the case of a National Health Service trust or a committee or subcommittee of such a trust, is a reference only to the chairman of the trust and such directors or (in the case of a committee or subcommittee) members as are not also employees of the trust.

(6) The powers conferred by this section on any NHS foundation trust may be exercised by any three or more persons authorised by the board of the trust in that behalf each of whom is neither an executive director of the board nor an employee of the trust.

Amendments. Words in subss (3), (4) and subss 5 inserted: National Health Service and Community Care Act 1990, s 66(1), Sch 9, para 24(3)(a)–(c). Words in subss (5) substituted: Health Authorities Act 1995, s 2(1), Sch 1, para 107(2). Words in subss (3) and (5) substituted: Health Act 1999 (Supplementary, Consequential etc Provisions) Order 2000, SI 2000 No. 90, arts 1, 3(1), Sch 1, para 16(1), (4)(a), (b). Words in subs (3) inserted: Health and Social Care (Community Health and

Standards) Act 2003, s 34, Sch 4, paras 50, 53(a), (c). Words in subs (5) substituted: National Health Service (Consequential Provisions) Act 2006, s 2, Sch 1, paras 62, 65. Words in subs (1) substituted, and subss (1A) and (1B) inserted: MHA 2007, s 32(4), Sch 3, paras 1, 10(1)–(3). Words in subss (2)(a), (b) substituted: MHA 2007, s 9(1), (6). Subss (2)(c) and (3A) inserted: MHA 2007, s 32(4), Sch 3, paras 1, 10(1), (4), (6). Words in subs (3) substituted: MHA 2007, s 32(4), Sch 3, paras 10(1), (5)(a), (b). Words in subs (6) substituted: MHA 2007, s 45(1). Words in subss (3) and 5 substituted: References to Health Authorities Order 2007, SI 2007 No. 961, arts 1(1), 3, Schedule, para 13(1), (2)(a), (d).

24 Visiting and examination of patients

(1) For the purpose of advising as to the exercise by the nearest relative of a patient who is liable to be detained or subject to guardianship under this Part of this Act, or who is a community patient, of any power to order his discharge, any registered medical practitioner or approved clinician authorised by or on behalf of the nearest relative of the patient may, at any reasonable time, visit the patient and examine him in private.

(2) Any registered medical practitioner or approved clinician authorised for the purposes of subsection (1) above to visit and examine a patient may require the production of and inspect any records relating to the detention or treatment of the patient in any hospital or to any after-care services provided for the patient under section 117 below.

(3) Where application is made by the Secretary of State or a Local Health Board, Special Health Authority, Primary Care Trust, National Health Service trust or NHS foundation trust to exercise, any power under section 23(3) above to make an order for a patient's discharge, the following persons, that is to say –

(a) any registered medical practitioner or approved clinician authorised by the Secretary of State or, as the case may be, that Local Health Board, Special Health Authority, Primary Care Trust, National Health Service trust or NHS foundation trust; and

(b) any other person (whether a registered medical practitioner or approved clinician or not) authorised under Part II of the Care Standards Act 2000 or Part 1 of the Health and Social Care Act 2008 to inspect the establishment in question;

may at any reasonable time visit the patient and interview him in private.

(4) Any person authorised for the purposes of subsection (3) above to visit a patient may require the production of and inspect any documents constituting or alleged to constitute the authority for the detention of the patient, or (as the case may be) for his liability to recall, under this Part of this Act; and any person so authorised, who is a registered medical practitioner or approved clinician, may examine the patient in private, and may require the production of and inspect any other records relating to the treatment of the patient in the establishment or to any after-care services provided for the patient under section 117 below.

Amendments. Words in subss (2), (4) inserted: Mental Health (Patients in the Community) Act 1995, s 1(2), Sch 1, para 1. Words in subs (3) substituted: Health Authorities Act 1995, s 2(1), Sch 1, para 107(3). Words in subs (3)(b) substituted: Care Standards Act 2000, s 116, Sch 4, para 9(1), (3). Words in subs (3) inserted: Health Act 1999 (Supplementary, Consequential etc Provisions) Order 2000, SI 2000 No. 90, art 3(1), Sch 1, para 16(1), (5). Words in subs (3) substituted: Health and Social Care (Community Health and Standards) Act 2003, s 34, Sch 4, paras 50, 54. Words in subs (1) inserted: MHA 2007, s 32(4), Sch 3, paras 1, 11(2). Words inserted in subss (1), (2), (3) and (4): MHA 2007, s 9(7). Words in subss (3) and (4) substituted: MHA 2007, s 32(4), Sch 3, paras 11(1), (3), (4)(b). Words in subs (4) inserted: MHA 2007, s 32(4), Sch 3, paras 11(1), (4)(a). Words in subs (3) substituted: References to Health Authorities Order 2007, SI 2007 No. 961, arts 1(1), 3, Schedule, para 13(1), (3). Words in subs (3)(b) inserted: Health and Social Care Act 2008 (Consequential Amendments No 2) Order 2010, SI 2010 No. 813, arts 1, 5(1), (2).

25 Restrictions on discharge by nearest relative

(1) An order for the discharge of a patient who is liable to be detained in a hospital shall not be made under section 23 above by his nearest relative except after giving not less than 72 hours' notice in writing to the managers of the hospital; and if, within 72 hours after such notice has been given, the responsible clinician furnishes to the managers a report certifying that in the opinion of that clinician the patient, if discharged, would be likely to act in a manner dangerous to other persons or to himself –

  (a)   any order for the discharge of the patient made by that relative in pursuance of the notice shall be of no effect; and
  (b)   no further order for the discharge of the patient shall be made by that relative during the period of six months beginning with the date of the report.

(1A) Subsection (1) above shall apply to an order for the discharge of a community patient as it applies to an order for the discharge of a patient who is liable to be detained in a hospital, but with the reference to the managers of the hospital being read as a reference to the managers of the responsible hospital.

(2) In any case where a report under subsection (1) above is furnished in respect of a patient who is liable to be detained in pursuance of an application for admission for treatment, or in respect of a community patient, the managers shall cause the nearest relative of the patient to be informed.

Amendments. Words in subss (1) and (2) inserted: MHA 2007, Sch 3 paras 12(1), (2), (4). Subs (1A) inserted: Sch 3 paras 12(1), (3). Words in subs (1) substituted: MHA 2007, s 9(1), (8)(a), (b).

Functions of relatives of patients

26 Definition of 'relative' and 'nearest relative'

(1) In this Part of this Act 'relative' means any of the following persons –

  (a)   husband or wife or civil partner;
  (b)   son or daughter;
  (c)   father or mother;
  (d)   brother or sister;
  (e)   grandparent;
  (f)   grandchild;
  (g)   uncle or aunt;
  (h)   nephew or niece.

(2) In deducing relationships for the purposes of this section, any relationship of the half-blood shall be treated as a relationship of the whole blood, and an illegitimate person shall be treated as the legitimate child of

(a)   his mother, and
(b)   if his father has parental responsibility for him within the meaning of section 3 of the Children Act 1989, his father.

(3) In this Part of this Act, subject to the provisions of this section and to the following provisions of this Part of this Act, the 'nearest relative' means the person first described in subsection (1) above who is for the time being surviving, relatives of the whole blood being preferred to relatives of the same description of the half-blood and the elder or eldest of two or more relatives described in any paragraph of that subsection being preferred to the other or others of those relatives, regardless of sex.

(4) Subject to the provisions of this section and to the following provisions of this Part of this Act, where the patient ordinarily resides with or is cared for by one or more of his relatives (or, if he is for the time being an in-patient in a hospital, he last ordinarily resided with or was cared for by one or more of his relatives) his nearest relative shall be determined –

(a)   by giving preference to that relative or those relatives over the other or others; and
(b)   as between two or more such relatives, in accordance with subsection (3) above.

(5) Where the person who, under subsection (3) or (4) above, would be the nearest relative of a patient –

(a)   in the case of a patient ordinarily resident in the United Kingdom, the Channel Islands or the Isle of Man, is not so resident; or
(b)   is the husband or wife or civil partner of the patient, but is permanently separated from the patient, either by agreement or under an order of a court, or has deserted or has been deserted by the patient for a period which has not come to an end; or
(c)   is a person other than the husband, wife, civil partner, father or mother of the patient, and is for the time being under 18 years of age;
(d)   (*repealed*)

(6) In this section 'husband', 'wife' and 'civil partner' include a person who is living with the patient as the patient's husband or wife or as if they were civil partners, as the case may be (or, if the patient is for the time being an in-patient in a hospital, was so living until the patient was admitted), and has been or had been so living for a period of not less than six months; but a person shall not be treated by virtue of this subsection as the nearest relative of a married patient or a patient in a civil partnership unless the husband, wife or civil partner of the patient is disregarded by virtue of paragraph (b) of subsection (5) above.

(7) A person, other than a relative, with whom the patient ordinarily resides (or, if the patient is for the time being an in-patient in a hospital, last ordinarily resided before he was admitted), and with whom he has or had been ordinarily

residing for a period of not less than five years, shall be treated for the purposes of this Part of this Act as if he were a relative but –

(a) shall be treated for the purposes of subsection (3) above as if mentioned last in subsection (1) above; and

(b) shall not be treated by virtue of this subsection as the nearest relative of a married patient or a patient in a civil partnership unless the husband, wife or civil partner of the patient is disregarded by virtue of paragraph (b) of subsection (5) above.

Amendments. Sub-paragraph (5)(d) repealed: Children Act 1989, s 108(6), (7), Sch 14, paras 1, 27, Sch 15. Words in subss (1), (5) inserted: MHA 2007, s 26(1)–(3). Words in subss (6), (7) substituted: MHA 2007, s 26(1), (4), (5).

27 Children and young persons in care

Where –

(a) a patient who is a child or young person is in the care of a local authority by virtue of a care order within the meaning of the Children Act 1989; or

(b) the rights and powers of a parent of a patient who is a child or young person are vested in a local authority by virtue of section 16 of the Social Work (Scotland) Act 1968,

the authority shall be deemed to be the nearest relative of the patient in preference to any person except the patient's husband or wife or civil partner (if any).

Amendments. Section substituted: Children Act 1989, s 108(5), (6), Sch 13, para 48(1), Sch 14, para 1. Words inserted: MHA 2007, s 26(6).

28 Nearest relative of minor under guardianship, etc

(1) Where –

(a) a guardian has been appointed for a person who has not attained the age of eighteen years; or

(b) a residence order (as defined by section 8 of the Children Act 1989) is in force with respect to such a person, the guardian (or guardians, where there is more than one) or the person named in the residence order shall, to the exclusion of any other person, be deemed to be his nearest relative.

(2) Subsection (5) of section 26 above shall apply in relation to a person who is, or who is one of the persons, deemed to be the nearest relative of a patient by virtue of this section as it applies in relation to a person who would be the nearest relative under subsection (3) of that section.

(3) In this section 'guardian' includes a special guardian (within the meaning of the Children Act 1989), but does not include a guardian under this Part of this Act.

(4) In this section 'court' includes a court in Scotland or Northern Ireland, and 'enactment' includes an enactment of the Parliament of Northern Ireland, a Measure of the Northern Ireland Assembly and an Order in Council under Schedule 1 of the Northern Ireland Act 1974.

Amendments. Subss (1), (3) substituted: Children Act 1989, s 108(5), (6), Sch 13, para 48, Sch 14, para 1. Words inserted in subss (3): Adoption and Children Act 2002, s 139(1), Sch 3, para 41.

29 Appointment by court of acting nearest relative

(1) The county court may, upon application made in accordance with the provisions of this section in respect of a patient, by order direct that the functions of the nearest relative of the patient under this Part of this Act and sections 66 and 69 below shall, during the continuance in force of the order, be exercisable by the person specified in the order.

(1A) If the court decides to make an order on an application under subsection (1) above, the following rules have effect for the purposes of specifying a person in the order –

   (a)   if a person is nominated in the application to act as the patient's nearest relative and that person is, in the opinion of the court, a suitable person to act as such and is willing to do so, the court shall specify that person (or, if there are two or more such persons, such one of them as the court thinks fit);

   (b)   otherwise, the court shall specify such person as is, in its opinion, a suitable person to act as the patient's nearest relative and is willing to do so.

(2) An order under this section may be made on the application of –

   (za) the patient;
   (a)   any relative of the patient;
   (b)   any other person with whom the patient is residing (or, if the patient is then an in-patient in a hospital, was last residing before he was admitted); or
   (c)   approved mental health professional.

(3) An application for an order under this section may be made upon any of the following grounds, that is to say –

   (a)   that the patient has no nearest relative within the meaning of this Act, or that it is not reasonably practicable to ascertain whether he has such a relative, or who that relative is;

   (b)   that the nearest relative of the patient is incapable of acting as such by reason of mental disorder or other illness;

   (c)   that the nearest relative of the patient unreasonably objects to the making of an application for admission for treatment or a guardianship application in respect of the patient;

(d)   that the nearest relative of the patient has exercised without due regard
       to the welfare of the patient or the interests of the public his power to
       discharge the patient under this Part of this Act, or is likely to do so;
       or

(e)   that the nearest relative of the patient is otherwise not a suitable
       person to act as such.

(4) If, immediately before the expiration of the period for which a patient is
liable to be detained by virtue of an application for admission for assessment,
an application under this section, which is an application made on the ground
specified in subsection (3)(c) or (d) above, is pending in respect of the patient,
that period shall be extended –

(a)   in any case, until the application under this section has been finally
       disposed of; and

(b)   if an order is made in pursuance of the application under this section,
       for a further period of seven days;

and for the purposes of this subsection an application under this section shall
be deemed to have been finally disposed of at the expiration of the time allowed
for appealing from the decision of the court or, if notice of appeal has been
given within that time, when the appeal has been heard or withdrawn, and
'pending' shall be construed accordingly.

(5) An order made on the ground specified in subsection (3)(a), (b) or (e) above
may specify a period for which it is to continue in force unless previously
discharged under section 30 below.

(6) While an order made under this section is in force, the provisions of this
Part of this Act (other than this section and section 30 below) and sections 66,
69, 132(4) and 133 below shall apply in relation to the patient as if for any
reference to the nearest relative of the patient there were substituted a reference
to the person having the functions of that relative and (without prejudice to
section 30 below) shall so apply notwithstanding that the person who was the
patient's nearest relative when the order was made is no longer his nearest
relative; but this subsection shall not apply to section 66 below in the case
mentioned in paragraph (h) of subsection (1) of that section.

Amendments. Words substituted in subs (1): MHA 2007, s 23(1), (2). Subs (1A) inserted:
MHA 2007, s 23(1), (3). Para inserted and words repealed in subs (2): MHA 2007, s 23(1), (4).
Words substituted in subs (2): MHA 2007, s 21, Sch 2, paras 1, 7(c). Word prospectively and para
inserted in subs (3): MHA 2007, s 23(1), (5), Sch 11, Pt 4. Words repealed in subs (3): MHA 2007,
ss 32(4), 55, Sch 3, paras 1, 13, Sch 11, Pt 5. Words substituted in subs (5): MHA 2007, s 23(1), (6).

30 Discharge and variation of orders under s 29

(1) An order made under section 29 above in respect of a patient may be
discharged by the county court upon application made –

(a)   in any case, by the patient or the person having the functions of the
       nearest relative of the patient by virtue of the order;

(b)   where the order was made on the ground specified in paragraph (a) or
       paragraph (b),(b) or (e) of section 29(3) above, or where the person

who was the nearest relative of the patient when the order was made has ceased to be his nearest relative, on the application of the nearest relative of the patient.

(1A) But, in the case of an order made on the ground specified in paragraph (e) of section 29(3) above, an application may not be made under subsection (1)(b) above by the person who was the nearest relative of the patient when the order was made except with leave of the county court.

(2) An order made under section 29 above in respect of a patient may be varied by the county court, on the application of the patient or of the person having the functions of the nearest relative by virtue of the order or on the application of an approved mental health professional, by substituting for the first mentioned person a local social services authority or any other person who in the opinion of the court is a proper person to exercise those functions, being an authority or person who is willing to do so another person for the person having those functions.

(2A) If the court decides to vary an order on an application under subsection (2) above, the following rules have effect for the purposes of substituting another person –

(a) if a person is nominated in the application to act as the patient's nearest relative and that person is, in the opinion of the court, a suitable person to act as such and is willing to do so, the court shall specify that person (or, if there are two or more such persons, such one of them as the court thinks fit);

(b) otherwise, the court shall specify such person as is, in its opinion, a suitable person to act as the patient's nearest relative and is willing to do so.

(3) If the person having the functions of the nearest relative of a patient by virtue of an order under section 29 above dies –

(a) subsections (1) and (2) above shall apply as if for any reference to that person there were substituted a reference to any relative of the patient, and

(b) until the order is discharged or varied under those provisions the functions of the nearest relative under this Part of this Act and sections 66 and 69 below shall not be exercisable by any person.

(4) An order made on the ground specified in paragraph (c) or (d) of section 29(3) above shall, unless previously discharged under subsection (1) above, cease to have effect as follows –

(a) if –

(i) on the date of the order the patient was liable to be detained or subject to guardianship by virtue of a relevant application, order or direction; or

(ii) he becomes so liable or subject within the period of three months beginning with that date; or

     (iii) he was a community patient on the date of the order, it shall cease to have effect when he is discharged under section 23 above or 72 below or the relevant application, order or direction otherwise ceases to have effect (except as a result of his being transferred in pursuance of regulations under section 19 above);

  (b)   otherwise, it shall cease to have effect at the end of the period of three months beginning with the date of the order.

(4A) In subsection (4) above, reference to a relevant application, order or direction is to any of the following –

  (a)   an application for admission for treatment;

  (b)   a guardianship application;

  (c)   an order or direction under Part 3 of this Act (other than under section 35, 36 or 38).

(4B) An order made on the ground specified in paragraph (a), (b) or (e) of section 29(3) above shall –

  (a)   if a period was specified under section 29(5) above, cease to have effect on expiry of that period, unless previously discharged under subsection (1) above;

  (b)   if no such period was specified, remain in force until it is discharged under subsection (1) above.

(5) The discharge or variation under this section of an order made under section 29 above shall not affect the validity of anything previously done in pursuance of the order.

Amendments. Words inserted and substituted in subs (1): MHA 2007, s 24(1), (2). Subs (1A) inserted: MHA 2007, s 24(1), (3). Words substituted in subs (2): MHA 2007, s 21, Sch 2, paras 1, 7(d). Words inserted and substituted in subs (2): MHA 2007, s 24(1), (4). Subs (2A) inserted: MHA 2007, s 24(1), (5). Words substituted in subs (4): MHA 2007, s 24(1), (6). Paras substituted in subs (4), and subs (4A) inserted: MHA 2007, s 32(4), Sch 3, paras 1, 14(1)–(3). Subs (4B) inserted: MHA 2007, s 24(1), (7).

Supplemental

31 Procedure on applications to county court

County court rules which relate to applications authorised by this Part of this Act to be made to a county court may make provision –

  (a)   for the hearing and determination of such applications otherwise than in open court;

  (b)   for the admission on the hearing of such applications of evidence of such descriptions as may be specified in the rules notwithstanding anything to the contrary in any enactment or rule of law relating to the admissibility of evidence;

  (c)   for the visiting and interviewing of patients in private by or under the directions of the court.

32 Regulations for purposes of Part II

(1) The Secretary of State may make regulations for prescribing anything which, under this Part of this Act, is required or authorised to be prescribed, and otherwise for carrying this Part of this Act into full effect.

(2) Regulations under this section may in particular make provision –

(a) for prescribing the form of any application, recommendation, report, order, notice or other document to be made or given under this Part of this Act;

(b) for prescribing the manner in which any such application, recommendation, report, order, notice or other document may be proved, and for regulating the service of any such application, report, order or notice;

(c) for requiring such bodies as may be prescribed by the regulations to keep such registers or other records as may be so prescribed in respect of patients liable to be detained or subject to guardianship under this Part of this Act or community patients, and to furnish or make available to those patients, and their relatives, such written statements of their rights and powers under this Act as may be so prescribed;

(d) for the determination in accordance with the regulations of the age of any person whose exact age cannot be ascertained by reference to the registers kept under the Births and Deaths Registration Act 1953; and

(e) for enabling the functions under this Part of this Act of the nearest relative of a patient to be performed, in such circumstances and subject to such conditions (if any) as may be prescribed by the regulations, by any person authorised in that behalf by that relative;

and for the purposes of this Part of this Act any application, report or notice the service of which is regulated under paragraph (b) above shall be deemed to have been received by or furnished to the authority or person to whom it is authorised or required to be furnished, addressed or given if it is duly served in accordance with the regulations.

(3) Without prejudice to subsections (1) and (2) above, but subject to section 23(4) and (6) above, regulations under this section may determine the manner in which functions under this Part of this Act of the managers of hospitals, local social services authorities, Local Health Board, Special Health Authorities, Primary Care Trusts, National Health Service trusts or NHS foundation trusts are to be exercised, and such regulations may in particular specify the circumstances in which, and the conditions subject to which, any such functions may be performed by officers of or other persons acting on behalf of those managers, boards, authorities and trusts.

Amendments. Words in subs (3) substituted: National Health Service and Community Care Act 1990, s 66(1), Sch 9, para 24(5). Words in subs (2)(c) substituted and inserted: Mental Health (Patients in the Community) Act 1995, s 1(2), Sch 1, para 2. Words in subs (3) substituted: Health Authorities Act 1995, s 2(1), Sch 1, para 107(4). Words in subs (3) inserted: Health Act 1999 (Supplementary, Consequential etc Provisions) Order 2000, SI 2000, No. 90, art 3(1), Sch 1, para 16(1), (6). Words repealed in subs (2)(c): MHA 2007, s 55, Sch 11, Pt 5. Words inserted in subs (2)(c): MHA 2007, s 32(4), Sch 3, paras 1, 15. Words inserted in subs (3): MHA 2007, s 45(2).

Words in subs (3) substituted: Health and Social Care (Community Health and Standards) Act 2003, s 34, Sch 4, paras 50, 55. Words in subs (3) substituted and inserted: References to Health Authorities Order 2007, SI 2007, No. 961, art 3, Schedule, para 13(1), (7)(a), (b).

33 Special provisions as to wards of court

(1) An application for the admission to hospital of a minor who is a ward of court may be made under this Part of this Act with the leave of the court; and section 11(4) above shall not apply in relation to an application so made.

(2) Where a minor who is a ward of court is liable to be detained in a hospital by virtue of an application for admission under this Part of this Act or is a community patient, any power exercisable under this Part of this Act or under section 66 below in relation to the patient by his nearest relative shall be exercisable by or with the leave of the court.

(3) Nothing in this Part of this Act shall be construed as authorising the making of a guardianship application in respect of a minor who is a ward of court, or the transfer into guardianship of any such minor.

(4) Where a community treatment order has been made in respect of a minor who is a ward of court, the provisions of this Part of this Act relating to community treatment orders and community patients have effect in relation to the minor subject to any order which the court makes in the exercise of its wardship jurisdiction; but this does not apply as regards any period when the minor is recalled to hospital under section 17E above.

Amendments. Words inserted in subs (2): s 32(4), Sch 3, paras 1, 16(1), (2). Subs (4) substituted (previously inserted: Mental Health (Patients in the Community) Act 1995, s 1(2), Sch 1, para 3: MHA 2007, s 32(4), Sch 3, paras 1, 16(1), (3).

34 Interpretation of Part II

(1) In this Part of this Act –

'the appropriate practitioner' means –
- (a) in the case of a patient who is subject to the guardianship of a person other than a local social services authority, the nominated medical attendant of the patient; and
- (b) in any other case, the responsible clinician;

'the nominated medical attendant', in relation to a patient who is subject to the guardianship of a person other than a local social services authority, means the person appointed in pursuance of regulations made under section 9(2) above to act as the medical attendant of the patient;
'registered establishment' means an establishment which would not, apart from subsection (2) below, be a hospital for the purposes of this Part and which –
- (a) in England, is a hospital as defined by section 275 of the National Health Service Act 2006 that is used for the carrying on of a regulated activity, within the meaning of Part 1 of the Health and Social Care Act 2008, which relates to the assessment

or medical treatment of mental disorder and in respect of which a person is registered under Chapter 2 of that Part; and

(b)   in Wales, is an establishment in respect of which a person is registered under Part 2 of the Care Standards Act 2000 as an independent hospital in which treatment or nursing (or both) are provided for persons liable to be detained under this Act;

'the responsible clinician' means –

(a)   in relation to a patient liable to be detained by virtue of an application for admission for assessment or an application for admission for treatment, or a community patient, the approved clinician with overall responsibility for the patient's case;

(b)   in relation to a patient subject to guardianship, the approved clinician authorised by the responsible local social services authority to act (either generally or in any particular case or for any particular purpose) as the responsible clinician;

(2) Except where otherwise expressly provided, this Part of this Act applies in relation to a registered establishment, as it applies in relation to a hospital, and references in this Part of this Act to a hospital, and any reference in this Act to a hospital to which this Part of this Act applies, shall be construed accordingly.

(3) In relation to a patient who is subject to guardianship in pursuance of a guardianship application, any reference in this Part of this Act to the responsible local social services authority is a reference –

(a)   where the patient is subject to the guardianship of a local social services authority, to that authority;

(b)   where the patient is subject to the guardianship of a person other than a local social services authority, to the local social services authority for the area in which that person resides.

Amendments. Definitions in subs (1) 'the community responsible medical officer' and 'the supervisor', and subs 1A, (all repealed) inserted: Mental Health (Patients in the Community) Act 1995, s 1(2), Sch 1, para 4(2), (4), (5). Words in subs (2) substituted: Care Standards Act 2000, s 116, Sch 4, para 9(1), (4)(b). Definition inserted in subs (1): MHA 2007, s 9(1), (9). Definitions and subs (1A) repealed: MHA 2007, s 55, Sch 11, Pt 5. Definition substituted: MHA 2007, s 9(1), (10). Definition in sub-s (1) substituted: Health and Social Care Act 2008 (Consequential Amendments No 2) Order 2010, SI 2010 No. 813, arts 1, 5(1), (3).

PART III
PATIENTS CONCERNED IN CRIMINAL PROCEEDINGS OR UNDER SENTENCE

Remands to hospital

35 Remand to hospital for report on accused's mental condition

(1) Subject to the provisions of this section, the Crown Court or a magistrates' court may remand an accused person to a hospital specified by the court for a report on his mental condition.

(2) For the purposes of this section an accused person is –

(a)   in relation to the Crown Court, any person who is awaiting trial before the court for an offence punishable with imprisonment or who has been arraigned before the court for such an offence and has not yet been sentenced or otherwise dealt with for the offence on which he has been arraigned;

(b)   in relation to a magistrates' court, any person who has been convicted by the court of an offence punishable on summary conviction with imprisonment and any person charged with such an offence if the court is satisfied that he did the act or made the omission charged or he has consented to the exercise by the court of the powers conferred by this section.

(3) Subject to subsection (4) below, the powers conferred by this section may be exercised if –

(a)   the court is satisfied, on the written or oral evidence of a registered medical practitioner, that there is reason to suspect that the accused person is suffering from mental disorder; and

(b)   the court is of the opinion that it would be impracticable for a report on his mental condition to be made if he were remanded on bail;

but those powers shall not be exercised by the Crown Court in respect of a person who has been convicted before the court if the sentence for the offence of which he has been convicted is fixed by law.

(4) The court shall not remand an accused person to a hospital under this section unless satisfied, on the written or oral evidence of the approved clinician who would be responsible for making the report or of some other person representing the managers of the hospital, that arrangements have been made for his admission to that hospital and for his admission to it within the period of seven days beginning with the date of the remand; and if the court is so satisfied it may, pending his admission, give directions for his conveyance to and detention in a place of safety.

(5) Where a court has remanded an accused person under this section it may further remand him if it appears to the court, on the written or oral evidence of the approved clinician responsible for making the report, that a further remand is necessary for completing the assessment of the accused person's mental condition.

(6) The power of further remanding an accused person under this section may be exercised by the court without his being brought before the court if he is represented by an authorised person who is given an opportunity of being heard.

(7) An accused person shall not be remanded or further remanded under this section for more than 28 days at a time or for more than 12 weeks in all; and the court may at any time terminate the remand if it appears to the court that it is appropriate to do so.

(8) An accused person remanded to hospital under this section shall be entitled to obtain at his own expense an independent report on his mental condition

from a registered medical practitioner or approved clinician chosen by him and to apply to the court on the basis of it for his remand to be terminated under subsection (7) above.

(9) Where an accused person is remanded under this section –

(a) a constable or any other person directed to do so by the court shall convey the accused person to the hospital specified by the court within the period mentioned in subsection (4) above; and

(b) the managers of the hospital shall admit him within that period and thereafter detain him in accordance with the provisions of this section.

(10) If an accused person absconds from a hospital to which he has been remanded under this section, or while being conveyed to or from that hospital, he may be arrested without warrant by any constable and shall, after being arrested, be brought as soon as practicable before the court that remanded him; and the court may thereupon terminate the remand and deal with him in any way in which it could have dealt with him if he had not been remanded under this section.

Amendments. Words substituted in subs (3)(a): MHA 2007, s 1(4), Sch 1, Pt 1, paras 1, 5. Words substituted in subss (4), (5): MHA 2007, s 10(1), (2)(a). Words inserted in subs (6): Legal Services Act 2007, s 208(1), Sch 21, paras 53, 54. Words inserted in subs (8): MHA 2007, s 10(1), (2)(b).

36 Remand of accused person to hospital for treatment

(1) Subject to the provisions of this section, the Crown Court may, instead of remanding an accused person in custody, remand him to a hospital specified by the court if satisfied, on the written or oral evidence of two registered medical practitioners, that

(a) he is suffering from mental disorder of a nature or degree which makes it appropriate for him to be detained in a hospital for medical treatment; and

(b) appropriate medical treatment is available for him.

(2) For the purposes of this section an accused person is any person who is in custody awaiting trial before the Crown Court for an offence punishable with imprisonment (other than an offence the sentence for which is fixed by law) or who at any time before sentence is in custody in the course of a trial before that court for such an offence.

(3) The court shall not remand an accused person under this section to a hospital unless it is satisfied, on the written or oral evidence of the approved clinician who would have overall responsibility for his case or of some other person representing the managers of the hospital, that arrangements have been made for his admission to that hospital and for his admission to it within the period of seven days beginning with the date of the remand; and if the court is so satisfied it may, pending his admission, give directions for his conveyance to and detention in a place of safety.

(4) Where a court has remanded an accused person under this section it may further remand him if it appears to the court, on the written or oral evidence of the responsible clinician, that a further remand is warranted.

(5) The power of further remanding an accused person under this section may be exercised by the court without his being brought before the court if he is represented by an authorised person who is given an opportunity of being heard.

(6) An accused person shall not be remanded or further remanded under this section for more than 28 days at a time or for more than 12 weeks in all; and the court may at any time terminate the remand if it appears to the court that it is appropriate to do so.

(7) An accused person remanded to hospital under this section shall be entitled to obtain at his own expense an independent report on his mental condition from a registered medical practitioner or approved clinician chosen by him and to apply to the court on the basis of it for his remand to be terminated under subsection (6) above.

(8) Subsections (9) and (10) of section 35 above shall have effect in relation to a remand under this section as they have effect in relation to a remand under that section.

Amendments. Subs (1)(a) substituted: MHA 2007, s 1(4), Sch 1, Pt 1, paras 1, 6. Subs (1)(b) and preceding word inserted: MHA 2007, s 5(1), (2). Words substituted in subss (3), (4), and words inserted in subs (7): MHA 2007, s 10(3)(a)–(c). Words inserted in subs (5): Legal Services Act 2007, s 208(1), Sch 21, paras 53, 55.

Hospital and guardianship orders

37 Powers of courts to order hospital admission or guardianship

(1) Where a person is convicted before the Crown Court of an offence punishable with imprisonment other than an offence the sentence for which is fixed by law, or is convicted by a magistrates' court of an offence punishable on summary conviction with imprisonment, and the conditions mentioned in subsection (2) below are satisfied, the court may by order authorise his admission to and detention in such hospital as may be specified in the order or, as the case may be, place him under the guardianship of a local social services authority or of such other person approved by a local social services authority as may be so specified.

(1A) In the case of an offence the sentence for which would otherwise fall to be imposed –

    (a)   under section 51A(2) of the Firearms Act 1968,
    (b)   under section 110(2) or 111(2) of the Powers of Criminal Courts (Sentencing) Act 2000,
    (c)   under any of sections 225 to 228 of the Criminal Justice Act 2003, or
    (d)   under section 29(4) or (6) of the Violent Crime Reduction Act 2006 (minimum sentences in certain cases of using someone to mind a weapon),

nothing in those provisions shall prevent a court from making an order under subs (1) above for the admission of the offender to a hospital.

(1B) References in subsection (1A) above to a sentence falling to be imposed under any of the provisions mentioned in that subsection are to be read in accordance with section 305(4) of the Criminal Justice Act 2003.

(2) The conditions referred to in subsection (1) above are that –

    (a)   the court is satisfied, on the written or oral evidence of two registered medical practitioners, that the offender is suffering from mental disorder and that either –

        (i)   the mental disorder from which the offender is suffering is of a nature or degree which makes it appropriate for him to be detained in a hospital for medical treatment and appropriate medical treatment is available for him, or

        (ii)   in the case of an offender who has attained the age of 16 years, the mental disorder is of a nature or degree which warrants his reception into guardianship under this Act; and

    (b)   the court is of the opinion, having regard to all the circumstances Including the nature of the offence and the character and antecedents of the offender, and to the other available methods of dealing with him, that the most suitable method of disposing of the case is by means of an order under this section.

(3) Where a person is charged before a magistrates' court with any act or omission as an offence and the court would have power, on convicting him of that offence, to make an order under subsection (1) above in his case, then, if the court is satisfied that the accused did the act or made the omission charged, the court may, if it thinks fit, make such an order without convicting him.

(4) An order for the admission of an offender to a hospital (in this Act referred to as 'a hospital order') shall not be made under this section unless the court is satisfied on the written or oral evidence of the approved clinician who would have overall responsibility for his case or of some other person representing the managers of the hospital that arrangements have been made for his admission to that hospital, and for his admission to it within the period of 28 days beginning with the date of the making of such an order; and the court may, pending his admission within that period, give such directions as it thinks fit for his conveyance to and detention in a place of safety.

(5) If within the said period of 28 days it appears to the Secretary of State that by reason of an emergency or other special circumstances it is not practicable for the patient to be received into the hospital specified in the order, he may give directions for the admission of the patient to such other hospital as appears to be appropriate instead of the hospital so specified; and where such directions are given –

    (a)   the Secretary of State shall cause the person having the custody of the patient to be informed, and

    (b)   the hospital order shall have effect as if the hospital specified in the directions were substituted for the hospital specified in the order.

(6) An order placing an offender under the guardianship of a local social services authority or of any other person (in this Act referred to as 'a guardianship order') shall not be made under this section unless the court is satisfied that that authority or person is willing to receive the offender into guardianship.

(7) *(repealed)*

(8) Where an order is made under this section, the court shall not –

(a)　pass sentence of imprisonment or impose a fine or make a community order (within the meaning of Part 12 of the Criminal Justice Act 2003) or a youth rehabilitation order (within the meaning of Part 1 of the Criminal Justice and Immigration Act 2008) in respect of the offence,

(b)　if the order under this section is a hospital order, make a referral order (within the meaning of the Powers of Criminal Courts (Sentencing) Act 2000) in respect of the offence, or

(c)　make in respect of the offender an order under section 150 of that Act (binding over of parent or guardian),

but the court may make any other order which it has power to make apart from this section; and for the purposes of this subsection 'sentence of imprisonment' includes any sentence or order for detention.

Amendments. Words in subs (1) (repealed) inserted, words in subs (4) repealed and words in subs (5) substituted: Crime (Sentences) Act 1997, s 49(1), 55, 56(2), Sch 4, para 12(1), (3), Sch 6. Words in subs (8) substituted: Youth Justice and Criminal Evidence Act 1999, s 67, Sch 4, para 11. Words in subs (8)(a), (c) substituted: Powers of Criminal Courts (Sentencing) Act 2000, Sch 9, paras 90(1), (6)(a), (b). Words in subs (1) repealed, subss (1A), (1B) substituted and words in subs 8 substituted: Criminal Justice Act 2003, s 304, Sch 32, Pt 1, paras 37, 38(a)–(c). Word in subs (1A)(b) repealed, subs (1A)(d) and immediately preceding word inserted: Violent Crime Reduction Act 2006, ss 49, 65, Sch 1, para 2, Sch 5. Words in subs (2)(a) substituted: MHA 2007, s 1(4), Sch 1, Pt 1, paras 1, 7(a). Words in subs (2)(a)(i) substituted: MHA 2007, s 4(1), (5). Words in subs (3) repealed: MHA 2007, ss 1(4), 55, Sch 1, Pt 1, paras 1, 7(b), Sch 11, Pt 1. Words in subs (4) substituted: MHA 2007, s 10(1), (4). Subs (7) prospectively repealed: MHA 2007, s 55, Sch 11, Pt 1. Words in subs (8)(a) inserted: Criminal Justice and Immigration Act 2008 s 6(2), Sch 4, Pt 1, para 30(a). Words in subs (8)(c) repealed: Criminal Justice and Immigration Act 2008 ss 6(2), 149, Sch 4, Pt 1, para 30(b), Sch 28, Part 1.

38　Interim hospital orders

(1) Where a person is convicted before the Crown Court of an offence punishable with imprisonment (other than an offence the sentence for which is fixed by law) or is convicted by a magistrates' court of an offence punishable on summary conviction with imprisonment and the court before or by which he is convicted is satisfied, on the written or oral evidence of two registered medical practitioners –

(a)　that the offender is suffering from mental disorder; and

(b)　that there is reason to suppose that the mental disorder from which the offender is suffering is such that it may be appropriate for a hospital order to be made in his case, the court may, before making a hospital order or dealing with him in some other way, make an order (in this Act referred to as 'an interim hospital order') authorising his admission to such hospital as may be specified in the order and his detention there in accordance with this section.

(2) In the case of an offender who is subject to an interim hospital order the court may make a hospital order without his being brought before the court if he is represented by an authorised person who is given an opportunity of being heard.

(3) At least one of the registered medical practitioners whose evidence is taken into account under subsection (1) above shall be employed at the hospital which is to be specified in the order.

(4) An interim hospital order shall not be made for the admission of an offender to a hospital unless the court is satisfied, on the written or oral evidence of the approved clinician who would have overall responsibility for his case or of some other person representing the managers of the hospital, that arrangements have been made for his admission to that hospital and for his admission to it within the period of 28 days beginning with the date of the order; and if the court is so satisfied the court may, pending his admission, give directions for his conveyance to and detention in a place of safety.

(5) An interim hospital order –

(a) shall be in force for such period, not exceeding 12 weeks, as the court may specify when making the order; but

(b) may be renewed for further periods of not more than 28 days at a time if it appears to the court, on the written or oral evidence of the responsible clinician, that the continuation of the order is warranted;

but no such order shall continue in force for more than twelve months in all and the court shall terminate the order if it makes a hospital order in respect of the offender or decides after considering the written or oral evidence of the responsible clinician, to deal with the offender in some other way.

(6) The power of renewing an interim hospital order may be exercised without the offender being brought before the court if he is represented by counsel or a solicitor and his counsel or solicitor is given an opportunity of being heard.

(7) If an offender absconds from a hospital in which he is detained in pursuance of an interim hospital order, or while being conveyed to or from such a hospital, he may be arrested without warrant by a constable and shall, after being arrested, be brought as soon as practicable before the court that made the order; and the court may thereupon terminate the order and deal with him in any way in which it could have dealt with him if no such order had been made.

Amendments. Words in subs (5) substituted: Crime (Sentences) Act 1997, s 49(1). Words in subs (1)(a) substituted: MHA 2007, s 1(4), Sch 1, Pt 1, paras 1, 8. Words in subss (4), (5) prospectively substituted: MHA 2007, s 10(1), (5)(a), (b). Words inserted in subs (2): Legal Services Act 2007, s 208, Sch 21, para 56.

39 Information as to hospitals

(1) Where a court is minded to make a hospital order or interim hospital order in respect of any person it may request –

(a)   the Primary Care Trust or Local Health Board for the area in which that person resides or last resided; or

(b)   the National Assembly for Wales or any other Primary Care Trust or Local Health Board that appears to the court to be appropriate,

to furnish the court with such information as that Primary Care Trust or Local Health Board or National Assembly for Wales have or can reasonably obtain with respect to the hospital or hospitals (if any) in their area or elsewhere at which arrangements could be made for the admission of that person in pursuance of the order, and that Primary Care Trust or Local Health Board or National Assembly for Wales shall comply with any such request.

(1A) In relation to a person who has not attained the age of 18 years, subsection (1) above shall have effect as if the reference to the making of a hospital order included a reference to a remand under section 35 or 36 above or the making of an order under section 44 below.

(1B) Where the person concerned has not attained the age of 18 years, the information which may be requested under subsection (1) above includes, in particular, information about the availability of accommodation or facilities designed so as to be specially suitable for patients who have not attained the age of 18 years.'

(2) (*repealed*)

Amendments. Words substituted in subs (1): Health Authorities Act 1995, s 2(1), Sch 1, para 107(1), (5)(ii)–(v). Subs (2) repealed: Health Authorities Act 1995, ss 2(1), 5(1), Sch 1, para 107(5), Sch 3. Words inserted in subs (1): National Health Service Reform and Health Care Professions Act 2002, s 2(5), Sch 2, Pt 2, paras 42, 46. Subss (1A), (1B) inserted: MHA 2007 s 31(1), (2). Words substituted and inserted in subs (1): References to Health Authorities Order 2007, SI 2007 No. 961, art 3, Schedule, para 13(1), (8)(a)–(d).

39A Information to facilitate guardianship orders

(1) Where a court is minded to make a hospital order or interim hospital order in respect of any offender it may request the local social services authority for the area in which the offender resides or last resided, or any other local social services authority which seems to the court to be appropriate –

(a)   to inform the court whether it on any person approved by it is willing to receive the offender into guardianship; and

(b)   if so, to give such information as it reasonably can about how it or the other person could be expected to exercise in relation to the offender the powers conferred by section 40(2) below

and that authority shall comply with any such request.

Amendments. Section inserted: Criminal Justice Act 1991, s 27(1).

40 Effect of hospital orders, guardianship orders and interim hospital orders

(1) A hospital order shall be sufficient authority –

(a)   for a constable, an approved mental health professional or any other person directed to do so by the court to convey the patient to the hospital specified in the order within a period of 28 days; and

(b)   for the managers of the hospital to admit him at any time within that period and thereafter detain him in accordance with the provisions of this Act.

(2) A guardianship order shall confer on the authority or person named in the order as guardian the same powers as a guardianship application made and accepted under Part II of this Act.

(3) Where an interim hospital order is made in respect of an offender –

(a)   a constable or any other person directed to do so by the court shall convey the offender to the hospital specified in the order within the period mentioned in section 38(4) above; and

(b)   the managers of the hospital shall admit him within that period and thereafter detain him in accordance with the provisions of section 38 above.

(4) A patient who is admitted to a hospital in pursuance of a hospital order, or placed under guardianship by a guardianship order, shall, subject to the provisions of this subsection, be treated for the purposes of the provisions of this Act mentioned in Part I of Schedule 1 to this Act as if he had been so admitted or placed on the date of the order in pursuance of an application for admission for treatment or a guardianship application, as the case may be, duly made under Part II of this Act, but subject to any modifications of those provisions specified in that Part of that Schedule.

(5) Where a patient is admitted to a hospital in pursuance of a hospital order, or placed under guardianship by a guardianship order, any previous application, hospital order or guardianship order by virtue of which he was liable to be detained in a hospital or subject to guardianship shall cease to have effect; but if the first-mentioned order, or the conviction on which it was made, is quashed on appeal, this subsection shall not apply and section 22 above shall have effect as if during any period for which the patient was liable to be detained or subject to guardianship under the order, he had been detained in custody as mentioned in that section.

(6) Where –

(a)   a patient admitted to a hospital in pursuance of a hospital order is absent without leave;

(b)   a warrant to arrest him has been issued under section 72 of the Criminal Justice Act 1967; and

(c)   he is held pursuant to the warrant in any country or territory other than the United Kingdom, any of the Channel Islands and the Isle of Man, he shall be treated as having been taken into custody under section 18 above on first being so held.

Amendments. Subs (6) inserted: Mental Health (Patients in the Community) Act 1995, s 2(4). Words in subs (1)(a) substituted: MHA 2007, s 21, Sch 2, paras 1, 7(e).

Restriction orders

41 Power of higher courts to restrict discharge from hospital

(1) Where a hospital order is made in respect of an offender by the Crown Court, and it appears to the court, having regard to the nature of the offence, the antecedents of the offender and the risk of his committing further offences if set at large, that it is necessary for the protection of the public from serious harm so to do, the court may, subject to the provisions of this section, further order that the offender shall be subject to the special restrictions set out in this section; and an order under this section shall be known as 'a restriction order'.

(2) A restriction order shall not be made in the case of any person unless at least one of the registered medical practitioners whose evidence is taken into account by the court under section 37(2)(a) above has given evidence orally before the court.

(3) The special restrictions applicable to a patient in respect of whom a restriction order is in force are as follows –

(a) none of the provisions of Part II of this Act relating to the duration, renewal and expiration of authority for the detention of patients shall apply, and the patient shall continue to be liable to be detained by virtue of the relevant hospital order until he is duly discharged under the said Part II or absolutely discharged under section 42, 73, 74 or 75 below;

(aa) none of the provisions of Part II of this Act relating to community treatment orders and community patients shall apply;

(b) no application shall be made to the appropriate tribunal in respect of a patient under section 66 or 69(1) below;

(c) the following powers shall be exercisable only with the consent of the Secretary of State, namely –

(i) power to grant leave of absence to the patient under section 17 above;

(ii) power to transfer the patient in pursuance of regulations under section 19 above or in pursuance of subsection (3) of that section; and

(iii) power to order the discharge of the patient under section 23 above; and if leave of absence is granted under the said section 17 power to recall the patient under that section shall vest in the Secretary of State as well as the responsible clinician; and

(d) the power of the Secretary of State to recall the patient under the said section 17 and power to take the patient into custody and return him under section 18 above may be exercised at any time; and in relation to any such patient section 40(4) above shall have effect as if it referred to Part II of Schedule 1 to this Act instead of Part I of that Schedule.

(4) A hospital order shall not cease to have effect under section 40(5) above if a restriction order in respect of the patient is in force at the material time.

(5) Where a restriction order in respect of a patient ceases to have effect while the relevant hospital order continues in force, the provisions of section 40 above and Part I of Schedule 1 to this Act shall apply to the patient as if he had been admitted to the hospital in pursuance of a hospital order (without a restriction order) made on the date on which the restriction order ceased to have effect.

(6) While a person is subject to a restriction order the responsible clinician shall at such intervals (not exceeding one year) as the Secretary of State may direct examine and report to the Secretary of State on that person; and every report shall contain such particulars as the Secretary of State may require.

Amendments. Subs (3)(aa) inserted: Mental Health (Patients in the Community) Act 1995, s 1(2), Sch 1, para 5. Words in subs (3)(c)(ii) inserted: Crime (Sentences) Act 1997, s 49(2). Words in subs (1) repealed: MHA 2007, ss 40(1), 55, Sch 11, Pt 8. Words in subss (3)(c), (6) substituted: MHA 2007, s 10(1), (6). Words in subs (3)(aa) substituted: MHA 2007, s 32(4), Sch 3, paras 1, 17. Words in subs (3)(c) substituted by Transfer of Tribunal Functions Order 2008, SI 2008 No. 2833 Art 9, Sch 3, paras 40, 41.

42 Powers of Secretary of State in respect of patients subject to restriction orders

(1) If the Secretary of State is satisfied that in the case of any patient a restriction order is no longer required for the protection of the public from serious harm, he may direct that the patient cease to be subject to the special restrictions set out in section 41(3) above; and where the Secretary of State so directs, the restriction order shall cease to have effect, and section 41(5) above shall apply accordingly.

(2) At any time while a restriction order is in force in respect of a patient, the Secretary of State may, if he thinks fit, by warrant discharge the patient from hospital, either absolutely or subject to conditions; and where a person is absolutely discharged under this subsection, he shall thereupon cease to be liable to be detained by virtue of the relevant hospital order, and the restriction order shall cease to have effect accordingly.

(3) The Secretary of State may at any time during the continuance in force of a restriction order in respect of a patient who has been conditionally discharged under subsection (2) above by warrant recall the patient to such hospital as may be specified in the warrant.

(4) Where a patient is recalled as mentioned in subsection (3) above –

    (a)   if the hospital specified in the warrant is not the hospital from which the patient was conditionally discharged, the hospital order and the restriction order shall have effect as if the hospital specified in the warrant were substituted for the hospital specified in the hospital order;

    (b)   in any case, the patient shall be treated for the purposes of section 18 above as if he had absented himself without leave from the hospital specified in the warrant.

(5) If a restriction order in respect of a patient ceases to have effect after the patient has been conditionally discharged under this section, the patient shall, unless previously recalled under subsection (3) above, be deemed to be absolutely discharged on the date when the order ceases to have effect, and shall cease to be liable to be detained by virtue of the relevant hospital order accordingly.

(6) The Secretary of State may, if satisfied that the attendance at any place in Great Britain of a patient who is subject to a restriction order is desirable in the interests of justice or for the purposes of any public inquiry, direct him to be taken to that place; and where a patient is directed under this subsection to be taken to any place he shall, unless the Secretary of State otherwise directs, be kept in custody while being so taken, while at that place and while being taken back to the hospital in which he is liable to be detained.

Amendments. Words in subs (4)(b) repealed: MHA 2007, ss 40(2), 55, Sch 11, Pt 8.

43 Power of magistrates' courts to commit for restriction order

(1) If in the case of a person of or over the age of 14 years who is convicted by a magistrates' court of an offence punishable on summary conviction with imprisonment –

(a) the conditions which under section 37(1) above are required to be satisfied for the making of a hospital order are satisfied in respect of the offender; but

(b) it appears to the court, having regard to the nature of the offence, the antecedents of the offender and the risk of his committing further offences if set at large, that if a hospital order is made a restriction order should also be made, the court may, instead of making a hospital order or dealing with him in any other manner, commit him in custody to the Crown Court to be dealt with in respect of the offence.

(2) Where an offender is committed to the Crown Court under this section, the Crown Court shall inquire into the circumstances of the case and may –

(a) if that court would have power so to do under the foregoing provisions of this Part of this Act upon the conviction of the offender before that court of such an offence as is described in section 37(1) above, make a hospital order in his case, with or without a restriction order;

(b) if the court does not make such an order, deal with the offender in any other manner in which the magistrates' court might have dealt with him.

(3) The Crown Court shall have the same power to make orders under sections 35, 36 and 38 above in the case of a person committed to the court under this section as the Crown Court has under those sections in the case of an accused person within the meaning of section 35 or 36 above or of a person convicted before that court as mentioned in section 38 above.

(4) The powers of a magistrates' court under section 3 or 3B of the Powers of Criminal Courts (Sentencing) Act 2000 (which enable such a court to commit

an offender to the Crown Court where the court is of the opinion, or it appears to the court, as mentioned in the section in question) shall also be exercisable by a magistrates' court where it is of that opinion (or it so appears to it) unless a hospital order is made in the offender's case with a restriction order.

Amendments. Words in subs (4) substituted: Powers of Criminal Courts (Sentencing) Act 2000, s 165(1), Sch 9, para 91

44 Committal to hospital under s 43

(1) Where an offender is committed under section 43(1) above and the magistrates' court by which he is committed is satisfied on written or oral evidence that arrangements have been made for the admission of the offender to a hospital in the event of an order being made under this section, the court may, instead of committing him in custody, by order direct him to be admitted to that hospital, specifying it, and to be detained there until the case is disposed of by the Crown Court, and may give such directions as it thinks fit for his production from the hospital to attend the Crown Court by which his case is to be dealt with.

(2) The evidence required by subsection (1) above shall be given by the approved clinician who would have overall responsibility for the offender's case or by some other person representing the managers of the hospital in question.

(3) The power to give directions under section 37(4) above, section 37(5) above and section 40(1) above shall apply in relation to an order under this section as they apply in relation to a hospital order, but as if references to the period of 28 days mentioned in section 40(1) above were omitted; and subject as aforesaid an order under this section shall, until the offender's case is disposed of by the Crown Court, have the same effect as a hospital order together with a restriction order.

Amendments. Words in subs (3) repealed subject to saving: MHA 2007, ss 40(3)(a), 55, Sch 11, Pt 8. For saving see MHA 2007, s 40(7). Words in subs (2) substituted: MHA 2007, s 10(1), (7).

45 Appeals from magistrates' courts

(1) Where on the trial of an information charging a person with an offence a magistrates' court makes a hospital order or guardianship order in respect of him without convicting him, he shall have the same right of appeal against the order as if it had been made on his conviction; and on any such appeal the Crown Court shall have the same powers as if the appeal had been against both conviction and sentence.

(2) An appeal by a child or young person with respect to whom any such order has been made, whether the appeal is against the order or against the finding upon which the order was made, may be brought by him or by his parent or guardian on his behalf.

Hospital and limitation directions

Amendment. Heading inserted by the Crime (Sentences) Act 1997, s 46.

45A Power of higher courts to direct hospital admission

(1) This section applies where, in the case of a person convicted before the Crown Court of an offence the sentence for which is not fixed by law –

    (a)   the conditions mentioned in subsection (2) below are fulfilled; and

    (b)   the court considers making a hospital order in respect of him before deciding to impose a sentence of imprisonment ('the relevant sentence') in respect of the offence.

(2) The conditions referred to in subsection (1) above are that the court is satisfied, on the written or oral evidence of two registered medical practitioners –

    (a)   that the offender is suffering from mental disorder;

    (b)   that the mental disorder from which the offender is suffering is of a nature or degree which makes it appropriate for him to be detained in a hospital for medical treatment; and

    (c)   that appropriate medical treatment is available for him.

(3) The court may give both of the following directions, namely –

    (a)   a direction that, instead of being removed to and detained in a prison, the offender be removed to and detained in such hospital as may be specified in the direction (in this Act referred to as a 'hospital direction'); and

    (b)   a direction that the offender be subject to the special restrictions set out in section 41 above (in this Act referred to as a 'limitation direction').

(4) A hospital direction and a limitation direction shall not be given in relation to an offender unless at least one of the medical practitioners whose evidence is taken into account by the court under subsection (2) above has given evidence orally before the court.

(5) A hospital direction and a limitation direction shall not be given in relation to an offender unless the court is satisfied on the written or oral evidence of the approved clinician who would have overall responsibility for his case, or of some other person representing the managers of the hospital that arrangements have been made –

    (a)   for his admission to that hospital; and

    (b)   for his admission to it within the period of 28 days beginning with the day of the giving of such directions;

and the court may, pending his admission within that period, give such directions as it thinks fit for his conveyance to and detention in a place of safety.

(6) If within the said period of 28 days it appears to the Secretary of State that by reason of an emergency or other special circumstances it is not practicable for the patient to be received into the hospital specified in the hospital direction, he may give instructions for the admission of the patient to such other hospital as appears to be appropriate instead of the hospital so specified.

(7) Where such instructions are given –

(a) the Secretary of State shall cause the person having the custody of the patient to be informed, and

(b) the hospital direction shall have effect as if the hospital specified in the instructions were substituted for the hospital specified in the hospital direction.

(8) Section 38(1) and (5) and section 39 above shall have effect as if any reference to the making of a hospital order included a reference to the giving of a hospital direction and a limitation direction.

(9) A hospital direction and a limitation direction given in relation to an offender shall have effect not only as regards the relevant sentence but also (so far as applicable) as regards any other sentence of imprisonment imposed on the same or a previous occasion.

(10), (11) *(repealed)*

Amendments. Section inserted: Crime (Sentences) Act 1997, s 46. Words in subs (1)(b) repealed: Criminal Justice Act 2003, ss 304, 332, Sch 32, Pt 1, paras 37, 39, Sch 37, Pt 7. Words in subs (2)(a) substituted: MHA, s 1(4), Sch 1, Pt 1, paras 1, 9. Subs (2)(c) substituted: MHA 2007, s 4(1), (6). Words in subs (5) substituted: MHA 2007, s 10(1), (8). Subss (10), (11) repealed: MHA 2007, s 55, Sch 11, Pt 1.

45B Effect of hospital and limitation directions

(1) A hospital direction and a limitation direction shall be sufficient authority –

(a) for a constable or any other person directed to do so by the court to convey the patient to the hospital specified in the hospital direction within a period of 28 days; and

(b) for the managers of the hospital to admit him at any time within that period and thereafter detain him in accordance with the provisions of this Act.

(2) With respect to any person –

(a) a hospital direction shall have effect as a transfer direction; and

(b) a limitation direction shall have effect as a restriction direction.

(3) While a person is subject to a hospital direction and a limitation direction the responsible medical officer responsible clinician shall at such intervals (not exceeding one year) as the Secretary of State may direct examine and report to the Secretary of State on that person; and every report shall contain such particulars as the Secretary of State may require.

Amendments. Section inserted: Crime (Sentences) Act 1997, s 46. Words in subs (3) substituted: MHA 2007, s 10(1), (9)(a).

46 *(repealed)*

Amendments. Section repealed: Armed Forces Act 1996, s 35(2), Sch 7, Pt III.

Transfer to hospital of prisoners etc

47 Removal to hospital of persons serving sentences of imprisonment, etc

(1) If in the case of a person serving a sentence of imprisonment the Secretary of State is satisfied, by reports from at least two registered medical practitioners –

    (a)   that the said person is suffering from mental disorder; and

    (b)   that the mental disorder from which that person is suffering is of a nature or degree which makes it appropriate for him to be detained in a hospital for medical treatment; and

    (c)   that appropriate medical treatment is available for him;

the Secretary of State may, if he is of the opinion having regard to the public interest and all the circumstances that it is expedient so to do, by warrant direct that that person be removed to and detained in such hospital as may be specified in the direction; and a direction under this section shall be known as 'a transfer direction'.

(2) A transfer direction shall cease to have effect at the expiration of the period of 14 days beginning with the date on which it is given unless within that period the person with respect to whom it was given has been received into the hospital specified in the direction.

(3) A transfer direction with respect to any person shall have the same effect as a hospital order made in his case.

(4) (*repealed*)

(5) References in this Part of this Act to a person serving a sentence of imprisonment include references –

    (a)   to a person detained in pursuance of any sentence or order for detention made by a court in criminal proceedings or service disciplinary proceedings (other than an order made in consequence of a finding of insanity or unfitness to stand trial or a sentence of service detention within the meaning of the Armed Forces Act 2006);

    (b)   to a person committed to custody under section 115(3) of the Magistrates' Courts Act 1980 (which relates to persons who fail to comply with an order to enter into recognisances to keep the peace or be of good behaviour); and

    (c)   to a person committed by a court to a prison or other institution to which the Prison Act 1952 applies in default of payment of any sum adjudged to be paid on his conviction.

(6) In subsection (5)(a) 'service disciplinary proceedings' means proceedings in respect of a service offence within the meaning of the Armed Forces Act 2006.

Amendments. Words in subs (4) repealed: Crime (Sentences) Act 1997, ss 49(3), 56(2), Sch 6. Words in subs (5)(a) substituted: Domestic Violence, Crime and Victims Act 2004, s 58(1), Sch 10, para 18. Words in subs (1)(a) substituted: MHA 2007, s 1(4), Sch 1, Pt 1, paras 1, 10. Words in subs (1)(b) repealed, and subs (1)(c) and preceding word inserted: MHA 2007, s 4(1), (7). Subs (4) repealed: s 55, Sch 11, Pt 1. Words in subs (5)(a) inserted, and subs (6) inserted: Armed Forces Act 2006, s 378(1), Sch 16, para 97(1)–(3).

48 Removal to hospital of other prisoners

(1) If in the case of a person to whom this section applies the Secretary of State is satisfied by the same reports as are required for the purposes of section 47 above that that person is suffering from mental illness or severe mental impairment of a nature or degree which makes it appropriate for him to be detained in a hospital for medical treatment and that he is in urgent need of such treatment,

    (a) that person is suffering from mental disorder of a nature or degree which makes it appropriate for him to be detained in hospital for medical treatment; and

    (b) he is in urgent need of such treatment; and

    (c) appropriate medical treatment is available for him;

the Secretary of State shall have the same power of giving a transfer direction in respect of him under that section as if he were serving a sentence of imprisonment.

(2) This section applies to the following persons, that is to say –

    (a) persons detained in a prison or remand centre, not being person serving a sentence of imprisonment or persons falling within the following paragraphs of this subsection;

    (b) persons remanded in custody by a magistrates' court;

    (c) civil prisoners, that is to say, persons committed by a court to prison for a limited term, who are not persons falling to be dealt with under section 47 above;

    (d) persons detained under the Immigration Act 1971 or under section 62 of the Nationality, Immigration and Asylum Act 2002 (detention by Secretary of State).

(3) Subsections (2) and (3) of section 47 above shall apply for the purposes of this section and of any transfer direction given by virtue of this section as they apply for the purposes of that section and of any transfer direction under that section.

Amendments. Words in subs (2)(d) inserted: Nationality, Immigration and Asylum Act 2002, s 62(10)(a). Words in subs (2)(c) repealed: Statute Law (Repeals) Act 2004 (no specific commencement provision). Words in subs (1) repealed and subs (1)(a), (b) substituted: MHA 2007, s 1(4), Sch 1, Pt 1, paras 1, 11(a); Subs(1)(c) inserted: MHA 2007, s 5(1), (3); Words in subs (3) substituted: s 1(4), Sch 1, Pt 1, paras 1, 11(b).

49 Restriction on discharge of prisoners removed to hospital

(1) Where a transfer direction is given in respect of any person, the Secretary of State, if he thinks fit, may by warrant further direct that that person shall be subject to the special restrictions set out in section 41 above; and where the Secretary of State gives a transfer direction in respect of any such person as is

described in paragraph (a) or (b) of section 48(2) above, he shall also give a direction under this section applying those restrictions to him.

(2) A direction under this section shall have the same effect as a restriction order made under section 41 above and shall be known as 'a restriction direction'.

(3) While a person is subject to a restriction direction the responsible clinician shall at such intervals (not exceeding one year) as the Secretary of State may direct examine and report to the Secretary of State on that person; and every report shall contain such particulars as the Secretary of State may require.

Amendments. Words in subs (3) substituted: MHA 2007, s 10(9)(b).

50 Further provisions as to prisoners under sentence

(1) Where a transfer direction and a restriction direction have been given in respect of a person serving a sentence of imprisonment and before his release date the Secretary of State is notified by the responsible clinician, any other approved clinician or the appropriate tribunal that that person no longer requires treatment in hospital for mental disorder or that no effective treatment for his disorder can be given in the hospital to which he has been removed, the Secretary of State may –

(a)   by warrant direct that he be remitted to any prison or other institution in which he might have been detained if he had not been removed to hospital, there to be dealt with as if he had not been so removed; or

(b)   exercise any power of releasing him on licence or discharging him under supervision which could have been exercisable if he had been remitted to such a prison or institution as aforesaid,

and on his arrival in the prison or other institution or, as the case may be, his release or discharge as aforesaid, the transfer direction and the restriction direction shall cease to have effect.

(2) A restriction direction in the case of a person serving a sentence of imprisonment shall cease to have effect, if it has not previously done so, on his release date.

(3) In this section, references to a person's release date are to the day (if any) on which he would be entitled to be released (whether unconditionally or on licence) from any prison or other institution in which he might have been detained if the transfer direction had not been given; and in determining that day there shall be disregarded –

(a)   any powers that would be exercisable by the Parole Board if he were detained in such a prison or other institution, and

(b)   any practice of the Secretary of State in relation to the early release under discretionary powers of persons detained in such a prison or other institution.

(4) For the purposes of section 49(2) of the Prison Act 1952 (which provides for discounting from the sentences of certain prisoners periods while they are

unlawfully at large) a patient who, having been transferred in pursuance of a transfer direction from any such institution as is referred to in that section, is at large in circumstances in which he is liable to be taken into custody under any provision of this Act, shall be treated as unlawfully at large and absent from that institution.

(5) The preceding provisions of this section shall have effect as if –

    (a)   the reference in subsection (1) to a transfer direction and a restriction direction having been given in respect of a person serving a sentence of imprisonment included a reference to a hospital direction and a limitation direction having been given in respect of a person sentenced to imprisonment;

    (b)   the reference in subsection (2) to a restriction direction included a reference to a limitation direction; and

    (c)   references in subsections (3) and (4) to a transfer direction included references to a hospital direction.

Amendments. Subs (5) inserted: Crime (Sentences) Act 1997, s 55, Sch 4, para 12(5). Words in subs (1)–(3) substituted: Criminal Justice Act 2003, s 294(1)–(3). Words substituted: MHA 2007, s 11(1), (2)(a), (b). Words in subs (1) substituted by Transfer of Tribunal Functions Order 2008, SI 2008 No 2833 Art 9, Sch 3, para 42.

51 Further provisions as to detained persons

(1) This section has effect where a transfer direction has been given in respect of any such person as is described in paragraph (a) of section 48(2) above and that person is in this section referred to as 'the detainee'.

(2) The transfer direction shall cease to have effect when the detainee's case is disposed of by the court having jurisdiction to try or otherwise deal with him, but without prejudice to any power of that court to make a hospital order or other order under this Part of this Act in his case.

(3) If the Secretary of State is notified by the responsible clinician, any other approved clinician or the appropriate tribunal at any time before the detainee's case is disposed of by that court –

    (a)   that the detainee no longer requires treatment in hospital for mental disorder; or

    (b)   that no effective treatment for his disorder can be given at the hospital to which he has been removed,

the Secretary of State may by warrant direct that he be remitted to any place where he might have been detained if he had not been removed to hospital, there to be dealt with as if he had not been so removed, and on his arrival at the place to which he is so remitted the transfer direction shall cease to have effect.

(4) If (no direction having been given under subsection (3) above) the court having jurisdiction to try or otherwise deal with the detainee is satisfied on the written or oral evidence of the responsible medical officer responsible clinician –

(a)   that the detainee no longer requires treatment in hospital for mental disorder; or

(b)   that no effective treatment for his disorder can be given at the hospital to which he has been removed,

the court may order him to be remitted to any such place as is mentioned in subsection (3) above or, subject to section 25 of the Criminal Justice and Public Order Act 1994, released on bail and on his arrival at that place or, as the case may be, his release on bail the transfer direction shall cease to have effect.

(5) If (no direction or order having been given or made under subsection (3) or (4) above) it appears to the court having jurisdiction to try or otherwise deal with the detainee –

(a)   that it is impracticable or inappropriate to bring the detainee before the court; and

(b)   that the conditions set out in subsection (6) below are satisfied,

the court may make a hospital order (with or without a restriction order) in his case in his absence and, in the case of a person awaiting trial, without convicting him.

(6) A hospital order may be made in respect of a person under subsection (5) above if the court –

(a)   is satisfied, on the written or oral evidence of at least two registered medical practitioners, that;
      (i)   the detainee is suffering from mental disorder of a nature or degree which makes it appropriate for the patient to be detained in a hospital for medical treatment; and
      (ii)   appropriate medical treatments is available for him; and

(b)   is of the opinion, after considering any depositions or other documents required to be sent to the proper officer of the court, that it is proper to make such an order.

(7) Where a person committed to the Crown Court to be dealt with under section 43 above is admitted to a hospital in pursuance of an order under section 44 above, subsections (5) and (6) above shall apply as if he were a person subject to a transfer direction.

Amendments. Words in subs (4) inserted: Criminal Justice and Public Order Act 1994, s 168(2), Sch 10, para 51. Words in subss (3), (4) substituted: MHA 2007, s 11(1), (3). Subs (6)(a)(i) substituted: MHA 2007, s 1(4), Sch 1, Pt 1, paras 1, 12. Subs (6)(a)(ii) and preceding word inserted: MHA 2007, s 5(1), (4). Reference to 'the appropriate tribunal' in subs (3)(c) substituted: Transfer of Tribunal Functions Order 2008, SI 2008 No 2833 Art 9(1), Sch 3, paras 39, 43.

52 Further provisions as to persons remanded by magistrates' courts

(1) This section has effect where a transfer direction has been given in respect of any such person as is described in paragraph (b) of section 48(2) above; and that person is in this section referred to as 'the accused'.

(2) Subject to subsection (5) below, the transfer direction shall cease to have effect on the expiration of the period of remand unless the accused is committed in custody to the Crown Court for trial or to be otherwise dealt with.

(3) Subject to subsection (4) below, the power of further remanding the accused under section 128 of the Magistrates' Courts Act 1980 may be exercised by the court without his being brought before the court; and if the court further remands the accused in custody (whether or not he is brought before the court) the period of remand shall, for the purposes of this section, be deemed not to have expired.

(4) The court shall not under subsection (3) above further remand the accused in his absence unless he has appeared before the court within the previous six months.

(5) If the magistrates' court is satisfied, on the written or oral evidence of the responsible clinician –

    (a)   that the accused no longer requires treatment in hospital for mental disorder; or

    (b)   that no effective treatment for his disorder can be given in the hospital

to which he has been removed, the court may direct that the transfer direction shall cease to have effect notwithstanding that the period of remand has not expired or that the accused is committed to the Crown Court as mentioned in subsection (2) above.

(6) If the accused is committed to the Crown Court as mentioned in subsection (2) above and the transfer direction has not ceased to have effect under subsection (5) above, section 51 above shall apply as if the transfer direction given in his case were a direction given in respect of a person falling within that section.

(7) The magistrates' court may, in the absence of the accused, send him to the Crown Court for trial under section 51 or 51A of the Crime and Disorder Act 1998 if –

    (a)   the court is satisfied, on the written or oral evidence of the responsible clinician, that the accused is unfit to take part in the proceedings; and

    (b)   the accused is represented by an authorised person.

Amendments. Words in subs (7) substituted: Criminal Justice Act 2003, s 41, Sch 3, Pt 2, para 55(1), (3)(d). Words in subs (7)(b) repealed: Criminal Justice Act 2003, ss 41, 332, Sch 3, Pt 2, para 55(1), (3)(d), Sch 37, Pt 4. Words in subss (5), (7)(a) substituted: MHA 2007, s 11(1), (4) Words inserted in subs (7)(b): Legal Services Act 2007, s 208(1), Sch 21, paras 53, 57.

53 Further provisions as to civil prisoners and persons detained under the Immigration Acts

(1) Subject to subsection (2) below, a transfer direction given in respect of any such person as is described in paragraph (c) or (d) of section 48(2) above shall

cease to have effect on the expiration of the period during which he would, but for his removal to hospital, be liable to be detained in the place from which he was removed.

(2) Where a transfer direction and a restriction direction have been given in respect of any such person as is mentioned in subsection (1) above, then, if the Secretary of State is notified by the responsible clinician, any other approved clinician or the appropriate tribunal at any time before the expiration of the period there mentioned –

   (a)   that that person no longer requires treatment in hospital for mental disorder; or
   (b)   that no effective treatment for his disorder can be given in the hospital to which he has been removed,

the Secretary of State may by warrant direct that he be remitted to any place where he might have been detained if he had not been removed to hospital, and on his arrival at the place to which he is so remitted the transfer direction and the restriction direction shall cease to have effect.

Amendments. Words in Section heading substituted: Nationality, Immigration and Asylum Act 2002, s 62(10)(b). Words in subs (2) substituted: MHA 2007, s 11(1), (5). Reference to 'the appropriate tribunal' in subs (2) substituted: Transfer of Tribunal Functions Order 2008, SI 2008 No. 2833 Art 9, Sch 3, para 44.

Supplemental

54 Requirements as to medical evidence

(1) The registered medical practitioner whose evidence is taken into account under section 35(3)(a) above and at least one of the registered medical practitioners whose evidence is taken into account under sections 36(1), 37(2)(a), 38(1), 45A(2) and 51(6)(a) above and whose reports are taken into account under sections 47(1) and 48(1) above shall be a practitioner approved for the purposes of section 12 above by the Secretary of State as having special experience in the diagnosis or treatment of mental disorder.

(2) For the purposes of any provision of this Part of this Act under which a court may act on the written evidence of any person, a report in writing purporting to be signed by that person may, subject to the provisions of this section, be received in evidence without proof of the following –

   (a)   the signature of the person; or
   (b)   his having the requisite qualifications or approval or authority or being of the requisite description to give the report.

(2A) But the court may require the signatory of any such report to be called to give oral evidence.

(3) Where, in pursuance of a direction of the court, any such report is tendered in evidence otherwise than by or on behalf of the person who is the subject of the report, then –

(a)   if that person is represented by an authorised person, a copy of the report shall be given tothat authorised person;

(b)   if that person is not so represented, the substance of the report shall be disclosed to him or, where he is a child or young person, to his parent or guardian if present in court; and

(c)   except where the report relates only to arrangements for his admission to a hospital, that person may require the signatory of the report to be called to give oral evidence, and evidence to rebut the evidence contained in the report may be called by or on behalf of that person.

Amendments. Number in subs (1) inserted: Crime (Sentences) Act 1997, s 55, Sch 4, para 12(6). Subss (2), (2A) substituted for previous subs (2): MHA 2007, s 11(1), (6). Words inserted in subs (3)(a): Legal Services Act 2007, s 208(1), Sch 21, paras 53, 58(a), (b).

54A Reduction of period for making hospital orders

(1) The Secretary of State may by order reduce the length of the periods mentioned in sections 37(4) and (5) and 38(4) above.

(2) An order under subsection (1) above may make such consequential amendments of sections 40(1) and 44(3) above as appear to the Secretary of State to be necessary or expedient.

Amendments. Section inserted: Criminal Justice Act 1991, s 27(2).

55 Interpretation of Part III

(1) In this Part of this Act –

'authorised person' means a person who, for the pruposes of the Legal services Act 2007, is an authorised person in relation to an activity hich constitutes the exercise of a right of audience (within the meaning of that Act);

'child' and 'young person' have the same meaning as in the Children and Young Persons Act 1933;

'civil prisoner' has the meaning given to it by section 48(2)(c) above;

'guardian', in relation to a child or young person, has the same meaning as in the Children and Young Persons Act 1933;

'place of safety', in relation to a person who is not a child or young person, means any police station, prison or remand centre, or any hospital the managers of which are willing temporarily to receive him, and in relation to a child or young person has the same meaning as in the Children and Young Persons Act 1933;

'responsible clinician', in relation to a person liable to be detained in a hospital within the meaning of Part 2 of this Act, means the approved clinician with overall responsibility for the patient's case.

(2) Any reference in this Part of this Act to an offence punishable on summary conviction with imprisonment shall be construed without regard to any prohibition or restriction imposed by or under any enactment relating to the imprisonment of young offenders.

(3) *(repealed)*

(4) Any reference to a hospital order, a guardianship order or a restriction order in section 40(2), (4) or (5), section 41(3) to (5), or section 42 above or section 69(1) below shall be construed as including a reference to any order or direction under this Part of this Act having the same effect as the firstmentioned order; and the exceptions and modifications set out in Schedule 1 to this Act in respect of the provisions of this Act described in that Schedule accordingly include those which are consequential on the provisions of this subsection.

(5) Section 34(2) above shall apply for the purposes of this Part of this Act as it applies for the purposes of Part II of this Act.

(6) References in this Part of this Act to persons serving a sentence of imprisonment shall be construed in accordance with section 47(5) above.

(7) Section 99 of the Children and Young Persons Act 1933 (which relates to the presumption and determination of age) shall apply for the purposes of this Part of this Act as it applies for the purposes of that Act.

Amendments. Definitions in subs (1) substituted: MHA 2007, s 11(1), (7). Subs (3) repealed: MHA 2007, s 55, Sch 11, Pt 1. Definition of 'authorised person' inserted in subs (1): Legal Services Act 2007, s 208, Sch 21, para 59.

PART IV
CONSENT TO TREATMENT

56 Patients to whom Part 4 applies

(1) Section 57 and, so far as relevant to that section, sections 59 to 62 below apply to any patient.

(2) Subject to that and to subsection (5) below, this Part of this Act applies to a patient only if he falls within subsection (3) or (4) below.

(3) A patient falls within this subsection if he is liable to be detained under this Act but not if –

   (a)   he is so liable by virtue of an emergency application and the second medical recommendation referred to in section 4(4)(a) above has not been given and received;
   (b)   he is so liable by virtue of section 5(2) or (4) or 35 above or section 135 or 136 below or by virtue of a direction for his detention in a place of safety under section 37(4) or 45A(5) above; or
   (c)   he has been conditionally discharged under section 42(2) above or section 73 or 74 below and he is not recalled to hospital.

(4) A patient falls within this subsection if –

   (a)   he is a community patient; and
   (b)   he is recalled to hospital under section 17E above.

(5) Section 58A and, so far as relevant to that section, sections 59 to 62 below also apply to any patient who –

(a)   does not fall within subsection (3) above;
(b)   is not a community patient; and
(c)   has not attained the age of 18 years.

Amendments. Section inserted: MHA 2007 s 34(1), (2).

57 Treatment requiring consent and a second opinion

(1) This section applies to the following forms of medical treatment for mental disorder –

(a)   any surgical operation for destroying brain tissue or for destroying the functioning of brain tissue; and
(b)   such other forms of treatment as may be specified for the purposes of this section by regulations made by the Secretary of State.

(2) Subject to section 62 below, a patient shall not be given any form of treatment to which this section applies unless he has consented to it and –

(a)   a registered medical practitioner appointed for the purposes of this Part of this Act by the regulatory authority (not being the responsible clinician (if there is one) in charge of the treatment in question) and two other persons appointed for the purposes of this paragraph by the regulatory authority (not being registered medical practitioners) have certified in writing that the patient is capable of understanding the nature, purpose and likely effects of the treatment in question and has consented to it; and
(b)   the registered medical practitioner referred to in paragraph (a) above has certified in writing that it is appropriate for the treatment to be given.

(3) Before giving a certificate under subsection (2)(b) above the registered medical practitioner concerned shall consult two other persons who have been professionally concerned with the patient's medical treatment, but of those persons:

(a)   one shall be a nurse and the other shall be neither a nurse nor a registered medical practitioner; and
(b)   neither shall be the responsible clinician (if there is one) or the person in charge of the treatment in question.

(4) Before making any regulations for the purpose of this section the Secretary of State shall consult such bodies as appear to him to be concerned.

Amendments. Words in subs (2)(a) substituted: MHA 2007, s 12(1), (2)(a). Words in subs (2)(b) substituted: MHA 2007, s 6(1), (2)(a). Words in subs (3) substituted: MHA 2007, s 12(1), (2)(b). References to regulatory authority in subs (2) substituted: Health and Social Care Act 2008, s 52, Sch 3, para 2.

Note. Subss 57(2)(a), (3) are amended to take account of the new responsible clinician status, and the old test in s 57(2)(b) that the treatment 'ought to be given, having regard to the likelihood that it will alleviate or prevent deterioration in the patient's condition' is replaced by the new test that it is 'appropriate for the treatment to be given'.

58 Treatment requiring consent or a second opinion

(1) This section applies to the following forms of medical treatment for mental disorder –

  (a)   such forms of treatment as may be specified for the purposes of this section by regulations made by the Secretary of State;

  (b)   the administration of medicine to a patient by any means (not being a form of treatment specified under paragraph (a) above or section 57 above or section 58A(1)(b) below) at any time during a period for which he is liable to be detained as a patient to whom this Part of this Act applies if three months or more have elapsed since the first occasion in that period when medicine was administered to him by any means for his mental disorder.

(2) The Secretary of State may by order vary the length of the period mentioned in subsection (1)(b) above.

(3) Subject to section 62 below, a patient shall not be given any form of treatment to which this section applies unless –

  (a)   he has consented to that treatment and either the approved clinician in charge of it or a registered medical practitioner appointed for the purposes of this Part of this Act by the regulatory authority has certified in writing that the patient is capable of understanding its nature, purpose and likely effects and has consented to it;

  (b)   a registered medical practitioner appointed as aforesaid (not being the responsible clinician or the approved clinician in charge of the treatment in question) has certified in writing that the patient is not capable of understanding the nature, purpose and likely effects of that treatment or 'being so capable' has not consented to it but that it is appropriate for the treatment to be given.

(4) Before giving a certificate under subsection (3)(b) above the registered medical practitioner concerned shall consult two other persons who have been professionally concerned with the patient's medical treatment, and of those persons one shall be a nurse and the other shall be neither a nurse nor a registered medical practitioner nor the responsible clinician.

(5) Before making any regulations for the purposes of this section the Secretary of State shall consult such bodies as appear to him to be concerned.

Amendments. Words in subs (1)(b) inserted: MHA 2007, s 28(1), (2)(a). Words in subs (3)(a) substituted: MHA 2007, s 12(1), (3)(a)(i). Words in subs (3)(b) substituted: MHA 2007, s 12(1), (3)(a)(ii). Words in subs (3)(b) inserted: MHA 2007, s 28(1), (2)(b). Words in subs (3)(b) substituted: MHA 2007, s 6(1), (2)(b). Words in subs (4) substituted: MHA 2007, s 12(1), (3)(b). References to regulatory authority in subs (3)(a) substituted: Health and Social Care Act 2008, s 52(5), Sch 3, paras 1, 3.

58A Electro-convulsive therapy, etc

(1) This section applies to the following forms of medical treatment for mental disorder –

(a) electro-convulsive therapy; and
(b) such other forms of treatment as may be specified for the purposes of this section by regulations made by the appropriate national authority.

(2) Subject to section 62 below, a patient shall be not be given any form of treatment to which this section applies unless he falls within subsection (3), (4) or (5) below.

(3) A patient falls within this subsection if –

(a) he has attained the age of 18 years;
(b) he has consented to the treatment in question; and
(c) either the approved clinician in charge of it or a registered medical practitioner appointed as mentioned in section 58(3) above has certified in writing that the patient is capable of understanding the nature, purpose and likely effects of the treatment and has consented to it.

(4) A patient falls within this subsection if –

(a) he has not attained the age of 18 years; but
(b) he has consented to the treatment in question; and
(c) a registered medical practitioner appointed as aforesaid (not being the approved clinician in charge of the treatment) has certified in writing –
   (i) that the patient is capable of understanding the nature, purpose and likely effects of the treatment and has consented to it; and
   (ii) that it is appropriate for the treatment to be given.

(5) A patient falls within this subsection if a registered medical practitioner appointed as aforesaid (not being the responsible clinician (if there is one) or the approved clinician in charge of the treatment in question) has certified in writing –

(a) that the patient is not capable of understanding the nature, purpose and likely effects of the treatment; but
(b) that it is appropriate for the treatment to be given; and
(c) that giving him the treatment would not conflict with –
   (i) an advance decision which the registered medical practitioner concerned is satisfied is valid and applicable; or
   (ii) a decision made by a donee or deputy or by the Court of Protection.

(6) Before giving a certificate under subsection (5) above the registered medical practitioner concerned shall consult two other persons who have been professionally concerned with the patient's medical treatment but, of those persons –

(a) one shall be a nurse and the other shall be neither a nurse nor a registered medical practitioner; and

(b)   neither shall be the responsible clinician (if there is one) or the approved clinician in charge of the treatment in question.

(7) This section shall not by itself confer sufficient authority for a patient who falls within section 56(5) above to be given a form of treatment to which this section applies if he is not capable of understanding the nature, purpose and likely effects of the treatment (and cannot therefore consent to it).

(8) Before making any regulations for the purposes of this section, the appropriate national authority shall consult such bodies as appear to it to be concerned.

(9) In this section –

(a)   a reference to an advance decision is to an advance decision (within the meaning of the Mental Capacity Act 2005) made by the patient;

(b)   'valid and applicable', in relation to such a decision, means valid and applicable to the treatment in question in accordance with section 25 of that Act;

(c)   a reference to a donee is to a donee of a lasting power of attorney (within the meaning of section 9 of that Act) created by the patient, where the donee is acting within the scope of his authority and in accordance with that Act; and

(d)   a reference to a deputy is to a deputy appointed for the patient by the Court of Protection under section 16 of that Act, where the deputy is acting within the scope of his authority and in accordance with that Act.

(10) In this section, 'the appropriate national authority' means –

(a)   in a case where the treatment in question would, if given, be given in England, the Secretary of State;

(b)   in a case where the treatment in question would, if given, be given in Wales, the Welsh Ministers.

Amendments. Section inserted by MHA 2007, s 27.

59 Plans of treatment

Any consent or certificate under section 57, 58 or 58A above may relate to a plan of treatment under which the patient is to be given (whether within a specified period or otherwise) one or more of the forms of treatment to which that section applies.

Amendments. Words substituted: MHA 2007, s 28(1), (3).

60 Withdrawal of consent

(1) Where the consent of a patient to any treatment has been given for the purposes of section 57, 58 or 58A above, the patient may, subject to section 62 below, at any time before the completion of the treatment withdraw his consent, and those sections shall then apply as if the remainder of the treatment were a separate form of treatment.

(1A) Subsection (1B) below applies where –

(a)   the consent of a patient to any treatment has been given for the purposes of section 57, 58 or 58A above; but

(b)   before the completion of the treatment, the patient ceases to be capable of understanding its nature, purpose and likely effects.

(1B) The patient shall, subject to section 62 below, be treated as having withdrawn his consent, and those sections shall then apply as if the remainder of the treatment were a separate form of treatment.

(1C) Subsection (1D) below applies where –

(a)   a certificate has been given under section 58 or 58A above that a patient is not capable of understanding the nature, purpose and likely effects of the treatment to which the certificate applies; but

(b)   before the completion of the treatment, the patient becomes capable of understanding its nature, purpose and likely effects.

(1D) The certificate shall, subject to section 62 below, cease to apply to the treatment and those sections shall then apply as if the remainder of the treatment were a separate form of treatment.

(2) Without prejudice to the application of subsections (1) to (1D) above to any treatment given under the plan of treatment to which a patient has consented, a patient who has consented to such a plan may, subject to section 62 below, at any time withdraw his consent to further treatment, or to further treatment of any description, under the plan.

Amendments. Words in subs (1) substituted: MHA 2007, s 28(1), (4). Subss (1A)–(1D) inserted: MHA 2007, s 29(1), (2). Words in subs (2) substituted: MHA 2007, s 29(1), (3).

61 Review of treatment

(1) Where a patient is given treatment in accordance with section 57(2), 58(3)(b) or 58A(4) or (5) above or by virtue of section 62A below in accordance with a Part 4A certificate (within the meaning of that section) a report on the treatment and the patient's condition shall be given by the approved clinician in charge of the treatment to the regulatory authority –

(a)   on the next occasion on which the responsible clinician furnishes a report under section 20(3), 20A(4) or 21B(2) above in respect of the patient; and

(b)   at any other time if so required by the regulatory authority.

(2) In relation to a patient who is subject to a restriction order, limitation direction or restriction direction subsection (1) above shall have effect as if paragraph (a) required the report to be made –

(a)   in the case of treatment in the period of six months beginning with the date of the order or direction, at the end of that period;

(b)   in the case of treatment at any subsequent time, on the next occasion on which the responsible clinician makes a report in respect of the patient under section 41(6), 45B(3) or 49(3) above.

(3) The regulatory authority may at any time give notice directing that, subject to section 62 below, a certificate given in respect of a patient under section 57(2), 58(3)(b) or 58A(4) or (5) above shall not apply to treatment given to him whether in England or Wales after a date specified in the notice and sections 57, 58 and 58A above shall then apply to any such treatment as if that certificate had not been given.

(3A) The notice under subsection (3) above shall be given to the approved clinician in charge of the treatment.

Amendments. Words in subs (1)(a) substituted: Mental Health (Patients in the Community) Act 1995, s 2(5). Words in subs (2) and reference in subs (2)(b) inserted: Crime (Sentences) Act 1997, s 55, Sch 4, para 12(7)(a), (b). Words in subs (1) substituted: MHA 2007, s 28(1), (5)(a). Words in subs (1) inserted: MHA 2007, s 34(1), (3)(a). Words in subs (1) substituted: MHA 2007, s 12(1), (4)(a)(i). Words in subs (1) substituted: MHA 2007, s 12(1), (4)(a)(ii). Words in subs (1)(a) prospectively substituted: MHA 2007, s 34(1), (3)(b). Words in subs (2)(b) substituted: MHA 2007, s 12(1), (4)(b). Words in subs (3) repealed: MHA 2007, ss 12(1), (4)(c), 55, Sch 11, Pt 3. Words in subs (3) substituted: MHA 2007, s 28(1), (5)(b)(i). Words in subs (3) substituted: MHA 2007, s 28(1), (5)(b)(ii). Subs (3A) inserted: MHA 2007, s 12(1), (4)(d). Words 'regulatory authority' in subs (1) and (3) substituted and words 'whether in England or Wales' inserted: Health and Social Care Act 2008, s 52(5), Sch 3, paras 1, 4(1)–(3).

62 Urgent treatment

(1) Sections 57 and 58 above shall not apply to any treatment –

    (a)   which is immediately necessary to save the patient's life; or

    (b)   which (not being irreversible) is immediately necessary to prevent a serious deterioration of his condition; or

    (c)   which (not being irreversible or hazardous) is immediately necessary to alleviate serious suffering by the patient; or

    (d)   which (not being irreversible or hazardous) is immediately necessary and represents the minimum interference necessary to prevent the patient from behaving violently or being a danger to himself or to others.

(1A) Section 58A above, in so far as it relates to electro-convulsive therapy by virtue of subsection (1)(a) of that section, shall not apply to any treatment which falls within paragraph (a) or (b) of subsection (1) above.

(1B) Section 58A above, in so far as it relates to a form of treatment specified by virtue of subsection (1)(b) of that section, shall not apply to any treatment which falls within such of paragraphs (a) to (d) of subsection (1) above as may be specified in regulations under that section.

(1C) For the purposes of subsection (1B) above, the regulations –

    (a)   may make different provision for different cases (and may, in particular, make different provision for different forms of treatment);

    (b)   may make provision which applies subject to specified exceptions; and

    (c)   may include transitional, consequential, incidental or supplemental provision.

(2) Sections 60 and 61(3) above shall not preclude the continuation of any treatment or of treatment under any plan pending compliance with section 57, 58 or 58A above if the approved clinician in charge of the treatment considers that the discontinuance of the treatment or of treatment under the plan would cause serious suffering to the patient.

(3) For the purposes of this section treatment is irreversible if it has unfavourable irreversible physical or psychological consequences and hazardous if it entails significant physical hazard.

Amendments. Subss (1A)–(1C) inserted: MHA 2007, s 28(1), (6). Words in subs (2) substituted: MHA 2007, ss 12(1), (5), 28(1), (7).

62A Treatment on recall of community patient or revocation of order

(1) This section applies where –

(a) a community patient is recalled to hospital under section 17E above; or
(b) a patient is liable to be detained under this Act following the revocation of a community treatment order under section 17F above in respect of him.

(2) For the purposes of section 58(1)(b) above, the patient is to be treated as if he had remained liable to be detained since the making of the community treatment order.

(3) But section 58 above does not apply to treatment given to the patient if –

(a) the certificate requirement is met (within the meaning of section 64C below); or
(b) as a result of section 64B(4) or 64E(4) below, the certificate requirement would not apply (were the patient a community patient not recalled to hospital under section 17E above).

(4) In a case where this section applies, the certificate requirement is met only in so far as –

(a) the Part 4A certificate expressly provides that it is appropriate for one or more specified forms of treatment to be given to the patient in that case (subject to such conditions as may be specified); or
(b) a notice having been given under subsection (4) of section 64H below, treatment is authorised by virtue of subsection (7) of that section.

(5) Subsection (4)(a) above shall not preclude the continuation of any treatment, or of treatment under any plan, pending compliance with section 58 above if the approved clinician in charge of the treatment considers that the discontinuance of the treatment, or of the treatment under the plan, would cause serious suffering to the patient.

(6) In a case where subsection (1)(b) above applies, subsection (3) above only applies pending compliance with section 58 above.

(7) In subsection (4) above –

'Part 4A certificate' has the meaning given in section 64H below; and 'specified', in relation to a Part 4A certificate, means specified in the certificate.

Amendments. Section inserted: MHA 2007, s 34(1), (4).

63 Treatment not requiring consent

The consent of a patient shall not be required for any medical treatment given to him for the mental disorder from which he is suffering, not being a form of treatment to which section 57, 58 or 58A above applies, if the treatment is given by or under the direction of the approved clinician in charge of the treatment.

Amendments. Words substituted: MHA 2007, ss 12(1), (6), 28(1), (8).

64 Supplementary provisions for Part 4

(1) In this Part of this Act 'the responsible clinician' means the approved clinician with overall responsibility for the case of the patient in question and 'hospital' includes a registered establishment.

(1A) References in this Part of this Act to the approved clinician in charge of a patient's treatment shall, where the treatment in question is a form of treatment to which section 57 above applies, be construed as references to the person in charge of the treatment.

(1B) References in this Part of this Act to the approved clinician in charge of a patient's treatment shall, where the treatment in question is a form of treatment to which section 58A above applies and the patient falls within section 56(5) above, be construed as references to the person in charge of the treatment.

(1C) Regulations made by virtue of section 32(2)(d) above apply for the purposes of this Part as they apply for the purposes of Part 2 of this Act.

(2) Any certificate for the purposes of this Part of this Act shall be in such form as may be prescribed by regulations made by the Secretary of State.

(3) For the purposes of this Part of this Act, it is appropriate for treatment to be given to a patient if the treatment is appropriate in his case, taking into account the nature and degree of the mental disorder from which he is suffering and all other circumstances of his case.

Amendments. Words in subs (1) substituted: Care Standards Act 2000, s 116, Sch 4, para 9(1), (2). Words in subs (1) substituted and subs (1A) inserted: MHA 2007, s 12(1), (7)(a), (b). Subss (1B), (1C) inserted: MHA 2007, s 28(1), (9). Subs (3) inserted: MHA 2007, s 6(1), (3).

PART 4A
TREATMENT OF COMMUNITY PATIENTS NOT RECALLED TO HOSPITAL

Amendment. Part heading inserted: MHA 2007, s 35(1).

64A Meaning of 'relevant treatment'

In this Part of this Act 'relevant treatment', in relation to a patient, means medical treatment which –

(a)   is for the mental disorder from which the patient is suffering; and

(b)   is not a form of treatment to which section 57 above applies.

Amendment. Section inserted: MHA 2007, s 35(1).

64B Adult community patients

(1) This section applies to the giving of relevant treatment to a community patient who –

(a)   is not recalled to hospital under section 17E above; and

(b)   has attained the age of 16 years.

(2) The treatment may not be given to the patient unless –

(a)   there is authority to give it to him; and

(b)   if it is section 58 type treatment or section 58A type treatment, the certificate requirement is met.

(3) But the certificate requirement does not apply if –

(a)   giving the treatment to the patient is authorised in accordance with section 64G below; or

(b)   the treatment is immediately necessary and –

    (i)   the patient has capacity to consent to it and does consent to it; or

    (ii)   a donee or deputy or the Court of Protection consents to the treatment on the patient's behalf.

(4) Nor does the certificate requirement apply in so far as the administration of medicine to the patient at any time during the period of one month beginning with the day on which the community treatment order is made is section 58 type treatment.

(5) The reference in subsection (4) above to the administration of medicine does not include any form of treatment specified under section 58(1)(a) above.

Amendment. Section inserted: MHA 2007, s 35(1).

64C Section 64B: supplemental

(1) This section has effect for the purposes of section 64B above.

(2) There is authority to give treatment to a patient if –

(a)   he has capacity to consent to it and does consent to it;

(b)   a donee or deputy or the Court of Protection consents to it on his behalf; or

(c)   giving it to him is authorised in accordance with section 64D or 64G below.

(3) Relevant treatment is section 58 type treatment or section 58A type treatment if, at the time when it is given to the patient, section 58 or 58A above (respectively) would have applied to it, had the patient remained liable to be detained at that time (rather than being a community patient).

(4) The certificate requirement is met in respect of treatment to be given to a patient if –

(a)   a registered medical practitioner appointed for the purposes of Part 4 of this Act (not being the responsible clinician or the person in charge of the treatment) has certified in writing that it is appropriate for the treatment to be given or for the treatment to be given subject to such conditions as may be specified in the certificate; and

(b)   if conditions are so specified, the conditions are satisfied.

(5) In a case where the treatment is section 58 type treatment, treatment is immediately necessary if –

(a)   it is immediately necessary to save the patient's life; or

(b)   it is immediately necessary to prevent a serious deterioration of the patient's condition and is not irreversible; or

(c)   it is immediately necessary to alleviate serious suffering by the patient and is not irreversible or hazardous; or

(d)   it is immediately necessary, represents the minimum interference necessary to prevent the patient from behaving violently or being a danger to himself or others and is not irreversible or hazardous.

(6) In a case where the treatment is section 58A type treatment by virtue of subsection (1)(a) of that section, treatment is immediately necessary if it falls within paragraph (a) or (b) of subsection (5) above.

(7) In a case where the treatment is section 58A type treatment by virtue of subsection (1)(b) of that section, treatment is immediately necessary if it falls within such of paragraphs (a) to (d) of subsection (5) above as may be specified in regulations under that section.

(8) For the purposes of subsection (7) above, the regulations –

(a)   may make different provision for different cases (and may, in particular, make different provision for different forms of treatment);

(b)   may make provision which applies subject to specified exceptions; and

(c)   may include transitional, consequential, incidental or supplemental provision.

(9) Subsection (3) of section 62 above applies for the purposes of this section as it applies for the purposes of that section.

Amendment. Section inserted: MHA 2007, s 35(1).

64D Adult community patients lacking capacity

(1) A person is authorised to give relevant treatment to a patient as mentioned in section 64C(2)(c) above if the conditions in subsections (2) to (6) below are met.

(2) The first condition is that, before giving the treatment, the person takes reasonable steps to establish whether the patient lacks capacity to consent to the treatment.

(3) The second condition is that, when giving the treatment, he reasonably believes that the patient lacks capacity to consent to it.

(4) The third condition is that –

  (a) he has no reason to believe that the patient objects to being given the treatment; or
  (b) he does have reason to believe that the patient so objects, but it is not necessary to use force against the patient in order to give the treatment.

(5) The fourth condition is that –

  (a) he is the person in charge of the treatment and an approved clinician; or
  (b) the treatment is given under the direction of that clinician.

(6) The fifth condition is that giving the treatment does not conflict with –

  (a) an advance decision which he is satisfied is valid and applicable; or
  (b) a decision made by a donee or deputy or the Court of Protection.

(7) In this section –

  (a) reference to an advance decision is to an advance decision (within the meaning of the Mental Capacity Act 2005) made by the patient; and
  (b) 'valid and applicable', in relation to such a decision, means valid and applicable to the treatment in question in accordance with section 25 of that Act.

Amendment. Section inserted: MHA 2007, s 35(1).

64E Child community patients

(1) This section applies to the giving of relevant treatment to a community patient who –

  (a) is not recalled to hospital under section 17E above; and
  (b) has not attained the age of 16 years.

(2) The treatment may not be given to the patient unless –

  (a) there is authority to give it to him; and
  (b) if it is section 58 type treatment or section 58A type treatment, the certificate requirement is met.

(3) But the certificate requirement does not apply if –

  (a) giving the treatment to the patient is authorised in accordance with section 64G below; or
  (b) in a case where the patient is competent to consent to the treatment and does consent to it, the treatment is immediately necessary.

(4) Nor does the certificate requirement apply in so far as the administration of medicine to the patient at any time during the period of one month beginning with the day on which the community treatment order is made is section 58 type treatment.

(5) The reference in subsection (4) above to the administration of medicine does not include any form of treatment specified under section 58(1)(a) above.

(6) For the purposes of subsection (2)(a) above, there is authority to give treatment to a patient if –

(a)   he is competent to consent to it and he does consent to it; or

(b)   giving it to him is authorised in accordance with section 64F or 64G below.

(7) Subsections (3) to (9) of section 64C above have effect for the purposes of this section as they have effect for the purposes of section 64B above.

(8) Regulations made by virtue of section 32(2)(d) above apply for the purposes of this section as they apply for the purposes of Part 2 of this Act.

Amendment. Section inserted: MHA 2007, s 35(1).

64F   Child community patients lacking competence

(1) A person is authorised to give relevant treatment to a patient as mentioned in section 64E(6)(b) above if the conditions in subsections (2) to (5) below are met.

(2) The first condition is that, before giving the treatment, the person takes reasonable steps to establish whether the patient is competent to consent to the treatment.

(3) The second condition is that, when giving the treatment, he reasonably believes that the patient is not competent to consent to it.

(4) The third condition is that –

(a)   he has no reason to believe that the patient objects to being given the treatment; or

(b)   he does have reason to believe that the patient so objects, but it is not necessary to use force against the patient in order to give the treatment.

(5) The fourth condition is that –

(a)   he is the person in charge of the treatment and an approved clinician; or

(b)   the treatment is given under the direction of that clinician.

Amendment. Section inserted: MHA 2007, s 35(1).

64G   Emergency treatment for patients lacking capacity or competence

(1) A person is also authorised to give relevant treatment to a patient as mentioned in section 64C(2)(c) or 64E(6)(b) above if the conditions in subsections (2) to (4) below are met.

(2) The first condition is that, when giving the treatment, the person reasonably believes that the patient lacks capacity to consent to it or, as the case may be, is not competent to consent to it.

(3) The second condition is that the treatment is immediately necessary.

(4) The third condition is that if it is necessary to use force against the patient in order to give the treatment –

 (a)   the treatment needs to be given in order to prevent harm to the patient; and
 (b)   the use of such force is a proportionate response to the likelihood of the patient's suffering harm, and to the seriousness of that harm.

(5) Subject to subsections (6) to (8) below, treatment is immediately necessary if –

 (a)   it is immediately necessary to save the patient's life; or
 (b)   it is immediately necessary to prevent a serious deterioration of the patient's condition and is not irreversible; or
 (c)   it is immediately necessary to alleviate serious suffering by the patient and is not irreversible or hazardous; or
 (d)   it is immediately necessary, represents the minimum interference necessary to prevent the patient from behaving violently or being a danger to himself or others and is not irreversible or hazardous.

(6) Where the treatment is section 58A type treatment by virtue of subsection (1)(a) of that section, treatment is immediately necessary if it falls within paragraph (a) or (b) of subsection (5) above.

(7) Where the treatment is section 58A type treatment by virtue of subsection (1)(b) of that section, treatment is immediately necessary if it falls within such of paragraphs (a) to (d) of subsection (5) above as may be specified in regulations under section 58A above.

(8) For the purposes of subsection (7) above, the regulations –

 (a)   may make different provision for different cases (and may, in particular, make different provision for different forms of treatment);
 (b)   may make provision which applies subject to specified exceptions; and
 (c)   may include transitional, consequential, incidental or supplemental provision.

(9) Subsection (3) of section 62 above applies for the purposes of this section as it applies for the purposes of that section.

Amendment. Section inserted: MHA 2007, s 35(1).

64H Certificates: supplementary provisions

(1) A certificate under section 64B(2)(b) or 64E(2)(b) above (a 'Part 4A certificate') may relate to a plan of treatment under which the patient is to be given (whether within a specified period or otherwise) one or more forms of section 58 type treatment or section 58A type treatment.

(2) A Part 4A certificate shall be in such form as may be prescribed by regulations made by the appropriate national authority.

(3) Before giving a Part 4A certificate, the registered medical practitioner concerned shall consult two other persons who have been professionally concerned with the patient's medical treatment but, of those persons –

    (a)   at least one shall be a person who is not a registered medical practitioner; and

    (b)   neither shall be the patient's responsible clinician or the person in charge of the treatment in question.

(4) Where a patient is given treatment in accordance with a Part 4A certificate, a report on the treatment and the patient's condition shall be given by the person in charge of the treatment to the regulatory authority if required by that authority.

(5) The regulatory authority may at any time give notice directing that a Part 4A certificate shall not apply to treatment given to a patient after a date specified in the notice, and the relevant section shall then apply to any such treatment as if that certificate had not been given.

(6) The relevant section is –

    (a)   if the patient is not recalled to hospital in accordance with section 17E above, section 64B or 64E above;

    (b)   if the patient is so recalled or is liable to be detained under this Act following revocation of the community treatment order under section 17F above –

        (i)   section 58 above, in the case of section 58 type treatment;

        (ii)   section 58A above, in the case of section 58A type treatment; (subject to section 62A(2) above).

(7) The notice under subsection (5) above shall be given to the person in charge of the treatment in question.

(8) Subsection (5) above shall not preclude the continuation of any treatment or of treatment under any plan pending compliance with the relevant section if the person in charge of the treatment considers that the discontinuance of the treatment or of treatment under the plan would cause serious suffering to the patient.

(9) In this section, 'the appropriate national authority' means –

    (a)   in relation to community patients in respect of whom the responsible hospital is in England, the Secretary of State;

    (b)   in relation to community patients in respect of whom the responsible hospital is in Wales, the Welsh Ministers.

Amendments. Section inserted: MHA 2007, s 35(1). Words 'regulatory authority' in subs (4) and (5) substituted: Heatlh and Social Care Act 2008, s 52(5), Sch 3, paras 1, 5.

64I Liability for negligence

Nothing in section 64D, 64F or 64G above excludes a person's civil liability for loss or damage, or his criminal liability, resulting from his negligence in doing anything authorised to be done by that section.

Amendment. Section inserted: MHA 2007, s 35(1).

64J Factors to be considered in determining whether patient objects to treatment

(1) In assessing for the purposes of this Part whether he has reason to believe that a patient objects to treatment, a person shall consider all the circumstances so far as they are reasonably ascertainable, including the patient's behaviour, wishes, feelings, views, beliefs and values.

(2) But circumstances from the past shall be considered only so far as it is still appropriate to consider them.

Amendment. Section inserted: MHA 2007, s 35(1).

64K Interpretation of Part 4A

(1) This Part of this Act is to be construed as follows.

(2) References to a patient who lacks capacity are to a patient who lacks capacity within the meaning of the Mental Capacity Act 2005.

(3) References to a patient who has capacity are to be read accordingly.

(4) References to a donee are to a donee of a lasting power of attorney (within the meaning of section 9 of the Mental Capacity Act 2005) created by the patient, where the donee is acting within the scope of his authority and in accordance with that Act.

(5) References to a deputy are to a deputy appointed for the patient by the Court of Protection under section 16 of the Mental Capacity Act 2005, where the deputy is acting within the scope of his authority and in accordance with that Act.

(6) Reference to the responsible clinician shall be construed as a reference to the responsible clinician within the meaning of Part 2 of this Act.

(7) References to a hospital include a registered establishment.

(8) Section 64(3) above applies for the purposes of this Part of this Act as it applies for the purposes of Part 4 of this Act.

Amendment. Section inserted: MHA 2007, s 35(1).

PART V
MENTAL HEALTH REVIEW TRIBUNALS

Constitution etc

65 Mental Health Review Tribunals for Wales

(1) There shall be a Mental Health Review Tribunal for Wales.

(1A) The purpose of that tribunal is to deal with applications and references by and in respect of patients under the provisions of this Act.

(2) The provisions of Schedule 2 to this Act shall have effect with respect to the constitution of the Mental Health Review Tribunal for Wales.

(3) Subject to the provisions of Schedule 2 to this Act, and to rules made by the Lord Chancellor under this Act, the jurisdiction of the Mental Health Review Tribunal for Wales may be exercised by any three or more of its members, and references in this Act to the Mental Health Review Tribunal for Wales shall be construed accordingly.

(4) The Welsh Ministers may pay to the members of the Mental Health Review Tribunal for Wales such remuneration and allowances as they may determine, and defray the expenses of that tribunal to such amount as they may determine, and may provide for that tribunal such officers and servants, and such accommodation, as that tribunal may require.

Amendments. Subss (1), (1A) substituted for subss (1), (1A)–(1C) (as substituted by the Health Authorities Act 1995 for sub-s (1) as originally enacted): MHA 2007, s 38(1), (2). Subs (4), words in heading, and words in subss (1), (1A), (2), (3) substituted: Transfer of Tribunal Functions Order 2008 SI 2008 No. 2833, art 9(1), Sch 3, paras 39, 45(a)–(f).

Applications and references concerning Part II patients

66 Applications to tribunals

(1) Where –

    (a)   a patient is admitted to a hospital in pursuance of an application for admission for assessment; or

    (b)   a patient is admitted to a hospital in pursuance of an application for admission for treatment; or

    (c)   a patient is received into guardianship in pursuance of a guardianship application; or

    (ca)   a community treatment order is made in respect of a patient; or

    (cb)   a community treatment order is revoked under section 17F above in respect of a patient; or

    (e)   a patient is transferred from guardianship to a hospital in pursuance of regulations made under section 19 above; or

    (f)   a report is furnished under section 20 above in respect of a patient and the patient is not discharged under section 23 above; or

    (fza)   a report is furnished under section 20A above in respect of a patient and the patient is not discharged under section 23 above; or (fa) a report is furnished under subsection (2) of section 21B above in respect of a patient and subsection (5) of that section applies (or subsections (5) and (6)(b) of that section apply) in the case of the report; or

(faa) a report is furnished under subsection (2) of section 21B above in respect of a community patient and subsection (6A) of that section applies (or subsections (6A) and (6B)(b) of that section apply) in the case of the report; or

(g) a report is furnished under section 25 above in respect of a patient who is detained in pursuance of an application for admission for treatment or a community patient; or

(h) an order is made under section 29 above on the ground specified in paragraph (c) or (d) of subsection (3) of that section in respect of a patient who is or subsequently becomes liable to be detained or subject to guardianship under Part II of this Act or who is a community patient,

an application may be made to the appropriate tribunal within the relevant period –

(i) by the patient (except in the cases mentioned in paragraphs (g) and (h) above, and

(ii) in the cases mentioned in paragraphs (g) and (h) above, by his nearest relative.

(2) In subsection (1) above 'the relevant period' means –

(a) in the case mentioned in paragraph (a) of that subsection, 14 days beginning with the day on which the patient is admitted as so mentioned;

(b) in the case mentioned in paragraph (b) of that subsection, six months beginning with the day on which the patient is admitted as so mentioned;

(c) in the case mentioned in paragraph (c) of that subsection, six months beginning with the day on which the application is accepted;

(ca) in the case mentioned in paragraph (ca) of that subsection, six months beginning with the day on which the community treatment order is made;

(cb) in the case mentioned in paragraph (cb) of that subsection, six months beginning with the day on which the community treatment order is revoked;

(d) in the case mentioned in paragraph (g) of that subsection, 28 days beginning with the day on which the applicant is informed that the report has been furnished;

(e) in the case mentioned in paragraph (e) of that subsection, six months beginning with the day on which the patient is transferred;

(f) in the case mentioned in paragraph (f) or (fa) of that subsection, the period or periods for which authority for the patient's detention or guardianship is renewed by virtue of the report;

(fza) in the cases mentioned in paragraphs (fza) and (faa) of that subsection, the period or periods for which the community treatment period is extended by virtue of the report;

(g) in the case mentioned in paragraph (h) of that subsection, 12 months beginning with the date of the order, and in any subsequent period of 12 months during which the order continues in force.

(2A) Nothing in subsection (1)(b) above entitles a community patient to make an application by virtue of that provision even if he is admitted to a hospital on being recalled there under section 17E above.

(3) Section 32 above shall apply for the purposes of this section as it applies for the purposes of Part II of this Act.

(4) In this Act 'the appropriate tribunal' means the First-tier Tribunal or the Mental Health Review Tribunal for Wales.

(5) For provision determining to which of those tribunals applications by or in respect of a patient under this Act shall be made, see section 77(3) and (4) below.

Amendments. Subs (1)(fa), (fb) inserted: Mental Health (Patients in the Community) Act 1995, s 2(6)(a). Subs (1)(ga)–(gc) inserted: Mental Health (Patients in the Community) Act 1995, s 1(2), Sch 1, para 7(1), (2). Words in subs (2)(f) substituted: Mental Health (Patients in the Community) Act 1995, ss 1(2), 2(6)(b), Sch 1, para 7(4). Subs (2)(fa) inserted: Mental Health (Patients in the Community) Act 1995, ss 1(2), 2(6)(b), Sch 1, para 7(4). Subs (1)(ca), (cb) inserted: MHA 2007, s 32(4), Sch 3, paras 1, 18(1), (2)(a). Subs (1)(d) repealed: MHA 2007, s 55, Sch 11, Pt 1. Words in subs (1)(f) inserted: MHA 2007, s 32(4), Sch 3, paras 1, 18(1), (2)(b). Subs (1)(fza) inserted: MHA 2007, s 32(4), Sch 3, paras 1, 18(1), (2)(c). Subs (1)(faa) inserted: MHA 2007, s 32(4), Sch 3, paras 1, 18(1), (2)(d). Subs (1)(fb) repealed: MHA 2007, s 55, Sch 11, Pt 1. Words in subs (1)(g) inserted: MHA 2007, s 32(4), Sch 3, paras 1, 18(1), (2)(e). Subs (1) paras (ga)–(gc) repealed: MHA 2007, s 55, Sch 11, Pt 5. Words in subs (1)(h) inserted: MHA 2007, s 25. Words in subs (1)(h) inserted: MHA 2007, s 32(4), Sch 3, paras 1, 18(1), (2)(f). Words in subs (1)(i) repealed: MHA 2007, s 55, Sch 11, Pt 5. Words in subs (2)(c) substituted: MHA 2007, s 36(1), (3). Subs (2)(ca), (cb) inserted: MHA 2007, s 32(4), Sch 3, paras 1, 18(1), (3)(a). Words in subs (2)(d) substituted: MHA 2007, s 1(4), Sch 1, Pt 1, paras 1, 13. Words in subs (2)(d) repealed: MHA 2007, s 55, Sch 11, Pt 5. Subs (2)(fza) inserted: MHA 2007, s 32(4), Sch 3, paras 1, 18(1), (3)(b). Subs (2)(fa) repealed: MHA 2007, s 55, Sch 11, Pt 5. Subs (2A) inserted: MHA 2007, s 32(4), Sch 3, paras 1, 18(1), (4). Words in subs (1) substituted and subss (4), (5): inserted: Transfer of Tribunal Functions Order 2008 SI 2008 No. 2833, art 9(1), Sch 3, paras 39, 46(a), (b).

67 References to tribunals by Secretary of State concerning Part II patients

(1) The Secretary of State may, if he thinks fit, at any time refer to the appropriate tribunal the case of any patient who is liable to be detained or subject to guardianship under Part II of this Act or of any community patient.

(2) For the purpose of furnishing information for the purposes of a reference under subsection (1) above any registered medical practitioner or approved clinician authorised by or on behalf of the patient may, at any reasonable time, visit the patient and examine him in private and require the production of and inspect any records relating to the detention or treatment of the patient in any hospital or to any after-care services provided for the patient under section 117 below.

(3) Section 32 above shall apply for the purposes of this section as it applies for the purposes of Part II of this Act.

Amendments. Words in subss (1), (2) inserted: Mental Health (Patients in the Community) Act 1995, s 1(2), Sch 1, para 8(1)–(3). Words in subs (1) repealed: MHA 2007, s 55, Sch 11, Pt 5. Words in subs (1) inserted: MHA 2007, s 32(4), Sch 3, paras 1, 19. Words in subs (2) inserted: MHA 2007, s 13(1), (2)(a). Words in subs (1) substituted: Transfer of Tribunal Functions Order 2008 SI 2008 No. 2833, art 9(1), Sch 3, paras 39, 47.

68 Duty of managers of hospitals to refer cases to tribunal

(1) This section applies in respect of the following patients –

(a)   a patient who is admitted to a hospital in pursuance of an application for admission for assessment;

(b)   a patient who is admitted to a hospital in pursuance of an application for admission for treatment;

(c)   a community patient;

(d)   a patient whose community treatment order is revoked under section 17F above;

(e)   a patient who is transferred from guardianship to a hospital in pursuance of regulations made under section 19 above.

(2) On expiry of the period of six months beginning with the applicable day, the managers of the hospital shall refer the patient's case to the appropriate tribunal.

(3) But they shall not do so if during that period –

(a)   any right has been exercised by or in respect of the patient by virtue of any of paragraphs (b), (ca), (cb), (e), (g) and (h) of section 66(1) above;

(b)   a reference has been made in respect of the patient under section 67(1) above, not being a reference made while the patient is or was liable to be detained in pursuance of an application for admission for assessment; or

(c)   a reference has been made in respect of the patient under subsection (7) below.

(4) A person who applies to a tribunal but subsequently withdraws his application shall be treated for these purposes as not having exercised his right to apply, and if he withdraws his application on a date after expiry of the period mentioned in subsection (2) above, the managers shall refer the patient's case as soon as possible after that date.

(5) In subsection (2) above, 'the applicable day' means –

(a)   in the case of a patient who is admitted to a hospital in pursuance of an application for admission for assessment, the day on which the patient was so admitted;

(b)   in the case of a patient who is admitted to a hospital in pursuance of an application for admission for treatment –

(i)   the day on which the patient was so admitted; or

    (ii)   if, when he was so admitted, he was already liable to be detained in pursuance of an application for admission for assessment, the day on which he was originally admitted in pursuance of the application for admission for assessment;

(c)   in the case of a community patient or a patient whose community treatment order is revoked under section 17F above, the day mentioned in sub-paragraph (i) or (ii), as the case may be, of paragraph (b) above;

(d)   in the case of a patient who is transferred from guardianship to a hospital, the day on which he was so transferred.

(6) The managers of the hospital shall also refer the patient's case to the appropriate tribunal if a period of more than three years (or, if the patient has not attained the age of 18 years, one year) has elapsed since his case was last considered by such a tribunal, whether on his own application or otherwise.

(7) If, in the case of a community patient, the community treatment order is revoked under section 17F above, the managers of the hospital shall also refer the patient's case to the appropriate tribunal as soon as possible after the order is revoked.

(8) For the purposes of furnishing information for the purposes of a reference under this section, a registered medical practitioner or approved clinician authorised by or on behalf of the patient may at any reasonable time –

(a)   visit and examine the patient in private; and

(b)   require the production of and inspect any records relating to the detention or treatment of the patient in any hospital or any after-care services provided for him under section 117 below.

(9) Reference in this section to the managers of the hospital –

(a)   in relation to a community patient, is to the managers of the responsible hospital;

(b)   in relation to any other patient, is to the managers of the hospital in which he is liable to be detained.

Amendments. Section substituted: MHA 2007, s 37(1), (3). Words in subss (2), (6), (7) substituted: Transfer of Tribunal Functions Order 2008, SI 2008 No. 2833, art 9(1), Sch 3, paras 39, 48.

68A Power to reduce periods under section 68

(1) The appropriate national authority may from time to time by order amend subsections (2) or (6) of section 68 above so as to substitute for a period mentioned there such shorter period as is specified in the order.

(2) The order may include such transitional, consequential, incidental or supplemental provision as the appropriate national authority thinks fit.

(3) The order may, in particular, make provision for a case where –

(a)   a patient in respect of whom subsection (1) of section 68 above applies is, or is about to be, transferred from England to Wales or from Wales to England; and

    (b)   the period by reference to which subsection (2) or (6) of that section operates for the purposes of the patient's case is not the same in one territory as it is in the other.

(4) A patient is transferred from one territory to the other if –

    (a)   he is transferred from a hospital, or from guardianship, in one territory to a hospital in the other in pursuance of regulations made under section 19 above;

    (b)   he is removed under subsection (3) of that section from a hospital or accommodation in one territory to a hospital or accommodation in the other;

    (c)   he is a community patient responsibility for whom is assigned from a hospital in one territory to a hospital in the other in pursuance of regulations made under section 19A above;

    (d)   on the revocation of a community treatment order in respect of him under section 17F above he is detained in a hospital in the territory other than the one in which the responsible hospital was situated; or

    (e)   he is transferred or removed under section 123 below from a hospital in one territory to a hospital in the other.

(5) Provision made by virtue of subsection (3) above may require or authorise the managers of a hospital determined in accordance with the order to refer the patient's case to the appropriate tribunal.

(6) In so far as making provision by virtue of subsection (3) above, the order

    (a)   may make different provision for different cases;

    (b)   may make provision which applies subject to specified exceptions.

(7) Where the appropriate national authority for one territory makes an order under subsection (1) above, the appropriate national authority for the other territory may by order make such provision in consequence of the order as it thinks fit.

(8) An order made under subsection (7) above may, in particular, make provision for a case within subsection (3) above (and subsections (4) to (6) above shall apply accordingly).

(9) In this section, 'the appropriate national authority' means –

    (a)   in relation to the managers of a hospital in England, the Secretary of State;

    (b)   in relation to the managers of a hospital in Wales, the Welsh Ministers.

Amendments. Section substituted with new s 68 for existing s 68: MHA 2007, s 37(1), (3). Words in subs (5) substituted: Transfer of Tribunal Functions Order 2008, SI 2008 No. 2833, art 9(1), Sch 3, paras 39, 49.

Applications and references concerning Part III patients

69 Applications to tribunals concerning patients subject to hospital and guardianship orders

(1) Without prejudice to any provision of section 66(1) above as applied by section 40(4) above, an application to the appropriate tribunal may also be made –

    (a)   in respect of a patient liable to be detained in pursuance of a hospital order or a community patient who was so liable immediately before he became a community patient, by the nearest relative of the patient in any period in which an application may be made by the patient under any such provision as so applied; and

    (b)   in respect of a patient placed under guardianship by a guardianship order –

        (i)   by the patient, within the period of six months beginning with the date of the order;

        (ii)   by the nearest relative of the patient, within the period of 12 months beginning with the date of the order and in any subsequent period of 12 months.

(2) Where a person detained in a hospital –

    (a)   is treated as subject to a hospital order, hospital direction or transfer direction by virtue of section 41(5) above, 82(2) or 85(2) below, or article 2(2) of the Mental Health (Care and Treatment) (Scotland) Act 2003 (Consequential Provisions) Order 2005 or section 80B(2), 82(2) or 85(2) below; or

    (b)   is subject to a direction having the same effect as a hospital order by virtue of section 47(3) or 48(3) above,

then, without prejudice to any provision of Part II of this Act as applied by section 40 above, that person may make an application to the appropriate tribunal in the period of six months beginning with the date of the order or direction mentioned in paragraph (a) above or, as the case may be, the date of the direction mentioned in paragraph (b) above.

(3) The provisions of section 66 above as applied by section 40(4) above are subject to subsection (4) below.

(4) If the initial detention period has not elapsed when the relevant application period begins, the right of a hospital order patient to make an application by virtue of paragraph (ca) or (cb) of section 66(1) above shall be exercisable only during whatever remains of the relevant application period after the initial detention period has elapsed.

(5) In subsection (4) above –

    (a)   'hospital order patient' means a patient who is subject to a hospital order, excluding a patient of a kind mentioned in paragraph (a) or (b) of subsection (2) above;

(b)   'the initial detention period', in relation to a hospital order patient, means the period of six months beginning with the date of the hospital order; and

(c)   'the relevant application period' means the relevant period mentioned in paragraph (ca) or (cb), as the case may be, of section 66(2) above.

Amendments. Reference in subs (2)(b) inserted: Crime (Sentences) Act 1997, s 55, Sch 4, para 12(8). Subs (1): para (a) prospectively substituted: MHA 2007, s 32(4), Sch 3, paras 1, 20(a). Words in subs –(2) inserted: MHA 2007, s 39(2), Sch 5, Pt 2, para 18(a). Words in subs (2)(a) prospectively substituted: MHA 2007, s 39(2), Sch 5, Pt 2, para 18(b). Reference in subs (2)(b) prospectively repealed: MHA 2007, ss 32(4), 55, Sch 3, paras 1, 20(b), Sch 11, Pt 5. Subss (3)–(5): prospectively inserted: MHA 2007, s 32(4), Sch 3, paras 1, 20(c). Words in subss (1), (2) substituted: Transfer of Tribunal Functions Order 2008, SI 2008 No. 2833, art 9(1), Sch 3, paras 39, 50.

70 Applications to tribunals concerning restricted patients

A patient who is a restricted patient within the meaning of section 79 below and is detained in a hospital may apply to the appropriate tribunal –

(a)   in the period between the expiration of six months and the expiration of 12 months beginning with the date of the relevant hospital order, hospital direction or transfer direction; and

(b)   in any subsequent period of 12 months.

Amendments. Words inserted: Crime (Sentences) Act 1997, s 55, Sch 4, para 12(9). Words substituted: Transfer of Tribunal Functions Order 2008, SI 2008 No. 2833, art 9(1), Sch 3, paras 39, 51.

71 References by Secretary of State concerning restricted patients

(1) The Secretary of State may at any time refer the case of a restricted patient to the appropriate tribunal.

(2) The Secretary of State shall refer to the appropriate tribunal the case of any restricted patient detained in a hospital whose case has not been considered by such a tribunal, whether on his own application or otherwise, within the last three years.

(3) The Secretary of State may by order vary the length of the period mentioned in subsection (2) above.

(3A) An order under subsection (3) above may include such transitional, consequential, incidental or supplemental provision as the Secretary of State thinks fit.

(4) Any reference under subsection (1) above in respect of a patient who has been conditionally discharged and not recalled to hospital shall be made to the tribunal for the area in which the patient resides.

(5), (6) (*repealed*)

Amendments. Subss (5), (6): repealed: Domestic Violence, Crime and Victims Act 2004, s 58(1), (2), Sch 10, para 20, Sch 11. Subs (3A) inserted: MHA 2007, s 37(1), (4). Words in subss (1), (2) substituted: Transfer of Tribunal Functions Order 2008, SI 2008 No. 2833, art 9(1), Sch 3, paras 39, 52.

Discharge of patients

72 Powers of tribunals

(1) Where application is made to the appropriate tribunal by or in respect of a patient who is liable to be detained under this Act or is a community patient, the tribunal may in any case direct that the patient be discharged, and –

    (a)   the tribunal shall direct the discharge of a patient liable to be detained under section 2 above if it is not satisfied –

        (i)   that he is then suffering from mental disorder or from mental disorder of a nature or degree which warrants his detention in a hospital for assessment (or for assessment followed by medical treatment) for at least a limited period; or

        (ii)   that his detention as aforesaid is justified in the interests of his own health or safety or with a view to the protection of other persons;

    (b)   the tribunal shall direct the discharge of a patient liable to be detained otherwise than under section 2 above if it is not satisfied –

        (i)   that he is then suffering from mental disorder or from mental disorder of a nature or degree which makes it appropriate for him to be liable to be detained in a hospital for medical treatment; or

        (ii)   that it is necessary for the health of safety of the patient or for the protection of other persons that he should receive such treatment; or

        (iia)   that appropriate medical treatment is available for him; or

        (iii)   in the case of an application by virtue of paragraph (g) of section 66(1) above, that the patient, if released, would be likely to act in a manner dangerous to other persons or to himself.

    (c)   the tribunal shall direct the discharge of a community patient if it is not satisfied –

        (i)   that he is then suffering from a mental disorder or mental disorder of a nature or degree which makes it appropriate for him to receive medical treatment; or

        (ii)   that it is necessary for his health or safety or for the protection of other persons that he should receive such treatment; or

        (iii)   that it is necessary that the responsible clinician should be able to exercise the power under s 17E(1) to recall the patient to hospital; or

        (iv)   that appropriate medical treatment is available for him; or

        (v)   in the case of an application by virtue of paragraph (g) of section 66(1) above, that the patient, if discharged, would be likely to act in a manner dangerous to other persons or to himself.

(1A) In determining whether the criterion in subsection (1)(c)(iii) above is met, the tribunal shall, in particular, consider, having regard to the patient's history of mental disorder and any other relevant factors, what risk there would be of a deterioration of the patient's condition if he were to continue not to be detained in a hospital (as a result, for example, of his refusing or neglecting to receive the medical treatment he requires for his mental disorder.

(2) *(repealed)*

(3) A tribunal may under subsection (1) above direct the discharge of a patient on a future date specified in the direction; and where a tribunal does not direct the discharge of a patient under that subsection the tribunal may –

(a)   with a view to facilitating his discharge on a future date, recommend that he be granted leave of absence or transferred to another hospital or into guardianship; and

(b)   further consider his case in the event of any such recommendation not being complied with.

(3A) Subsection (1) above does not require a tribunal to direct the discharge of a patient just because it thinks it might be appropriate for the patient to be discharged (subject to the possibility of recall) under a community treatment order; and a tribunal –

(a)   may recommend that the responsible clinician consider whether to make a community treatment order; and

(b)   may (but need not) further consider the patient's case if the responsible clinician does not make an order.

(4) Where application is made to the appropriate tribunal by or in respect of a patient who is subject to guardianship under this Act, the tribunal may in any case direct that the patient be discharged, and shall so direct if it is satisfied –

(a)   that he is not then suffering from mental disorder; or

(b)   that it is not necessary in the interests of the welfare of the patient, or for the protection of other persons, that the patient should remain under such guardianship.

(4A), (5) *(repealed)*

(6) Subsections (1) to (4) above apply in relation to references to the appropriate tribunal as they apply in relation to applications made to the appropriate tribunal by or in respect of a patient.

(7) Subsection (1) above shall not apply in the case of a restricted patient except as provided in sections 73 and 74 below.

Amendments. Subss (3A), (4A): inserted: Mental Health (Patients in the Community) Act 1995, s 1(2), Sch 1, para 10(1)–(3). Subs (1) substituted: Mental Health Act 1983 (Remedial) Order 2001, SI 2001 No. 3712, art 3. Words in subs (1) inserted: MHA 2007, s 32(4), Sch 3, paras 1, 21(1), (2)(a) Words in subs (1)(b)(i) substituted: MHA 2007, s 1(4), Sch 1, Pt 1, paras 1, 14(a). Para (1)(b)(iia) inserted: MHA 2007, s 4(1), (8)(a). Para (1)(c) inserted: MHA 2007, s 32(4), Sch 3, paras 1, 21(1), (2)(b). Subs (1A) inserted: MHA 2007, s 32(4), Sch 3, paras 1, 21(1), (3). Subs (2) repealed: MHA 2007, ss 4(1), (8)(b), 55, Sch 11, Pt 2. Subs (3A) substituted: MHA 2007, s 32(4), Sch 3, paras 1, 21(1), (4). Words in subs (4)(a) substituted: MHA 2007, s 1(4), Sch 1, Pt 1, paras 1, 14(b). Subs (4A) repealed: MHA 2007, s 55, Sch 11, Pt 5. Subs (5) repealed: MHA 2007, s 55, Sch 11, Pt 1. Reference in subs (6) substituted: MHA 2007, s 1(4), Sch 1, Pt 1, paras 1, 14(c). Words in subss (1), (3), (3A), (4), (6) substituted: Transfer of Tribunal Functions Order 2008, SI 2008 No. 2833, art 9(1), Sch 3, paras 39, 53(a)–(e).

73 Power to discharge restricted patients

(1) Where an application to the appropriate tribunal is made by a restricted patient who is subject to a restriction order, or where the case of such a patient is referred to the appropriate tribunal, the tribunal shall direct the absolute discharge of the patient if –

(a)   the tribunal is not satisfied as to the matters mentioned in paragraph (b)(i), (ii) or (iia) of section 72(1) above;
(b)   the tribunal is satisfied that it is not appropriate for the patient to remain liable to be recalled to hospital for further treatment.

(2) Where in the case of any such patient as is mentioned in subsection (1) above –

(a)   paragraph (a) of that subsection applies; but
(b)   paragraph (b) of that subsection does not apply, the tribunal shall direct the conditional discharge of the patient.

(3) Where a patient is absolutely discharged under this section he shall thereupon cease to be liable to be detained by virtue of the relevant hospital order, and the restriction order shall cease to have effect accordingly.

(4) Where a patient is conditionally discharged under this section –

(a)   he may be recalled by the Secretary of State under subsection (3) of section 42 above as if he had been conditionally discharged under subsection (2) of that section; and
(b)   the patient shall comply with such conditions (if any) as may be imposed at the time of discharge by the tribunal or at any subsequent time by the Secretary of State.

(5) The Secretary of State may from time to time vary any condition imposed (whether by the tribunal or by him) under subsection (4) above.

(6) Where a restriction order in respect of a patient ceases to have effect after he has been conditionally discharged under this section the patient shall, unless previously recalled, be deemed to be absolutely discharged on the date when the order ceases to have effect and shall cease to be liable to be detained by virtue of the relevant hospital order.

(7) A tribunal may defer a direction for the conditional discharge of a patient until such arrangements as appear to the tribunal to be necessary for that purpose have been made to its satisfaction; and where by virtue of any such deferment no direction has been given on an application or reference before the time when the patient's case comes before the tribunal on a subsequent application or reference, the previous application or reference shall be treated as one on which no direction under this section can be given.

(8) This section is without prejudice to section 42 above.

Amendments. Subss (1), (2) substituted: Mental Health Act 1983 (Remedial) Order 2001, SI 2001 No. 3712, art 4. Words in subs (1)(a) substituted: MHA 2007, s 4(1), (9). Words in subss (1), (7) substituted: Transfer of Tribunal Functions Order 2008, SI 2008 No. 2833, art 9(1), Sch 3, paras 39, 54(a)(i)–(iii), (b).

74 Restricted patients subject to restriction directions

(1) Where an application to the appropriate tribunal is made by a restricted patient who is subject to a limitation direction or restriction direction, or where the case of such a patient is referred to the appropriate tribunal the tribunal –

    (a)   shall notify the Secretary of State whether, in its opinion, the patient would, if subject to a restriction order, be entitled to be absolutely or conditionally discharged under section 73 above; and

    (b)   if the tribunal notifies him that the patient would be entitled to be conditionally discharged, may recommend that in the event of his not being discharged under this section he should continue to be detained in hospital.

(2) If in the case of a patient not falling within subsection (4) below –

    (a)   the tribunal notifies the Secretary of State that the patient would be entitled to be absolutely or conditionally discharged; and

    (b)   within the period of 90 days beginning with the date of that notification the Secretary of State gives notice to the tribunal that the patient may be so discharged,

the tribunal shall direct the absolute or, as the case may be, the conditional discharge of the patient.

(3) Where a patient continues to be liable to be detained in a hospital at the end of the period referred to in subsection (2)(b) above because the Secretary of State has not given the notice there mentioned, the managers of the hospital shall, unless the tribunal has made a recommendation under subsection (1)(b) above, transfer the patient to a prison or other institution in which he might have been detained if he had not been removed to hospital, there to be dealt with as if he had not been so removed.

(4) If, in the case of a patient who is subject to a transfer direction under section 48 above, the tribunal notifies the Secretary of State that the patient would be entitled to be absolutely or conditionally discharged, the Secretary of State shall, unless the tribunal has made a recommendation under subsection (1)(b) above, by warrant direct that the patient be remitted to a prison or other institution in which he might have been detained if he had not been removed to hospital, there to be dealt with as if he had not been so removed.

(5) Where a patient is transferred or remitted under subsection (3) or (4) above the relevant hospital direction and the limitation direction or, as the case may be, the relevant transfer direction and the restriction direction shall cease to have effect on his arrival in the prison or other institution.

(5A) Where the tribunal has made a recommendation under subsection (1)(b) above in the case of a patient who is subject to a restriction direction or a limitation direction –

    (a)   the fact that the restriction direction or limitation direction remains in force does not prevent the making of any application or reference to the Parole Board by or in respect of him or the exercise by him of any power to require the Secretary of State to refer his case to the Parole Board, and

(b)   if the Parole Board make a direction or recommendation by virtue of which the patient would become entitled to be released (whether unconditionally or on licence) from any prison or other institution in which he might have been detained if he had not been removed to hospital, the restriction direction or limitation direction shall cease to have effect at the time when he would become entitled to be so released.

(6) Subsections (3) to (8) of section 73 above shall have effect in relation to this section as they have effect in relation to that section, taking references to the relevant hospital order and the restriction order as references to the hospital direction and the limitation direction or, as the case may be, to the transfer direction and the restriction direction.

(7) This section is without prejudice to sections 50 to 53 above in their application to patients who are not discharged under this section.

Amendments. Words in subss (1), (5), (6) inserted: Crime (Sentences) Act 1997, s 55, Sch 4, para 12(10)–(12). Subs (5A) inserted: Criminal Justice Act 2003, s 295. Words in subss (1), (2), (3), (4), (5A) substituted: Transfer of Tribunal Functions Order 2008, SI 2008 No. 2833, art 9(1), Sch 3, paras 39, 55(a)(iii), (iv), (b), (c)).

75 Applications and references concerning conditionally discharged restricted patients

(1) Where a restricted patient has been conditionally discharged under section 42(2), 73 or 74 above and is subsequently recalled to hospital –

(a)   the Secretary of State shall, within one month of the day on which the patient returns or is returned to hospital, refer his case to the appropriate tribunal; and

(b)   section 70 above shall apply to the patient as if the relevant hospital order, hospital direction or transfer direction had been made on that day.

(2) Where a restricted patient has been conditionally discharged as aforesaid but has not been recalled to hospital he may apply to the appropriate tribunal –

(a)   in the period between the expiration of 12 months and the expiration of two years beginning with the date on which he was conditionally discharged; and

(b)   in any subsequent period of two years.

(3) Sections 73 and 74 above shall not apply to an application under subsection (2) above but on any such application the tribunal may –

(a)   vary any condition to which the patient is subject in connection with his discharge or impose any condition which might have been imposed in connection therewith; or

    (b)   direct that the restriction order, limitation direction or restriction direction to which he is subject shall cease to have effect;

and if the tribunal gives a direction under paragraph (b) above the patient shall cease to be liable to be detained by virtue of the relevant hospital order, hospital direction or transfer direction.

Amendments. Words in subs (1)(b) inserted: Crime (Sentences) Act 1997, s 55, Sch 4, para 12(13). Words in subs (3) inserted: MHA 2007, s 41(a), (b). Words in subss (1)(a), (2), (3) substituted: Transfer of Tribunal Functions Order 2008, SI 2008 No. 2833, art 9(1), Sch 3, paras 39, 56(a), (b).

General

76 Visiting and examination of patients

(1) For the purpose of advising whether an application to the appropriate tribunal should be made by or in respect of a patient who is liable to be detained or subject to guardianship under Part II of this Act or a community patient, or of furnishing information as to the condition of a patient for the purposes of such an application, any registered medical practitioner or approved clinician authorised by or on behalf of the patient or other person who is entitled to make or has made the application –

    (a)   may at any reasonable time visit the patient and examine him in private, and

    (b)   may require the production of and inspect any records relating to the detention or treatment of the patient in any hospital or to any after-care services provided for the patient under section 117 below.

(2) Section 32 above shall apply for the purposes of this section as it applies for the purposes of Part II of this Act.

Amendments. Words in subs (1) inserted: Mental Health (Patients in the Community) Act 1995, s 1(2), Sch 1, para 11(a), (b). Words in subs (1) repealed: MHA 2007, s 55, Sch 11, Pt 5. Words in subs (1) inserted: MHA 2007, s 32(4), Sch 3, paras 1, 22. Words in subs (1) inserted: MHA 2007, s 13(1), (2)(b). Words in subs (1) substituted: Transfer of Tribunal Functions Order 2008 SI 2008 No. 2833, art 9(1), Sch 3, paras 39, 57.

77 General provisions concerning tribunal applications

(1) No application shall be made to the appropriate tribunal by or in respect of a patient under this Act except in such cases and at such times as are expressly provided by this Act.

(2) Where under this Act any person is authorised to make an application to the appropriate tribunal within a specified period, not more than one such application shall be made by that person within that period but for that purpose there shall be disregarded any application which is withdrawn in accordance with Tribunal Procedure Rules or rules made under section 78 below.

(3) Subject to subsection (4) below an application to a tribunal authorised to be made by or in respect of a patient under this Act shall be made by notice in writing addressed

(a)   in the case of a patient who is liable to be detained in a hospital, to the First-tier Tribunal where that hospital is in England and to the Mental Health Review Tribunal for Wales where that hospital is in Wales;

(b)   in the case of a community patient, to the First-tier Tribunal where the responsible hospital is in England and to the Mental Health Review Tribunal for Wales where that hospital is in Wales;

(c)   in the case of a patient subject to guardianship, to the First-tier Tribunal where the patient resides in England and to the Mental Health Review Tribunal for Wales where the patient resides in Wales.

(4) Any application under section 75(2) above shall be made to the First-tier Tribunal where the patient resides in England and to the Mental Health Review Tribunal for Wales where the patient resides in Wales.

Amendments. Subs (3)(a)–(c) substituted for existing words: MHA 2007, s 32(4), Sch 3, paras 1, 23. Words in subss (1), (3)(a)–(c), (4) substituted: Transfer of Tribunal Functions Order 2008, SI 2008 No. 2833, art 9(1), Sch 3, paras 39, 58(a), (b), (c)(i)–(iv), (d). Words in subs (2) inserted: Transfer of Tribunal Functions (Lands Tribunal and Miscellaneous Amendments) Order 2009, SI 2009 No. 1307, art 5(1), (2), Sch 1, paras 160, 161.

78 Procedure of tribunals

(1) The Lord Chancellor may make rules with respect to the making of applications to the Mental Health Review Tribunal for Wales and with respect to the proceedings of that tribunal and matters incidental to or consequential on such proceedings.

(2) Rules made under this section may in particular make provision –

(a)   for enabling the tribunal, or the chairman of the tribunal, to postpone the consideration of any application by or in respect of a patient, or of any such application of any specified class, until the expiration of such period (not exceeding 12 months) as may be specified in the rules from the date on which an application by or in respect of the same patient was last considered and determined under this Act by the tribunal or the First-tier Tribunal;

(b)   for the transfer of proceedings to or from the Mental Health Review Tribunal for Wales in any case where, after the making of the application, the patient is moved into or out of Wales;

(c)   for restricting the persons qualified to serve as members of the tribunal for the consideration of any application, or of an application of any specified class;

(d)   for enabling the tribunal to dispose of an application without a formal hearing where such a hearing is not requested by the applicant or it appears to the tribunal that such a hearing would be detrimental to the health of the patient;

(e)   for enabling the tribunal to exclude members of the public, or any specified class of members of the public, from any proceedings of the tribunal, or to prohibit the publication of reports of any such proceedings or the names of any persons concerned in such proceedings;

(f)   for regulating the circumstances in which, and the persons by whom, applicants and patients in respect of whom applications are made to the tribunal may, if not desiring to conduct their own case, be represented for the purposes of those applications;

(g)   for regulating the methods by which information relevant to an application may be obtained by or furnished to the tribunal, and in particular for authorising the members of the tribunal, or any one or more of them, to visit and interview in private any patient by or in respect of whom an application has been made;

(h)   for making available to any applicant, and to any patient in respect of whom an application is made to the tribunal, copies of any documents obtained by or furnished to the tribunal in connection with the application, and a statement of the substance of any oral information so obtained or furnished except where the tribunal considers it undesirable in the interests of the patient or for other special reasons;

(i)   for requiring the tribunal, if so requested in accordance with the rules, to furnish such statements of the reasons for any decision given by the tribunal as may be prescribed by the rules, subject to any provision made by the rules for withholding such a statement from a patient or any other person in cases where the tribunal considers that furnishing it would be undesirable in the interests of the patient or for other special reasons;

(j)   for conferring on the tribunal such ancillary powers as the Lord Chancellor thinks necessary for the purposes of the exercise of its functions under this Act;

(k)   for enabling any functions of the tribunal which relate to matters preliminary or incidental to an application to be performed by the chairman of the tribunal.

(3) Subsections (1) and (2) above apply in relation to references to the Mental Health Review Tribunal for Wales as they apply in relation to applications to that tribunal by or in respect of patients.

(4) Rules under this section may make provision as to the procedure to be adopted in cases concerning restricted patients and, in particular –

(a)   for restricting the persons qualified to serve as president of the tribunal for the consideration of an application or reference relating to a restricted patient;

(b)   for the transfer of proceedings to or from the tribunal in any case where, after the making of a reference or application in accordance with section 71(4) or 77(4) above, the patient begins or ceases to reside in Wales.

(5) Rules under this section may be so framed as to apply to all applications or references or to applications or references of any specified class and may make different provision in relation to different cases.

(6) Any functions conferred on the chairman of the Mental Health Review Tribunal for Wales by rules under this section may be exercised by another member of that tribunal appointed by him for the purpose.

(7) The Mental Health Review Tribunal for Wales may pay allowances in respect of travelling expenses, subsistence and loss of earnings to any person attending the tribunal as an applicant or witness, to the patient who is the subject of the proceedings if he attends otherwise than as the applicant or a witness and to any person (other than an authorised person (within the meaning of Part 3) who attends as the representative of an applicant.

(8) *(repealed)*

(9) Part I of the Arbitration Act 1996 shall not apply to any proceedings before The Mental Health Review Tribunal for Wales except so far as any provisions of that Act may be applied, with or without modifications, by rules made under this section.

Amendments. Words in subs (9) substituted: Arbitration Act 1996, s 107(1), Sch 3, para 40. Words in subs (2)(a) substituted: MHA 2007, s 38(1), (3)(a), (b). Words in subs (2)(b) substituted: MHA 2007, s 38(1), (3)(c). Words in subs (2)(k) substituted: MHA 2007, s 38(1), (3)(a). Words in subs (4)(a) substituted: MHA 2007, s 38(1), (3)(d). Words in subs (4)(b) substituted: MHA 2007, s 38(1), (3)(c). Words in subs (6) substituted: MHA 2007, s 38(1), (3)(a). Words in subs (6) repealed: MHA 2007, ss 38(1), (3)(e), 55, Sch 11, Pt 6. Words in subs (7) substituted: Legal Services Act 2007, s 208(1), Sch 21, paras 53, 60.Words in section heading substituted: Transfer of Tribunal Functions Order 2008, SI 2008 No. 2833, art 9(1), Sch 3, paras 39, 59(1). Words in subss (1)–(4), (6), (7), (9) substituted: Transfer of Tribunal Functions Order 2008, SI 2008 No. 2833, art 9(1), Sch 3, paras 39, 59(2)(a), (b), (3)(a), (b), (d)(i), (ii), (4)(a), (b), (5)(a), (6), (7), (9). Subs (2)(b) substituted: Transfer of Tribunal Functions Order 2008, SI 2008 No. 2833, art 9(1), Sch 3, paras 39, 59(3)(c). Subs (4)(b) substituted: Transfer of Tribunal Functions Order 2008, SI 2008 No. 2833, art 9(1), Sch 3, paras 39, 59(5)(b). Subs (8) repealed: Transfer of Tribunal Functions Order 2008, SI 2008 No. 2833, art 9(1), Sch 3, paras 39, 59(8).

78A Appeal from the Mental Health Review Tribunal for Wales to the Upper Tribunal

(1) A party to any proceedings before the Mental Health Review Tribunal for Wales may appeal to the Upper Tribunal on any point of law arising from a decision made by the Mental Health Review Tribunal for Wales in those proceedings.

(2) An appeal may be brought under subsection (1) above only if, on an application made by the party concerned, the Mental Health Review Tribunal for Wales or the Upper Tribunal has given its permission for the appeal to be brought.

(3) Section 12 of the Tribunals, Courts and Enforcement Act 2007 (proceedings on appeal to the Upper Tribunal) applies in relation to appeals to the Upper Tribunal under this section as it applies in relation to appeals to it under section 11 of that Act, but as if references to the First-tier Tribunal were references to the Mental Health Review Tribunal for Wales.

Amendments. Section inserted: Transfer of Tribunal Functions Order 2008 SI 2008 No. 2833, art 9(1), Sch 3, paras 39, 60.

79 Interpretation of Part V

(1) In this Part of this Act 'restricted patient' means a patient who is subject to a restriction order, limitation direction or restriction direction and this Part of this Act shall, subject to the provisions of this section, have effect in relation to any person who –

  (a) is treated by virtue of any enactment as subject to a hospital order and a restriction order; or

  (b) (*repealed*)

  (c) is treated as subject to a hospital order and a restriction order, or to a hospital direction and a limitation direction, or to a transfer direction and a restriction direction, by virtue of any provision of Part 6 of this Act (except section 80D(3), 82A(2) or 85A(2) below),

as it has effect in relation to a restricted patient.

(2) Subject to the following provisions of this section, in this Part of this Act 'the relevant hospital order', 'the relevant hospital direction' and 'the relevant transfer direction', in relation to a restricted patient, mean the hospital order, the hospital direction or transfer direction by virtue of which he is liable to be detained in a hospital.

(3) In the case of a person within paragraph (a) of subsection (1) above, references in this Part of this Act to the relevant hospital order or restriction order shall be construed as references to the direction referred to in that paragraph.

(4) In the case of a person within paragraph (b) of subsection (1) above, references in this Part of this Act to the relevant hospital order or restriction order shall be construed as references to the order under the provisions mentioned in that paragraph.

(5) In the case of a person within paragraph (c) of subsection (1) above, references in this Part of this Act to the relevant hospital order, the relevant hospital direction, the relevant transfer direction, the restriction order, limitation direction or the restriction direction or to a transfer direction under section 48 above shall be construed as references to the hospital order, hospital direction, transfer direction, restriction order, limitation direction, restriction direction or transfer direction under that section to which that person is treated as subject by virtue of the provisions mentioned in that paragraph.

(5A) Section 75 above shall, subject to the modifications in subsection (5C) below, have effect in relation to a qualifying patient as it has effect in relation to a restricted patient who is conditionally discharged under section 42(2), 73 or 74 above.

(5B) A patient is a qualifying patient if he is treated by virtue of section 80D(3), 82A(2) or 85A(2) below as if he had been conditionally discharged and were subject to a hospital order and a restriction order, or to a hospital direction and a limitation direction, or to a transfer direction and a restriction direction.

(5C) The modifications mentioned in subsection (5A) above are –

(a) references to the relevant hospital order, hospital direction or transfer direction, or to the restriction order, limitation direction or restriction direction to which the patient is subject, shall be construed as references to the hospital order, hospital direction or transfer direction, or restriction order, limitation direction or restriction direction, to which the patient is treated as subject by virtue of section 80D(3), 82A(2) or 85A(2) below; and

(b) the reference to the date on which the patient was conditionally discharged shall be construed as a reference to the date on which he was treated as conditionally discharged by virtue of a provision mentioned in paragraph (a) above.

(6) In this Part of this Act, unless the context otherwise requires, 'hospital' means a hospital, and 'the responsible clinician' means the responsible clinician within the meaning of Part II of this Act.

(7) *(repealed)*

Amendments. Words in subss (1), (2) inserted: Crime (Sentences) Act 1997, s 55, Sch 4, para 12(14), (15)(a), (b). Subs (1)(a) substituted: Domestic Violence, Crime and Victims Act 2004, s 58(1), Sch 10, para 21(a). Subs (1)(b) repealed: Domestic Violence, Crime and Victims Act 2004, s 58(1), (2), Sch 10, para 21(b), Sch 11. Subs (1)(c) substituted: MHA 2007, s 39(2), Sch 5, Pt 2, para 19(1), (2). Words in subs (5) inserted: MHA 2007, s 39(2), Sch 5, Pt 2, para 19(1), (3)(a)–(d). Subss (5A)–(5C) inserted: MHA 2007, s 39(2), Sch 5, Pt 2, para 19(1), (4). Words in subs (6) substituted: MHA 2007, s 13(1), (3). Subs (7) (previously inserted: Health Authorities Act 1995, s 2(1), Sch 1, para 107(7)) repealed: Transfer of Tribunal Functions Order 2008, SI 2008 No. 2833, art 9(1), Sch 3, paras 39, 61.

PART VI
REMOVAL AND RETURN OF PATIENTS WITHIN UNITED KINGDOM, ETC

Removal to and from Scotland

Amendments. Cross-heading substituted: Mental Health Act 2007, s 39(2), Sch 5, Pt 1, paras 1, 2.

80 Removal of patients to Scotland

(1) If it appears to the Secretary of State, in the case of a patient who is for the time being liable to be detained under this Act (otherwise than by virtue of section 35, 36 or 38 above), that it is in the interests of the patient to remove him to Scotland, and that arrangements have been made for admitting him to a hospital there or, where he is not to be admitted to a hospital, for his detention in hospital to be authorised by virtue of the Mental Health (Care and Treatment) (Scotland) Act 2003 or the Criminal Procedure (Scotland) Act 1995 the Secretary of State may authorise his removal to Scotland and may give any necessary directions for his conveyance to his destination.

(2)–(6) *(repealed in relation to England and Wales)*

(7) In this section 'hospital' has the same meaning as in the Mental Health (Care and Treatment) (Scotland) Act 2003.

(8) Reference in this section to a patient's detention in hospital being authorised by virtue of the Mental Health (Care and Treatment) (Scotland) Act 2003 or the Criminal Procedure (Scotland) Act 1995 shall be read as including reference to a patient in respect of whom a certificate under one of the provisions listed in section 290(7)(a) of the Act of 2003 is in operation.

Amendments. Words in subs (6) substituted: Mental Health (Amendment) (Scotland) Act 1983, s 39(2), Sch 2, para 1. Subs (8): inserted, in relation to England and Wales: Mental Health (Care and Treatment) (Scotland) Act 2003 (Consequential Provisions) Order 2005, SI 2005/2078, art 15, Sch 1, para 2(1), (4)(c). Words in subs (1) inserted, in relation to England and Wales: Mental Health (Care and Treatment) (Scotland) Act 2003 (Consequential Provisions) Order 2005, SI 2005 No. 2078, art 15, Sch 1, para 2(1), (4)(a). Subss (2)–(6) repealed in relation to England and Wales: Mental Health (Care and Treatment) (Scotland) Act 2003 (Consequential Provisions) Order 2005, SI 2005 No. 2078, art 16(1), Sch 3; a corresponding amendment (repealing sub-ss (2)–(5) and subs (6) in part) has been made in relation to Scotland by SSI 2005/465, art 3, Sch 2. Words in subs (7) substituted in relation to England and Wales: Mental Health (Care and Treatment) (Scotland) Act 2003 (Consequential Provisions) Order 2005, SI 2005 No. 2078, art 15, Sch 1, para 2(1), (4)(b) and in relation to Scotland by SSI 2005/465, art 2, Sch 1, para 13(1), (2).Words in subs (1) repealed: MHA 2007, ss 39(2), 55, Sch 5, Pt 1, paras 1, 2, Sch 11, Pt 7.

80ZA Transfer of responsibility for community patients to Scotland

(1) If it appears to the appropriate national authority, in the case of a community patient, that the conditions mentioned in subsection (2) below are met, the authority may authorise the transfer of responsibility for him to Scotland.

(2) The conditions are –

(a)   a transfer under this section is in the patient's interests; and
(b)   arrangements have been made for dealing with him under enactments in force in Scotland corresponding or similar to those relating to community patients in this Act.

(3) The appropriate national authority may not act under subsection (1) above while the patient is recalled to hospital under section 17E above.

(4) In this section, 'the appropriate national authority' means –

(a)   in relation to a community patient in respect of whom the responsible hospital is in England, the Secretary of State;
(b)   in relation to a community patient in respect of whom the responsible hospital is in Wales, the Welsh Ministers.

Amendments. Section inserted: MHA 2007, s 39(2), Sch 5, Pt 1, paras 1, 3.

80A Transfer of responsibility for conditionally discharged patients to Scotland

(1) If it appears to the Secretary of State, in the case of a patient who –

(a)   is subject to a restriction order under section 41 above; and
(b)   has been conditionally discharged under section 42 or 73 above,

that a transfer under this section would be in the interests of the patient, the Secretary of State may, with the consent of the Minister exercising corresponding functions in Scotland, transfer responsibility for the patient to that Minister.

(2), (3) (*repealed*)

Amendments. Section Inserted: Crime (Sentences) Act 1997, s 48, Sch 3, para 1. Section heading substituted, in relation to England and Wales: MHA 2007, s 39(2), Sch 5, Pt 1, paras 1, 4. Subss (2), (3): repealed in relation to England and Wales: Mental Health (Care and Treatment) (Scotland) Act 2003 (Consequential Provisions) Order 2005, SI 2005 No. 2078, art 16(1), Sch 3 and in relation to Scotland: SSI 2005/465, art 3, Sch 2.

80B Removal of detained patients from Scotland

(1) This section applies to a patient if –

- (a) he is removed to England and Wales under regulations made under section 290(1)(a) of the Mental Health (Care and Treatment) (Scotland) Act 2003 ('the 2003 Act');
- (b) immediately before his removal, his detention in hospital was authorised by virtue of that Act or the Criminal Procedure (Scotland) Act 1995; and
- (c) on his removal, he is admitted to a hospital in England or Wales.

(2) He shall be treated as if, on the date of his admission to the hospital, he had been so admitted in pursuance of an application made, or an order or direction made or given, on that date under the enactment in force in England and Wales which most closely corresponds to the enactment by virtue of which his detention in hospital was authorised immediately before his removal.

(3) If, immediately before his removal, he was subject to a measure under any enactment in force in Scotland restricting his discharge, he shall be treated as if he were subject to an order or direction under the enactment in force in England and Wales which most closely corresponds to that enactment.

(4) If, immediately before his removal, the patient was liable to be detained under the 2003 Act by virtue of a transfer for treatment direction, given while he was serving a sentence of imprisonment (within the meaning of section 136(9) of that Act) imposed by a court in Scotland, he shall be treated as if the sentence had been imposed by a court in England and Wales.

(5) If, immediately before his removal, the patient was subject to a hospital direction or transfer for treatment direction, the restriction direction to which he is subject by virtue of subsection (3) above shall expire on the date on which that hospital direction or transfer for treatment direction (as the case may be) would have expired if he had not been so removed.

(6) If, immediately before his removal, the patient was liable to be detained under the 2003 Act by virtue of a hospital direction, he shall be treated as if any sentence of imprisonment passed at the time when that hospital direction was made had been imposed by a court in England and Wales.

(7) Any directions given by the Scottish Ministers under regulations made under section 290 of the 2003 Act as to the removal of a patient to which this section applies shall have effect as if they were given under this Act.

(8) Subsection (8) of section 80 above applies to a reference in this section as it applies to one in that section.

(9) In this section –

'hospital direction' means a direction made under section 59A of the Criminal Procedure (Scotland) Act 1995; and 'transfer for treatment direction' has the meaning given by section 136 of the 2003 Act.

Amendments. Section inserted, in relation to England and Wales: MHA 2007, s 39(2), Sch 5, Pt 1, paras 1, 4.

80C Removal of patients subject to compulsion in the community from Scotland

(1) This section applies to a patient if –

  (a) he is subject to an enactment in force in Scotland by virtue of which regulations under section 289(1) of the Mental Health (Care and Treatment) (Scotland) Act 2003 apply to him; and
  (b) he is removed to England and Wales under those regulations.

(2) He shall be treated as if on the date of his arrival at the place where he is to reside in England or Wales –

  (a) he had been admitted to a hospital in England or Wales in pursuance of an application or order made on that date under the corresponding enactment; and
  (b) a community treatment order had then been made discharging him from the hospital.

(3) For these purposes –

  (a) if the enactment to which the patient was subject in Scotland was an enactment contained in the Mental Health (Care and Treatment) (Scotland) Act 2003, the corresponding enactment is section 3 of this Act;
  (b) if the enactment to which he was subject in Scotland was an enactment contained in the Criminal Procedure (Scotland) Act 1995, the corresponding enactment is section 37 of this Act.

(4) 'The responsible hospital', in the case of a patient in respect of whom a community treatment order is in force by virtue of subsection (2) above, means the hospital to which he is treated as having been admitted by virtue of that subsection, subject to section 19A above.

(5) As soon as practicable after the patient's arrival at the place where he is to reside in England or Wales, the responsible clinician shall specify the conditions to which he is to be subject for the purposes of section 17B(1) above, and the conditions shall be deemed to be specified in the community treatment order.

(6) But the responsible clinician may only specify conditions under subsection (5) above which an approved mental health professional agrees should be specified.

Amendments. Section inserted, in relation to England and Wales: MHA 2007, s 39(2), Sch 5, Pt 1, paras 1, 4.

80D Transfer of conditionally discharged patients from Scotland

(1) This section applies to a patient who is subject to –

    (a)   a restriction order under section 59 of the Criminal Procedure (Scotland) Act 1995; and

    (b)   a conditional discharge under section 193(7) of the Mental Health (Care and Treatment) (Scotland) Act 2003 ('the 2003 Act').

(2) A transfer of the patient to England and Wales under regulations made under section 290 of the 2003 Act shall have effect only if the Secretary of State has consented to the transfer.

(3) If a transfer under those regulations has effect, the patient shall be treated as if –

    (a)   on the date of the transfer he had been conditionally discharged under section 42 or 73 above; and

    (b)   he were subject to a hospital order under section 37 above and a restriction order under section 41 above.

(4) If the restriction order to which the patient was subject immediately before the transfer was of limited duration, the restriction order to which he is subject by virtue of subsection (3) above shall expire on the date on which the first-mentioned order would have expired if the transfer had not been made.

Amendments. Section inserted, in relation to England and Wales: MHA 2007, s 39(2), Sch 5, Pt 1, paras 1, 4.

Removal to and from Northern Ireland

81 Removal of patients to Northern Ireland

(1) If it appears to the Secretary of State, in the case of a patient who is for the time being liable to be detained or subject to guardianship under this Act (otherwise than by virtue of section 35, 36 or 38 above), that it is in the interests of the patient to remove him to Northern Ireland, and that arrangements have been made for admitting him to a hospital or, as the case may be, for receiving him into guardianship there, the Secretary of State may authorise his removal to Northern Ireland and may give any necessary directions for his conveyance to his destination.

(2) Subject to the provisions of subsections (4) and (5) below, where a patient liable to be detained under this Act by virtue of an application, order or direction under any enactment in force in England and Wales is removed under this section and admitted to a hospital in Northern Ireland, he shall be treated as if on the date of his admission he had been so admitted in pursuance of an

application made, or an order or direction made or given, on that date under the corresponding enactment in force in Northern Ireland, and, where he is subject to a hospital order and a restriction order or a transfer direction and a restriction direction under any enactment in this Act, as if he were subject to a hospital order and a restriction order or a transfer direction and a restriction direction under the corresponding enactment in force in Northern Ireland.

(3) Where a patient subject to guardianship under this Act by virtue of an application, order or direction under any enactment in force in England and Wales is removed under this section and received into guardianship in Northern Ireland, he shall be treated as if on the date on which he arrives at the place where he is to reside he had been so received in pursuance of an application, order or direction under the corresponding enactment in force in Northern Ireland, and as if the application had been accepted or, as the case may be, the order or direction had been made or given on that date.

(4) Where a person removed under this section was immediately before his removal liable to be detained by virtue of an application for admission for assessment under this Act, he shall, on his admission to a hospital in Northern Ireland, be treated as if he had been admitted to the hospital in pursuance of an application for assessment under Article 4 of the Mental Health (Northern Ireland) Order 1986 made on the date of his admission.

(5) Where a person removed under this section was immediately before his removal liable to be detained by virtue of an application for admission for treatment under this Act, he shall, on his admission to a hospital in Northern Ireland, be treated as if he were detained for treatment under Part II of the Mental Health (Northern Ireland) Order 1986 by virtue of a report under Article 12(1) of that Order made on the date of his admission.

(6) Where a patient removed under this section was immediately before his removal liable to be detained under this Act by virtue of a transfer direction given while he was serving a sentence of imprisonment (within the meaning of section 47(5) above) imposed by a court in England and Wales, he shall be treated as if the sentence had been imposed by a court in Northern Ireland.

(7) Where a person removed under this section was immediately before his removal subject to a restriction direction of limited duration, the restriction direction to which he is subject by virtue of subsection (2) above shall expire on the date on which the first-mentioned restriction direction would have expired if he had not been so removed.

(8) In this section 'hospital' has the same meaning as in the (Northern Ireland) Order 1986.

Amendments. Words in subss (4), (5), (7), (8) substituted: Mental Health (Northern Ireland Consequential Amendments) Order 1986, SI 1986 No. 596, art 2(1), (3)–(6). Words in subs (2) substituted: MHA 2007, s 39(2), Sch 5, Pt 1, paras 1, 5. Words in subs (7) repealed: MHA 2007, ss 40(4), 55, Sch 11, Pt 8.

81ZA Removal of community patients to Northern Ireland

(1) Section 81 above shall apply in the case of a community patient as it applies in the case of a patient who is for the time being liable to be detained under this Act, as if the community patient were so liable.

(2) Any reference in that section to the application, order or direction by virtue of which a patient is liable to be detained under this Act shall be construed, for these purposes, as a reference to the application, order or direction under this Act in respect of the patient.

Amendments. Section inserted: MHA 2007, s 39(2), Sch 5, Pt 1, paras 1, 6.

81A Transfer of responsibility for patients to Northern Ireland

(1) If it appears to the Secretary of State, in the case of a patient who –

   (a) is subject to a hospital order under section 37 above and a restriction order under section 41 above or to a transfer direction under section 47 above and a restriction direction under section 49 above; and
   (b) has been conditionally discharged under section 42 or 73 above, that a transfer under this section would be in the interests of the patient, the Secretary of State may, with the consent of the Minister exercising corresponding functions in Northern Ireland, transfer responsibility for the patient to that Minister.

(2) Where responsibility for such a patient is transferred under this section, the patient shall be treated –

   (a) as if on the date of the transfer he had been conditionally discharged under the corresponding enactment in force in Northern Ireland; and
   (b) as if he were subject to a restriction order or restriction direction a hospital order and a restriction order, or to a transfer direction and a restriction direction, under the corresponding enactment in force in Northern Ireland.

(3) Where a patient responsibility for whom is transferred under this section was immediately before the transfer subject to a restriction direction of limited duration, the restriction direction to which he is subject by virtue of subsection (2) above shall expire on the date on which the first-mentioned order or direction would have expired if the transfer had not been made.

Amendments. Section inserted: Crime (Sentences) Act 1997, s 48, Sch 3, para 2. Subs (1)(a) and words in subs (2)(b) substituted: MHA 2007, s 39(2), Sch 5, Pt 1, paras 1, 7(1)–(3). Words in subs (3) repealed: MHA 2007, ss 40(5)(a), (b), 55, Sch 11, Pt 8.

Note. In subs (3) the words 'restriction order or' are repealed because, when the 2007 Act comes into force, all restriction orders will be without limit of time, but the provision does apply to time limited restriction orders made prior to the 2007 Act coming into force as well as to orders made outside England and Wales, which have the effect of a time limited restriction order.

82 Removal to England and Wales of patients from Northern Ireland

(1) If it appears to the responsible authority, in the case of a patient who is for the time being liable to be detained or subject to guardianship under the (Northern Ireland) Order 1986 (otherwise than by virtue of Article 42, 43 or 45 of that Order), that it is in the interests of the patient to remove him to England and Wales, and that arrangements have been made for admitting him to a hospital or, as the case may be, for receiving him into guardianship there, the responsible authority may authorise his removal to England and Wales and may give any necessary directions for his conveyance to his destination.

(2) Subject to the provisions of subsections (4) and (4A) below, where a patient who is liable to be detained under the Mental Health (Northern Ireland) Order 1986 by virtue of an application, order or direction under any enactment in force in Northern Ireland is removed under this section and admitted to a hospital in England and Wales, he shall be treated as if on the date of his admission he had been so admitted in pursuance of an application made, or an order or direction made or given, on that date under the corresponding enactment in force in England and Wales and, where he is subject to a hospital order and a restriction order or a transfer direction and a restriction direction under any enactment in that Order, as if he were subject to a hospital order and a restriction order or a transfer direction and a restriction direction under the corresponding enactment in force in England and Wales.

(3) Where a patient subject to guardianship under the Mental Health (Northern Ireland) Order 1986 by virtue of an application, order or direction under any enactment in force in Northern Ireland is removed under this section and received into guardianship in England and Wales, he shall be treated as if on the date on which he arrives at the place where he is to reside he had been so received in pursuance of an application, order or direction under the corresponding enactment in force in England and Wales and as if the application had been accepted or, as the case may be, the order or direction had been made or given on that date.

(4) Where a person removed under this section was immediately before his removal liable to be detained for treatment by virtue of a report under Article 12(1) or 13 of the Mental Health (Northern Ireland) Order 1986, he shall be treated, on his admission to a hospital in England and Wales, as if he had been admitted to the hospital in pursuance of an application for admission for treatment made on the date of his admission.

(4A) Where a person removed under this section was immediately before his removal liable to be detained by virtue of an application for assessment under Article 4 of the Mental Health (Northern Ireland) Order 1986, he shall be treated, on his admission to a hospital in England and Wales, as if he had been admitted to the hospital in pursuance of an application for admission for assessment made on the date of his admission.

(5) Where a patient removed under this section was immediately before his removal liable to be detained under the Mental Health (Northern Ireland) Order 1986 by virtue of a transfer direction given while he was serving a

sentence of imprisonment (within the meaning of Article 53(5) of that Order) imposed by a court in Northern Ireland, he shall be treated as if the sentence had been imposed by a court in England and Wales.

(6) Where a person removed under this section was immediately before his removal subject to a restriction order or restriction direction of limited duration, the restriction order or restriction direction to which he is subject by virtue of subsection (2) above shall expire on the date on which the first-mentioned restriction order or restriction direction would have expired if he had not been so removed.

(7) In this section 'the responsible authority' means the Department of Health and Social Services for Northern Ireland or, in relation to a patient who is subject to a restriction order or restriction direction, the Department of Justice in Northern Ireland.

Amendments. Words in subss (1)–(3), (5)–(7) substituted: Mental Health (Northern Ireland Consequential Amendments) Order 1986, SI 1986 No. 596, arts 2(1), (7)–(9), (11)–(13). Subss (4), (4A): substituted, for sub-s (4) as originally enacted: SI 1986 No. 596, art 2(1), (10). Words in subs (2) substituted: MHA 2007, s 39(2), Sch 5, Pt 1, paras 1, 8. Words in subs (7) substituted: Northern Ireland Act 1998 (Devolution of Policing and Justice Functions) Order 2010, SI 2010 No. 976, art 12, Sch 14, para 28(1), (2).

82A Transfer of responsibility for conditionally discharged patients to England and Wales from Northern Ireland

(1) If it appears to the Department of Justice in Northern Ireland, in the case of a patient who –

   (a)   is subject to a restriction order or restriction direction under Article 47(1) or 55(1) of the Mental Health (Northern Ireland) Order 1986; and
   (b)   has been conditionally discharged under Article 48(2) or 78(2) of that Order,

that a transfer under this section would be in the interests of the patient, the Department of Justice in Northern Ireland may, with the consent of the Secretary of State, transfer responsibility for the patient to the Secretary of State.

(2) Where responsibility for such a patient is transferred under this section, the patient shall be treated –

   (a)   as if on the date of the transfer he had been conditionally discharged under section 42 or 73 above; and
   (b)   as if he were subject to a hospital order under section 37 above and a restriction order under section 41 above or to a transfer direction under section 47 above and a restriction direction under section 49 above.

(3) Where a patient responsibility for whom is transferred under this section was immediately before the transfer subject to a restriction order or restriction direction of limited duration, the restriction order or restriction direction to

which he is subject by virtue of subsection (2) above shall expire on the date on which the first-mentioned order or direction would have expired if the transfer had not been made.

(4) (*repealed*)

Amendments. Section inserted: Crime (Sentences) Act 1997, s 48, Sch 3, para 3. Section heading and subs (2)(b) substituted: MHA 2007, s 39(2), Sch 5, Pt 1, paras 1, 9. Words in subss (1) substituted and sub-s (4) repealed: Northern Ireland Act 1998 (Devolution of Policing and Justice Functions) Order 2010, SI 2010 No. 976, art 12, Sch 14, para 28(1), (3)(a), (b).

Removal to and from Channel Islands and Isle of Man

83 Removal of patients to Channel Islands or Isle of Man

If it appears to the Secretary of State, in the case of a patient who is for the time being liable to be detained or subject to guardianship under this Act (otherwise than by virtue of section 35, 36 or 38 above), that it is in the interests of the patient to remove him to any of the Channel Islands or to the Isle of Man, and that arrangements have been made for admitting him to a hospital or, as the case may be, for receiving him into guardianship there, the Secretary of State may authorise his removal to the island in question and may give any necessary directions for his conveyance to his destination.

83ZA Removal or transfer of community patients to Channel Islands or Isle of Man

(1) Section 83 above shall apply in the case of a community patient as it applies in the case of a patient who is for the time being liable to be detained under this Act, as if the community patient were so liable.

(2) But if there are in force in any of the Channel Islands or the Isle of Man enactments ('relevant enactments') corresponding or similar to those relating to community patients in this Act –

  (a) subsection (1) above shall not apply as regards that island; and
  (b) subsections (3) to (6) below shall apply instead.

(3) If it appears to the appropriate national authority, in the case of a community patient, that the conditions mentioned in subsection (4) below are met, the authority may authorise the transfer of responsibility for him to the island in question.

(4) The conditions are –

  (a) a transfer under subsection (3) above is in the patient's interests; and
  (b) arrangements have been made for dealing with him under the relevant enactments.

(5) But the authority may not act under subsection (3) above while the patient is recalled to hospital under section 17E above.

(6) In this section, 'the appropriate national authority' means –

(a)   in relation to a community patient in respect of whom the responsible hospital is in England, the Secretary of State;

(b)   in relation to a community patient in respect of whom the responsible hospital is in Wales, the Welsh Ministers.

Amendments. Section inserted: MHA 2007, s 39(2), Sch 5, Pt 1, paras 1, 10.

83A   Transfer of responsibility for conditionally discharged patients to Channel Islands or Isle of Man

If it appears to the Secretary of State, in the case of a patient who –

(a)   is subject to a restriction order or restriction direction under section 41 or 49 above; and

(b)   has been conditionally discharged under section 42 or 73 above, that a transfer under this section would be in the interests of the patient, the Secretary of State may, with the consent of the authority exercising corresponding functions in any of the Channel Islands or in the Isle of Man, transfer responsibility for the patient to that authority.

Amendments. Section inserted: Crime (Sentences) Act 1997, s 48, Sch 3, para 4. Section heading substituted: Mental Health Act 2007, s 39(2), Sch 5, Pt 1, paras 1, 10.

84   Removal to England and Wales of offenders found insane in Channel Islands and Isle of Man

(1) The Secretary of State may by warrant direct that any offender found by a court in any of the Channel Islands or in the Isle of Man to be insane or to have been insane at the time of the alleged offence, and ordered to be detained during Her Majesty's pleasure, be removed to a hospital in England and Wales.

(2) A patient removed under subsection (1) above shall, on his reception into the hospital in England and Wales, be treated as if he were subject to a hospital order together with a restriction order.

(3) The Secretary of State may by warrant direct that any patient removed under this section from any of the Channel Islands or from the Isle of Man be returned to the island from which he was so removed, there to be dealt with according to law in all respects as if he had not been removed under this section.

Amendments. Words in subs (2) substituted: Domestic Violence, Crime and Victims Act 2004, s 58(1), Sch 10, para 22. Words in subs (2) repealed: MHA 2007, ss 40(3)(b), 55, Sch 11, Pt 8.

85   Patients removed from Channel Islands or Isle of Man

(1) This section applies to any patient who is removed to England and Wales from any of the Channel Islands or the Isle of Man under a provision corresponding to section 83 above and who immediately before his removal was liable to be detained or subject to guardianship in the island in question under a provision corresponding to an enactment contained in this Act (other than section 35, 36 or 38 above).

(2) Where the patient is admitted to a hospital in England and Wales he shall be treated as if on the date of his admission he had been so admitted in pursuance of an application made, or an order or direction made or given, on that date under the corresponding enactment contained in this Act and, where he is subject to an order or direction restricting his discharge, as if he were subject to a restriction order or restriction direction to a hospital order and a restriction order or to a hospital direction and a limitation direction or to a transfer direction and a restriction direction.

(3) Where the patient is received into guardianship in England and Wales, he shall be treated as if on the date on which he arrives at the place where he is to reside he had been so received in pursuance of an application, order or direction under the corresponding enactment contained in this Act and as if the application had been accepted or, as the case may be, the order or direction had been made or given on that date.

(4) Where the patient was immediately before his removal liable to be detained by virtue of a transfer direction given while he was serving a sentence of imprisonment imposed by a court in the island in question, he shall be treated as if the sentence had been imposed by a court in England and Wales.

(5) Where the patient was immediately before his removal subject to an order or direction restricting his discharge, being an order or direction of limited duration, the restriction order or restriction direction to which he is subject by virtue of subsection (2) above shall expire on the date on which the first-mentioned order or direction would have expired if he had not been removed.

(6) While being conveyed to the hospital referred to in subsection (2) or, as the case may be, the place referred to in subsection (3) above, the patient shall be deemed to be in legal custody, and section 138 below shall apply to him as if he were in legal custody by virtue of section 137 below.

(7) In the case of a patient removed from the Isle of Man the reference in subsection (4) above to a person serving a sentence of imprisonment includes a reference to a person detained as mentioned in section 60(6)(a) of the Mental Health Act 1974 (an Act of Tynwald).

Amendment. Words in subs (2) substituted: MHA 2007, s 39(2), Sch 5, Pt 1, paras 1, 11.

85ZA Responsibility for community patients transferred from Channel Islands or Isle of Man

(1) This section shall have effect if there are in force in any of the Channel Islands or the Isle of Man enactments ('relevant enactments') corresponding or similar to those relating to community patients in this Act.

(2) If responsibility for a patient is transferred to England or Wales under a provision corresponding to section 83ZA(3) above, he shall be treated as if on the date of his arrival at the place where he is to reside in England or Wales –

    (a)   he had been admitted to the hospital in pursuance of an application made, or an order or direction made or given, on that date under the enactment in force in England and Wales which most closely corresponds to the relevant enactments; and

(b)   a community treatment order had then been made discharging him from the hospital.

(3) 'The responsible hospital', in his case, means the hospital to which he is treated as having been admitted by virtue of subsection (2), subject to section 19A above.

(4) As soon as practicable after the patient's arrival at the place where he is to reside in England or Wales, the responsible clinician shall specify the conditions to which he is to be subject for the purposes of section 17B(1) above, and the conditions shall be deemed to be specified in the community treatment order.

(5) But the responsible clinician may only specify conditions under subsection (4) above which an approved mental health professional agrees should be specified.

Amendment. Section inserted: MHA 2007, s 39(2), Sch 5, Pt 1, paras 1, 12.

85A Responsibility for conditionally discharged patients transferred from Channel Islands or Isle of Man

(1) This section applies to any patient responsibility for whom is transferred to the Secretary of State by the authority exercising corresponding functions in any of the Channel Islands or the Isle of Man under a provision corresponding to section 83A above.

(2) The patient shall be treated –

(a)   as if on the date of the transfer he had been conditionally discharged under section 42 or 73 above; and

(b)   as if he were subject to a hospital order under section 37 above and a restriction order under section 41 above, or to a hospital direction and a limitation direction under section 45A above, or to a transfer direction under section 47 above and a restriction direction under section 49 above.

(3) Where the patient was immediately before the transfer subject to an order or direction restricting his discharge, being an order or direction of limited duration, the restriction order, limitation direction or restriction direction to which he is subject by virtue of subsection (2) above shall expire on the date on which the first-mentioned order or direction would have expired if the transfer had not been made.

Amendments. Section inserted: Crime (Sentences) Act 1997, s 48, Sch 3, para 5. Section heading substituted: MHA 2007, s 39(2), Sch 5, para 12. Subs (2)(b) substituted: MHA 2007, s 39(2), Sch 5, Pt 1, paras 1, 13(1), (2). Words in subs (3) inserted: MHA 2007, s 39(1), Sch 5, Pt 1, paras 1, 13(1), (3).

Removal of aliens

86 Removal of alien patients

(1) This section applies to any patient who is neither a British citizen nor a Commonwealth citizen having the right of abode in the United Kingdom by virtue of section 2(1)(b) of the Immigration Act 1971, being a patient who is receiving treatment for mental disorder as an in-patient in a hospital in England and Wales or a hospital within the meaning of the Mental Health (Northern Ireland) Order 1986 and is detained pursuant to –

   (a)   an application for admission for treatment or a report under Article 12(1) or 13 of that Order;
   (b)   a hospital order under section 37 above or Article 44 of that Order; or
   (c)   an order or direction under this Act (other than under section 35, 36 or 38 above) or under that Order (other than under Article 42, 43 or 45 of that Order) having the same effect as such a hospital order.

(2) If it appears to the Secretary of State that proper arrangements have been made for the removal of a patient to whom this section applies to a country or territory outside the United Kingdom, the Isle of Man and the Channel Islands and for his care or treatment there and that it is in the interests of the patient to remove him, the Secretary of State may, subject to subsection (3) below –

   (a)   by warrant authorise the removal of the patient from the place where he is receiving treatment as mentioned in subsection (1) above, and
   (b)   give such directions as the Secretary of State thinks fit for the conveyance of the patient to his destination in that country or territory and for his detention in any place or on board any ship or aircraft until his arrival at any specified port or place in any such country or territory.

(3) The Secretary of State shall not exercise his powers under subsection (2) above in the case of any patient except with the approval of the appropriate tribunal or, as the case may be, of the Mental Health Review Tribunal for Northern Ireland.

(4) In relation to a patient receiving treatment in a hospital within the meaning of the Mental Health (Northern Ireland) Order 1986, the reference in subsection (1) above to mental disorder shall be construed in accordance with that Order and any reference in subsection (2) or (3) to the Secretary of State shall be construed as a reference to the Department of Justice in Northern Ireland.

Amendments. Words in subs (1) (1)(c) substituted: Mental Health (Northern Ireland Consequential Amendments) Order 1986, SI 1986 No. 596, art 2(14). Words in subs (1) substituted and subs (4) inserted: MHA 2007, s 1(4), Sch 1, Pt 1, paras 1, 15(1)–(3). Words in subs (3) substituted: Transfer of Tribunal Functions Order 2008, SI 2008 No. 2833, art 9(1), Sch 3, paras 39, 62. Words in subs (4) inserted: Northern Ireland Act 1998 (Devolution of Policing and Justice Functions) Order 2010, SI 2010 No. 976, art 12, Sch 14, para 28(1), (4).

Return of patients absent without leave

87 Patients absent from hospitals in Northern Ireland

(1) Any person who –

  (a)   under Article 29 or 132 of the Mental Health (Northern Ireland) Order 1986 (which provide, respectively, for the retaking of patients absent without leave and for the retaking of patients escaping from custody); or

  (b)   under the said Article 29 as applied by Article 31 of the said Order (which makes special provision as to persons sentenced to imprisonment);

may be taken into custody in Northern Ireland, may be taken into custody in, and returned to Northern Ireland from, England and Wales by an approved mental health professional, by any constable or by any person authorised by or by virtue of the said Order to take him into custody.

(2) This section does not apply to any person who is subject to guardianship.

Amendments. Words in subs (1) substituted: Mental Health (Northern Ireland Consequential Amendments) Order 1986, SI 1986 No. 596, art 2(15). Words in subs (1) substituted: MHA 2007, s 21, Sch 2, paras 1, 7(f).

88 *(repealed)*

Amendments. Section repealed: Adult Support and Protection (Scotland) Act 2007, s 74.

89 Patients absent from hospitals in the Channel Islands or Isle of Man

(1) Any person who under any provision corresponding to section 18 above or 138 below may be taken into custody in any of the Channel Islands or the Isle of Man may be taken into custody in, and returned to the island in question from, England and Wales by an approved mental health professional or a constable.

(2) This section does not apply to any person who is subject to guardianship.

Amendments. Words in subs (1) substituted: MHA 2007, s 21, Sch 2, paras 1, 7(h).

General

90 Regulations for purposes of Part VI

Section 32 above shall have effect as if references in that section to Part II of this Act included references to this Part of this Act, so far as this Part of this Act applies to patients removed to England and Wales or for whom responsibility is transferred to England and Wales.

Amendments. Words substituted: MHA 2007, s 39(2), Sch 5, Pt 1, paras 1, 15.

91 General provisions as to patients removed from England and Wales

(1) Subject to subsection (2) below, where a patient liable to be detained or subject to guardianship by virtue of an application, order or direction under Part II or III of this Act (other than section 35, 36 or 38 above) is removed from England and Wales in pursuance of arrangements under this Part of this Act, the application, order or direction shall cease to have effect when he is duly received into a hospital or other institution, or placed under guardianship or, where he is not received into a hospital but his detention in hospital is authorised by virtue of the Mental Health (Care and Treatment) (Scotland) Act 2003 or the Criminal Procedure (Scotland) Act 1995, in pursuance of those arrangements.

(2) Where the Secretary of State exercises his powers under section 86(2) above in respect of a patient who is detained pursuant to a hospital order under section 37 above and in respect of whom a restriction order is in force, those orders shall continue in force so as to apply to the patient if he returns to England and Wales.

(2A) Where responsibility for a community patient is transferred to a jurisdiction outside England and Wales (or such a patient is removed outside England and Wales) in pursuance of arrangements under this Part of this Act, the application, order or direction mentioned in subsection (1) above in force in respect of him shall cease to have effect on the date on which responsibility is so transferred (or he is so removed) in pursuance of those arrangements.

(3) Reference in this section to a patient's detention in hospital being authorised by virtue of the Mental Health (Care and Treatment) (Scotland) Act 2003 or the Criminal Procedure (Scotland) Act 1995 shall be read as including references to a patient in respect of whom a certificate under one of the provisions listed in section 290(7)(a) of the Act of 2003 is in operation.

Amendment. Words in subs (1) and subs 3 inserted, in relation to England and Wales: Mental Health (Care and Treatment) (Scotland) Act 2003 (Consequential Provisions) Order 2005, SI 2005 No. 2078, art 15, Sch 1, para 2(1), (7)(a), (b). Words in subs (2) repealed: MHA 2007, ss 40(6), 55, Sch 11, Pt 8. Subs (2A) inserted: MHA 2007, s 39(2), Sch 5, Pt 1, paras 1, 16.

92 Interpretation of Part VI

(1) References in this Part of this Act to a hospital, being a hospital in England and Wales, shall be construed as references to a hospital within the meaning of Part II of this Act.

(1A) References in this Part of this Act to the responsible clinician shall be construed as references to the responsible clinician within the meaning of Part 2 of this Act.

(2) Where a patient is treated by virtue of this Part of this Act as if he had been removed to a hospital in England and Wales in pursuance of a direction under Part III of this Act, that direction shall be deemed to have been given on the date of his reception into the hospital.

(3) (*repealed*)

(4) Sections 80 to 85A above shall have effect as if –

    (a)   any hospital direction under section 45A above were a transfer direction under section 47 above; and

    (b)   any limitation direction under section 45A above were a restriction direction under section 49 above.

(5) Sections 80(5), 81(6) and 85(4) above shall have effect as if any reference to a transfer direction given while a patient was serving a sentence of imprisonment imposed by a court included a reference to a hospital direction given by a court after imposing a sentence of imprisonment on a patient.

Amendments. Subss (4), (5) inserted: Crime (Sentences) Act 1997, s 55, Sch 4, para 12(16). Subs (1A) inserted: MHA 2007, s 39(2), Sch 5, Pt 1, paras 1, 17. Subs (3) repealed: MHA 2007, s 55, Sch 11, Pt 1.

PART VII (*REPEALED*)

Amendments. Part repealed: Mental Capacity Act 2005, ss 66(1)(a), (2), 67(2), Sch 7.

PART VIII
MISCELLANEOUS FUNCTIONS OF LOCAL AUTHORITIES AND THE SECRETARY OF STATE

Approved mental health professionals

Amendments. Cross heading substituted: Mental Health Act 2007, s 18.

114 Approval by local social services authority

(1) A local social services authority may approve a person to act as an approved mental health professional for the purposes of this Act.

(2) But a local social services authority may not approve a registered medical practitioner to act as an approved mental health professional.

(3) Before approving a person under subsection (1) above, a local social services authority shall be satisfied that he has appropriate competence in dealing with persons who are suffering from mental disorder.

(4) The appropriate national authority may by regulations make provision in connection with the giving of approvals under subsection (1) above.

(5) The provision which may be made by regulations under subsection (4) above includes, in particular, provision as to –

    (a)   the period for which approvals under subsection (1) above have effect;
    (b)   the courses to be undertaken by persons before such approvals are to be given and during the period for which such approvals have effect;
    (c)   the conditions subject to which such approvals are to be given; and
    (d)   the factors to be taken into account in determining whether persons have appropriate competence as mentioned in subsection (3) above.

(6) Provision made by virtue of subsection (5)(b) above may relate to courses approved or provided by such person as may be specified in the regulations (as well as to courses approved under section 114A below).

(7) An approval by virtue of subsection (6) above may be in respect of a course in general or in respect of a course in relation to a particular person.

(8) The power to make regulations under subsection (4) above includes power to make different provision for different cases or areas.

(9) In this section 'the appropriate national authority' means –

    (a)   in relation to persons who are or wish to become approved to act as approved mental health professionals by a local social services authority whose area is in England, the Secretary of State;

    (b)   in relation to persons who are or wish to become approved to act as approved mental health professionals by a local social services authority whose area is in Wales, the Welsh Ministers.

(10) In this Act 'approved mental health professional' means –

    (a)   in relation to acting on behalf of a local social services authority whose area is in England, a person approved under subsection (1) above by any local social services authority whose area is in England, and

    (b)   in relation to acting on behalf of a local social services authority whose area is in Wales, a person approved under that subsection by any local social services authority whose area is in Wales.'

Amendment. Section substituted: MHA 2007, s 18.

114A Approval of courses etc for approved mental health professionals

(1) The relevant Council may, in accordance with rules made by it, approve courses for persons who are or wish to become approved mental health professionals.

(2) For that purpose –

    (a)   subsections (2) to (4)(a) and (7) of section 63 of the Care Standards Act 2000 apply as they apply to approvals given, rules made and courses approved under that section; and

    (b)   sections 66 and 71 of that Act apply accordingly.

(3) In subsection (1), 'the relevant Council' means –

    (a)   in relation to persons who are or wish to become approved to act as approved mental health professionals by a local social services authority whose area is in England, the General Social Care Council;

    (b)   in relation to persons who are or wish to become approved to act as approved mental health professionals by a local social services authority whose area is in Wales, the Care Council for Wales.

(4) The functions of an approved mental health professional shall not be considered to be relevant social work for the purposes of Part 4 of the Care Standards Act 2000.

(5) The General Social Care Council and the Care Council for Wales may also carry out, or assist other persons in carrying out, research into matters relevant to training for approved mental health professionals.

Amendment. Section inserted: MHA 2007, s 19.

115 Powers of entry and inspection

(1) An approved mental health professional may at all reasonable times enter and inspect any premises (other than a hospital) in which a mentally disordered patient is living, if he has reasonable cause to believe that the patient is not under proper care.

(2) The power under subsection (1) above shall be exercisable only after the professional has produced, if asked to do so, some duly authenticated document showing that he is an approved mental health professional.

Amendment. Section substituted: MHA 2007, s 21, Sch 2, paras 1, 8.

Visiting patients

116 Welfare of certain hospital patients

(1) Where a patient to whom this section applies is admitted to a hospital, independent hospital or care home in England and Wales (whether for treatment for mental disorder or for any other reason) then, without prejudice to their duties in relation to the patient apart from the provisions of this section, the authority shall arrange for visits to be made to him on behalf of the authority, and shall take such other steps in relation to the patient while in the hospital, independent hospital or care home as would be expected to be taken by his parents.

(2) This section applies to –

    (a)   a child or young person –
        (i)   who is in the care of a local authority by virtue of a care order within the meaning of the Children Act 1989, or
        (ii)   in respect of whom the rights and powers of a parent are vested in a local authority by virtue of section 16 of the Social Work (Scotland) Act 1968;
    (b)   a person who is subject to the guardianship of a local social services authority under the provisions of this Act; or
    (c)   a person the functions of whose nearest relative under this Act are for the time being transferred to a local social services authority.

Amendments. Subs (2)(a) substituted: Courts and Legal Services Act 1990, s 116, Sch 16, para 42. Words in subs (1) substituted, in relation to England and Wales: Care Standards Act 2000, s 116, Sch 4, para 9(1), (5). Words in subs (2)(b), (c) repealed in relation to England and Wales: Mental Health (Care and Treatment) (Scotland) Act 2003 (Consequential Provisions) Order 2005, SI 2005 No. 2078, art 16(1), Sch 3 and in relation to Scotland by virtue of SSI 2005/465, art 3, Sch 2.

After-care

117 After-care

(1) This section applies to persons who are detained under section 3 above, or admitted to a hospital in pursuance of a hospital order made under section 37 above, or transferred to a hospital in pursuance of a hospital direction made under section 45A above or a transfer direction made under section 47 or 48 above, and then cease to be detained and (whether or not immediately after so ceasing) leave hospital.

(2) It shall be the duty of the Primary Care Trust or Local Health Board and of the local social services authority to provide, in co-operation with relevant voluntary agencies, after-care services for any person to whom this section applies until such time as the Primary Care Trust or Local Health Board and the local social services authority are satisfied that the person concerned is no longer in need of such services; but they shall not be so satisfied in the case of a community patient while he remains such a patient.

(2A) *(repealed)*

(2B) Section 32 above shall apply for the purposes of this section as it applies for the purposes of Part II of this Act.

(2C) References in this Act to after-care services provided for a patient under this section include references to services provided for the patient –

    (a)   in respect of which direct payments are made under regulations under section 57 of the Health and Social Care Act 2001 or section 12A(4) of the National Health Service Act 2006, and

    (b)   which would be provided under this section apart from the regulations.

(3) In this section 'the Primary Care Trust or Local Health Board' means the Primary Care Trust or Local Health Board, and 'the local social services authority' means the local social services authority, for the area in which the person concerned is resident or to which he is sent on discharge by the hospital in which he was detained.

Amendments. Words in subs (3) substituted: Health Authorities Act 1995, s 2(1), Sch 1, para 107(1), (8)(b). Subss (2A), (2B) and words in subss (1), (2) inserted: Mental Health (Patients in the Community) Act 1995, s 1(2), Sch 1, para 15(1)–(4). Words in subs (1) inserted: Crime (Sentences) Act 1997, s 55, Sch 4, para 12(17). Words in subss (2), (3) inserted: National Health Service Reform and Health Care Professions Act 2002, s 2(5), Sch 2, Pt 2, paras 42, 47. Words in subs (2) substituted: MHA 2007, s 32(4), Sch 3, paras 1, 24. Subs (2A) repealed: MHA 2007, s 55, Sch 11, Pt 5. Words in subs (2), (3) substituted: References to Health Authorities Order 2007, SI 2007 No. 961, art 3, Schedule, para 13(1), (9). Subs (2C): inserted: Health Act 2009, s 13, Sch 1, para 3.

Note. Existing subs (2A) provides that: '(2A) It shall be the duty of the Primary Care Trust or Local Health Board to secure that at all times while a patient is subject to after-care under supervision – (a) a person who is a registered medical practitioner approved for the purposes of section 12 above by the Secretary of State as having special experience in the diagnosis or treatment of mental disorder is in charge of the medical treatment provided for the patient as part of the after-care services provided for him under this section; and (b) a person professionally concerned with any of the after-care services so provided is supervising him with a view to securing that he receives the after-care services so provided.'

Functions of the Secretary of State

118 Code of practice

(1) The Secretary of State shall prepare, and from time to time revise, a code of practice –

    (a)   for the guidance of registered medical practitioners, approved clinicians, managers and staff of hospitals, independent hospitals and care homes and approved mental health professionals in relation to the admission of patients to hospitals and registered establishments under this Act and to guardianship and community patients under this Act; and

    (b)   for the guidance of registered medical practitioners and members of other professions in relation to the medical treatment of patients suffering from mental disorder.

(2) The code shall, in particular, specify forms of medical treatment in addition to any specified by regulations made for the purposes of section 57 above which in the opinion of the Secretary of State give rise to special concern and which should accordingly not be given by a registered medical practitioner unless the patient has consented to the treatment (or to a plan of treatment including that treatment) and a certificate in writing as to the matters mentioned in subsection (2)(a) and (b) of that section has been given by another registered medical practitioner, being a practitioner appointed for the purposes of this section by the regulatory authority.

(2A) The code shall include a statement of the principles which the Secretary of State thinks should inform decisions under this Act.

(2B) In preparing the statement of principles the Secretary of State shall, in particular, ensure that each of the following matters is addressed –

    (a)   respect for patients' past and present wishes and feelings,
    (b)   respect for diversity generally including, in particular, diversity of religion, culture and sexual orientation (within the meaning of section 35 of the Equality Act 2006),
    (c)   minimising restrictions on liberty,
    (d)   involvement of patients in planning, developing and delivering care and treatment appropriate to them,
    (e)   avoidance of unlawful discrimination,
    (f)   effectiveness of treatment,
    (g)   views of carers and other interested parties,
    (h)   patient wellbeing and safety, and
    (i)   public safety.

(2C) The Secretary of State shall also have regard to the desirability of ensuring –

    (a)   the efficient use of resources, and
    (b)   the equitable distribution of services.

(2D) In performing functions under this Act persons mentioned in subsection (1)(a) or (b) shall have regard to the code.'

(3) Before preparing the code or making any alteration in it the Secretary of State shall consult such bodies as appear to him to be concerned.

(4) The Secretary of State shall lay copies of the code and of any alteration in the code before Parliament; and if either House of Parliament passes a resolution requiring the code or any alteration in it to be withdrawn the Secretary of State shall withdraw the code or alteration and, where he withdraws the code, shall prepare a code in substitution for the one which is withdrawn.

(5) No resolution shall be passed by either House of Parliament under subsection (4) above in respect of a code or alteration after the expiration of the period of 40 days beginning with the day on which a copy of the code or alteration was laid before that House; but for the purposes of this subsection no account shall be taken of any time during which Parliament is dissolved or prorogued or during which both Houses are adjourned for more than four days.

(6) The Secretary of State shall publish the code as for the time being in force.

(7) The Care Quality Commission may at any time make proposals to the Secretary of State as to the content of the code of practice which the Secretary of State must prepare, and from time to time revise, under this section in relation to England.

Amendments. Words in subs (1)(a) inserted: Mental Health (Patients in the Community) Act 1995, s 1(2), Sch 1, para 16. Words in subs (1)(a) substituted: Care Standards Act 2000, s 116, Sch 4, para 9(1), (6). Words in subs (1) inserted: MHA 2007, s 14(1), (2). Words in subs (1)(a) substituted: MHA 2007, s 21, Sch 2, paras 1, 9. Words in subs (1)(a) substituted: MHA 2007, s 32(4), Sch 3, paras 1, 25. Subss (2A)–(2D) inserted: MHA 2007, s 8.

119 Practitioners approved for Part IV and s 118

(1) The regulatory authority may make such provision as it may with the approval of the Treasury determine for the payment of remuneration, allowances, pensions or gratuities to or in respect of registered medical practitioners appointed by the authority for the purposes of Part IV of this Act and section 118 above and to or in respect of other persons appointed for the purposes of section 57(2)(a) above.

(2) A registered medical practitioner or other person appointed for the purposes of the provisions mentioned in subsection (1) above may, for the purpose of exercising his functions under those provisions or under Part 4A of this Act, at any reasonable time –

    (a)   visit and interview and, in the case of a registered medical practitioner, examine in private any patient detained in a hospital or registered establishment or any community patient in a hospital or regulated establishment (other than a hospital) or (if access is granted) other place; and

(b) require the production of and inspect any records relating to the treatment of the patient there.

(3) In this section 'regulated establishment' means –

(a) an establishment in respect of which a person is registered under Part 2 of the Care Standards Act 2000; or

(b) premises used for the carrying on of a regulated activity, within the meaning of Part 1 of the Health and Social Care Act 2008, in respect of which a person is registered under Chapter 2 of that Part.

Amendments. Words in subs (1) substituted: Health and Social Care Act 2008, s 52(5), Sch 3, paras 1, 7(1), (2)(a)–(c). Words in subs (2) repealed: Health and Social Care Act 2008, ss 52(5), 166, Sch 3, paras 1, 7(1), (3), Sch 15, Pt 1. Words in subs (2) inserted: MHA 2007, s 35(2)(a)(i). Words in subs (2)(a) substituted: MHA 2007, s 35(2)(a)(ii). Words in subs (2)(b) substituted: MHA 2007, s 35(2)(a)(iii). Subs (3) and words in subs (2)(a) substituted: Health and Social Care Act 2008 (Consequential Amendments No 2) Order 2010, SI 2010 No. 813, art 5(1), (4)(a), (b).

120 General protection of relevant patients

(1) The regulatory authority must keep under review and, where appropriate, investigate the exercise of the powers and the discharge of the duties conferred or imposed by this Act so far as relating to the detention of patients or their reception into guardianship or to relevant patients.

(2) Relevant patients are –

(a) patients liable to be detained under this Act,
(b) community patients, and
(c) patients subject to guardianship.

(3) The regulatory authority must make arrangements for persons authorised by it to visit and interview relevant patients in private –

(a) in the case of relevant patients detained under this Act, in the place where they are detained, and

(b) in the case of other relevant patients, in hospitals and regulated establishments and, if access is granted, other places.

(4) The regulatory authority must also make arrangements for persons authorised by it to investigate any complaint as to the exercise of the powers or the discharge of the duties conferred or imposed by this Act in respect of a patient who is or has been detained under this Act or who is or has been a relevant patient.

(5) The arrangements made under subsection (4) –

(a) may exclude matters from investigation in specified circumstances, and

(b) do not require any person exercising functions under the arrangements to undertake or continue with any investigation where the person does not consider it appropriate to do so.

(6) Where any such complaint as is mentioned in subsection (4) is made by a Member of Parliament or a member of the National Assembly for Wales, the results of the investigation must be reported to the Member of Parliament or member of the Assembly.

(7) For the purposes of a review or investigation under subsection (1) or the exercise of functions under arrangements made under this section, a person authorised by the regulatory authority may at any reasonable time –

  (a)   visit and interview in private any patient in a hospital or regulated establishment,

  (b)   if the authorised person is a registered medical practitioner or approved clinician, examine the patient in private there, and

  (c)   require the production of and inspect any records relating to the detention or treatment of any person who is or has been detained under this Act or who is or has been a community patient or a patient subject to guardianship.

(8) The regulatory authority may make provision for the payment of remuneration, allowances, pensions or gratuities to or in respect of persons exercising functions in relation to any review or investigation for which it is responsible under subsection (1) or functions under arrangements made by it under this section.

(9) In this section 'regulated establishment' means

  (a)   an establishment in respect of which a person is registered under Part 2 of the Care Standards Act 2000, or

  (b)   premises used for the carrying on of a regulated activity (within the meaning of Part 1 of the Health and Social Care Act 2008) in respect of which a person is registered under Chapter 2 of that Part.

Amendments. Section substituted: Health and Social Care Act 2008, s 52(5), Sch 3, paras 1, 8.

120A Investigation reports

(1) The regulatory authority may publish a report of a review or investigation carried out by it under section 120(1).

(2) The Secretary of State may by regulations make provision as to the procedure to be followed in respect of the making of representations to the Care Quality Commission before the publication of a report by the Commission under subsection (1).

(3) The Secretary of State must consult the Care Quality Commission before making any such regulations.

(4) The Welsh Ministers may by regulations make provision as to the procedure to be followed in respect of the making of representations to them before the publication of a report by them under subsection (1).

Amendments. Section inserted: Health and Social Care Act 2008, s 52(5), Sch 3, paras 1, 9.

120B Action statements

(1) The regulatory authority may direct a person mentioned in subsection (2) to publish a statement as to the action the person proposes to take as a result of a review or investigation under section 120(1).

(2) The persons are –

    (a)   the managers of a hospital within the meaning of Part 2 of this Act;
    (b)   a local social services authority;
    (c)   persons of any other description prescribed in regulations.

(3) Regulations may make further provision about the content and publication of statements under this section.

(4) 'Regulations' means regulations made –

    (a)   by the Secretary of State, in relation to England;
    (b)   by the Welsh Ministers, in relation to Wales.

Amendments. Section inserted: Health and Social Care Act 2008, s 52(5), Sch 3, paras 1, 9.

120C Provision of information

(1) This section applies to the following persons –

    (a)   the managers of a hospital within the meaning of Part 2 of this Act;
    (b)   a local social services authority;
    (c)   persons of any other description prescribed in regulations.

(2) A person to whom this section applies must provide the regulatory authority with such information as the authority may reasonably request for or in connection with the exercise of its functions under section 120.

(3) A person to whom this section applies must provide a person authorised under section 120 with such information as the person so authorised may reasonably request for or in connection with the exercise of functions under arrangements made under that section.

(4) This section is in addition to the requirements of section 120(7)(c).

(5) 'Information' includes documents and records.

(6) 'Regulations' means regulations made –

    (a)   by the Secretary of State, in relation to England;
    (b)   by the Welsh Ministers, in relation to Wales.

Amendments. Section inserted: Health and Social Care Act 2008, s 52(5), Sch 3, paras 1, 9.

120D Annual reports

(1) The regulatory authority must publish an annual report on its activities in the exercise of its functions under this Act.

(2) The report must be published as soon as possible after the end of each financial year.

(3) The Care Quality Commission must send a copy of its annual report to the Secretary of State who must lay the copy before Parliament.

(4) The Welsh Ministers must lay a copy of their annual report before the National Assembly for Wales.

(5) In this section 'financial year' means –

    (a)   the period beginning with the date on which section 52 of the Health and Social Care Act 2008 comes into force and ending with the next 31 March following that date, and

    (b)   each successive period of 12 months ending with 31 March.

Amendments. Section inserted: Health and Social Care Act 2008, s 52(5), Sch 3, paras 1, 9.

121 (*repealed*)

Amendments. Section repealed: Health and Social Care Act 2008, s 166, Sch 15, Pt 1.

122 Provision of pocket money for in-patients in hospital

(1) The Secretary of State may pay to persons who are receiving treatment as inpatients (whether liable to be detained or not) in hospitals wholly or mainly used for the treatment of persons suffering from mental disorder, such amounts as he thinks fit in respect of their occasional personal expenses where it appears to him that they would otherwise be without resources to meet those expenses.

(2) For the purposes of the National Health Service Act 2006 and the National Health Service (Wales) Act 2006, the making of payments under this section to persons for whom hospital services are provided under either of those Acts shall be treated as included among those services.

Amendments. Words 'special hospitals or other hospitals being' in subs (1) repealed: Health Act 1999, s 65, Sch 4, paras 65, 66, Sch 5 (prospective in relation to Scotland: Health Act 1999, s 67(1), (2)). Words in subs (2) substituted: National Health Service (Consequential Provisions) Act 2006, s 2, Sch 1, paras 62, 67(a). Words in subs (2) substituted: National Health Service (Consequential Provisions) Act 2006, s 2, Sch 1, paras 62, 67(b).

123 Transfers to and from special hospitals

(1) Without prejudice to any other provisions of this Act with respect to the transfer of patients, any patient who is for the time being liable to be detained under this Act (other than under section 35, 36 or 38 above) in a hospital at which high security psychiatric services are provided may, upon the directions of the Secretary of State, at any time be removed into any other hospital at which those services are provided.

(2) Without prejudice to any such provision, the Secretary of State may give directions for the transfer of any patient who is for the time being liable to be so detained into a hospital at which those services are not provided.

(3) Subsections (2) and (4) of section 19 above shall apply in relation to the transfer or removal of a patient under this section as they apply in relation to the transfer or removal of a patient from one hospital to another under that section.

Amendments. Words in subs (1) repealed: Health Act 1999, s 65, Sch 4, paras 65, 67(a), Sch 5. Words in subs (1) inserted: Health Act 1999, s 65, Sch 4, paras 65, 67(a). Words in subss (1), (2) substituted: Health Act 1999, s 65, Sch 4, paras 65, 67(a), (b).

124 (*repealed*)

Amendments. Section repealed: National Health Service and Community Care Act 1990, s 66(2), Sch 2

125 (*repealed*)

Amendments. Section repealed: Inquiries Act 2005, ss 48(1), 49(2), Sch 2, Pt 1, para 9, Sch 3.

PART IX
OFFENCES

126 Forgery, false statements, etc

(1) Any person who without lawful authority or excuse has in his custody or under his control any document to which this subsection applies, which is, and which he knows or believes to be, false within the meaning of Part I of the Forgery and Counterfeiting Act 1981, shall be guilty of an offence.

(2) Any person who without lawful authority or excuse makes, or has in his custody or under his control, any document so closely resembling a document to which subsection (1) above applies as to be calculated to deceive shall be guilty of an offence.

(3) The documents to which subsection (1) above applies are any documents purporting to be –

(a)   an application under Part II of this Act;
(b)   a medical or other recommendation or report under this Act; and
(c)   any other document required or authorised to be made for any of the purposes of this Act.

(4) Any person who –

(a)   wilfully makes a false entry or statement in any application, recommendation, report, record or other document required or authorised to be made for any of the purposes of this Act; or
(b)   with intent to deceive, makes use of any such entry or statement which he knows to be false, shall be guilty of an offence.

(5) Any person guilty of an offence under this section shall be liable –

(a)   on summary conviction, to imprisonment for a term not exceeding six months or to a fine not exceeding the statutory maximum, or to both;

(b)   on conviction on indictment, to imprisonment for a term not exceeding two years or to a fine of any amount, or to both.

Amendments. Words in subs (3)(b) inserted: Mental Health (Patients in the Community) Act 1995, s 1(2), Sch 1, para 17.

127 Ill-treatment of patients

(1) It shall be an offence for any person who is an officer on the staff of or otherwise employed in, or who is one of the managers of, a hospital, independent hospital or care home –

(a)   to ill-treat or wilfully to neglect a patient for the time being receiving treatment for mental disorder as an in-patient in that hospital or home; or

(b)   to ill-treat or wilfully to neglect, on the premises of which the hospital or home forms part, a patient for the time being receiving such treatment there as an out-patient.

(2) It shall be an offence for any individual to ill-treat or wilfully to neglect a mentally disordered patient who is for the time being subject to his guardianship under this Act or otherwise in his custody or care (whether by virtue of any legal or moral obligation or otherwise).

(2A) *(repealed)*

(3) Any person guilty of an offence under this section shall be liable –

(a)   on summary conviction, to imprisonment for a term not exceeding six months or to a fine not exceeding the statutory maximum, or to both;

(b)   on conviction on indictment, to imprisonment for a term not exceeding five years or to a fine of any amount, or to both.

(4) No proceedings shall be instituted for an offence under this section except by or with the consent of the Director of Public Prosecutions.

Amendments. Subs (2A) inserted: Mental Health (Patients in the Community) Act 1995, s 1(2), Sch 1, para 18. Words in subs (1) substituted: Care Standards Act 2000, s 116, Sch 4, para 9(1), (8). Subs (2A) repealed: MHA 2007, s 55, Sch 11, Pt 5. Words in subs (3)(b) substituted: MHA 2007, s 42.

128 Assisting patients to absent themselves without leave, etc

(1) Where any person induces or knowingly assists another person who is liable to be detained in a hospital within the meaning of Part II of this Act or is subject to guardianship under this Act or is a community patient to absent himself without leave he shall be guilty of an offence.

(2) Where any person induces or knowingly assists another person who is in legal custody by virtue of section 137 below to escape from such custody he shall be guilty of an offence.

(3) Where any person knowingly harbours a patient who is absent without leave or is otherwise at large and liable to be retaken under this Act or gives him

any assistance with intent to prevent, hinder or interfere with his being taken into custody or returned to the hospital or other place where he ought to be he shall be guilty of an offence.

(4) Any person guilty of an offence under this section shall be liable –

    (a)   on summary conviction, to imprisonment for a term not exceeding six months or to a fine not exceeding the statutory maximum, or to both;

    (b)   on conviction on indictment, to imprisonment for a term not exceeding two years or to a fine of any amount, or to both.

Amendments. Words in subs (1) inserted: MHA 2007, s 32(4), Sch 3, paras 1, 28 Section repealed: Adult Support and Protection (Scotland) Act 2007, s 74.

129 Obstruction

(1) Any person who without reasonable cause –

    (a)   refuses to allow the inspection of any premises; or

    (b)   refuses to allow the visiting, interviewing or examination of any person by a person authorised in that behalf by or under this Act or to give access to any person to a person so authorised; or

    (c)   refuses to produce for the inspection of any person so authorised any document or record the production of which is duly required by him; or

    (ca)   fails to comply with a request made under section 120C; or

    (d)   otherwise obstructs any such person in the exercise of his functions,

shall be guilty of an offence.

(2) Without prejudice to the generality of subsection (1) above, any person who insists on being present when required to withdraw by a person authorised by or under this Act to interview or examine a person in private shall be guilty of an offence.

(3) Any person guilty of an offence under this section shall be liable on summary conviction to imprisonment for a term not exceeding three months or to a fine not exceeding level 4 on the standard scale or to both.

Amendments. Words in subs (1)(b) inserted: Mental Health (Patients in the Community) Act 1995, s 1(2), Sch 1, para 19. Subs (1)(ca) inserted: Health and Social Care Act 2008, s 52(5), Sch 3, paras 1, 10.

130 Prosecutions by local authorities

A local social services authority may institute proceedings for any offence under this Part of this Act, but without prejudice to any provision of this Part of this Act requiring the consent of the Director of Public Prosecutions for the institution of such proceedings.

PART X
MISCELLANEOUS AND SUPPLEMENTARY

Miscellaneous provisions

130A Independent mental health advocates

(1) The appropriate national authority shall make such arrangements as it considers reasonable to enable persons ('independent mental health advocates') to be available to help qualifying patients.

(2) The appropriate national authority may by regulations make provision as to the appointment of persons as independent mental health advocates.

(3) The regulations may, in particular, provide –

    (a)   that a person may act as an independent mental health advocate only in such circumstances, or only subject to such conditions, as may be specified in the regulations;

    (b)   for the appointment of a person as an independent mental health advocate to be subject to approval in accordance with the regulations.

(4) In making arrangements under this section, the appropriate national authority shall have regard to the principle that any help available to a patient under the arrangements should, so far as practicable, be provided by a person who is independent of any person who is professionally concerned with the patient's medical treatment.

(5) For the purposes of subsection (4) above, a person is not to be regarded as professionally concerned with a patient's medical treatment merely because he is representing him in accordance with arrangements –

    (a)   under section 35 of the Mental Capacity Act 2005; or

    (b)   of a description specified in regulations under this section.

(6) Arrangements under this section may include provision for payments to be made to, or in relation to, persons carrying out functions in accordance with the arrangements.

(7) Regulations under this section –

    (a)   may make different provision for different cases;

    (b)   may make provision which applies subject to specified exceptions;

    (c)   may include transitional, consequential, incidental or supplemental provision.

Amendments. Section inserted: MHA 2007, s 30(1), (2); for transitional provisions and savings see s 53, Sch 10, paras 1, 8 thereto.

130B Arrangements under section 130A

(1) The help available to a qualifying patient under arrangements under section 130A above shall include help in obtaining information about and understanding –

    (a)   the provisions of this Act by virtue of which he is a qualifying patient;

(b)   any conditions or restrictions to which he is subject by virtue of this Act;

(c)   what (if any) medical treatment is given to him or is proposed or discussed in his case;

(d)   why it is given, proposed or discussed;

(e)   the authority under which it is, or would be, given; and

(f)   the requirements of this Act which apply, or would apply, in connection with the giving of the treatment to him.

(2) The help available under the arrangements to a qualifying patient shall also include –

(a)   help in obtaining information about and understanding any rights which may be exercised under this Act by or in relation to him; and

(b)   help (by way of representation or otherwise) in exercising those rights.

(3) For the purpose of providing help to a patient in accordance with the arrangements, an independent mental health advocate may –

(a)   visit and interview the patient in private;

(b)   visit and interview any person who is professionally concerned with his medical treatment;

(c)   require the production of and inspect any records relating to his detention or treatment in any hospital or registered establishment or to any after-care services provided for him under section 117 above;

(d)   require the production of and inspect any records of, or held by, a local social services authority which relate to him.

(4) But an independent mental health advocate is not entitled to the production of, or to inspect, records in reliance on subsection (3)(c) or(d) above unless –

(a)   in a case where the patient has capacity or is competent to consent, he does consent; or

(b)   in any other case, the production or inspection would not conflict with a decision made by a donee or deputy or the Court of Protection and the person holding the records, having regard to such matters as may be prescribed in regulations under section 130A above, considers that –
   (i)   the records may be relevant to the help to be provided by the advocate; and
   (ii)   the production or inspection is appropriate.

(5) For the purpose of providing help to a patient in accordance with the arrangements, an independent mental health advocate shall comply with any reasonable request made to him by any of the following for him to visit and interview the patient –

(a)   the person (if any) appearing to the advocate to be the patient's nearest relative;

(b)   the responsible clinician for the purposes of this Act;

(c)   an approved mental health professional.

(6) But nothing in this Act prevents the patient from declining to be provided with help under the arrangements.

(7) In subsection (4) above –

(a) the reference to a patient who has capacity is to be read in accordance with the Mental Capacity Act 2005;

(b) the reference to a donee is to a donee of a lasting power of attorney (within the meaning of section 9 of that Act) created by the patient, where the donee is acting within the scope of his authority and in accordance with that Act;

(c) the reference to a deputy is to a deputy appointed for the patient by the Court of Protection under section 16 of that Act, where the deputy is acting within the scope of his authority and in accordance with that Act.

Amendments. Section inserted: MHA 2007, s 30(1), (2); for transitional provisions and savings see s 53, Sch 10, paras 1, 8 thereto.

130C Section 130A: supplemental

(1) This section applies for the purposes of section 130A above.

(2) A patient is a qualifying patient if he is –

(a) liable to be detained under this Act (otherwise than by virtue of section 4 or 5(2) or (4) above or section 135 or 136 below);

(b) subject to guardianship under this Act; or

(c) a community patient.

(3) A patient is also a qualifying patient if –

(a) not being a qualifying patient falling within subsection (2) above, he discusses with a registered medical practitioner or approved clinician the possibility of being given a form of treatment to which section 57 above applies; or

(b) not having attained the age of 18 years and not being a qualifying patient falling within subsection (2) above, he discusses with a registered medical practitioner or approved clinician the possibility of being given a form of treatment to which section 58A above applies.

(4) Where a patient who is a qualifying patient falling within subsection (3) above is informed that the treatment concerned is proposed in his case, he remains a qualifying patient falling within that subsection until –

(a) the proposal is withdrawn; or

(b) the treatment is completed or discontinued.

(5) References to the appropriate national authority are –

(a) in relation to a qualifying patient in England, to the Secretary of State;

(b) in relation to a qualifying patient in Wales, to the Welsh Ministers.

(6) For the purposes of subsection (5) above –

(a)   a qualifying patient falling within subsection (2)(a) above is to be regarded as being in the territory in which the hospital or registered establishment in which he is liable to be detained is situated;

(b)   a qualifying patient falling within subsection (2)(b) above is to be regarded as being in the territory in which the area of the responsible local social services authority within the meaning of section 34(3) above is situated;

(c)   a qualifying patient falling within subsection (2)(c) above is to be regarded as being in the territory in which the responsible hospital is situated;

(d)   a qualifying patient falling within subsection (3) above is to be regarded as being in the territory determined in accordance with arrangements made for the purposes of this paragraph, and published, by the Secretary of State and the Welsh Ministers.

Amendments. Section inserted: MHA 2007, s 30(1), (2); for transitional provisions and savings see s 53, Sch 10, paras 1, 8 thereto.

130D   Duty to give information about independent mental health advocates

(1) The responsible person in relation to a qualifying patient (within the meaning given by section 130C above) shall take such steps as are practicable to ensure that the patient understands –

(a)   that help is available to him from an independent mental health advocate; and

(b)   how he can obtain that help.

(2) In subsection (1) above, 'the responsible person' means –

(a)   in relation to a qualifying patient falling within section 130C(2)(a) above (other than one also falling within paragraph (b) below), the managers of the hospital or registered establishment in which he is liable to be detained;

(b)   in relation to a qualifying patient falling within section 130C(2)(a) above and conditionally discharged by virtue of section 42(2), 73 or 74 above, the responsible clinician;

(c)   in relation to a qualifying patient falling within section 130C(2)(b) above, the responsible local social services authority within the meaning of section 34(3) above;

(d)   in relation to a qualifying patient falling within section 130C(2)(c) above, the managers of the responsible hospital;

(e)   in relation to a qualifying patient falling within section 130C(3) above, the registered medical practitioner or approved clinician with whom the patient first discusses the possibility of being given the treatment concerned.

(3) The steps to be taken under subsection (1) above shall be taken –

(a)   where the responsible person falls within subsection (2)(a) above, as soon as practicable after the patient becomes liable to be detained;

(b)   where the responsible person falls within subsection (2)(b) above, as soon as practicable after the conditional discharge;

(c)   where the responsible person falls within subsection (2)(c) above, as soon as practicable after the patient becomes subject to guardianship;

(d)   where the responsible person falls within subsection (2)(d) above, as soon as practicable after the patient becomes a community patient;

(e)   where the responsible person falls within subsection (2)(e) above, while the discussion with the patient is taking place or as soon as practicable thereafter.

(4) The steps to be taken under subsection (1) above shall include giving the requisite information both orally and in writing.

(5) The responsible person in relation to a qualifying patient falling within section 130C(2) above (other than a patient liable to be detained by virtue of Part 3 of this Act) shall, except where the patient otherwise requests, take such steps as are practicable to furnish the person (if any) appearing to the responsible person to be the patient's nearest relative with a copy of any information given to the patient in writing under subsection (1) above.

(6) The steps to be taken under subsection (5) above shall be taken when the information concerned is given to the patient or within a reasonable time thereafter.'

Amendments. Section inserted: MHA 2007, s 30(1), (2); for transitional provisions and savings see s 53, Sch 10, paras 1, 8 thereto.

131   Informal admission of patients

(1) Nothing in this Act shall be construed as preventing a patient who requires treatment for mental disorder from being admitted to any hospital or registered establishment in pursuance of arrangements made in that behalf and without any application, order or direction rendering him liable to be detained under this Act, or from remaining in any hospital or registered establishment in pursuance of such arrangements after he has ceased to be so liable to be detained.

(2) Subsections (3) and (4) below apply in the case of a patient aged 16 or 17 years who has capacity to consent to the making of such arrangements as are mentioned in subsection (1) above.

(3) If the patient consents to the making of the arrangements, they may be made, carried out and determined on the basis of that consent even though there are one or more persons who have parental responsibility for him.

(4) If the patient does not consent to the making of the arrangements, they may not be made, carried out or determined on the basis of the consent of a person who has parental responsibility for him.

(5) In this section –

(a)   the reference to a patient who has capacity is to be read in accordance with the Mental Capacity Act 2005; and

(b) 'parental responsibility' has the same meaning as in the Children Act 1989.'

Amendments. Words in subs (2) substituted: Children Act 1989, s 108(5), (6), Sch 13, para 48(5), Sch 14, para 1. Words in sub-s (1) substituted by the Care Standards Act 2000, s 116, Sch 4, para 9(1), (2). Subs (2) substituted by subss (2)–(5): MHA 2007, s 43, with effect from 1 January 2008.

131A Accommodation, etc for children

(1) This section applies in respect of any patient who has not attained the age of 18 years and who –

(a) is liable to be detained in a hospital under this Act; or
(b) is admitted to, or remains in, a hospital in pursuance of such arrangements as are mentioned in section 131(1) above.

(2) The managers of the hospital shall ensure that the patient's environment in the hospital is suitable having regard to his age (subject to his needs).

(3) For the purpose of deciding how to fulfil the duty under subsection (2) above, the managers shall consult a person who appears to them to have knowledge or experience of cases involving patients who have not attained the age of 18 years which makes him suitable to be consulted.

(4) In this section, 'hospital' includes a registered establishment.'

Amendment. Section inserted: MHA 2007, s 31(1), (3).

132 Duty of managers of hospitals to give information to detained patients

(1) The managers of a hospital or registered establishment in which a patient is detained under this Act shall take such steps as are practicable to ensure that the patient understands –

(a) under which of the provisions of this Act he is for the time being detained and the effect of that provision; and
(b) what rights of applying to a tribunal are available to him in respect of his detention under that provision;

and those steps shall be taken as soon as practicable after the commencement of the patient's detention under the provision in question.

(2) The managers of a hospital or registered establishment in which a patient is detained as aforesaid shall also take such steps as are practicable to ensure that the patient understands the effect, so far as relevant in his case, of sections 23, 25, 56 to 64, 66(1)(g), 118 and 120 above and section 134 below; and those steps shall be taken as soon as practicable after the commencement of the patient's detention in the hospital or establishment.

(3) The steps to be taken under subsections (1) and (2) above shall include giving the requisite information both orally and in writing.

(4) The managers of a hospital or registered establishment in which a patient is detained as aforesaid shall, except where the patient otherwise requests, take

such steps as are practicable to furnish the person (if any) appearing to them to be his nearest relative with a copy of any information given to him in writing under subsections (1) and (2) above; and those steps shall be taken when the information is given to the patient or within a reasonable time thereafter.

Amendments. Word in subss (1), (2), (4) substituted: Care Standards Act 2000, s 116, Sch 4, para 9(1), (2). Words in subs (2) substituted: MHA 2007, s 32(4), Sch 3, paras 1, 29. Word in subs (1)(b) substituted: Transfer of Tribunal Functions Order 2008, SI 2008 No. 2833, art 9(1), Sch 3, paras 39, 63.

132A Duty of managers of hospitals to give information to community patients

(1) The managers of the responsible hospital shall take such steps as are practicable to ensure that a community patient understands –

   (a)   the effect of the provisions of this Act applying to community patients; and

   (b)   what rights of applying to a tribunal are available to him in that capacity;

and those steps shall be taken as soon as practicable after the patient becomes a community patient.

(2) The steps to be taken under subsection (1) above shall include giving the requisite information both orally and in writing.

(3) The managers of the responsible hospital shall, except where the community patient otherwise requests, take such steps as are practicable to furnish the person (if any) appearing to them to be his nearest relative with a copy of any information given to him in writing under subsection (1) above; and those steps shall be taken when the information is given to the patient or within a reasonable time thereafter.

Amendments. Section inserted: MHA 2007, s 32(4), Sch 3, paras 1, 30. Word in subs (1)(b) substituted: Transfer of Tribunal Functions Order 2008, SI 2008 No. 2833, art 9(1), Sch 3, paras 39, 64.

133 Duty of managers of hospitals to inform nearest relatives of discharge

(1) Where a patient liable to be detained under this Act in a hospital or registered establishment is to be discharged otherwise than by virtue of an order for discharge made by his nearest relative, the managers of the hospital or registered establishment shall, subject to subsection (2) below, take such steps as are practicable to inform the person (if any) appearing to them to be the nearest relative of the patient; and that information shall, if practicable, be given at least seven days before the date of discharge.

(1A) The reference in subsection (1) above to a patient who is to be discharged includes a patient who is to be discharged from hospital under section 17A above.

(1B) Subsection (1) above shall also apply in a case where a community patient is discharged under section 23 or 72 above (otherwise than by virtue of an order for discharge made by his nearest relative), but with the reference in that subsection to the managers of the hospital or registered establishment being read as a reference to the managers of the responsible hospital.

(2) Subsection (1) above shall not apply if the patient or his nearest relative has requested that information about the patient's discharge should not be given under this section.

Amendments. Words in subs (1) substituted: Care Standards Act 2000, s 116, Sch 4, para 9(1), (2). Subss (1A), (1B) inserted: MHA 2007, s 32(4), Sch 3, paras 1, 31.

134 Correspondence of patients

(1) A postal packet addressed to any person by a patient detained in a hospital under this Act and delivered by the patient for dispatch may be withheld from the postal operator concerned –

  (a) if that person has requested that communications addressed to him by the patient should be withheld; or
  (b) subject to subsection (3) below, if the hospital is one at which high security psychiatric services are provided and the managers of the hospital consider that the postal packet is likely –
       (i)   to cause distress to the person to whom it is addressed or to any other person (not being a person on the staff of the hospital); or
       (ii) to cause danger to any person;

and any request for the purposes of paragraph (a) above shall be made by a notice in writing given to the managers of the hospital, the approved clinician with overall responsibility for the patient's case or the Secretary of State.

(2) Subject to subsection (3) below, a postal packet addressed to a patient detained under this Act in a hospital at which high security psychiatric services are provided may be withheld from the patient if, in the opinion of the managers of the hospital, it is necessary to do so in the interests of the safety of the patient or for the protection of other persons.

(3) Subsections (1)(b) and (2) above do not apply to any postal packet addressed by a patient to, or sent to a patient by or on behalf of –

  (a)   any Minister of the Crown or the Scottish Ministers or Member of either House of Parliament or member of the Scottish Parliament or of the Northern Ireland Assembly;
  (aa) any of the Welsh Ministers, the Counsel General to the Welsh Assembly Government or a member of the National Assembly for Wales;
  (b)   any judge or officer of the Court of Protection, any of the Court of Protection Visitors or any person asked by that Court for a report under section 49 of the Mental Capacity Act 2005 concerning the patient;
  (c)   the Parliamentary Commissioner for Administration, the Scottish Public Services Ombudsman, the Public Services Ombudsman for

Wales, the Health Service Commissioner for England or a Local Commissioner within the meaning of Part III of the Local Government Act 1974;

(ca)   the Care Quality Commission;

(d)   the First-tier Tribunal or the Mental Health Review Tribunal for Wales;

(e)   a Strategic Health Authority, Local Health Board, Special Health Authority or Primary Care Trust, a local social services authority, a Community Health Council, a local probation board established under section 4 of the Criminal Justice and Court Services Act 2000 or a provider of probation services;

(ea)   a provider of a patient advocacy and liaison service for the assistance of patients at the hospital and their families and carers;

(eb)   a provider of independent advocacy services for the patient;

(f)   the managers of the hospital in which the patient is detained;

(g)   any legally qualified person instructed by the patient to act as his legal adviser; or

(h)   the European Commission of Human Rights or the European Court of Human Rights.

and for the purposes of paragraph (d) above the reference to the First-tier Tribunal is a reference to that tribunal so far as it is acting for the purposes of any proceedings under this Act or paragraph 5(2) of the Schedule to the Repatriation of Prisoners Act 1984.

(3A) In subsection (3) above –

(a)   'patient advocacy and liaison service' means a service of a description prescribed by regulations made by the Secretary of State, and

(b)   'independent advocacy services' means services provided under –

(i)   arrangements under section 130A above;

(ii)   arrangements under section 248 of the National Health Service Act 2006 or section 187 of the National Health Service (Wales) Act 2006; or

(iii) arrangements of a description prescribed as mentioned in paragraph (a) above.

(4) The managers of a hospital may inspect and open any postal packet for the purposes of determining –

(a)   whether it is one to which subsection (1) or (2) applies, and

(b)   in the case of a postal packet to which subsection (1) or (2) above applies, whether or not it should be withheld under that subsection; and the power to withhold a postal packet under either of those subsections includes power to withhold anything contained in it.

(5) Where a postal packet or anything contained in it is withheld under subsection (1) or (2) above the managers of the hospital shall record that fact in writing.

(6) Where a postal packet or anything contained in it is withheld under subsection (1)(b) or (2) above the managers of the hospital shall within seven

days give notice of that fact to the patient and, in the case of a packet withheld under subsection (2) above, to the person (if known) by whom the postal packet was sent; and any such notice shall be given in writing and shall contain a statement of the effect of section 134A(1) to (4).

(7) The functions of the managers of a hospital under this section shall be discharged on their behalf by a person on the staff of the hospital appointed by them for that purpose and different persons may be appointed to discharge different functions.

(8) The Secretary of State may make regulations with respect to the exercise of the powers conferred by this section.

(9) In this section and section 134A 'hospital' has the same meaning as in Part II of this Act and 'postal operator' and 'postal packet' have the same meaning as in the Postal Services Act 2000.

Amendments. Words in subs (3)(a) inserted: Northern Ireland Act 1998, s 99, Sch 13, para 5(1), (2). Words in subss (1)(b), (2) substituted: Health Act 1999, s 65, Sch 4, paras 65, 68(a), (b). Words in subs (3)(a) inserted: Scotland Act 1998 (Consequential Modifications) (No 2) Order 1999, SI 1999 No. 1820, art 4, Sch 2, Pt I, para 71(1), (2). Words in subs (1) substituted: Postal Services Act 2000, s 127(4), Sch 8, Pt II, para 19(1), (2). Words in subs (9) inserted and substituted: Postal Services Act 2000, s 127(4), Sch 8, Pt II, para 19(1), (3)(a)–(c). Words in subs (9) repealed: Postal Services Act 2000, s 127(6), Sch 9. Words in subs (3)(e) substituted: Criminal Justice and Court Services Act 2000, s 74, Sch 7, Pt II, paras 72, 74. Subs (3A) and words in subs (3)(ea), (eb) inserted: Health and Social Care Act 2001, s 67(1), Sch 5, Pt 1, para 6(1)–(3). Words in subs (3)(e) omitted inserted: National Health Service Reform and Health Care Professions Act 2002, s 19(6). Words in subs (3)(e) substituted:Health Act 1999 (Supplementary, Consequential etc Provisions) Order 2000, SI 2000 No. 90, art 3(1), Sch 1, para 16(1), (7). Words in subs (3)(e) inserted: National Health Service Reform and Health Care Professions Act 2002 (Supplementary, Consequential etc Provisions) Regulations 2002, SI 2002 No. 2469, reg 4, Sch 1, Pt 1, para 10(1), (2). Words in subs (3)(c) inserted: Scottish Public Services Ombudsman Act 2002 (Consequential Provisions and Modifications) Order 2004, SI 2004 No. 1823, art 9. Subs (3)(b) substituted: Mental Capacity Act 2005, s 67(1), Sch 6, para 29(1), (2). Words in subs (3)(c) substituted (for words as inserted by the Government of Wales Act 1998, s 125, Sch 12, para 22): Public Services Ombudsman (Wales) Act 2005, s 39(1), Sch 6, para 21(a). Words in subs (3)(c) repealed: Public Services Ombudsman (Wales) Act 2005, s 39(1), Sch 6, para 21(b), Sch 7. W ords in subs (1) substituted: MHA 2007, s 14(1), (4). Subs (3A)(b) substituted: MHA 2007, s 30(1), (3). Words in subs (3)(e) repealed: Local Government and Public Involvement in Health Act 2007, s 241, Sch 18, Pt 18. Words in subs (3)(e) substituted: References to Health Authorities Order 2007, SI 2007 No. 961, art 3, Schedule, para 13(1), (10). Subs (3)(aa) inserted: Government of Wales Act 2006 (Consequential Modifications and Transitional Provisions) Order 2007, SI 2007 No. 1388, art 3, Sch 1, para 18. Subs (3)(ca) inserted: Health and Social Care Act 2008, s 52(5), Sch 3, paras 1, 11(1), (2). Words in subs (6) substituted: Health and Social Care Act 2008, s 52(5), Sch 3, paras 1, 11(1), (3). Words in subs (9) inserted: Health and Social Care Act 2008, s 52(5), Sch 3, paras 1, 11(1), (4). Words in subs (3)(e) substituted and inserted: Offender Management Act 2007 (Consequential Amendments) Order 2008, SI 2008 No. 912, art 3, Sch 1, Pt 1, para 7. Words in subs (3) inserted and words in subs (3)(d) substituted: Transfer of Tribunal Functions Order 2008, SI 2008 No. 2833, art 9(1), Sch 3, paras 39, 65(a), (b).

134A Review of decisions to withhold correspondence

(1) The regulatory authority must review any decision to withhold a postal packet (or anything contained in it) under subsection (1)(b) or (2) of section 134 if an application for a review of the decision is made –

(a) in a case under subsection (1)(b) of that section, by the patient; or
(b) in a case under subsection (2) of that section, either by the patient or by the person by whom the postal packet was sent.

(2) An application under subsection (1) must be made within 6 months of receipt by the applicant of the notice referred to in section 134(6).

(3) On an application under subsection (1), the regulatory authority may direct that the postal packet (or anything contained in it) is not to be withheld.

(4) The managers of the hospital concerned must comply with any such direction.

(5) The Secretary of State may by regulations make provision in connection with the making to and determination by the Care Quality Commission of applications under subsection (1), including provision for the production to the Commission of any postal packet which is the subject of such an application.

(6) The Welsh Ministers may by regulations make provision in connection with the making to them of applications under subsection (1), including provision for the production to them of any postal packet which is the subject of such an application.

Amendments. Section inserted: Health and Social Care Act 2008, s 52(5), Sch 3, paras 1, 12.

135 Warrant to search for and remove patients

(1) If it appears to a justice of the peace, on information on oath laid by an approved mental health professional, that there is reasonable cause to suspect that a person believed to be suffering from mental disorder –

(a) has been, or is being, ill-treated, neglected or kept otherwise than under proper control, in any place within the jurisdiction of the justice, or
(b) being unable to care for himself, is living alone in any such place,

the justice may issue a warrant authorising any constable to enter, if need be by force, any premises specified in the warrant in which that person is believed to be, and, if thought fit, to remove him to a place of safety with a view to the making of an application in respect of him under Part II of this Act, or of other arrangements for his treatment or care.

(2) If it appears to a justice of the peace, on information on oath laid by any constable or other person who is authorised by or under this Act or under article 8 of the Mental Health (Care and Treatment) (Scotland) Act 2003 (Consequential Provisions) Order 2005 to take a patient to any place, or to take into custody or retake a patient who is liable under this Act or under the said article 8 to be so taken or retaken –

(a) that there is reasonable cause to believe that the patient is to be found on premises within the jurisdiction of the justice; and

(b)   that admission to the premises has been refused or that a refusal of such admission is apprehended, the justice may issue a warrant authorising any constable to enter the premises, if need be by force, and remove the patient.

(3) A patient who is removed to a place of safety in the execution of a warrant issued under this section may be detained there for a period not exceeding 72 hours.

(3A) A constable, an approved mental health professional or a person authorised by either of them for the purposes of this subsection may, before the end of the period of 72 hours mentioned in subsection (3) above, take a person detained in a place of safety under that subsection to one or more other places of safety.

(3B) A person taken to a place of safety under subsection (3A) above may be detained there for a period ending no later than the end of the period of 72 hours mentioned in subsection (3) above.

(4) In the execution of a warrant issued under subsection (1) above, a constable shall be accompanied by an approved mental health professional and by a registered medical practitioner, and in the execution of a warrant issued under subsection (2) above a constable may be accompanied –

(a)   by a registered medical practitioner;
(b)   by any person authorised by or under this Act or under article 8 of the Mental Health (Care and Treatment) (Scotland) Act 2003 (Consequential Provisions) Order 2005 to take or retake the patient.

(5) It shall not be necessary in any information or warrant under subsection (1) above to name the patient concerned.

(6) In this section 'place of safety' means residential accommodation provided by a local social services authority under Part III of the National Assistance Act 1948, a hospital as defined by this Act, a police station, an independent hospital or care home for mentally disordered persons or any other suitable place the occupier of which is willing temporarily to receive the patient.

Amendments. Words in subss (1), (2) repealed: Police and Criminal Evidence Act 1984, s 119, Sch 7, Part I. Words in sub (4) substituted: Police and Criminal Evidence Act 1984, s 119, Sch 6, Part I. Words in subs (2), (4)(b) substituted: Mental Health (Scotland) Act 1984, s 127(1), Sch 3, para 56. Words in subs (6) repealed: National Health Service and Community Care Act 1990, s 66(2), Sch 10. Words in subs (6) substituted: Care Standards Act 2000, s 116, Sch 4, para 9(1), (9). Words in subss (2), (4)(b) substituted, in relation to England and Wales: Mental Health (Care and Treatment) (Scotland) Act 2003 (Consequential Provisions) Order 2005, SI 2005 No. 2078, art 15, Sch 1, para 2(1), (9)(a)(i), (ii), (b). Words in subss (1) and (4) substituted: MHA 2007, s 21, Sch 2, paras 1, 10(a). Subss (3A), (3B) inserted: MHA 2007, s 44(1), (2).

136 Mentally disordered persons found in public places

(1) If a constable finds in a place to which the public have access a person who appears to him to be suffering from mental disorder and to be in immediate need of care or control, the constable may, if he thinks it necessary to do so in

the interests of that person or for the protection of other persons, remove that person to a place of safety within the meaning of section 135 above.

(2) A person removed to a place of safety under this section may be detained there for a period not exceeding 72 hours for the purpose of enabling him to be examined by a registered medical practitioner and to be interviewed by an approved mental health professional and of making any necessary arrangements for his treatment or care.

(3) A constable, an approved mental health professional or a person authorised by either of them for the purposes of this subsection may, before the end of the period of 72 hours mentioned in subsection (2) above, take a person detained in a place of safety under that subsection to one or more other places of safety.

(4) A person taken to a place of a safety under subsection (3) above may be detained there for a purpose mentioned in subsection (2) above for a period ending no later than the end of the period of 72 hours mentioned in that subsection.

Amendments. Words in subs (2) substituted: MHA 2007, s 21, Sch 2, paras 1, 10(b). Subss (3), (4) inserted: MHA 2007, s 44(1), (3).

137 Provisions as to custody, conveyance and detention

(1) Any person required or authorised by or by virtue of this Act to be conveyed to any place or to be kept in custody or detained in a place of safety or at any place to which he is taken under section 42(6) above shall, while being so conveyed, detained or kept, as the case may be, be deemed to be in legal custody.

(2) A constable or any other person required or authorised by or by virtue of this Act to take any person into custody, or to convey or detain any person shall, for the purposes of taking him into custody or conveying or detaining him, have all the powers, authorities, protection and privileges which a constable has within the area for which he acts as constable.

(3) In this section 'convey' includes any other expression denoting removal from one place to another.

138 Retaking of patients escaping from custody

(1) If any person who is in legal custody by virtue of section 137 above escapes, he may, subject to the provisions of this section, be retaken –

(a) in any case, by the person who had his custody immediately before the escape, or by any constable or approved mental health professional;

(b) if at the time of the escape he was liable to be detained in a hospital within the meaning of Part II of this Act, or subject to guardianship under this Act, or a community patient who was recalled to hospital under section 17E above, by any other person who could take him into custody under section 18 above if he had absented himself without leave.

(2) A person to whom paragraph (b) of subsection (1) above applies shall not be retaken under this section after the expiration of the period within which he could be retaken under section 18 above if he had absented himself without leave on the day of the escape unless he is subject to a restriction order under Part III of this Act or an order or direction having the same effect as such an order; and subsection (4) of the said section 18 shall apply with the necessary modifications accordingly.

(3) A person who escapes while being taken to or detained in a place of safety under section 135 or 136 above shall not be retaken under this section after the expiration of the period of 72 hours beginning with the time when he escapes or the period during which he is liable to be so detained, whichever expires first.

(4) This section, so far as it relates to the escape of a person liable to be detained in a hospital within the meaning of Part II of this Act, shall apply in relation to a person who escapes –

    (a)   while being taken to or from such a hospital in pursuance of regulations under section 19 above, or of any order, direction or authorisation under Part III or VI of this Act (other than under section 35, 36, 38, 53, 83 or 85) or under section 123 above; or

    (b)   while being taken to or detained in a place of safety in pursuance of an order under Part III of this Act (other than under section 35, 36 or 38 above) pending his admission to such a hospital, as if he were liable to be detained in that hospital and, if he had not previously been received in that hospital, as if he had been so received.

(5) In computing for the purposes of the power to give directions under section 37(4) above and for the purposes of sections 37(5) and 40(1) above the period of 28 days mentioned in those sections, no account shall be taken of any time during which the patient is at large and liable to be retaken by virtue of this section.

(6) Section 21 above shall, with any necessary modifications, apply in relation to a patient who is at large and liable to be retaken by virtue of this section as it applies in relation to a patient who is absent without leave and references in that section to section 18 above shall be construed accordingly.

Amendments. Words in subs (1)(a) substituted: MHA 2007, s 21, Sch 2, paras 1, 10(c). Words in subs (1)(b) inserted: MHA 2007, s 32(4), Sch 3, paras 1, 32.

139 Protection for acts done in pursuance of this Act

(1) No person shall be liable, whether on the ground of want of jurisdiction or on any other ground, to any civil or criminal proceedings to which he would have been liable apart from this section in respect of any act purporting to be done in pursuance of this Act or any regulations or rules made under this Act, unless the act was done in bad faith or without reasonable care.

(2) No civil proceedings shall be brought against any person in any court in respect of any such act without the leave of the High Court; and no criminal

proceedings shall be brought against any person in any court in respect of any such act except by or with the consent of the Director of Public Prosecutions.

(3) This section does not apply to proceedings for an offence under this Act, being proceedings which, under any other provision of this Act, can be instituted only by or with the consent of the Director of Public Prosecutions.

(4) This section does not apply to proceedings against the Secretary of State or against a Strategic Health Authority, Local Health Board, Special Health Authority or Primary Care Trust or against a National Health Service trust established under the National Health Service Act 2006 or the National Health Service (Wales) Act 2006 or NHS foundation trust or against the Department of Justice in Northern Ireland.

(5) In relation to Northern Ireland the reference in this section to the Director of Public Prosecutions shall be construed as a reference to the Director of Public Prosecutions for Northern Ireland.

Amendments. Words in subs (4) inserted: National Health Service and Community Care Act 1990, s 66(1), Sch 9, para 24(7). Words in subs (4) substituted: Health Act 1999 (Supplementary, Consequential etc Provisions) Order 2000, SI 2000 No. 90, art 3(1), Sch 1, para 16(1), (8). Words in subs (4) inserted: National Health Service Reform and Health Care Professions Act 2002 (Supplementary, Consequential etc Provisions) Regulations 2002, SI 2002 No. 2469, reg 4, Sch 1, Pt 1, para 10(1), (3). Words in subs (4) inserted: Health and Social Care (Community Health and Standards) Act 2003, s 34, Sch 4, paras 50, 56. Words in subs (1) repealed: Mental Capacity Act 2005, s 67(1), (2), Sch 6, para 29(1), (3), Sch 7. Words in subs (4) substituted: National Health Service (Consequential Provisions) Act 2006, s 2, Sch 1, paras 62, 69. Words in subs (4) substituted: References to Health Authorities Order 2007, SI 2007 No. 961, art 3, Schedule, para 13(1), (11). Words in subs (4) inserted: Northern Ireland Act 1998 (Devolution of Policing and Justice Functions) Order 2010, SI 2010 No. 976, art 12, Sch 14, para 28(1).

140 Notification of hospitals having arrangements for special cases

It shall be the duty of every Primary Care Trust and of every Local Health Board to give notice to every local social services authority for an area wholly or partly comprised within the area of the Primary Care Trust or Local Health Board specifying the hospital or hospitals administered by or otherwise available to the Primary Care Trust or Local Health Board in which arrangements are from time to time in force –

(a)   for the reception of patients in cases of special urgency;

(b)   for the provision of accommodation or facilities designed so as to be specially suitable for patients who have not attained the age of 18 years.'

Amendments. Words inserted: National Health Service and Community Care Act 1990, s 66(1), Sch 9, para 24(8). Words substituted: Health Authorities Act 1995, s 2(1), Sch 1, para 107(1), (12(c). Words inserted and substituted: National Health Service Reform and Health Care Professions Act 2002, s 2(5), Sch 2, Pt 2, paras 42, 48(a–(c). Section heading substituted, and paras (a), (b) substituted for existing words: MHA 2007, s 31(1), (4). Words substituted: References to Health Authorities Order 2007, SI 2007 No. 961, art 3, Schedule, para 13(1), (12).

141 Members of Parliament suffering from mental illness

(1) Where a member of the House of Commons is authorised to be detained under a relevant enactment on the ground (however formulated) that he is suffering from mental disorder, it shall be the duty of the court, authority or person on whose order or application, and of any registered medical practitioner upon whose recommendation or certificate, the detention was authorised, and of the person in charge of the hospital or other place in which the member is authorised to be detained, to notify the Speaker of the House of Commons that the detention has been authorised.

(2) Where the Speaker receives a notification under subsection (1) above, or is notified by two members of the House of Commons that they are credibly informed that such an authorisation has been given, the Speaker shall cause the member to whom the notification relates to be visited and examined by two registered medical practitioners appointed in accordance with subsection (3) below.

(3) The registered medical practitioners to be appointed for the purposes of subsection (2) above shall be appointed by the President of the Royal College of Psychiatrists and shall be practitioners appearing to the President to have special experience in the diagnosis or treatment of mental disorders.

(4) The registered medical practitioners appointed in accordance with subsection (3) above shall report to the Speaker whether the member is suffering from mental disorder and is authorised to be detained under a relevant enactment as such.

(5) If the report is to the effect that the member is suffering from mental disorder and authorised to be detained as aforesaid, the Speaker shall at the expiration of six months from the date of the report, if the House is then sitting, and otherwise as soon as may be after the House next sits, again cause the member to be visited and examined by two such registered medical practitioners as aforesaid, and the registered medical practitioners shall report as aforesaid.

(6) If the second report is that the member is suffering from mental disorder and authorised to be detained as mentioned in subsection (4) above, the Speaker shall forthwith lay both reports before the House of Commons, and thereupon the seat of the member shall become vacant.

(6A) For the purposes of this section, the following are relevant enactments –

    (a)   this Act;
    (b)   the Criminal Procedure (Scotland) Act 1995 and the Mental Health (Care and Treatment) (Scotland) Act 2003 ('the Scottish enactments'); and
    (c)   the Mental Health (Northern Ireland) Order 1986 ('the 1986 Order').

(6B) In relation to an authorisation for detention under the Scottish enactments or the 1986 Order, the references in this section to mental disorder shall be construed in accordance with those enactments or that Order (as the case may be).

(6C) References in this section to a member who is authorised to be detained shall not include a member who is a community patient (whether or not he is recalled to hospital under section 17E above).

(7) Any sums required for the payment of fees and expenses to registered medical practitioners acting in relation to a member of the House of Commons under this section shall be defrayed out of moneys provided by Parliament.

(8) This section also has effect in relation to members of the Scottish Parliament but as if –

    (a)   any references to the House of Commons or the Speaker were references to the Scottish Parliament or (as the case may be) the Presiding Officer, and

    (b)   subsection (7) were omitted.

(9) This section also has effect in relation to members of the National Assembly for Wales but as if –

    (a)   references to the House of Commons were to the Assembly and references to the Speaker were to the presiding officer, and

    (b)   in subsection (7), for 'defrayed out of moneys provided by Parliament' there were substituted 'paid by the National Assembly for Wales Commission'.

(10) This section also has effect in relation to members of the Northern Ireland Assembly but as if –

    (a)   references to the House of Commons were to the Assembly and references to the Speaker were to the Presiding Officer; and

    (b)   in subsection (7), for 'provided by Parliament' there were substituted 'appropriated by Act of the Assembly'.

Amendments. Subs (8) inserted: the Scotland Act 1998, s 125, Sch 8, para 19. Subs (9) inserted: Government of Wales Act 1998, s 125, Sch 12, para 23. Subs (10) inserted Northern Ireland Act 1998, s 99, Sch 13, para 5(1), (3). Word in subs (9)(b) inserted: Government of Wales Act 2006, s 160(1), Sch 10, para 13. Words in subs (1) inserted and substituted: MHA 2007, s 1(4), Sch 1, Pt 1, paras 1, 16(1), (2). Words in subs (4) substituted and inserted: MHA 2007, s 1(4), Sch 1, Pt 1, paras 1, 16(1), (3). Words in subs (5) substituted: MHA 2007, s 1(4), Sch 1, Pt 1, paras 1, 16(1), (4). Words in subs (6) substituted: MHA 2007, s 1(4), Sch 1, Pt 1, paras 1, 16(1), (4). Subss (6A), (6B) inserted: MHA 2007, s 1(4), Sch 1, Pt 1, paras 1, 16(1), (5). Subs (6C) inserted: MHA 2007, s 32(4), Sch 3, paras 1, 33.

142 (*repealed*)

Amendments. Repealed by Mental Capacity At 2005, s 67(1), Sch 6, para 29(5), (6) and: Adult Support and Protection (Scotland) Act 2007, s 77(2), Sch 2.

142A Regulations as to approvals in relation to England and Wales

The Secretary of State jointly with the Welsh Ministers may by regulations make provision as to the circumstances in which –

    (a)   a practitioner approved for the purposes of section 12 above, or

(b)   a person approved to act as an approved clinician for the purposes of this Act, approved in relation to England is to be treated, by virtue of his approval, as approved in relation to Wales too, and vice versa.

Amendment. Section inserted: MHA 2007, s 17.

142B Delegation of powers of managers of NHS foundation trusts

(1) The constitution of an NHS foundation trust may not provide for a function under this Act to be delegated otherwise than in accordance with provision made by or under this Act.

(2) Paragraph 15(3) of Schedule 7 to the National Health Service Act 2006 (which provides that the powers of a public benefit corporation may be delegated to a committee of directors or to an executive director) shall have effect subject to this section.

Amendments. Section inserted: MHA 2007, s 45(3).

Supplemental

143 General provisions as to regulations, orders and rules

(1) Any power of the Secretary of State or the Lord Chancellor to make regulations, orders or rules under this Act shall be exercisable by statutory instrument.

(2) Any Order in Council under this Act or any order made by the Secretary of State under section 54A or 68A(7) above and any statutory instrument containing regulations made by the Secretary of State, or rules made, under this Act shall be subject to annulment in pursuance of a resolution of either House of Parliament.

(3) No order shall be made by the Secretary of State under section 45A(10), 68(4) 68A(1) or 71(3) above unless a draft of it has been approved by a resolution of each House of Parliament.

(3A) Subsections (3B) to (3D) apply where power to make regulations or an order under this Act is conferred on the Welsh Ministers (other than by or by virtue of the Government of Wales Act 2006).

(3B) Any power of the Welsh Ministers to make regulations or an order shall be exercisable by statutory instrument.

(3C) Any statutory instrument containing regulations made by the Welsh Ministers, or an order under section 68A(7) above, made by the Welsh Ministers shall be subject to annulment in pursuance of a resolution of the National Assembly for Wales.

(3D) No order shall be made under section 68A(1) above by the Welsh Ministers unless a draft of it has been approved by a resolution of the National Assembly for Wales.

(3E) In this section –

(a) references to the Secretary of State include the Secretary of State and the Welsh Ministers acting jointly; and

(b) references to the Welsh Ministers include the Welsh Ministers and the Secretary of State acting jointly.

(4) This section does not apply to rules which are, by virtue of section 108 of this Act, to be made in accordance with Part 1 of Schedule 1 to the Constitutional Reform Act 2005.

Amendments. Words in subs (2) inserted: Criminal Justice Act 1991, s 27(3). Words in subs (2) omitted inserted: Health Authorities Act 1995, s 2(1), Sch 1, para 107(13). Reference to '45A(10)' in subs (3) inserted: Crime (Sentences) Act 1997, s 55, Sch 4, para 12(18). Subs (4) inserted: Constitutional Reform Act 2005, s 12(2), Sch 1, Pt 2, paras 14, 16. Words in subs (2) inserted: MHA 2007, s 37(1), (5)(a)(i), (ii). Words in subs (2) repealed: MHA 2007, s 55, Sch 11, Pt 6. Words in subs (2) substituted: MHA 2007, s 47(1), (2). Words in subs (3) inserted. MHA 2007, s 37(1), (5)(b)(i). Reference in subs (3) substituted: MHA 2007, s 37(1), (5)(b)(ii). Subss (3A)–(3E) inserted: MHA 2007, s 47(1), (3).

144 Power to amend local Acts

Her Majesty may by Order in Council repeal or amend any local enactment so far as appears to Her Majesty to be necessary in consequence of this Act.

145 Interpretation

(1) In this Act, unless the context otherwise requires –

'absent without leave' has the meaning given to it by section 18 above and related expressions (including expressions relating to a patient's liability to be returned to a hospital or other place) shall be construed accordingly;

'application for admission for assessment' has the meaning given in section 2 above;

'application for admission for treatment' has the meaning given in section 3 above;

'the appropriate tribunal' has the meaning given by section 66(4) above;

'approved clinician' means a person approved by the Secretary of State (in relation to England) or by the Welsh Ministers (in relation to Wales) to act as an approved clinician for the purposes of this Act;

'approved mental health professional' has the meaning given in section 114 above;

'care home' has the same meaning as in the Care Standards Act 2000;

'community patient' has the meaning given in section 17A above;

'community treatment order' and 'the community treatment order' have the meanings given in section 17A above;

'the community treatment period' has the meaning given in section 20A above;

'high security psychiatric services' has the same meaning as in section 4 of the National Health Service Act 2006 or section 4 of the National Health Service (Wales) Act 2006;

'hospital' means –

(a)   any health service hospital within the meaning of the National Health Service Act 2006 or the National Health Service (Wales) Act 2006; and

(b)   any accommodation provided by a local authority and used as a hospital by or on behalf of the Secretary of State under that Act; and

(c)   any hospital as defined by section 206 of the National Health Service (Wales) Act 2006 which is vested in a Local Health Board; and 'hospital within the meaning of Part II of this Act' has the meaning given in section 34 above;

'hospital direction' has the meaning given in section 45A(3)(a) above;

'hospital order' and 'guardianship order' have the meanings respectively given in section 37 above;

'independent hospital' –

(a)   in relation to England, means a hospital as defined by section 275 of the National Health Service Act 2006 that is not a health service hospital as defined by that section, and

(b)   in relation to Wales, has the same meaning as in the Care Standards Act 2000;

'interim hospital order' has the meaning given in section 38 above;

'limitation direction' has the meaning given in section 45A(3)(b) above;

'Local Health Board' means a Local Health Board established under section 11 of the National Health Services (Wales) Act 2006;

'local social services authority' means a council which is a local authority for the purpose of the Local Authority Social Services Act 1970;

'the managers' means –

(a)   in relation to a hospital vested in the Secretary of State for the purposes of his functions under the National Health Service Act 2006, or in the Welsh Ministers for the purposes of their functions under the National Health Service (Wales) Act 2006, and in relation to any accommodation provided by a local authority and used as a hospital by or on behalf of the Secretary of State under the National Health Service Act 2006, or of the Welsh Ministers under the National Health Service (Wales) Act 2006, the Primary Care Trust, Strategic Health Authority, Local Health Board or Special Health Authority responsible for the administration of the hospital;

(bb)   in relation to a hospital vested in a Primary Care Trust or a National Health Service trust, the trust;

(bc)   in relation to a hospital vested in an NHS foundation trust, the trust;

(bd)   in relation to a hospital vested in a Local Health Board, the Board;

(c)   in relation to a registered establishment –

(i)   if the establishment is in England, the person or persons registered as a service provider under Chapter 2 of Part 1 of the Health and Social Care Act 2008 in respect of the regulated activity (within the meaning of that Part) relating to the assessment or medical treatment of mental disorder that is carried out in the establishment, and

(ii) if the establishment is in Wales, the person or persons registered in respect of the establishment under Part 2 of the Care Standards Act 2000;

and in this definition 'hospital' means a hospital within the meaning of Part II of this Act;

'medical treatment' includes nursing, psychological intervention and specialist mental health habilitation, rehabilitation and care (but see also subsection (4) below);

'mental disorder' has the meaning given in section 1 above (subject to sections 86(4) and 141(6B));

'nearest relative', in relation to a patient, has the meaning given in Part II of this Act;

'patient' means a person suffering or appearing to be suffering from mental disorder;

'Primary Care Trust' means a Primary Care Trust established under section 18 of the National Health Service Act 2006;

'registered establishment' has the meaning given in section 34 above;

'the regulatory authority' means –

(a) in relation to England, the Care Quality Commission;

(b) in relation to Wales, the Welsh Ministers;

'the responsible hospital' has the meaning given in section 17A above;

'restriction direction' has the meaning given to it by section 49 above;

'restriction order' has the meaning given to it by section 41 above;

'Special Health Authority' means a Special Health Authority established under section 28 of the National Health Service Act 2006, or section 22 of the National Health Service (Wales) Act 2006;

'Strategic Health Authority' means a Strategic Health Authority established under section 13 of the National Health Service Act 2006;

'transfer direction' has the meaning given to it by section 47 above.

(1AA) Where high security psychiatric services and other services are provided at a hospital, the part of the hospital at which high security psychiatric services are provided and the other part shall be treated as separate hospitals for the purposes of this Act.

(1AB) References in this Act to appropriate medical treatment shall be construed in accordance with section 3(4) above.

(1AC) References in this Act to an approved mental health professional shall be construed as references to an approved mental health professional acting on behalf of a local social services authority, unless the context otherwise requires.

(1A), (2) (*repealed*)

(3) In relation to a person who is liable to be detained or subject to guardianship or a community patient by virtue of an order or direction under Part III of this Act (other than under section 35, 36 or 38), any reference in this

Act to any enactment contained in Part II of this Act or in section 66 or 67 above shall be construed as a reference to that enactment as it applies to that person by virtue of Part III of this Act.

(4) Any reference in this Act to medical treatment, in relation to mental disorder, shall be construed as a reference to medical treatment the purpose of which is to alleviate, or prevent a worsening of, the disorder or one or more of its symptoms or manifestations.

Amendments. Subs (1) definition, 'the managers', para (bb) inserted: National Health Service and Community Care Act 1990, s 66(1), Sch 9, para 24(9). Subs (1) definition, 'standard scale' repealed: Statute Law (Repeals) Act 1993. Subs (2) repealed: Statute Law (Repeals) Act 1993. Words in subs (1) definition, 'the managers', para (bb) repealed: Mental Health (Amendment) Act 1994, s 1. Subs (1) definition, 'Health Authority' (omitted) inserted: Health Authorities Act 1995, s 2(1), Sch 1, para 107(14). Words in subs (1) definition, 'the managers', para (a) substituted: Health Authorities Act 1995, s 2(1), Sch 1, para 107(14). Subs (1) definition, 'Special Health Authority' inserted: Health Authorities Act 1995, s 2(1), Sch 1, para 107(14). Subs (1): definition, 'supervision application' (omitted) inserted: Mental Health (Patients in the Community) Act 1995, s 1(2), Sch 1, para 20(2). Subs (1A) inserted: Mental Health (Patients in the Community) Act 1995, s 1(2), Sch 1, para 20(3). Subs (1) definition, 'the responsible after-care bodies' (omitted) inserted: Mental Health (Patients in the Community) Act 1995, s 1(2), Sch 1, para 20(2). Subs (1) definition, 'hospital direction' inserted: Crime (Sentences) Act 1997, s 55, Sch 4, para 12(19)(a). Subs (1) definition, 'limitation direction' inserted: Crime (Sentences) Act 1997, s 55, Sch 4, para 12(19)(b). Subs (1) definition, 'high security psychiatric services' inserted: Health Act 1999, s 65, Sch 4, paras 65, 69(1), (2)(a). Subs (1AA) inserted: Health Act 1999, s 65, Sch 4, paras 65, 69(1), (3). Subs (1) definition, 'care home' inserted: Care Standards Act 2000, Sch 4, para 9(1), (10)(a). Subs (1) definition, 'mental nursing home' repealed: Care Standards Act 2000, s 117(2), Sch 6. Subs (1) definition, 'registered establishment' inserted: Care Standards Act 2000, s 116, Sch 4, para 9(1), (10)(d). Words in subs (1) definition, 'the managers', para (bb) inserted: Health Act 1999 (Supplementary, Consequential etc Provisions) Order 2000, SI 2000 No. 90, art 3(1), Sch 1, para 16(1), (9)(a). Subs (1) definition, 'Primary Care Trust' inserted: Health Act 1999 (Supplementary, Consequential etc Provisions) Order 2000, SI 2000 No. 90, art 3(1), Sch 1, para 16(1), (9)(b). Words in subs (1) definition, 'the managers' para (a), inserted: National Health Service Reform and Health Care Professions Act 2002, s 2(5), Sch 2, Pt 2, paras 42, 49. Words in subs (1) definition, 'the managers', para (a), inserted and subs (1) definition, 'Strategic Health Authority' inserted: National Health Service Reform and Health Care Professions Act 2002 (Supplementary, Consequential etc Provisions) Regulations 2002, SI 2002 No. 2469, reg 4, Sch 1, Pt 1, para 10(1), (4)(a), (b). Subs (1) definition, 'the managers', para (bc) inserted: Health and Social Care (Community Health and Standards) Act 2003, s 34, Sch 4, paras 50, 57. Words in sub-s (1) definition, 'patient' repealed: Mental Capacity Act 2005, s 67(1), (2), Sch 6, para 29(1), (7), Sch 7. Words in subs (1) definition, 'high security psychiatric services' substituted: National Health Service (Consequential Provisions) Act 2006, s 2, Sch 1, paras 62, 70(b). Subs (1) definition, 'Health Authority' repealed: National Health Service (Consequential Provisions) Act 2006, s 2, Sch 1, paras 62, 70(a). Words in subs (1) definition, 'hospital', para (a), substituted: National Health Service (Consequential Provisions) Act 2006, s 2, Sch 1, paras 62, 70(c). Words in subs (1) definition, 'the managers', para (a), substituted: National Health Service (Consequential Provisions) Act 2006, s 2, Sch 1, paras 62, 70(d)(i), (ii). Words in subs (1) definition, 'Primary Care Trust' substituted: National Health Service (Consequential Provisions) Act 2006, s 2, Sch 1, paras 62, 70(e). Words in subs (1) definition, 'Special Health Authority' substituted: National Health Service (Consequential Provisions) Act 2006, s 2, Sch 1, paras 62, 70(f). Words in subs (1) definition, 'Strategic Health Authority' substituted: National Health Service (Consequential Provisions) Act 2006, s 2, Sch 1, paras 62, 70(g).P ara (c) and preceding word inserted in definition 'hospital' in subs (1): MHA 2007, s 46(1), (3)(a). Para (bd) inserted in definition 'the managers' in subs (1): MHA 2007, s 46(1), (3)(b). Words in definition 'absent without leave' in subs (1) inserted: MHA 2007, s 32(4), Sch 3, paras 1, 34(1), (2). Definition 'approved clinician' in subs (1) inserted: MHA 2007, s 14(1), (5). Definition 'approved mental health professional' in subs (1) substituted for definition 'approved social worker': MHA 2007, s 21, Sch 2, paras 1, 11(1), (2). Definition 'community patient' in subs (1) inserted: MHA 2007, s 32(4), Sch 3, paras 1, 34(1), (3). Definitions 'community treatment order' and 'the community treatment order" inserted: MHA 2007, s 32(4), Sch 3, paras 1, 34(1), (3). Definition 'the community treatment period' in subs (1) inserted: MHA 2007, s 32(4), Sch 3, paras 1, 34(1), (3). Subs (1) definition, 'hospital', para (c) and word immediately preceding it inserted: MHA 2007, s 46(1), (3)(a). Subs (1) definition, 'the managers', para (bd) inserted: Mental Health Act 2007, s 46(1), (3)(b). Words in definition 'medical treatment' in subs (1) substituted: MHA 2007, s 7(1), (2). Definition 'mental disorder' in subs (1) substituted for definitions 'mental disorder', 'severe mental impairment', 'mental impairment' and 'psychopathic disorder': MHA 2007, s 1(4), Sch 1, Pt 1, paras 1, 17. Definition 'the regulatory authority' inserted: Definition 'the responsible after-care bodies' in subs (1) repealed: MHA 2007, s 55, Sch 11, Pt 5. Definition 'the responsible hospital' in subs (1) inserted: MHA 2007, s 32(4), Sch 3, paras 1, 34(1), (3). Definition 'supervision application' in subs (1) repealed: MHA 2007, s 55, Sch 11, Pt 5. Subs (1AB) inserted: MHA 2007, s 4(1), (10). Subs (1AC) inserted: MHA 2007, s 21, Sch 2, paras 1, 11(1), (3). Subs (1A) repealed: MHA 2007, s 55, Sch 11, Pt 5. Words in subs (3) inserted: MHA 2007, s 32(4), Sch 3, paras 1, 34(1), (4). Subs (4) inserted: MHA 2007, s 7(1), (3). Subs (1) definition, 'Local Health Board' inserted: References to Health Authorities Order 2007, SI 2007 No. 961, art 3, Schedule, para 13(1), (13)(i). Words in subs (1) definition, 'the managers', para (a) substituted: References to Health Authorities Order 2007, SI 2007 No. 961, art 3, Schedule, para 13(1), (13)(ii). Subs (1) definition, 'the regulatory authority' inserted: Health and Social Care Act 2008, s 52(5), Sch 3, paras 1, 13. Subs (1) definition 'the appropriate tribunal' inserted: Transfer of Tribunal Functions Order 2008, SI 2008 No 2833, art 9(1), Sch 3, paras 39, 66. Subs (1) definitions, 'independent hospital' and 'the managers', para (c) substituted by Health and Social Care Act 2008 (Consequential Amendments No 2) Order 2010, SI 2010 No. 813, art 5(1), (5)(a), (b).

146 Application to Scotland

Sections 42(6), 80, 116, 122, 137, 139(1), 141, 142, 143 (so far as applicable to any Order in Council extending to Scotland) and 144 above shall extend to Scotland together with any amendment or repeal by this Act of or any provision of Schedule 5 to this Act relating to any enactment which so extends; but, except as aforesaid and except so far as it relates to the interpretation or commencement of the said provisions, this Act shall not extend to Scotland.

Amendments. Words repealed in relation to England and Wales: MHA 2007, ss 32(4), 39(2), 55, Sch 3, paras 1, 35, Sch 5, Pt 2, para 20, Sch 11, Pts 5, 7.

147 Application to Northern Ireland

Sections 81, 82, 86, 87, 88 (and so far as applied by that section sections 18, 22 and 138), section 128 (except so far as it relates to patients subject to guardianship), 137, 139, 141, 142, 143 (so far as applicable to any Order in Council extending to Northern Ireland) and 144 above shall extend to Northern Ireland together with any amendment or repeal by this Act of or any provision of Schedule 5 to this Act relating to any enactment which so extends; but except as aforesaid and except so far as it relates to the interpretation or commencement of the said provisions, this Act shall not extend to Northern Ireland.

Amendments. Words repealed: Mental Capacity Act 2005, s 67(1), (2), Sch 6, para 29(1), (9), Sch 7.

148 Consequential and transitional provisions and repeals

(1) Schedule 4 (consequential amendments) and Schedule 5 (transitional and saving provisions) to this Act shall have effect but without prejudice to the operation of sections 15 to 17 of the Interpretation Act 1978 (which relate to the effect of repeals).

(2) Where any amendment in Schedule 4 to this Act affects an enactment amended by the Mental Health (Amendment) Act 1982 the amendment in Schedule 4 shall come into force immediately after the provision of the Act of 1982 amending that enactment.

(3) The enactments specified in Schedule 6 to this Act are hereby repealed to the extent mentioned in the third column of that Schedule.

149 Short title, commencement and application to Scilly Isles

(1) This Act may be cited as the Mental Health Act 1983.

(2) Subject to subsection (3) below and Schedule 5 to this Act, this Act shall come into force on 30th September 1983.

(3) (*repealed*)

(4) Section 130(4) of the National Health Service Act 1977 (which provides for the extension of that Act to the Isles of Scilly) shall have effect as if the references to that Act included references to this Act.

Amendments. Subs repealed: Statute Law (Repeals) Act 2004.

****

Schedule 1
Application of Certain Provisions to Patients Subject to Hospital and Guardianship Orders

Sections 40(4), 41(3), (5), 55(4)

PART I
PATIENTS NOT SUBJECT TO SPECIAL RESTRICTIONS

1

Sections 9, 10, 17 to 17C, 17E, 17F, 20A, 21 to 21B, 24(3) and (4), 26 to 28, 31, 32, 34, 67 and 76 shall apply in relation to the patient without modification.

2

Sections 17D, 17G, 18 to 20, 20B, 22, 23, 66 and 68 shall apply in relation to the patient with the modifications specified in paragraphs 2A to 10 below.

2A

In section 17D(2)(a) for the reference to section 6(2) above there shall be substituted a reference to section 40(1)(b) below.

2B

In section 17G –

(a)   in subsection (2) for the reference to section 6(2) above there shall be substituted a reference to section 40(1)(b) below;

(b)   in subsection (4) for paragraphs (a) and (b) there shall be substituted the words 'the order or direction under Part 3 of this Act in respect of him were an order or direction for his admission or removal to that other hospital'; and

(c)   in subsection (5) for the words from 'the patient' to the end there shall be substituted the words 'the date of the relevant order or direction under Part 3 of this Act were the date on which the community treatment order is revoked'.

3 *(repealed)*

4

In section 18 subsection (5) shall be omitted.

5

In section 19(2) for the words from 'as follows' to the end of the subsection there shall be substituted the words 'as if the order or direction under Part III of this Act by virtue of which he was liable to be detained or subject to guardianship before being transferred were an order or direction for his admission or removal to the hospital to which he is transferred, or placing him under the guardianship of the authority or person into whose guardianship he is transferred, as the case may be'.

5A

In section 19A(2), paragraph (b) shall be omitted.

6

In section 20 –

(a)   in subsection (1) for the words from 'day on which he was' to 'as the case may be' there shall be substituted the words 'date of the relevant order or direction under Part III of this Act';

(b)   *(repealed)*

6A

In section 20B(1), for the reference to the application for admission for treatment there shall be substituted a reference to the order or direction under Part 3 of this Act by virtue of which the patient is liable to be detained.

7

In section 22 for references to an application for admission or a guardianship application there shall be substituted references to the order or direction under Part III of this Act by virtue of which the patient is liable to be detained or subject to guardianship.

8

In section 23(2) –

(a) in paragraph (a) the words 'for assessment or' shall be omitted; and
(b) in paragraphs (a) to (c) the references to the nearest relative shall be omitted.

8A *(repealed)*

9

In section 66 –

(a) in subsection (1), paragraphs (a), (b), (c), (g) and (h), the words in parenthesis in paragraph (i) and paragraph (ii) shall be omitted; and
(b) in subsection (2), paragraphs (a), (b), (c) and (g), and in paragraph (d) ', (g)', shall be omitted.

10

In section 68 –

(a) in subsection (1) paragraph (a) shall be omitted; and
(b) subsections (2) to (5) shall apply if the patient falls within paragraph (e) of subsection (1), but not otherwise.

Amendments: Words in para 1 substituted: Mental Health (Patients in the Community) Act 1995, ss 1(2), 2(8), Sch 1, para 6(a). Para 8A: inserted: Mental Health (Patients in the Community) Act 1995, s 1(2), Sch 1, para 6(c). Words in para 9(b) substituted: Mental Health (Patients in the Community) Act 1995, s 1(2), Sch 1, para 14. Words substituted: Mental Health Act 2007, s 32(4), Sch 3, paras 1, 36(1), (2). Para 1 reference substituted: MHA 2007, s 36(1), (4). Definitions in para 1 repealed and subsequent reference substituted, MHA 2007, s 55, Sch 11, Pt 1, Para 2 reference repealed and subsequent words substituted MHA 2007, s 32(4), Sch 3, paras 1, 36(1), (3)(a), (b), s 37(1), (6) (a)(i), (ii); Para 2: reference repealed: MHA 2007, s 55, Sch 11, Pt 5. Paras (2A), (2B) inserted by MHA 2007, s 32(4), Sch 3, paras 1, 36(1), (4). Para 3 repealed by MHA 2007, s 55, Sch 11, Pt 1, para (5A) inserted by MHA 2007, s 32(4), Sch 3, paras 1, 36(1), (5), para 6 words repealed and subsequent words substituted by MHA 2007, s 53, Sch 3, paras 1, 2; Para 6(b) and preceding word repealed: Mental Health Act 2007, s 55, Sch 11, Pt 1.para (6A), inserted by MHA 2007, s 32(4), Sch 3, paras 1, 36(1), (6); para (8) words repealed and subsequent words substituted by MHA 2007, s 32(4), Sch 3, paras 1, 36(1), (7); para (8A) repealed: MHA 2007, s 55, Sch 11, Pt 5; para (10) inserted by MHA 2007, s 37 (1), (6)(b).

PART II
PATIENTS SUBJECT TO SPECIAL RESTRICTIONS

1

Sections 24(3) and (4), 32 and 76 shall apply in relation to the patient without modification.

2

Sections 17, 18, 19, 22, 23 and 34 shall apply in relation to the patient with the modifications specified in paragraphs 3 to 8 below.

3

In section 17 –

(a) in subsection (1) after the word 'may' there shall be inserted the words 'with the consent of the Secretary of State';

(aa) subsections (2A) and (2B) shall be omitted;

(b) in subsection (4) after the words 'the responsible clinician' and after the words 'that clinician' there shall be inserted the words 'or the Secretary of State'; and

(c) in subsection (5) after the word 'recalled' there shall be inserted the words 'by the responsible clinician', and for the words from 'he has ceased' to the end of the subsection there shall be substituted the words 'the expiration of the period of twelve months beginning with the first day of his absence on leave'.

4

In section 18 there shall be omitted –

(a) in subsection (1) the words 'subject to the provisions of this section'; and

(b) subsections (3), (4) and (5).

5

In section 19 –

(a) in subsection (1) after the word 'may' in paragraph (a) there shall be inserted the words 'with the consent of the Secretary of State', and the words from 'or into' to the end of the subsection shall be omitted; ...

(b) in subsection (2) for the words from 'as follows' to the end of the subsection there shall be substituted the words 'as if the order or direction under Part III of this Act by virtue of which he was liable to be detained before being transferred were an order or direction for his admission or removal to the hospital to which he is transferred'; and

(c) in subsection (3) after the words 'may at any time' there shall be inserted the words ', with the consent of the Secretary of State,'.

6

In section 22, subsections (1) and (5) shall not apply.

7

In section 23 –

(a)   in subsection (1) references to guardianship shall be omitted and after the word 'made' there shall be inserted the words 'with the consent of the Secretary of State and'; and

(b)   in subsection (2) –

(i)   in paragraph (a) to the words 'for assessment or' and 'or by the nearest relative of the patient' shall be omitted; and

(ii)   paragraph (b) shall be omitted.

8

In section 34, in subsection (1) the definition of 'the nominated medical attendant' and subsection (3) shall be omitted.

Amendments. Words in para 5(a) repealed: Crime (Sentences) Act 1997, ss 49(4), 56(2), Sch 6. Para 5(c) and preceding word inserted: Crime (Sentences) Act 1997, s 49(4). Words in para 2 substituted: MHA 2007, s 32(4). Sch 3, paras 1, 37(1), (2), para 3 (aa) inserted by MHA 2007, s 33 (1), (3), para 3(b), (c) words substituted MHA 2007, s 11(1), (8)(a), (b); para 6 substituted by MHA 2007, s 32(4), Sch 3, paras 1, 37 (1), (3).

Schedule 2
Mental Health Review Tribunal for Wales

Section 65(2)

1

The Mental Health Review Tribunal for Wales shall consist of –

(a)   a number of persons (referred to in this Schedule as 'the legal members') appointed by the Lord Chancellor and having such legal experience as the Lord Chancellor considers suitable;

(b)   a number of persons (referred to in this Schedule as 'the medical members') being registered medical practitioners appointed by the Lord Chancellor; and

(c)   a number of persons appointed by the Lord Chancellor and having such experience in administration, such knowledge of social services or such other qualifications or experience as the Lord Chancellor considers suitable.

1A

As part of the selection process for an appointment under paragraph 1(b) or (c) the Judicial Appointments Commission shall consult the Secretary of State.

2

Subject to paragraph 2A below the members of the Mental Health Review Tribunal for Wales shall hold and vacate office under the terms of the instrument under which they are appointed, but may resign office by notice in writing to the Lord Chancellor; and any such member who ceases to hold office shall be eligible for re-appointment.

2A

A member of the Mental Health Review Tribunal for Wales shall vacate office on the day on which he attains the age of 70 years; but this paragraph is subject to section 26(4) to (6) of the Judicial Pensions and Retirement Act 1993 (power to authorise continuance in office up to the age of 75 years).

3

(1) (*repealed*)

(2) The Lord Chancellor shall appoint one of the legal members of the Mental Health Review Tribunal for Wales to be the President of that tribunal.

4

Subject to rules made by the Lord Chancellor under section 78(2)(c) above, the members who are to constitute the Mental Health Review Tribunal for Wales for the purposes of any proceedings or class or group of proceedings under this Act shall be appointed by the chairman of the tribunal or by another member of the tribunal appointed for the purpose by the chairman; and of the members so appointed –

(a)   one or more shall be appointed from the legal members;

(b)   one or more shall be appointed from the medical members; and

(c)   one or more shall be appointed from the members who are neither legal nor medical members.

5

(1) A member of the First-tier Tribunal who is eligible to decide any matter in a case under this Act may, at the request of the President of the Mental Health Review Tribunal for Wales and with the approval of the Senior President of Tribunals, act as a member of the Mental Health Review Tribunal for Wales.

(2) Every person while acting under this paragraph may perform any of the functions of a member of the Mental Health Review Tribunal for Wales.

(3) Until section 38(7) of the Mental Health Act 2007 comes into force, the reference in sub-paragraph (1) to the President of the Mental Health Review Tribunal for Wales is to be read as a reference to the chairman of the tribunal.

6

Subject to any rules made by the Lord Chancellor under section 78(4)(a) above, where the chairman of the tribunal is included among the persons appointed under paragraph 4 above, he shall be president of the tribunal; and in any other case the president of the tribunal shall be such one of the members so appointed (being one of the legal members) as the chairman may nominate.

Amendments. Words in para 2 inserted: Judicial Pensions and Retirement Act 1993, s 26, Sch 6, para 40. Para 2A inserted: Judicial Pensions and Retirement Act 1993, s 26, Sch 6, para 40. Words in para 1(b), (c) repealed: Constitutional Reform Act 2005, ss 15(1), 146, Sch 4, Pt 1, paras 150, 158(1), (2), Sch 18, Pt 2. Para 1A inserted: Constitutional Reform Act 2005, s 15(1), Sch 4, Pt 1, paras 150, 158(1), (3). Words in para 4 repealed: Mental Health Act 2007, ss 38(1), (5), (7)(b), 55, Sch 11, Pt 6. Words in schedule heading substituted: Transfer of Tribunal Functions Order 2008, SI 2008 No 2833, art 9(1), Sch 3, paras 39, 67(a). Words Paras 1, 2, 2A substituted: Transfer of Tribunal Functions Order 2008, SI 2008 No, 2833, art 9(1), Sch 3, paras 39, 67(b)–(d). Words substituted into prospectively inserted new para 3: Transfer of Tribunal Functions Order 2008, SI 2008 No, 2833, art 9(1), Sch 3, paras 39, 67(e). Previous para 3 (as substituted by the Mental Health Act 2007, s 38(1), (5), (6)): sub-para (1) repealed: Transfer of Tribunal Functions Order 2008, SI 2008 No, 2833, art 9(1), Sch 3, paras 39, 67(f). Words in para 4 substituted: Transfer of Tribunal Functions Order 2008, SI 2008 No, 2833, art 9(1), Sch 3, paras 39, 67(g). Para 5 (as originally enacted) repealed: Transfer of Tribunal Functions Order 2008, SI 2008 No, 2833, art 9(1), Sch 3, paras 39, 67(h). Para 5: inserted: Transfer of Tribunal Functions (Lands Tribunal and Miscellaneous Amendments) Order 2009, SI 2009 No. 1307, art 5(1), (2), Sch 1, paras 160, 162.

Schedule 3 *(repealed)*

Amendments. Repealed by the Mental Capacity Act 2005, s 67(2), Sch 7.

Schedule 4 *(repealed)*

Schedule 5
Transitional and Saving Provisions

Section 148

1

Where any period of time specified in an enactment repealed by this Act is current at the commencement of this Act, this Act shall have effect as if the corresponding provision of this Act had been in force when that period began to run.

2

Nothing in this Act shall affect the interpretation of any provision of the Mental Health Act 1959 which is not repealed by this Act and accordingly sections 1 and 145(1) of this Act shall apply to any such provision as if it were contained in this Act.

3

Where, apart from this paragraph, anything done under or for the purposes of any enactment which is repealed by this Act would cease to have effect by virtue of that repeal it shall have effect as if it had been done under or for the purposes of the corresponding provision of this Act.

4–5 *(repealed)*

6

This Act shall apply in relation to any authority for the detention or guardianship of a person who was liable to be detained or subject to guardianship under the Mental Health Act 1959 immediately before 30th September 1983 as if the provisions of this Act which derive from provisions amended by sections 1 or 2 of the Mental Health (Amendment) Act 1982 and the amendments in Schedule 3 to that Act which are consequential on those sections were included in this Act in the form the provisions from which they derive would take if those amendments were disregarded but this provision shall not apply to any renewal of that authority on or after that date.

7–8 *(repealed)*

9

(1) *(repealed)*

(2) Section 20(2) of this Act shall have effect in relation to any authority renewed before 1st October 1983 with the substitution for the words 'six months' of the words 'one year' and for the words 'one year' in both places they occur of the words 'two years'.

(3) *(repealed)*

10–14 *(repealed)*

15

The provisions of this Act which derive from sections 24 to 27 of the Mental Health (Amendment) Act 1982 shall have effect in relation to a transfer direction given before 30th September 1983 as well as in relation to one given later, but where, apart from this paragraph, a transfer direction given before 30th September 1983 would by virtue of the words in section 50(3) of this Act which are derived from section 24(3) of the Mental Health (Amendment) Act 1982 have ceased to have effect before that date it shall cease to have effect on that date.

16

The words in section 42(1) of this Act which derive from the amendment of section 66(1) of the Mental Health Act 1959 by section 28(1) of the Mental Health (Amendment) Act 1982 and the provisions of this Act which derive from section 28(3) of and Schedule 1 to that Act have effect in relation to a restriction order or, as the case may be, a restriction direction made or given before 30th September 1983 as well as in relation to one made or given later, but –

(a)   any reference to a tribunal under section 66(6) of the said Act of 1959 in respect of a patient shall be treated for the purposes of subsections (1) and (2) of section 77 of this Act in their application to sections 70 and 75(2) of this Act as an application made by him; and

(b)   sections 71(5) and 75(1)(a) of this Act do not apply where the period in question has expired before 30th September 1983.

17

Section 91(2) of this Act shall not apply in relation to a patient removed from England and Wales before 30th September 1983.

18–19 (*repealed*)

20

The repeal by the Mental Health (Amendment) Act 1982 of section 77 of the Mental Health Act 1959 does not affect subsection (4) of that section in its application to a transfer direction given before 30th September 1983, but after the coming into force of this Act that subsection shall have effect for that purpose as if for the references to subsection (6) of section 60, Part IV of that Act and the provisions of that Act there were substituted respectively references to section 37(8), Part II and the provisions of this Act.

21

Any direction to which section 71(4) of the Mental Health Act 1959 applied immediately before the commencement of this Act shall have the same effect as a hospital order together with a restriction order, made without limitation of time.

22 (*repealed*)

23

For any reference in any enactment, instrument, deed or other document to a receiver under Part VIII of the Mental Health Act 1959 there shall be substituted a reference to a receiver under Part VII of this Act.

24

Nothing in this Act shall affect the operation of the proviso to section 107(5) of the Mental Health Act 1959 in relation to a charge created before the commencement of this Act under that section.

25

Nothing in this Act shall affect the operation of subsection (6) of section 112 of the Mental Health Act 1959 in relation to a charge created before the commencement of this Act by virtue of subsection (5) of that section.

26 (*repealed*)

27

Nothing in this Act shall affect the operation of section 116 of the Mental Health Act 1959 in relation to orders made, directions or authorities given or other instruments issued before the commencement of this Act.

28

References to applications, recommendations, reports and other documents in section 126 of this Act shall include those to which section 125 of the Mental Health Act 1959 applied immediately before the commencement of this Act and references in section 139 of this Act to the Acts to which that section applies shall include those to which section 141 of the said Act of 1959 applied at that time.

29

The repeal by the Mental Health Act 1959 of the Mental Treatment Act 1930 shall not affect any amendment effected by section 20 of that Act in any enactment not repealed by the said Act of 1959.

30

The repeal by the Mental Health Act 1959 of the provisions of the Lunacy Act 1890 and of the Mental Deficiency Act 1913 relating to the superannuation of officers or employees shall not affect any arrangements for the payment of allowances or other benefits made in accordance with those provisions and in force on 1st November 1960.

31

(1) Any patient who immediately before the commencement of this Act was liable to be detained in a hospital or subject to guardianship by virtue of paragraph 9 of Schedule 6 to the Mental Health Act 1959 shall unless previously discharged continue to be so liable for the remainder of the period of his treatment current on 1st November 1960.

(2) The patient may before the expiration of the period of treatment referred to in sub-paragraph (1) above apply to a Mental Health Review Tribunal.

32

Any patient who immediately before the commencement of this Act was liable to be detained or subject to guardianship by virtue of an authority which had been renewed under paragraph 11 of Schedule 6 to the Mental Health Act 1959 shall unless previously discharged continue to be so liable during the period for which that authority was so renewed.

33

(1)   This paragraph applies to patients who at the commencement of this Act are liable to be detained or subject to guardianship by virtue of paragraph 31 or 32 above.

(2)   Authority for the detention or guardianship of the patient may on the expiration of the relevant period, unless the patient has previously been discharged, be renewed for a further period of two years.

(3)   Sections 20(3) to (10) and 66(1)(f) of this Act shall apply in relation to the renewal of authority for the detention or guardianship of a patient under this paragraph as they apply in relation to the renewal of authority for the detention or guardianship of the patient under section 20(2).

(4)   In this paragraph 'the relevant period' means –

   (a)   in relation to a patient liable to be detained or subject to guardianship by virtue of the said paragraph 31, the period of his treatment referred to in that paragraph;

   (b)   in relation to a patient detained by virtue of the said paragraph 32, the period for which authority for the detention or guardianship of the patient has been renewed under paragraph 11 of Schedule 6 to the 1959 Act;

   (c)   in relation to a patient the authority for whose detention or guardianship has previously been renewed under this paragraph, the latest period for which it has been so renewed.

34

(1)   Any patient who is liable to be detained in a hospital or subject to guardianship by virtue of paragraph 31 above shall (subject to the exceptions and modifications specified in the following provisions of this paragraph) be treated as if he had been admitted to the hospital in pursuance of an application for admission for treatment under Part II of this Act or had been received into guardianship in pursuance of a guardianship application under the said Part II and had been so admitted or received as a patient suffering from the form or forms of mental disorder recorded under paragraph 7 of Schedule 6 to the Mental Health Act 1959 or, if a different form or forms have been specified in a report under section 38 of that Act as applied by that paragraph, the form or forms so specified.

(2)   Section 20 of this Act shall not apply in relation to the patient, but the provisions of paragraph 33 above shall apply instead.

(3)   Any patient to whom paragraph 9(3) of Schedule 6 to the Mental Health Act 1959 applied at the commencement of this Act who fell within paragraph (b) of that paragraph shall cease to be liable to be detained on attaining the age of 25 years unless, during the period of two months ending on the date when he attains that age, the responsible medical officer records his opinion under the following provisions of this Schedule that the patient is unfit for discharge.

(4) If the patient was immediately before 1st November 1960 liable to be detained by virtue of section 6, 8(1) or 9 of the Mental Deficiency Act 1913, the power of discharging him under section 23 of this Act shall not be exercisable by his nearest relative, but his nearest relative may make one application in respect of him to the appropriate tribunal in any period of 12 months.

35

(1) The responsible medical officer may record for the purposes of paragraph 34(3) above his opinion that a patient detained in a hospital is unfit for discharge if it appears to the responsible medical officer –

(a) that if that patient were released from the hospital he would be likely to act in a manner dangerous to other persons or to himself, or would be likely to resort to criminal activities; or

(b) that that patient is incapable of caring for himself and that there is no suitable hospital or other establishment into which he can be admitted and where he would be likely to remain voluntarily;

and where the responsible medical officer records his opinion as aforesaid he shall also record the grounds for his opinion.

(2) Where the responsible medical officer records his opinion under this paragraph in respect of a patient, the managers of the hospital or other persons in charge of the establishment where he is for the time being detained or liable to be detained shall cause the patient to be informed, and the patient may, at any time before the expiration of the period of 28 days beginning with the date on which he is so informed, apply to a Mental Health Review Tribunal.

(3) On any application under sub-paragraph (2) above the tribunal shall, if satisfied that none of the conditions set out in paragraphs (a) and (b) of sub-paragraph (1) above are fulfilled, direct that the patient be discharged, and subsection (1) of section 72 of this Act shall have effect in relation to the application as if paragraph (b) of that subsection were omitted.

36

Any person who immediately before the commencement of this Act was deemed to have been named as the guardian of any patient under paragraph 14 of Schedule 6 to the Mental Health Act 1959 shall be deemed for the purposes of this Act to have been named as the guardian of the patient in an application for his reception into guardianship under Part II of this Act accepted on that person's behalf by the relevant local authority.

37

(1) This paragraph applies to patients who immediately before the commencement of this Act were transferred patients within the meaning of paragraph 15 of Schedule 6 to the Mental Health Act 1959.

(2) A transferred patient who immediately before the commencement of this Act was by virtue of sub-paragraph (2) of that paragraph treated for the purposes of that Act as if he were liable to be detained in a hospital in pursuance of a direction under section 71 of that Act shall be treated as if he were so liable in pursuance of a hospital order together with a restriction order, made without limitation of time.

(3) A transferred patient who immediately before the commencement of this Act was by virtue of sub-paragraph (3) of that paragraph treated for the purposes of that Act as if he were liable to be detained in a hospital by virtue of a transfer direction under section 72 of that Act and as if a direction restricting his discharge had been given under section 74 of that Act shall be treated as if he were so liable by virtue of a transfer direction under section 47 of this Act and as if a restriction direction had been given under section 49 of this Act.

(4) Section 84 of this Act shall apply to a transferred patient who was treated by virtue of sub-paragraph (5) of that paragraph immediately before the commencement of this Act as if he had been removed to a hospital under section 89 of that Act as if he had been so removed under the said section 84.

(5) Any person to whom sub-paragraph (6) of that paragraph applied immediately before the commencement of this Act shall be treated for the purposes of this Act as if he were liable to be detained in a hospital in pursuance of a transfer direction given under section 48 of this Act and as if a restriction direction had been given under section 49 of this Act.

38

Any patient who immediately before the commencement of this Act was treated by virtue of sub-paragraph (1) of paragraph 16 of Schedule 6 to the Mental Health Act 1959 as if he had been conditionally discharged under section 66 of that Act shall be treated as if he had been conditionally discharged under section 42 of this Act and any such direction as is mentioned in paragraph (b) of that sub-paragraph shall be treated as if it had been given under the said section 42.

39 (*repealed*)

40

A person who immediately before the commencement of this Act was detained by virtue of paragraph 19 of Schedule 6 to the Mental Health Act 1959 may continue to be detained until the expiration of the period of his treatment current on 1st November 1960 or until he becomes liable to be detained or subject to guardianship under this Act, whichever occurs first, and may be so detained in any place in which he might have been detained under that paragraph.

41

Any opinion recorded by the responsible medical officer under the foregoing provisions of this Schedule shall be recorded in such form as may be prescribed by regulations made by the Secretary of State.

42

(1) In the foregoing provisions of this Schedule –

  (a) references to the period of treatment of a patient that was current on 1st November 1960 are to the period for which he would have been liable to be detained or subject to guardianship by virtue of any enactment repealed or excluded by the Mental Health Act 1959, or any enactment repealed or replaced by any such enactment as aforesaid, being a period which began but did not expire before that date; and

  (b) 'the responsible medical officer' means –

    (i) in relation to a patient subject to guardianship, the medical officer authorised by the local social services authority to act (either generally or in any particular case or for any particular purpose) as the responsible medical officer;

    (ii) in relation to any other class of patient, the registered medical practitioner in charge of the treatment of the patient.

(2) Subsection (2) of section 34 of this Act shall apply for the purposes of the foregoing provisions of this Schedule as it applies for the purposes of Part II of this Act.

(3) The sentence or other period of detention of a person who was liable to be detained or subject to guardianship immediately before 1st November 1960 by virtue of an order under section 9 of the Mental Deficiency Act 1913 shall be treated for the purposes of the foregoing provisions of this Schedule as expiring at the end of the period for which that person would have been liable to be detained in a prison or other institution if the order had not been made.

(4) For the purposes of the foregoing provisions of this Schedule, an order sending a person to an institution or placing a person under guardianship made before 9th March 1956 on a petition presented under the Mental Deficiency Act 1913 shall be deemed to be valid if it was so deemed immediately before the commencement of this Act by virtue of section 148(2) of the Mental Health Act 1959.

43–46 (*repealed*)

Amendments: Para 46: repealed: Health Authorities Act 1995, s 5(1), Sch 3. Paras 4, 5, 7, 8, 10–14, 18, 19, 22, 26: repealed: Statute Law (Repeals) Act 2004. Para 9(1), (3) repealed: Statute Law (Repeals) Act 2004. Para 21 substituted: Domestic Violence, Crime and Victims Act 2004, s 58(1), Sch 10, para 23(1), (2). Paras 43–45 repealed: Mental Capacity Act 2005, s 67(2), Sch 7. Words in para 37(5) repealed: Mental Health Act 2007, s 55, Sch 11, Pt 1. Para 39 repealed: Mental Health Act 2007, s 55, Sch 11, Pt 1. Words in para 34(4) substituted: Transfer of Tribunal Functions Order 2008, SI 2008 No. 2833, art 9(1), Sch 3, paras 39, 68.

****

INDEX

References are to paragraph numbers.